'ARMED ATTACK' AND ARTICLE 51 OF THE UN CHARTER

This book examines to what extent the right of self-defence, as laid down in Article 51 of the Charter of the United Nations, permits States to launch military operations against other States. In particular, it focuses on the occurrence of an 'armed attack' – the crucial trigger for the activation of this right. In light of the developments since 9/11, the author analyses relevant physical and verbal customary practice, ranging from the 1974 Definition of Aggression to recent incidents such as the 2001 US intervention in Afghanistan and the 2006 Israeli intervention in Lebanon. The notion of 'armed attack' is examined from a threefold perspective. What acts can be regarded as an 'armed attack'? When can an 'armed attack' be considered to take place? And from whom must an 'armed attack' emanate? By way of conclusion, the different findings are brought together in a draft 'Definition of Armed Attack'.

DR TOM RUYS is a lawyer with Stibbe, Brussels, and a senior member of the Leuven Centre for Global Governance Studies. He also teaches Public International Law as a substitute lecturer at the Catholic University of Leuven.

'ARMED ATTACK' AND ARTICLE 51 OF THE UN CHARTER: EVOLUTIONS IN CUSTOMARY LAW AND PRACTICE

TOM RUYS

CAMBRIDGE UNIVERSITY PRESS
Cambridge, New York, Melbourne, Madrid, Cape Town, Singapore,
São Paulo, Delhi, Dubai, Tokyo, Mexico City

Cambridge University Press
The Edinburgh Building, Cambridge CB2 8RU, UK

Published in the United States of America by Cambridge University Press, New York

www.cambridge.org
Information on this title: www.cambridge.org/9780521766647

© Tom Ruys 2010

This publication is in copyright. Subject to statutory exception
and to the provisions of relevant collective licensing agreements,
no reproduction of any part may take place without the written
permission of Cambridge University Press.

First published 2010

A catalogue record for this publication is available from the British Library

Library of Congress Cataloguing in Publication data
Ruys, Tom. "Armed attack" and Article 51 of the UN Charter :
customary law and practice / Tom Ruys.
p. cm.
ISBN 978-0-521-76664-7 (hardback)
1. Self-defense (International law) 2. Aggression (International law)
I. Title.
KZ6374.R89   2010
341.6′2–dc22
2010019534

ISBN 978-0-521-76664-7 Hardback

Cambridge University Press has no responsibility for the persistence or
accuracy of URLs for external or third-party Internet websites referred to
in this publication, and does not guarantee that any content on such
websites is, or will remain, accurate or appropriate.

"POWER ALONE CANNOT PROTECT US, NOR DOES IT
ENTITLE US TO DO AS WE PLEASE."

Barack Obama, 44th President of the United States, Inaugural Speech,
Washington DC, 20 January 2009

TABLE OF CONTENTS

Acknowledgment page x
Table of abbreviations and abbreviated citations xi
Selected case law, legislation and related documents xviii

Introduction 1

1 **The methodological debate and the quest for custom** 6

   1.1 Treaty vs. custom 7
      1.1.1 The Charter and pre-existing custom 7
      1.1.2 The role of custom in treaty interpretation and modification 19

   1.2 State practice vs. *opinio iuris* 29
      1.2.1 Introduction: the methodological debate 29
      1.2.2 The evidentiary weight of words and deeds 31
      1.2.3 Observations concerning the density of customary practice 44
      1.2.4 Conclusion 51

2 **'Armed attack' and other conditions of self-defence** 53

   2.1 The 'armed attack' requirement as an integral part of Article 51 UN Charter 53
      2.1.1 Self-preservation and self-defence prior to 1945 53
      2.1.2 Article 51 UN Charter – primary means of interpretation 55
      2.1.3 The preparatory works of the UN Charter 60

   2.2 Other conditions of self-defence 68
      2.2.1 'Procedural' obligations 68
      2.2.2 Necessity and proportionality 91

TABLE OF CONTENTS

3 The 'armed attack' requirement *ratione materiae*   126

  3.1   Armed attack and aggression   127
      3.1.1   Two sides of the same coin   127
      3.1.2   The negotiations within the Fourth Special Committee on the Question of Defining Aggression (1968–74)   129
      3.1.3   Value of the Definition of Aggression   136

  3.2   General factors determining the existence of an 'armed attack'   139
      3.2.1   The 'most grave' forms of the use of force and the *de minimis* controversy   139
      3.2.2   The *'animus aggressionis'* and accumulation of events   158
      3.2.3   Connecting the dots: the panoply of scenarios and the role of context   175

  3.3   Small-scale incursions by land, sea or air   184

  3.4   Attacks against external manifestations of the State   199
      3.4.1   Military units and military installations abroad   199
      3.4.2   Embassies and diplomatic envoys   201
      3.4.3   Civilian aircraft and merchant vessels   204
      3.4.4   Protection of nationals   213

4 The 'armed attack' requirement *ratione temporis*   250

  4.1   Anticipatory self-defence: the never-ending saga (1945–2001)   255
      4.1.1   The doctrinal debate – a brief appraisal   255
      4.1.2   Customary precedents: evidence *in concreto*   267
      4.1.3   Customary evidence *in abstracto*   294

  4.2   The shockwaves of 9/11   305
      4.2.1   The 2002 US National Security Strategy and the intervention in Iraq in 2003   305
      4.2.2   Shifting positions of States and scholars: a defeat of *preventive* self-defence at the expense of an embrace of *pre-emptive* self-defence?   318

  4.3   Exceptions and borderline cases   342
      4.3.1   The prospective dimension of the necessity standard   342
      4.3.2   Possible exceptions?   343
      4.3.3   Interceptive self-defence at the tactical level: on-the-spot reaction   346

5 The 'armed attack' requirement *ratione personae* 368

5.1 Indirect military aggression in the decolonization era 369
- 5.1.1 Formulation of the problem 369
- 5.1.2 The debate on 'indirect aggression' within the Fourth Special Committee on the Question of Defining Aggression 382
- 5.1.3 State practice 394
- 5.1.4 Indirect aggression in the wake of the ICJ's *Nicaragua* case 406

5.2 Self-defence against non-State actors in the age of international terrorism and State failure 419
- 5.2.1 Prelude to 9/11: shifting context, shifting practice? 419
- 5.2.2 9/11: awakening to a new security environment 433
- 5.2.3 Customary practice after 9/11 447
- 5.2.4 The response of the International Court of Justice 472
- 5.2.5 Conclusion: can non-State actors commit 'armed attacks'? 485

6 What future for the 'armed attack' criterion? 511

6.1 The customary boundaries of self-defence 511
- 6.1.1 A word of caution 511
- 6.1.2 The correlation between Article 51 UN Charter and other primary or secondary rules, and the 'pre-existing custom' paradigm 514
- 6.1.3 Preconditions of individual self-defence other than the 'armed attack' requirement 517
- 6.1.4 *Ratione materiae*: the basic ingredients of an 'armed attack' 520
- 6.1.5 The 'armed attack' *ratione temporis* 524
- 6.1.6 *Ratione personae*: attacks by non-State actors and the right of self-defence 528
- 6.1.7 The slippery slope of self-defence 532

6.2 Towards a UNGA 'Definition of Armed Attack'? 535
- 6.2.1 Resuming an ancient project 535
- 6.2.2 A blueprint 539
- 6.2.3 Post-scriptum: strengthening the compliance pull of the *Ius ad Bellum* 545

Index 551

ACKNOWLEDGMENT

The present volume is the product of several years of research at the Institute for International Law of the Catholic University of Leuven, culminating in the defence of a doctoral thesis in October 2009.

It has been made possible through the valued financial support of the Fund for Scientific Research Flanders (Fonds voor Wetenschappelijk Onderzoek Vlaanderen) as well as the even more valued moral support of my ever-energetic supervisor, Professor Jan Wouters. I thank my colleagues at the Institute for International Law and the Leuven Centre for Global Governance Studies for a very fruitful and most gratifying cooperation, in particular the former occupants of the 'International House' Dominic, Bruno, and Maarten, as well as Bart, Sten, Cedric, Fred and Viviane.

I also wish to specifically thank several persons, who, in various ways, supported or inspired me during the task ahead, notably Ambassador Johan Verbeke and his former team at the Belgian Permanent Representation at the United Nations in New York, Professor Michael Reisman of Yale Law School, Professors Christine Gray (Cambridge), Olivier Corten (Université Libre de Bruxelles) and Dino Kritsiotis (University of Nottingham), as well as the Leuven faculty members who, with Professor Wouters, granted me the honour of serving on my doctoral jury, Stephan Parmentier and Luc Reychler.

My warmest thanks to my parents for their unremitting support and for instilling in me sufficient perseverance to cope with prolonged sojourns in the dusty catacombs of the Leuven university library.

Last but not least, I express my gratitude to my wife, Isabelle, who was the first to read the present work in its entirety, and whose invaluable logistical and moral support always kept the ship on course. It is to her and our two wonderful boys, Mathias and Laurens, that I dedicate this work.

TABLE OF ABBREVIATIONS AND ABBREVIATED CITATIONS

1. Abbreviations

ADF	Allied Democratic Forces
ASIL	American Society of International Law
AU	African Union
CNA	Computer Network Attack
DASR	International Law Commission Draft Articles on State Responsibility (2001)
DRC	Democratic Republic of the Congo
ECtHR	European Court of Human Rights
ESS	European Security Strategy
ETA	Euskadi Ta Askatasuna
EU	European Union
(ex-)FAR	Forces armées rwandaises
FARC	Revolutionary Armed Forces of Colombia
G8	Group of Eight
IAEA	International Atomic Energy Agency
ICAO	International Civil Aviation Organization
ICC	International Criminal Court
ICJ	International Court of Justice
ICTY	International Criminal Tribunal for the former Yugoslavia
IDF	Israeli Defence Forces
IDI	Institut de Droit International
IGAD	Intergovernmental Authority on Development
IHL	International Humanitarian Law
ILA	International Law Association
ILC	International Law Commission
IO	International Organization
IRA	Irish Republican Army
ITLOS	International Tribunal for the Law of the Sea
KRG	Kurdistan Regional Government

LRA	Lord's Resistance Army
LTTE	Liberation Tigers of Tamil Eelam
MONUC	United Nations Organization Mission in the Democratic Republic of the Congo
NAFTA	North American Free Trade Agreement
NATO	North Atlantic Treaty Organization
NEO	Non-Combatant Evacuation Operation
NSS	National Security Strategy of the United States
OAS	Organization of American States
OAU	Organization of African Unity (now African Union)
ODA	Official Development Assistance
OECS	Organization of Eastern Caribbean States
OPT	Occupied Palestinian Territories
OSCE	Organization for Security and Cooperation in Europe
P–5	Permanent Members of the United Nations Security Council
PCA	Permanent Court of Arbitration
PCIJ	Permanent Court of International Justice
PKK	Kurdistan Workers' Party
PLO	Palestine Liberation Organization
ROE	Rules of Engagement
SOFA	Status of Forces Agreement
SWAPO	South West Africa People's Organization
TFG	Transitional Federal Government (Somalia)
UAR	United Arab Republic
UIC	Union of Islamic Courts
UN	United Nations
UNCIO	United Nations Conference on International Organization (San Francisco Conference)
UNCLOS	United Nations Convention on the Law of the Sea
UNEF	United Nations Emergency Force
UNGA	United Nations General Assembly
UNMOVIC	United Nations Monitoring, Verification and Inspections Commission
UNSC	United Nations Security Council
UNSG	United Nations Secretary-General
UNTSO	United Nations Truce Supervision Organization
VCLT	Vienna Convention on the Law of Treaties (1969)
WMD	Weapons of Mass Destruction
WTO	World Trade Organization

2. Journals and related materials

AASL	Annals of Air and Space Law
ABNYC Rec	Record of the Association of the Bar of the City of New York
ADI	Anuario de Derecho Internacional
AdV	Archiv des Völkerrechts
AFDI	Annuaire français de Droit International
AFP	Agence France Press
AFReII	Annuaire Français de Relations Internationales
African YBIL	African Yearbook of International Law
Air Force L Rev	Air Force Law Review
AJIL	American Journal of International Law
Alberta L Rev	Alberta Law Review
American Un IL Rev	American University International Law Review
American Un JILP	American University Journal of International Law and Policy
American Un L Rev	American University Law Review
Ann IDI	Annuaire de L'Institut de Droit International
ARIEL	Austrian Review of International and European Law
Arizona JICL	Arizona Journal of International and Comparative Law
ASDI	Annuaire Suisse de Droit International
ASIL Proc	Proceedings of the American Society of International Law
Australian YBIL	Australian Yearbook of International Law
Baltic YBIL	Baltic Yearbook of International Law
Berkeley JIL	Berkeley Journal of International Law
BFSP	British and Foreign State Papers
Boston College ICL Rev	Boston College International and Comparative Law Review
Brooklyn JIL	Brooklyn Journal of International Law
BYBIL	British Yearbook of International Law
California Western ILJ	California Western International Law Journal
California Western L Rev	California Western Law Review
Cal L Rev	California Law Review
Cambridge LJ	Cambridge Law Journal
Cambridge Student L Rev	Cambridge Student Law Review
Can YBIL	Canadian Yearbook of International Law
Case Western JIL	Case Western Journal of International Law

Chinese JIL	Chinese Journal of International Law
Columbia JTL	Columbia Journal of Transnational Law
Col L Rev	Columbia Law Review
Cornell ILJ	Cornell International Law Journal
Cornell L Rev	Cornell Law Review
Denver JILP	Denver Journal of International Law and Policy
Denver LJ	Denver Law Journal
Dickinson L Rev	Dickinson Law Review
Duke JCIL	Duke Journal of Comparative and International Law
EJIL	European Journal of International Law
EJIRel	European Journal of International Relations
EPIL	Max Planck Encyclopaedia of Public International Law
EuGRZ	Europäische Grundrechte-Zeitschrift
Finnish YBIL	Finnish Yearbook of International Law
Georgia JICL	Georgia Journal of International and Comparative Law
Georgetown LJ	Georgetown Law Journal
German LJ	German Law Journal
GYBIL	German Yearbook of International Law
Hastings ICL Rev	Hastings International and Comparative Law Review
HJL Public Policy	Harvard Journal of Law and Public Policy
HILJ	Harvard International Law Journal
HL Rev	Harvard Law Review
ICJ Rep	ICJ Reports
ICLQ	International and Comparative Law Quarterly
ICL Rev	International Community Law Review
IHT	International Herald Tribune
ILF	International Law Forum
ILM	International Legal Materials
ILR	International Law Reports
ILSA JICL	ILSA Journal of International and Comparative Law
Indian JIL	Indian Journal of International Law
Indiana ICL Rev	Indiana International and Comparative Law Review
IO	International Organization
Iowa L Rev	Iowa Law Review

IRRC	International Review of the Red Cross
Israeli L Rev	Israeli Law Review
Israeli YBHR	Israeli Yearbook of Human Rights
Italian YBIL	Italian Yearbook of International Law
JACL	Journal of Armed Conflict Law
JALC	Journal of Air Law and Commerce
Japanese Annual IL	Japanese Annual of International Law
JCSL	Journal of Conflict and Security Law
JICJ	Journal of International Criminal Justice
J Int'l L & Economics	Journal of International Law and Economics
JTLP	Journal of Transnational Law and Policy
Keesing's	Keesing's Contemporary Archives/Keesing's Record of World Events
LNTS	League of Nations Treaty series
Leiden JIL	Leiden Journal of International Law
Melbourne JIL	Melbourne Journal of International Law
Mercer L Rev	Mercer Law Review
Michigan JIL	Michigan Journal of International Law
Michigan L Rev	Michigan Law Review
Modern L Rev	Modern Law Review
MPYBUNL	Max Planck Yearbook of United Nations Law
Naval L Rev	Naval Law Review
NILR	Netherlands International Law Review
North Carolina JIL Comm Reg.	North Carolina Journal of International Law and Commercial Regulation
Northwestern UNL Rev	Northwestern University Law Review
NYBIL	Netherlands Yearbook of International Law
NYL School JICL	New York Law School Journal of International and Comparative Law
NY Times	New York Times
NYUJILP	New York University Journal of International Law and Politics
OJ	Official Journal of the European Union
Ottawa L Rev	Ottawa Law Review
Pace IL Rev	Pace International Law Review
Penn State IL Rev	Penn State International Law Review
RBDI	Revue Belge de Droit International
RdC	Recueil des Cours
RDMDG	Revue de Droit Militaire et de Droit de la Guerre
REDI	Revista Española de Derecho Internacional
Regent JIL	Regent Journal of International Law

RGDIP	Revue Générale de Droit International Public
RHDI	Revue Hellénique de Droit International
RIAA	Reports of International Arbitral Awards
RQDI	Revue québécoise de Droit International
RSDI	Revue Suisse de Droit International
San Diego ILJ	San Diego International Law Journal
San Diego L Rev	San Diego Law Review
Singapore YBIL	Singapore Yearbook of International Law
South African LJ	South African Law Journal
South African YBIL	South African Yearbook of International Law
Stanford JIL	Stanford Journal of International Law
Stanford L Rev	Stanford Law Review
Stat	United States Statutes at Large
Syracuse L Rev	Syracuse Law Review
SZIER	Schweizerisches Zeitschrift für internationales und europäisches Recht
Temple ICLJ	Temple International and Comparative Law Journal
Texas JIL	Texas Journal of International Law
Texas L Rev	Texas Law Review
Tilburg Foreign L Rev	Tilburg Foreign Law Review
UCLA JILFA	UCLA Journal of International Law and Foreign Affairs
Un Chicago L Rev	University of Chicago Law Review
UNCIO	United Nations Conference on International Organization
Un Pittsburgh L Rev	University of Pittsburgh Law Review
UNTS	United Nations Treaty Series
UNYB	United Nations Yearbook
UST	United States Treaties and Other International Agreements
Valparaiso Un L Rev	Valparaiso University Law Review
Vanderbilt L Rev	Vanderbilt Law Review
Vanderbilt JTL	Vanderbilt Journal of Transnational Law
Villanova L Rev	Villanova Law Review
Virginia JIL	Virginia Journal of International Law
Washington L Rev	Washington Law Review
West Virginia L Rev	West Virginia Law Review
Whittier L Rev	Whittier Law Review
Yale HRDev LJ	Yale Human Rights and Development Law Journal
Yale LJ	Yale Law Journal

YBIHC	Yearbook of International Human Rights Law
YBILC	Yearbook of the International Law Commission
YJIL	Yale Journal of International Law
ZaöRV	Zeitschrift für ausländisches öffentliches Recht und Völkerrecht
ZöR	Zeitschrift für öffentliches Recht

SELECTED CASE LAW, LEGISLATION AND RELATED DOCUMENTS

1. International Case Law (ordered chronologically)

ICJ

ICJ, *Corfu Channel (United Kingdom v. Albania)*, Judgment of 9 April 1949, (1949) ICJ Rep 4–38

ICJ, *Case concerning United States diplomatic and consular staff in Tehran (United States of America v. Islamic Republic of Iran)*, Judgment of 24 May 1980, (1980) ICJ Rep 3–46

ICJ, *Case concerning military and paramilitary activities in and against Nicaragua (Nicaragua v. United States of America)* (Admissibility), Judgment of 26 November 1984 on the jurisdiction of the Court, (1984) ICJ Rep 392

ICJ, *Case concerning military and paramilitary activities in and against Nicaragua (Nicaragua v. United States of America)* (Merits), Judgment of 27 June 1986, (1986) ICJ Rep 14–150

ICJ, *Legality of the threat or use of nuclear weapons*, Advisory opinion of 8 July 1996, (1996) ICJ Rep 226–67

ICJ, *Case concerning the aerial incident of 10 August 1999 (Pakistan v. India)*, Judgment of 21 June 2000, (2000) ICJ Rep 12–35

ICJ, *Case concerning the land and maritime boundary between Cameroon and Nigeria (Cameroon v. Nigeria; Equatorial Guinea intervening)*, Judgment of 10 October 2002, (2002) ICJ Rep 303–458

ICJ, *Case concerning oil platforms (Islamic Republic of Iran v. United States of America)*, Judgment of 6 November 2003, (2003) ICJ Rep 161–219

ICJ, *Legal consequences of the construction of a wall in the Occupied Palestinian Territory*, Advisory Opinion of 9 July 2004, (2004) ICJ Rep 163

ICJ, *Case concerning armed activities on the territory of the Congo (Democratic Republic of the Congo v. Uganda)*, Judgment of 19 December 2005, (2005) ICJ Rep 116–220

ICJ, *Application of the Convention on the Prevention and Punishment of the Crime of Genocide (Bosnia and Herzegovina v. Serbia and Montenegro)*, Judgment of 26 February 2007, reprinted in (2007) 46 ILM 188–310

Arbitration (ordered chronologically)

I'm Alone case (*Canada* v. *United States of America*), (1935) 3 RIAA 1609
Red Crusader case (Commission of Enquiry, *Denmark* v. *United Kingdom*), (1962) 35 ICR 485
Ethiopia–Eritrea Claims Commission, Partial Award *Jus ad Bellum*, Ethiopia Claims 1–8, 19 December 2005, reprinted in (2006) 45 ILM 430
Guyana v. *Suriname*, Arbitral award of 17 September 2007, available at www.pca-cpa.org/upload/files/Guyana-Suriname%20Award.pdf

Other (ordered chronologically)

Judgment of the International Military Tribunal at Nuremberg, (1946) 1 *Trial of German Major War Criminals before the International Military Tribunal*, 208 (1947)
ICTY Appeals Chamber, *Prosecutor* v. *Dusko Tadić*, Decision on the defence motion for interlocutory appeal on jurisdiction, 2 October 1995, reprinted in (1996) 35 ILM 32
ICTY Appeals Chamber, *Prosecutor* v. *Dusko Tadić*, Case No. IT-94-1-A, Judgment of 15 July 1999
ICTY Trial Chamber, *Prosecutor* v. *Furundžija*, Judgment of 10 December 1998, reprinted in (1999) 38 ILM 349
ITLOS, *The M/V 'Saiga' Case (No.2)* (*Saint Vincent and the Grenadines* v. *Guinea*), Judgment of 1 July 1999, (1999) 38 ILM 1323–64

2. Selected practice of the UN bodies

Security Council (ordered chronologically)

SC Res. 38 (1948) of 17 January 1948 (India–Pakistan)
SC Res. 39 (1948) of 20 January 1948 (India–Pakistan)
SC Res. 47 (1948) of 21 April 1948 (India–Pakistan)
SC Res. 51 (1948) of 3 June 1948 (India–Pakistan)
SC Res. 82 (1950) of 25 June 1950 (Korean War)
SC Res. 83 (1950) of 27 June 1950 (Korean War)

SC Res. 84 (1950) of 7 July 1950 (Korean War)
SC Res. 95 (1951) of 1 September 1951 (Israel–Egypt)
SC Res. 101 (1953) of 24 November 1953 (Middle East)
SC Res. 111 (1956) of 19 January 1956 (Lake Tiberias incident)
SC Res. 128 (1958) of 11 June 1958 (Lebanon)
SC Res. 129 (1958) of 7 August 1958 (Middle East)
SC Res. 143 (1960) of 13 July 1960 (Congo)
SC Res. 145 (1960) of 22 July 1960 (Congo)
SC Res. 178 (1963) of 24 April 1963 (Portugal)
SC Res. 188 (1964) of 9 April 1964 (Harib Fort; UK–Yemen)
SC Res. 204 (1965) of 19 May 1965 (Portugal)
SC Res. 233 (1967) of 6 June 1967 (Six Day War)
SC Res. 234 (1967) of 7 June 1967 (Six Day War)
SC Res. 235 (1967) of 9 June 1967 (Six Day War)
SC Res. 236 (1967) of 11 June 1967 (Six Day War)
SC Res. 239 (1967) of 10 July 1967 (Democratic Republic of the Congo)
SC Res. 241 (1967) of 15 November 1967 (Democratic Republic of the Congo)
SC Res. 242 (1967) of 22 November 1967 (Middle East)
SC Res. 248 (1968) of 23 March 1968 (Israel)
SC Res. 252 (1968) of 21 May 1968 (Middle East)
SC Res. 256 (1968) of 16 August 1968 (Israel)
SC Res. 262 (1968) of 31 December 1968 (Israel)
SC Res. 267 (1969) of 3 July 1969 (Middle East)
SC Res. 268 (1969) of 28 July 1969 (Portugal)
SC Res. 273 (1969) of 9 December 1969 (Portugal)
SC Res. 275 (1969) of 22 December 1969 (Portugal)
SC Res. 280 (1970) of 12 May 1970 (Israel)
SC Res. 316 (1972) of 26 June 1972 (Israel)
SC Res. 332 (1973) of 19 April 1973 (Israel)
SC Res. 360 (1974) of 16 August 1974 (Turkey–Cyprus)
SC Res. 393 (1976) of 30 July 1976 (South Africa–Zambia)
SC Res. 403 (1977) of 14 January 1977 (Botswana–Southern Rhodesia)
SC Res. 405 (1977) of 14 April 1977 (Mercenary attacks against Benin)
SC Res. 418 (1977) of 4 November 1977 (South Africa–neighbouring States)
SC Res. 419 (1977) of 24 November 1977 (Benin)
SC Res. 447 (1979) of 28 March 1979 (Angola–South Africa)
SC Res. 450 (1979) of 14 June 1979 (Israel)
SC Res. 454 (1979) of 2 November 1979 (Angola–South Africa)

SC Res. 455 (1979) of 23 November 1979 (Southern Rhodesia–Zambia)
SC Res. 466 (1980) of 11 April 1980 (South Africa–Zambia)
SC Res. 467 (1980) of 24 April 1980 (Israel)
SC Res. 475 (1980) of 27 June 1980 (Angola–South Africa)
SC Res. 479 (1980) of 28 September 1980 (Iran–Iraq War)
SC Res. 487(1981) of 19 June 1981 (Osiraq raid)
SC Res. 496 (1981) of 15 December 1981 (Seychelles)
SC Res. 502 (1982) of 3 April 1982 (Falklands War)
SC Res. 507 (1982) of 28 May 1982 (Seychelles)
SC Res. 508 (1982) of 5 June 1982 (Israel–Lebanon)
SC Res. 509 (1982) of 6 June 1982 (Israel–Lebanon)
SC Res. 527 (1982) of 15 December 1982 (Lesotho–South Africa)
SC Res. 545 (1983) of 20 December 1983 (Angola–South Africa)
SC Res. 546 (1984) of 6 January 1984 (Angola–South Africa)
SC Res. 567 (1985) of 20 June 1985 (Angola–South Africa)
SC Res. 568 (1985) of 21 June 1985 (South Africa–neighbouring States)
SC Res. 571 (1985) of 20 September 1985 (Angola–South Africa)
SC Res. 572 (1985) of 30 September 1985 (Botswana–South Africa)
SC Res. 573 (1985) of 4 October 1985 (Israel)
SC. Res. 574 (1985) of 7 October 1985 (Angola–South Africa)
SC Res. 577 (1985) of 6 December 1985 (Angola–South Africa)
SC Res. 580 (1985) of 30 December 1985 (Lesotho–South Africa)
SC Res. 581 (1986) of 13 February 1986 (South Africa)
SC Res. 598 (1987) of 20 July 1987 (Iran–Iraq War)
SC Res. 602 (1987) of 25 November 1987 (Angola–South Africa)
SC Res. 606 (1987) of 22 December 1987 (Angola–South Africa)
SC Res. 660 (1990) of 2 August 1990 (Iraq–Kuwait)
SC Res. 661 (1990) of 6 August 1990 (Iraq–Kuwait)
SC Res. 662 (1990) of 9 August 1990 (Iraq–Kuwait)
SC Res. 664 (1990) of 18 August 1990 (Iraq–Kuwait)
SC Res. 665 (1990) of 25 August 1990 (Iraq–Kuwait)
SC Res. 670 (1990) of 25 September 1990 (Iraq–Kuwait)
SC Res. 678 (1990) of 29 November 1990 (Iraq–Kuwait)
SC Res. 1177 (1998) of 26 June 1998 (Ethiopia–Eritrea)
SC Res. 1189 (1998) of 13 August 1998 (International terrorism)
SC Res. 1193 (1998) of 28 August 1998 (Afghanistan)
SC Res. 1214 (1998) of 8 December 1998 (Afghanistan)
SC Res. 1226 (1999) of 29 January 1999 (Ethiopia–Eritrea)
SC Res. 1234 (1999) of 9 April 1999 (DRC)
SC Res. 1267 (1999) of 15 October 1999 (Afghanistan)
SC Res. 1304 (2000) of 16 June 2000 (DRC)
SC Res. 1333 (2000) of 19 December 2000 (Afghanistan)

SC Res. 1368 (2001) of 12 September 2001 (9/11 attacks)
SC Res. 1373 (2001) of 28 September 2001 (9/11 attacks and international terrorism)
SC Res. 1438 (2002) of 14 October 2002 (terrorist attacks)
SC Res. 1440 (2002) of 24 October 2002 (terrorist attacks)
SC Res. 1441 (2002) of 8 November 2002 (Iraq)
SC Res. 1450 (2002) of 13 December 2002 (Terrorist attacks)
SC Res. 1465 (2003) of 13 February 2003 (Terrorist attacks)
SC Res. 1516 (2003) of 20 November 2003 (Terrorist attacks)
SC Res. 1530 (2004) of 11 March 2004 (Terrorist attacks)
SC Res. 1540 (2004) of 28 April 2004 (WMD proliferation)
SC Res. 1566 (2004) of 8 October 2004 (Terrorist attacks)
SC Res. 1559 (2004) of 2 September 2004 (Lebanon)
SC Res. 1583 (2005) of 28 January 2005 (Lebanon)
SC Res. 1614 (2005) of 29 July 2005 (Lebanon)
SC Res. 1655 (2006) of 31 January 2006 (Lebanon)
SC Res. 1674 (2006) of 28 April 2006 (Referring to R2P)
SC Res. 1680 (2006) of 17 May 2006 (Lebanon)
SC Res. 1701 (2006) of 11 August 2006 (Israel–Lebanon)
SC Res. 1706 (2006) of 31 August 2006 (Darfur)
SC Res. 1737 (2006) of 23 December 2006 (Iran)
SC Res. 1747 (2007) of 24 March 2007 (Iran)
SC Res. 1776 (2007) of 19 September 2007 (Afghanistan)
SC Res. 1803 (2008) of 3 March 2008 (Iran)
SC Res. 1874 (2009) of 12 June 2009 (North Korea)
SC Res. 1887 (2009) of 24 September 2009 (Nuclear non-proliferation)

General Assembly (ordered chronologically)

GA Res. 377 (V) of 3 November 1950 (Uniting for Peace)
GA Res. 498 (V) of 1 February 1951 (Korean War)
GA Res. 500 (V) of 18 May 1951 (Korean War)
GA Res. 1125 (XI) of 2 February 1957 (UNEF I)
GA Res. 1237 (ES-III) of 21 August 1958 (Middle East)
GA Res. 1514 (XV) of 14 December 1960 (Declaration on the Granting of Independence to Colonial Countries and Peoples)
GA Res. 2131 (XX) of 21 December 1965 (Declaration on the Inadmissibility of Intervention in the Domestic Affairs of States and the Protection of their Independence and Sovereignty)
GA Res. 2625 (XXV) of 24 October 1970 (Friendly Relations Declaration)
GA Res. 2734 (XXV) of 16 December 1970 (Declaration on the Strengthening of International Security)

GA Res. 3070 (XXVIII) of 30 November 1973 (Self-determination)
GA Res. 3246 (XXIX) of 29 November 1974 (Self-determination)
GA Res. 3314 (XXIX) of 14 December 1974 (Definition of Aggression)
GA Res. 3382 (XXX) of 10 November 1975 (Self-determination)
GA Res. 31/34 of 30 November 1976 (Self-determination)
GA Res. 36/27 of 13 November 1981 (Osiraq raid)
GA Res. 36/103 of 9 December 1981 (Declaration on the Inadmissibility of Intervention and Interference in the Internal Affairs of States)
GA Res. 36/172 of 17 December 1981 (South Africa)
GA Res. 37/101 of 14 December 1982 (South Africa–Lesotho)
GA Res. 37/233 of 20 December 1982 (Question of Namibia)
GA Res. 38/7 of 2 November 1983 (US–Grenada)
GA Res. 41/38 of 20 November 1986 (US–Libya)
GA Res. 42/22 of 18 November 1987 (Declaration on the Enhancement of the Effectiveness of the Principle of Refraining from the Threat or Use of Force in International Relations)
GA Res. 44/240 of 29 December 1989 (US–Panama)
GA Res. 46/87 of 16 December 1991 (Self-determination)
GA Res. 47/82 of 16 December 1992 (Self-determination)
GA Res. 48/94 of 20 December 1993 (Self-determination)
GA Res. 49/60 of 9 December 1994 (Declaration on Measures to Eliminate Terrorism)
GA Res. 49/151 of 23 December 1994 (Self-determination)
GA Res. A/RES/ES-10/14 of 8 December 2003 (Palestinian Wall)
GA Res. 60/1 of 16 September 2005 (World Summit Outcome)
GA Res. 60/147 of 16 December 2005 (Basic Principles and Guidelines on the Right to a Remedy and Reparation for Victims of Gross Violations of International Human Rights Law and Serious Violations of International Humanitarian Law)

International Law Commission (ordered chronologically)

ILC, 'Draft Articles on the Law of Treaties with Commentaries', (1966-II) YBILC

ILC, 'Draft Code of Crimes against the Peace and Security of Mankind 1996', (1996-II) YBILC, part two, 26–74.

ILC, 'Commentary on the Draft Articles on the Responsibility of States for Internationally Wrongful Acts', (2001-II) YBILC

ILC, 'Draft Articles on Diplomatic Protection with Commentaries 2006', at http://untreaty.un.org/ilc/texts/instruments/english/commentaries/9_8_2006.pdf

3. Treaties (ordered chronologically)

Hague Convention (I) for the Pacific Settlement of International Disputes, 29 July 1899, 91 BFSP 970; revised 18 October 1907, (1971) UKTS No. 6 (Cmnd. 4575)

Hague Convention (II) Respecting the Limitation of the Employment of Force for the Recovery of Contract Debts, 18 October 1907, (1910) UKTS No. 7 (Cmnd. 5028)

Covenant of the League of Nations, (1919) UKTS No. 4 (Cmnd. 153)

General Treaty for the Renunciation of War, 27 August 1928, 94 LNTS 57

Inter-American Reciprocal Assistance and Solidarity (Act of Chapultepec), Mexico, 6 March 1945, 60 Stat 1831

United Nations Charter and Statute of the International Court of Justice, San Franciso, 26 June 1945, 1 UNTS xvi

Treaty of Friendship and Mutual Assistance between Yugoslavia and Albania, Tirana, 9 July 1946, 1 UNTS No. 15

Inter-American Treaty of Reciprocal Assistance, Rio de Janeiro, 1947, 21 UNTS 77

Charter of the Organization of American States, Bogotá, 30 April 1948 2 UST 2394

North Atlantic Treaty, Washington DC, 4 April 1949, 34 UNTS 243

Australia, New Zealand, United States Security Treaty 1951 (ANZUS), 131 UNTS 83

Treaty of Peace with Japan, San Francisco, 8 September 1951, 136 UNTS No. 1832

Mutual Defence Treaty between the United States and the Republic of China 1954, 248 UNTS 213

Warsaw Security Pact, Warsaw, 14 May 1955, 219 UNTS 25

Treaty of Guarantee, signed between Cyprus, Greece, Turkey and the UK (1960) 382 LNTS 5475

International Covenant on Civil and Political Rights (1966) 999 UNTS 171

International Covenant on Economic, Social and Cultural Rights (1966) 993 UNTS 3

Treaty on the Non-Proliferation of Nuclear Weapons, New York, 1 July 1968, 729 UNTS 161

Vienna Convention on the Law of Treaties, Vienna, 23 May 1969, 1155 UNTS 331

Convention on the Prevention and Punishment of Crimes against Diplomatic Agents and Other Internationally Protected Persons, New York, 14 December 1973, (1977) UNTS No. 15410

Conference on Security and Cooperation in Europe, Helsinki Final Act, Helsinki, 1 August 1975 (1975) 14 ILM 1292

International Convention against the Taking of Hostages, 17 December 1979, GA Res. 34/146 (adopted by consensus), 1316 UNTS 205

UN Convention on the Law of the Sea, Montego Bay, 10 December 1982, 1833 UNTS 31363

Treaty on Conventional Armed Forces in Europe, Paris 19 November 1990, (1991) 30 ILM 1

Rome Statute of the International Criminal Court, Rome, 17 July 1998, UN Doc. A/CONF.183/9, reprinted in (1998) 37 ILM 1002–69

Constitutive Act of the African Union, Lome, 11 July 2000, 2158 UNTS I-37733

4. National case-law (ordered chronologically)

Germany

- Judgment of the Bundesverfassungsgericht of 12 July 1994, translated in (1994) 106 ILR, 320.
- Judgment of the Bundesverwaltungsgericht of 21 June 2005, BVerwG, 2 WD 12.04.

Israel

- Israeli Supreme Court, sitting as High Court of Justice, *Beit Sourik Village Council v. Israel*, Judgment of 30 June 2004, HCJ 2056/04
- Israeli Supreme Court, sitting as High Court of Justice, *Mara'abe v. Prime Minister of Israel*, Judgment of 15 September 2005, HCJ 7957/04
- Israeli Supreme Court, sitting as High Court of Justice, *Bassiouni v. Prime Minister*, Judgment of 30 January 2008, HCJ 9132/07

United Kingdom

- UK Court of Appeal, *Jones, Milling, Olditch, Pritchard and Richards v. Gloucester Crown Prosecution Service*, (2004) EWCA 1981
- UK House of Lords, *R v. Jones*, Judgment of 29 March 2006, (2006) UKHL 16

United States

- US Court of Appeals, District of Columbia Circuit, *El-Shifa Pharmaceutical Industries Co.* v. *United States of America*, 27 March 2009, 559 F.3d 578

5. Selected regional and national materials (ordered chornologically)

African Union

- Solemn Declaration on a Common African Defence and Security Policy, 2nd Extraordinary Session of the African Union, Sirte, 28 February 2004
- African Union Non-Aggression and Common Defence Pact, Abuja, 31 January 2005

Australia

- *Australian Defence Doctrine Publication ADDP 3.10, Evacuation Operations*, April 2004

Canada

- *Canadian Joint Doctrine Manual on Non-Combatant Evacuation Operations*, B-GJ-005-307/FP-050, 16 October 2003

European Union

- European Security Strategy, 'A Secure Europe in a Better World', approved by the European Council on 12 December 2003
- EU General Affairs and External Relations Council, 'Paper for the Submission to the High-Level Panel on Threats, Challenges and Change', 17–18 May 2004

France

- French Ministry of Defence, 'Loi de Programmation militaire 2003–2008', September 2002, Annex, Chapter 3
- Secrétariat Général de la Défense Nationale, *La France face au terrorisme: Livre Blanc du Gouvernement sur la sécurité intérieure face au terrorisme* (Paris: La Documentation française, 2006)

- French Ministry of Defense, Secrétariat Général pour l'administration, *Manuel de droit des conflits armés* (undated), available at www.defense. gouv.fr/defense/enjeux_defense/defense_et_droit/droit_des_conflicts_ ames/manuel_de_droit_des_conflicts_armes,%20at%2045.

Germany

- German Bundestag, 'Gesetz über die parlamentarische Beteiligung bei der Entscheidung bewaffneter Streitkräfte im Ausland', (2005) 1 *Bundesgesetzblatt* 775

Italy

- *Chief of the Italian Defence Staff Strategic Concept*, April 2005

Japan

- Japanese Ministry of Defense, *Defense of Japan 2008*

The Netherlands

- Dutch Ministry of Defence, *Netherlands Defence Doctrine*, 1 September 2005

North Atlantic Treaty Organization

- Statement by the North Atlantic Council, 12 September 2001, NATO Press Release No. 124
- Secretary-General Lord Robertson, Statement of 2 October 2001, reprinted in (2001) 41 ILM 1267
- North Atlantic Council, Prague Summit Declaration, Prague, 21 November 2002, NATO Press Release (2002) 127

Organization of American States

- OAS Council, Adoption of Necessary Measures to Prevent Cuba from Threatening the Peace and Security of the Continent, Resolution of 23 October 1962, Annex A, Doc. OEA/Ser.G/V/C-d-1024 Rev.2
- OAS Meeting of Consultation of Ministers of Foreign Affairs, Terrorist Threat to the Americas, Resolution of 21 September 2001, Doc. OEA/Ser.F/II.24 RC.24/Res.1/01

- OAS Meeting of Consultation of Ministers of Foreign Affairs, Support for the Measures of Individual and Collective Self-defense Established in Resolution RC.24/Res.1/01, 16 October 2001, Doc. OEA/Ser.F/II.24 – CS/TIAR/Res.1/01
- OAS Permanent Council, Convocation of the Meeting of Consultation of Ministers of Foreign Affairs and Appointment of a Commission, 5 March 2008, Doc. OEA/Ser.G, CP.RES.930 (1632/08)
- OAS Meeting of Consultation of Ministers of Foreign Affairs, 'Report of the OAS Commission that visited Ecuador and Colombia', 16 March 2008, Doc. OEA/Ser.F/II.25, RC.25/doc.7/08
- OAS Meeting of Consultation of Ministers of Foreign Affairs, Resolution of 17 March 2008, Doc. OEA/Ser.F/iI.25, RC.25/RES.1/08 rev.1

Organization for Security and Cooperation in Europe

- OSCE Ministerial Council, OSCE Strategy to Address Threats to Security and Stability in the Twenty-First Century, Maastricht, 1–2 December 2003

Russia

- Russian Foreign Ministry, 'Information and press department commentary regarding a Russian media question concerning possible preventive strikes at terrorists' bases', 3 February 2005

Turkey

- Note verbale from the Permanent Mission of Turkey to the Human Rights Council, 26 March 2008, UN Doc. A/HRC/7/G/15

United Kingdom

- UK Ministry of Defence, *Joint Warfare Publication 3-51*, August 2000
- UK Press Release, Office of the Prime Minister, 'Responsibility for the terrorist atrocities in the United States, 11 September 2001', 4 October 2001

United States

- US State Department, 'The legality of United States participation in the defense of Viet-Nam', 4 March 1966, reprinted in (1966) 60 AJIL 564–85

- US Senate and House of Representatives, Joint Resolution concerning the War Powers of Congress and the President, 93rd Congress, 7 November 1973, H.J. Res. 542, Public Law 93–148, 87 Stat 555 (1973)
- US Department of Defence, *Report of the Commission on Beirut International Airport Terrorist Act*, 20 December 1983
- White House, National Security Decision Directive 138, 3 April 1984
- US State Department, 'Statement on the US withdrawal from the ICJ proceedings in *Nicaragua*', 18 January 1985, reprinted in (1985) 24 ILM 246
- White House, National Security Decision Directive 207, 'The National Program for Combatting Terrorism', 20 January 1986
- US Department of the Army, *Field Manual FM 90–29*, 17 October 1994, available at www.globalsecurity.org/military/library/policy/army/fr/90-29/index.html
- US Senate and House of Representatives, Joint Resolution to Authorize the Use of United States Armed Forces against those Responsible for the Recent Attacks launched against the United States, 18 September 2001, reprinted in (2002) 40 ILM 1282
- White House, *National Security Strategy of the United States of America*, Washington DC, 17 September 2002 http://georgewbush-whitehouse.archives.gov/nsc/nss/2002/index.html
- US Senate and House of Representatives, Joint Resolution to Authorize the Use of Military Force against Iraq, 16 October 2002, H.J. Res. 542, Public Law 107–243, 116 Stat 1497–502
- US, National Commission on terrorist attacks upon the United States of America, *The 9/11 Commission Report*, 22 July 2004
- White House, *National Security Strategy of the United States of America*, Washington DC March 2006
- US Joint Chiefs of Staff, *Joint Publication JP 3–68 on Noncombatant Evacuation Operations*, 22 January 2007 www.fas.org/irp/doddir/dod/jp3-68.pdf
- US Department of the Navy and US Department of Homeland Security, *The Commander's Handbook of the Law of Naval Operations*, July 2007, NWP 1–14M
- US Senate, Resolution Condemning Hezbollah and Hamas and their State Sponsors and Supporting Israel's Exercise of its Right to Self-defense, 18 July 2006, 109th Congress, 2nd Session, S. Res. 534
- US House of Representatives, Draft Resolution expressing the Unequivocal Support of the House of Representatives for Israel's Right to Self-defense in the Face of an Imminent Nuclear or Military Threat from Syria, introduced by Mr Wexler and referred to the

Committee on Foreign Affairs, 24 September 2007, 110th Congress, 1st Session, H. Res. 674

6. Other materials (ordered chronologically)

- Adviesraad International Vraagstukken/Advisory Council on International Affairs (AIV), *Pre-emptive action*, Advisory Report No. 36, July 2004, 33 papes
- *San Remo Manual on International Law Applicable to Armed Conflicts at Sea*, 12 June 1994, reproduced in A. Roberts and R. Guelff (eds.), *Documents on the laws of war*, 3rd edn (Oxford University Press, 2000), pp. 573–606
- International Law Association, '*Final Report of the Committee. Statement of Principles applicable to the Formation of General Customary International Law*', Report of the 69th Conference. London (London: ILA, 2000), pp. 712–77
- Report of the International Commission on Intervention and State Sovereignty, '*The Responsibility to Protect*', December 2001, 91 p.
- Institut de Droit International, 'Declaration on the Use of Force', Bruges, 2 September 2003
- Report of the UN Secretary-General's High-level Panel on Threats, Challenges and Change, '*A More Secure World: Our Shared Responsibility*', 2 December 2004, UN Doc. A/59/565
- UN Secretary-General Kofi Annan, 'In Larger Freedom: Towards Development, Security and Human Rights for All', 21 March 2005, UN Doc. A/59/2005
- Institut de Droit International, Tenth Commission – present problems of the use of armed force in international law – self-defence, Provisional Draft of Rapporteur Emmanuel Roucounas and comments', (2007) Ana IDI 67–165
- Institut de Droit International, Tenth Commission – present problems of the use of force in international law – intervention by invitation, Preliminary Draft of Rapporteur Gerhard Hafner and comments, (2007) Ann IDI 227–67
- Institut de Droit International, Tenth Commission – Present Problems of the Use of Armed Force in International Law – Self-Defence, Resolution of 27 October 2007, Santiago available at www.idi-iil.org/idiE/resolutionsE/2007_san02_en.pdf
- *Report of the Independent International Fact-Finding Commission on the Conflict in Georgia*, September 2009

Introduction

On 27 June 1986, the International Court of Justice pronounced its much-anticipated judgment in the *Nicaragua* case. For the first time in its history, it gave a direct and elaborate ruling on issues pertaining to the international law on the use of force (*Ius ad Bellum*), including on the conditions for the exercise of States' right of self-defence. If the Court's approach merits praise for unequivocally affirming that disputes involving the recourse to force are inherently justiciable, it is somewhat puzzling what led the Hague Judges to conclude that '[t]here appears now to be general agreement on the nature of the acts which can be treated as constituting armed attacks', triggering the right of self-defence.[1] Whether it was naïvety, over-confidence or bluff on their part is open to speculation, yet one need not possess the combined legal skills of Grotius and Vattel to understand that it did not completely reflect normative reality.

Indeed, ever since the creation of the United Nations in 1945, scholars have been deeply divided over the purport of Article 51 UN Charter, which enshrines the right of self-defence 'if an armed attack occurs'. Opinions differ as to whether the latter phrase extends to 'protection of nationals' abroad; whether it sanctions defensive measures against small-scale attacks or 'imminent' attacks; whether it permits military action against States engaged in so-called 'indirect aggression', et cetera. The confusion over the 'armed attack' requirement is further compounded by additional sources of controversy, in particular the relationship between Article 51 and the general prohibition on inter-State use of force of Article 2(4) UN Charter, and the relationship between Article 51 and the customary right of self-defence.

Despite this bleak picture, the distinct lack of 'general agreement' proved reasonably manageable for most of the Charter era. A majority

---

[1] ICJ, *Case concerning military and paramilitary activities in and against Nicaragua (Nicaragua v. United States of America)*, (Merits) Judgment of 27 June 1986, (1986) ICJ Rep 14–150, § 195.

of international lawyers consistently stuck to an extensive interpretation of the prohibition on the use of force along with a more or less restrictive reading of self-defence. More importantly, save rare exceptions, States refrained from eroding the scope of Article 51 UN Charter by asserting new or contested applications of the right of self-defence. Most often, whether as a matter of legal conviction or as an effort to minimize exposure to international criticism, States engaging in military intervention abroad stayed on safe legal grounds.[2] When, in spite thereof, controversial legal questions surfaced, States generally circumvented these conundrums, instead focusing on the necessity and proportionality of the interventions under consideration.

The delicate equilibrium that existed was, however, fundamentally disturbed by the 9/11 attacks and their aftermath. All of a sudden, the slumbering academic controversies were pushed to the forefront of public attention. Several countries expressly argued that the Charter rules on the use of force were no longer suitable to deal with 'new' twenty-first century security threats such as transnational terrorism, proliferation of weapons of mass destruction and the collapse of governmental authority in 'failed' or 'failing' States. Military manuals and security doctrines were adapted to integrate a more expansive interpretation of self-defence.[3] International lawyers for their part were anything but insensitive to shifts in customary practice. Some have gone as far as to qualify the US response to the 9/11 attacks (viz. the intervention in Afghanistan and the promulgation of the 'Bush doctrine') as 'instant custom' modifying the existing norms.

Almost a decade later, there now exists a significant amount of subsequent practice and *opinio iuris* that allows us to put into perspective the various claims. These evidentiary elements admittedly affirm that some of the more radical suggestions raised in the immediate aftermath of 9/11 were made on the spur of the moment, without necessarily corresponding to actual changes in the normative groundwork. At the same time, if States recognized in the 2005 World Summit Outcome Document that 'the relevant provisions of the Charter are sufficient to address the full range of threats to international peace and security,' it would seem rather

---

[2] C. Gray, *International law and the use of force*, 3rd edn. (Oxford University Press, 2008), p. 118.
[3] See in particular White House, National Security Strategy of the United States of America, Washington DC, 17 September 2002, available at http://georgewbush-whitehouse.archives.gov/nsc/nss/2002/index.html (accessed 6 May 2009).

naïve to take for granted the status quo. Against this background, the key research question the present study intends to tackle is whether and to what extent recent evolutions have altered the customary boundaries of the right of self-defence, both *de lege lata* and *de lege ferenda*. Has the storm radically changed the landscape of the *Ius ad Bellum*; has it dwindled without doing any damage; or has it merely torn out a few sloping trees?

Since recent controversy has focused first and foremost on various aspects of the 'armed attack' requirement, it is precisely this precondition that is at the centre of our analysis. More specifically, the thesis examines its meaning from a threefold perspective: *ratione materiae*, *ratione temporis*, and *ratione personae*. Each angle raises a different set of thorny interpretative questions. As regards the material aspect, we mainly identify what sort of acts qualify as 'armed attack'; whether there exists a *de minimis* threshold under which no self-defence is permitted; and, if so, whether various small-scale attacks may be 'accumulated' so as to reach this threshold (Chapter 3). The *ratione temporis* aspect addresses the long-standing controversy as to whether self-defence may be exercised only *after* an armed attack has taken place, or whether, and to what extent, such attack may be intercepted or anticipated (Chapter 4). Finally, the *ratione personae* aspect relates to the question from 'whom' the armed attack must emanate in order to trigger the right of self-defence (Chapter 5). Should an armed attack be attributable to a State, or does it equally cover attacks by non-State actors, such as terrorist groups? At the same time, the thesis takes account of the remaining conditions of self-defence, in particular the customary standards of necessity and proportionality (Chapter 2). Because of their inextricable link to the 'armed attack' criterion, a proper understanding of the purport and application of these two standards is indispensable to tackle the questions raised above.

However, it should be noted that this study does not have the ambition to cover the whole area of the *Ius ad Bellum*. Collective security is beyond the scope of our survey, implying that (consensual) peace-keeping and Security Council authorized enforcement action are not considered. Furthermore, of the various modalities of unilateral recourse to force,[4] we will only look at those related to the 'inherent' right of self-defence.

---

[4] This term is hereby understood as covering all enforcement action that is not authorized by the UN Security Council. It includes not only military interventions undertaken by one or more individual States, but also action undertaken by regional arrangements or

Other legal constructions, such as humanitarian intervention, intervention by invitation or pro-democratic intervention, which are sometimes claimed to fall outside the prohibition on the use of force, will not be scrutinized.

Underlying our research are a number of considerations that merit briefly being restated. First, while it is premature to declare the death of Articles 2(4) and 51 UN Charter, the wide variety of challenges to their scope does threaten the 'determinacy' of these rules, i.e., their ability to generate an ascertainable understanding of what is permitted or prohibited.[5] Indeed, the confusion on the shared normative framework renders it increasingly difficult to come to a reasoned consensus on the legality of a particular intervention through the exchange of claims and counter-claims at the international level. The implication is an erosion of the 'compliance pull' of the *Ius ad Bellum*, which can only be remedied by a much-needed clarification of the law.

Second, on a more methodological level, the present thesis starts from the premise that the evolution of the *Ius ad Bellum* is essentially a State-driven process (Chapter 1). Customary practice has a crucial role in clarifying and supplementing the precise content of Article 51 UN Charter, and may inspire evolutions in its interpretation. For this reason, the primary material guiding the analysis consists in the customary practice of States, both concrete – viz. the justificatory discourse pertaining to specific interventions – as well as abstract – viz. general statements on the content of the norms under consideration. Conversely, the case law of the ICJ and legal doctrine are only considered a subsidiary source of interpretation, the evidentiary value of which is reduced by inconsistencies and disagreement.

Third, the various aspects of self-defence, and in particular the different dimensions of the 'armed attack' requirement, are ultimately interlinked and cannot be examined in strict isolation. For example, one cannot scrutinize the debate on anticipatory self-defence without examining the prospective dimension of the necessity standard; nor can one grasp the *de minimis* controversy without at the same time considering the 'accumulation of events' doctrine. Whether one accepts a stricter or more flexible approach to one aspect of self-defence inevitably impacts

---

regional agencies in contravention of Article 53(1) UN Charter (which requires authorization by the Council for such action).

[5] T. M. Franck, *Fairness in international law and institutions* (Oxford: Clarendon Press, 1995), pp. 30–4.

on the desirability or risk of interpreting other aspects in a similar fashion. For this reason, the present thesis tries to make correlations where needed and concludes with a more integrated picture of Article 51 (Chapter 6).

The analysis of relevant customary practice was concluded in December 2009.

1

The methodological debate and the quest for custom

Legal rules are not static, but are capable of evolving over time. This holds all the more true for a multilateral convention such as the UN Charter, which spells out a broad array of open-textured principles intended to regulate the relations between States for an indefinite period of time. The Charter regime indeed constitutes 'a living, growing, and above all discursive system for applying the rules on a reasoned, principled, case-by-case basis'.[1]

In the present chapter, we intend to shed further light on how this process of change operates in relation to the legal regime on the use of force. It may be noted at the outset that several excellent monographs attempt to identify the substance of the present-day *Ius ad Bellum* by analysing relevant state practice and *opinio iuris*, albeit without explaining at much length *why* or *how* (changing) custom influences the law on the use of force. Nonetheless, both issues are of crucial importance. The methodological approach one adopts to a large degree determines the outcome of any inquiry into the substantive content of the law on the use of force.[2] A different approach may lead one author to acknowledge the legality of pre-emptive self-defence or humanitarian intervention, while leading another to reject it. Hence, for the sake of intellectual honesty and academic accuracy, the issue of methodology should not lightly be passed over.

Hereafter, we will first examine the interaction between treaty law and custom in order to understand the impact of customary practice through the distinct processes of interpretation and modification (Section 1.1). Subsequently, we will briefly spell out some considerations in relation to

---

[1] T. M. Franck, *Fairness in international law and institutions* (Oxford: Clarendon Press, 1995), p. 260.
[2] See O. Corten, 'The controversies over the customary prohibition on the use of force: a methodological debate', (2006) 16 EJIL 803–22, at 803.

the identification and assessment of state practice and *opinio iuris* in the field of the *Ius ad Bellum* (Section 1.2).

1.1 Treaty vs. custom

1.1.1 The Charter and pre-existing custom

The obvious starting point for an analysis into the boundaries of self-defence is the ICJ's *Nicaragua* case, which is widely perceived as the Bible of the *Ius ad Bellum* (if now only the Old Testament). *In casu*, the Court for the first time engaged in an in-depth examination of the substantive content of the law on the use of force. At the same time, the judgment is significant from a methodological perspective, since the Court pronounced on the interaction between the Charter and customary law on the use of force. The immediate cause for this was the fact that the United States had adopted a reservation (the so-called 'Vandenberg reservation') which withheld from the Court's jurisdiction 'disputes arising under a multilateral treaty, unless (1) all the parties to the treaty affected by the decision are also parties to the case before the Court, or (2) the [United States] specially agrees to jurisdiction'.[3]

In the US view, the reservation barred the Court from looking into Nicaragua's claims concerning the alleged use of armed force on the grounds that it prohibited the Court from applying any rule of customary international law the content of which was also the subject of provision in the relevant multilateral treaties.[4] Contrary to Nicaragua's position, the US claimed that the Charter provisions and the customary rules were identical, leaving no room for 'other customary and general international law' on which Nicaragua could rest its claims.[5]

The Court, however, refused to follow this line of reasoning.[6] On the one hand, it found that the incorporation of a customary norm into treaty law did not deprive it of its applicability as distinct from that of the treaty norm, *even if the two rules would be completely identical*.[7] On the other hand, the Court disagreed with the United States' view that the two

---

[3] See ICJ, *Case concerning military and paramilitary activities in and against Nicaragua* (*Nicaragua* v. *United States of America* (Merits)), Judgment of 27 June 1986, (1986) ICJ Rep 14–150, § 42.
[4] *Ibid.*, § 173.   [5] *Ibid.*, §§ 173, 187.
[6] ICJ, *Case concerning military and paramilitary activities in and against Nicaragua* (*Nicaragua* v. *United States of America* (Admissibility)), Judgment of 26 November 1984 on the jurisdiction of the Court, (1984) ICJ Rep 392, § 73.
[7] ICJ, *Nicaragua* case (Merits), §§ 177–9.

sources of law necessarily overlapped: 'On a number of points, the areas governed by the two sources of law do not exactly overlap, and the substantive rules in which they are framed are not identical in content.'[8] The Court recognized that the UN Charter by no means covered the whole area of the regulation of the use of force in international relations. It regarded the reference to the 'inherent' character of self-defence in Article 51 UN Charter as an affirmation of the relevance of customary law. It moreover stressed that a definition of 'armed attack' was not provided in the Charter or elsewhere in treaty law, and should therefore be sought in custom. The Court furthermore noted that the criteria of necessity and proportionality were not enshrined in Article 51 UN Charter but formed part of the customary right of self-defence.[9] Last but not least, it considered whether the obligation under Article 51 to report measures taken in self-defence to the Security Council also existed in customary law. Given that this procedure was 'so closely dependent on the content of a treaty commitment and of the institutions established by it', the question was answered in the negative.[10]

Regardless of whether one finds the Court's circumvention of the 'Vandenberg reservation' artificial or not,[11] the *Nicaragua* judgment raises important questions vis-à-vis the overlapping and, more importantly, the possible discrepancies between the Charter provisions and customary international law on the use of force. Indeed, even if it did not explicitly affirm or exclude the existence of *substantive discrepancies* between the two sources of law,[12] the Court's approach acquires particular meaning when tested against the long-standing doctrinal

---

[8] Ibid., §§ 175–6.   [9] Ibid., § 194.   [10] Ibid., § 199.

[11] Remark: the ICJ's disregard for the 'Vandenberg reservation' was one of the reasons why the US withdrew from the case and revoked its acceptance of compulsory jurisdiction. The US Legal Adviser, Judge Sofaer, declared before the Senate Foreign Relations Committee: 'We carefully considered modifying our 1946 declaration as an alternative to its termination, but we concluded that modification would not meet our concerns. No limiting language that we could draft would prevent the Court from asserting jurisdiction if it wanted to take a particular case, as the Court's treatment of our multilateral treaty reservation in the Nicaragua case demonstrates.' The Court's approach was strongly criticized by Judge Schwebel: ICJ, *Nicaragua* case, (Admissibility), Separate opinion of Judge Schwebel, § 88; ICJ, *Nicaragua* case (Merits), Separate opinion of Judge Schwebel, §§ 95–6.

[12] Remark: when referring to customary law to clarify the meaning of the phrase 'armed attack' or to identify the criteria of necessity and proportionality, the Court was clearly not deviating from, but interpreting and supplementing, the Charter regime. The same criteria were used in later judgments in which the Court addressed issues of the *Ius ad Bellum* without being barred from applying the UN Charter. See, e.g., ICJ, *Case*

schism between the so-called 'restrictionist' school and the 'counter-restrictionist' (or 'expansionist') school.

On the one hand, a considerable group of scholars (the 'restrictionists') have consistently argued that the inclusion in the UN Charter of Articles 2 (4) and 51 has left unaffected pre-existing customary law on the use of force.[13] According to these authors, the reference to the 'inherent' nature of self-defence illustrates that Article 51 was only intended to give particular emphasis, *in a declaratory manner*, to self-defence in the case of an armed attack. McDougal, for example, argues that there is 'not the slightest evidence' that the framers of the UN Charter intended to impose new limitations upon the traditional right of self-defence.[14] Rather, the insertion of Article 51 aimed at clarifying the position of collective security arrangements, like the Act of Chapultepec. In this view, the right enshrined in Article 51 UN Charter is merely part of a much broader customary right to self-defence. Regardless of the text of Article 51, these authors claim a right to use force against imminent or non-imminent threats of attack, to protect nationals abroad, to resort to armed reprisals or even to protect economic interests in a foreign country.

It should be observed that this approach is clearly distinct from the one adopted by the parties to the *Nicaragua* case. As mentioned before, the United States proceeded on the basis that there existed a complete identity of the relevant customary rules with the provisions of the Charter.[15] Nicaragua similarly asserted that the rules incorporated in the UN Charter corresponded 'in essentials' to those found in customary

---

concerning armed activities on the territory of the Congo (Democratic Republic of the Congo v. Uganda), Judgment of 19 December 2005, (2005) ICJ Rep 116–220, § 147; ICJ, Case concerning oil platforms (Islamic Republic of Iran v. United States of America), Judgment of 6 November 2003, (2003) ICJ Rep 161–219, § 43. The only real 'discrepancy' between the two sources of law expressly identified in the *Nicaragua* case concerned the existence of a duty to report under Article 51 UN Charter. However, this is merely a procedural obligation, linked to the monitoring of treaty commitments by an institution established by the treaty, rather than a substantive rule.

[13] See for example: D. W. Bowett, *Self-defence in international law* (Manchester University Press, 1958), pp. 187 *et seq.*; J. E. S. Fawcett, 'Intervention in international law: a study of some recent cases', (1961-II) 103 RdC 343–423, at 360 *et seq.*; M. S. McDougal, 'The Soviet–Cuban quarantine and self-defense', (1963) 57 AJIL 597–604, at 599–600; J. N. Moore, 'The secret war in Central America and the future world order', (1986) 80 AJIL 43–127, at 82–3; S. M. Schwebel, 'Aggression, intervention and self-defence in modern international law', (1972-II) 136 RdC 411–97, at 479–83; C. H. M. Waldock, 'The regulation of the use of force by individual states in international law', (1952-II) 81 RdC 451–517, at 496–9.

[14] McDougal, 'The Soviet–Cuban quarantine', 599.

[15] See ICJ, *Nicaragua* case (Merits), § 181.

law.[16] The idea that pre-existing custom has continued to exist *unaltered* alongside the Charter provisions is furthermore hard to reconcile with the Court's opinion that customary international law has developed under the influence of the Charter.[17]

A majority of scholars (the 'counter-restrictionists') reject the parallel subsistence of pre-existing custom diverging from the Charter provisions.[18] Ago, for example, has stressed that 'it is right to dismiss at the outset so unconvincing an idea as that two really divergent notions of self-defence, based respectively on general international law and on the United Nations system, could co-exist'.[19] And according to Dinstein, it 'can be taken for granted that pre-Charter customary international law was swayed by the Charter and that, *grosso-modo*, customary and Charter *Ius ad Bellum* have converged'.[20] Last but not least, in 1966, the International Law Commission observed that 'the great majority of international lawyers today unhesitatingly hold that Article 2, paragraph 4, together with other provisions of the Charter, authoritatively declares the modern customary law regarding the threat or use of force'.[21]

Scholars of the majority group have occasionally discarded the views of the 'restrictionist' group by arguing that they were in reality referring to custom as it existed in the nineteenth century, rather than to custom as it had developed in the period immediately prior to the UN Charter.[22] Brownlie, for example, rejects the anachronistic and 'episodic reference to the *Caroline* incident and the related correspondence of the years

---

[16] Ibid., § 187 iuncto 188. [17] Ibid., §§ 176, 181.
[18] See, *inter alia*: R. Ago, 'Addendum to the 8th Report on State Responsibility', (1980-II) 32 YBILC, Part One, 63; I. Brownlie, 'The principle of non-use of force in contemporary international law', in W. E. Butler (ed.), *The non-use of force in international law* (Dordrecht: Martinus Nijhoff, 1989), pp. 17–27, at 19; I. Brownlie, 'The use of force in self-defence', (1961) 37 BYBIL 183–268, at 239 *et seq.*; A. Constantinou, *The right of self-defence under customary international law and Article 51 of the UN Charter* (Brussels: Bruylant, 2000), p. 204; Y. Dinstein, *War, aggression and self-defence*, 4th edn (Cambridge University Press, 2005), p. 96; T. Gazzini, *The changing rules on the use of force in international law* (Manchester University Press, 2005), pp. 121–2; C. Gray, *International law and the use of force*, 3rd edn (Oxford University Press, 2008), pp. 98–9. For other references, see: A. Randelzhofer, 'Article 51', in B. Simma, in collabaration with H. Mosler, A. Randelzhofer, C. Tomuschat and R. Wolfrüm (eds.), *The Charter of the United Nations: a commentary*. Vol. I (Oxford University Press, 2002), pp. 788–806, at 792, footnotes 24–5; A. Cassese, 'Article 51', in J.-P. Cot and A. Pellet (eds.), *La Charte des Nations Unies*, 3rd edn (Paris: Economica, 2005), pp. 1329–61, at 1336, footnote 4.
[19] Ago, 'Addendum', 63. [20] Dinstein, *War, aggression and self-defence*, p. 96.
[21] ILC, 'Reports of the Commission to the General Assembly', (1966-II) YBILC 247.
[22] See Cassese, 'Article 51', p. 1336.

1838–1842' as proof of the continuing validity of a broad right of anticipatory self-defence during the Charter era.[23] Nonetheless, few have attempted to provide a more theoretical answer to the challenge of pre-existing custom.[24]

In principle, the claim that pre-existing custom has remained valid despite the adoption of the UN Charter could theoretically be founded on two different grounds. First, it could be argued on a general basis that the introduction of the Charter rules on the use of force has left unabridged pre-existing customary rules, even if the latter would seem incompatible with the Charter provisions. According to such view, there would simultaneously exist two *substantially divergent* frameworks for the use of force. A second option would be to argue more specifically that the pre-existing customary right of self-defence was not limited by the introduction of Article 51 of the Charter, since the latter provision explicitly foresees the unimpaired survival of pre-existing custom by stressing the 'inherent' nature thereof. The latter argument hinges on the interpretation of Article 51 and will be examined below in Section 2.1, where we will also take account of the *travaux préparatoires* of the Charter. In the present section, we will focus on the first argument, by briefly examining the normative relationship between the Charter and the customary rules on the use of force.

At the outset, it may be observed that it is as such uncontroversial that, *at the time of its adoption*, the UN Charter did constitute a marked departure from pre-existing custom. This view was expressed by several individual judges in the *Nicaragua* case and finds support among authors in both the aforementioned groups.[25] Indeed, up until the end of the nineteenth century, the predominant conviction was that every State had a customary right, inherent in sovereignty itself, to embark upon war whenever it pleased.[26] While some modest initiatives were taken at the beginning of the twentieth century to impose conventional restrictions, it

---

[23] E.g., Brownlie, 'The principle of non-use of force', p. 19.
[24] Cf. M. H. Mendelson, 'The *Nicaragua* case and customary international law', in Butler (ed.), *The non-use of force*, pp. 85–99.
[25] See for example: ICJ, *Nicaragua* case (Admissibility), Dissenting opinion of Judge Schwebel, § 88. ICJ, *Nicaragua* case (Merits), Dissenting opinion of Judge Jennings, 530–2; Separate opinion of President Singh, 151–3; Separate opinion of Judge Ago, § 6. Also Gray, *The use of force*, p. 6; H. Kelsen, *The law of the United Nations: a critical analysis of its fundamental problems* (London: Stevens, 1950), pp. 108, 110; Mendelson, 'The *Nicaragua* case', p. 91.
[26] E.g., H. W. Briggs, *The law of nations*, 2nd edn (New York: Appleton-Century-Crofts) 1952), p. 976.

was not until the adoption of the Pact of Paris in 1928 [27] that a comprehensive prohibition on the recourse to war came into being. Even if one accepts that the Kellogg–Briand Pact had a significant influence on the practice of States during the interwar period and that it had become part of customary international law by 1945,[28] the fact remains that one of the very aims of the UN Charter was to address some crucial loopholes which the Pact left open and which had become clear with the outbreak of the Second World War.[29] This is illustrated by the inclusion of the much broader prohibition on the threat or use of 'force' (instead of 'war') and the creation of a review procedure for self-defence claims by the UN Security Council. In the end, leaving aside the precise extent to which the Charter codified or 'progressively developed' the pre-existing customary rules, it may safely be assumed that important discrepancies existed between the two.

Starting from this presumption, to what extent did the adoption of the Charter remove contradictory customary rules on the use of force? In order to answer this question, it must first be stressed that the overwhelming majority of authors nowadays agree that there exists no generally established hierarchy between treaty and custom, because both are equivalent expressions of States' (direct or indirect) consent to be bound.[30] This position seems to be supported by the *travaux* of the

---

[27] General Treaty for the Renunciation of War, 27 August 1928, 94 LNTS 57.
[28] See I. Brownlie, *International law and the use of force by States* (Oxford University Press, 1963), pp. 75–80.
[29] E.g., Dinstein, *War, aggression and self-defence*, p. 85; Mendelson, 'The *Nicaragua* case', p. 91.
[30] N. Kontou, *The termination and revision of treaties in the light of new customary international law* (Oxford: Clarendon Press, 1994), p. 20. See *inter alia*: M. Bos, 'The hierarchy among the recognized manifestations ("sources") of international law', (1978) 25 NILR 334–44; I. Brownlie, *Principles of public international law*, 6th edn (Oxford University Press, 2003), p. 5; W. Czaplinski and G. Danilenko, 'Conflicts of norms in international law', (1990) 21 NYBIL 3–42, at 7–8; W. Czaplinski, 'Sources of international law in the *Nicaragua* case', (1989) 38 ICLQ 151–66, at 162–5; N. Q. Dinh, P. Daillier and A. Pellet, *Droit international public*, 7th edn (Paris: Librairie générale de droit et jurisprudence, 2002), p. 114; P.-M. Dupuy, *Droit international public*, 3rd edn (Paris: Dalloz, 1992), pp. 14–16; G. Fitzmaurice, 'Some problems regarding the formal sources of international law', in J. H. W. Verzijl, *Symbolae Verzijl* (The Hague: Martinus Nijhoff, 1958), pp. 153–76, at 173; T. Schweisfurth, *Völkerrecht* (Tübingen: Mohr Siebeck, 2006), p. 83; H. Thirlway, 'The sources of international law', in M. D. Evans (ed.), *International law*, 2nd edn (Oxford University Press, 2006), pp. 115–40, at 133; J. Verhoeven, *Droit international public* (Brussels: Larcier, 2000), p. 337; K. Wolfke, *Custom in present international law*, 2nd edn (Dordrecht: Martinus Nijhoff, 1993) pp. 110 *et seq.*

Advisory Committee of Jurists that drafted Article 38 of the ICJ Statute.[31] *Ergo*, treaties and customary rules are autonomous sources of international law that are equally binding, implying that treaties may in principle derogate from customary rules and vice versa.

Absent the existence of a *lex superior*, and notwithstanding certain exceptions,[32] it is generally accepted that conflicts between the two sources of law must be settled according to the techniques of *lex specialis derogat generali* and *lex posterior derogat priori*.[33] *In casu*, it is obvious that the Charter rules constitute the *lex posterior* in comparison to customary law as it has evolved prior to the Second World War. Those authors stressing the importance of pre-existing custom seem to base their idea on the absence of express statements during the drafting stages of the UN Charter indicating States' intention to depart from pre-existing custom.[34] As such, their position reflects Akehurst's suggestion that there is a presumption against the replacement of customary rules by treaties (and vice versa).[35] Such presumption may well play a role when it comes to interpreting obscurities in conventional rules or to fill the gaps in a treaty regime. However, given the equal normative power of custom and treaty law and the fact that a State cannot simultaneously be bound by contradictory norms, it cannot be upheld when confronted with actual incompatibilities between the two sources of law. Rather, it may be presumed that the parties to a treaty were aware of the existing customary rule, and that through the express statement of a new rule in a text, they intended to exclude other, incompatible customary rules on the same subject matter.[36] In accordance with the *lex posterior*

---

[31] See D. Harris, *Cases and materials on international law*, 5th edn (London: Sweet & Maxwell, 1998), p. 23; Wolfke, *Custom*, pp. 110–12.

[32] Cf. according to Article 103 UN Charter, the obligations of UN Members under the Charter prevail over conflicting obligations under other international agreements. Furthermore, pursuant to Article 53 VCLT, treaties are void if, at the time of their conclusion, they conflict with a peremptory norm of general international law.

[33] E.g., Bos, 'The hierarchy', 337; Czaplinski and Danilenko, 'Conflicts of norms', 8; Dinh, Daillier and Pellet, *Droit international public*, p. 116; Kontou, *The termination and revision of treaties*, pp. 19–20; Schweisfurth, *Völkerrecht*, p. 83; M. N. Shaw, *International law* (Cambridge University Press, 2003), p. 116; A. Verdross and B. Simma, *Universelles Völkerrecht: Theorie und Praxis*, 3rd edn (Berlin: Dunker Humblot, 1984), p. 414.

[34] See, e.g., McDougal, 'The Soviet–Cuban quarantine', 599; Moore, 'The secret war', 82.

[35] M. Akehurst, 'The hierarchy of the sources of international law', (1974–5) 47 *BYBIL* 273–85, at 275.

[36] Bos, 'The hierarchy', 74; Jennings, 'The progressive development of international law and its codification', (1947) 24 *BYBIL* 301–29, at 305; Thirlway, 'The sources of international law', p. 133.

principle, the incompatible customary norms become inapplicable (at least) as long as the treaty is valid.[37] As a result, *for States that ratified the UN Charter after 1945, incompatible rules of pre-existing custom on the recourse to force must be considered to have been abrogated.*[38]

Having determined that incompatible rules of pre-existing custom can no longer apply between parties to the UN Charter, we must now turn to the question whether they continued to apply after 1945 vis-à-vis those States that had not (yet) become Members of the United Nations. Several authors have signalled that the adoption of a treaty derogating from pre-existing custom may constitute 'negative' *opinio iuris*, eroding away the binding nature of the customary rule.[39] Thus, when a multilateral treaty that is partially incompatible with pre-existing custom gains wide acceptance, this may set in motion a gradual erosion of the contradictory custom, due to the fact that it initiates a shift in *opinio iuris* and provides the basis for new directions in State practice.[40] Clearly, there can be no legal limbo whereby non-UN Members would be bound neither by the Charter rules (because they would lack support in State practice) nor by pre-existing custom (due to a lack of *opinio iuris*), thus effectively returning to the nineteenth-century *compétence de guerre*. Hence, the erosion of contradictory custom is inextricably linked to the question whether the Charter rules on the use of force themselves have acquired the status of customary law (or, expressed differently, whether they have modified pre-existing custom so as to remove any incompatibilities

---

[37] E.g., R. Bernhardt, 'Custom and treaty in the law of the sea', (1987-V) 205 *RdC* 251–330, at 271. *A contrario*: J. Combacau and S. Sur, *Droit international public*, 6th edn (Paris: Montchrestien, 2004), p. 72; Wolfke, *Custom*, p. 115; K. Wolfke, 'Some persistent controversies regarding customary international law', (1993) 24 NYBIL 1–16, at 11.

[38] In a similar vein: G. Abi-Saab, 'Cours général de droit international public', (1987-III) 207 RdC 9–463, at 370; T. Christakis, 'Vers une reconnaissance de la notion de guerre préventive?', in K. Bannelier, T. Christakis, O. Corten and P. Klein (eds.), *L'intervention en Irak et le droit international* (Paris: Pedone, 2004), pp. 9–45, at 19, footnote 11; O. Corten, *Le droit contre la guerre; l'interdiction du recours à la force en droit international contemporain* (Paris: Pedone, 2008), p. 623.

[39] E.g., L. Ferrari Bravo, 'Méthodes de recherche de la coutume internationale dans la pratique des Etats', (1985-III) 192 RdC 233–330, at 275–6; M. E. Villiger, *Customary international law and treaties: a manual on the theory and practice of the interrelation of sources*, 2nd edn (The Hague: Kluwer Law International, 1997), p. 160, §§ 243–5.

[40] I. Brownlie, *The rule of law in international affairs: international law at the fiftieth anniversary of the United Nations* (The Hague: Martinus Nijhoff, 1998), p. 28; ILA, *Final Report of the Committee. Statement of principles applicable to the formation of general customary international law*, Report of the 69th Conference London (London: ILA, 2000), pp. 712–77, at 757.

between them). Given the quasi-universal membership of the United Nations and the fact that incompatible pre-existing custom is in any event abrogated *inter partes*, this question might at first sight appear largely irrelevant. Still, it must be recalled that the UN has not always been a quasi-universal organization. Moreover, the issue has practical consequences, for example not only because the customary status of the provisions may entail jurisdictional consequences in certain domestic legal systems, but also because it determines the applicable law after expiry of the conventional rules.

In the end, regardless of the view one takes in respect of the generation of custom on the basis of treaty provisions – whether one accepts the immediate passage of treaties into customary law by virtue of the 'controlling' impact of a treaty text,[41] or to the contrary insists on the need for adequate proof of State practice and *opinio iuris outside of the application of the treaty in question*[42] – it cannot be denied that the evidence in support of the customary status of the Charter provisions on the use of force is overwhelming. First, it is clear that they are of a *'fundamentally norm-creating character, such as could be regarded as forming the basis of a general rule of law'*.[43] Second, the intent to generalize these provisions to third States is clear from Article 2(6) UN Charter. According to this provision, the United Nations shall ensure that non-Members act in accordance with the Principles set out in Article 2 UN Charter, so far as may be necessary for the maintenance of international peace and security. Another indication of universality is provided by the inclusion of the Charter prohibition on the use of force and/or the rule enshrined in Article 51 UN Charter in numerous instruments, such as the Inter-American Treaty of Reciprocal Assistance (1947), the OAS Charter (1948), the North Atlantic Treaty (1949), the Helsinki Final Act (1975),

---

[41] A. D'Amato, *The concept of custom in international law* (Ithaca, NY: Cornell University Press, 1971), p. 110.
[42] R. R. Baxter, 'Treaties and customs', (1970-I) 129 RdC 27–105, at 64 *et seq.*; G. M. Danilenko, *Law-making in the international community* (Dordrecht: Martinus Nijhoff, 1993), pp. 154, 158 *et seq.*; See also J.-M. Henckaerts and L. Doswald-Beck, *Customary international humanitarian law.* Vol. 1 (Cambridge University Press, 2005), p. xliv; ILA, *The formation of general customary international law*, p.758; O. Schachter, 'Entangled treaty and custom', in Y. Dinstein (ed.), *International law at a time of perplexity: essays in honour of Shabtai Rosenne* (Dordrecht: Martinus Nijhoff, 1989), pp. 717–38, at 718, 725.
[43] ICJ, *North Sea Continental Shelf (Federal Republic of Germany v. Denmark and the Netherlands)*, Judgment of 20 February 1969, (1969) ICJ Rep 3, § 72 (emphasis added).

the Constitutive Act of the African Union (2000), et cetera.[44] Furthermore, relevant *opinio iuris* can be found in individual statements by State representatives acknowledging the customary status of Article 2 (4) UN Charter.[45] Such statements were *inter alia* made by the United States, both during the *Nicaragua* proceedings and on other occasions.[46] Significantly, similar declarations have also been made by States that were not (yet) UN Members. Thus, both German States accepted the principles of the Charter before becoming members of the UN.[47] In addition, the Charter provisions relating to inter-State recourse to force were incorporated in several bilateral and multilateral treaties with non-Member States such as the 1951 Treaty of Peace with Japan,[48] or the 1946 Treaty of Friendship and Mutual Assistance between Yugoslavia and Albania.[49]

Important evidence can also be distilled from a number of UNGA resolutions reaffirming the applicability of the Charter provisions on the use of force to '*all* States'.[50] Of particular relevance is the 'Friendly Relations Declaration', adopted in 1970 without a vote.[51] This resolution

---

[44] Articles 1 and 3(1), Inter-American Treaty of Reciprocal Assistance, Rio de Janeiro, 1947, 82 UNTS 330; Article 22, Charter of the Organization of American States, Bogotá, 2 UST 2394, at 2420; Articles 1 and 5, North Atlantic Treaty, Washington DC, 4 April 1949, 34 UNTS 243; Conference on Security and Cooperation in Europe, Helsinki Final Act, Helsinki, 1 August 1975 (1975) 14 ILM 1292; Article 4(f), Constitutive Act of the African Union, Lome, 11 July 2000, 2158 UNTS I-37733.

[45] See ICJ, *Nicaragua* case (Merits), § 190.

[46] *Ibid.*, § 187; M. M. Whiteman, *Digest of international law*. Vol. 12 (Washington DC: US Department of State Publications, 1968), p. 122.

[47] See Czaplinski, 'The *Nicaragua* case', 157.

[48] Treaty of Peace with Japan, San Francisco, 8 September 1951, 136 UNTS 1832, Article 5. Japan only became a UN Member in 1956.

[49] Treaty of Friendship and Mutual Assistance between Yugoslavia and Albania, Tirana, 9 July 1946, 1 UNTS 15. Albania only acceded to the UN in 1955. Remark: for other examples, see Brownlie, *The use of force by States*, Appendix II, pp. 127–9.

[50] E.g., Definition of Aggression, Annex to GA Res. 3314 (XXIX) of 14 December 1974 (according to Article 1, the term 'State' in the definition is used 'without prejudice to questions of recognition or to whether a State is a [UN] member'.); Declaration on the Inadmissibility of Intervention in the Domestic Affairs of States and the Protection of their Independence and Sovereignty, GA Res. 2131 (XX), 21 December 1965; Declaration on the Strengthening of International Security, GA Res. 2734 (XXV), 16 December 1970; Declaration on the Inadmissibility of Intervention and Interference in the Internal Affairs of States, GA Res. 36/103, 9 December 1981.

[51] Declaration on Principles of International Law concerning Friendly Relations and Cooperation among States in accordance with the Charter of the United Nations, GA Res. 2625 (XXV), 24 October 1970 (1970) UNYB 787.

aims at proclaiming and elaborating seven basic principles of international law. The first principle copies the wording of Article 2(4) UN Charter, yet deliberately replaces the reference to 'all Members' by the phrase 'every State'. The resolution recognizes that 'nothing in the foregoing paragraphs shall be construed as enlarging or diminishing in any way the scope of the provisions of the Charter concerning cases in which the use of force is lawful'. In the *Nicaragua* case, the ICJ recognized that the 'Friendly Relations Declaration' was not merely a reiteration or elucidation of the treaty commitments undertaken in the Charter, but reflected *opinio iuris* in support of a customary rule prohibiting the threat or use of force in inter-State relations.[52]

Another important resolution, again adopted without a vote, is the 1987 Declaration on the Enhancement of the Effectiveness of the Principle of Refraining from the Threat or Use of Force in International Relations.[53] Apart from reproducing the prohibition on the use of force in the same way as the 'Friendly Relations Declaration', this resolution states that the principle is 'universal in character and is binding, regardless of each State's political, economic, social or cultural system or relations of alliance', while adding that States have 'the inherent right of individual or collective self-defence if an armed attack occurs, *as set forth in the Charter*'.[54]

Furthermore, in light of the difficulty of obtaining evidence of State practice of non-parties in relation to treaties that have been ratified quasi-universally,[55] the Final Report of the ILA Committee on the formation of customary law acknowledges that there may be exceptional situations where multilateral treaties may, 'of their own impact' give rise to new customary rules – as suggested in *North Sea Continental Shelf* – 'provided that it is their clear intention to accept more than a merely conventional norm'.[56] While stressing that such cases will be rare, the

---

[52] ICJ, *Nicaragua* case (Merits), § 188. According to Cassese, the Friendly Relations Declaration provided 'the final indication of a gradual transformation of Article 2(4) into a general rule of international law'. A. Cassese, *International law in a divided world* (Oxford: Clarendon Press, 1986), pp. 137–8.
[53] Declaration on the Enhancement of the Effectiveness of the Principle of Refraining from the Threat or Use of Force in International Relations, GA Res. 42/22, 18 November 1987.
[54] *Ibid.*, §§ 2, 13 (emphasis added).
[55] On the so-called 'Baxter paradox', see Baxter, 'Treaties and customs', 64; H. Thirlway, *International customary law and codification: an examination of the continuing role of custom in the present period of codification of international law* (Leiden: Sijthoff, 1972), pp. 90–1; Villiger, *Customary international law and treaties*, p. 155.
[56] ILA *The formation of general customary international law*, p. 763.

Committee specifies that: 'One such example is probably ... Article 2(4) of the UN Charter'.[57]

In the end, on the basis of our previous considerations, a number of conclusions seem warranted. First, in accordance with the equal normative power of treaty and customary law and the *lex posterior* principle, incompatible rules of pre-existing custom have been abrogated after 1945 as for the Members of the United Nations. Second, as the ILC[58] as well as the overwhelming majority of international lawyers affirm, the prohibition on the threat or use of force, enshrined in Article 2(4) UN Charter, must be considered an integral part of customary international law, binding upon UN Members and non-Members alike.[59] Insofar as pre-existing custom was substantially different from the content of Article 2(4), it was modified subsequent to the adoption of the Charter. Third, Article 51 UN Charter has likewise acquired customary status,[60] and excludes the preservation of a customary right of self-defence incompatible with the Charter framework. Some of the proponents of a broad reading of self-defence implicitly recognize this by arguing that pre-existing custom continues to exist 'except in so far as obligations inconsistent with those existing rights are assumed under the Charter'.[61] Hence, the crucial question is what interpretation should be given to the terms of Article 51 UN Charter, in particular the reference to the 'inherent' nature of self-defence and the controversial phrase 'if an armed attack occurs' (this is dealt with in Section 2.1). As with Article 2(4) UN Charter, pre-existing custom relating to self-defence must be

---

[57] Ibid.

[58] According to the ILC: 'The great majority of international lawyers today unhesitatingly hold that Article 2, paragraph 4, together with other provisions of the Charter, authoritatively declares the modern customary law regarding the threat or use of force.' ILC, 'Reports of the Commission to the General Assembly', 247.

[59] E.g., American Law Institute, *Restatement of the law – Third. The Foreign Relations Law of the United States* (St. Paul, MN: American Law Institute Publishers, 1990), p. 382; M. Bossuyt and J. Wouters, *Grondlijnen van internationaal recht* (Antwerp: Intersentia, 2005), p. 517; Cassese, *International law in a divided world*, pp. 137–8; Dinstein, *War, aggression and self-defence*, p. 92; ILA *The formation of general customary international law*, p.757; P. Malanczuk and M. Akehurst, *Akehurst's modern introduction to international law*, 7th edn (London: Routledge, 1997), p. 309; M. N. Shaw, *International law*, 4th edn (Cambridge University Press, 1997), p. 781.

[60] E.g., American Law Institute, *The Foreign Relations Law of the United States*, p. 382; ILA, *The formation of general customary international law*, p.757; ILC, 'Reports of the Commission to the General Assembly', 247.

[61] Bowett, *Self-defence in international law*, pp. 184–5. In a similar vein: Schwebel, 'Aggression, intervention and self-defence', 480.

THE METHODOLOGICAL DEBATE AND THE QUEST FOR CUSTOM 19

considered modified insofar as it contradicts the outcome of this interpretation process.

In sum, the idea that the adoption of the UN Charter gave rise to the parallel existence of two *substantially divergent* tracks for the international law on the use of force (one Charter-based, the other custom-based) is artificial and theoretically unsustainable.[62] We may thus rephrase the statement by Dinstein previously cited as follows: it can be taken for granted that pre-Charter customary international law is swayed by the Charter *insofar as it is incompatible with (the interpretation of) the Charter rules on the use of force*, and that, *grosso modo*, customary and Charter *Ius ad Bellum* have converged.[63] If this implies that the Charter provisions provide our point of departure in any case, it does not necessarily mean that custom (or better: custom extraneous to the Charter provisions) has no role to play whatsoever. Indeed, as pointed out in *Nicaragua*, the Charter by no means covers the whole area of the regulation of the use of force in international relations.[64] Custom plays an important supplementary role in interpreting its provisions. Moreover, if post-Charter State practice and *opinio iuris* gradually turn away from the actual content of these provisions, this could possibly result in a modification of the law on the use of force. Both aspects – interpretation and modification – require further examination.

1.1.2 The role of custom in treaty interpretation and modification

1.1.2.a Interpretation

The interpretation of treaties does not take place in a normative vacuum, but is influenced by other relevant rules of international law. Today Article 31(3)(c) VCLT explicitly recognizes that 'any relevant rules of international law applicable in the relations between the parties' 'shall be taken into account'. Unlike the supplementary means of Article 32 VCLT, these rules form part of the mandatory interpretation process. The wording covers all sources of international law, including general principles, other treaty law, as well as custom.

---

[62] E.g., Ago, 'Addendum', 63; Constantinou, *The right of self-defence*, p. 54; Gazzini, *The changing rules*, pp. 120–1.
[63] See Dinstein, *War, aggression and self-defence*, p. 96.
[64] ICJ, *Nicaragua* case (Merits), § 176.

The ILC admits that, in principle, there would be no room to refer to other rules of international law unless the treaty itself gave rise to a problem in its interpretation.[65] Reference to customary international law is considered of particular relevance especially where the treaty rule is unclear or open-textured and its meaning can be determined by reference to a developed body of international law, or where the terms used in the treaty have a recognized meaning in customary international law, to which the parties can therefore be taken to have intended to refer.[66] Obviously, Article 31(3)(c) not only applies to 'relevant rules' with a different substantive content, but *a fortiori* permits the reference to customary rules that partially overlap with the treaty provision requiring interpretation.[67]

A related, but more controversial, aspect of treaty interpretation concerns the question whether the 'relevant rules' are those applicable at the time the treaty was adopted, or whether one should rather look at the normative climate at the time of interpretation. Originally, the draft of Article 31(3)(c) VCLT, proposed by Waldock in 1964, referred to 'the rules of international law *in force at the time of the conclusion of the treaty*'.[68] This approach is in line with the traditional principle of contemporaneity in treaty interpretation, as famously espoused by Judge Huber in the *Island of Palmas* arbitration.[69] However, other members of the ILC as well as a number of governments criticized Waldock's proposal for being overly restrictive.[70] Eventually, the Commission decided to omit a reference to the temporal element and amended the Article accordingly.

---

[65] ILC, Report of the 56th session, 2004, UN Doc. A/59/10, § 347.

[66] Report of the Study Group of the International Law Commission, Fragmentation of International Law: Difficulties Arising from the Diversification and Expansion of International Law, 13 April 2006, UN Doc. A/CN.4/L.682, § 467; ILC, Report of the 57th session, 2005, UN Doc. A/60/10, § 471. D. French, 'Treaty interpretation and the incorporation of extraneous legal rules', (2006) 55 ICLQ 281–314, at 303–4; C. McLachlan, 'The principle of systematic integration and Article 31(3)(c) of the Vienna Convention', (2005) 54 ICLQ 279–320, at 312.

[67] I. Sinclair, *The Vienna Convention on the Law of Treaties*, 2nd edn (Manchester University Press, 1984), p. 258.

[68] H. Waldock, 'Third Report on the Law of Treaties', (1964-II) YBILC 5–65, at 52 (emphasis added).

[69] PCA, *The Island of Palmas Case (or Miangas) (United States of America v. The Netherlands)*, Award of 4 April 1928, (1928) 2 RIAA 829, at 845: 'a juridical fact must be appreciated in the light of the law contemporary with it, and not of the law in force at the time when a dispute in regard to it arises or falls to be settled.'

[70] ILC, 'Draft Articles on the Law of Treaties with Commentaries', (1966-II) YBILC 222.

A rigid application of the principle of contemporaneity is nowadays rejected by judicial practice. In the *Namibia* case, for instance, the ICJ held that the interpretation of the treaty under consideration could not remain unaffected 'by the subsequent development of law, through the Charter of the United Nations and by way of customary law'.[71] Particularly explicit is the statement by the Arbitral Tribunal in the *Iron Rhine* arbitration that 'an evolutive interpretation, which would ensure an application of the treaty that would be effective in terms of its object and purpose, will be preferred to a strict application of the intertemporal rule'.[72] This was considered particularly important when the treaty was not intended as a treaty of limited or fixed duration.[73]

In the end, while caution is needed, subsequent developments in the law may be taken into account *if* it can be established that the parties to the treaty so intended.[74] Concrete evidence of this intention can be found in the material sources referred to in Articles 31 and 32 VCLT, namely the text itself, the context, the object and purpose, or, where necessary, the *travaux préparatoires*.[75] In particular, judicial practice suggests that the treaty language itself may sometimes create a presumption in favour of evolutive interpretation,[76] for example, when it uses a term which is not static but evolutionary,[77] or when the treaty sets up an obligation for further progressive development for the parties.[78] This presumption also

---

[71] ICJ, *Legal consequences for States of the continued presence of South Africa in Namibia (South West Africa) notwithstanding Security Council Resolution 276 (1970)*, Advisory opinion of 21 June 1971, (1971) ICJ Rep 16–66, § 53. Also, e.g., ICJ, *Case concerning the Gabčíkovo-Nagymaros Project (Hungary v. Slovakia)*, Judgment of 25 September 1997, (1997) ICJ Rep 7–84, § 112.

[72] Arbitration regarding the Iron Rhine ('Ijzeren Rijn') Railway (Belgium v. The Netherlands), Award of 24 May 2005, 27 RIAA 35–125, §§ 79–81.

[73] *Ibid.*, § 82.

[74] E.g., H. Thirlway, 'The law and procedure of the International Court of Justice 1960–1989', (1990) 61 BYBIL 1–133, 57. See also the comments made by Jimenéz de Aréchaga in the ILC in 1964: 'Law of Treaties' (1964-I) YBILC 34, § 10; Institut de Droit International, The Intertemporal Problem in Public International Law, Resolution of 11 August 1975, Wiesbaden, at § 4, available at www.idi-iil.org/idiE/resolutionsE/1975_wies_01_en.pdf (accessed 15 April 2009).

[75] ILC, Report of the 57th session, 2005, UN Doc. A/60/10, § 474.

[76] See ILC, Report of the ILC Study Group, Fragmentation of International Law, § 478; C. McLachlan, 'Systematic integration and Article 31(3)(c) of the Vienna Convention', 299, 317.

[77] E.g., ICJ, *Namibia* case, § 53; ICJ, *Agean Sea Continental Shelf* case (Greece v. Turkey), Judgment of 19 December 1978, (1978) ICJ Rep 3–45, § 77.

[78] E.g., ICJ, *Gabčíkovo-Nagymaros Project* case, § 112.

covers the description of obligations in very general terms that must take account of changing circumstances.[79]

Turning back to the Charter rules on the use of force and recalling the ICJ's finding that these provisions by no means cover the whole of the *Ius ad Bellum*, custom clearly is of crucial importance in tackling the lacunae and ambiguities left open by the Charter. Such use of custom for purposes of treaty interpretation is undisputed. Furthermore, a strong case can be made in favour of an evolutive approach to interpretation. Apart from the lack of a fixed duration of the Charter or the fact that a dynamic interpretation was already envisaged during the San Francisco Conference,[80] one can point to the very general nature of the obligation enshrined in Article 2(4) UN Charter, or the inclusion of general notions, such as the 'use of force' or 'armed attack', which were not defined in the Charter itself but must be qualified by reference to the broader normative context. This means *inter alia* that whereas the meaning of 'armed attack' must be sought in customary international law, one should not stick to a static interpretation of the concept as it may have stood in 1945, but must pay attention to evolutions in State practice and *opinio iuris* subsequent to the adoption of the UN Charter.

1.1.2.b   Modification

Having established that relevant custom may be used for the (evolutive) interpretation of the Charter provisions on the use of force, we still need to ascertain whether it constitutes a valid mechanism for *modification* of the latter rules. Indeed, as the ILC acknowledges, interpretation and modification of a treaty are two distinct legal processes:[81] contrary to modification, authentic interpretation does not in principle alter the legal rights or obligations enshrined in the treaty provisions. Moreover, while authentic interpretation in principle operates retroactively, modification normally only generates consequences for the future.[82]

---

[79] See ILC, Report of the ILC Study Group, Fragmentation of International Law, § 478; C. McLachlan, 'Systematic integration and Article 31(3)(c) of the Vienna Convention', 299, 317.

[80] See G. Ress, 'Interpretation', in B. Simma *et al.* (eds.), *The Charter of the United Nations*, pp. 13–32, at 24–5.

[81] ILC, 'Draft Articles on the Law of Treaties with Commentaries', 236. See also: G. Scelle, *Théorie juridique de la revision des traits* (Paris: Sirey, 1936), p. 11.

[82] See, e.g., S. Sur, *L'interprétation en droit international public* (Paris: Librairie générale de droit et de jurisprudence, 1974), p. 202; M.K. Yasseen, 'L'interprétation des traités d'après la Convention de Vienne sur le droit des Traités', (1976-III) 151 RdC 1–114, at 47, 52.

At the outset, it should be emphasized that in practice no sharp division exists between interpretation and modification. The key criterion is (in)compatibility: if the customary norm and the treaty provision can be applied simultaneously, then this falls within the scope of interpretation.[83] If, however, a conflict between the two normative contents arises, so that a choice must be made between them, then we leave the realm of interpretation and enter that of modification. Determining whether a situation of incompatibility exists is itself a matter of interpretation, which may give rise to diverging views among different interpreters.[84] In this regard, one must take account of the aforementioned possibility of dynamic treaty interpretation and of the fact that a treaty term may possess many 'ordinary meanings'. Modification can arguably be defined as the situation where the new rule cannot be fit into *any* of the plausible meanings that could be given to the treaty text, nor into the special meaning which the parties intended to give to the text at the time of its adoption. The picture that emerges is that of an interpretive continuum, whereby parties may, in their interpretation, gradually wander from the original text and intention towards adjusting or updating the content, and, eventually, to the creation of a new rule through modification.[85]

While modification of treaties by subsequent custom was originally explicitly foreseen in the 1964 draft Convention on the Law of Treaties, this reference was removed from later drafts.[86] Several States suggested that the matter should be omitted because they foresaw difficulties in determining the precise moment at which a customary rule arose, or because they considered the issue to reside outside the scope of the law of treaties.[87] This, however, does not necessarily evidence genuine opposition to the rule itself. To the contrary, a number of States expressly or

---

[83] ILC, 'Conclusions of the work of the Study Group on the Fragmentation of International Law: difficulties arising from the diversification and expansion of international law', included in ILC, Report of the 58th session, 2006, UN Doc. A/61/10, 407-8. See F. Capotorti, 'L'extinction et la suspension des traités', (1971-III) 134 RdC 417-587, at 517; Sur, *L'interprétation en droit international public*, p. 209; Villiger, *Customary international law and treaties*, p. 205.

[84] ILC, Report of the ILC Study Group, Fragmentation of International law, § 412.

[85] French, 'Treaty interpretation', 283; Villiger, *Customary international law and treaties*, p. 213.

[86] ILC, 'Draft Articles on the Law of Treaties', (1964-II) YBILC 198 (Art. 68). Cf. ILC, 'Draft Articles on the Law of Treaties with Commentaries', 236 (Art. 38); Articles 39 *et seq.* VCLT, Vienna, 23 May 1969, 1155 UNTS 331.

[87] See Villiger, *Customary international law and treaties*, p. 195.

implicitly affirmed that subsequent custom may modify treaties.[88] Today, most scholars accept the possibility of treaty modification as a result of the emergence of incompatible custom.[89] This view is consistent with the equal normative power of treaty and customary law and the application of the *lex posterior* axiom,[90] and has on occasion been confirmed by judicial practice.[91]

On the other hand, given the gradual and unpredictable development of customary law, as well as the fact that treaties normally provide for their formal revision or denunciation, it is usually emphasized that this form of modification should remain an exception.[92] Several authors even argue there is a presumption against such process and claim it can only take place if there is clear evidence that the parties so intended.[93] Express statements to this end will evidently provide the clearest evidence. Explicit objections to breaches of the conventional rules will avert or retard the process.[94] Still, express statements are not indispensable. In accordance with their equal normative status, when a multilateral treaty provision is clearly incompatible with a subsequent rule of general custom, which is supported by generally consistent State practice and corresponding *opinio iuris*, modification will in principle result.[95]

In relation to the Charter provisions on the use of force, a second hurdle should moreover be identified. Indeed, there is credible support for the view that the Charter provisions on the use of force are not merely

---

[88] *Ibid.*
[89] Danilenko, *Law-making*, pp. 165 *et seq.*; Kontou, *The termination and revision of treaties*, p. 36; Thirlway, *International customary law and codification*, p. 131; Villiger, *Customary international law and treaties*, pp. 196, 203 *et seq.* See also: ILC, Report of the ILC Study Group, 'Fragmentation of international law', § 224. Akehurst, 'The hierarchy of the sources', 276; Czaplinski and Danilenko, 'Conflicts of norms', 37-9.
[90] Capotorti, 'L'extinction et la suspension des traités', 516; Kontou, *The termination and revision of treaties*, pp. 19-20, 23-4; Villiger, *Customary international law and treaties*, pp. 206-7.
[91] *Delimitation of the Continental Shelf between the United Kingdom of Great Britain and Northern Ireland, and the French Republic (United Kingdom v. France)*, Arbitral Decision of 30 June 1977, 18 RIAA 3, § 47. See also ICJ, *Fisheries Jurisdiction* case (*United Kingdom v. Iceland*), Judgment of 25 July 1974, (1974) ICJ Rep 3-44, §§ 49-54.
[92] See Danilenko, *Law-making*, pp. 162-5.
[93] Akehurst, 'The hierarchy of the sources', 275-6; Czaplinski and Danilenko, 'Conflicts of norms', 40; Danilenko, *Law-making*, pp. 169-70; Kontou, *The termination and revision of treaties*, pp. 28-9, 145-6.
[94] Villiger, *Customary international law and treaties*, p. 211.
[95] See *Ibid.*, §§ 343-5. Also: Danilenko, *Law-making*, p. 170; Kontou, *The termination and revision of treaties*, pp. 146-8.

part of customary international law, but are also part of *ius cogens*. Article 53 VCLT describes the latter concept as referring to norms 'accepted and recognized by the international community of States as a whole as a norm from which no derogation is permitted and which can be modified only by a subsequent norm of general international law having the same character'. Admittedly, it is not possible to make a conclusive assessment of the peremptory character of the Charter rules on the use of force on the basis of Article 53 VCLT as such: the definition provides no simple objective criteria for identifying *ius cogens* and encloses a disturbing degree of circularity. Still, it is striking that while the ILC thought it undesirable to draw up a list of examples of peremptory norms, it pointed out that 'the law of the Charter concerning the prohibition of the use of force' constitutes 'a conspicuous example' of such a norm.[96] The ICJ quoted this statement in the *Nicaragua* case,[97] putting the argument in a 'seemingly favourable light'.[98] The peremptory character of the prohibition was moreover subscribed to by several individual judges of the ICJ.[99] In a similar vein, various States have explicitly lent support to this view in the course of the *travaux pré paratoires* of the Vienna Convention on the Law of Treaties[100] and the ILC Draft Articles on State Responsibility,[101] and on other occasions.[102] Further evidence can be found in several other national and international

---

[96] ILC, 'Draft Articles on the Law of Treaties with Commentaries', 247–8.
[97] ICJ, *Nicaragua* case (Merits), § 190.
[98] I. D. Seiderman, *Hierarchy in international law: the human rights dimension* (Antwerp: Intersentia, 2001), p. 61.
[99] ICJ, *Nicaragua* case (Merits), Separate opinion of Judge Singh, 153; Separate opinion of Judge Sette-Camara, 199. ICJ, *Oil Platforms* case, Separate opinion of Judge Simma, § 9; Separate opinion of Judge Kooijmans, § 44; Dissenting opinion of Judge Elaraby, 291. ICJ, *Legal Consequences of the construction of a wall in the occupied Palestinian territory*, Advisory opinion of 9 July 2004, (2004) ICJ Rep 163, Separate opinion of Judge Elaraby, § 3.1.
[100] See for instance: (1966-II) YBILC 285 (Cyprus); (1966- II) YBILC 354 (US). See also: UN, *Conférence sur le droit des traités. Deuxième session. Vienne, 9 avril–22 mai 1969* (New York: United Nations) (1970), 96, § 66 (Ecuador); 102, § 26 (the Federal Republic of Germany); 103, § 42 (Cuba); 112, § 48 (Belarus). For other examples, see Sinclair, *The Vienna Convention*, p. 218.
[101] See for instance UN Doc. A/CN.4/488, 138 (Czech Republic); UN Doc. A/C.6/35/SR.51, § 62 (Iraq); UN Doc. A/C.6/35/SR.53, § 51 (Jamaica).
[102] E.g., remarks of Nicaragua and the US in the *Nicaragua* case (Merits), § 187. For other references, see L. Hannikainen, *Peremptory norms (jus cogens) in international law. Historical development, criteria, present status* (Helsinki: Lakimiesliiton Kustannus, 1988), p. 324, footnote 3.

judgments.[103] Not insignificantly, another corollary of *ius cogens* norms, namely the non-recognition of situations created by a serious breach of a peremptory norm,[104] has received ample support in important General Assembly resolutions affirming that no territorial acquisition resulting from the threat or use of force shall be recognized as legal.[105]

Some authors reserve the *ius cogens* qualification for the prohibition of 'aggression',[106] while others – probably the large majority – extend it to the prohibition on the use of force (Article 2(4)),[107] or to the Charter provisions on the use of force as a whole, including *both* Article 2(4) and Article 51 (the right to self-defence).[108] The former position does not always appear to reflect a conscious distinction, yet some scholars do argue that the peremptory character is confined to an established 'hard core', limited to those instances of inter-State force amounting to 'aggression'.[109] This approach is founded primarily on the idea that violations in

---

[103] US Court of Appeals, District of Columbia Circuit, *Committee of US Citizens Living in Nicaragua v. Reagan*, 14 October 1988, 859 F.2d 929, at 941; Judgment of the Bundesverwaltungsgericht of 21 June 2005, BVerwG, 2 WD 12.04; ICTY Trial Chamber, *Prosecutor v. Furundžija*, Judgment of 10 December 1998, reprinted in (1999) 38 ILM 349, § 147.

[104] ILC, 'Commentary on the Draft Articles on the Responsibility of States for Internationally Wrongful Acts', (2001-II) YBILC 114 (regarding Article 41(2) DASR)).

[105] E.g., Friendly Relations Declaration, GA Res. 2625 (XXV), Principle 1, § 11; Declaration on the Enhancement of the Effectiveness of the Principle of Refraining from the Threat or Use of Force in International Relations, GA Res. 42/22, Part I, § 10. Consider also, for example: SC Res. 242 (1967) of 22 November 1967; SC Res. 662 (1990) of 9 August 1990.

[106] E.g., Hannikainen, *Peremptory norms*, p. 356; P. H. Kooijmans, *Internationaal publiekrecht in vogelvlucht* (Groningen: Wolters-Noordhoff, 1996), p. 29. This was also the formulation used by the ILC in its 'Commentary on the Draft Articles on the Responsibility of states for Internationally Wrongful Acts, (2001-II) YBILC 283.

[107] E.g., A. Aust, *Modern treaty law and practice* (Cambridge University Press, 2000), p. 257; Bossuyt and Wouters, *Grondlijnen*, p. 92; M. Bothe, 'Das Gewaltverbot imm allgemeinen', in W. Schaumann and M. Bothe (eds.), *Völkerrechtliches Gewaltverbod und Friedenssicherung* (Baden-Baden: Nomos, 1971), pp. 11–30, at 26; Brownlie, *Principles of public international law*, p. 489; A. Cassese, *International law*, 2nd edn (Oxford University Press, 2005), p. 202; D. Schindler and K. Hailbronner, *Die Grenzen des völkerrechtlichen Gewaltverbots* (Heidelberg: Müller Juristischer Verlag, 1986), p. 14; Seiderman, *Hierarchy in international law*, p. 62; Shaw, *International law*, p. 97; Sur, *L'interprétation en droit international public*, p. 177.

[108] E.g., A. Cassese, 'Article 51', p. 1357; C. Kahgan, '*Jus cogens* and the inherent right to self-defense', (1996-7) 3 ILSA JICL 767–827, at 820–7; A. Orakelashivili, *Peremptory norms in international law* (Oxford University Press, 2006), p. 51. See also: ILC, Report of the ILC Study Group, 'Fragmentation of international law', § 374.

[109] See in particular Ago, 'Addendum', 44: '[W]e hesitate to ascribe the same force of *jus cogens* as must, in our view, be accorded to the prohibition of aggression.' For an elaborate discussion, see: Hannikainen, *Peremptory norms*, pp. 323–56.

State practice and diverging views on the authentic interpretation of the Charter provisions prevent the provisions from acquiring peremptory character as a whole. With respect, these reservations are unconvincing. First, occasional breach of the rules does not automatically prevent them from acquiring the status of *ius cogens*. Thus, in spite of the regrettable fact that the prohibition on torture is frequently infringed, it is undoubtedly among the rules most widely recognized as *ius cogens*. Furthermore, problems of interpretation do not necessarily imply that a norm cannot fulfil the requirements of Article 53 VCLT. Like any legal norm, *ius cogens* norms require further interpretation, a process which may entail differences of opinion.[110] It is not necessary 'that every aspect be fully defined and universally agreed upon'.[111] The better view is therefore that the peremptory character of prohibition on the use of force relates to the scope of Article 2(4) as it stands.[112] Given the fact that Article 51 UN Charter – whether considered an exception or a supplement to Article 2 (4) – is inextricably linked to the Charter prohibition on the use of force, it should arguably be endowed with the same normative status.[113] In sum, it appears plausible that both Article 2(4) and Article 51 form part of *ius cogens*.[114]

If we accept this assumption, the implication is that Articles 2(4) and 51 UN Charter can be modified 'only by a subsequent norm of general international law having the same character' (Article 53 VCLT). According to the ILC, it would be wrong to regard rules of *ius cogens* as immutable and incapable of modification in the light of future developments.[115] The Commission argued that modification of *ius cogens* would today most probably be effected through a general multilateral treaty,[116] albeit that there are inherent problems related to this

---

[110] This is as much true for the concept of 'aggression' as for the concept of 'use of force'. Even if one would employ the UNGA Definition of Aggression, this document leaves plenty of room for interpretative disagreement. In other words, reserving *ius cogens* status to the prohibition of aggression is an inadequate remedy to avoid disagreement on the precise content of the peremptory obligation.

[111] US District Court, D. Massachusetts, *Xuncax v. Gramajo*, 12 April 1995, 886 F.Supp. 62, at 187.

[112] Orakelashivili, *Peremptory norms*, p. 68.

[113] See *ibid.*, pp. 50–1, 68, 72, 81. See also Cassese, 'Article 51', p.1357; ILC, Report of the ILC Study Group, 'Fragmentation of international law', § 95.

[114] In a similar vein: American Law Institute, *The Foreign Relations Law of the United States*, p. 382.

[115] ILC, 'Draft Articles on the Law of Treaties with Commentaries', 248.

[116] *Ibid.* Consider also the report of Special Rapporteur Waldock: (1963-II) YBILC 52.

process.[117] It is submitted that modification of *ius cogens* could also occur as a result of subsequent custom.[118] For this to be the case, the normal evidentiary standard for the formation of custom, viz. 'a uniform and generally consistent practice accepted as law', will not be sufficient. Rather, the practice must also be 'accepted and recognized by the international community of States as a whole'.[119] No single State has a right of veto in the determination of a *ius cogens* norm, yet the contrary practice by a number of States will substantially weaken the evidential position. Again, however, modification through subsequent custom would pose certain difficulties. Indeed, State practice directed towards the change of *ius cogens* would initially be invalid as a breach of the existing peremptory norm.[120] However, if this practice would come to be accepted and recognized by the *opinio iuris* of the international community as a whole, it could possibly sow the seeds of a new peremptory norm.[121] This is evidently an imperfect process, accompanied by a good deal of legal uncertainty. A determinate resolution by the UN General Assembly or an international conference, declaring expressly in normative terms the modification of the peremptory norm, could be of help,[122] offering a useful starting point to examine the necessary State practice and *opinio iuris*. Given the high evidentiary burden, this process of modification through custom is considered 'hardly conceivable'. Practice offers no credible examples.[123] Still, on a theoretical basis, it cannot be excluded altogether.

In any event, in light of the different evidentiary thresholds, it is important to take account of the sliding scale between interpretation and modification. Again, this distinction constitutes an interpretative continuum, whereby parties may gradually wander from the original text and intention towards adjusting or updating the content, to the creation of a new rule through modification. This continuum is well illustrated by the different views on the *ratione temporis* aspect of the 'armed attack'

---

[117] See Danilenko, *Law-making*, p. 251; Sinclair, *The Vienna Convention*, p. 226.
[118] E.g., Brownlie, *Principles of public international law*, p. 488.
[119] See Hannikainen, *Peremptory norms*, pp. 210–12; Orakelashivili, *Peremptory norms*, p. 129; C. L. Rozakis, *The concept of jus cogens in the law of treaties* (Amsterdam: North Holland, 1976), p. 79.
[120] Danilenko, *Law-making*, pp. 250–1.
[121] E.g., Orakelashivili, *Peremptory norms*, p. 129; G. J. H. Van Hoof, *Rethinking the sources of international law* (Deuentes: Kluwer, 1983), p. 167.
[122] Dinstein, *War, aggression and self-defence*, p. 102; Hannikainen, *Peremptory norms*, pp. 247, 266.
[123] Orakelashivili, *Peremptory norms*, p. 130.

requirement of Article 51 UN Charter. A first point of view holds that self-defence can only be exercised if an armed attack has taken place, objective evidence of which includes human casualties, territorial intrusions and/or destruction of property. A second approach holds that Article 51 applies as soon as an attack has been 'initiated', even if it has not yet resulted in any of the aforementioned objective elements. Third, a related line of thought suggests that self-defence can be exercised pre-emptively, when there exists an imminent threat of an armed attack. Finally, some have also expressed support for the 'preventive' recourse to self-defence, in response to a 'non-imminent' threat of an attack (here the link to an armed attack is virtually abandoned).

It is not our purpose at present to identify which of these views falls within the scope of interpretation and which enters into the realm of modification. This presupposes an in-depth examination of Article 51 UN Charter in accordance with Articles 31 and 32 VCLT and will be examined later on (see *infra* Chapter 4). However, the controversy illustrates the difficulty in distinguishing the two processes. In this regard, the guiding principle must be that the more we move up the interpretive continuum towards overt modification, the higher the evidentiary standard that must be reached in terms of State practice and *opinio iuris*.

1.2 State practice vs. *opinio iuris*

1.2.1 Introduction: the methodological debate

Having established the importance of custom in relation to the interpretation and possibly the modification of the Charter rules, we must now turn to the difficult enterprise of its identification. In other words, the question how to execute our quest for custom arises, having regard to the peculiarities of inter-State use of force.

The identification of the two constitutive elements of custom, viz. State practice and *opinio iuris*,[124] in the area of inter-State use of force is not without problems. According to Corten, 'specialists in international law are radically opposed to each other on the methodological level, in particular when it comes to making sense of customary rules'.[125]

---

[124] Cf. Article 38(1) Statute of the International Court of Justice, San Francisco, 26 June 1945, 1 UNTS, xvi; ICJ, *Continental Shelf* case (*Libyan Arab Jamahiriya* v. *Malta*), Judgment of 3 June 1985, (1985) ICJ Rep 13, § 27.
[125] Corten, 'A methodological debate', 821.

Corten discerns an extensive approach to the customary rules on the use of force, mainly supported by US authors, and a restrictive one, to which most European and other non-US scholars subscribe. In essence, the former approach considers practice as the dominant element of custom, focuses in particular on the practice of the more powerful States in the international community and accepts that custom may evolve very rapidly. In marked contrast, the extensive approach focuses on the subjective element rather than on the objective element, recognizes that all States can contribute equally to the formation of custom and stresses the gradual (as opposed to instant) development of custom. While the picture presented is of course a simplification of the complex variety in methodological approaches, Corten is correct in identifying a methodological schism, which carries important consequences for the actual interpretation of the legal boundaries on inter-State use of force.[126]

At the outset, it is admitted that the quest for custom is not a matter of exact science. There is, unfortunately, no mathematical formula that allows one to derive (the content of) a customary rule from a specific quantity of practice in combination with a fixed degree of *opinio iuris*. Much depends on the specific circumstances of the practice under consideration, on the normative or regulatory character of the rule, on the paucity or plenitude of verbal and non-verbal practice, on the number of States that are affected by the rule, and on the character of the rule (whether it constitutes an obligation, a permission or a prohibition). Some authors argue that the process of ascertaining customary rules is purely arbitrary, or merely establishes the individual perception of the interpreter.[127] Such criticism is perhaps understandable given the non-transparency of the ICJ's case law on the matter. Nonetheless, by expressing and applying a systematic methodology rather than a random 'pick-and-choose' strategy, we can to a great extent avoid the pitfall of arbitrariness.

Against this background, the present section will spell out a number of considerations regarding the identification and qualification of State practice and *opinio iuris* in the area of the *Ius ad Bellum*, building on the case law of the International Court of Justice and the final report of

---

[126] *Ibid.*, 803.
[127] E.g., P. Haggenmacher, 'La doctrine des deux éléments du droit coutumier dans la pratique de la Cour internationale', (1986) 90 RGDIP 5–125, at 117; M. Koskenniemi, *From apology to Utopia: the structure of international legal argument* (Helsinki: Lakimiesliiton Kustannus, 1989), p. 363, 388–9.

the ILA Committee on the formation of customary international law (2000).[128] In this context, it is worth recalling the famous dictum of the ICJ in the *Nicaragua* case, according to which inconsistent conduct must ultimately be assessed by reference to the State's justification of its conduct and the reactions of other States:

> In order to deduce the existence of customary rules, the Court deems it sufficient that the conduct of States should, in general, be consistent with such rules, and that instances of State conduct inconsistent with a given rule should generally have been treated as breaches of that rule, not as indications of the recognition of a new rule. If a State acts in a way prima facie incompatible with a recognized rule, but defends its conduct by appealing to exceptions or justifications contained within the rule itself, then whether or not the State's conduct is in fact justifiable on that basis, the significance of that attitude is to confirm rather than to weaken the rule.[129]

1.2.2 The evidentiary weight of words and deeds

One of the main stumbling blocks in the doctrinal controversy surrounding the formation and ascertaining of customary international law pertains to the apparent contrast between words and deeds. Thus, one group of scholars sees physical acts as the main element of State practice, because they are more 'against the interest' than the mere acceptance of a theoretical rule, or because they are allegedly less likely to conflict than claims and other statements.[130] Other scholars oppose this emphasis on physical practice, on the grounds that it is artificial to try to distinguish between what States do and say, and that physical acts do not necessarily produce a more consistent picture than statements do.[131] Some even go as far as to suggest that the actual conduct of States in their relations with other nations is 'only a subsidiary means' to ascertain customary rules.[132]

---

[128] See ILA, *The formation of general customary international law.*
[129] ICJ, *Nicaragua* case (Merits), § 186.
[130] Thirlway, *International customary law and codification*, p. 57; H. C. M. Charlesworth, 'Customary international law and the *Nicaragua* case', (1984-7) 11 Australian YBIL 1-31, at 28-9; D'Amato, *The concept of custom in international law*, pp. 50-1. See also A. Cassesse and J. H. H. Weiler (eds.), *Change and stability in international law-making* (Berlin: Walter de Gruyter, 1988), p. 24.
[131] E.g., M. Akehurst, 'Custom as a source of international law', (1977) 47 BYBIL 1-53, at 3.
[132] R. R. Baxter, 'Multilateral treaties as evidence of customary international law', (1965-66) 41 BYBIL 275-300, at 300.

This discussion is also one of the key dividing lines between the extensive and the restrictive approach to the customary prohibition on the use of force.[133] According to the former, 'talk is cheap' and only the 'real' conduct of States reflects what they consider binding as law. The latter group, however, concentrates on the verbal discourse provoked by the material act, rather than the material act as such. Which of the two holds the upper hand?

On the one hand, it could indeed be argued that physical acts are usually less non-committal than statements.[134] For this reason, positive actions of competent State organs, as well as the implementation of legislative acts have arguably more probative value than acts devoid of practical measures in their execution, or contradictory verbal statements made by state organs.[135] By analogy, the recourse to force accompanied by a claim that such action is legally permissible in a given situation will generally have a greater impact on the customary process than the mere assertion by a State that the resort to force is permitted in the situation at hand. Furthermore, customary rules can never be *purely* paper rules.[136] Apart from the fact that some collective expressions of views – e.g., the inclusion of a fundamental norm in a universally ratified treaty – may exceptionally create a presumption in favour of the required State practice, in principle no customary rule can arise unless supported by a minimal degree of physical practice.

On the other hand, in the field of the *Ius ad Bellum*, oral and written statements are readily available, especially in the records of the Security Council and the General Assembly. Such statements provide the only *explicit* evidence of States' *opinio iuris*. By contrast, isolated 'acts' involving inter-State use of force require legal qualification in order to assess their contribution to the customary process.[137] If a military intervention

---

[133] See Corten, 'A methodological debate', 810–2, 817–18.
[134] ILA, *The formation of general customary international law*, p. 724; M. H. Mendelson, 'The formation of customary international law', (1998) 272 RdC 155–410, 205.
[135] V. D. Degan, *Sources of international law* (The Hague: Martinus Nijhoff, 1997), p. 160.
[136] G. M. Danilenko, 'The theory of international customary law', (1988) 31 GYBIL 9–47, at 24.
[137] Remark: the ILA Committee on the Formation of General Customary International Law observes that: 'In practice international tribunals, and, it seems, States, do not specifically look for evidence of *opinio iuris* unless there is reason to believe … that practice … does not "count" towards the formation of customary law.' At the same time, the ILA Committee acknowledges that there are certain situations where the conduct will only 'count' if there is positive evidence that the State or States concerned intended, understood or accepted that a customary rule could result from, or lay behind, the conduct in question. This is firstly the case when dealing with omissions, which are

is not verbally defended by the intervening State it will often remain unclear whether it considers itself to be acting lawfully, and, if so, on what legal basis. Imagine for instance that the US, the UK and Australia had provided no verbal justification whatsoever for their military intervention in Iraq in 2003. In such scenario, at least theoretically, several legal qualifications could have been put forward by members of the interpretative community: some might have considered the intervention as an example of pre-emptive or preventive self-defence in reaction to Saddam Hussein's endeavours to acquire weapons of mass destruction; others might have labelled it a humanitarian intervention, inspired by the violent repression of the Kurdish minority; still others might have qualified the Iraq war as a 'pro-democratic intervention' against the dictatorial Baathist regime; a fourth group might have identified the war as a counter-terrorist operation, since the Iraqi regime was (wrongly) suspected of maintaining relations with Al Qaeda.[138] In reality, however, the intervening countries (mainly) relied on a wholly distinct justification, namely the presence of a (revived) Security Council authorization.[139] This example illustrates that, amidst the fog of war, the legal qualification of a concrete instance of inter-State use of force is a complex undertaking, the appreciation of which is to a greater or lesser degree in the eye of the beholder. The implication is that acts of States are of greater use for purposes of ascertaining the content of customary rules when they are accompanied by verbal statements. Such statements enable us to establish whether the intervening State intended to set a precedent or not, and to gain insight in its interpretation of the law. Other recourses to force are not excluded from our analysis of State practice and *opinio iuris*, yet one should proceed extremely carefully in ascribing legal views to the intervening States that they themselves have not expressly subscribed to. Furthermore, as in the field of human rights and humanitarian law, it is very difficult to weigh instances of compliance against instances of violation[140] – violations are much more visible than practice respecting

---

often ambiguous as to their legal relevance. The same is true for other forms of ambiguous conduct, 'the basis of which remains speculative'. In such situations separate proof of *opinio iuris* is deemed necessary. See ILA, *The formation of general customary international law*, pp. 745–9.

[138] See, e.g., D. Kritsiotis, 'Arguments of mass confusion', (2004) 15 EJIL 233–78, at 246 *et seq.*
[139] See Letters to the President of the Security Council, 20 March 2003, UN Doc. S/2003/350 (UK); UN Doc. S/2003/351 (US); UN Doc. S/2003/352 (Australia).
[140] R. Kolb, 'Selected problems in the theory of customary international law', (2003) 50 NILR 119–50, at 124–5, 128–9. In relation to IHL and human rights law, see: T. Meron,

the prohibition on the use of force.[141] Hence, an emphasis on (verbally expressed) *opinio iuris* helps to steer clear of misjudging the impact of breaches of the law.

Ultimately, in order to gain a better understanding of the respective roles of words and deeds, it is necessary to grasp the dynamic nature of the customary process, which in essence is governed by the interaction of claims and responses given thereto.[142] Again, customary law does not consist of a static set of rules, but constitutes a continuous process whereby States advance through their organs unilateral claims, which are subsequently appraised by other members of the international community by means of protest, acceptance or acquiescence.[143]

The exchange of claims and counter-claims is usually catalysed by a single 'incident',[144] *in casu* the recourse to force by one State against another. Broadly speaking, the development of the *Ius ad Bellum* presupposes two things: first, one or more States must rely 'on a novel right or an unprecedented exception' to the prohibition on the use of force; and second, this argument must in principle be shared by other States.[145] Both conditions merit a closer look.

As regards the former precondition, it is first of all clear that – in accordance with the general requirements for State practice – the recourse to force must be public to some extent and that the intervening State must take responsibility for its actions.[146] This will not be the case if

Human rights and humanitarian norms as customary law (Oxford: Clarendon Press, 1989), p. 61.

[141] E.g., G. P. Buzzini, 'Les comportements passifs des Etats et leur incidence sur la réglémentation de l'emploi de la force en droit international général', in E. Cannizzaro and P. Palchetti (eds.), *Customary international law on the use of force* (Dordrecht: Martinus Nijhoff, 2005), pp. 79–117, at 83.

[142] E.g., K. Skubiszewski, 'Elements of custom and the Hague Court', (1971) 31 ZaöRV 810–54, at 824; ICJ, *North Sea Continental Shelf* case, Dissenting opinion of Judge Lachs, 231.

[143] E.g., M. S. McDougal, 'The hydrogen bomb tests and international law of the sea', (1955) 49 AJIL 356–61, at 357–8; Wolfke, *Custom*, p. 56.

[144] Cf. W. M. Reisman, 'The incident as a decisional unit in international law', (1954–85) 10 YJIL 1–20, at 13.

[145] ICJ, *Nicaragua* case (Merits), § 207. See O. Corten, 'Breach and evolution of customary international law on the use of force', in Cannizzaro and Palchetti (eds.), *Customary international law on the use of force*, pp. 119–44.

[146] Henckaerts and Doswald-Beck, *Customary international humanitarian law*, p. xxxiv; ILA, *The formation of general customary international law*, p. 720, 726; Mendelson, 'Customary international law', 204; Villiger, *Customary international law and treaties*, p. 17. Acts that are never disclosed cannot influence the evolution of custom, since other States must in principle be given the opportunity to react to the behaviour within a reasonable period of time. Hence, when a State stages a secret military operation to

an attack is clouded in secrecy and it cannot be established who directed it. Likewise, if a State simply denies the allegations, the recourse to force will carry no evidential weight in terms of State practice. This is a rather common scenario, especially in relation to military support of irregular forces or terrorist groups.[147] In September 2007, Israel carried out an air strike in northern Syria that, according to some sources, was directed against a nuclear-related facility that North Korea was helping to equip (an accusation Syria and North Korea denied).[148] In the days following the operation, several anonymous Israeli and American officials confirmed the attack in the media. Nonetheless, the Israeli government initially remained shrouded in official silence, refusing either to acknowledge or to deny the facts.[149] Syria submitted a letter of complaint to the Security Council in which it condemned the incident as 'an aggression in clear and brazen defiance of international law'.[150] Only several weeks after the operation did the Israeli Army radio report that Israeli planes attacked a military target 'deep inside Syria', without, however, offering further details or providing some sort of legal justification.[151] As long as the perpetrator denies the facts or adopts a highly evasive attitude, its recourse to force can hardly qualify as a precedent in favour of 'a novel right or unprecedented exception', although the protests or declarations of support expressed in reaction thereto may provide an indication of the relevant States' *opinio iuris*.

Furthermore, once it is established that the State or States involved assume responsibility for the attack, the evidentiary weight of the acts on the customary process hinges on the explicitness and the content of the legal justification in which the operation is couched: the legal qualification by the intervening State determines the interpretative or precedential value of the incident. For instance, in the hypothesis that a State declares itself to be acting in self-defence to protect its nationals abroad,

---

eliminate a terrorist leader abroad, this will probably not constitute an example of the material element. Even if the act is discovered, it will generally not count as State practice unless the State tries to assert that its conduct was legally justified. Remark: it should also be noted that only *conscious* conduct may qualify, implying, for instance, that the unintentional entering of another State's territory by a military unit will have no bearing on the customary law on the use of force.

[147] See Corten, 'Breach and evolution', pp.123–4.   [148] See *infra*, Section 4.3.4.
[149] Initially, the (then) Israeli opposition leader, Benjamin Netanyahu, was the sole public figure to confirm reports of the operation, a démarche for which he faced heavy criticism.
[150] UN Doc. S/2007/537, 9 September 2007 (Syria).
[151] 'Israel admits air strike on Syria', *BBC News* 2 October 2007.

its intervention should not be considered as a case of humanitarian intervention, even if it de facto resulted in the halting of grave human rights abuses. One should not ascribe to States legal views which they themselves do not advance.[152] Neither does it matter that the State may have been led by an additional motive, other than that officially proclaimed.[153] This is of crucial importance, since on most occasions States simply rely on the 'classical' justifications of self-defence, Security Council authorization or State consent, rather than entering the murky waters of 'novel rights or unprecedented exceptions'.[154] Whatever the reason for this attitude (whether the fear of creating objectionable precedents, the desire to attract maximum support, or simply the conviction that this 'classical' label is most befitting), such incidents will not generally inspire a fundamental reappraisal of the *Ius ad Bellum*. On the other hand, an apparently traditional legal justification may very well disguise an attempt to re-interpret or even modify altogether the existing customary rules on the use of force,[155] and merit the same attention as any open departure from the conventional justifications.

Moreover, what matters are the justifications of a *legal* character, not statements of international policy or morality that virtually always surround instances of inter-State use of force and are aimed at various (domestic or foreign) audiences.[156] This presupposes firstly a textual analysis of the declarations involved. In principle there must be some express reference to legal considerations, for example to a formal source of law, or to a legal concept or institution.[157] If explicit reference is made to a treaty provision, e.g., to Articles 2(4) or 51 UN Charter or to Article V North Atlantic Treaty, the legal nature stands beyond doubt. Moreover, the statement may also refer to concepts with a clear legal connotation, such as self-defence, humanitarian intervention, et cetera. If no such concepts are used but the intervening State expresses its 'desire to prevent a humanitarian catastrophe' or to 'defend its territory', the legal qualification of the action may be deduced implicitly. Apart from

---

[152] ICJ, *Nicaragua* case (Merits), § 207.
[153] *Ibid.*, § 127: 'The existence of an additional motive, other than that officially proclaimed by the United States, could not deprive the latter of its right to resort to collective self-defence.'
[154] Corten, 'Breach and evolution', pp. 129–30; Gray, *The use of force*, p. 118.
[155] E.g., Corten, 'Breach and evolution', pp. 129–30.
[156] In this sense: ICJ, *South West Africa* cases (*Ethiopia v. South Africa*; *Liberia v. South Africa*), Judgment of 18 July 1966, (1966) ICJ Rep 6–58, § 49.
[157] Corten, 'Breach and evolution', p. 125.

the text, much depends on the context or the setting in which the statements are made. In general, statements made at the international level give a better indication of the State's legal position than statements made for domestic audiences. Furthermore, official statements in formal fora provide better evidence than, for instance, television interviews or press communiqués.[158] When available, the intervening State's report to the UN Security Council is likely to offer the best starting point to examine its legal case. Other valuable sources of information are statements made during the subsequent debates of the Security Council or the General Assembly, as well as arguments submitted during proceedings of the ICJ. It is possible that the intervening State changes its legal case in the course of time or that it adopts an 'elements' approach based on a panoply of possible justifications.[159] Such attitudes sometimes reflect a degree of uncertainty on behalf of the State vis-à-vis the lawfulness of the intervention. The more explicit and the more consistent the legal justification, the greater its probative value will be. A distinction must moreover be upheld between *opinio de lege lata* and *opinio de lege ferenda*. Indeed, although declarations that something 'ought to be law' would also seem to contribute to the development of the *opinio iuris*, they would not suffice on their own. Such statements might even be taken as *a contrario* evidence to deny the existence of a customary rule, since they implicitly recognize that the rule has *not yet* crystallized.

The second aspect of the exchange of claims and counter-claims concerns the reaction of other States to the initial 'incident'. In this regard, it should first be pointed out that not all recourse to force triggers an intensive justificatory discourse at the international level. Many small-scale interventions immediately pass into oblivion, without giving rise to official reactions by third States.[160] By contrast, other episodes, such as the NATO intervention in Kosovo in 1999 and the US-led intervention in Iraq in 2003, were debated at length in the Security Council and the General Assembly. While episodes of the former type should not be excluded from our analysis, it is especially the latter interventions that are of crucial importance due to the fact that they allow us to gain an insight into the legal position of a great number of members of the international community, and may thus shed light on the precise content of the customary rules on the use of force.

---

[158] See Kritsiotis, 'Arguments of mass confusion', 241 *et seq.*   [159] *Ibid.*, 243, 272.
[160] Corten, 'Breach and evolution', p. 132; Gray, *The use of force*, p. 11.

Instances of 'meaningful silence' by third States are extremely difficult to qualify.[161] Acquiescence vis-à-vis an alleged violation of a rule of international law may signal a third State's approval *de lege lata* or *de lege ferenda*, it may imply the recognition of a derogatory regime or it may be inspired by a desire to leave the existing legal regime unaffected.[162] It may also be considered as a renunciation of legal claims against the alleged perpetrator of the violation. Other possible motives include mere indifference, fear from sanctions when criticism is uttered, et cetera. No clear-cut criteria exist to evaluate acquiescence.[163] It is true that the ICJ has on occasion referred to the 'general toleration' of a certain conduct, or the acquiescence of specially affected States.[164] From this it may be inferred that acquiescence matters most when it emanates from States directly concerned with a concrete recourse to force (for instance the State against which self-defence is exercised or neighbouring States) or from a large number of States.[165]

Caution is also needed when dealing with expressions of acceptance or opposition. Indeed, while the approval of an intervention by other States provides implicit proof of their support of the *legal* case, this attitude may also be inspired by considerations of courtesy, political alliance, economic interest, et cetera,[166] especially when the State confines itself to expressing 'sympathy' or 'understanding' for the intervention. Thus, some authors have suggested that the broad approval for the US operation against Afghanistan in 2001 may have been motivated by the worldwide atmosphere of solidarity with the United States following the 9/11 terrorist attacks, and therefore did not necessarily reflect equally widespread support for the legal basis of the operation.[167] Even more than acceptance, opposition may be inspired by a range of motivations. A State that is at loggerheads with the intervening State is obviously more

---

[161] On the 'polysemy' of acquiescence, see Buzzini, 'Les comportements passifs des Etats', pp. 84–117.
[162] *Ibid.*, pp. 87–92.
[163] See *ibid.*, pp. 92–116.
[164] ICJ, *Fisheries* case (*United Kingdom v. Norway*), Judgment of 18 December 1951, (1951) ICJ Rep 116–44, 139–40; PCIJ, *The case of the* 'SS Lotus' (*France v. Turkey*), Judgment of 7 September 1927, Series A No 10, 23, 29.
[165] E.g., Buzzini, 'Les comportements passifs des Etats', pp. 85–6, 104.
[166] Corten, 'Breach and evolution', p.135.
[167] E.g., M. G. Kohen, 'The use of force by the United States after the end of the Cold War, and its impact on international law', in M. Byers and G. Nolte (eds.), *United States hegemony and the foundations of international law* (Cambridge University Press, 2003), pp. 197–231, at 221–6. See *infra* Section 5.2.2.

likely to condemn the recourse to force than a political ally. For this reason, condemnation of another State by a State with whom it normally maintains close relations offers exceptionally strong evidence of illegality.[168] A condemnation may also be inspired by other aspects of the intervening State's policy apart from the actual recourse to force. For instance, throughout the 1970s and 1980s it seems that some States *a priori* regarded any self-defence claim of South Africa, Israel or Portugal as defective because of these countries' policies of apartheid and illegal occupation, rather than to judge each incident on its own merits.[169] Finally, a condemnation may express disagreement with the way in which the intervention was carried out, rather than with the legal basis as such. For example, a closer look at the Security Council debates following Israel's intervention in Lebanon in the summer of 2006 reveals that several, if not most, States accepted that Israel was entitled to exercise its right to self-defence following the attack by Hezbollah on an Israeli border patrol.[170] Nonetheless, many of those States expressed concern or even outright condemnation of the disproportionate character of Israel's reaction.[171] Hence, if one would merely 'count' the number of supporting and opposing States without further analysis, this would result in a misinterpretation of the precedential value of the incident.

By analogy, the same is true for resolutions of the Security Council or the General Assembly. On the one hand, the condemnation[172] of a particular use of force by the Security Council or by the General Assembly (or both) provides persuasive prima facie evidence as to illegality.[173] Still, in the former case, it is important to also take account of the reactions of other States apart from the fifteen members of the Council. In both situations, caution is needed. When the resolution identifies the recourse to force as an 'act of aggression' or a violation of Article 2(4) UN Charter, the situation will be clear. However, in the more likely scenario that the resolution simply condemns in general terms the

---

[168] Gray, *The use of force*, pp. 20–1.   [169] Ibid. See *infra* Section 5.1.3.b.
[170] UN Security Council, 61st session, 5489th meeting, 14 July 2006, UN Doc. S/PV.5489; UN Security Council, 61st session, 5493th meeting, 21 July 2006, UN Doc. S/PV.5493.
[171] See T. Ruys, 'Crossing the Thin Blue Line: an inquiry into Israel's recourse to self-defense against Hezbollah', (2007) 43 Stanford JIL 265–94, at 270–1. Also *infra* Section 6.2.3.b.
[172] Remark: explicit approbations of an exercise of the right to self-defence by either of the two UN organs are virtually non-existent.
[173] E.g., Gray, *The use of force*, p. 20.

actions of a certain State,[174] it is important to verify this presumption by reference to the statements surrounding the adoption of the resolution. A failure to condemn should not automatically be considered evidence of the legality of the use of force.[175] Often, an incident involving inter-State use of force is simply never inscribed on the agenda of either body. Inaction may be influenced by political motivations or may reflect the disagreement between members of the international community regarding the application of the law on the use of force. In the case of the Security Council, the failure to condemn may even be explained by a single permanent Member's veto. An in-depth examination of the debates is therefore crucial.

In sum, one must avoid taking expressions of acceptance or opposition at face value. Even if one accepts Franck's finding that, apart from the superpowers and their close allies, States have generally voted in a principled way in responding to the use of force,[176] it is still important to look for explicit statements concerning the *legal* case under consideration. Such statements are primarily found in the debates before the General Assembly and especially the Security Council convened to discuss particular uses of force. These debates are governed by the shared normative framework enshrined in the Charter provisions on the use of force. This does not mean that observations made throughout the debates will always make explicit or implicit reference to the relevant Charter provisions or to legal concepts involved. Again, they may not always use legal language, but may be confined to mere political statements. Gray observes for example that:

> [T]he UK, in its reaction to controversial uses of force by the USA, has from time to time adopted forms of words that allow it to offer support or sympathy but to stop short of unequivocal endorsement of the legal argument of the USA; to a casual observer this statement may appear to offer support for the US legal argument, but in fact it does not go so far.[177]

The statements may also concern disagreement on the particular *facts* surrounding the recourse to force, rather than on the interpretation of the law.[178] Still, these debates provide the most useful source to gain

---

[174] E.g., G. Cahin, 'Le rôle des organes politiques des Nations Unies', in Cannizzaro and Palchetti (eds.), *Customary international law on the use of force*, pp. 147–77, at 166–8.
[175] See *ibid.*, pp. 168–71; Gray, *The use of force*, pp. 21–3.
[176] T. M. Franck, 'Of gnats and camels: is there a double standard at the United Nations?', (1984) 78 AJIL 811–33, at 811.
[177] Gray, *The use of force*, p. 19.   [178] *Ibid.*, p. 11.

insight into States' interpretation of the customary rules on the use of force and of their position in relation to the doctrinal divides involved.

In the end, turning back to our initial question concerning the relative value of words and deeds, the present study holds that, in light of the characteristics of the law on the use of force, the actual incidents only provide the raw material of the customary process. An approach that bases itself almost exclusively on physical practice presents far greater risks of arbitrariness than one that focuses on what States say. It tends to ignore rule-compliant behaviour and to downplay the (positive and negative) reactions of third States. Furthermore, it implies a great risk of subjectiveness in the sense that the interpreter will examine the practice through the lens of what he believes the State *could* or *should* have said to justify its conduct, which could lead to manifestly absurd results (imagine again that the US-led intervention in Iraq in 2003 were considered a precedent for lawful intervention to protect one's economic interests). To gain true insight into the legal qualification and evaluation of these incidents by States, one must systematically examine the verbal discourse which they may (to greater or lesser extent) provoke. Thus, contrary to the suggestion of Judge Read in the *Fisheries* case that 'claims are important as starting points', but that only physical practice can provide convincing evidence,[179] the present study holds that concrete incidents involving the use of force provide important starting points, but that convincing evidence must mainly be sought in the ensuing exchange of claims and counter-claims.

It must be noted that the justificatory discourse is not exclusively triggered by actual recourses to force. Sometimes a mere declaration not directly connected to a concrete incident may fuel a debate touching upon the customary rules on the use of force. In particular, the promulgation of the 2002 US National Security Strategy,[180] proclaiming a broad right of anticipatory self-defence, not only stirred academic debates, but also had a significant impact on security doctrines worldwide. A few months after its adoption, the Australian Prime Minister suggested that the Charter provision regarding self-defence should be rewritten.[181] France, in a 2006 White Paper on counter-terrorism, acknowledged the

---

[179] ICJ, *Fisheries* case, Dissenting opinion of Judge Read, 191.
[180] White House, The National Security Strategy of the United States of America, Washington DC, 17 September 2002, at http://georgewbush-whitehouse.archives.gov/nsc/nss/2002/index.html (accessed 6 May 2009). See *infra* Section 5.2.1.a.
[181] 'Australia ready to strike abroad', *BBC News* 1 December 2002.

possibility under Article 51 UN Charter of 'pre-emptive action' against explicit and confirmed terrorist threats.[182] And at the European level, the matter was discussed intensively during the drafting of the European Security Strategy.[183] These declarations are all examples of State practice, which may implicitly or explicitly embody States' *opinio iuris*. Again, care must be taken not to conflate legal statements with politically-oriented ones. Compare for instance the following illustrations. In 1998 the Clinton Administration proclaimed that the United States 'must always be prepared to act alone when that is [its] most advantageous course'.[184] Four years later, the US National Security Strategy stated as follows:

> For centuries, international law has recognized that nations need not suffer an attack before they can lawfully take action to defend themselves against forces that present an imminent danger of attack. Legal scholars and international jurists often conditioned the legitimacy of pre-emption on the existence of an imminent threat. ... We must adapt the concept of imminent threat to the capabilities and objectives of today's adversaries ... The greater the threat, the greater is the risk of inaction – and the more compelling the case for taking anticipatory action to defend ourselves, even if uncertainty remains as to the time and place of the enemy's attack.[185]

While the former quote presents only a very general political statement without any legal bearing, the latter reflects a deliberate intent to broaden the scope of self-defence.

Last but not least, within international fora debates may occasionally take place which do not pronounce on specific use of force-related incidents, but which address aspects of the *Ius ad Bellum* from a more abstract or theoretical perspective. Examples can be found in particular in the practice of the General Assembly (e.g., statements submitted throughout the drafting stage of the 1974 Definition of Aggression),

---

[182] Secrétariat Général de la Défense Nationale, *La France face au terrorisme: Livre Blanc du Gouvernement sur la sécurité intérieure face au terrorisme* (Paris: La Documentation française, 2006), p. 62.

[183] European Security Strategy, 'A secure Europe in a better world', approved by the European Council on 12 December 2003, available at http://ue.eu.int/uedocs/cmsUpload/78367.pdf (accessed 15 April 2009). See J. Wouters and T. Ruys, 'The legality of anticipatory military action after 9/11: the slippery slope of self-defense', (2006) 59 *Studia Diplomatica* 45–67.

[184] White House, 'A national security strategy for a new century', Washington DC, October 1998, available at http://clinton2.nara.gov/WH/EOP/NSC/html/documents/nssr.pdf (accessed 15 April 2009), 2.

[185] White House, National Security Strategy 2002, 15.

THE METHODOLOGICAL DEBATE AND THE QUEST FOR CUSTOM 43

and also in the practice of other bodies, such as the ILC (e.g., statements submitted during the preparatory stages of the Draft Articles on Diplomatic Protection) or the ICC Special Working Group on the Crime of Aggression. Some authors object that such statements *in abstracto* are of lesser importance than those connected to some concrete dispute (actual or potential), since the latter will be of a more practical character.[186] Others hold the opposite view and suggest that so-called abstract statements are often given more careful preparation than 'speedily drafted protest notes', and are less likely to be influenced by considerations of convenience or political alliance.[187] As Akehurst suggests, the two arguments tend to cancel one another out.[188] Even assuming that the distinction is feasible,[189] both types of statements should be taken into account to determine the State's legal position as well as the uniformity thereof. In sum, subject to the reservations made above – i.e., that statements combined with physical practice have a greater impact on the customary process and that some degree of physical practice is in principle indispensable for a change of the customary rules to take place – all of these statements constitute State practice which may embody the State's *opinio*.[190]

Thus, in the realm of the *Ius ad Bellum*, relevant verbal practice covers a wide range of oral and written statements. Apart from statements made in various international fora, as well as observations in the course of proceedings before the ICJ, the following examples may be mentioned: inter-State diplomatic correspondence, official statements before national parliaments,[191] press communiqués and interviews; opinions of national legal advisers expressed in their position as representative of

---

[186] See, e.g., Thirlway, *International customary law and codification*, p. 58.
[187] Brownlie, *The rule of law in international affairs*, p. 20; Corten, 'Breach and evolution', p. 138.
[188] Akehurst, 'Custom as a source of international law', 21.
[189] Cf. *ibid.*, 4.
[190] For the sake of completeness, it may be observed that the relevance of 'verbal' State practice has repeatedly been recognized by the ICJ. See, e.g., ICJ, *Fisheries* case, §§ 55–8; ICJ, *Continental Shelf* case, 45; ICJ, *Nicaragua* case (Merits), § 190; Ago, 'Addendum to the eighth report on State responsibility, 34 *et seq*. Also: ILC, 'Report of the International Law Commission to the General Assembly', (1950-II) YBILC 368 *et seq.*; ILA, *The formation of general customary international law*, p. 725.
[191] Remark: it may be recalled that (subject to the general requirements) all State organs can contribute to the formation of customary law, regardless of whether they belong to the executive, legislative or judicial branch (e.g., ILA, *The formation of general customary international law*, pp. 728–9). Thus, a resolution authorizing the use of military force or a parliamentary declaration of war will both constitute acts of State practice, as

the government; or national military manuals and security doctrines (insofar as they are not strictly confidential).

1.2.3 Observations concerning the density of customary practice

It is well-known that, in order to give rise to general custom, a certain 'density' of practice is indispensable. First of all, State practice must be virtually *uniform*.[192] This means that the acts must indicate a certain similarity or consistency.[193] A second requirement is that practice must also be *'extensive'*.[194] As the ILA report notes, practice does not need to be universal for all States to be bound by it: 'general' practice suffices.[195] A few dissenting States will not normally prevent the formation of a rule of general customary law. The third and last aspect of the density of State practice concerns the temporal element, i.e., the *time lapse* during which a practice must substantiate to give rise to general custom.

With regard to the second factor, it is impossible to fix a quantitative level of (active or passive) support that must be attained for the creation of a customary rule. Rather, the 'generality' criterion should be considered a qualitative standard, fulfilment of which depends on the context and the nature of the conduct under consideration.[196] In the *North Sea Continental Shelf* cases, the ICJ made reference to 'widespread and *representative* participation', as well as to the role of 'States whose interests were specially affected'.[197] In accordance herewith, it is accepted that primary attention should go to the actions of those States which are in a position to participate in the practice under consideration and/or which

> will a parliamentary decision to support the military efforts of a third State by allowing the use of its territory. Hypothetically, if a national Court were to condemn the executive's decision to resort to military force or a government member for the crime of aggression, this would equally constitute a relevant act of State practice for present purposes. However, national laws generally provide very little leeway for judicial control over executive war powers and domestic courts themselves have been highly reluctant to enforce substantive restraints on the use of force. See, however: Judgment of the Bundesverwaltungsgericht of 21 June 2005, BVerwG, 2 WD 12.04, 95.

[192] E.g., ICJ, *North Sea Continental Shelf* case, § 75.
[193] ICJ, *Fisheries* case 131, 138; ICJ, *Asylum* case (*Colombia v. Peru*), Judgment of 20 November 1950, (1951) ICJ Rep 266–89, at 277. Absolute consistency is not required. Some violations of the rule are inevitable. The ICJ has affirmed that 'too much importance need not be attached to [a] few uncertainties or contradictions, real or apparent'. ICJ, *Fisheries* case, 138. Also ICJ, *Nicaragua* case (Merits), § 186.
[194] ICJ, *North Sea Continental Shelf* case, § 74.
[195] ILA, *The formation of general customary international law*, p. 735.
[196] Akehurst, 'Custom as a source of international law', 18–19.
[197] ICJ, *North Sea Continental Shelf* case, § 73.

THE METHODOLOGICAL DEBATE AND THE QUEST FOR CUSTOM 45

have an interest in the subject matter.[198] For instance, in the *North Sea Continental Shelf* cases, coastal nations possessing a continental shelf were identified as 'specially affected', whereas landlocked States had no interest in becoming parties to the 1958 Geneva Convention on the Continental Shelf.[199] On the other hand, this does not mean that the concept of 'specially affected States' is applicable in each and every situation – certain treaties such as the Vienna Convention on the Law of Treaties or the Vienna Conventions on Diplomatic and Consular Relations would seem to be of equal importance to all members of the international community.

The impact of specially affected States on the customary process is twofold.[200] On the negative side, if these States do not accept the practice under consideration, it will be prevented from maturing into a rule of general customary law. On the positive side, if all specially affected States are represented, it is not quintessential for a majority of States to have actively participated, although they must at least have acquiesced in the practice of the former States.[201]

Some authors interpret the concept of specially affected States as implying that the practice of more powerful or dominant States would have a greater impact on the development of customary rules.[202] In accordance with the principle of sovereign equality, there is no *intrinsic* reason why larger States should exercise a greater influence on the customary process.[203] There are, however, practical reasons why this may be so.[204] First of all, given the scope of their interests, major States are more likely to be 'specially affected' in a wide variety of international legal domains. They possess the resources to engage in physical practice for which smaller States may not have the necessary capabilities (e.g., vis-

---

[198] See Danilenko, 'The theory of international customary law', 29; Skubiszewski, 'Elements of custom', 827; Villiger, *Customary international law and treaties*, p. 32. See also M. Sørensen, 'Principes de droit international public', (1960-III) 101 RdC 1–254, at 40.
[199] ICJ, *North Sea Continental Shelf* case, § 73. For other examples, see Skubiszewski, 'Elements of custom', 830; Villiger, *Customary international law and treaties*, p. 31.
[200] ILA, *The formation of general customary international law*, p. 737.
[201] Akehurst, 'Custom as a source of international law', 22; Henckaerts and Doswald-Beck, *Customary international humanitarian law*, p. xxxviii.
[202] Baxter, 'Treaties and customs', 66. Also Mendelson, 'Customary international law', 225.
[203] See Akehurst, 'Custom as a source of international law', 22–3; ILA, *The formation of general customary international law*, p. 737; Villiger, *Customary international law and treaties*, pp. 32–3.
[204] See, *inter alia*, M. Byers, *Custom, power and the power of rules: international relations and customary international law* (Cambridge University Press, 1999), pp. 19, 36–40, 152–3.

à-vis the use of outer space), or to do so on a more frequent basis. Second, the practice of major States is likely to be more public than that of smaller States, and is more likely to be publicized and to be readily accessible. Still, the idea that the practice of great powers is invariably more important must be rejected.[205] This ultimately depends on the context and on the availability of State practice. Several authors have moreover stressed that the creation of general customary rules must in one way or another include States with different political, economic and legal systems and States of all continents.[206]

What are the implications for the ascertainment of customary rules on the use of force? As mentioned at the outset, the role of dominant States is one of the key stumbling blocks between what Corten identified as the extensive and the restrictive approaches to the customary prohibition on the use of force.[207] The former approach pays predominant attention to the practice of powerful States. The latter, however, asserts that all States can contribute equally to the customary process. In the present author's view, however, the truth lies somewhere in the middle. On the one hand, there are a number of reasons why the major powers should be accorded a primary role in relation to the *Ius ad Bellum*. First, it is obvious that they have a greater *capacity* to participate in relevant physical practice than smaller States. A State such as Luxembourg does not possess the military capacity to engage in any significant inter-State use of force. Conversely, the United States operates over half of the twenty-some aircraft carriers that cruise the world's oceans, and its military expenditure outstrips those of the next fifteen countries combined. It would therefore seem naïve and unjustified to attach the same weight to their respective positions. Furthermore, given the mandate of the Security Council vis-à-vis the maintenance of international peace and security, it could be argued that its permanent members qualify as 'specially affected States' for present purposes. Parallel to their veto right, the P–5 have a primary responsibility to lead the work of the Security Council. In this capacity, they can be considered as having a special interest in the customary law on the use of force.

---

[205] Akehurst, 'Custom as a source of international law', 23.
[206] ICJ, *North Sea Continental Shelf* case, Dissenting opinion of Judge Lachs, 227. Also Danilenko, 'The theory of international customary law', 30; Villiger, *Customary international law and treaties*, p. 29.
[207] Corten, 'A methodological debate', 810–12, 816–21.

On the other hand, like international humanitarian law,[208] the *Ius ad Bellum* is by definition an area of law that affects each and every member of the international community. Every State, no matter how big or how small, has an interest in not becoming the victim of a military intervention, and, more generally, in the orderly and peaceful conduct of international relations. For this reason, the practice of all States must be taken into account, whether or not they are 'specially affected' in the strict sense of that term. In sum, while a purely numerical approach of 'one State, one vote' should be avoided, one must equally avoid an exclusive focus on the practice and *opinio iuris* of the five permanent members of the Security Council and other major powers.[209] Instead, an equilibrium must be sought, attempting to map the position of as many members of the international community as possible, while recognizing that some States' practice will carry relatively greater weight.

In relation to the third aspect of 'density', viz. the need for a certain time lapse for a certain practice to give rise to general custom, legal doctrine accepts that this element has become much less important than it once was, and that custom can now arise in a very short time[210] – a position that apparently finds support in the *North Sea Continental Shelf* cases[211] as well as the individual opinions of several ICJ judges.[212] This accelerated pace of customary law-making is explained by the development of modern means of communication and the proliferation of international fora, which enable States to express their views on various international legal problems and to learn the views of other States without a substantial cost of time.[213] It may also be observed in this context that the three different aspects of the 'density' of customary law are closely interrelated, in the sense that a lack of time lapse may to some extent be compensated for by a greater uniformity and generality, and so on.[214]

---

[208] See Henckaerts and Doswald-Beck, *Customary international humanitarian law*, p. xxxix.
[209] Brownlie, *The rule of law in international affairs*, p. 33.
[210] E.g., Akehurst, 'Custom as a source of international law', 16; Baxter, 'Treaties and customs', 67; Wolfke, *Custom*, pp. 65, 59; Villiger, *Customary international law and treaties*, p. 46.
[211] ICJ, *North Sea Continental Shelf* case, § 74.
[212] E.g., *ibid.*, Dissenting opinion of Judge Tanaka, 177; Dissenting opinion of Judge Lachs, 230; Dissenting opinion of Judge Sørensen, 244.
[213] Danilenko, 'The theory of international customary law', 30.
[214] Ferrari Bravo, 'Méthodes de recherche', 250; ILA, *The formation of general customary international law*, p. 731; Skubiszewski, 'Elements of custom', 837; Villiger, *Customary international law and treaties*, p. 45. See also: Kolb, 'Selected problems', 133–5.

Does this mean that one single act of State practice could inspire a shift in the customary boundaries of the *Ius ad Bellum*, provided it would be supported (actively or passively) by a broad majority of the international community? On the one hand, inter-State use of force by its very nature is not the kind of behaviour that lends itself to frequent application. States are obliged to settle their disputes peacefully; inter-State use of force is subject to a comprehensive prohibition; and self-defence is only permitted on an exceptional basis. If each year perhaps a handful of opportunities present themselves where States could possibly appeal to the right to self-defence, over the same period of time States produce a vast quantity of active practice in relation to commercial shipping, treatment of foreign nationals, et cetera. The obvious inference is that more importance should probably be attached to a conscious and public exercise of the right to self-defence (from the perspective of the formation/modification of customary law) than to a single act of the latter type. Accordingly, there would seem to be no need to insist on a continual repetition vis-à-vis the customary boundaries on the use of force, on condition that the active practice would be met by a very extensive support among the members of the international community, in turn providing proof of a high degree of uniformity as to the precise content and the legally binding character of the practice at the collective level.[215] On the other hand, as the ILA report emphasizes, in the nature of things some time will normally need to elapse before a practice matures into a rule:[216]

> [E]ven in the present era of easy and instantaneous communications, if a State or group of States adopts a practice, others will need to consider how (if at all) they wish to respond. These responses may give rise to further responses, and so on. All of this will usually involve some delay.[217]

A certain time lapse may also serve to clarify whether the practice and the concomitant reaction of third States was inspired by a sense of legal conviction,[218] or whether States' positions were, for instance, motivated by factual or circumstantial particularities. In sum, while so-called 'instant custom' – controversial though it may be – must not *a priori*

---

[215] Consider also Akehurst, 'Custom as a source of international law', 14.
[216] ILA *The formation of general customary international law*, p. 731; Villiger, *Customary international law and treaties*, p. 46.
[217] ILA, *The formation of general customary international law*, p. 732. Also Byers, *Custom, power and the power of rules*, pp. 161, 165.
[218] Villiger, *Customary international law and treaties*, p. 46.

be excluded from a theoretical perspective, in practice it would seem highly unlikely that a single instance of active State practice would, without any repetition or significant time lapse, give rise to the formation or modification of a rule of general customary international law.

The present author does not believe that a single Security Council resolution, such as the famous resolution 1368 (2001), adopted the day after the 9/11 attacks, could *of itself* give rise to new custom.[219] On the one hand, it is true that the Security Council is endowed with the primary competence in dealing with the maintenance of international peace and may adopt binding decisions. Several international judgments moreover pay heed to its practice to determine the applicability of rules of international law.[220] When evaluating the impact of Security Council resolutions it is nonetheless important to keep in mind that these documents represent the position of those voting for them. Insofar as they represent the practice and corresponding *opinio iuris* of (maximum) fifteen UN Members, including several 'specially affected States' (most notably the P-5), Security Council resolutions may constitute important evidence of customary practice. Together with other practice they may result in the formation or development of customary norms, be it that one must again take account of the exact content of the resolution, as well as of the opinions expressed during the debates. Unlike General Assembly resolutions, however, they can never represent the position of the international community as a whole due to a lack of generality. The emergence of 'instant custom' from a single Council resolution is therefore excluded.

As for General Assembly resolutions, the ICJ has repeatedly recognized that they 'can, in certain circumstances, provide evidence important for establishing the existence of a rule or the emergence of an *opinio iuris*'.[221] Furthermore, Article 13(1) UN Charter explicitly acknowledges that the General Assembly shall make recommendations for the progressive development of international law and its codification. On the other hand, when pronouncing on matters of *Ius ad Bellum*, the

---

[219] See, e.g., B. Langille, 'It's "instant custom": how the Bush doctrine became law after the terrorist attacks of September 11, 2001', (2003) 26 Boston College ICL Rev 145–56.

[220] ICTY Appeals Chamber, *Prosecutor* v. *Dusko Tadić*, Decision on the defence motion for interlocutory appeal on jurisdiction, 2 October 1995, reprinted in (1996) 35 ILM 32, §§ 114, 133; ICJ, *Legal Consequences of the construction of a wall in the Occupied Palestinian Territory*, Advisory opinion of 9 July 2004, (2004) ICJ Rep 163, §§ 99, 139. On the reference to resolution 1368 (2001) in the latter case, see *infra* Section 5.2.4.a.

[221] ICJ, *Legality of the threat or use of nuclear weapons*, Advisory opinion of 8 July 1996, (1996) ICJ Rep 226–67, §§ 70 *et seq.*; ICJ, *Nicaragua* case (Merits), § 188.

Assembly only acts as the forum through which the participating States express their views and not 'in its own capacity'. Hence, when a resolution is adopted by majority its content only represents the practice of those States voting in favour. What then about resolutions adopted by consensus or even unanimity, which in theory would represent the practice of virtually the whole international community, and which, when touching upon a Charter provision, could be considered an interpretation of the latter provisions by the whole UN membership? Without entering at length into the long-standing (and politically laden) debate as to these resolutions' impact vis-à-vis the customary process,[222] some considerations urge a cautious approach. First, the idea that the Assembly may create customary rules 'out of nothing' is hard to reconcile with the fact that its resolutions are, in principle, recommendatory.[223] Second, while in theory a resolution adopted by consensus or unanimity may represent the practice of the combined Member States of the United Nations and may simultaneously be used to deduce their *opinio iuris*, this will not always be so. A careful analysis of the text is indispensable to verify whether its provisions were inspired by legal considerations, or by political or other non-legal ones.[224] Likewise, if the resolution claims that something *ought to be* the law, this is not the same as asserting that it *is* law already.[225] Apart from the text itself, one must also take account of the surrounding verbal practice, such as reservations or vote explanations. If the pressure for consensus may stop an individual Member State from formally opposing the resolution, the latter documents may sometimes reflect important differences of opinion between the participating States. Third, even if no such differences of opinion appear to exist and the text is drafted in unambiguous legal terminology, in principle there would need to be some degree of physical practice, although it could be argued that the resolution may, exceptionally, create a rebuttable presumption that such practice exists.[226] In sum, the various General Assembly resolutions of a normative character which touch upon aspects

---

[222] See, e.g., G. Arangio-Ruiz, 'The normative role of the General Assembly of the United Nations and the development of Principles of Friendly Relations', (1972-III) RdC 419-72; ILA, *The formation of general customary international law*, pp. 765-76.
[223] E.g., Danilenko, 'The theory of international customary law', 26.
[224] E.g., ILA, *The formation of general customary international law*, p. 773; Villiger, *Customary international law and treaties*, p. 52.
[225] E.g., Akehurst, 'Custom as a source of international law', 7.
[226] De facto, the possibility of 'instant custom' is therefore not excluded, although technically it is not the resolution alone which would create the customary rule. See ILA, *The formation of general customary international law*, pp. 768-70, 772-6.

of the *Ius ad Bellum*, such as the Definition of Aggression[227] or the Declaration on the Non-Use of Force,[228] undeniably play a role for the purpose of ascertaining the content of the customary rules on the use of force and their development. Nonetheless, their importance must be assessed by reference to the context of their adoption as well as other relevant practice. The existence of a General Assembly resolution is no excuse for not looking at other (and possibly contradictory) evidence. In any event, since textual ambiguity is typically the price for consensus,[229] the debates preceding the vote will often be of greater interest for present purposes than the resolution itself.

1.2.4 Conclusion

In the end, the thorny quest for custom cannot be tackled simply by subscribing to an extensive or a restrictive approach. What is needed is a balanced approach, starting from all available evidence of State practice and *opinio iuris*, and proceeding to a cautious evaluation thereof. The physical practice of States, i.e., actual instances of inter-State recourse to force, constitutes the raw material of the customary process and will be our main point of departure. These incidents must be assessed by means of an analysis of States' relevant claims and counter-claims, which are primarily (but not exclusively) found in the records of the Security Council and, to a lesser extent, the General Assembly. On the other hand, incidents that have not fuelled significant legal debates as well as abstract legal debates not inspired by any particular incident must be included in our assessment. An equilibrium must be sought, not only between 'words' and 'deeds', but also between 'abstract' and 'concrete' statements; between the various aspects of density of State practice (uniformity, extensiveness and duration); between the (relatively more influential) practice of powerful States and that of other members of the international community; or between the practice of the Security Council and that of the General Assembly. Rapid and possibly far-reaching evolutions in the customary law on the use of force are thereby not excluded, yet they presuppose the furnishing of credible and compelling

---

[227] Definition of Aggression, Annex to GA Res. 3314 (XXIX).
[228] Declaration on the Enhancement of the Effectiveness of the Principle of Refraining from the Threat or Use of Force in International Relations, GA Res. 42/22 (XLII) of 18 November 1987.
[229] Gray, *The use of force*, pp. 9–10. Also Cahin, 'Le rôle des organes politiques des Nations Unies', 153.

evidence. This is the equilibrium we will seek to uphold. It must be stressed that, given their close interrelation, we will not in the remainder of this study attempt to separate out expressly in each case the material and the subjective element, but instead use the term 'customary practice' as a generic one, referring to varying degrees of evidence of both elements.

As for our examination of the customary boundaries of the right to self-defence, for the first fifty years of the Charter era we will, for practical reasons, confine ourselves mainly to those instances of inter-State use of force which have generated debates in the Security Council and on relevant General Assembly resolutions of a more normative character (in particular the Definition of Aggression and its *travaux*). In relation to more recent years, especially the post-9/11 era, we will broaden our analysis to also include incidents which have not been subject to the scrutiny of the international community in New York (here press statements may sometimes provide the main lead to establish the circumstances of and justifications for the use of force), as well as national security strategies and military doctrines, decisions of national parliaments, et cetera. It should at all times be kept in mind that the customary process is steered by *States* themselves – it is their words and deeds we need to scrutinize.

It stands beyond doubt that the case law of the ICJ dealing with the law on the use of force plays a central role in any analysis of the customary boundaries of self-defence and carries considerable authority. At the same time, it must be kept in mind that this case law does not of itself contribute to the formation of customary law, but rather constitutes a 'subsidiary means for the determination of the law', as recognized in Article 38 ICJ Statute.[230] Likewise, the writings of ('the most highly qualified') legal scholars provide a helpful tool to put into perspective the customary practice, but one of only subsidiary nature. Inconsistencies between different findings of the ICJ inevitably reduce the probative value of its dicta. By analogy, the same is true for doctrinal divides between groups of scholars. In short, if discrepancies arise between the 'law in the books' and the 'law in practice', precedence must be given to the latter.

---

[230] E.g., ILA, *The formation of general customary international law*, p. 729–30.

2

'Armed attack' and other conditions of self-defence

Having spelt out the methodological assumptions on which the present study is founded, we may now proceed to the actual analysis of the law on the use of force. In this context, it must be recalled that the focus of this study lies in particular on the aspect of self-defence that has raised most controversy in recent years, namely the need for an armed attack to occur before self-defence may lawfully be exercised. As explained in the Introduction, Chapters 3 to 5 are dedicated to an analysis of customary practice relevant for the notion of 'armed attack'.

Before turning to the various dimensions of the 'armed attack' requirement, however, it is first necessary to gain a better insight into the preconditions of self-defence in general. To this end, the present chapter briefly examines the text and the *travaux* of Article 51 UN Charter, in order to determine whether the 'armed attack' requirement actually constitutes an integral part thereof (section 2.1). This constitutes an important step to determine the 'baseline' against which customary practice is to be tested, and to distinguish interpretative from modificatory practice. Subsequently, we will proceed to an analysis of the various conventional and/or customary preconditions for the exercise of self-defence, other than the armed attack criterion (section 2.2).

2.1 The 'armed attack' requirement as an integral part of Article 51 UN Charter

2.1.1 Self-preservation and self-defence prior to 1945

If the UN Charter was the first international instrument to regulate in general terms the exercise of the right of self-defence, reference to the concept was made long before 1945. Thus, while the *compétence de guerre* was regarded as an obvious corollary of State sovereignty throughout the nineteenth century, States rarely went to war without invoking 'some stereotyped plea' to a right of self-preservation, necessity, self-help or self-defence.[1] Still, the wide variety of *casus belli* invoked, the unchecked discretion of States[2] and the lack of a coherent terminology all make clear that no legal regime of self-defence could be said to exist at the time.[3]

This gradually began to change in the transitional period between 1920 and 1945, when self-defence became the predominant concept and was increasingly linked to imminent or actual violence.[4] Several treaties referred to 'legitimate defence' or provided for recourse to force in 'collective defence'. The 1928 General Treaty for the Renunciation of War,[5] which first introduced a comprehensive ban on the recourse to war, did not include an express provision on self-defence. Still, numerous States submitted express reservations relating to this end.[6] These reservations generally framed self-defence in terms of 'protection against attack and foreign invasion.'[7] A US note of 23 June 1928, for example, stated that: 'There is nothing in the... treaty which restricts or impairs in any way the right of self-defence. That right is inherent in every sovereign state and is implicit in every treaty. Every nation is free at all times and regardless of treaty provisions to defend its territory from attack or invasion'.[8]

At the same time, despite apparent shifts in customary practice, writers remained very much divided on the scope of self-defence,[9] some still linking it to the nineteenth-century concept of self-preservation and others confining it to a reaction against an attack on the State's territory. Up to this date, legal scholars continue to disagree on the scope of self-defence as it stood in pre-Charter customary law. Many

---

[1] See I. Brownlie, 'The use of force in self-defence', (1961) 37 BYBIL 183–268, at 184 *et seq.*
[2] *Ibid.*, 190. See also: J. Westlake, *International law* Vol. I (Cambridge University Press, 1904), p. 299.
[3] Brownlie, 'The use of force in self-defence', 191; I. Brownlie, *International law and the use of force by states* (Oxford: Clarendon Press, 1963), p. 48. See also E. Giraud, 'La théorie de la légitime défense', (1934-III) 49 RdC 687–868, at 720.
[4] See Brownlie, 'The use of force in self-defence', 191 *et seq.*; Giraud, 'La légitime défense', 691, 720.
[5] General Treaty for the Renunciation of War, 27 August 1928, 94 LNTS 57.
[6] See Giraud, 'La légitime défense', 702 (Belgium), 713 (Italy); D. H. Miller, *The Peace Pact of Paris: a study of the Briand–Kellogg Treaty* (New York: Putnam's Sons, 1928), p. 43 (France), p. 196 (UK), p. 203 (Japan), p. 211 (South Africa), p. 213 (US), p. 240 (Czechoslovakia); D. P. Myers, *Origin and conclusion of the Paris Pact. The renunciation of war as an instrument of national policy* (Boston, MA: World Peace Foundation, 1929), p. 166 (Persia), p. 167 (Romania).
[7] See, e.g., the reservations of the UK, the US, Czechoslovakia and Romania.
[8] Reproduced in Miller, *The Peace Pact of Paris*, p. 213.
[9] See Brownlie, 'The use of force in self-defence', 210–11, 218–19. Aso Giraud, 'La légitime défense'.

argue that it was significantly broader than what is currently provided for under the terms of Article 51 UN Charter.[10] On the other hand, Brownlie has denounced these claims as 'references to the nebulous doctrines of the nineteenth century', and instead makes a strong case that the customary norm as it had evolved by 1945 had a content closely resembling the right expressed in Article 51 UN Charter.[11]

2.1.2 Article 51 UN Charter – primary means of interpretation

When the founding Members of the United Nations met in San Francisco in 1945, they ordained that 'all Members shall refrain in their international relations from the threat or use of force against the territorial integrity or political independence of any State, or in any other manner inconsistent with the Purposes of the United Nations' (Article 2 (4) UN Charter). By doing so, they extended the outlawry of *war* introduced by the Kellogg–Briand Pact to small-scale uses of force, effectively sanctioning armed reprisals short of war, as well as threats to use such force. While the precise meaning of the term 'force' has occasionally inspired debates in the UN General Assembly,[12] it is generally accepted in legal literature that it refers to the use of 'armed' or 'physical' force only.[13] This interpretation is apparently confirmed by

---

[10] See, e.g.: D. W. Bowett, *Self-defence in international law* (Manchester University Press, 1958), pp. 187 *et seq.*; J. L. Kunz, 'Individual and collective self-defense in Article 51 of the Charter of the United Nations', (1947) 41 AJIL 872–9, at 877; R. S. J. Macdonald, 'The *Nicaragua* case: new answers to old question?', (1986) 24 Can YBIL 127–60, at 147; S. M. Schwebel, 'Aggression, intervention and self-defence in modern international law', (1972-II) 136 RdC 411–97, at 479–83; C. H. M. Waldock, 'The regulation of the use of force by individual States in international law', (1952-II) 81 RdC 451–517, at 496–9.

[11] See Brownlie, *The use of force by states*, inter alia pp. 274, 280. See also M. Lachs, 'The development and general trends of international law in our time', (1980-IV) 169 RdC 9–377, at 162; H. Wehberg, 'L'interdiction du recours à la force. Le principe et les problèmes qui se posent', (1951-I) 78 RdC 1–121, at 84. Remark: Giraud in 1934 argued that the positive law of self-defence had evolved considerably in the first decennia of the twentieth century and no longer allowed for military action in order to defend a State's legal rights. On the other hand, Giraud recognized that, while the relevant law had developed considerably, this development was only recent and *yet incomplete*. See Giraud, 'La légitime défense', 691, 722 *et seq.*

[12] E.g., Macdonald, 'The *Nicaragua* case', 131 *et seq.*; P. Malanczuk and M. Akehurst, *Akehurst's modern introduction to international law*, 7th edn (London: Routledge, 1997), p. 310.

[13] E.g., American Law Institute, *Restatement of the Law – Third. The Foreign Relations Law of the United States* (St. Paul, MN: American Law Institute Publishers, 1990), p. 383; A. Constantinou, *The right of self-defence under customary international law and Article*

customary practice[14] and by the Charter's *travaux* – a Brazilian proposal to include economic aggression was rejected in San Francisco.[15] Furthermore, contrary to what some authors and some (limited) customary practice suggest,[16] the prohibition on the threat or use of force is not confined to force that is directed against a State's territorial integrity (most notably conquest or occupation) or its political independence (most notably regime overthrow). Rather, the final phrase, which speaks of force 'inconsistent with the purposes of the UN Charter', serves as a

51 *of the UN Charter* (Brussels: Bruylant, 2000), pp. 36–7; Y. Dinstein, *War, aggression and self-defence*, 4th edn (Cambridge University Press, 2005), p. 86; L. M. Goodrich and E. Hambro, *Charter of the United Nations: commentary and documents* (Boston, MA: World Peace Foundation, 1946), p. 70; R. Higgins, *Problems and process: international law and how we use it* (Oxford: Clarendon Press, 1994), at 248; D. Kritsiotis, 'Topographies of force', in Y. Dinstein and M. N. Schmitt (eds.), *International law and armed conflict exploring the faultlines: essays in honour of Yoram Dinstein* (Leiden: Martinus Nijhoff, 2007), pp. 29–77, at 68; Lachs, 'General trends of international law', 160; A. Randelzhofer, 'Article 2(4)', in B. Simma in collaboration with H. Mosler, A. Randelzhofer, C. Tomuschat and R. Wolfrüm (eds.), *The Charter of the United Nations: a commentary*. Vol. I (Oxford University Press, 2002), pp. 114–37, at 117–18; B. V. A. Röling, 'The ban on the use of force and the U.N. Charter', in A. Cassese (ed.), *The current legal regulation of the use of force* (Dordrecht: Martinus Nijhoff, 1986), pp. 3–8, at 3; M. Virally, 'Article 2: paragraphe 4', in J.-P. Cot and A. Pellet, *La Charte des Nations Unies*, 2nd edn (Paris: Economica, 1991), pp. 115–28, at 122–3; Waldock, 'The use of force by individual states', 492; Wehberg, 'L'interdiction du recours à la force', 68–9.

[14] See, e.g., T. J. Farer, 'Political and economic coercion in contemporary international law', (1985) 79 AJIL 405–13.

[15] UN, *Documents of the Conference on International Organization* (hereafter UNCIO), Vol. 6, 339, 340, 609. Remark: this interpretation also finds support in the reference in the Charter's preamble that 'armed force shall not be used, save in the common interest, as well as in the reference to the 'use of force' in Article 44 in a context clearly equating this concept with the use of *armed* force.

[16] E.g., the United Kingdom relied on the allegedly restrictive connotation of the phrase 'territorial integrity or political independence' before the ICJ to justify its mine-sweeping operation in Albanian territorial waters. The argument was nonetheless rejected by the Court. See: ICJ, *Corfu Channel (United Kingdom v. Albania)*, Judgment of 9 April 1949, (1949) ICJ Rep 4–38. For some other (hesitant) indications of such reading of Article 2 (4), see C. Gray, *International law and the use of force*, 3rd edn (Oxford University Press, 2008), pp. 32–3.

Among legal scholars, the argument was most staunchly defended by D'Amato. In relation to Israel's strike against the Iraqi nuclear reactor at Osiraq in 1981, D'Amato argued that: 'In its pre-emptive strike that lasted all of two minutes, Israel sought no annexation of any of Iraq's territory. Nor did Israel interfere with the Iraqi government or its legal standing vis-à-vis other nations. Thus, although Israel's strike was certainly a use of force, it arguably was not directed against Iraq's territorial integrity or political independence.' See A. D'Amato, *International law: process and prospect* (Dobbs Ferry, NY: Transnational Publishers, 1987), pp. 79 *et seq.* See also Bowett, *Self-defence in international law*, pp. 152, 185–6; J. Stone, *Aggression and world order: a critique of United Nations theories of aggression* (London: Stevens & Sons, 1958), pp. 95–6.

residual 'catch-all' provision, making clear that Article 2(4) constitutes a comprehensive ban against all uses or threats of force, regardless of their impact and gravity.[17] As the US asserted, the intention was to state in the broadest terms an absolute all-inclusive prohibition; the phrase 'or in any other manner' was designed to ensure that there should be no loopholes.[18]

While the precise meaning of the prohibition on the threat or use of force is beyond the scope of our analysis,[19] it must be observed that Article 2(4) is inextricably linked to two supplementary legal mechanisms enshrined in Chapter VII of the UN Charter. First, as the organ endowed with the primary responsibility for the maintenance of international peace and security, the Security Council is awarded the power to adopt enforcement measures whenever it determines that a threat to the peace, a breach of the peace, or an act of aggression has occurred (Article 39 UN Charter). In such case, the Council may *inter alia* impose economic or diplomatic enforcement measures (Article 41). Should the latter prove inadequate, the Council may resort to military enforcement (Article 42). Second, recognizing that the Council might not always be capable of responding in due course to acts of aggression, the drafters of the Charter included an express provision dealing with self-defence. Article 51 reads in full:

---

[17] See, e.g., T. M. Franck, *Recourse to force: State action against threats and armed attacks* (Cambridge University Press, 2002), p. 12. According to Franck, the Australian amendment adding the words 'against the territorial integrity or political independence' unintentionally created an opening for some to argue that the prohibition against force did not extend to 'minor' or 'temporary' invasions that stopped short of actually threatening the territorial integrity of the victim State or its independence. However, 'such reading of Article 2(4) is utterly incongruent with the evident intent of the sponsors of this amendment.' In a similar vein: Brownlie, *The use of force by states*, pp. 265–8; Constantinou, *The right of self-defence*, p. 49; Dinstein, *War, aggression and self-defence*, p. 87; P. Ducheine, *Krijgsmacht, geweldgebruik en terreurbestrijding* (Nijmegen: Wolf Legal Publishers, 2008), pp. 126–39; C. Greenwood, 'International law and the pre-emptive use of force: Afghanistan, Al-Qaida, and Iraq', (2003) 4 San Diego ILJ 7–37, at 10–11; L. Henkin, *International law: politics and values* (Dordrecht: Martinus Nijhoff, 1995), pp. 115–16; D. Kritsiotis, 'When States use armed force', in C. Reus-Smit, *The politics of international law* (Cambridge University Press, 2004), pp. 45–79, at 58–9; Malanczuk and Akehurst, *Akehurst's modern introduction*, p. 310; Wehberg, 'L'interdiction du recours à la force', 70.

[18] UNCIO Vol. 6, 334–5.

[19] For example, proponents of humanitarian intervention and/or pro-democratic intervention sometimes argue that the latter types of interventions do not contravene the prohibition of Article 2(4), since they are in fact aimed at promoting the very purposes of the United Nations. Both constructs fall beyond the scope of the present study.

> Nothing in the present Charter shall impair the inherent right of individual or collective self-defence if an armed attack occurs against a Member of the United Nations, until the Security Council has taken measures necessary to maintain international peace and security. Measures taken by Members in the exercise of this right of self-defence shall be immediately reported to the Security Council and shall not in any way affect the authority and responsibility of the Security Council under the present Charter to take at any time such action as it deems necessary in order to maintain or restore international peace and security.

It clearly follows from the text that self-defence was only considered a temporary measure, available pending appropriate reaction by the Council. States allegedly exercising this right were obliged to inform the Council of their actions and the reasons therefor, in order to enable it to assess the situation and to take any measures deemed necessary. Upon adoption, such measures terminate the need for and permissibility of a unilateral response by the relevant State.

The key interpretative problem lies in the first part of the first sentence. The phrase 'nothing ... shall impair' and the reference to the 'inherent' right of self-defence have been invoked by several scholars as evidence that the Charter did not impose any limitations on the pre-existing customary right of self-defence.[20] According to these authors, the phrase 'if an armed attack occurs' was only intended to give particular emphasis in a declaratory manner, for self-defence in the case of an armed attack.[21] Hence, Article 51 was not incompatible with the broader customary right of self-defence, which allegedly allowed for self-defence in certain situations in which no armed attack had occurred, and which was simply left unabridged. Most proponents of this approach support the legality of anticipatory self-defence, before an actual attack is launched. Some also claim that self-defence is available in other situations, for instance to enforce legal rights, to undertake armed reprisals or even to protect economic interests abroad.[22]

---

[20] See, e.g.: Bowett, *Self-defence in international law*, pp. 187 et seq.; M. S. McDougal, 'The Soviet–Cuban quarantine and self-defense', (1963) 57 AJIL 597–604, at 599–600; J. N. Moore, 'The secret war in Central America and the future world order', (1986) 80 AJIL 43–127, at 82–3; Schwebel, 'Aggression, intervention and self-defence', 479–83; Waldock, 'The use of force by individual States', 496–9.

[21] See A. Randelzhofer, 'Article 51', in B. Simma et al. (eds.), *The Charter of the United Nations*, pp. 788–806, at 792–3.

[22] Bowett, for example, held that Article 51 permitted the protection of certain substantive rights: 'Action undertaken for the purpose of, and limited to, the defence of a State's

Even if the ICJ apparently considered the word 'inherent' to refer to customary law,[23] it is difficult to see how the phrase 'if an armed attack occurs' could be of a merely declaratory or illustrative nature. To the contrary, each of the three primary elements of interpretation listed in Article 31(1) VCLT suggests that it can only be interpreted as a characterization of the scope of permissible self-defence. First, as regards the ordinary meaning of the words, 'if an armed attack occurs' – 'dans le cas où un Membre des Nations Unies est l'objet d'une agression armée' in the equally authentic French version; 'en caso de ataque armado' in the Spanish version – prima facie points to a precondition for the exercise of self-defence. Taking into account the principle of effectiveness or *effet utile*, it is hard to imagine that the drafters merely desired to state the obvious – that self-defence is lawful against an armed attack – while leaving unaffected other, much more controversial, opportunities for lawful self-defence. In such case, one could have expected the drafters to have stressed that self-defence was available '*for example*, if an armed attack occurs', or simply not to have included the phrase at all: *expressio unius est exclusio alterius*. Second, as far as the contextual element is concerned, Article 51 must be read in conjunction with Articles 2(4), 39, 42 and 53. The picture that emerges is that of a comprehensive regime, consisting of an absolute ban on the unilateral use of force by States, supplemented by the creation of a sort of world police, the UN Security Council, the sole body endowed with the power to engage in military enforcement action to maintain international peace and security. Against this background, the legal regime enshrined in Article 51 can only be perceived as a provisional and exceptional regime, which must be interpreted in a restrictive manner. It should moreover be noted that while Article 51 only refers to an 'armed attack', Article 2(4) outlaws both the *use* and the *threat* of force. The gap between the two provisions is striking and cannot merely be passed off as bad draftsmanship. Third, the 'objects and purpose' of the UN Charter only reinforce this picture. Indeed, as a product of the horrors of the Second World War inspired by the desire to end the 'scourge of war', the whole object of the Charter was precisely to

---

political independence, territorial integrity, the lives and property of its nationals (and even to protect its economic independence) cannot by definition involve a threat or use of force "against the territorial integrity or political independence" of any other State.' Bowett, *Self-defence in international law*, pp. 185–6.

[23] ICJ, *Case concerning military and paramilitary activities in and against Nicaragua (Nicaragua v. United States of America)* (Merits), Judgment of 27 June 1986, (1986) ICJ Rep 14–150, § 176.

limit the scope for unilateral use of force as much as possible and to subject it to the control of the Security Council. It is no coincidence that Article 2(4) forms part of the purposes of the Charter and is immediately preceded by a provision which orders States to settle their disputes peacefully (Article 2(3)). In sum, all of the primary interpretative elements indicate that the phrase 'if an armed attack occurs' forms an integral part of, and essential condition for, the exercise of the right of self-defence.

In a normal situation, this would settle the controversy regarding the original meaning of Article 51: the primary means of interpretation cannot be said to leave the meaning ambiguous or obscure. Nonetheless, proponents of a broad reading of self-defence have occasionally pointed out that a restrictive reading of the provision would lead to 'manifestly absurd' results, since States would be forced to suffer a 'first strike' before being able to respond.[24] This passivity, it is argued, can hardly be demanded from a threatened State, as a first strike can inflict appalling and possibly decisive destruction, an argument that has become all the more compelling in the nuclear era. From a theoretical perspective, this argument merits further scrutiny and warrants an examination of the preparatory works of the UN Charter as a supplementary means of interpretation (Article 32 VCLT).

2.1.3 *The preparatory works of the UN Charter*

In May–June 1945, the Conference on International Organization, held in San Francisco, brought together some 300 official delegates, representing fifty different nations, charged with the drafting of the founding document of the new world organization. The delegates proceeded on the basis of the Dumbarton Oaks proposals,[25] which had been agreed upon in 1944 by the Big Four (the US, the UK, USSR and the (then) Republic of China). While the proposals already included an elaborate blueprint of the competences of the Security Council, as well as a prohibition on 'the threat or use of force in any manner inconsistent with the purposes of the Organization', the provision on self-defence was only inserted at San Francisco. Information relating to its drafting can be

---

[24] E.g., Schwebel, 'Aggression, intervention and self-defence', 479–81; Waldock, 'The use of force by individual States', 498.
[25] 'Proposals for the establishment of a general international organization', *US Department of State Bulletin* 11, 368.

found in two different sources: the official records of the Conference on International Organization (UNCIO) (in particular those regarding the proceedings of Committee III/4 ('regional arrrangements'))[26] and the US Diplomatic Papers of the Conference.[27]

Starting with the official UNCIO records, some brief references to self-defence can be found in the course of the discussions within Committee I/1, where the drafting of Article 2(4) took place. In response to an Australian amendment substantially identical with the final text of Article 2(4),[28] Norway sought to prohibit in general terms any use of force not approved by the Security Council. Explaining why the Norwegian amendment was rejected, the Committee Rapporteur reported that:

> The sense of approval was considered ambiguous because it might mean approval before or after the use of force. It might thus curtail the right of States to use force in legitimate self-defence, while it was clear to the subcommittee that the right of self-defence against aggression should not be impaired or diminished.[29]

'The subsequent Committee report reflected a similar view: 'The Committee likes it to be stated in view of the Norwegian amendment ... that the unilateral use of force or similar coercive measures is not authorized or admitted. The use of arms in legitimate self-defence remains admitted and unimpaired.'[30]

The two aforementioned statements are sometimes invoked as evidence that the drafters did not intend to *regulate* self-defence, but chose to leave pre-existing custom 'unimpaired'.[31] However, the significance of these statements should not be overestimated. They were expressed as side comments in a discussion concerning the scope of Article 2(4) and not during a discussion of Article 51. It is to the latter provision's drafting we must turn.

---

[26] Remark: at San Francisco, the preparatory work was divided between four main commissions (General Provisions (I); General Assembly (II); Security Council (III); and Judicial Organization (IV)), each consisting of a number of technical committees and subcommittees. In exceptional cases, the drafts worked out by these commissions were subject to review by the Coordinating Committee and/or the Advisory Committee of Jurists (*ibid.*, 10). Once a text had been cleared by the Coordinating Committee, it was up to the Steering Committee to submit it to the Plenary Assembly for adoption.

[27] US Department of State, *Foreign Relations of the United States, Diplomatic Papers. (1945) General: the United Nations* (1967), pp. 425 *et seq.* Remark: the US delegation was directly responsible for the drafting of Article 51.

[28] UNCIO, Vol. 6, 557.   [29] UNCIO, Vol. 6, 721.   [30] UNCIO, Vol. 6, 418.

[31] See, e.g., C. Kahgan, 'Jus Cogens and the inherent right to self-defense', (1996–7) 3 ILSA JICL 767–827, at 802–3.

It is well-known that the inclusion of Article 51 was motivated first and foremost by the wish of certain States expressly to affirm the compatibility with the UN Charter of existing and future collective defence arrangements. In particular, the Article aimed at accommodating concerns among Latin-American States that, despite the rule that regional arrangements should not undertake enforcement action without authorization by the Security Council (Article 53), they would still be allowed to engage in collective defence in accordance with the Act of Chapultepec.[32] Immediately following the approval within Subcommittee III/4/9 of the American draft Article 51, the Colombian delegate hastened to stress that the approval of this article implied that the Act of Chapultepec was not in contravention of the Charter[33] – a view numerous Latin-American countries expressly associated with.[34] The focus on 'collective defence' by regional arrangements or mutual defence alliances was also present in numerous other statements.[35] Uruguay, for example, observed that the right of collective self-defence referred not only to the Act of Chapultepec, but also to any other regional arrangement which might be established in the future.[36] Egypt stated that it should certainly extend to the newly established League of Arab States.[37]

Does this *raison d'être* of Article 51 imply that the Article did not purport to define the right of self-defence, as some contend?[38] The UNCIO records do not seem to warrant such a conclusion. It may be observed that several delegations expressly referred to both collective *and*

---

[32] Inter-American Reciprocal Assistance and Solidarity (Act of Chapultepec), Mexico, 6 March 1945, 60 Stat 1831. The Act of Chapultepec became the progenitor of the Inter-American Treaty of Reciprocal Assistance 2 September 1947, Rio de Janeiro, 1947, 21 UNTS 77.
[33] UNCIO Vol. 12, 680–1: 'The Latin American countries understood . . . that the origin of the term "collective self-defense" is identified with the necessity of preserving regional systems like the Inter-American one. The Charter . . . legitimizes the right of collective self-defense to be carried out in accord with the regional pacts so long as they are not opposed to the purposes and principles . . . expressed in the Charter. . . . [T]he approval of this article implies that the Act of Chapultepec is not in contravention of the Charter.'
[34] UNCIO, Vol. 12, 681 (Mexico, Costa Rica, Paraguay, Venezuela, Chile, Ecuador, Bolivia, Panama, Uruguay, Peru, Guatemala, El Salvador, Brazil, Honduras and Cuba).
[35] E.g., statements by France (UNCIO, Vol. 1, 437; UNCIO, Vol. 3, 379, 387; UNCIO, Vol. 6, 681) and Turkey (UNCIO, Vol. 12, 781; UNCIO, Vol. 3, 483).
[36] UNCIO, Vol. 12, 681.   [37] *Ibid.*, 682.
[38] E.g., Kahgan, 'The inherent right to self-defense', 803 *et seq.*; T. L. H. McCormack, *Self-defense in international law: the Israeli raid on the Iraqi nuclear reactor* (New York: St. Martin's Press, 1996), pp. 150–85; Waldock, 'The use of force by individual states', 497.

individual self-defence throughout the discussions of draft Article 51.[39] In the words of US Senator Vandenberg:

> [W]e here recognize the inherent right of self-defence, whether individual or collective, which permits any sovereign State among us or any qualified regional group of States to ward off attack pending adequate action by the parent body.[40]

The discussions vis-à-vis the location of Article 51 point in the same direction. While Committee III/4 had suggested that the Article be placed as a separate section following the Chapter on 'Regional Arrangements',[41] both the Advisory Committee of Jurists and the Coordination Committee insisted that it be incorporated under Chapter VII, dealing with the Security Council.[42] On the one hand, it was argued that the provision was closely connected with the powers given to the Security Council in that Chapter. On the other hand, placing the Article after Chapter VIII was considered undesirable, on the grounds that it might have the effect of limiting the right of self-defence only to regional arrangements, a conclusion that was clearly not to be permitted.[43] As one US delegate put it: 'the desire to emphasize a general right of individual or collective self-defence would be better realized at the end of Chapter VII rather than with Chapter VIII, where it would only have a bearing on the regional system'.[44] From this it appears that, despite the original motive for its inclusion, Article 51 intended to regulate on equal footing the exercise of both collective and individual self-defence. Numerous statements illustrate that the exercise of both forms of self-defence was subjected to a double procedural check: first, recourse to self-defence had to be reported to the Security Council with the least possible delay; and, second, the exercise of the right was terminated with the adoption of appropriate measures by the Council. No delegation made any attempt to assert the permissibility of self-defence in situations other than those involving an armed attack. To the contrary, several delegates expressly linked self-defence with the

---

[39] E.g., UNCIO, Vol. 3, 681–2 (Czechoslovakia), 687 (Colombia). Also UNCIO, Vol. 1, 453; UNCIO, Vol. 3, 483 (Turkey).
[40] UNCIO, Vol. 11, 53.   [41] E.g., UNCIO, Vol. 18, 272.
[42] See in particular: UNCIO, Vol. 17, 286–8.
[43] Statement by Mr Golunsky: *ibid.*, 287. See also the statement by Chairman Pasvolsky: 'There is a residual and inherent right of self-defense which can be applied by nations individually or collectively. Having said that it can be applied collectively in Chapter VII, Chapter VIII makes provision for the actual application of that right.'
[44] Statement by Mr Jebb: *ibid.*, 288.

warding off of an armed attack pending adequate action by the Security Council, or with the repression of aggression, two concepts that were sometimes used interchangeably.[45]

What additional evidence can be distilled from the US Diplomatic Papers? Admittedly, the discussions within the US delegation confirm the view that Article 51 was inserted to accommodate the concerns of the signatories of the Act of Chapultepec. The idea apparently came from Governor Stassen. According to the minutes of a meeting of 10 May 1945:

> Mr. Stassen pointed out that ... the basic objection to the present plan was the inability of a regional organization to act in the event of an arbitrary veto of one of the major powers. He said that he had come to the conclusion that it might be best to spell out in the Charter the right of self-defense, in order to meet the recurrent criticism on this question.[46]

Nonetheless, subsequent draft versions of the Article all dealt with both collective and individual self-defence and defined the right as a response to an 'attack', an 'armed attack' or 'aggression'. One of the first drafts read as follows:

> In the event of an attack by any State against a Member State, such Member shall possess the right to take measures of self-defence. The right to take measures of self-defence against armed attack shall apply to arrangements, like those embodied in the Act of Chapultepec, under which all members of a group of States agree to consider an attack against any one of them as an attack against all of them...[47]

Upon suggestion of US Delegate Pasvolsky, the word 'inherent' was inserted before the phrase 'right to self-defence', apparently without any debate taking place on the intent or meaning of the word.[48] In response to objections by the British and French, the US worked out a

---

[45] E.g., UNCIO, Vol. 11, 6–7 (US, referring to the warding off of an attack and to the 'repression of aggression'); UNCIO, Vol. 3, 483 (Turkey, referring to 'legitimate defense against a surprise attack by another State'); UNCIO, Vol. 12, 680–1 (Colombia); UNCIO, Vol. 12, 687 (Colombia: "But if at any time an armed attack should ensue, that is, an aggression against a State which is a member of the regional group, self-defense, whether individual or collective ... shall operate automatically ... until such time as the Security Council may take the appropriate punitive measures ...').

Remark: on the intitiative of the Canadian member of the Coordination Committee, some minor textual revisions of Article 51 were accepted by the Coordination Committee. The phrase 'if an armed attack occurs' was left unchanged. See UNCIO, Vol. 17, 26, 286.

[46] *Foreign Relations of the United States, Diplomatic Papers* (1945), p. 659.
[47] Ibid., p. 674 (deleted wording).
[48] Ibid., pp. 670, 674. See also Kaghan, 'The inherent right to self-defense', 813, footnote 179.

new draft, which made self-defence dependent on the lack of a decision by the Security Council.[49] According to this version: 'should the Security Council not succeed in preventing aggression, and should aggression occur by any State against any member State, such Member State possesses the inherent right to take necessary measures for self-defence ...'. Both drafts stressed that measures for self-defence had to be reported immediately to the Security Council and left the latter body's authority and responsibility unaffected.

The British delegation nonetheless expressed strong discomfort that regional organizations would be given too much leeway and that this might impair the effectiveness of the international organization.[50] More specifically, the UK expressed concern at the use of the term 'aggression', 'a concept which no-one had been able to define in 30 years'. In reply, US delegates assured that regional organizations were not accorded a broad freedom of action; there would only be the 'right of action in self-defence against armed attack'.[51] Mr Dulles moreover noted that the latest US proposal specifically used the terms 'armed attack' in an attempt to circumvent the problem of trying to define aggression as such.[52] A British proposal that would link self-defence to disputes or situations involving a 'breach of the peace' was quickly abandoned.[53] Later (US and USSR) draft versions no longer referred to 'aggression', but only spoke of 'armed attack'.[54] No substantive discussion took place in relation to the content of the latter concept. Nonetheless, when, during a meeting of the US delegation, one member warned that the draft 'greatly qualified' the right of self-defence by limiting it to the occasion of an armed attack, Governor Stassen replied that 'this was intentional', since 'we did not want exercised the right of self-defence before an armed attack had occurred'.[55] Significantly, when another delegate asked what action could be undertaken 'in case a fleet had started from abroad against an American republic but had not yet attacked', Stassen replied that 'we could not under this provision attack the fleet but we could send a fleet of our own and be ready in case an attack came'.[56]

At the seventh Five-Power Informal Consultative Meeting on Proposed Amendments, a slightly modified draft was discussed, which included the clause that self-defence could be exercised 'until the Security

---

[49] *Foreign Relations of the United States, Diplomatic Papers* (1945), pp. 675–7 et seq., 683–834.
[50] *Ibid.*, p. 692.   [51] *Ibid.*, p. 694.   [52] *Ibid.*, p. 700.   [53] *Ibid.*, p. 699.
[54] See *ibid.*, pp. 705, 813–20.   [55] *Ibid.*, p. 818.   [56] *Ibid.*, p. 709.

Council has taken the measures necessary'.[57] The latter draft was greeted with enthusiastic support *inter alia* by the Latin-American ambassadors. No substantial changes were proposed during the debates in the UNCIO subcommittee or committee.[58]

In the end, what may be inferred from the *travaux*? Nothing in the preparatory works suggests that Article 51 was merely perceived as an example of a broader, pre-existing and unimpaired customary right of self-defence. No explicit reference was made to pre-existing custom, nor to any alleged right of self-defence in circumstances not involving an armed attack. The word was added without any substantive discussion concerning its implications. In light of the French version of the text, which refers to a '*droit naturel*', we may assume that it is merely a remnant of the natural law origin of the concept of self-defence.[59] Indeed, the word recalls the works of famous scholars, such as Grotius or Vattel, who framed self-defence or self-preservation as an absolute, natural right of the State.[60] Similar language was and is on occasion used by States in official pronouncements.[61] Upon adoption of the Kellogg–Briand Pact, for example, South Africa issued a reservation regarding the 'natural right of legitimate self-defence'.[62] The US explanatory note of 23 June 1928 likewise referred to the 'natural right of self-defence', which was 'inherent in every sovereign State and implicit in every treaty'.[63] However, if the perception of self-defence as an 'inherent right' implies that it was considered to be tacitly reserved in every treaty, this does not

---

[57] *Ibid.*, pp. 823–4.   [58] UNCIO, Vol. 17, 286.
[59] Dinstein, *War, aggression and self-defence*, p. 180. See also: Kunz, 'Individual and collective self-defense', 876. According to Kunz: 'The phrase "inherent right" can only serve to obscure the legal meaning. As a legal right, granted by positive international law, it has to be defined by this positive law. Only thus can its legal meaning be discovered; only thus can we see whether Art. 51 constitutes a progressive development ...'. See also H. Kelsen, *The law of the United Nations: a critical analysis of its fundamental problems* (London: Stevens, 1950), pp. 791–2: '[Article 51] presupposes the existence of the right of self-defence as established, not by positive international law, but by natural law, for it speaks of an "inherent" right. This is a theoretical opinion of the legislator which has no legal importance. The effect of Article 51 would not change if the term "inherent" were dropped.'
[60] Grotius, for example, wrote that 'the right of self-defence ... has its origin directly, and chiefly, in the fact that nature commits to each his own protection ...'. H. Grotius, *De Jure Belli ac Paci* (Carnegie Endowment translation of 1925, 1646), Book II, Chapter II, Pt. III, at 172. Also E. de Vattel, *Le droit des gens* 1863 edn (Paris: Guillaumin, 1863), Book II, Chapter IV, p. 49.
[61] See S. Smis and K. Van der Borght, 'The advisory opinion on the legality of the threat or use of nuclear weapons', (1998–9) 27 Georgia JICL 345–87, at 367.
[62] See Miller, *The Peace Pact of Paris*, p. 211.   [63] *Ibid.*, p. 213.

mean that it was considered to be beyond legal qualification.[64] Indeed, the widespread recognition in the nineteenth century of the liberty of States to go to war clearly did not prevent States from subjecting this sovereign prerogative to legal regulation in the first half of the twentieth century, most notably as a result of the Kellogg–Briand Pact. In a similar vein, the reference to the 'inherent' right of self-defence in Article 51 cannot outweigh the clear intent of the Charter's authors to subject the exercise of self-defence to legal regulation, *inter alia* by imposing a review by the Security Council. Hence, we may agree with the majority of legal doctrine that the term simply means that, contrary to what the text of Article 51 might suggest, this right is also vested in States other than UN Members.[65]

In general, an analysis of the *travaux* affirms our initial interpretation, according to which Article 51 qualifies the exercise of individual and collective self-defence by imposing a double procedural condition, as well as a substantive condition, namely the incidence of an 'armed attack'. The 'armed attack' requirement thus constitutes an integral part of Article 51; no self-defence can be exercised if no armed attack occurs.[66]

On the other hand, if the reference to 'armed attack' aimed at avoiding the problems of definition associated with the controversial concept of 'aggression', no substantial discussion took place as to its precise scope, thus leaving many questions unanswered. For example, while the first versions of Article 51 referred to attack 'by any State against any Member State',[67] the drafters of the Charter apparently did not envisage the possibility of attacks being carried out by irregular forces or armed bands. It remains unclear from the text of Article 51 and from the

---

[64] See, e.g., O. Schachter, *International law in theory and practice* (Dordrecht: Martinus Nijhoff, 1991), pp. 135 *et seq.* Contra: Kelsen, *The law of the United Nations*, pp. 791–2. Kelsen argued that the right of self-defence was supposed to be established by a *ius cogens* norm so that it could not be affected by any treaty. At the same time, he observed that 'the Charter does not maintain very consistently the presupposed idea of an "inherent" right of self-defence, which implies that this right ... cannot be altered by it. For the Charter extends this right in one respect and limits it in the other.'

[65] See, e.g., Randelzhofer, 'Article 51', p. 792; Wehberg, 'L'interdiction du recours à la force', 81–2. See also Constantinou, *The right of self-defence*, pp. 53–6.

[66] For a similar reading of the preparatory works: e.g., Lachs, 'General trends of international law', 162; L.-A. Sicilianos, *Les réactions décentralisées à l'illicité: des contre-mesures à la légitime défense* (Paris: Librairie générale de droit et de jurisprudence, 1990), pp. 299–300. Contra: McCormack, *Self-defense in international law*, pp. 150–85.

[67] *Foreign Relations of the United States, Diplomatic Papers* (1945), pp. 664, 674, 834. See also: UNCIO, Vol. 3, 483 (Turkey; referring to a 'surprise attack by another State').

travaux to what extent self-defence would be available to a State falling victim to such attacks. In a similar vein, while some statements referred to an armed attack '*having occurred*'[68] (instead of '*occurring*'), there was no direct discussion regarding the possibility of 'intercepting' or 'preventing' an attack. In this context, it must be stressed that while we have rejected the idea that Article 51 is but part of a broader pre-existing customary right of self-defence, this does not necessarily mean that substantial claims regarding a broad reading of 'armed attack' should automatically be rejected. Yet, relevant claims ought to be tested against present day customary practice, rather than against pre-Charter custom (whatever its content).

2.2 Other conditions of self-defence

2.2.1 'Procedural' obligations

2.2.1.a The reporting obligation

Apart from the 'armed attack' requirement, the exercise of the right of self-defence is bound by several other conditions, some of which are enshrined in Article 51 UN Charter and others required by customary international law. First, in accordance with Article 51, '[m]easures taken by Members in the exercise of [the] right of self-defence shall be immediately reported to the Security Council and shall not in any way affect the authority and responsibility of the Security Council ... to take at any time such action as it deems necessary in order to maintain or restore international peace and security'.[69]

The purport of this obligation was discussed by the ICJ in the *Nicaragua* case.[70] *In casu*, the United States claimed that its support to the Contras and subsequent actions, such as attacks on Nicaraguan oil factories, constituted lawful measures of self-defence, even though these actions had never been reported to the Security Council. The Court – precluded from directly applying the Charter provisions as a result of the

---

[68] *Foreign Relations of the United States, Diplomatic Papers* (1945), pp. 705 (draft Article), 818 (comment by Governor Stassen).

[69] This phrase was inserted at an early stage of the drafting process of the provision and was copied without modification in subsequent American and Russian drafts. E.g., *Foreign Relations of the United States, Diplomatic Papers* (1945), pp. 683, 705, 813, 823–4. See also, e.g., UNCIO, Vol. 3, 379 (France); UNCIO, Vol. 11, 58 (US).

[70] ICJ, *Nicaragua* case (Merits), §§ 200, 235.

'Vandenberg reservation'[71] – observed that the reporting procedure was 'closely dependent on the content of a treaty commitment and of the institutions established by it'.[72] Consequently, 'whatever the influence the Charter may have had on customary international law', the absence of a report on the part of the US was not of itself a breach of a customary norm applicable to the dispute. At the same time, even within the framework of international custom, the absence of a report was found to constitute *one of the factors indicating* whether the State in question was itself convinced that it was acting in self-defence.[73] The lack of a report on behalf of the United States was therefore hard to reconcile with 'its avowed conviction that it was acting in the context of collective self-defence as consecrated by Article 51 of the UN Charter'.[74]

Considering that the ICJ in *Nicaragua* examined the reporting obligation from the perspective of customary law, the question remains to what extent the obligation is of a mandatory or directory nature under the treaty provision of Article 51 UN Charter as such.[75] Two options can be distinguished. Either it could be considered a substantive precondition in the absence of which self-defence cannot be invoked; *or* it could be identified as a separate procedural obligation, the violation of which would also provide a rebuttable indication that the State did not consider itself to be acting in self-defence. While some have interpreted the

---

[71] See *supra*, Section 1.1.1.
[72] ICJ, *Nicaragua* case (Merits), § 200. Remark: it could moreover be argued that the reporting requirement is admittedly not of a 'fundamentally norm-creating character such as could be regarded as forming the basis of a general rule of law', in the sense of the North Sea Continental Shelf case. ICJ, *North Sea Continental Shelf* (*Federal Republic of Germany* v. *Denmark and the Netherlands*), Judgment of 20 February 1969, (1969) ICJ Rep 3, § 72.
[73] ICJ, *Nicaragua* case (Merits), § 200.   [74] *Ibid.*, § 235.
[75] Remark: in the *DRC* v. *Uganda* case, the Court – directly applying the Charter provisions on the use of force – observed that Uganda had not reported to the Security Council any events that it had regarded as requiring it to act in self-defence. It further noted that Uganda did not ever argue that it had been subjected to an armed attack by the armed forces of the DRC. '*For all these reasons*, the Court [found] that the legal and factual circumstances for the exercise of a right of self-defence by Uganda against the DRC were not present (emphasis added).' This dictum reaffirms that the failure to report counts as an element to be taken into account to determine the (il)legality of alleged measures of self-defence. The question whether such failure could, of its own, render defensive measures unlawful is, however, not conclusively settled by this ruling. ICJ, *Case concerning armed activities on the territory of the Congo* (*Democratic Republic of the Congo* v. *Uganda*), Judgment of 19 December 2005, (2005) ICJ Rep 116–220, §§ 145–7. Consider also: Ethiopia–Eritrea Claims Commission, Partial Award *Jus ad Bellum*, Ethiopia Claims 1–8, 19 December 2005, reprinted in (2006) 45 ILM 430, § 11.

Nicaragua judgment in the former sense,[76] Greig objects that it is hardly possible to have a mandatory provision in the Charter relating to the exercise of a power available under both sources, to which there is no counterpart in customary law.[77] This view, he argues, is inconsistent with the Court's own approach to the relationship between the customary and treaty rules relating to the recourse to force.[78] Indeed, although the Court recognized that the two sources do not overlap exactly, it apparently excluded the possibility of major discrepancies.[79] Nonetheless, if the duty to report were seen as a substantive precondition under Article 51, this could mean that a single recourse to force by a UN Member State could be lawful under the customary rules on the use of force, yet unlawful under the Charter provisions.

If Greig's argument hinges on the somewhat artificial and contested dicta of the Court on the relationship between treaty and customary *Ius ad Bellum*, other, more convincing, arguments support the view that the duty to report is only a procedural and evidentiary obligation, rather than a substantive one. First of all, a teleological interpretation of Article 51 leaves little doubt that its insertion was linked to the conception of self-defence as a temporary safeguard pending appropriate measures by the Security Council. Its object and purpose is to permit the Security Council to exert its supervening authority in a timely way, not to predetermine the validity of the recourse to self-defence before the Security Council has had a chance to pronounce on the situation.[80] The sequence of events also suggests that it cannot constitute a substantive obligation: as the obligation does not arise until measures of self-defence have been taken, it would seem illogical that compliance therewith could determine the (il)legality of the initiation of an operation.[81]

---

[76] E.g., Dinstein, *War, aggression and self-defence*, p. 216.

[77] D. W. Greig, 'Self-defence and the Security Council: what does Article 51 require?', (1991) 40 ICLQ 366–402, at 380.

[78] Ibid., 379–86.

[79] ICJ, *Nicaragua* case (Merits), § 181: 'The differences which may exist between the specific content of each are not, in the Court's view, such as to cause a judgment confined to the field of customary international law to be ineffective or inappropriate, or a judgment not susceptible of compliance or execution.'

[80] As Judge Schwebel observes: 'the international community at large, as represented by the Security Council, has an interest in the maintenance of international peace and security which should not be pre-empted by the failure of a State to report its defensive measures to the Security Council'. *Ibid.*, Dissenting opinion of Judge Schwebel, § 227. Also Greig, 'Self-defence and the Security Council', 368.

[81] M. Knisbacher, 'The Entebbe operation: a legal analysis of Israel's rescue action', (1977–8) 12 J Int'l L of Economics 57–83, at 79.

CONDITIONS OF SELF-DEFENCE 71

Furthermore, customary practice generally supports the view that (1) the failure to report does not automatically bar the invocation of self-defence, (2) but nonetheless provides an indication in assessing the legality of the measures allegedly taken in self-defence. In support of the former conclusion it suffices to note that there do not appear to be any statements in the practice of the Security Council whereby States have claimed that the actions undertaken were unlawful merely because of the absence of a report, and that, conversely, States have sometimes supported the legality of unilateral interventions that were not reported to the Council.[82] In support of the latter conclusion, it may be observed that States have occasionally praised the filing of a report as a token of 'good faith', and, more importantly, have repeatedly suggested that the failure to do so weakens a State's legal case.[83] For example, as the ICJ in *Nicaragua* was keen to point out, in relation to the 1979 Soviet intervention in Afghanistan, the United States itself took the view that failure to observe the requirement to make a report contradicted a State's claim to be acting on the basis of collective self-defence.[84] According to the US representative: 'That neither the Soviet Union nor the puppet regime it has installed in Afghanistan [had] given the required notice to the Security Council under Article 51 [was] itself evidence of the hollowness of the Soviet Union's refuge in the Charter.'[85] In a similar vein, the UK representative asked 'why, if such external attacks had been going on, Afghanistan and the USSR had not brought the matter to the United Nations attention'.[86] Both Libya and the United States raised identical arguments in relation to clashes between them in 1986.[87] The significance of the reporting obligation was also stressed by India in relation to

---

[82] In 2008, for example, the Dutch Foreign Minister expressed support for Turkey's exercise of self-defence in response to PKK attacks emanating from northern Iraqi territory, even though Turkey never reported its actions to the Security Council. Statement by Dutch Foreign Minister Maxime Verhagen, 'Beantwoording vragen van het lid Van Bommel over een Turkse invasie in Noord-Irak', 3 March 2008, available at www.minbuza.nl/nl/actueel/brievenparlement,2008/03/Beantwoording-vragen-van-het-lid-Van-Bommel-over-e.html (accessed 27 April 2009). See also *infra*, Section 5.2.3.c.
[83] See Gray, *The use of force*, p. 122. E.g., UN Doc. S/PV.1200, 5 May 1965, § 9 (Jordan); UN Doc. S/PV.2288, 19 June 1981, § 141 (Uganda); (1964) UNYB 148 (UK, in relation to the Gulf of Tunkin incident, noting that 'it was proper that the United States had reported to the Council on the measures which it had felt compelled to undertake in the exercise of the right to self-defence').
[84] ICJ, *Nicaragua* case (Merits), § 235.
[85] UN Doc. S/PV.2187, 6 January 1980, 3. [86] (1980) UNYB 300.
[87] E.g., UN Doc. S/PV.2671, 31 March 1986, 38 (US); UN Doc. S/PV.2674, 15 April 1986 (Libya).

alleged Pakistani attacks against its territory in 1950,[88] as well as by the USSR in relation to the UK raid against Yemen in 1964.[89]

The view that the duty to report is a procedural obligation with an evidential impact, but not an integral part of the substantive conditions of self-defence is shared by a majority of scholars.[90] In sum, if the Charter provisions on the recourse to force are technically not applicable, a failure to report may nonetheless cast doubt on the legality of the State's actions. If, on the other hand, the Charter is technically applicable – as will normally be the case – the absence of a report will not only negatively influence a State's legal case, but will also constitute a violation of a separate legal obligation of a procedural nature, linked to the effective exercise of the Security Council's powers.

Legal scholars have often argued that the duty to report is seldom observed in practice.[91] Combacau, for instance, only finds a handful of cases of compliant behaviour in the Repertoire of the Security Council up until 1974.[92] On the other hand, Gray argues that, after the *Nicaragua* judgment, it can no longer be maintained that the requirement is *rarely* complied with.[93] To the contrary, she asserts that there is sometimes even a tendency to over-report in the sense that participants in a prolonged conflict often report each episode separately, instead of confining themselves to report to the Security Council at the start of the conflict.[94]

---

[88] United Nations Department of Political and Security Council Affairs, *Repertoire of the Practice of the Security Council 1946–1951* (New York, 1954), pp. 448–9.

[89] See (1964) UNYB 184.

[90] E.g., Constantinou, *The right of self-defence*, pp. 194–5. See also Dinstein, *War, aggression and self-defence*, pp. 217–18 ('a failure ... to formally invoke self-defence should not be fatal, provided that the substantive conditions for the exercise of this right are met'); Gray, *The use of force*, p. 122; Greig, 'Self-defence and the Security Council', 384; R. Higgins, *The development of international law through the political organs of the United Nations* (Oxford University Press, 1963), p. 207; Knisbacher, 'The Entebbe operation', 79; N. Ronzitti, 'The expanding law of self-defence', (2006) 11 JCSL 343–59, at 356; ICJ, *Nicaragua* case (Merits), Dissenting opinion of Judge Schwebel, §§ 227–30.

[91] E.g., Ronzitti, 'The expanding law of self-defence', 356; Schachter, *International law in theory and practice*, p. 138.

[92] J. Combacau, 'The exception of self-defence in U.N. practice', in Cassese (ed.), *The use of force*, pp. 9–38, at 15–16. Contra: Gray, *The use of force*, p. 123, footnote 35 (questioning Combacau's methodology).

[93] Gray, *The use of force*, pp. 121–2.

[94] See *ibid.*, at 123–4. Such tendency to over-report was marked *inter alia* in the practice of Iran and Iraq during their 1980–8 conflict and in the practice of the UK and Argentina in the Falklands conflict. The US similarly submitted subsequent reports in relation to its involvement in the Iran–Iraq War as well as the Vietnam War. As Gray suggests, over-reporting partly seems to play a propaganda role; by doing so, States may attempt to

CONDITIONS OF SELF-DEFENCE 73

Gray's appraisal may be slightly over-optimistic. Even in recent years, numerous instances of inter-State recourse to force were not reported to the Council. Notable examples are the Turkish intervention in northern Iraq in 2007–8, the Colombian raid in Ecuador in 2008 or the Ethiopian intervention in Somalia during the same year.[95] Compliance with the reporting obligation is most problematic vis-à-vis small-scale incidents and interventions of controversial legality. Still, a quick scan of the UN documentation database reveals that after 2000 several dozens of self-defence claims were indeed submitted to the Council. For instance, in the aftermath of the 9/11 attacks, communications were submitted by the US, the UK, Canada, France, Australia, Germany, the Netherlands, New Zealand and Poland.[96] Other recent self-defence reports were made *inter alia* by Iraq,[97] Israel,[98] Iran,[99] Ethiopia and Eritrea,[100] Liberia,[101] the DRC (against Rwanda),[102] et cetera. Often States merely intend to bring the situation to the attention of the Security Council, while expressly *reserving* their right to self-defence or *warning* about the possible exercise thereof.[103] Notification may also take the form of a self-defence claim made during the course of a debate before the Security

portray themselves as victims. It may also signal an effort to rely on the *Ius ad Bellum* instead of applicable rules of IHL.

[95] See on these three cases, *infra* Section 5.2.3. For another example, see: ICJ, *DRC v. Uganda*, §§ 145–7 (Uganda failed to report its intervention in the DRC to the Council).

[96] UN Doc. S/2001/946, 7 October 2001 (US); UN Doc. S/2001/947, 7 October 2001 (UK); UN Doc. S/2001/1005, 24 October 2001 (Canada); UN Doc. S/2001/1091, 16 November 2001 (Chile); UN Doc. S/2001/1103, 23 November 2001 (France); UN Doc. S/2001/1104, 23 November 2001 (Australia); UN Doc. S/2001/1127, 29 November 2001 (Germany); UN Doc. S/2001/1171, 6 December 2001 (Netherlands); UN Doc. S/2001/1193, 17 December 2001 (New Zealand); UN Doc. S/2002/275, 15 March 2002 (Poland).

[97] E.g., UN Doc. S/2000/1, 4 January 2000; UN Doc. S/2001/248, 20 March 2001; UN Doc. S/2001/370, 13 April 2001; UN Doc. S/2001/692, 12 July 2001.

[98] E.g., UN Doc. S/2006/515, 12 July 2006; UN Doc. S/2007/69, 8 February 2007.

[99] UN Doc. S/2001/381, 18 April 2001.

[100] E.g., UN Doc. S/2000/523, 2 June 2000 (Ethiopia); UN Doc. S/2000/554, 9 June 2000 (Eritrea).

[101] UN Doc. S/2002/310, 20 March 2002.

[102] UN Doc. S/2002/198, 25 February 2002; UN Doc. S/2004/489, 10 June 2004.

[103] E.g., UN Doc. S/2000/48, 23 January 2000 (Pakistan re alleged attacks by Indian forces); UN Doc. S/2000/216, 13 March 2000 (Iran re alleged attacks by an Iraqi-sponsored terrorist group); UN Doc. S/2003/148, 4 February 2003 (Lebanon re Israeli violations of Lebanese airspace); UN Doc. S/2001/362, 16 April 2001 (*Syria v. Israel*); UN Doc. S/2000/512, 31 May 2000 (Israel re Lebanon); UN Doc. S/2002/1012, 11 September 2002 (Russia re Georgia); UN Doc. S/2003/327, 16 March 2003 (Iraq re the military build-up by the US and the UK); UN Doc. S/2001/474, 11 May 2001 (Liberia); UN Doc. S/2001/562, 4 June 2002 (Liberia); UN Doc. S/2005/620, 3 October 2005 (*DRC v. Uganda*).

Council.[104] On the other hand, if a State only raises the self-defence claim in response to accusations of aggression by other States instead of informing the Council on its own initiative, this might amount to a technical violation of the duty to report and could again cast (refutable) doubts on the lawfulness of the operation.

2.2.1.b The 'until clause'

Apart from the reporting obligation, Article 51 UN Charter contains a second limitation of a more 'procedural' nature. The provision makes clear that self-defence constitutes an exceptional, provisional regime, only available 'until the Security Council has taken measures necessary to maintain international peace and security'.[105] For most of the UN era the temporal limitation of Article 51 has been of little practical significance.[106] Indeed, while States emphasized the requirement from time to time during Council debates,[107] and while its validity per se was never called into question, the Cold War deadlock impeded the Security Council from taking any significant action in the overwhelming majority

---

[104] Combacau, 'The exception of self-defence in U.N. practice', 16. E.g., following a Lebanese request for military support in 1958, the United States called for an emergency meeting of the Security Council, during which it announced that it had responded positively to that request 'and wished the Council to be officially advised of that fact'. (1958) UNYB 38.

[105] Contrary to the reporting obligation, the so-called 'until clause' was inserted at a later stage of the drafting process. The first US drafts merely asserted that the taking of measures of self-defence 'shall not affect the authority and responsibility of the Security Council' to take such action as it may deem necessary (e.g., *Foreign Relations of the United States, Diplomatic Papers* (1945), pp. 664, 674, 834). Asked whether the Council could take cognizance of a situation in which there had been an attack followed by a counter-attack by other States acting in self-defence, US Delegate Dulles observed that States were not obligated to discontinue their actions in such situation (*ibid.*, 666). Rather, there was 'concurrent power'. Subsequent drafts substantially qualified the idea of 'concurrent power'. Alternative proposals referred to the right of self-defence 'prior to undertaking the measures necessary for the maintenance of international peace and security' (*ibid.*, 705 (US draft); 813 (USSR draft); 817 (US draft)). In the end, the wording was changed to the 'until clause' as reproduced above. Throughout the UNCIO debates, several delegations emphasized the temporary character of individual or collective self-defence (UNCIO, Vol. 3, 379 (France); UNCIO, Vol. 12, 687 (Colombia)).

[106] E.g., Randelzhofer, 'Article 51', p. 804.

[107] UN Department of Political and Security Council Affairs, *Repertoire of the practice of the Security Council 1946–1951* (New York, 1954), pp. 449 (Egypt), 450 (UK, the Netherlands); UN Department of Political and Security Council Affairs, *Repertoire of the Practice of the Security Council 1956–1958* (New York, 1959), p. 174 (France); (1956) UNYB 27 (Egypt).

of cases.[108] Even in the face of blatant aggression, the Council failed to determine who had actually attacked whom, let alone to adopt economic sanctions or military enforcement measures.

The revitalization of the Council at the end of the twentieth century may have initiated a more frequent implementation of the 'until clause'. A recent example is provided by Israel's incursion in southern Lebanon in the summer of 2006,[109] which resulted in intense fighting between Israeli forces and Hezbollah fighters. One month after the outbreak of the conflict, the Security Council adopted resolution 1701 (2006) which abrogated Israel's self-defence claim via a three-phased approach.[110] First, it called for a *full cessation of hostilities* based upon the immediate cessation by Hezbollah of all attacks and the immediate cessation by Israel of all *offensive* military operations. Second, *upon full cessation of hostilities*, it called upon the Government of Lebanon and the (upgraded) UN peace-keeping operation UNIFIL to deploy their forces together throughout southern Lebanon. Third, *as that deployment began*, the Council called upon Israel to withdraw all of its forces from southern Lebanon in parallel.

While the aforementioned resolution offers a model of how the 'until clause' may be implemented, the text of Article 51 UN Charter leaves ample room for interpretation. Two main issues can be discerned. First, *what* is meant by 'measures necessary'? Second, *who* determines when the right to self-defence is terminated?

As regards the first issue, some States have occasionally suggested that the exercise of self-defence is suspended if and while the Security Council is seized of a situation.[111] Although this approach is not completely

---

[108] See, e.g., Dinstein, *War, aggression and self-defence*, pp. 214–15; Greig, 'Self-defence and the Security Council', 399, 401; Ronzitti, 'The expanding law of self-defence', 352. See also: W. M. Reisman, 'Allocating competences to use coercion in the post-Cold War World: practices, conditions, and prospects', in L. F. Damrosch and D. J. Scheffer (eds.), *Law and force in the new international order* (Boulder, CO: Westview Press, 1991), pp. 26–48, at 43–4.

[109] Cf. UN Doc. S/2006/515, 12 July 2006 (Israel).

[110] SC Res. 1701 (2006) of 11 August 2006.

[111] E.g., UN Department of Political and Security Council Affairs, *Repertoire of the Practice of the Security Council 1985–1988* (New York, 2000), p. 431 (Algeria); UN Department of Political and Security Council Affairs, *Repertoire of the Practice of the Security Council 1989–1992* (New York, 2006), p. 940: following the Iraqi invasion of Kuwait, the Iraqi representative argued that no State had the right to use force unilaterally against his country as the Security Council was seized of the situation (note 540).

without doctrinal support,[112] it is hard to imagine that the mere inclusion of an issue on the Council's agenda ends the right to self-defence. If such were the case, this might lead to the absurd result that an aggressor would bring its own unlawful actions to the attention of the Council and consequently be shielded (at least theoretically) from a counter-attack in self-defence (which is to some extent what Iraq attempted to do in 1990).[113] Moreover, the plain meaning of the word 'measures' in Article 51 suggests that there needs to be an affirmative decision of the Council.[114] Consequently, should the Council fail to adopt a resolution, for instance as a result of the exercise of the veto power, then defensive action may continue (provided all other conditions are respected).[115]

A second view holds that the adoption of *any* resolution by the Council, regardless of its content or impact, suffices to end the exercise of self-defence. This approach seems to be implicitly followed by some scholars.[116] Nonetheless, compelling evidence indicates that only measures 'adequate' or 'effective' to 'restore' international peace and security affect the right of self-defence.[117] First, if the mere promulgation of a resolution would qualify, this would mean for example that if an aggressor State would simply ignore a call for unconditional withdrawal by the Council, the victim State would no longer be allowed to defend itself. Common sense suggests that the effectiveness of the measures must to

---

[112] E.g., A. Chayes, 'The Use of Force in the Persian Gulf', in Damrosch and Scheffer (eds.), *Law and force*, pp. 3–12, at 5; R. Mullerson, quoted in E. V. Rostow, 'Until what? Enforcement action or collective self-defense?', (1991) 85 AJIL 506–16, at 511.

[113] See UN Department of Political and Security Council Affairs, *Repertoire of the Practice of the Security Council 1989–1992* (New York, 2006), p. 940 (note 540).

[114] E.g., Bowett, *Self-defence in international law*, p. 196; Kelsen, *The law of the United Nations*, p. 804; Waldock, 'The use of force by individual states', 495–6.

[115] E.g., Dinstein, *War, aggression and self-defence*, p. 215.

[116] E.g., T. M. Franck and F. Patel, 'UN Police Action in lieu of war: the old order changeth', (1991) 85 AJIL 63–74, at 63. Cf. M. Halberstam, 'The right to self-defence once the Security Council takes action', (1995–6) 17 Michigan JIL 229–48, at 234. More recently, however, Franck has adopted the view that the potential coexistence of collective measures with continued measures in self-defence has become accepted as a result of subsequent practice (referring to the 1990 Gulf conflict and the 9/11 attacks). See Franck, *Recourse to force*, pp. 49–50.

[117] This is the approach followed by most authors. E.g., Greig, 'Self-defence and the Security Council', 389; Halberstam, 'The right to self-defence', 238 *et seq.*; Kelsen, *The law of the United Nations*, p. 800; Rostow, 'Enforcement action or collective self-defense?', 511; Sicilianos, *Des contre-mesures à la légitime défense*, pp. 306–7. See also: O. Corten, *Le droit contre la guerre; l'interdiction du recours à la force en droit international contemporain* (Paris: Pedone, 2008), pp. 711, 713; Ducheine, *Geweldgebruik en terreurbestrijding*, p. 235.

some extent be taken into account.[118] The addition after 'measures' of the phrase 'necessary to maintain international peace and security' reinforces this interpretation. Indeed, '[w]hile the Security Council might take measures which it regards as necessary to terminate the armed attack, whether they do have that effect only time will tell. If they do not have that consequence, then clearly additional measures are '"necessary".'[119] The legislative history of Article 51 points in the same direction.[120] Throughout the drafting sessions within the US delegation, various delegates repeatedly stressed that the right of self-defence continued until the Security Council took 'adequate measures to restore international peace and security', 'effective action', or 'all necessary measures'.[121]

Subsequent statements by the US Secretary of State[122] and the UK Foreign Office[123] uphold the view that the right of self-defence continues until international peace and security had been restored. Customary practice provides additional evidence: on several occasions, States allegedly acting in self-defence insisted that this right only ceased when the Security Council had taken measures that were actually effective.[124]

---

[118] E.g., Greig, 'Self-defence and the Security Council', 389; Sicilianos, *Des contre-mesures à la légitime défense*, p. 307.

[119] Greig, 'Self-defence and the Security Council', 389. See also Halberstam, 'The right to self-defence', 239.

[120] See *ibid.*, 240–4.

[121] *Foreign Relations of the United States, Diplomatic Papers* (1945), p. 817; Hearings before the Senate Committee on Foreign Relations, 79th Cong., 1st Sess., pt. 1 (1945), 304. Remark: when the Great Powers discussed the final proposal, which referred to measures necessary to 'maintain or restore' international peace and security', the Soviet delegate suggested deleting the word 'restore'. The UK delegate objected that the word should be retained, since the right of self-defence 'should continue during the period of restoration.' The Soviet delegate did not disagree on the substance, but took the view that the word 'maintain' encompassed the (then) concept of 'restore', making an express reference thereto unnecessary. The Republic of China and France also indicated a preference for 'restore', yet, in the end, upon suggestion of the UK, it was agreed to use the word 'maintain' in order not to split the delegation. See: *Foreign Relations of the United States, Diplomatic Papers* (1945), pp. 823–4.

[122] 'Report on the San Francisco Conference', (1945) 12 *Department of State Bulletin* 1009.

[123] 'In the event of the Security Council failing to take any action, or if such action as it does take is clearly inadequate, the right of self-defence could be invoked by any member or Group of members as justifying any action they thought fit to take.' Quoted in G. Schwarzenberger, 'The fundamental principles of international law', (1955-I) 87 RdC 191–385, at 336.

[124] E.g., (1965) UNYB 164 (Pakistan, asserting its right of self-defence 'until the Security Council took effective measures to vacate India's aggression against Pakistan and Jammu and Kashmir'); UN Department of Political and Security Council Affairs,

Several bilateral and multilateral treaties, such as the North Atlantic Treaty[125] and the Warsaw Pact,[126] moreover expressly affirm the continuing of the right of self-defence until the Security Council has taken the measures necessary to effectively restore international peace and security.[127]

What then are the 'necessary measures' envisaged by the 'until clause'? First, it may be assumed that this concept only covers measures that aim directly at tackling the concrete case at hand, rather than measures of a more general nature. Indeed, when shortly after the 9/11 attacks, the Security Council decreed resolution 1373 (2001),[128] imposing wide-ranging counter-terrorism measures, many authors stressed that this resolution did not in any way diminish the United States' right of self-defence because of its general nature.[129] This view was apparently shared by the international community, in that support for the subsequent US intervention in Afghanistan was quasi-unanimous. It should, however, be observed in all honesty that the preamble of resolution 1373 (2001) expressly '[reaffirmed] the inherent right of individual or collective self-defence as recognized by the [UN] Charter.'[130]

Repertoire of the Practice of the Security Council 1981–1984 (New York, 1992), p. 326 (UK argument re the Falklands war).

[125] Article 5(2) of the North Atlantic Treaty, Washington DC, 4 April 1949, 34 UNTS 243 ('measures necessary to restore and maintain international peace and security') .

[126] Article 4(2) Warsaw Security Pact, Warsaw, 14 May 1955, 219 UNTS 25 ('necessary measures to restore and maintain international peace and security').

[127] See Sicilianos, *Des contre-mesures à la légitime défense*, p. 307 (footnotes 347–9). Sicilianos refers amongst others to Article 4 of the 1951 Australia, New Zealand, United States Security Treaty (ANZUS) (131 UNTS 83); Article 5 of the 1954 Mutual Defence Treaty between the United States and the Republic of China (248 UNTS 213); and Article 5 of the 1960 Cooperation and Mutual Defence Treaty between the United States and Japan (373 UNTS 179).

[128] SC Res. 1373 (2001) of 28 September 2001.

[129] See M. Byers, 'Terrorism, the use of force and international law after September 11', (2002) 51 ICLQ 401–14, at 412; T. M. Franck, 'Terrorism and the right of self-defense', (2001) 95 AJIL 839–42, at 841–2; N. Schrijver, 'Responding to international terrorism: moving the frontiers of international law for "Enduring Freedom"?', (2001) 48 NILR 271–91, at 281–2; J. Verhoeven, 'Les "étirements" de la légitime défense', (2002) 48 AFDI 49–80, at 71. Also C. Greenwood, 'International law and the pre-emptive use of force: Afghanistan, Al-Qaida, and Iraq', (2003) 4 San Diego ILJ 7–37, at 22; M. E. O'Connell, 'Lawful self-defense to terrorism', (2002) 63 Un Pittsburgh L Rev 889–908, at 892–3.

[130] A similar recognition of the right of self-defence was inserted in SC Res. 1368 (2001) of 12 September 2001. Interestingly, in the latter resolution, the Security Council expressly declared its 'readiness to take all necessary steps to respond to the terrorist attacks of 11 September 2001 ... in accordance with its responsibilities under the [UN] Charter'.

As far as possible *concrete* measures are concerned, it stands beyond doubt that the imposition of military enforcement measures in accordance with Article 42 UN Charter suspends the exercise of the right to self-defence.[131] A majority of legal scholars take the view that economic sanctions under Article 41 of the Charter would likewise trigger the 'until clause'.[132] Support for this approach is implicit in the reaction of the international community following Iraq's invasion of Kuwait in 1991. Indeed, on 2 August 1990, on the very day Iraq invaded Kuwait, the Security Council adopted resolution 660 (1990), which condemned the Iraqi invasion; demanded that Iraq withdraw immediately and unconditionally all of its forces; and called upon Iraq and Kuwait to begin peaceful negotiations.[133] Iraq's refusal to comply led to the adoption, four days later, of resolution 661 (1990), imposing an economic sanctions regime.[134] At the same time, a number of Western States, led by the United States, decided to take further steps to secure observance of the sanctions regime and sent warships to the area with instructions to stop and search vessels suspected of travelling to Iraq or Kuwait.[135] Several States expressed concern at these unilateral measures, undertaken 'without considering the role assumed by the Security Council',[136] and Cuba and Iraq expressly took the view that they were incompatible with the

---

This paragraph *a contrario* concedes that the Council had not yet taken the 'necessary measures' in the sense of Article 51 UN Charter (also: Corten, *Le droit contre la guerre*, p. 713). On the other hand, in light of the Council's stated willingness to act, several scholars have criticized the US for not obtaining the express authorization of the Security Council for its intervention. On Operation 'Enduring Freedom', see also *infra* Section 5.2.2.a.ii.

[131] See, e.g., Halberstam, 'The right to self-defence', 246; Schrijver, 'Responding to international terrorism', 281.

[132] E.g., G. Abi-Saab, 'Cours général de droit international public', (1987-III) 207 RdC 9–463, at 372; Constantinou, *The right of self-defence*, p. 199; K. S. Elliott, 'The New World Order and the right of self-defense in the United Nations Charter', (1991–2) 15 Hastings ICL Rev 55–81, at 68; L. C. Green, 'Iraq, the U.N. and the law', (1991) 29 Alberta L Rev 560–83, at 565; Schrijver, 'Responding to international terrorism', 281; Sicilianos, *Des contre-mesures à la légitime défense*, p. 308. Contra: Dinstein, *War, aggression and self-defence*, p. 215; Halberstam, 'The right to self-defence', 246.

[133] SC Res. 660 (1990) of 2 August 1990.

[134] SC Res. 661 (1990) of 6 August 1990.

[135] See Green, 'Iraq, the U.N. and the law', 567.

[136] E.g., UN Doc. S/PV.2937, 18 August 1990, 6 (Yemen); 13–14 (PRC). Remark: Constantinou even finds that 'these statements of *opinio iuris* reveal uniformity of opinion concerning the cessation of action in self-defence once the Security Council had taken measures under Article 41 [UN Charter].' Constantinou, *The right of self-defence*, p. 201.

'until clause'.[137] Significantly, in response thereto, the US and the UK did not argue that economic sanctions did not qualify as 'measures necessary' in terms of Article 51. Rather, they emphasized that resolution 661 (1990) expressly reaffirmed the right of individual or collective self-defence in response to the armed attack by Iraq against Kuwait and could therefore not be taken to end that right.[138] In the end, the enforcing powers secured passage of Security Council resolution 665 (1990), which explicitly authorized the halting of maritime shipping in order to ensure strict implementation of resolution 660 (1990).[139]

Furthermore, it has sometimes been argued that the right of self-defence may also be terminated due to Security Council action other than the imposition of enforcement measures under Articles 41 and 42 UN Charter, for example by a provisional demand directed at an aggressor State to withdraw its armed forces from the victim State's territory, or by the creation of subsidiary organs charged with the surveillance of a ceasefire.[140] Customary practice provides some corroborating evidence. In 1951, for example, India argued that Pakistan could not invoke Article 51, since:

---

[137] Ibid., 31 (Cuba), 42 (Iraq: 'Article 51 grants the right of individual or collective self-defence 'until the Security Council has taken measures necessary to maintain international peace and security'. The Security Council took such measures by its hasty and unjust resolution 661 (1990) ...').

[138] Ibid., 33–4 (US); UN Doc. S/PV.2934, 9 August 1990, 8 (US), 18 (UK).

[139] SC Res. 665 (1990) of 25 August 1990; see Green, 'Iraq, the U.N. and the law', 568. Some three months later, the Council adopted resolution 678 (1990), authorizing Member States to use all necessary means to restore peace and security in the area. SC Res. 687 (1990) of 29 November 1990.

Remark: legal scholars are divided on the legality of the naval interdiction regime prior to the adoption of resolution 665 (1990). Even if one follows the reasoning of the US and the UK that resolution 660 reaffirmed the right of self-defence, it must be conceded that following resolution 660 two subsequent Council resolutions (SC Res. 662 (1990) of 9 August 1990 and SC Res. 664 (1990) of 18 August 1990) were adopted, none of which referred to the right of self-defence. On the other hand, neither of the latter resolutions imposed sanctions in the sense of Articles 41 or 42 of the Charter.

Authors apparently regarding the naval interdiction as (temporarily) unlawful: e.g., Constantinou, *The right of self-defence*, pp. 200–1; Elliott, 'The New World Order', 63–4, 81; Green, 'Iraq, the U.N. and the law', 568; Randelzhofer, 'Article 51', p. 804. Regarding it as lawful: e.g., Franck, *Recourse to force*, p. 49; Rostow, 'Enforcement action or collective self-defense?'.

[140] E.g., Dinstein, *War, aggression and self-defence*, p. 214; Sicilianos, *Des contre-mesures à la légitime défense*, p. 308. Uncertain: Abi-Saab, 'Cours général', 372; Kelsen, *The law of the United Nations*, pp. 801–2 (Kelsen refers to action under Articles 39 (recommendations), 41 and 42 UN Charter).

[T]he Security Council, through the United Nations Commission for India and Pakistan, took the necessary measures and, in fact, the Commission succeeded in getting the parties to agree to [two] resolutions ... Under these resolutions a ceasefire has been achieved, a ceasefire line has been demarcated, and there are military observers to supervise the observance of the ceasefire order.[141]

In a similar vein, during the 1982 Falklands War, Argentina claimed that the United Kingdom could no longer rely on Article 51 after the adoption of Security Council resolution 502 (1982).[142] The latter resolution demanded an immediate cessation of hostilities and an immediate withdrawal of all Argentine forces from the Falklands, and called upon the governments of Argentina and the UK to seek a diplomatic solution to their differences.[143] The UK in turn objected that Argentina had not withdrawn its armed forces from the Falklands as required by resolution 502. Hence, the decision of the Security Council had not 'in fact, been effective to restore international peace and security because of Argentina's refusal to comply'.[144] Another example concerns a 1958 complaint by Lebanon of armed incursions from the United Arab Republic (UAR), which led the Council to dispatch an observation group to Lebanon 'so as to ensure that no illegal infiltration of personnel or supply of arms or other *matériel* took place across the Lebanese borders'.[145] Approximately one month later, the United States informed the Security Council that it had responded positively to a request for military support from the Lebanese government.[146] The representatives of the Soviet Union and the UAR objected that the US intervention violated Article 51, since the Council was already acting vis-à-vis the situation.[147] Lebanon and the US, on the other hand, objected that the Council had not yet taken effective measures to thwart the infiltrations.[148] Both countries insisted that the Council adopt additional measures, and assured that US forces would be withdrawn if such were the case. The representatives of Canada, the (then) Republic of China, France and the UK all accepted that the US action was in full accord with the UN Charter.[149]

The quoted precedents provide some evidence that Council measures, other than those provided for in Articles 41 and 42 UN Charter may call a halt to the exercise of self-defence *if* they are effective. This finding,

---

[141] UN Department of Political and Security Council Affairs, *Repertoire of the Practice of the Security Council 1946–1951* (New York, 1954), p. 449.
[142] UN Doc. S/15014, 30 April 1982 (Argentina).   [143] SC Res. 502 (1982) of 3 April 1982.
[144] UN Doc. S/15017, 30 April 1982 (UK).   [145] SC Res. 128 (1958) of 11 June 1958.
[146] (1958) UNYB 38.   [147] (1958) UNYB 39–40.   [148] *Ibid.*   [149] (1958) UNYB 39.

however, inevitably raises a second question as to who is to decide whether the measures taken have been adequate. Article 51 itself does not settle the issue.[150] In light of the aim of the clause – i.e., to make clear that self-defence is a provisional remedy, subject to the control of the Security Council – as well as the discretionary power of the Council to determine the existence of a threat to the peace, a breach of the peace or an act of aggression, it seems logical that it is up to the Council to determine when the 'necessary measures' have been taken.[151] On the other hand, in some situations, States have apparently considered it their own prerogative to judge whether Council measures were sufficiently 'adequate',[152] as is illustrated by the aforementioned examples of the Falklands War[153] and the 1958 conflict between Lebanon and the United Arab Republic.[154]

A possible reading of customary practice would be to distinguish between enforcement measures under Articles 41 and 42 UN Charter, on the one hand, and provisional measures under Article 40, on the other hand. When measures of the former type are adopted, it could be argued that States are no longer allowed to undertake action in self-defence, since they are by nature considered to be 'measures necessary' in the sense of Article 51 and signal the intent of the Council to take over the situation at hand. Continued action in self-defence would only (temporarily) remain lawful if the Council indicated so, for example, by 'recalling' or '(re)affirming' the inherent right of individual or collective self-defence, as it

---

[150] Goodrich and Hambro, *Charter of the United Nations*, p. 178.
[151] E.g., Constantinou, *The right of self-defence*, p. 196; Elliott, 'The New World Order', 68; Sicilianos, *Des contre-mesures à la légitime défense*, p. 310. More cautious: Greig, 'Self-defence and the Security Council', 390–2. See also Kelsen, *The law of the United Nations*, pp. 801–3 (cf. Green, 'Iraq, the U.N. and the law', 566 and Halberstam, 'The right to self-defence', 244). Kelsen concluded that the issue had 'not unambiguously [been] expressed in Article 51.' Bowett suggests that 'whether the necessary measures have been taken must be determined objectively, as a question of fact, and that both the [Security Council] and the defending State are able to reach their own decisions on this. Should these decisions conflict then the individual member admittedly runs the risk of its continued action being characterized as a "threat to the peace, breach of the peace, or act of aggression" under [Article] 39.' See Bowett, *Self-defence in international law*, p. 196.
[152] See, e.g., Higgins, *The development of international law*, pp. 206–7. With regard to the 1956 Suez crisis, for example, the UK did not regard the resolutions calling for a cessation of hostilities as a sufficient guarantee to withdraw its troops. However, Higgins observes that 'the repeated condemnation of the United Kingdom by the vast majority of States would seem to indicate that it is not for the State allegedly taking action in self-defence to decide whether the Security Council has taken the measures necessary to secure peace and security, but that it is for the UN itself to decide.'
[153] UN Doc. S/15017, 30 April 1982 (UK).   [154] (1958) UNYB 39.

did in resolution 661 (1990) vis-à-vis the Gulf crisis (cf. *supra*).[155] Otherwise, the right would only be reactivated in case of a new *casus foederis*, i.e., a new armed attack. In relation to measures of the latter type, it is less clear that the Security Council has taken over the situation. In light of customary practice, it might be argued that if provisional measures are adopted, it is up to the States themselves – subject to the judgment of the international community and possibly to judicial scrutiny – to decide in good faith whether they have been adequate. In the case of a call for withdrawal, the situation is more or less clear. If an aggressor State were to withdraw its forces as ordered by the Council, this would effectively remove the need for action in self-defence. If it refuses to comply, it would be for the international community, through the Security Council, to decide upon the consequences, yet the victim State's right to self-defence would (at least temporarily) remain unaffected.

2.2.1.c Collective self-defence

Although the duty to report and the 'until clause' are the only 'procedural' obligations incorporated in Article 51 UN Charter, the ICJ in the *Nicaragua* case identified additional customary obligations, applicable only to *collective* self-defence. According to the Court, this right is not only subject to the same criteria as individual self-defence, but must also meet two further requirements: it can only be exercised if there has been a request for support by the State which regards itself as the victim of an armed attack; and the latter State should have publicly declared itself to have been attacked.[156] Nonetheless, this part of the judgment has been heavily criticized by numerous authors, as well as by two dissenting Judges.[157] The criticism can be broken down in three parts. First, some have complained at the manifest lack of evidence provided by the Court in support of the alleged customary status of the aforementioned conditions. On a more

---

[155] E.g., preamble of SC Res. 661 (1990) of 6 August 1990. See also SC Res. 1234 (1999) of 9 April 1999 (regarding the DRC); SC Res. 1368 (2001) of 12 September 2001 (regarding the 9/11 terrorist attacks); SC Res. 1373 (2001) of 28 September 2001 (regarding the 9/11 terrorist attacks). The same inference can arguably be made if a defensive operation is somehow applauded by the Security Council (e.g., SC Res. 1776 (2007) of 19 September 2007 (in relation to Operation 'Enduring Freedom')).
[156] E.g., ICJ, *Nicaragua* case (Merits), §§ 195, 199, 211.
[157] E.g., *ibid.*, Dissenting opinion of Judge Schwebel, §§ 221 *et seq.*; Dissenting opinion of Judge Jennings, 544–6; Dinstein, *War, aggression and self-defence*, pp. 269–70; Greig, 'Self-defence and the Security Council', 369 *et seq.*; J. N. Moore, 'The *Nicaragua* case and the deterioration of world order', (1987) 81 AJIL 151–9, at 155; Macdonald, 'The *Nicaragua* case', 149–50; Randelzhofer, 'Article 51', p. 803.

fundamental level, a number of authors disagree with the conception of collective self-defence as the collective exercise of a single State's individual right of self-defence. Last but not least, the *Nicaragua* case has been attacked for creating an overly 'formalistic' model of collective self-defence.

As for the first criticism, it is difficult not to share some authors' deception at the lack of a convincing legal basis on behalf of the Court for articulating the two requirements.[158] No evidence of customary practice whatsoever was provided in support of the need for a public statement by the victim State that it is subject to armed attack. The only shred of evidence of an alleged need for a formal request for support consisted in the Court's reference to Article 3(2) Inter-American Treaty of Reciprocal Assistance (the 'Rio Treaty'), which states that:

> On the request of the State or States directly attacked and until the decision of the Organ of Consultation of the Inter-American System, each one of the Contracting Parties may determine the immediate measures which it may individually take in fulfilment of the obligation [to assist the victim State(s)] . . . .[159]

The Court's summary argumentation stands in striking contrast with the fact that at the time of adoption of the Charter, the concept of 'collective self-defence' was a relatively novel one, by and large inspired by the adoption only months earlier of the Act of Chapultepec (cf. *supra*).[160] In light thereof, one cannot escape a sense of arbitrariness in examining why the Court considered these requirements to be part of customary law, while holding that the reporting obligation of Article 51 was not.[161]

---

[158] E.g., Gray, *The use of force*, p. 184; Greig, 'Self-defence and the Security Council', 375–6; Macdonald, 'The *Nicaragua* case', 149–50.

[159] Article 3(2) Inter-American Treaty of Reciprocal Assistance. This provision actually organizes the implementation of the Act of Chapultepec, which had called for a treaty establishing procedures for the regional exercise of collective self-defence by the American Republics and which was the main *raison d'être* for the inclusion of Article 51 UN Charter (cf. *supra*).

[160] Inter-American Reciprocal Assistance and Solidarity (Act of Chapultepec). As Brownlie observes: 'The express recognition of a right of collective self-defence . . . gave the right a precise legal status which it had perhaps lacked previously. Jurists have [previously] asserted the existence of such a collective right although not with any great frequency and without much examination of the problems involved.' Brownlie, *The use of force by states*, p. 329. In a similar vein: Kunz, 'Individual and collective self-defense', 874; Macdonald, 'The *Nicaragua* case', 143.

[161] Greig, 'Self-defence and the Security Council', 376. Gray suggests that, in spite of the 'Vandenberg reservation', the Court was probably influenced by the fact that the parties concerned were actually bound by the requirement of Article 3(2) of the Rio Treaty that the victim State request assistance. Gray, *The use of force*, p. 184.

A second, more fundamental criticism concerns the nature of the so-called right of 'collective self-defence.' According to a majority opinion, the term 'collective *self-defence*' is a misnomer and would more correctly be described as 'collective *defence*'.[162] Adherents of this view consider it not as defence of the 'self', but as a defence of the 'other', exercised in favour of a State which has suffered an armed attack and which consequently has a right of individual self-defence. Unless States have agreed otherwise by means of a mutual defence alliance or some collective defence agreement, the possibility to aid a victim State in the exercise of its right of individual self-defence is a right and not a duty. Given the link to the attacked State's individual right of self-defence, it is the victim State and not the assisting State that has the discretion to determine *a priori* whether the conditions for collective self-defence are present.[163] In other words, collective self-defence cannot be exercised against the wishes of the victim State, implying *inter alia* that if the latter chooses to renounce the exercise of the right, for example to avoid escalation, third States cannot engage in a military response instead. The various dicta of the Court in the *Nicaragua* case – such as the finding that 'there is no rule in customary international law permitting another State to exercise the right of collective self-defence on the basis of its own assessment of the situation',[164] or the declaration that 'if the victim wishes another State to come to its help in the exercise of the right of collective self-defence, it will normally make an express request to that effect'[165] – can only be seen as an endorsement of this approach of 'collective defence'.

It needs no wonder then that the Court's judgment was strongly opposed by those who perceive collective self-defence as the defence of the 'self', rather than the 'other'. This view was elaborated by Bowett, who equated 'collective self-defence' with the collective exercise of States' individual right of self-defence.[166] In his view, there exist two

---

[162] E.g., Brownlie, *The use of force by states*, pp. 329–31; Kelsen, *The law of the United Nations*, p. 792; Kunz, 'Individual and collective self-defense', 875. Also Gray, *The use of force*, p. 184.

[163] Constantinou, *The right of self-defence*, p. 176; J. Verhoeven, *Droit international public* (Brussels: Larcier, 2000), pp. 687–8.

[164] ICJ, *Nicaragua* case (Merits), § 195.   [165] *Ibid.*, § 232.

[166] See D. W. Bowett, 'Collective self-defence under the Charter of the United Nations', (1955-6) 32 BYBIL 130–61. Bowett explicitly rejects the idea that the right to go to the assistance of any State acting in self-defence is within the meaning of 'collective self-defence' (at 138). See also: Higgins, *The development of international law*, pp. 208–9; H. Lauterpacht (ed.), *Oppenheim's international law: a treatise*. Vol. II. 7th edn. (London: Longmans, 1952), p. 155.

requirements for the exercise of collective self-defence: 'first, that each participating State has an individual right of self-defence, and, second, that there exists an agreement between the participating States to exercise their rights collectively'.[167] Bowett's interpretation cannot properly be understood without taking account of his broad approach to the right of *individual* self-defence. According to him, the latter right is not only activated when a State is the direct victim of an armed attack, but also whenever it is faced with a serious threat to its security. The implication is that an attack on a third State may simultaneously constitute such a threat to the State's national security and trigger the possibility of a collective exercise of different States' right of indivual self-defence.[168] Bowett adds that this link between the original armed attack and the resulting security threat cannot be stretched to the fiction that 'an attack against one is an attack against all', but presupposes some sort of (political or geographical) 'proximate relationship' between the victim of the armed attack and the third State.[169] Several other scholars have built further on Bowett's ideas, retaining certain elements while adjusting others. Judge Jennings, for instance, in his dissenting opinion in *Nicaragua* agreed that the victim State must both be in real need of assistance and must want it.[170] On the other hand, he denounced the perception of collective self-defence as 'an idea of vicarious defence by champions', suggesting instead that the assisting State must surely in some measure be defending itself.[171] Dinstein too emphasizes that collective self-defence is above all the defence of self.[172] He furthermore takes the position that whenever an attack against a State threatens the security of a 'third' State, the latter State is entitled to resort to counter-force under Article 51, regardless of whether the direct victim agrees.[173] Only when the 'third' State's actions extend to the territory of the victim State is the latter's approval required.

While important differences exist between the various scholars belonging to this second group, two elements regularly surface, which

---

[167] Bowett, 'Collective self-defence', 139–40.   [168] *Ibid.*, 140.
[169] *Ibid.*, 150 *et seq.* Even the availability of a collective defence agreement does not remove the need for this proximate relationship. Bowett admits that the greater the scale of the attack, the wider the range of neighbouring States imperilled by the attack and able to invoke their right of self-defence. This right would not, however, justify a general right of intervention; States not individually in a state of self-defence would have no right to take action or to join in a collective action (159).
[170] ICJ, *Nicaragua* case (Merits), Dissenting opinion of Judge Jennings, 545.
[171] *Ibid.* See also Macdonald, 'The *Nicaragua* case', 146, 151.
[172] Dinstein, *War, aggression and self-defence*, p. 269.   [173] *Ibid.*, 270.

make this interpretation of collective self-defence at the same time broader and narrower than the previous one. It is broader to the extent that several supporters relinquish the need for approval of the State which is the direct victim of the attack. It is also narrower, due to a number of authors' insistence that – even if a formal request for assistance would have been made and/or a pre-existing mutual defence treaty exists – a relationship of (geographical, political, economical or cultural) proximity must exist between the victim and the assisting State.

Nonetheless, for several reasons, this conception of collective *self-defence* must be rejected. First of all, on a theoretical basis, once it is established that individual self-defence presupposes an *attack* against the State acting in self-defence (*supra* Section 2.1), rather than a mere security threat, collective self-defence can no longer be framed as the collective exercise of several States' right of individual self-defence as Bowett claimed. Second, the proximity criterion seems so vague and subjective that it can hardly be said to have any constraining effect at all.[174] According to Bowett, this criterion could not be stretched as far as to justify collective self-defence by the UK or Turkey in response to an armed attack against Chile or one of its South American neighbours.[175] However, the (uncontested) invocation of collective self-defence in the aftermath of the 9/11 attacks by countries ranging from New Zealand and Australia to Canada, Poland and the Netherlands illustrates that a 'proximity criterion' would merely constitute an empty shell.[176] This brings us to the third and decisive reason why the conception of collective 'defence of the other', endorsed by the ICJ and a majority of legal scholars, holds the upper hand over the 'defence of the self' approach: customary practice provides virtually no support either for the requirement that a proximity relationship should exist, or for the idea that collective self-defence may be exercised absent the approval of the actual victim State.[177] On the contrary, practice convincingly shows that a State which is the subject of an attack has a legal right to ask for military

---

[174] Brownlie, *The use of force by states*, p. 330.
[175] Bowett, 'Collective self-defence', 151.
[176] UN Doc. S/2001/1005, 24 October 2001 (Canada); UN Doc. S/2001/1104, 23 November 2001 (Australia); UN Doc. S/2001/1171, 6 December 2001 (Netherlands); UN Doc. S/2001/1193, 17 December 2001 (New Zealand); UN Doc. S/2002/275, 15 March 2002 (Poland).
[177] See Brownlie, *The use of force by states*, pp. 330–1; Constantinou, *The right of self-defence*, p. 178; Gray, *The use of force*, pp. 186–8; Malanczuk and Akehurst, *Akehurst's modern introduction*, p. 317. Contra: Macdonald, 'The *Nicaragua* case', 151.

assistance. In 1958, for instance, responding to a request for military support from Jordan, the United Kingdom declared that: 'Jordan's appeal for assistance from friendly Governments in maintaining its independence was natural and entirely justified in the circumstances. ... [The British forces] were in Jordan to help preserve its political independence and territorial integrity. They were not there for any military purpose of their own ...'.[178] A large number of Council members moreover supported the legality of Lebanon's request for military aid in response to alleged military infiltrations from abroad as well as of the US's positive response thereto.[179] The United States for its part stressed that its forces were in Lebanon 'for the sole purpose of helping the Government of Lebanon, at its request, in its efforts to stabilize the situation ...'.[180] No UN Member made any reference to an alleged need for a proximate relationship between the victim and the assisting State. In 1965, the US representative reported to the Security Council that 'the Republic of Vietnam and, at its request, the Government of the United States and other Governments [were] resisting [the] systematic and continuing aggression [by the Hanoi regime]'. This action was allegedly undertaken in accordance with the US's 'public commitment to assist the Republic of Vietnam against aggression from the North'.[181] Likewise, in relation to the 1956 Hungarian question, the USSR claimed that its troops were in Hungarian territory with the approval of the Hungarian government – a fact contested by most other UN Members – and would be withdrawn 'as soon as the Hungarian government recognized that to be necessary'.[182] As regards the Soviet interventions in Czechoslovakia (1968) an Afghanistan (1980), the USSR did make some allusion to a certain self-interest – in the former case it referred *inter alia* to the threat created by foreign and domestic reaction to the socialist order,[183] in the latter to the danger to the security threat to the southern border of the USSR.[184] Nonetheless, in both cases these were only subsidiary observations. The Soviet Union primarily argued that it was assisting the two countries.[185] The crux of the debate centred on the question whether the host State had genuinely consented to the presence of Soviet troops. In sum, in each case, what was deemed crucial was whether the actual victim State had a right of individual self-defence, and whether it approved of the actions of the assisting State. Of course, the assisting State will most often have

---

[178] (1958) UNYB 41. [179] (1958) UNYB 39. [180] (1958) UNYB 38.
[181] UN Doc. S/6174, 7 February 1965. [182] (1956) UNYB 68. [183] (1968) UNYB 298.
[184] (1980) UNYB 299. [185] (1968) UNYB 298; (1980) UNYB 299.

some sort of interest in responding to the victim's request; States seldom engage in military action out of pure altruism. Yet, practice makes clear that a proximate relationship is not a legal criterion; only the victim State's approval is.[186]

This in turn raises the question whether the latter's approval should take the form of a formal request or may otherwise be expressed. As mentioned before, the ICJ took a restrictive position and demanded both a formal request for support and a public declaration by the victim State that it had been attacked. The insistence on a formal request was heavily criticized for subjecting collective self-defence to unwarranted formalism.[187] It was considered unrealistic, for example, because it rendered covert self-defence impossible, or did not envisage the possibility of a State being suddenly overrun by an invading army. Still, customary practice generally supports this requirement.[188] Not only is it incorporated in a number of collective defence treaties and mutual defence alliances,[189] it has also played a prominent role in various Security Council debates. The US claimed to be acting at the request of Lebanon and the Republic of Vietnam respectively in 1958 and 1965.[190] The UK invoked a request from Jordan in 1958.[191] In 1981, Libya claimed that the presence of its military forces in Chad had been requested by the Chadian government.[192] A request for assistance was similarly available in relation to military support to Kuwait prior to the actual Security Council authorization to use force.[193] The Soviet Union also invoked a request for assistance in relation to its interventions in Hungary (1956), Czechoslovakia (1968) and Afghanistan (1980).[194] In the latter cases, however, numerous States took the position that the invitiations were invalid because they emanated from a puppet regime installed by Soviet

---

[186] Remark: it is from the victim State's perspective that the fulfilment of the necessity and proportionality standards must be assessed.
[187] E.g., Macdonald, 'The *Nicaragua* case', 151; Moore, 'The *Nicaragua* case', 155; Randelzhofer, 'Article 51', p. 803. ICJ, *Nicaragua* case (Merits), Dissenting opinion of Judge Schwebel, §§ 222 *et seq.*; Dissenting opinion of Judge Jennings, 545.
[188] See, e.g., Constantinou, *The right of self-defence*, pp. 178–80; Gray, *The use of force*, pp. 186–8.
[189] E.g., Article 3(2) Inter-American Treaty of Reciprocal Assistance. See Gray, *The use of force*, p. 186, footnote 96 (referring to the 1950 Arab League Treaty of Joint Defence and the 1982 France-Djibouti Protocol).
[190] (1958) UNYB 39; (1958) UNYB 38; UN Doc. S/6174, 7 February 1965.
[191] (1958) UNYB 40.   [192] (1981) UNYB 223.   [193] (1990) UNYB 195.
[194] (1956) UNYB 67 *et seq.*; (1968) UNYB 298; (1980) UNYB 297.

troops in the course of the intervention.[195] The discussions concerning the validity of the request were undeniably at the heart of the legality assessment. Does this mean that a formal invitation is not only a sufficient but also a necessary precondition for collective self-defence? Some caution is needed. First, the Court's reasoning is rather ambiguous.[196] If the Court initially creates the impression that the requirement is mandatory in nature,[197] these stringent demands are apparently eased in their actual application to the situation at hand:

> [I]t is evident that it is the victim State, being the most directly aware of [the occurrence of an armed attack], which is likely to draw general attention to its plight. It is also evident that if the victim State wishes another State to come to its help in the exercise of the right of collective self-defence, it will *normally* make an express request to that effect.[198]

Some scholars have interpreted this statement as implying that the Court simply took the absence of a declaration or a request for assistance as a confirmation that there had been no armed attack, rather than a *sine qua non*.[199] Furthermore, the frequent reference to a formal request for assistance in customary practice does not necessarily imply that this constitutes an absolute condition. Thus, while the discussion on the legality of the Soviet interventions in Hungary, Czechoslovakia and Afghanistan by and large focused on the presence of a (valid) request, it should be kept in mind that in these cases there were important prima facie indications that the intervention took place against the wishes of the respective governments. In 1956, for example, before being replaced by a 'Revolutionary Workers' and Peasants' Government', the Government of Hungarian Prime Minister Nagy strongly protested at the incursions by

---

[195] Remark: the validity of the request hinges on the same conditions as in the case of a so-called intervention by invitation. This implies amongst others that the request should be made by the government which de facto controls the territory of the State or which is generally recognized as the legitimate authority. See on this: L. Doswald-Beck, 'The legal validity of military intervention by invitation of the government', (1985) 56 BYBIL 189–252.

[196] See, e.g., Gray, *The use of force*, pp. 185–6; Greig, 'Self-defence and the Security Council', 377–8.

[197] ICJ, *Nicaragua* case (Merits), § 199: 'At all events, the Court finds that ... there is no rule permitting the exercise of collective self-defence in the absence of a request by the State which regards itself as the victim of an armed attack. The Court concludes that the requirement of a request is additional to the requirement that such a State should have declared itself to have been attacked.'

[198] *Ibid.*, § 232 (emphasis added). See also § 195 ('it is to be expected that ...').

[199] Gray, *The use of force*, p. 186; Greig, 'Self-defence and the Security Council', 378.

Soviet troops.[200] A similar scenario unfolded when the USSR entered Czechoslovakia in 1968.[201] Some practice illustrates that prior 'consultation' may also validly indicate the consent of the victim State.[202] In the end, it should be kept in mind that the request criterion is primarily aimed at securing the approval of the victim State. If this approval can be established in some other way, for example if it is clear that the States' military actions are closely coordinated or if the States jointly submit a report to the Security Council, a flexible interpretation should arguably prevail.[203]

Finally, if customary practice demonstrates that victim States have generally asserted that they have been the victim of an armed attack,[204] it would seem unwarranted to conclude that such declaration is mandatory. The absence or presence of a declaration was apparently never decisive to determine the legality of the exercise of collective self-defence. It is interesting to note that in its more recent judgment in the *Oil Platforms* case, the ICJ again conditioned collective self-defence upon the making of a request 'by the State which regards itself as the victim of an armed attack,' but did not explicitly reiterate the requirement of a public declaration to this end.[205] Whether or not this signals a shift in the Court's reasoning, it appears that – like the reporting obligation of Article 51 – the absence or presence of a public declaration has at best indicative value in considering the lawfulness of the recourse to force.

2.2.2 Necessity and proportionality

2.2.2.a General

In order to be lawful, recourse to self-defence must finally abide by two substantive criteria, the customary nature of which has consistently been affirmed by the International Court of Justice,[206] namely the principles of

---

[200] (1956) UNYB 68–9.   [201] (1968) UNYB 299.
[202] E.g., in relation to the 2001 intervention in Afghanistan: (2001) UNYB 65. A number of collective defence agreements similarly require 'consultation' or 'agreement'. See Gray, *The use of force*, p. 186, footnote 96 (referring to the 1968 UK/Mauritius Agreement on Mutual Defence and Assistance, the 1964 UK/Malta Agreement on Mutual Defence and the 1959 USA/Liberia Agreement on Cooperation).
[203] E.g., Abi-Saab, 'Cours général', 373. Also Ducheine, *Geweldgebruik en terreurbestrijding*, p. 292.
[204] Gray, *The use of force*, p. 186.
[205] ICJ, *Case concerning oil platforms (Islamic Republic of Iran v. United States of America)*, Judgment of 6 November 2003, (2003) ICJ Rep 161–219, § 51.
[206] ICJ, *Nicaragua* case (Merits), §§ 194, 237; ICJ, *Oil Platforms* case, §§ 51, 73–7; ICJ, *Legality of the threat or use of nuclear weapons*, Advisory opinion of 8 July 1996, (1996) ICJ Rep 226–67, §§ 41 *et seq.*

necessity and proportionality. The two standards were authoritatively expressed in the course of the diplomatic exchange of views relating to the famous 1837 *Caroline* incident.[207] Following the sinking by British forces of the *Caroline*, US Secretary of State Webster called upon the British government to show that its actions were inspired by a 'necessity of self-defence, instant, overwhelming, leaving no choice of means, and no moment for deliberation.' Webster furthermore insisted that the action should have involved 'nothing unreasonable or excessive; since the act, justified by the necessity of self-defence, must be limited by that necessity and kept clearly within it'. In reply, UK Foreign Minister Ashburton accepted the proposed standard of evaluation, yet claimed that the British action had been in conformity therewith. Whether the *Caroline* incident should be identified as the historical origin of the two criteria is highly unlikely. Long before the advent of the nineteenth century, necessity and proportionality already formed part of just war theory.[208] Furthermore, it could well be argued that the *Caroline* incident constituted an episode of self-help or self-preservation, rather than an instance of what is today termed self-defence.[209] In any event, irrespective of the incident's precedential value, it cannot be denied that the two interlinked standards formed an integral part of the concept of self-defence when it emerged as a legal doctrine throughout the nineteenth century.[210]

It is admitted that, even after the adoption of the UN Charter, the role of the two principles has sometimes been questioned by legal scholars.[211] A number of States have moreover (on rare occasions) expressed doubts as to the customary nature of the proportionality principle. During the

---

[207] See, e.g., R. Jennings, 'The *Caroline* and *McLeod* cases', (1938) 32 AJIL 82–99, at 85; 29 BFSP 1137; 30 BFSP 195–6.

[208] See, e.g., J. Gardam, *Necessity, proportionality and the use of force by States* (Cambridge University Press, 2004), pp. 28 *et seq.* On the difference between the interpretation of the proportionality requirement in the *bellum justum* doctrine and modern law on self-defence: *ibid.*, p. 33; C. Greenwood, 'Self-defence and the conduct of international armed conflict', in Y. Dinstein (ed.), *International law at a time of perplexity: essays in honour of Shabtai Rosenne* (Dordrecht: Martinus Nijhoff, 1989), pp. 273–88, at 274.

[209] Cf. ILC, *Commentary on the Draft Articles on the Responsibility of States for Internationally Wrongful Acts*, (2001-II) YBILC 81 (qualifying the *Caroline* correspondence as an invocation of 'the plea of necessity at a time when the law concerning the use of force had a quite different basis than it has at present').

[210] See Brownlie, 'The use of force in self-defence', 229; Gardam, *Necessity, proportionality*, pp. 4–6, 28 *et seq.*; Sicilianos, *Des contre-mesures à la légitime défense*, p. 312.

[211] E.g., Kunz, 'Individual and collective self-defense', 877, 878; see also the remarks by Bindschedler, Castrén and Chaumont in (1975) 56 Ann IDI 73–6.

negotiations on the Definition of Aggression some States (*inter alia* the Soviet Union) strongly opposed the reference to proportionality as a precondition for the exercise of self-defence, primarily on the grounds that this principle would benefit potential aggressors.[212] On the other hand, as will be examined below, it seems that these objections and doubts generally concerned the *content* of the proportionality requirement, rather than its validity as such.[213] A broad majority of participating States has explicitly emphasized the binding character of the criterion.[214] Furthermore, Security Council practice demonstrates that States have on numerous occasions discussed the necessity and/or proportionality of incidents involving the recourse to force (often making explicit reference to the '*Caroline* formula').[215] States allegedly implementing their right of self-defence have generally asserted that the

---

[212] E.g., UN Doc. A/AC.134/SR.67–78, 19 October 1970, 85 (USSR: 'It seemed unreasonable to try to limit the victim's choice of weapons and scale of defensive response, when it was the aggressor who should be bound hand and foot.'); 86 (Ghana); 87 (Syria); 91 (Ghana).

[213] R. Ago, 'Addendum to the 8th Report on State Responsibility', (1980-II) 32 YBILC, Part One, 69. Some States nonetheless questioned the legal nature of the proportionality requirement. The USSR, for instance, warned that the principle was 'not universally accepted in international law' (UN Doc. A/AC.134/SR.79-91, 36). In a similar vein: UN Doc. A/AC.134/SR.67-78, 86 (Ghana); UN Doc. A/AC.134/SR.67-78, 87 (Syria).

[214] E.g., UN Doc. A/AC.134/SR.52-66, 19 October 1970, 43 (Turkey), 61 (Yugoslavia); UN Doc. A/AC.134/SR.67-78, 19 October 1970, 81-2 (Cango); 83 (Iraq); 84 (UK); 86 (US); 87 (Romania); 88 (Guyana); 89 (Cyprus, Bulgaria, Italy); 90 (Ecuador); UN Doc. A/AC.134/SR.79-91, 7 June 1971, 21 (Mexico). See B. B. Ferencz, *Defining international aggression. The search for world peace: a documentary history and analysis.* Vol. II (Dobbs Ferry, NY: Oceana, 1975), p. 46. Remark: given the uncertainty regarding the precise content of the proportionality requirement as well as the insistence of several States (e.g., UK, US, Australia) that the Definition of Aggression should not touch upon the scope of self-defence, the reference to proportionality was ultimately abandoned. See also *infra* Section 3.1.2.

[215] E.g., UN Doc. S/PV.748, 30 October 1956, 4, 7 (Suez crisis); UN Doc. S/PV.749, 30 October 1956, 22, 29; UN Doc. S/PV.1106, 2 April 1964, 15 (UK raid against Harib Fort); UN Doc. S/PV.1107, 3 April 1964, 4, 5, 13; UN Doc. S/PV.1108, 6 April 1964, 6-8, 10, 20; UN Doc. S/PV.1939, 9 July 1976; (1976) UNYB 319 (Entebbe raid); UN Doc. S/PV.2282, 15 June 1981, § 15-16 (Osiraq raid), § 95, § 106; UN Doc. S/PV.2283, 15 June 1981, § 148 (Sierra Leone); UN Department of Political and Security Council Affairs, *Repertoire of the Practice of the Security Council 1985-1988* (New York, 2000), 428 (United Arab Emirates); UN Doc. S/PV.2611, 2 October 1985, §§ 44, 111 (Israeli air raid on the PLO headquarters in Tunis); UN Doc. S/PV.2615, 4 October 1985, §§ 60, 194; UN Doc. S/PV.1643, 26 February 1972, §§ 20, 166 (Israeli actions against Lebanon); UN Doc. S/PV.1644, 27–28 February 1972, §§ 24-9; UN Doc. S/PV.1649, 24 June 1972, § 158; 26 UN Doc. S/PV.1650, June 1972, § 10.

measures undertaken respected the two criteria.[216] These considerations have repeatedly played a decisive role in assessing concrete self-defence claims. When Israel launched a large-scale military operation against Lebanon in 2006 following the abduction by Hezbollah of two Israeli soldiers, for example, most States accepted that Israel could exercise its right of self-defence, but rejected the disproportionate character of Israel's operation.[217] In sum, the two criteria have not only been upheld in the case law of the ICJ, but are relatively consistently supported (in compliance or breach) in customary practice.[218] Legal doctrine today is moreover virtually unanimous in confirming the view that any action undertaken in self-defence must abide by the necessity and proportionality principles.[219]

Notwithstanding the broad consensus as to their limiting role, the necessity and proportionality criteria have generated relatively little (in-depth) academic interest.[220] It is generally accepted in customary practice and legal doctrine that they essentially imply that measures should be geared towards the halting or repelling of an armed attack and should not exceed this goal.[221] Otherwise, the action undertaken will involve a

---

[216] E.g., (1986) UNYB 248 (US justification for military strikes against Libya); (1993) UNYB 431 (US justification for military strikes against Iraq); UN Doc. S/PV.1106, 2 April 1964, 12–13 (UK justification for the raid against Harib Fort in Yemen); UN Doc. S/PV.1939, 9 July 1976, § 115 (Israeli justification for the Entebbe raid); UN Doc. S/PV.2280, 12 June 1981, §§ 59, 95–102 (Osiraq raid); (1998) UNYB 295 (Iranian military action against Taleban militia in Afghanistan); (1998) UNYB 262 (US military action against Iraq); UN Department of Political and Security Council Affairs, *Repertoire of the Practice of the Security Council 1985–1988* (New York, 2000), 428 (South African justification in relation to cross-border actions against 'ANC terrorists').

[217] See UN Doc. S/PV.5489, 13 July 2006; UN Doc. S/PV.5493, 21 July 1972. See also *infra*, Section 5.2.3.b.

[218] E.g., Gray, *The use of force*, pp. 148–9.

[219] E.g., Abi-Saab, 'Cours général', 371; Ago, 'Addendum', 69; American Law Institute, *Restatement of the law – Third. The Foreign Relations Law of the United States*, p. 383; A. Cassese, 'Article 51', in J.-P. Cot and A. Pellet, *La Charte des Nations Unies*, 3rd edn. (Paris: Economica, 2005), pp. 1329–61, at 1333; Constantinou, *The right of self-defence*, p. 157; Dinstein, *War, aggression and self-defence*, pp. 208–11; Malanczuk and Akehurst, *Akehurst's modern introduction*, pp. 316–17; Randelzhofer, 'Article 51', p. 805; D. Rodin, *War and self-defense* (Oxford: Clarendon Press, 2002), pp. 111–12; O. Schachter, 'The lawful resort to unilateral use of force', (1984–5) 10 YJIL 291–4, at 292.

[220] Brownlie, 'The use of force in self-defence', 229; Gray, *The use of force*, p. 150; Gardam, *Necessity, proportionality*, p. 20 (Gardam's book is one of the rare in-depth analyses of the two principles).

[221] E.g., Abi-Saab, 'Cours général', 371; Ago, 'Addendum', 69; Cassese, 'Article 51', p. 1333; Gray, *The use of force*, p. 150; Randelzhofer, 'Article 51', p. 805; UN Doc. A/AC.134/SR.52-66, 53 (Ecuador); UN Doc. A/AC.134/SR.67-78, 81 (Cango); ICJ, *DRC v. Uganda*, Mémoire de la République Démocratique du Congo, 6 July 2000, § 5.26.

CONDITIONS OF SELF-DEFENCE 95

punitive or retialiatory character and will be qualified as a reprisal, rather than as self-defence. In times of peace, such reprisals involving the use of armed force are considered unlawful[222] – this view has been confirmed by the ICJ,[223] the General Assembly[224] and the Security Council.[225] As we will see, the distinction between lawful self-defence and unlawful reprisals is a very delicate one. Nonetheless, the overarching axiom that defensive action should be limited to what is necessary to halt or repel an attack provides a useful starting point to discern and analyse the various aspects of the necessity and proportionality requirements.

2.2.2.b Necessity

2.2.2.b.i Self-defence as a last resort Starting with the necessity criterion – not to be confused with the distinct legal construct of 'necessity' as a ground precluding wrongfulness of State conduct[226] – a first component that can be identified is the need for self-defence to be a last resort. This implies that a State can only resort to armed force against another State when there are no realistic alternative means of redress available. In other words, self-defence is permissible only when peaceful means have reasonably been exhausted, or when diplomatic enterprises would clearly be futile. This precondition has long played a major role in the writings of *bellum justum* theorists, and enjoys unanimous support in present-day legal doctrine.[227]

---

[222] See e.g., Brownlie, *The use of force by states*, p. 281: 'The provisions of the Charter ... are universally regarded as prohibiting reprisals which involve the use of force.' Remark: in the course of an ongoing armed conflict, (belligerent) reprisals are not prohibited as such, but are nevertheless subjected to numerous stringent limitations by the Geneva Conventions and the Additional Protocols. See F. Kalshoven, *Belligerent reprisals*, 2nd edn. (Leiden: Martinus Nijhoff, 2005).

[223] ICJ, *Nuclear Weapons care*, Advisory opinion, § 46.

[224] Declaration on Principles of International Law Concerning Friendly Relations and Cooperation among States, Annex to GA Res. 2625 (XXV) of 24 October 1970; Declaration on the Inadmissibility of Intervention and Interference in the Internal Affairs of States, GA Res. 36/103, 9 December 1981.

[225] In 1953, the Council condemned the 'retaliatory action' at Qibya undertaken by Israeli armed forces, which was considered inconsistent with the UN Charter, SC Res. 101 (1953) of 24 November 1953. Again in response to the British raid against Harib Fort in Yemen in 1964, the Security Council *condemned* reprisals as incompatible with the principles and purposes of the United Nations, and *deplored* the British military action (SC Res. 188 (1964) of 9 April 1964). At the same time, it deplored *all* attacks and incidents which had occurred in the area.

[226] See *infra* Section 5.1.1.b.

[227] See, e.g., Ago, 'Addendum', 69; Dinstein, *War, aggression and self-defence*, pp. 209–10; Gardam, *Necessity, proportionality*, pp. 150–1; T. Gazzini, *The changing rules on the use of force in international law* (Manchester University Press, 2005), p. 144; Rodin, *War and self-defense*, p. 111.

In his report to the ILC on State Responsibility, Ago expressed the view that this requirement is 'self-evident and generally recognized'. Hence, 'it require[d] no further discussion'.[228] Nonetheless, upon closer look, customary practice sheds very little light on what peaceful initiatives are 'reasonably expected' from States in concrete situations. It is true that States resorting to self-defence have often insisted that peaceful measures had been tested and proven unsuccessful, as the US did in relation to strikes against Iraq in 1993 and 1998.[229] Likewise, the 'last resort' component has sometimes surfaced in the submissions of third States in Security Council debates. In 1986, for instance, Ghana criticized the US military action against Libya on the grounds that the United States 'had not bothered to exhaust the Charter provisions for settling disputes'.[230] And during the 1956 Suez crisis, Yugoslavia claimed that the *fedayeen* raids against Israel should have been dealt with through the armistice machinery, rather than through an Israeli military offensive against Egypt.[231] However, in those situations where the issue was raised, it was referred to as only one element amongst many others, without the criterion having played a primary role in the legality assessment. By contrast, on several other occasions where questions could potentially have been raised vis-à-vis the attacked States' dedication to peaceful diplomacy, no reference was made to the need for self-defence to be a last resort.[232] One of the very rare instances where this aspect of the necessity requirement did play a crucial role concerns the Israeli raid against the Iraqi nuclear reactor of Osiraq in 1981.[233] *In casu*, Israel

---

[228] Ago, 'Addendum', 69.

[229] E.g., (1993) UNYB 431: 'Based on the pattern of Iraqi behaviour, including the disregard for international law and Council resolutions, the [US] concluded that there was no reasonable prospect that new diplomatic initiatives or economic measures could influence the Iraqi Government to cease planning attacks against the United States. As a last resort, the United States had decided to respond by striking at an Iraqi military and intelligence target involved in such attacks.' see also (1998) UNYB 262. Remark: the US similarly attempted to demonstrate that it had exhausted peaceful means in the *Oil Platforms* case: ICJ, *Oil Platforms* case, Counter-memorial submitted by the United States of America, 23 June 1997, §§ 4.23–4.26. In a similar vein: ICJ, *DRC* v.*Uganda*, Mémoire de la République Démocratique du Congo, 6 July 2000, § 5.29.

[230] (1986) UNYB 256. See also: UN Doc. S/PV.1644, 27–28 February 1972, § 25.

[231] UN Doc. S/PV.748, 30 October 1956, 4.

[232] E.g., G. Redsell, 'Illegitimate, unnecessary and disproportionate: Israel's use of force in Lebanon', (2007) Cambridge Student L Rev 70–85, at 80 (vis-à-vis the Second Lebanon War).

[233] Remark: another incident where this issue seems to have played an important (albeit less explicit) role concerns the Council consideration of the 1976 Entebbe raid. Several

emphasized that it had tried to halt the nuclear threat against its existence by diplomatic means. However, as the latter efforts bore no fruit and the reactor was about to go 'hot' any time, Israel saw no choice but to destroy the site in the exercise of its right of self-defence.[234] Israel's justification received no support whatsoever in the course of the Council debates. Intervening States were undivided in denouncing the operation as unlawful[235] and the Council unanimously condemned the Israeli military attack 'in clear violation of the [UN] Charter'.[236] Several States expressly argued that Israel should first have submitted its concerns to the Security Council, rather than taking the law in its own hands.[237] Japan suggested that if, in spite of the IAEA inspections (the latest of which had taken place only months before the raid), Israel suspected that Iraq intended to produce atomic bombs, it should 'have sought to settle the manner by peaceful means, for example by submitting it to the IAEA for consideration'.[238] The United States even stated that its condemnation of the operation 'was based solely on the conviction that Israel had failed to exhaust peaceful means'.[239]

However, when dealing with the Osiraq raid, one ought not to lose sight of the distinctive features of the particular case. Indeed, what Israel was doing was not so much responding to a prior armed attack as originally envisaged under Article 51 UN Charter, but rather relying on a broad reading of self-defence allowing for 'pre-emptive' or even 'preventive' self-defence.[240] Thus, the heightened attention for the last resort criterion should be seen in the light of the broader discussion concerning anticipatory self-defence, which strongly influenced States' assessment of the Osiraq incident.[241] We will come back to this conundrum at greater length when dealing with the temporal aspect of the armed attack concept (*infra*, Chapter 4). For now, it is merely established that in those (traditional) cases in which States exercised self-defence in response to a prior armed attack, the 'last resort' condition has been of relatively little

    States indeed questioned the raid on the grounds that negotiations with the hijackers were still going on when Israeli commandos raided the Ugandan airport of Entebbe to secure the hostages, and/or disagreed with Israel's view that President Idi Amin was in fact helping the terrorists. See (1976) UNYB 315–20.

[234] See UN Doc. S/PV.2280, 12 June 1981, §§ 59, 95.
[235] See UN Doc.S/PV.2281 – UN Doc. S/PV.2284, 13–16 June 1981.
[236] SC Res. 487 (1981) of 19 June 1981.
[237] UN Doc.S/PV.2281, 13 June 1981, § 70 (Pakistan); UN Doc. S/PV.2283, 15 June 1981, § 15 (Sierra Leone).
[238] UN Doc. S/PV.2282, 15 June 1981, § 95. [239] (1981) UNYB 276.
[240] See the justification of Israel: UN Doc. S/PV.2280, 12 June 1981, §§ 97–101.
[241] For an elaborate analysis of the Osiraq strike, see *infra* Section 4.1.2.c.

practical significance. Ago correctly finds that it 'would be particularly important if the idea of preventive self-defence were admitted. It would obviously be of lesser importance if only self-defence following the attack was regarded as lawful.'[242] Schachter puts it even more strongly by denying that there always is an overriding obligation to seek peaceful settlement first in case of an ongoing armed attack: 'a State is not obliged to turn the other cheek when attacked'.[243] Practice indeed indicates that the need to exhaust peaceful means only plays a subsidiary role for the assessment of self-defence claims in response to a prior attack, and that unlawfulness will only result when a manifest unwillingness to address diplomatic channels can be demonstrated. Whether the defending State has in good faith complied with this requirement must be assessed on a case-by-case basis, taking account *inter alia* of the compliance or non-compliance with earlier Security Council resolutions, and the outcome of past bilateral or multilateral initiatives.[244] In any event, the obligation only requires a bona fide utilization of diplomatic channels; the attacked State is not under an obligation to compromise its sovereignty.[245]

---

[242] Ago, 'Addendum', 69. *Idem* M. N. Schmitt, 'Preemptive strategies in international law', (2002–3) 24 Michigan JIL 513–48, at 530–1.

[243] Schachter, 'Unilateral use of force', 292. See also Schachter, *International law in theory and practice*, pp. 154–5. Gardam links the need to exhaust peaceful means to the requirement of immediacy (cf. *infra*), in the sense that the longer the period between the armed attack and the response, the more pressure there will be on the State concerned to resolve the matter by peaceful means. See Gardam, *Necessity, proportionality*, pp. 150 (footnote 58), 151, 152–3.

[244] Remark: in the *Oil Platforms* case, the United States not only referred to the fact that Iran had refused to moderate its behaviour, but also its 'constant denials of involvement' in the alleged attacks (ICJ, *Oil Platforms* case, Counter-memorial and counter-claim submitted by the United States of America, 23 June 1997, § 4.26). In his dissenting opinion in the *Nicaragua* case (Merits), Judge Schwebel drew attention to the following factors to 'mitigate' the view that the US had failed to exhaust peaceful means: the US had maintained a readiness to negotiate with Nicaragua; it had taken part in a substantial multilateral effort at peaceful settlement which Nicaragua rebuffed; it gave active support to the Contadora peace process; and it had actively taken part in the Security Council's handling of the matter (ICJ, *Nicaragua* case (Merits), Dissenting opinion of Judge Schwebel, § 204).

Remark: according to Corten, in practice, the necessity requirement is generally interpreted in a relatively flexible manner. Action in self-defence need not be strictly '*indispensable*' to repel the armed attack(s), but must be 'essential, important'. See Corten, *Le droit contre la guerre*, pp. 718–23.

[245] Remark: in relation to the Entebbe incident, the US pointed out that the fact 'that Israel might have secured the release of its nationals by complying with the terrorists' demands does not alter [the legality assessment]'. UN Doc. S/PV.1941, 12 July 1976, § 32. See Knisbacher, 'The Entebbe operation', 71–2.

2.2.2.b.ii Immediacy

A second component of the necessity criterion[246] concerns the 'immediacy' of action undertaken in self-defence. Indeed, it is generally accepted that for such action to be lawful, it should in principle be undertaken while the original armed attack which triggered it is still in progress and that there should be a close proximity in time between the start of the latter attack and the response in self-defence.[247] Again, this condition is inevitably subject to a degree of uncertainty, as no precise limit can be fixed. Still, the basic idea behind the need for a temporal link is sound, for without such limitation self-defence would theoretically be available to sanction countless past acts of aggression or conquest.[248] The immediacy aspect thus serves as an important factor to distinguish lawful self-defence and unlawful armed reprisals and makes clear that hostilities may not be re-opened at a much later stage without the occurrence of a new *casus foederis*.[249]

The need for a temporal link finds support in customary practice.[250] In the Council debates following the UK raid against the Yemeni Harib Fort in 1964, for instance, some States expressed concern at the fact that the UK raid had been launched after the aerial incursion(s) into the territory of the Federation of South Arabia had ended. The Iraqi delegate noted that:

> A proper defensive measure against such alleged incursions would have been to try to chase the aircraft and helicopters or even shoot at them if they had indeed violated the air space of the Federation. Instead, a whole day passed, and then eight aircraft were sent from Aden to demolish the police station at Harib.[251]

In the *Nicaragua* case, the ICJ by way of *obiter dicta* rejected the necessity of the US measures against Nicaragua on the grounds that they were taken months after the major offensive of the opposition against the government of El Salvador had been completely repulsed.[252]

---

[246] Some authors identify this as a separate customary condition next to necessity and proportionality. E.g., Constantinou, *The right of self-defence*, pp. 159–61; Dinstein, *War, aggression and self-defence*, p. 242; Gazzini, *The changing rules*, pp. 143–6.

[247] E.g., Ago, 'Addendum', 70; Cassese, 'Article 51', p. 1334; Gardam, *Necessity, proportionality*, pp. 150–3; Malanczuk and Akehurst, *Akehurst's modern introduction*, p. 317–18; Redsell, 'Israel's use of force in Lebanon', 80.

[248] Schachter, 'Unilateral use of force', 292.   [249] Gazzini, *The changing rules*, p. 147.

[250] E.g., UN Doc. S/PV.1644, 27–28 February 1972, § 25.

[251] UN Doc. S/PV.1107, 3 April 1964, § 17. See also UN Doc. S/PV.1110, 8 April 1964, § 24 (Czechoslovakia).

[252] ICJ, *Nicaragua* case (Merits), § 237.

At the same time, a double reservation must be made. First, when assessing the temporal proximity between the beginning of the armed attack and the initation of action in self-defence, this condition should not be construed too strictly.[253] A certain degree of flexibility is needed. Thus, if the premeditated nature of the response has sometimes been perceived as evidence of its retaliatory character,[254] this is not always so.[255] There is no clear-cut distinction between 'premeditated' reprisals and 'spontaneous' self-defence. Some level of preparation may be needed for the attacked State to mount an appropriate and coordinated response or to collect intelligence on the source and specifics of the attack. The attacked State may also postpone resort to force until negotiations have failed,[256] or it may engage in a time-consuming political decision-making process at the domestic level before actually giving a green light to the armed forces. In a noteworthy reply to criticism of the premeditated nature of the raid at Harib Fort, the UK delegate objected that:

> This [was] as it should be. Defensive measures undertaken by a responsible Government require preparation and the proper approval just as much as any other measures. In the present case, such planning and approval was necessary to ensure that only those responsible ... were

---

[253] E.g., Constantinou, *The right of self-defence*, pp. 160–1; Dinstein, *War, aggression and self-defence*, p. 210; Ducheine, *Geweldgebruik en terreurbestrijding*, pp. 247–8; Gardam, *Necessity, proportionality*, pp. 150–1; Gazzini, *The changing rules*, p. 144; Malanczuk and Akehurst, *Akehurst's modern introduction*, p. 317; Redsell, 'Israel's use of force in Lebanon', 80; J. Verhoeven, 'Les "étirements" de la légitime défense', (2002) 48 AFDI 49–80, at 65–6.

[254] UN Doc. S/PV.1107, 3 April 1964, § 15 (Iraq), § 48 (UAR). Also UN Doc. A/36/PV.56, 13 November 1981, § 25 (Algeria: 'legitimate defence and premeditation are mutually exclusive').

During the *Oil Platforms* case, Iran moreover argued as follows: 'Whilst States are entitled to prepare for necessary measures in self-defence, ... it is clear that where responsive measures are pre-meditated and pre-planned, then ... they cannot be truly protective. This is for the reason that they will rarely be limited to the necessities of the case, for the "case", the actual location, size and nature of the attack is not known.' ICJ, *Oil Platforms* case, Memorial submitted by the Islamic Republic of Iran, 8 June 1993, §§ 4.36, 4.37. Implicitly: Ethiopia–Eritrea Claims Commission, Partial Award *Jus ad Bellum*, Ethiopia Claims 1–8, 19 December 2005, reprinted in (2006) 45 ILM 430, § 19.

[255] E.g., D. Bowett, 'Reprisals involving recourse to armed force', (1972) 66 AJIL 1–36, at 7.

[256] Remark: Judge Schwebel nonetheless seems to stretch this concession excessively far by asking the rhetorical question whether the US 'really is to be faulted for asking the time to pursue prior recourse to measures of peaceful settlement'. *In casu*, a year had passed between the 1981 'final offensive' of the Salvadoran insurgents and the covert application of force by the US. ICJ, *Nicaragua* case (Merits), Dissenting opinion of Judge Schwebel, § 209.

involved in the attack and that civilians in the town of Harib were not affected by it in any way.[257]

Similarly, when justifying the US strike against Iraq in 1993 following the thwarting of an attempt to assassinate former President Bush during a visit to Kuwait City, Secretary of State Albright explained that the two-month time lapse between the Bush visit and the military raid was due to the intensive investigation into the assassination plot.[258] None of the States intervening in the debate suggested that this time lapse rendered the operation unlawful. Many indeed supported the US reliance on Article 51 UN Charter.[259] The same is true by analogy vis-à-vis the two-week span between the Al Qaeda attacks against the US embassies in Nairobi and Dar Es Salaam and the US strikes against Sudan and Afghanistan in 1998.[260] Thus, 'premeditation' may sometimes be qualified more positively as 'preparation' and escape the label of 'reprisal'. The temporal link should be assessed on a case-by-case basis, taking account of the circumstances at hand. Especially in relation to armed attacks of an ongoing nature, primarily those involving the occupation or annexation of territory, legal doctrine and customary practice seem to allow a leeway of time for the initiation of defensive action. The most well-known example concerns the 1982 Falklands conflict.[261] *In casu*, the United

---

[257] UN Doc. S/PV.1109, 7 April 1964, §§ 23–4.
[258] UN Doc. S/PV.3245, 27 June 1993, 3: 'Over the next two months, American law enforcement, forensic and intelligence professionals conducted a meticulous and exhaustive investigation of this incident. They conducted detailed forensic examinations of the bombs and devices. Through the cooperation of the Kuwaiti government, they had independent access to all the suspects in the case. They interviewed all involved several times. The process took time. There was no rush to judgement.'
[259] E.g., *ibid.*, 13 (France), 15 (Japan), 18 (Hungary), 19–20 (UK), 20 (Russia), 21 (New Zealand), 22 (Spain).
[260] The terrorist bombings took place on 7 August 1998. The military strikes were launched on 20 August 1998. See (1998) UNYB 1219–20; UN Doc. S/1998/780, 20 August 1998 (US).
Remark: in response to PKK attacks from northern Iraq in October 2007, Turkey engaged in aerial raids as well as a small-scale hot pursuit operation. In February 2008, Turkey eventually launched a major ground offensive (Operation 'Sun') on Iraqi territory. There was no explicit criticism of the time lapse. To the contrary, some statements indicate that Operation 'Sun' was regarded as consistent with the necessity and proportionality standards. See *infra* Section 5.2.3.c.
[261] Another example that is frequently cited in legal literature to underscore the flexible character of the immediacy requirement is the 1990–1 Gulf crisis (e.g., Dinstein, *War, aggression and self-defence*, p. 210; Gardam, *Necessity, proportionality*, p. 151). In this case, however, the precedential value of the time lapse (between the invasion of Kuwait and Operation 'Desert Storm') is less unequivocal due to the presence of an authorization by the Security Council to 'use all necessary means'.

Kingdom allowed several weeks to pass between the invading by Argentine forces of the contested Falklands Islands and the initiating of active military operations against Argentina.[262] This apparent lack of immediacy, which may in part be explained by the geographically distant location of the attack, was not raised by third States in the course of the Council debates. There appeared to be implicit support among many States for the view that the UK retained the right to self-defence for some time after the initial attack.[263] Still, as time went on, States increasingly expressed concern at the escalation of the conflict and urged both States to engage in peaceful negotiations. This may indicate that the longer the period between the armed attack and the response, the more pressure there will be on the State concerned to resolve the matter by peaceful means.[264]

In relation to isolated attacks, not of an ongoing nature, a second reservation has to be made. While in principle a State can no longer claim to be acting in self-defence after the attack – whether for instance an aerial incursion or a cross-border raid by ground forces – has ended, this is not always the case. According to Ago: 'if the attack in question consisted of a number of successive acts, the requirement of the immediacy of the self-defensive action would have to be looked at in the light of those acts as a whole'.[265] What Ago is actually defending here is the view that if there has been a series of attacks and there is convincing proof that further attacks will follow, the attacked State is not obliged to confine itself to an on-the-spot reaction to the armed attack, but may also exercise its right to self-defence after the latest attack has factually ended. In such situations it is accepted that measures of self-defence may also serve to impede further attacks.

Customary practice is replete with examples where the attacked State has (partially) justified its actions by relying on the need to prevent *further* attacks – i.e., a scenario not to be confused with the pure pre-emptive or preventive model, where no prior armed attack has occurred whatsoever.[266] The need to prevent further attacks was, for example, invoked by the United States in relation to the strikes against Libya in 1986 – framed as a response to an 'an ongoing pattern' of Libyan-sponsored

---

[262] See (1982) UNYB 1320–46. Remark: it must be admitted that although the actual counter-attack by UK forces took place almost a month after the invasion, the UK had immediately ordered the Royal Navy to leave for the area of conflict.
[263] Gardam, *Necessity, proportionality*, p. 151.
[264] *Ibid.*, pp. 150–1.　[265] Ago, 'Addendum', 70.　[266] See also *infra* Section 4.3.1.

terrorist attacks[267] – and the military strikes against targets in Sudan and Afghanistan in response to the bombing of the US embassies in Nairobi and Dar Es Salaam.[268] In the latter case, the American Ambassador to the UN declared as follows:

> In response to these terrorist attacks, and to prevent and deter their continuation, United States armed forces today struck at a series of camps and installations used by the Bin Ladin organization to support terrorist actions against the United States and other countries.... [W]e have convincing evidence that further such attacks were in preparation from these terrorist facilities. The United States, therefore, had no choice but to use armed force to prevent these attacks from continuing.[269]

The same argument was *inter alia* used in relation to the 1964 Gulf of Tunkin incident,[270] the 1975 Israeli intervention in Lebanon,[271] the South African incursions into Lesotho in 1982[272] and the 1993 US strikes against Iraq.[273]

While it is true that several of the cited interventions were criticized in or even condemned by the UN, negative reactions were generally related to factual circumstances and other aspects of the incidents concerned and should therefore not be read as a principled rejection of *post facto* defensive measures. For example, the widespread censure of the South African raid into Lesotho in 1982 was founded on the loss of innocent lives, the reprehensible nature of the apartheid regime, as well as the lack of evidence that South Africa had been the victim of any armed attack.[274] Again, even if some States expressed concern at the 'preventive' nature of Israel's intervention in Lebanon in 1975,[275] condemnations were mainly inspired by the disproportionate nature of the actions and the

---

[267] UN Doc. S/17990; (1986) UNYB 252. [268] UN Doc. S/1998/780, 20 August 1998 (US).
[269] *Ibid.* [270] (1964) UNYB 147. [271] UN Doc. S/PV.1859, § 119.
[272] UN Doc. S/PV.2409, §§ 137–45. [273] UN Doc. S/PV.3245, 27 June 1993, 6 (US).
[274] See UN Docs. S/PV.2406-9, 14–16 December 1982; UN Doc. S/PV.2406, 16–17 (Lesotho); UN Doc. S/PV.2407, § 6 (Libya), § 19 (Zaire), §§ 36–7 (Togo), §§ 75–7 (France), §§ 84–9 (Ireland), §§ 101–2 (Japan), § 111 (Uganda), §§ 128–9 (PRC), § 135 (Jordan), § 150 (USSR), § 165 (Spain); UN Doc. S/PV.2408, 19 (US), 29, 33 (Angola), 44 (Algeria), 76–8 (Sierra Leone: 'South Africa ... has not demonstrated by an iota of evidence that any attack has been launched against it from Lesotho'), 93–4 (Zambia), 111 (Swaziland); UN Doc. S/PV.2409, § 7 (Panama), §§ 18–27 (Botswana), §§ 36–8 (Kenya), § 88 (Zimbabwe), § 64 (Tanzania), § 105 (Yemen). South Africa was eventually condemned by both the General Assembly (GA Res. 37/101 of 14 December 1982, adopted without vote) and the Security Council (SC Res. 527 (1982) of 15 December 1982, adopted unanimously).
[275] See UN Doc. S/PV.1859, 4 December 1975, § 99 (Lebanon), § 119 (Egypt), § 145 (Syria); UN Doc. S/PV.1861, 8 December 1975, §§ 31–2 (France).

considerable number of civilian casualties.[276] States criticizing the 1986 US strikes against Tripoli referred first and foremost to the loss of innocent lives as well as to the lack of evidence that Libya had been involved in armed attacks against US targets.[277]

Conversely, Security Council debates dealing with the concerned interventions sometimes offer fairly straightforward support for the prospective dimension of the necessity standard. With regard to the 1964 Gulf of Tunkin incident and the 1986 US strike against Libya, for example, the UK argued that the US had the right to take action to prevent the recurrence of attacks on its ships in accordance with Article 51 UN Charter.[278] Again, following the 1993 US strike against the Iraqi intelligence headquarters, several Council Members quoted with approval the US justification that the action was designed to prevent and deter further attacks.[279]

Last but not least, in the aftermath of the 9/11 attacks, the US and the UK announced that in accordance with the inherent right of self-defence, their forces had initiated 'actions designed to prevent and deter further attacks' from the same source.[280] No country seriously contended that the military response was not necessary since the 9/11 attacks were

---

[276] See UN Doc. S/PV.1860, 5 December 1975, § 32 (Japan); UN Doc. S/PV.1861, §§ 13, 18 (Cameroon), § 23 (Sweden), § 32 (France), § 38 (PRC), § 44 (Mauritania); UN Doc. S/PV.1862, 8 December 1975, § 3 (Belarus), §§ 35-6 (Tanzania), §§ 120-2 (Italy), § 139 (UK). Remark: Israel did not submit any justification of its actions to the Security Council and did not intervene in the Council debates. A resolution condemning Israel obtained thirteen votes in favour, but was vetoed by the US ((1975) UNYB 229).

[277] See, e.g., UN Docs. S/PV.2674-83, 15-24 April 1986; UN Doc. S/PV.2675, §§ 11-12, 18 (Syria), §§ 24-5 (Oman), §§ 37-8 (Cuba), § 42 (Yemen), § 48 (India); UN Doc. S/PV.2676, § 4 (Algeria), § 7 (Yugoslavia), § 12 (Ukraine), §§ 24-5 (German Democratic Republic); UN Doc. S/PV.2677, § 31 (Hungary); UN Doc. S/PV.2680, 7 (Belarus), 32-6 (Ghana); UN Doc. S/PV.2682, 6 (Pakistan), 14-6 (Uganda), 21 (Malta), 32 (Denmark), et cetera. But see UN Doc. S/PV.2677, 6-7 (Qatar, denouncing the US actions as a form of pre-emptive self-defence), 12-13 (Madagascar). A Security Council resolution condemning the US was vetoed by France, the UK and the US ((1986) UNYB 254).

[278] UN Doc. S/PV.1140, 5 August 1964, 12 ('It seems ... that, having regard to the repeated nature of these attacks and their mounting scale, the [US] had a right, in accordance with the principle of self-defence ..., to take action directed to prevent the recurrence of such attacks on its ships. Preventive action in accordance with that aim is an essential right which is embraced by any definition of that principle of self-defence. It ... is fully consistent with Article 51 of the Charter'); UN Doc. S/PV.2679, 26-7 ('the right of self-defence is not an entirely passive right. It plainly includes the right ... to discourage and prevent further violence').

[279] E.g., UN Doc. S/PV.3245, 27 June 1993, 17 (Brazil), 19-20 (Hungary), 21-2 (UK).

[280] UN Doc. S/2001/946, 7 October 2001 (US); UN Doc. S/2001/947, 7 October 2001 (UK).

factually 'over'. To the contrary, practically the entire international community endorsed the recourse to self-defence.[281]

In the *Oil Platforms* case, Iran in its initial memorial admitted that there might be circumstances in which a victim State has experienced a series of attacks, and apprehends further attacks, 'so that the measures taken, although taken after the last actual attack, are designed to protect the State against future attacks'.[282] On the other hand, Iran stressed that such instances of self-defence had generally been rejected by the Security Council, and 'rightly so, because the apprehended future attacks, if not imminent, are hypothetical; and in any event the measures tend to be designed to "teach a lesson"'.[283] In its reply to the US counter-memorial, Iran took an even more restrictive approach. It interpreted the principle of immediacy as implying that, in cases of single armed attacks, self-defence could not be exercised when the incident was over.[284] *In casu*, both the attacks on the *Sea Isle City* and on the *Samuel B. Roberts* had terminated when the counter-force was exercised.[285] Hence, the US actions did not constitute an act of self-defence, but a reprisal. The US, however, vigorously objected to the Iranian interpretation, arguing instead that the right to use force in self-defence is not strictly limited to the repelling of an attack in progress, but may extend to the use of force to remove continuing threats to its security:

> Such a limited view would render self-defence illusory in cases like this. The armed attacks here lasted only a few seconds. They involved mines secretly hidden in the sea and anti-ship missiles that struck anonymously and with little warning. Following such attacks, the ***status quo ante*** could not be restored simply by driving an attacking force back across the

---

[281] See, *inter alia*, (2001) UNYB 65–6. Also *infra*, Section 5.2.2.a.ii.
  Remark: another example that would seem to support the possibility of invoking self-defence to prevent *further* attacks is the Turkish intervention in Iraq in 2007–8. See *infra* Section 5.2.3.c.
[282] ICJ, *Oil Platforms* case, Memorial submitted by the Islamic Republic of Iran, 8 June 1993, § 4.32–33: 'An illustration would be in the destruction of bases from which attacks had occurred in the past, and from which future attacks were anticipated.'
[283] *Ibid.*
[284] ICJ, *Oil Platforms* case, Reply and defence to counter-claim submitted by the Islamic Republic of Iran, 10 March 1999, § 7.47: 'it means that the employment of counter-force must be temporally interlocked with the armed attack triggering it. In the case of the invasion of another State's territory, in principle an attack still exists as long as the occupation continues. But in cases of single armed attacks . . . , the attack is terminated when the incident is over. In such a case the subsequent use of counter-force constitutes a reprisal and not an exercise of self-defence.'
[285] *Ibid.*

border from whence they came.... The threat of further attacks against US vessels and their naval escorts continued.[286]

In the end, as we know, the ICJ found that the US actions were incompatible with the necessity criterion[287] – some judges explicitly labelling them as unlawful reprisals.[288] However, upon closer reading, the Court did not pronounce on whether the immediacy requirement excluded measures of self-defence aimed at preventing future armed attacks. Rather, the verdict was mainly inspired by the fact that it did not consider proven that the US had been victim of an armed attack, let alone a series of armed attacks, as well as by the US's choice of targets (cf. *infra*).

In all, customary practice indicates that if a State has been subject not to an isolated attack, but to a series of armed attacks, and if there is a considerable likelihood that more attacks will imminently follow, then self-defence is not automatically excluded.[289] This seems altogether rather logical, since the opposite position would imply that States would have little defence against consecutive pin-prick attacks whereby opposing forces withdraw immediately after having carried out an attack.

---

[286] ICJ, *Oil Platforms* case, Counter-memorial and counter-claim submitted by the United States of America, 23 June 1997, §§ 4.27–4.29. See also: ICJ, *Oil Platforms* case, Rejoinder submitted by the United States of America, 23 March 2001, § 5.33: 'Iran's arguments are, without exception, designed to fit neatly into its stealthy, one-by-one method of attack. Thus, Iran's contention that "[o]nly reaction to an existing, ongoing attack constitutes self-defence" only adds a new condition to the customary requirements of self-defense. It is also another of Iran's ploys to avoid responsibility for its special brand of sneak attacks on neutral shipping, since the Iranian attacks at issue in this case occurred – started, ended, caused damage and casualties – in but an instant, leaving no opportunity to the victim State to respond during that brief moment. Similarly, Iran's suggestion that only action taken against "a missile launching site" or "mine-laying boats" would be legitimate cannot withstand scrutiny. Article 51 cannot be read to require such constricting results, which would surely encourage aggressors to carry out attacks in such a manner. In a situation of armed attacks and the explicit threat of continuing armed attacks, Article 51 does not foreclose the victim State's right to take other necessary and proportionate measures in self-defence.'

[287] ICJ, *Oil Platforms* case, §§ 73–6.

[288] *Ibid.*, §§ 63–4, 72, 74–6. See also Separate opinion of Judge Simma, § 15; Dissenting opinion of Judge Elaraby, § 1.2; Separate opinion of Judge Kooijmans, §§ 62–3.

[289] Cf. Corten, *Le droit contre la guerre*, pp. 725–8; Dinstein, *War, aggression and self-defence*, pp. 228, 231; Franck, 'Terrorism and the right of self-defense', 840; T. Gazzini, 'The rules on the use of force at the beginning of the XXI century', (2006) 11 JCSL 319–42, at 331; M.E. O'Connell, 'Lawful self-defense to terrorism', 893–4; C. Stahn, 'International law at crossroads?: the impact of September 11', (2002) 62 ZaöRV 183–255, at 233. Cautiously: Verhoeven, 'Les "étirements" de la légitime défense', 65. Critical: L. Condorelli, 'Les attentats du 11 Septembre et leurs suites: où va le droit international?', (2001) 105 RGDIP 829–48, at 838–9.

This is particularly important in the context of attacks by non-State actors (see *infra* Chapter 5), since these groups often rely on hit-and-run tactics.

The result hereof is an inevitable blurring of the distinction between self-defence and unlawful reprisals – some scholars even use phrases such as 'defensive armed reprisals' to describe the situations of permissible self-defence discussed above.[290] A remarkable example in this regard is the 1993 US raid in Iraq, prompted by the discovery of an Iraqi plot to assassinate former President Bush. Indeed, even though the US asserted that its actions served to deter further attacks and a number of States intervening in the Council debates underscored this preventive/deterrent effect,[291] when looking at the facts of the case, it is difficult not to see the operation as a classical punitive expedition.[292] Nonetheless, the

---

[290] Dinstein, *War, aggression and self-defence*, pp. 221–31: ('[D]efensive armed reprisals must be future-oriented, and not limited to a desire to punish past transgressions. At bottom, the issue is whether the unlawful use of force by the other side is likely to repeat itself' (at 227)); Schachter, *International law in theory and practice*, p. 154 (referring to 'defensive retaliation', which is considered lawful when its prime motive is protective). See also A. D. Surchin, 'Terror and the law: the unilateral use of force and the June 1993 bombing of Baghdad', (1994–5) 5 Duke JCIL 457–97, at 487–93. Contra: Gazzini, *The changing rules*, p. 204; Ronzitti, 'The expanding law of self-defence', 354–5; ICJ, *Oil Platforms* case, Reply and defence to counter-claim submitted by the Islamic Republic of Iran, 10 March 1999, § 7.56.

Remark: in his 1972 AJIL article, analysing the Council practice, Bowett observed that the norm prohibiting armed reprisals suffered from a credibility gap, due to the divergence between the norm and the actual practice of States. He suggested that the Council should adopt a broader view of self-defence, but thought it more likely that the Council would move towards a partial acceptance of 'reasonable' reprisals (i.e., subject to a number of criteria such as proportionality). However, Bowett starts from the idea that military action against 'completed' attacks cannot fall under the heading of self-defence, but must necessarily amount to a form of reprisal. See Bowett, 'Reprisals', (in particular) at 3, 21–2. See also Y. Z. Blum, 'State response to acts of terrorism', (1976) 19 GYBIL 223–37, at 226–9. Blum agrees with Bowett that the distinction between reprisals and self-defence is blurred. Observing that recourse to armed reprisals has repeatedly been condemned by States and international organizations, he proposes a broadening of the rubric of self-defence, rather than a (partial) acceptance of 'armed reprisals', even though he notes that this shift from reprisals to self-defence is probably no more than 'an exercise in semantics' (229).

[291] UN Doc. S/PV.3245, 27 June 1993, 6 (US), 18 (Hungary), 19–20 (UK).

[292] In a similar vein: L. Condorelli, 'A propos de l'attaque américaine contre l'Irak du 26 juin 1993: lettre d'un professeur désemparé aux lecteurs du JEDI', (1994) 5 EJIL 134–44; J. Quigley, 'Missiles with a message: the legality of the United States raid on Iraq's intelligence headquarters', (1993–94) 17 Hastings ICLRev 241–74; W. M. Reisman, 'The Baghdad bombing: self-defence or reprisals?', (1994) 5 EJIL 120–33, at 125. Less unequivocal: Surchin, 'Terror and the law', 458, 474.

US self-defence claim gained wide support among Council members.[293] This attitude may perhaps have been inspired by the particularly reprehensible nature of the attack (the foiled murder attempt) and by Iraq's pariah status following the 1990–1 Gulf War,[294] yet it does illustrate the delicate distinction between self-defence and reprisals, a distinction which can only be made after taking account of all relevant circumstances. In any event, in spite of interpretative difficulties, States are keen to maintain the legal barrier between permissible self-defence and unlawful reprisals in order to limit possible abuses.[295]

2.2.2.b.iii Targeting   A final aspect of the necessity criterion concerns the choice of targets of the defensive action. Indeed, the use of force must not only comply with the relevant rules of international humanitarian law (IHL),[296] but must also be *adequate* for the repelling of an armed attack. For this reason, it is not sufficient that the target is a legitimate military objective; it must also be connected with the force to be repelled.[297] In short, the action undertaken (e.g., aerial strikes, artillery shelling, et cetera) should in principle be directed against the source(s) of the armed attack(s).

This requirement surfaces rather consistently in customary practice. In relation to the Harib Fort incident, for instance, the United Kingdom insisted that the fort was a military installation with artillery and armaments, kown to be a 'centre for subversion and aggressive activities across

---

[293] See UN Doc. S/PV.3245, 27 June 1993. Several other States similarly expressed support. See. Quigley, 'Missiles with a message', 271–2; Surchin, 'Terror and the law', 467–8.

[294] Also Quigley, 'Missiles with a message', 270–1.

[295] Thus, when in 1974 Yale Professor Rostow suggested to US Secretary of State Rush that the US endorse the right of military reprisal under the UN Charter, the latter responded as follows: 'Of course we recognize that the practice of States is not always consistent with [the prohibition of armed reprisals] and that it may sometimes be difficult to distinguish the exercise of proportionate self-defence from an act of reprisal. Yet, essentially for reasons of the abuse to which the doctrine of reprisals particularly lends itself, we think it desirable to endeavor to maintain the distinction between acts of lawful self-defense and unlawful reprisals.' Reproduced in (1974) 68 AJIL 736.

[296] E.g., ICJ, *Nuclear Weapons* case, Advisory opinion, § 42.

[297] E.g., Constantinou, *The right of self-defence*, pp. 170–1; Redsell, 'Israel's use of force in Lebanon', 80. Remark: some authors see this as an element of the proportionality criterion rather than the necessity criterion. The present author follows the approach of the *Oil Platforms* case where targeting formed part of the necessity assessment (ICJ, *Oil Platforms* case, §§ 74–6). At the same, it is noted that targeting cannot be exclusively brought under a single of the two criteria, but inevitably touches upon both. (Remark: in *Nicaragua*, the Court qualified the targeting of ports, oil installations et cetera as disproportionate. ICJ, *Nicaragua* case (Merits), § 237.)

the border into the South Arabian Federation'.[298] In the Security Council, Yugoslavia criticized the fact that the attack was directed against a land objective, which had nothing to do with the alleged raids by Yemeni aircraft and helicopters.[299] In 1993, the US stressed that its military raid against Iraq 'was aimed at a target directly linked to the operation against President Bush'.[300] Likewise, during its 2006 intervention in Lebanon, Israel argued that it was concentrating its response carefully, mainly on Hezbollah strongholds, positions and infrastructure.[301] However, in light of the widespread destruction of civilian infrastructure, the bombing of the Beirut airport and the instalment of a blockade on the Lebanese coast, an overwhelming majority of States condemned the excessive use of force by Israel, which went far beyond the stated objective of dismantling Hezbollah.[302] Conversely, in relation to Turkey's Operation 'Sun' in northern Iraq in February 2008, a number of States praised the fact that the operation was precisely aimed only at PKK targets in the region.[303]

As mentioned before, the choice of targets played an important role in the ICJ's necessity assessment in the *Oil Platforms* case. According to the United States, the Iranian oil platforms targeted by the US navy formed legitimate targets for action in self-defence since evidence showed that the platforms collected intelligence concerning passing vessels, acted as a military communication link coordinating Iranian naval forces and served as actual staging bases to launch helicopter and small boat attacks on neutral commercial shipping.[304] Iran recognized the presence of limited military personnel and equipment on the plaforms, but insisted that their purpose was exclusively defensive and justified by previous Iraqi attacks on its oil production facilities.[305] Eventually, the Court did not find the evidence submitted by the US sufficiently convincing.[306] It added that even if it would have held otherwise, there was no evidence that the US had actually complained to Iran of the military activities of

---

[298] E.g., UN Doc. S/PV.1108, 6 April 1964, § 112; UN Doc. S/PV.1109, 7 April 1964, § 30. This allegation was categorically denied by Yemen, which asserted that the fort was merely the police headquarters of the town of Harib (UN Doc. S/PV.1106, 2 April 1964, § 105).
[299] UN Doc. S/PV.1108, 8 April 1964, § 24.   [300] UN Doc. S/PV.3245, 27 June 1993, 6.
[301] UN Doc. S/PV.5489, 14 July 2006, 6.
[302] See *ibid.*; UN Doc. S/PV.5493, 21 July 2006. Remark: most States labelled Israel's reaction as 'disproportionate.' This again illustrates the difficulty of making a clear analytical distinction between the necessity and proportionality assessments.
[303] See *infra* Section 5.2.3.c.   [304] ICJ, *Oil Platforms* case, § 74.
[305] *Ibid.*, § 75.   [306] *Ibid.*, § 76.

the platforms, in the same way as it had complained of mine-laying and attacks on neutral shipping. This was seen as an indication that the US merely regarded the oil platforms as 'targets of opportunity', the destruction of which would harm Iran economically and thus teach it a lesson.[307]

2.2.2.c Proportionality

2.2.2.c.i The quantitative vs. the functional approach This brings us to the second customary criterion that the exercise of self-defence must comply with, namely the proportionality principle, whose function is to serve as a constraint on the scale and effects of defensive action. It should be noted from the outset that this principle has generated far more doctrinal controversy than the previous one, and that the identification of guidelines for its assessment is hampered for a number of reasons. First, while States themselves have consistently upheld the basic standard, they have seldom made explicit any concrete guidelines.[308] A second complicating factor is the fact that proportionality operates in two separate legal regimes, which are parallelly applicable to the use of force in self-defence, namely the *Ius ad Bellum* and IHL.[309] The legal evaluation is substantially different under the two regimes. What matters for IHL purposes is the precise conduct of the individual attacks by military personnel on the ground: whether care was taken not to directly target civilian infrastructure and to avoid disproportionate collateral damage among the civilian population; whether or not the State used weapons that are specifically prohibited under IHL or used weapons in an indiscriminate manner, et cetera. In terms of the *Ius ad Bellum*, it is the forceful response as a whole that must be scrutinized, instead of singling out specific attacks, implying that one should often look at strategic and political decisions at the highest levels of command.[310] Commentators find it difficult to cope with the partially overlapping

---

[307] *Ibid.* See also Separate opinion of Judge Simma, §§ 14–15; Separate opinion of Judge Kooijmans, § 59; Dissenting opinion of Judge Elaraby, § 1.2.

[308] E.g., Gardam, *Necessity, proportionality*, p. 20; Sicilianos, *Des contre-mesures à la légitime défense*, p. 315; R. Van Steenberghe, 'La légitime defense en droit international: une évolution à la suite du conflit israélo-libanais?', (2007) *Journal des Tribunaux* 421–6, at 423.

[309] See Gardam, *Necessity, proportionality*, pp. 10–11, 20 *et seq.*; Van Steenberghe, 'La légitime defense', 424.

[310] In the *Oil Platforms* case, for instance, the ICJ found that the proportionality of the US attacks against the Salman and Nasr complexes should not be considered in isolation but 'against the broader background of US operation 'Praying Mantis' of which they formed part.' ICJ, *Oil Platforms* case, § 77.

proportionality assessment, and have seemingly given preference to assessing the humanitarian impact of the use of force by reference to the more specific rules of the *Ius in Bello*.[311] States themselves generally do not distinguish between the two legal frameworks when pronouncing on the (dis)proportionate nature of concrete recourses to force.[312] Finally, the most important reason why the proportionality standard is so difficult to handle is its inherently contextual nature. Indeed, a magical template applicable to all instances of defensive action simply does not exist, since so much resides in the contingencies of the situation.[313] With these reservations in mind, we shall briefly identify the main doctrinal approaches and their support in customary practice, as well as a number of factors affecting the proportionality analysis.

In essence, the controversy boils down to one question: what must the scale and effects of the defensive action be proportionate to? In other words: what is on the other side of the balance? A first, quantitative approach holds that there must be some sort of equation between the gravity of the armed attack and the defensive response, in terms of relative casualties, damage caused and weapons used.[314] An overly rigid interpretation thereof is universally rejected: scholars agree that there is no need for the defensive action to be restricted to exactly the same weapons or the same number of armed forces as the armed attack.[315] Lachs argues in a more flexible manner that the defensive measures should not be identical, but should be *eiusdem generis*, implying for instance that if the attack did not amount to incursion into the territory of another State, the same should be true of the corresponding act of self-defence.[316]

---

[311] Gardam, *Necessity, proportionality*, p. 17. See also Greenwood, 'Self-defence', pp. 278–9.

[312] Remark: the Security Council debates dealing with the 2006 conflict between Israel and Lebanon provide a good example. *In casu*, a broad majority of States condemned the large-scale destruction of the Lebanese civilian infrastructure as a disproportionate use of force, albeit without distinguishing between the proportionality standard under *Ius ad Bellum* and *Ius in Bello*. See UN Doc. S/PV.5489, 14 July 2006; UN Doc. S/PV.5493, 21 July 2006.

[313] Constantinou, *The right of self-defence*, p. 162; Gardam, *Necessity, proportionality*, pp. 21–2; D. P. O'Connell, *The influence of law on sea power* (Manchester University Press, 1975), p. 34.

[314] E.g., B. Levenfeld, 'Israeli counter-fedayeen tactics in Lebanon: self-defence and reprisal under modern international law', (1982–3) 21 Columbia JTL 1–48, at 41; Randelzhofer, 'Article 51', p. 805.

[315] E.g., Gray, *The use of force*, p. 150; Malanczuk and Akehurst, *Akehurst's modern introduction*, p. 317; Randelzhofer, 'Article 51', p. 805.

[316] Lachs, 'General trends of international law', 164.

A majority of doctrine nonetheless rejects the idea that the defensive action should necessarily be commensurate with the initial attack, holding that this would deprive the victim State of effective protection. Instead, a functional approach is proposed, according to which proportionality must be evaluated by reference to the *aim* of the defensive action. Thus, as Ago argued in his report to the ILC: 'The action ... may well have to assume dimensions disproportionate to those of the attack suffered. What matters in this respect is the result to be achieved by the "defensive" action, and not the forms, substance and strength of the action itself.'[317] When considered from this perspective, the proportionality condition actually becomes an element of the broader necessity requirement, so that the two assessments largely merge into one. Today, Ago's theory that proportionality should be examined by reference to the 'objective' of self-defence has gained broad support among legal scholars.[318] Still, the question remains: what is the permissible objective of self-defence? Ago and several others refer to the classical notion of the 'halting and repelling of the attack',[319] whilst others include the deterring of future attacks.[320] Still others expand the proportionality concept to allow for the 'eliminating of the danger', thereby relying on the rather indeterminate notion of 'threat'.[321]

Does customary practice favour one approach over the other? The evidence is not unequivocal. Some elements seem to give preference to

---

[317] Ago, 'Addendum', 69.

[318] E.g., Gazzini, *The changing rules*, p. 148; Gray, *The use of force*, p. 150; Macdonald, 'The Nicaragua case', 153; M. S. McDougal and F. P. Feliciano, *Law and minimum world public order: the legal regulation of international coercion* (New Haven, CT: Yale University Press, 1961), p. 242; J. P. Rowles, '"Secret Wars", self-defense and the Charter – a reply to Professor Moore', (1986) 80 AJIL 568–83, at 575; R. Van Steenberghe, 'L'arrêt de la Cour Internationale de Justice dans l'affaire des Activités Armées sur le Territoire du Congo et le recours à la force', (2006) 39 RBDI 671–702, at 691; Waldock, 'The use of force by individual states', 464; ICJ, *Nicaragua* case (Merits), Dissenting opinion of Judge Schwebel, §§ 213–14. See also Greenwood, 'Self-defence', p. 274. See also on a more general level: E. Cannizzaro, 'The role of proportionality in the law of international countermeasures', (2001) 12 EJIL 889–916, at 909–10.

[319] E.g., Ago, 'Addendum', 69; Gazzini, *The changing rules*, p. 148; Gray, *The use of force*, p. 150.

[320] E.g., Henkin, *Politics and values*, p. 121; Schmitt, 'Preemptive strategies', 532.

[321] E.g., Brownlie, *The use of force by states*, p. 229; Greenwood, 'Self-defence', p. 274. See also Articles 4–5 San Remo Manual on International Law Applicable to Armed Conflicts at Sea, 12 June 1994, reproduced in A. Roberts and R. Guelff (eds.), *Documents on the laws of war*, 3rd edn (Oxford University Press, 2000), pp. 573–606. Contra: Gazzini, *The changing rules*, p. 148; Sicilianos, *Des contre-mesures à la légitime défense*, pp. 316–17.

the functional approach. The negotiations within the UNGA Committee on the Question of Defining Aggression are illustrative. States initially referred in general terms to the need for self-defence to be proportionate to the armed attack.[322] When the matter was discussed more thoroughly, it quickly became clear that most opposed a rigid quantitative approach and that many States insisted on the need for a flexible case-by-case approach.[323] The reluctance of the USSR and several others to incorporate into the Definition of Aggression a reference to proportionality was apparently inspired by their fear that a quantitative construction thereof would benefit the attacking State and unduly restrict the victim's choice of weapons and the scale of the defensive response.[324] Furthermore, a number of States explicitly claimed that proportionality should be measured against the objective of self-defence.[325] This was also the view taken by Capotorti, the Italian delegate, who instructively distinguished between proportionality as traditionally applied to armed reprisals and self-defence.[326] In the former context, proportionality had been perceived in terms of a quantitative equity between the two acts. In the latter case, however, it was the purpose of self-defence that was decisive.[327]

Corroborating evidence is found in the arguments submitted by the States parties in the *DRC v. Uganda* and *Oil Platforms* cases. In the latter case, Iran implicitly relied on Ago's standard, by denouncing the fact that the US attacks against Iranian oil platforms were justified by the 'actual needs' of self-defence.[328] In its reply, however, Iran subsequently shifted

---

[322] E.g., UN Doc. A/AC.134/SR.52-66, 19 October 1970, 43 (Turkey), 61 (Yugoslavia).
[323] E.g., UN Doc. A/AC.134/SR.67-78, 19 October 1970, 83 (Iraq: stressing that no exact balance was required, but that everything depended on the circumstances), 88 (Guyana), 90 (Ecuador); UN Doc. A/AC.134/SR.92-9, 5 June 1972, 74-5 (US). Contra: UN Doc. A/AC.134/SR.52-66, 91 (Cyprus).
[324] E.g., UN Doc. A/AC.134/SR.67-78, 85 (USSR), 86 (Ghana), 87 (Syria). Interestingly, the USSR claimed that 'the word "necessary" contained the idea of proportionality' (91).
[325] E.g., UN Doc. A/AC.134/67-78, 83 (Iraq), 84 (UK). See also UN Doc. A/AC.134/79-91, 7 June 1971, 49 (Colombia).
[326] See UN Doc. A/AC.134/79-91, 43-4; UN Doc. A/AC.134/67-78, 89.
[327] At the same time, Capotorti recognized that it was difficult to establish at what stage the aim had been achieved: 'whether it was when the attack had been repulsed or when the security of the victim had been ensured'. UN Doc. A/AC.134/67-78, 89.
[328] ICJ, *Oil Platforms* case, Memorial submitted by the Islamic Republic of Iran, 8 June 1993, § 4.21: 'The concept of proportionality suggests an equation. On the one side of this question is the action taken in self-defence. But on the other side of the equation there are two possibilities: either the size and scope of the aggression, or the actual needs of self-defence. It was the singular contribution of Roberto Ago's study that he insisted that self-defence must be proportionate to the latter'.

to a more quantitative approach.[329] The US literally stated that 'like Iran', it agreed with the functional approach and subsequently went on to demonstrate that its attacks had been carefully calibrated to achieve the objective 'of defeating and deterring Iranian attacks'.[330] In *DRC v. Uganda*, the DRC used the same standard, arguing that Uganda's invasion and occupation of large parts of its territory had far exceeded the goal of repelling aggression.[331] Uganda did not disagree on the principle itself, but only on its application to the facts, arguing that it its actions had been 'directly related to defensive objectives'.[332]

At the same time, when discussing concrete self-defence claims in Council debates, States regularly fall back on an equation between the scale and effects of the armed attack(s) and of the response, be it in the more flexible *eiusdem generis* version as described by Lachs (especially in relation to attacks by non-State actors).[333] During the 1956 Suez crisis, for instance, many States condemned the repeated attacks by *fedayeen* operating from Egypt, but at the same time considered it disproportionate that Israel had attacked with massed forces and had penetrated deep into Egyptian territory.[334] Again, in 1964, the UK raid against Yemen was judged by several States to far exceed previous frontier incidents,[335] even though some took a more moderate stance in light of the culmination of the series of events.[336] The two approaches to proportionality also

---

[329] ICJ, *Oil Platforms* case, Reply and defence to counter-claim submitted by the Islamic Republic of Iran, 10 March 1999, § 7.62: 'It is an uncontroversial requirement of self-defence that counter-force must not be excessive in relation to the first use of force. This means that the damage done by the counter-force must be commensurate with or generally comparable to that caused by the first use of force.'

[330] ICJ, *Oil Platforms* case, Counter-memorial submitted by the United States of America, 23 June 1997, §§ 4.32 *et seq.*; ICJ, *Oil Platforms* case, Rejoinder submitted by the United States of America, 23 March 2001, §§ 5.48–5.51. In its report to the Security Council, the US had declared that it had taken defensive action 'necessary and proportionate to the threat posed by ... Iranian actions'. UN Doc. S/19791, 18 April 1988.

[331] ICJ, *DRC v. Uganda*, Memorial of the Democratic Republic of the Congo, 6 July 2000, §§ 5.26 *et seq.*; Reply of the Democratic Republic of the Congo, 29 May 2002, §§ 3.159 *et seq.*

[332] ICJ, *DRC v. Uganda*, Rejoinder of Uganda, 6 December 2002, §§ 278 *et seq.*

[333] See, e.g., Van Steenberghe, 'La légitime defense', 423.

[334] UN Doc. S/PV.748, 30 October 1956, 4 (Yugoslavia), 5 (USSR), 7 (Australia); UN Doc. S/PV.749, 30 October 1956, 22 (Republic of China).

[335] UN Doc. S/PV.1106, 2 April 1964, § 67 (Iraq); UN Doc. S/PV.1108, 6 April 1964, §§ 32, 35 (Morocco); §§ 48–50 (Ivory Coast); UN Doc. S/PV.1109, 7 April 1964, § 58 (Iraq); UN Doc. S/PV.1110, 8 April 1964, § 20 (Czechoslovakia).

[336] UN Doc. S/PV.1111, 9 April 1964, § 5 (US), § 11 (Republic of China).

CONDITIONS OF SELF-DEFENCE 115

surfaced during the Council debates on the 1985 Israeli air raid on the PLO headquarters in Tunis. According to the representative of Thailand:

> While we regret the loss of 15 Israeli lives during the past few weeks, we also regret deeply the loss of over 60 lives in Tunisia – a figure which is evident proof of the lack of proportionality on this matter.[337]

Israel, however, vigorously responded that 'if the question of proportionality is raised, we must take into account not only the thousands who have already fallen victim, but also the many thousands more who will fall if this nerve-centre of terror is allowed to operate undisturbed'.[338] Similar issues were raised in numerous other Council debates, for instance those dealing with the 1965 US intervention in the Dominican Republic[339] or the Israeli interventions in Lebanon in 1972,[340] 1982[341] and 2006.[342] Furthermore, even though the ICJ has not clarified its position on the precise content of the proportionality requirement, there is apparently a quantitative element involved in its concrete assessments thereof.[343]

---

[337] UN Doc. S/PV.2611, 2 October 1985, § 44. The raid was also explicitly labelled as disproportionate by the UK (*ibid.*, § 111) and Indonesia (UN Doc. S/PV.2615, 4 October 1985, § 60).

[338] UN Doc. S/PV.2615, § 194.

[339] (1965) UNYB 142 (France). See also *infra*, Section 3.4.4.b.ii.

[340] E.g., UN Doc. S/PV.1643, 26 February 1972, § 20 (Lebanon), § 166 (Belgium); UN Doc. S/PV.1644, 27–28 February 1972, § 26 (Argentina: '[T]he measures adopted in self-defence must be of a similar nature or reasonably in keeping with the means used in the illegal act against which action is being taken. Any use of force on a considerably larger scale or on a scale which goes beyond the events or the provocative circumstances obviously exceeds the general framework of self-defence ...').

[341] See for example the statements of the UK and Ireland in UN Doc. S/PV.2374, 5 June 1982, §§ 31, 35–6. Both countries identified the attempted assassination of the Israeli ambassador in London as the immediate cause of Israel's actions, but found that this despicable act did not in any way justify the massive attacks on Lebanese towns and villages by the Israeli air force, 'attacks which have already inflicted major loss of life, casualties and damage to property' and which had 'also led to the collapse of the precarious ceasefire'.

[342] E.g., UN Doc. S/PV.5493 (resumption), 21 July 2006, 8 (Ghana referring to the 'asymmetry in the death toll').

[343] In *Nicaragua*, for instance, the Court drew a comparison between the scale of the aid received by the Salvadorian armed opposition from Nicaragua and the US activities (ICJ, *Nicaragua* case (Merits), § 327). Similarly, in *Oil Platforms*, the Court compared the damage caused by the mining of a US warship to the ensuing Operation 'Praying Mantis' (ICJ, *Oil Platforms* case, § 77, although the Court made reference to the specific 'circumstances of this case'). Ochoa-Ruiz and Salamanca-Aguado observe that the ICJ focuses on the size and scope of the aggression, rather than on the objectives of self-defence. See N. Ochoa-Ruiz and E. Salamanca-Aguado, 'Exploring the limits of

What lessons can be drawn from these instances? It would seem inaccurate to hold that States have consistently embraced the objective approach and wholly discarded the quantitative one. True, on a more theoretical level, Ago's reading has gained considerable support. Yet, one cannot deny that the idea of an equation between the armed attack and the defensive action somehow persists in the concrete evaluations of self-defence claims. In this respect, several differentiations are warranted. First of all, the equation has been applied in a flexible manner, requiring no exact balance between the amount of force used in the attack and the response. Second, proportionality has arguably been assessed not merely by reference to the armed attack which constituted the immediate cause for the defensive action, but, where appropriate, to the chain of attacks that preceded it, provided the attacks were linked in time, source and cause.[344] Finally, as was observed in our examination of the requirement of 'immediacy', if there exists a great likelihood that a chain of successive attacks will persist in the immediate future, then self-defence may be warranted in order to prevent further attacks against the victim State. The implication is that the proportionality requirement must be construed to include, as appropriate, both a retrospective and a prospective element.

2.2.2.c.ii Assessing the proportionality of defensive action In the end, the best approach is probably the one followed by those authors who do not consider the functional and the quantitative approach as diametrically opposed, but combine aspects of both.[345] The most appropriate point of departure seems to be that in principle any defensive action must be reasonably proportionate in scale and nature to the armed attack that provoked it. Any deviation needs to be justified by the defending State by reference to the imperative necessities of the defensive action, or, more specifically, by the specific objective that the defensive

---

international law relating to the use of force in self-defence', (2005) 16 EJIL 499–524, at 520–1. In the same sense Van Steenberghe, 'La légitime defense', 424.

[344] This is one branch of the so-called 'accumulation of events' theory, which was originally framed by Israel to justify territorial incursions and strikes against 'pin prick attacks' emanating from neighbouring countries. The other branch concerns the question whether different smaller attacks may be 'accumulated' to determine whether the gravity threshold of an 'armed attack' has been reached. Both aspects are elaborated on in Section 3.2.2.b.

[345] E.g., Dinstein, *War, aggression and self-defence*, pp. 219 *et seq.*; Higgins, *Problems and process*, p. 232; Schachter, *International law in theory and practice*, p. 153; Sicilianos, *Des contre-mesures à la légitime défense*, p. 316.

action is designed to meet. The primary determinant is of course the nature and gravity of the armed attack. In case of a small-scale isolated attack, the defensive action should be limited to the repelling thereof by using no more force than necessary – force is hereby measured in terms of the relative casualties and damage caused, the weapons used and the number of troops deployed. The defending State would not necessarily always be obliged to limit its reaction to its own territory,[346] but neither would it be permitted to engage in a large-scale ground operation against the attacker. Action undertaken after the completion or repulsion of the attack would amount to an unlawful armed reprisal. If the armed attack were to assume a much larger scale, or if it were to form part of a series of successive attacks, then a more flexible evaluation of the proportionality criterion becomes incumbent. Indeed, the more an attack or a series of attacks threaten the existence of a State, the greater the need to tackle the source of the attacks itself.[347] In extreme cases (for instance, if one State were to commence an all-out war against another), this would even warrant the defending State pursuing a total military defeat of the attacking State or the removal of its regime.[348] Yet, such cases remain very much the exception. The broad support for the massive US intervention in Afghanistan (2001) must be seen in light of the exceptional circumstances involved: the universal condemnation of the 9/11 terrorists attacks against the political, military and financial epicentres of the United States, the brutal murder of 3,000 civilians and the tacit acceptance of the international community that the only way to eliminate the source of the repeated attacks was to tackle both Al Qaeda and the Taleban regime. Obviously, States did not feel that the US's concern to protect the safety of its citizens in the Dominican Republic warranted the overthrow of the left-wing regime in 1965.[349] Temporary occupation of another State's territory may exceptionally be permissible, but only if there are no other means possible to avert and prevent the continuation of the armed attack(s).[350] Occupation must end as soon as the direct source of the attacks has been neutralized; prolonged occupation or annexation is never justified.[351] Furthermore, when evaluating the proportionality, one should take account of the fact that a reciprocal

---

[346] E.g., P. Cahier, 'Changements et continuité du droit international', (1985-VI) 195 RdC 9–374, at 77; Randelzhofer, 'Article 51', p. 805;.
[347] Cf. UN Doc. A/AC.134/SR.92-9, 5 June 1972, 74–5 (US).
[348] E.g., Cahier, 'Changements et continuité', 77.   [349] Cf. (1965) UNYB 142.
[350] Cahier, 'Changements et continuité', 77; Cassese, 'Article 51', p. 1333.
[351] Cassese, 'Article 51', p. 1333; Gray, The use of force, pp. 154–5.

escalation may take place on the ground.[352] For example, in the context of the 2006 Israeli intervention in Lebanon, Israeli forces initially responded to the abduction by Hezbollah of two Israeli soldiers with artillery fire, air strikes and a naval bombardment focused on several Hezbollah strongholds in southern Lebanon.[353] Israel also targeted roads and bridges in an attempt to keep Hezbollah from moving the captured soldiers further north and sent troops into southern Lebanon to retrieve them. Over the next days and weeks, however, the crisis rapidly escalated as Hezbollah launched hundreds of missiles against cities in northern Israel and Israeli troops engaged in fierce combat with Hezbollah fighters in southern Lebanon. In this regard, the proportionality of Israel's ground campaign should not purely be tested against the initial Hezbollah attack of 12 July, but against the mutually reinforcing cycle of violence that ensued. Thus, the fact that the campaign developed into an all-out war with Hezbollah militias did not automatically render it disproportionate. On the other hand, the imposition of a naval blockade on Lebanon, and the widespread targeting of civilian infrastructure (resulting in the destruction of some 15,000 Lebanese houses and 630 kilometres of roads) and Lebanese military bases can hardly be qualified other than as a substantial unilateral escalation of the conflict, in complete disregard of the proportionality principle (and in violation of the *Ius in Bello*).

When testing the nature and gravity of the armed attack(s) against that of the defensive response, several factors moreover merit special attention. A first factor concerns the geographical aspect of the actions. Indeed, contrary to what was the case before 1945,[354] it is today generally accepted that forceful actions should be confined to the area of the attack(s) that they are designed to repel.[355] In the context of naval hostilities, the majority of State practice since 1945 seems to be consistent with this idea.[356] Thus, Portugal did not react to India's seizure of Goa in 1961 by seizing Indian shipping in European waters where Portugal

---

[352] E.g., Dinstein, *War, aggression and self-defence*, p. 221.
[353] See *infra*, Section 5.2.3.b.
[354] See Lauterpacht, *Oppenheim's international law*, p. 225.
[355] Constantinou, *The right of self-defence*, pp. 171–2; Gardam, *Necessity, proportionality*, pp. 162–5; Greenwood, 'Self-defence', 274; Redsell, 'Israel's use of force in Lebanon', 84. Contra: Dinstein, *War, aggression and self-defence*, pp. 240–2 (arguing that no geographical limitations apply in case of a defensive war (as opposed to cases of what Dinstein describes as defensive measures 'short of war')).
[356] D. P. O'Connell, *The influence of law on sea power*, p. 65.

enjoyed naval superiority.[357] Neither did the British naval forces engage Argentine warships in areas far removed from the Falklands.[358] Furthermore, it is clear that the conflict over the remote Falkland Islands would not have justified large-scale military operations against the Argentine mainland (or, vice versa, Argentine attacks against the British mainland).[359] In February 2008, Turkey similarly insisted that its ground operation in Iraq was 'limited in scope, *geography* and duration', and, accordingly, confined its actions to the border region in northern Iraq from which PKK fighters were conducting cross-border attacks.[360] The geographical limitation is most relevant when dealing with localized border and territorial disputes. Its importance was underscored by the ICJ in the *DRC* v. *Uganda* case. *In casu*, the Court found by way of *obiter dicta* that 'the taking of airports and towns many hundreds of kilometers from Uganda's border would not seem proportionate to the series of transborder attacks it claimed had given rise to the right of self-defence, nor to be necessary to that end'.[361] At the same time, it must be conceded that any geographical limitation must be interpreted in a flexible manner. Especially in case of repeated and/or large-scale attacks which threaten the very existence of the State, or in the case of a reciprocal escalation of the armed conflict, this factor may gradually lose its constraining function.

Another factor to be taken into consideration concerns the duration of the defensive action. In this regard, customary practice supports the view that self-defence may not continue past the point in time that is necessary to deal effectively with the armed attack(s).[362] Thus, in reaction to the US intervention in the Dominican Republic in 1965, France insisted that any operation to evacuate citizens 'should be limited in objective, *duration*

---

[357] Greenwood, 'Self-defence', 274.   [358] *Ibid.*
[359] Remark: according to Greenwood, it is unclear whether the British abstention from attacking air bases on the Argentine mainland from which air attacks upon the British task force were being launched was inspired by the belief that such extension of the conflict would have been disproportionate, or whether it was inspired by political or military considerations (*ibid.*). According to Higgins, however, 'any bombing of the Argentinean air force or navy while in Argentina or in port would have been regarded as disproportionate.' Higgins, *Problems and process*, p. 232.
[360] Note verbale from the Permanent Mission of Turkey to the Human Rights Council, 26 March 2008, UN Doc. A/HRC/7/G/15 (emphasis added). See also *infra*, Section 5.2.3.c.
[361] ICJ, *DRC* v. *Uganda*, § 147. See also: Reply of the Democratic Republic of the Congo, 29 May 2002, §§ 3.168 *et seq.*
[362] Gardam, *Necessity, proportionality*, pp. 167–8; Greenwood, 'Self-defence', 275–6.

and scale'.³⁶³ In 1972, Argentina condemned the Israeli intervention against Lebanon in the following terms: 'Proportion has not been respected, either in terms of the scale of the action, or even in terms of the duration.... [W]e must conclude that the events... are in the nature of a punitive expedition... completely incompatible with the purposes, principles and tenets of the Charter'.³⁶⁴ Furthermore, in *Nicaragua*, the ICJ found that the US forceful reaction had 'continued long after the period in which any presumed armed attack by Nicaragua could reasonably be contemplated'.³⁶⁵ Finally, in *DRC* v. *Uganda*, the DRC referred to the excessive duration of the Ugandan intervention – Ugandan forces occupied parts of eastern Congo from August 1998 to April 2003 – as a clear indication of its disproportionate character.³⁶⁶ Again, the temporal aspect is less relevant in the face of continuing hostilities or when successive armed attacks continue to be committed. It is particularly important when the defensive action does not meet with any armed resistance or when hostilities have de facto ceased. In such situations, once the armed attack has been successfully repelled, the defending State cannot actively resume or reopen hostilities, regardless of the doctrine of belligerent rights.³⁶⁷ As noted above, prolonged occupation and annexation cannot be justified on grounds of self-defence. It must be observed that, in recent years, this temporal aspect of the proportionality criterion has to some extent come under strain, in particular in the context of repeated terrorist attacks. Thus, while Turkey stressed that Operation 'Sun' (2008) was 'limited in scope, geography and *duration*', and while the ground operation was concluded after a week, Turkey continued to launch aerial strikes within Iraqi territory in subsequent months.³⁶⁸ In a similar vein, the resumption of the US-led Operation 'Enduring

---

[363] (1965) UNYB 142 (emphasis added). In a similar vein, Gardam observes that even if the US intervention in Grenada (1983) could meet the other criteria for legitimacy under the Charter system as an exercise to protect US nationals, 'the fact that the forces remained in place some period after the initial invasion was regarded as disproportionate.' Gardam, *Necessity, proportionality*, p. 167.

[364] UN Doc. S/PV.1644, 27–28 February 1972, § 29.

[365] ICJ, *Nicaragua* case (Merits), § 237.

[366] ICJ, *DRC* v. *Uganda*, Reply of the Democratic Republic of the Congo, 29 May 2002, §§ 3.173 *et seq.*

[367] See Gardam, *Necessity, proportionality*, p. 168; Greenwood, 'Self-defence', 275–6. Apparently contra: Dinstein, *War, aggression and self-defence*, pp. 47–8 (regarding the Israeli strike against the Osiraq reactor (1981)). However, contra Dinstein: Kritsiotis, 'Topographies of force', pp. 37–40.

[368] Note verbale from the Permanent Mission of Turkey to the Human Rights Council, 26 March 2008, UN Doc. A/HRC/7/G/15 (emphasis added). See also: *infra*, Section 5.2.3.c.

Freedom' (OEF) long after the 9/11 attacks (both as a ground operation in Afghan territory and as a counter-terrorist maritime interdiction operation) raises difficult questions of proportionality. On the one hand, it may be pointed out that the Security Council has repeatedly expressed support for the operation; that the ground operation in Afghanistan is apparently supported by the internationally recognized government of Afghanistan; and that the maritime interdiction operation has not ostensibly resulted in violent encounters in breach of Article 2(4) UN Charter.[369] On the other hand, it is difficult to disagree with Gray and others that the further Operation 'Enduring Freedom' continues, the further it is detached from its initial basis in self-defence.[370]

A third factor that is frequently identified as influencing the proportionality evaluation concerns the range of targets of the defensive action.[371] This aspect was previously discussed in the context of the necessity criterion, but (like other aspects) equally fits into the proportionality framework.[372] It should again be emphasized that defensive action must respect the rules of IHL, including those pertaining to targeting and distinction. Defensive action resulting in large numbers of civilian casualties has unvariably evoked strong negative reactions from the international community and has frequently been condemned

---

[369] E.g., SC Res. 1589 (2005) of 24 March 2005; SC Res. 1659 (2006) of 15 February 2006; SC Res. 1707 (2006) of 12 September 2006; SC Res. 1776 (2007) of 19 September 2007; SC Res. 1833 (2008) of 22 September 2008. See Gray, *The use of force*, pp. 206-7; P. Jimenez Kwast, 'Maritime law enforcement and the use of force: reflections on the categorization of forcible action at sea in the light of the *Guyana/Suriname* Award', (2008) 13 JCSL 49-91, at 67-8. Remark: the US and other participating States have been careful to avoid elaborating on the precise legal basis of the operation after the instalment of the Security Council mandated NATO International Security Assistance Force. Other States have similarly been reluctant to question its legality.

[370] See Gray, *The use of force*, pp. 206-7; C. Gray, 'The Bush doctrine revisited: the 2006 National Security Strategy of the USA', (2006) 5 Chinese JIL 555-78; E. Myjer, 'Afghanistan, the erosion of the right to self-defence and the case of the missing immediacy', in I. Boerefijn and J. Goldschmidt (eds.), *Changing perceptions of sovereignty and human rights: essays in honour of Cees Flinterman* (Antwerp: Intersentia, 2008), pp. 529-50, at 538-40; S. Talmon, 'Changing views on the use of force: the German position', (2005) 5 Baltic YBIL 41-76, at 59-60. However, strongly defending the legality of the OEF Maritime Interdiction Component: W. Heintschel von Heinegg, 'Legality of maritime interception operations within the framework of Operation Enduring Freedom', in M. Bothe, M. E. O'Connell and N. Ronzitti (eds.), *Redefining sovereignty: the use of force after the Cold War* (Ardsley: Transnational Publishers, 2005), pp. 365-85.

[371] See Constantinou, *The right of self-defence*, p. 170; Gardam, *Necessity, proportionality*, pp. 171-2; Greenwood, 'Self-defence', 278-9.

[372] Cf. *supra*, footnote 297.

by the Security Council and/or the General Assembly.[373] Furthermore, customary practice relatively consistently upholds the view that only military objectives directly linked to the armed attack(s) may be targeted, be it that the gravity of the armed attack(s) or the escalation of the conflict may warrant a more flexible interpretation. Two controversial incidents nonetheless illustrate the difficulties of applying this limitation to concrete cases. A first case concerns the Israeli commando raid at the Ugandan airport of Entebbe in 1976.[374] During this operation, Israeli forces not only successfully ended the hijacking of the Air France plane, but also destroyed a number of Ugandan fighter jets located at the airport, killed several Ugandan soldiers and caused serious damage to the airport installations. Israel claimed it had acted in self-defence to protect its nationals from mortal danger.[375] It accused Uganda of complicity in the hijacking and argued that the fighter jets were destroyed lest they be used to pursue the Israeli commandos.[376] Several third States vigorously condemned the operation as a violation of Uganda's sovereignty and territorial integrity, thereby invoking the aforementioned elements as aggravating facts.[377] A number of Western States nonetheless showed sympathy for the Israeli action.[378] The Security Council was thus effectively split in two camps, resulting in the absence of any formal action. A second example concerns the sinking of the Argentine cruiser *General Belgrano* by a British submarine during the Falklands war outside of the UK-established 200 mile exclusion zone around the Falkland Islands.[379] In light of the heavy loss of life – far exceeding the total casualties on both sides up to that date – the ongoing diplomatic efforts to end the conflict and the fact that the *Belgrano* was sailing away from the Falklands, the torpedoing of the *Belgrano* resulted in considerable international criticism (even if States refrained from explicitly labelling

---

[373] See, e.g., (1971) UNYB 178; (1978) UNYB 298; (1979) UNYB 219–20 (US), 225; (1982), UNYB 311–12, 315.
[374] See UN Docs. S/PV.13939–1941, 9–12 July 1976; (1976) UNYB 315–20.
[375] See *infra*, Section 3.4.4.b.iv.   [376] See Knisbacher, 'The Entebbe operation', 73.
[377] E.g., S/PV.1939, § 210 (Cameroon), § 223 (PRC); S/PV.1941, § 132 (Pakistan), § 152 (USSR).
[378] E.g. S/PV.1940, § 99 (UK), § 122 (Sweden); S/PV.1941, § 54 (Federal Republic of Germany), §§ 77–81 (US).
[379] See M. Middlebrook, *The fight for the 'Malvinas': the Argentine forces in the Falklands War* (London: Viking, 1989). Remark: the UK had earlier informed the Argentine authorities that it did not regard the establishment of the maritime exclusion zone as limiting its right of self-defence.

the attack as unlawful).[380] While these two examples illustrate that the targeting limitation may be difficult to apply, they equally illustrate the importance attached thereto. Targeting is of particular significance in relation to self-defence against attacks by non-State actors, in the sense that the defensive action should in principle only be directed against the latter (cf. *infra*).[381]

Several authors also identify the type of weapons used as a factor that affects the proportionality analysis.[382] This, however, is an aspect which is more concretely dealt with under IHL.[383] As was stressed earlier, the defending State is not required to use the same or even similar weapons as the attacker.[384] Apart from the rules laid down in IHL, no weapon is excluded per se under the right of self-defence – arguably not even nuclear weapons.[385] Everything depends on whether the resort to a particular weapon can, in the concrete circumstances of the case, be said to constitute a considerable escalation of the hostilities.[386]

2.2.2.d Conclusion

In conclusion, it is fair to say that the proportionality and necessity criteria are truly two sides of the same coin,[387] both bound by the overarching aim that defensive action should be constrained to the halting and repelling of an attack, and exceptionally, in the case of successive and interlinked armed attacks, to the preventing of their reoccurrence. There exists no neat separation between the two, in the sense that necessity

---

[380] E.g., Gardam, *Necessity, proportionality*, pp. 171–2; Greenwood, 'Self-defence', 279. According to Greenwood, 'on balance, it is thought that the sinking was lawful, but the terms in which it is debated, and the intensity of that debate, show that the concept of self-defence may impose serious restrictions upon the right of a State to attack what, in terms of the *jus in bello*, is a legitimate military target'.

[381] See *infra*, Chapter 5, in particular Section 5.2.5.b.ii.

[382] See Constantinou, *The right of self-defence*, pp. 164–6; Gardam, *Necessity, proportionality*, pp. 168–71; Greenwood, 'Self-defence', 279–81.

[383] See ICJ, *Nuclear Weapons case* care, Advisory opinion, § 39: 'The Charter neither expressly prohibits, nor permits, the use of any specific weapon, including nuclear weapons. A weapon that is already unlawful per se, whether by treaty or custom, does not become lawful by reason of its being used for a legitimate purpose under the Charter.'

[384] Gray, *The use of force*, p. 150; Randelzhofer, 'Article 51', p. 805.

[385] See ICJ, *Nuclear Weapons case* care, Advisory opinion, §§ 42–3, 97. See, e.g., Randelzhofer, 'Article 51', p. 805 ; Sicilianos, *Des contre-mesures à la légitime défense*, pp. 317–18.

[386] E.g., Gardam, *Necessity, proportionality*, p. 171.

[387] Ago, 'Addendum', 69; Corten, *Le droit contre la guerre*, p. 729.

would determine *when* defensive action would be permissible, whereas proportionality would be the standard to evaluate *what* could be done in self-defence: to the contrary, both standards must constantly be kept under review[388] and overlap to a certain degree. In spite of the ICJ's finding that the necessity requirement 'is strict and objective, leaving no room for any "measure of discretion"',[389] customary practice and legal doctrine allow a certain flexibility when evaluating necessity and proportionality in specific cases. This is especially true when the attack assumes an increasingly grave character or forms part of a cumulative series of armed attacks. Proportionality and necessity must be assessed on a case-by-case basis by reference to all relevant contextual aspects.[390] It must be conceded that the lack of more precise guidelines may sometimes render it difficult to apply the proportionality and necessity criteria to concrete self-defence claims. Yet, this does not alter the fact that their substantial validity is today universally recognized, nor the fact that the two criteria (in particular the proportionality requirement) have frequently played a pivotal role. This is especially true with regard to some of the more controversial cases of self-defence. As Gray observes: 'In Security Council debates States have thus been able to avoid becoming involved in doctrinal disputes as to whether self-defence is wide or narrow; they can simply say that the use of force was not necessary and proportionate and therefore illegal.'[391] The reverse side of this attitude is that the proportionality and necessity criteria are at the same time the crucial toolbox used by proponents of a broad reading of self-defence to 'sell' their views. In this sense, the two customary standards are inextricably linked to the three aspects of the 'armed attack' requirement which will be discussed below. Indeed, as for the *ratione temporis* aspect, States and authors defending the lawfulness of varying degrees of anticipatory self-defence do so on the grounds that the necessity standard ought to provide sufficient protection against abuse and hence warrants the abandoning of a strictly 'reactive' view of self-defence. In a similar

---

[388] Gazzini, *The changing rules*, pp. 146–7. [389] ICJ, *Oil Platforms* case, § 73.
[390] Apart from the aspects identified in the foregoing pages, other factors may bear an influence too. Thus, the extent to which the defensive action adversely affects third States (for example, as a result of the overflight of aircraft and missiles, or the disturbance of neutral shipping) may play a role, although the interaction between the traditional law of neutrality and the Charter rules on the use of force remains highly problematic. See Gardam, *Necessity, proportionality*, pp. 173–9; Greenwood, 'Self-defence', 283–5.
[391] Gray, *The use of force*, p. 154.

vein, as far as the *ratione materiae* aspect is concerned, some favour a strict adherence to the proportionality criterion over the idea that the concept of 'armed attack' is subject to some sort of *de minimis* threshold: on this view, any use of force, regardless of its scale, would enable the victim State to exercise its right of self-defence, provided it did so in a proportionate manner. Last but not least, it has equally been suggested that a reliance on the proportionality and necessity standards cancels out the concerns relating to the possibility of engaging in defensive actions against non-State actors, such as terrorist groups (i.e., the *ratione personae* element).[392] Whether or not these arguments have been accepted in the customary practice of States, and whether they require a differentiated application of the necessity and proportionality requirements are questions we must now turn to.

---

[392] See, e.g., M. C. Bonafede, 'Here, there and everywhere: assessing the proportionality doctrine and U.S. uses of force in response to terrorism after the September 11 attacks', (2002) 88 Cornell L Rev 155–214; K. N. Trapp, 'Back to basics: necessity, proportionality, and the right of self-defence against non-state terrorist actors', (2007) 56 ICLQ 141–56.
Remark: this argument was raised by the United States during the negotiations on the Definition of Aggression in order to convince other States to incorporate indirect aggression into the definition. E.g., UN Doc. A/AC.134/SR.52–66, 116. Cf. *infra* Section 3.1.2.

3

The 'armed attack' requirement
ratione materiae

As explained in the Introduction, the present study analyses the armed attack requirement from a threefold perspective: *ratione materiae* – what acts count as armed attacks?; *ratione temporis* – when does an armed attack take place?; and *ratione personae* – from whom must the attack emanate?[1] The present chapter will begin by focusing on the *ratione materiae* aspect, making abstraction of the temporal and personal aspects.[2]

As recent controversies have generally concerned the legality of self-defence against non-State actors (the *ratione personae* element) and of anticipatory self-defence (the *ratione temporis* element), one might be inclined to conclude that the *ratione materiae* element is the least problematic of the three. Still, it raises important matters which are crucial for the evaluation of any self-defence claim. Against this backdrop, a first section will examine to what extent the UNGA Definition of Aggression is determinative of the scope of lawful self-defence (Section 3.1). Second, we will examine whether there exists some sort of *de minimis* threshold, i.e., a minimum level of scale and effects required for an attack to qualify as an 'armed attack' in the sense of Article 51 UN Charter. To this end, we will consider the distinction between 'armed attacks' and 'mere frontier incidents', and examine the

---

[1] A similar approach is adopted by Abi-Saab in G. Abi-Saab, 'Cours général de droit international public', (1987-III) 207 RdC 9–463, at 371–3.
[2] This does not mean that practice involving so-called indirect aggression is entirely excluded from our analysis. Rather, we will extract from such situations relevant *opinio iuris* relating to the type of acts that may be considered to constitute an 'armed attack', while reserving our opinion on the need for State involvement in the attack. For instance, as regards the Israeli intervention in Lebanon in 2006, it can be deduced from the reaction of the international community that the attack by Hezbollah on an Israeli border patrol was conceived as an armed attack in the *ratione materiae* sense. This finding carries relevance for the present chapter. Issues related to the link between Hezbollah and the Lebanese government, however, are taken up in Chapter 5.

relevance of the intent of the attacker, as well as the 'cumulative' impact of repeated attacks (Section 3.2). Sections 3.3 and 3.4 deal respectively with the challenges arising from small-scale incursions by land, sea or air, and with the extent to which certain attacks beyond the territory of the State activate the right of self-defence.

3.1 Armed attack and aggression

3.1.1 Two sides of the same coin

The UN Charter uses three different terms which have a bearing on inter-State recourse to force. Article 2(4) spells out a prohibition against the threat or use of *force*. In relation to the competence of the Security Council to adopt enforcement measures, reference is made in Article 39 to threats to the peace, breaches of the peace and *acts of aggression*.[3] Finally, Article 51 reserves the inherent right of self-defence 'if an *armed attack* occurs'. The (equally authentic) French version instead uses the phrase '*agression armée*'.

The use of these different labels, and the unfortunate discrepancy between the authentic versions, raises the question what the precise relationship is between 'armed attack' and 'aggression'. This question bears particular relevance if one takes account of the adoption by consensus by the UN General Assembly of the 1974 Definition of Aggression.[4] Should the two concepts be considered identical, this resolution would indeed provide an authoritative interpretation of the 'armed attack' criterion for purposes of establishing the scope of self-defence under Article 51. Interestingly, in *Nicaragua* and *DRC v. Uganda*, the ICJ used Article 3(g) of the resolution as the yardstick for self-defence against indirect aggression.[5] Some authors expand this

---

[3] Remark: 'aggression' also surfaces in Articles 1(1) and 53(1) of the UN Charter. In both cases it is used in relation to the UN collective security system.
[4] Definition of Aggression, Annex to GA Res. 3314 (XXIX) of 14 December 1974.
[5] See ICJ, *Case concerning military and paramilitary activities in and against Nicaragua (Nicaragua v. United States of America)* (Merits), Judgment of 27 June 1986, (1986) ICJ Rep 14–150, § 195; ICJ, *Case concerning armed activities on the territory of the Congo (Democratic Republic of the Congo v. Uganda)*, Judgment of 19 December 2005, (2005) ICJ Rep 116–220, § 146. See on this: D. Kritsiotis, 'Topographies of force', in Y. Dinstein and M. N. Schmitt (eds.), *International law and armed conflict. Exploring the faultlines: essays in honour of Yoram Dinstein* (Leiden: Martinus Nijhoff, 2007), pp. 29–77, at 58–60.

equation to the various other examples of (direct) aggression listed in the resolution.[6] Before rushing to such conclusion, however, a closer look at its origins is needed.

Going back to the pre-Charter period, Brownlie finds that the concept of aggression appeared as the vague right of self-preservation fell into disrepute.[7] Aggression and self-defence were by and large seen as two different sides of the same coin: recourse to force either constituted justified action in self-defence or it amounted to unlawful aggression.[8] In objection to a French proposal to include an explicit reference to the right of self-defence in the Pact of Paris, the US noted that: 'Express recognition by the treaty of this inalienable right ... gives rise to the same difficulty encountered in any effort to define aggression. It is the identical question approached from the other side.'[9] This brief quote confirms that self-defence and aggression were seen as correlative terms. On the other hand, it illustrates that the precise meaning of 'aggression' remained uncertain. Indeed, while numerous bilateral, regional and multilateral treaties made reference to 'aggression', they did so in different ways (some speaking of 'aggressive war' and 'acts of aggression', others using phrases such as 'external aggression' or 'policy of aggression')[10] and without dealing with its contents in a clear manner.[11] Throughout the 1930s, this ambiguity inspired a series of Soviet-led negotiations aimed at defining the legal concept of aggression.[12] The proposal eventually worked out by the USSR received support from a considerable number of States, but was strongly opposed by others who doubted that it was at all possible to lay down universal criteria applicable in each particular set of

---

[6] E.g., Abi-Saab, 'Cours général', 362–3; J. Zourek, 'La définition de l'agression et le droit international: développements récents de la question', (1958) 92 RdC 755–855, at 817. See also: R. S. J. Macdonald, 'The *Nicaragua* case: new answers to old question?', (1986) 24 Can YBIL 127–60, at 154.

[7] I. Brownlie, 'The use of force in self-defence', (1961) 37 BYBIL 183–268, at 222.

[8] *Ibid.*; D. W. Bowett, *Self-defence in international law* (Manchester University Press, 1958), p. 249.

[9] Note of the Government of the United States, 23 June 1928; text in J. T. Shotwell, *War as an instrument of national policy and its renunciation in the Pact of Paris* (New York: Harcourt, 1929), p. 297.

[10] See Report of the UN Secretary-General, 3 October 1952, UN Doc. A/2211, §§ 177 *et seq.*

[11] O. Solera, *Defining the crime of aggression* (London: Cameron May, 2007), p. 38. See also Brownlie, 'The use of force in self-defence', 210.

[12] Solera, *Defining the crime of aggression*, pp. 17–42.

circumstances, and who feared that States acting in self-defence would be branded as aggressors.[13]

Jumping to the *travaux préparatoires* of the UN Charter, several statements again indicate that States considered aggression and self-defence to be complementary. Some delegates framed self-defence as the 'repression of aggression', whereas others equated the terms 'aggression' and 'armed attack'.[14] A number of draft versions of Article 51 moreover relied on the notion of 'aggression' to trigger the right to self-defence.[15] In response to British warnings that 'no one had been able to define aggression in thirty years',[16] the US explained that the term 'armed attack' was used *specifically in an attempt to circumvent the problem of trying to define aggression as such.*[17] Apparently, it was thought that the plain meaning of 'armed attack' would cause fewer problems. Several countries did again press for a definition of aggression during the San Francisco Conference.[18] However, these initiatives were driven primarily by a desire to clarify the role and competence of the Security Council rather than to define States' legal responsibility for aggression and eventually failed to obtain sufficient support.[19]

3.1.2 The negotiations within the Fourth Special Committee on the Question of Defining Aggression (1968–74)

As the adoption of the Charter failed to settle the matter, efforts to clarify the purport of aggression continued, first within the ILC and subsequently within the General Assembly.[20] It is beyond the purview of the present study to engage in an elaborate overview of the whole process,

---

[13] *Ibid.*, p. 36. In the end, no agreement could be reached, although the efforts arguably contributed to developing the legal ideas on the use of force and set the stage for later discussions under the auspices of the General Assembly (*ibid.*, p. 38). Also: B. B. Ferencz, *Defining international aggression. The search for world peace.* Vol. I (Dobbs Ferry, NY: Oceana, 1975), pp. 53–6.
[14] See, e.g., UNCIO, Vol. 6, 721; UNCIO, Vol. 11, 6–7 (US), 58 (France); UNCIO, Vol. 12, 680–1, 687 (Colombia).
[15] E.g., US Department of State, *Foreign Relations of the United States, Diplomatic Papers. (1945) General: the United Nations* (New York, 1967), p. 676.
[16] *Ibid.*, 692. [17] *Ibid.*, 700.
[18] Proposals thereto were submitted by Czechoslovakia, Bolivia and the Philipinnes.
[19] See B. Broms, 'The definition of aggression', (1977-I) 154 RdC 299–400, at 315–6; Solera, *Defining the crime of aggression*, pp. 49–79.
[20] See Broms, 'The definition of aggression', 79–206.

which has aptly been analysed in scholarly writings.[21] Instead, in order to gain a better understanding of the impact of the 1974 Definition of Aggression (or Resolution 3314 (XXIX)) on the scope of self-defence, we will make a leap in time and briefly examine the final stages of the negotiations within the Fourth Special Committee on the Question of Defining Aggression (1968–74). By this period, the time and energy invested in the whole endeavour and the strong pressure from developing countries had led to a point where those Western States who had long questioned the desirability of a definition no longer dared to oppose the process as such.[22] Nonetheless, States held widely diverging conceptions about the fundamental tenets of aggression and its impact on permissible self-defence. These differences are obvious from scanning the three proposals around which the debates revolved.[23]

First, the Thirteen-Power proposal, submitted by Colombia, Cyprus, Ecuador, Ghana, Guyana, Haiti, Iran, Madagascar, Mexico, Spain, Uganda, Uruguay and Yugoslavia, was clearly geared towards a definition of 'armed attack' in the sense of Article 51 UN Charter.[24] This intention was made explicit in the second preambular paragraph: 'Convinced that armed attack (armed aggression) is the most serious and dangerous form of aggression and that it is proper at this stage to proceed to a definition of this form of aggression, ...'.

Article 2 subsequently defined 'aggression' as 'the use of armed force by a State against another State, including its territorial waters or air space, or in any way affecting the territorial integrity, sovereignty or political independence of such State, save [in self-defence] or when undertaken by or under the authority of the Security Council'. Apart from this general definition, the Thirteen-Power proposal set out a number of acts, which, 'when committed by a State first against another

---

[21] See e.g. ibid.; T. Bruha, *Die Definition der Aggression* (Berlin: Duncker & Humblot, 1980); Ferencz, *Defining international aggression*. Vol. I; A. M. Rifaat, *International aggression: a study of the legal concept* (Stockholm: Almqvist & Wiksell International, 1979); S. M. Schwebel, 'Aggression, intervention and self-defence in modern international law', (1972-II) 136 RdC 411–97; J. Stone, *Conflict through consensus: United Nations approaches to aggression* (Baltimore, MD: John Hopkins University Press, 1977); J. Stone, *Aggression and world order* (London: Stevens & Sons, 1958); Zourek, 'La définition de l'agression'.

[22] E.g., Solera, *Defining the crime of aggression*, p. 148.

[23] See Special Committee on the Question of Defining Aggression, Comparative table of draft proposals submitted to the Special Committee at its 1969 and 1970 sessions, 16 July 1970, UN Doc. A/AC.134/L.22.

[24] UN Doc. A/AC.134/L.16 (and Corr. 1).

State in violation of the Charter' shall constitute 'acts of aggression', including, for example, the declaration of war by one State against another State. Several other provisions touched upon self-defence:

- Article 3 emphasized that '[t]he inherent right of ... self-defence of a State can be exercised only in case of the occurrence of armed attack (armed aggression) by another State in accordance with Article 51 of the Charter';
- Article 6 asserted that the right of self-defence did not entitle States to take measures which are not 'reasonably proportionate' to the armed attack against it; and
- last but not least, Article 7 rejected self-defence against so-called 'indirect aggression'.

In all, despite the references in the text to '(armed) aggression', the proposal seemed more concerned with putting forward a restrictive interpretation of self-defence than with clarifying 'acts of aggression' in the context of Article 39 UN Charter. That, by contrast, was exactly the primary focus of the Six-Power proposal, submitted by Australia, Canada, Italy, Japan, the United Kingdom and the United States.[25] Article 1 stated that:

> Under the Charter of the United Nations, 'aggression', is a term to be applied by the Security Council when appropriate in the exercise of its primary responsibility for the maintenance of international peace and security under Article 24 and its functions under Article 39.

'Aggression' was subsequently defined as 'the use of force in international relations, overt or covert, direct or indirect, by a State against the territorial integrity or political independence of any other State, or in any other manner inconsistent with the purposes of the United Nations' (Article 2). Article 2(A) linked such use of force to a number of goals, such as the securing of changes in the government of another State, or the inflicting of harm of any sort. Article 2(B) non-exhaustively listed several means through which such use of force could be perpetrated, including several forms of indirect aggression. The only reference to 'the use of force in ... self-defence' was the simple affirmation in Article 3 that it '[did] not constitute aggression'.

Finally, the Soviet proposal[26] defined '*armed* aggression' 'direct or indirect', as 'the use by a State, first, of armed force against another

---

[25] UN Doc. A/AC.134/L.17 (and Corr. 1).   [26] UN Doc. A/AC.134/L.12 (and Corr. 1).

State contrary to the purposes, principles and provisions of the [UN] Charter' (Article 1). After listing several examples of 'direct' aggression, Article 2(C) gave a definition of 'indirect aggression'. The proposal concluded by acknowledging that '[n]othing in the foregoing shall prevent the use of armed force in accordance with the [UN] Charter ...' (Article 6).

Thus, while at face value States were engaged in a process to agree the definition of aggression, the negotiations were undeniably influenced by the awareness that a broader or narrower conception thereof could have important repercussions on the scope of self-defence.[27] Indeed, some of the key obstacles that for many years impeded consensus were essentially related to self-defence, rather than to the enforcement competences of the Security Council. The main stumbling block concerned the question to what extent self-defence was permissible against various forms of indirect aggression, such as subversive or terrorist acts by irregular, volunteer or armed bands organized, supported or directed by another State (as opposed to direct attacks by another State's armed forces).[28] The position of the Thirteen Powers on the issue was clear. Article 7 of their proposal excluded the exercise of self-defence in such situations, a position that was vigorously defended throughout the Committee debates.[29] Conversely, the Six Powers persistently refused to agree to any definition of aggression that would not include (certain cases of) indirect aggression.[30]

The scope of self-defence also arose in relation to the Soviet proposal that the State which was the first to commit a specified unlawful act would automatically be identified as the aggressor, i.e., the principle of priority or 'first use'.[31] Several States supported the principle as a valuable confirmation that self-defence could not be exercised preventively.[32] Others objected that a rigid application of the principle

---

[27] E.g., UN Doc. A/AC.134/SR.52–66, 37 (Norway: '[A]ny enlargement of the definition of aggression would entail a corresponding enlargement of the concept of self-defence.'), 59 (UAR).

[28] For an elaborate analysis of this aspect of the negotiations, see *infra*, Section 5.1.2.

[29] E.g., UN Doc. A/AC.134/SR.52–66, 32 (Uruguay), 55 (Ecuador), 86 (Mexico), 90 (Cyprus), 113 (Colombia), 117 (Uruguay), 126 (Guyana); UN Doc. A/AC.134/SR.67–78, 17 (Cyprus), 112 (Uruguay).

[30] E.g., UN Doc. A/AC.134/SR.52–66, 20–1 (Italy), 40–1 (Japan), 66, 116 (US).

[31] Articles 1 and 2 of the Soviet proposal, UN Doc. A/AC.134/L.12 (and Corr. 1). For an elaborate analysis of this aspect of the negotiations, see *infra*, Sections 3.2.2.a and 4.1.3.

[32] E.g., UN Doc. A/AC.134/SR.52–66, 46 (Bulgaria), 79 (Iraq), 134 (USSR), 135 (Ghana), 136 (UAR). See also: UN Doc. A/AC.134/SR.79–91, 39 (Syria).

could lead to undesirable results in particular circumstances and that it might be difficult to collect convincing evidence to establish which party was the first to act.[33] The Six Powers especially stressed that in determining who was the aggressor, one should look at the intentions of the State committing certain acts, rather than to fixate on priority.[34] The latter view in turn inspired criticism from States that preferred an objective element over a subjective analysis of a State's motives.[35]

A third element that played a considerable role in the debates concerned the proportionality criterion. Article 6 of the Thirteen-Power proposal asserted that the right of self-defence did not entitle States to take measures which were not 'reasonably proportionate' to the armed attack against it.[36] However, as examined earlier, a number of States, most notably the Soviet Union, strongly opposed the reference to proportionality as a precondition for self-defence, primarily because they feared that it would overly tie the hands of victims of aggression and benefit potential aggressor States.[37]

The scope of self-defence was also raised in relation to other elements, such as the required gravity for acts to qualify as aggression, or vis-à-vis specific acts, like declarations of war.[38] Still, the main divisions were those listed above: first, a partition on the legality of self-defence against indirect aggression, mainly between the Thirteen Powers and the Six Powers; second, a partition on the role of the 'first use' and 'intentions' criteria, mainly between the Soviet Union and the Six Powers; and third, a partition on the proportionality principle between the Soviet Union and the Thirteen Powers.

In light of these complex and interrelated issues, several delegates pointed out that no breakthrough was possible, unless there was a basic understanding about the *kind* of concept the Committee was to define: 'armed aggression'/'armed attack' in the sense of Article 51 UN Charter

---

[33] E.g., UN Doc. A/AC.134/SR.52–66, 36 (France), 37 (Norway), 43 (Turkey).
[34] Article II (A), UN Doc. A/AC.134/L.17 (and Corr.1). E.g., UN Doc. A/AC. 134/SR.52–66, 41 (Japan).
[35] E.g., UN Doc. A/AC.134/SR.52–66, 79 (Iraq), 86 (Mexico).
[36] UN Doc. A/AC.134/L.16 (and Corr. 1).
[37] E.g., UN Doc. A/AC.134/SR.67–78, 85 (USSR); 86, 91 (Ghana); 87 (Syria). See *supra* Section 2.2.2.
[38] See *infra*, Sections 3.2.1.c and 4.1.3.b. E.g., UN Doc. A/AC.134/SR.67–78, 54–60, 19 (France), 50 (UAR).

or 'act of aggression' in the sense of Article 39.[39] If some States occasionally insisted that the concepts were one and the same,[40] most agreed that there existed a cascading relationship between the terms 'use of force', 'aggression' and 'armed attack'. As one delegate noted: 'Article 2, paragraph 4, prohibited also the threat of force and was therefore concerned with a broader concept than the use of armed force. A more limited concept was invoked in Article 1 and 39 of the Charter, and a still more limited one of 'armed attack' in Article 51.'[41] In other words, it was generally accepted that the concepts used in Article 39 and 51 were not identical and that no single definition could be drafted that would simultaneously cover both.[42]

Against this background, several paths lay open to the negotiators. The Thirteen Powers[43] suggested that the Committee should 'for the time being' refrain from dealing with indirect aggression – which proved simply too controversial – and instead confine itself to defining direct aggression.[44] Given the Thirteen Powers' position on self-defence against indirect aggression, and the slim prospects for obtaining a separate definition thereof at some later stage, it needs no wonder that the Six Powers showed little enthusiasm for this idea.[45] On the contrary, the Six Powers persistently argued that the concept of aggression was indivisible and could not simply be split in two halves, one allowing for self-defence and another excluding

---

[39] E.g., UN Doc. A/AC.134/SR.52–66, 104 (Yugoslavia: 'the USSR draft referred to armed aggression, in the meaning of Article 51 of the Charter, whereas the thirteen-Power and six-Power drafts referred simply to aggression, in the meaning of Article 39 of the Charter, i.e. a much broader meaning ... It was therefore essential for the Committee to know exactly what it was discussing').

[40] E.g., UN Doc. A/AC.134/SR.52–66, 90 (Cyprus); UN Doc. A/AC.134/SR.67–78, 12 (Ecuador); UN Doc. A/AC.134/SR.79–91, 12 (Cyprus).

[41] UN Doc. A/AC.134/SR.52–66, 118 (Cyprus). See also: UN Doc. A/AC.134/SR.67–78, 5 (UK), 7 (Japan), 112 (Uruguay); UN Doc. A/AC.134/SR.79–91, 35 (USSR), 47 (France), 48 (Colombia); UN Doc. A/AC.134/SR.100–109, 16 (USSR).

[42] E.g., A/AC.134/SR.52–66, 44 (Turkey).

[43] E.g., UN Doc. A/AC.134/SR.52–66, 98 (Syria), 118 (Cyprus); UN Doc. A/AC.134/SR.79–91, 62 (Ghana).

[44] E.g., UN Doc. A/AC.134/SR.52–66, 46 (Bulgaria), 57, 113 (Colombia), 99 (Ghana); UN Doc. A/AC.134/SR.67–78, 49 (Cyprus), 52 (Syria)

[45] E.g., UN Doc. A/AC.134/SR.52–66, 117 (US).
Remark: a second approach proposed more generally that the Definition distinguish between cases of aggression triggering the exercise of self-defence and those cases not justifying such action. E.g., UN Doc. A/AC.134/SR.67–78, 108 (France), 113 (Uruguay); UN Doc. A/AC.134/SR.79–91, 48 (Colombia).

it.[46] They stressed that it was *unrealistic* to think that a definition of 'armed attack' was achievable. The United Kingdom especially firmly stressed that States had long been divided between two schools of thought – one seeing Article 51 UN Charter as part of a broader customary right of self-defence, and another viewing Article 51 as the exclusive regulation of self-defence – and that any definition of aggression should be acceptable to both. Furthermore, it was considered *unnecessary* to examine the scope of self-defence in any detail, since the Committee was only called upon to establish the meaning of 'aggression' for the purpose of clarifying the competences of the UN Security Council under Article 39 UN Charter, the latter provision serving a wholly different purpose than Article 51. In the end, the Six Powers claimed that it was too simplistic to regard self-defence as the mere obverse of aggression. Self-defence was only of incidental relevance to aggression. For this reason, a general provision confirming that the exercise of self-defence would not constitute aggression was all that was needed.

Throughout the debates, a certain convergence of positions did take place.[47] Nonetheless, the differences of opinion vis-à-vis the right of self-defence ultimately proved too deep to overcome.[48] As part of a broader compromise (involving other controversial issues, such as the purport of the right of self-determination), it was agreed that the Definition should include a reference to indirect aggression (Article 3(g)), and should at the same time merely be conceived as defining 'acts

---

[46] E.g., UN Doc. A/AC.134/SR.67–78, 5–6 (UK: ' [A]ny attempt to define aggression in terms of self-defence might cause more trouble than it would save.... [The Committee] should safeguard, in the definition of aggression, the inherent right of self-defence as recognized in the Charter, but in a way acceptable to both schools of thought ...'), 6–7 (Japan), 8–9, 111 (Australia), 15 (Canada), 114 (US); UN Doc. A/AC.134/SR.79–91, 18–9 (US: '[T]he Special Committee should now avoid engaging in an inconclusive conceptual debate on whether the term used in Article 1 and Article 39 of the Charter on the one hand, and the different term used in Article 51 on the other, were necessarily identical or equivalent.... The terms used were different and the context was different. Any attempt to merge those two concepts would produce a distortion of the legal regime embodied in the Charter.'), 30 (Australia), 34 (Japan), 42 (Italy), 50 (UK); UN Doc. A/AC.134/SR.100–9, at 17 (US). See also: UN Doc. A/AC.134/SR.79–91, 61 (Turkey).

[47] Several of the Thirteen Powers, for example, expressed more moderate positions concerning self-defence against indirect aggression: e.g., UN Doc. A/AC.134/SR.52–66, 99 (Ghana), 118 (Cyprus). There was also a growing recognition that the criteria of priority and intent were not necessarily incompatible: e.g., UN Doc. A/AC.134/SR.79–91, at 14 (DRC), 18 (US), 36 (USSR), 48 (France).

[48] Ferencz, *Defining international aggression*. Vol. II, p. 46.

of aggression' in the sense of Article 39 UN Charter.[49] As for the scope of self-defence, the resolution confined itself to the observation that: 'Nothing in this Definition shall be construed as in any way enlarging or diminishing the scope of the Charter, including its provisions concerning cases in which the use of force is lawful.'[50] According to the Soviet delegate, the inclusion of the latter provision constituted a 'success', 'particularly bearing in mind that that question had divided the Special Committee for years ... [T]he Committee had acted reasonably by confining itself to a formulation that could not cause any divergence of views ...'.[51]

3.1.3. Value of the Definition of Aggression

Despite the Soviet statement, it is hard to be wildly enthusiastic about the consensus text. The resolution as such only serves as guidance for the Security Council to determine the existence of an act of aggression in the sense of Article 39 UN Charter. Article 4 makes clear that its provisions are not in any way binding upon the Security Council. The preamble voices the belief that the definition 'ought to have the effect of deterring a potential aggressor, would simplify the determination of acts of aggression and the implementation of measures to suppress them and would also facilitate ... the rendering of assistance to, the victim'.[52] In retrospect, however, it may be doubted whether these noble intentions were truly fostered by Resolution 3314 (XXIX). On the one hand, the Definition has had very little concrete impact on the practice of the United Nations' political organs. References to '(acts of) aggression' in Security Council resolutions have been so extremely rare,[53] that one author notes an 'institutional allergy' to making such determination.[54] The General Assembly has explicitly referred to the Definition of

---

[49] Cf. the UK delegate observed after the adoption of the final text that 'it was always necessary to remember just what the definition was. ... [It constituted] valuable guidance to the Security Council – no less and no more – in performing its functions under Article 39 of the Charter.' UN Doc. A/AC.134/SR.110–13, 18 July 1974, 39.

[50] Article 6, Definition of Aggression, Annex to General Assembly Resolution 3314 (XXIX) of 14 December 1974. Article 6 was on the whole well received. See Broms, 'The definition of aggression', 367.

[51] UN Doc. A/AC.134/SR.100–9, 47.

[52] See also, e.g., UN Doc. A/AC.134/SR.92–9, 31 (Uruguay).

[53] For some of the rare exceptions, see: SC Res. 405 (1977) of 14 April 1977; SC Res. 418 (1977) of 4 November 1977; and SC Res. 546 (1984) of 6 January 1984.

[54] Kritsiotis, 'Topographies of force', p. 62.

Aggression only in relation to the occupation of Namibia by South Africa and Israel's occupation of the Golan Heights; the Security Council has so far not mentioned it a single time.[55] Moreover, the price for consensus also meant that while the project was originally envisaged as an attempt to draft a *legal definition* of aggression, this idea was gradually abandoned.[56] However, developments in this area emanating from the Assembly of States Parties to the Rome Statute are referred to in chapter 6.[57]

It is admitted that our succinct discussion of the Definition's *travaux* does not do justice to the wide array of issues on the negotiation table, and the difficult political compromise that was finally reached. Still, it is hard to avoid the impression that the major Western powers successfully managed to 'defuse' the project by steering it from a binding document with legal implications to a political instrument which they could all too easily ignore. Again, the use of the phrase 'acts of aggression' in Articles 2 and 3, in combination with the text of the aforementioned Article 6, makes clear that the consensus resolution does not *directly* restrict or expand the scope for lawful self-defence, a conviction that is shared by a majority of legal doctrine.[58]

On the other hand, it would be wrong to conclude from the foregoing that the resolution is of no value whatsoever for present purposes.[59] First, as we have seen, many aspects relating to the scope of self-defence were the subject of intense discussion throughout the negotiations. The positions voiced by States in this context provide valuable elements of customary practice and merit close consideration. This is all the more so because the *travaux* provide insights into States' positions *in abstracto*

---

[55] See Solera, *Defining the crime of aggression*, pp. 201–2.
[56] *Ibid.*, p. 203. On the negotiations within the Assembly of State Parties to the Rome Statute on the activation of the embryonic jurisdiction for the crime of aggression, see, N. Weisbord, 'Prosecuting aggression', (2008) 49 HILJ 161–220. These negotiations culminated in the adoption on 11 June 2010 of an amendment to the ICC Rome Statute. ICC Assembly of States Parties, Resolution RC/Res.6, 13th plenary meeting, 11 June 2010 (adopted by consensus). See also: www.icc-cpi.int/Menus/ASP/Crime+of+Aggression/; www.icc-cpi.int/Menus/ASP/ReviewConference/Crime+of+Aggression.htm.
[57] See, in particular, pp. 546–7.
[58] E.g., Bowett, *Self-defence in international law*, pp. 261–2; Broms, 'The definition of aggression', 358; A. Randelzhofer, 'Article 51', in B. Simma in collaboration with H. Mosler, A. Randelzhofer, C. Tomuschat and R. Wolfrüm (eds.), *The Charter of the United Nations: a commentary*. Vol. I (Oxford University Press, 2002), pp. 788–806, at 795; M. Virally, 'Article 2: paragraphe 4', in J.-P. Cot and A. Pellet, *La Charte des Nations Unies*, 2nd edn. (Paris: Economica, 1991), pp. 115–28, at 118. Contra: Abi-Saab, 'Cours général', 362–3; Kritsiotis, 'Topographies of force', p. 59; P. Rambaud, 'La definition de l'agression par l'Organisation des Nations Unies', (1976) 80 RGDIP 835–81, at 878.
[59] R. Ago, 'Addendum to the 8th Report on State Responsibility', (1980-II) 32 YBILC, Part One, 68.

and therefore function as a sort of 'mirror' to compare with the way States have applied Article 51 in concrete cases and to examine how positions have developed after 1974. Second, the negotiations confirm the view, supported by a majority of legal doctrine,[60] that, in general, a cascading relationship exists between the terms 'force', 'aggression', and 'armed attack'.[61] The implication would be that any 'armed attack' in the sense of Article 51 would normally also constitute an 'act of aggression' in the sense of Article 39. More importantly, the reverse would mean that any limitation on 'acts of aggression' identified by the UNGA Definition of Aggression would *a fortiori* apply to the concept of 'armed attack'.[62] This finding potentially carries important consequences. Consider for example the fact that in accordance with Article 1, 'aggression' presupposes the *actual* use of armed force and, contrary to Article 2(4) UN Charter does not extend to threats thereof; that Article 1–3 all define 'aggression' as an act committed *by a State* against another State (even under the indirect aggression scenario of Article 3(g)); or that Article 2 makes reference to the need for a 'sufficient gravity'. However, in light of the complex relationship between the different terms and the different purposes served by each, one should avoid reading the relationship

---

[60] E.g., M. Bothe, 'Das Gewaltverbot imm allgemeinen', in W. Schaumann and M. Bothe (eds.), *Völkerrechtliches Gewaltverbod und Friedenssicherung* (Baden-Baden: Nomos, 1971), pp. 11–30, at 16; A. Constantinou, *The right of self-defence under customary international law and Article 51 of the UN Charter* (Brussels: Bruylant, 2000), at 66; M. Knopf and C. Kreß, 'Der Nicaragua-Fall des IGH im Spannungsfeld zwischen Gewalverbot und Interventionslust', (1990) 41 Österreiches Zeitschrift für öffentliches unde Völkerrecht, pp. 9–55, at 16; C. A. Pompe, *Aggressive war: an international crime* (The Hague: Martinus Nijhoff) (1953), at 99; Randelzhofer, 'Article 51', p.795; B. V. A. Röling, 'The 1974 U.N. Definition of Aggression', in A. Cassese (ed.), *The current legal regulation of the use of force* (Dordrecht: Martinus Nijhoff, 1986), pp. 413–21, at 416, 419. Contra: D. Fleck, 'Rules of engagement of maritime forces and the limitation of the use of force under the UN Charter', (1989) 31 GYBIL 165–86, at 175; J. L. Hargrove, 'The *Nicaragua* judgment and the future of the law of force and self-defense', (1987) 81 AJIL 135–43, at 139, footnote 15.

[61] See, e.g., UN Doc. A/AC.134/SR.52–66, 104 (Yugoslavia), 118–19 (Cyprus); UN Doc. A/AC.134/SR.67–78, 5 (UK), 7 (Japan), 112 (Uruguay); UN Doc. A/AC.134/SR.79–91, 35 (USSR), 47 (France), 48 (Colombia); UN Doc. A/AC.134/SR.100–9, 16 (USSR). In a similar vein, see the second preambular paragraph of the Thirteen-Power proposal: 'Convinced that armed attack (armed aggression) is the most serious and dangerous form of aggression ...' UN Doc. A/AC.134/L.16 (and Corr. 1). The preamble of the Definition of Aggression moreover explicitly considers aggression as 'the most serious and dangerous form of the illegal use of force'. GA Res. 3314 (XXIX) of 14 December 1974.

[62] See, for instance, Constantinou, *The right of self-defence*, pp. 66 *et seq.*

between the two as strictly linear, holding the limitations on the former to be automatically applicable to the latter. The provisions of the Definition of Aggression provide a good point of departure to indirectly examine the scope of self-defence,[63] *on condition that* due consideration is paid to the *travaux* of the resolution and to other elements of customary practice. Hence, pending closer examination, one should refrain from excluding per se the recourse to self-defence against acts not constituting acts of aggression in the sense of Articles 1–3 of the Definition of Aggression, and keep open the theoretical possibility that the concept of 'armed attack' could in certain respects actually be broader than the one defined in Resolution 3314 (XXIX).

3.2 General factors determining the existence of an 'armed attack'

3.2.1 The 'most grave' forms of the use of force and the de minimis controversy

Now that we have shed some light on the general relationship between 'force', 'aggression' and 'armed attack', it becomes necessary to identify the factors that allow us to distinguish between 'armed attacks' and other forcible acts not triggering the right of self-defence. Such factors may potentially be objective in nature, or they may be subjective. As for the former, one could envisage the scale of the attacks (e.g., the amount of force used, the duration of the attack or its locale) and/or its effects (e.g., the damage or casualties caused) as relevant variables. As for the latter, possible variables would comprise the intention of the attacker (e.g., is the attack deliberate or accidental?) and/or his motives (e.g., territorial conquest, regime change, et cetera). Which of these factors do play a role, and which are irrelevant?

In attempting to answer this question, we will first examine whether there exists a certain gravity threshold which must be reached before an attack can qualify as an 'armed attack' in the sense of Article 51 UN Charter. The present section will address the view of the ICJ and the criticism expressed by legal scholars, and will subsequently test the various views against relevant customary practice.

---

[63] E.g., affirming that the Definition may serve as a helpful guideline vis-à-vis the right of self-defence: UN Doc. A/C.6/SR.1477, § 19 (UK); UN Doc. A/C.6/SR.1478, § 16 (Federal Republic of Germany); UN Doc. A/C.6/SR.1482, § 52 (Spain).

3.2.1.a The approach of the International Court of Justice

While the Court in *Nicaragua* refrains from defining the concept of 'armed attack', it does pronounce on the relationship between 'use of force' and 'armed attack'. It asserts that there exists a gap between Articles 2(4) and 51, and that it is necessary 'to distinguish the most grave forms of the use of force (those constituting an armed attack) from other less grave forms'.[64] By reference to the 'Friendly Relations Declaration',[65] it spells out a number of rules bearing on these less grave forms of the use of force.[66] These include *inter alia*: the duty to refrain from the threat or use of force to violate existing international boundaries; the duty to refrain from acts of reprisal involving the use of force; the duty to refrain from organizing or encouraging the organization of irregular forces of armed bands for incursion into the territory of another State, et cetera. In paragraph 195, the Court explains that the difference between 'armed attacks' and less grave forms of the use of force is primarily one of 'scale and effects'. Relying on Article 3(g) of the Definition of Aggression, the Court affirms that an armed attack should be conceived not only in terms of action by regular armed forces across an international border, but can also cover 'the sending by a State of armed bands to the territory of another State, *if such an operation, because of its scale and effects, would have been classified as an armed attack rather than as a mere frontier incident had it been carried out by regular armed forces*'.[67] This phrase implies a subscription to some form of *de minimis* threshold, which not only applies to 'indirect' aggression (as some have suggested),[68] but also – as the reference to 'mere frontier incidents' indicates – to attacks by regular armed forces. At the same time, the Court identifies a category of acts which do not in its view constitute armed attacks, but which can nonetheless qualify as less grave forms of the use of force, viz. 'assistance to rebels in the form of the provision of weapons or logistical or other support'.[69]

The picture emerging from these dicta is seriously complicated when the Court subsequently reflects on the question whether a State may use force 'in reaction to measures which do not constitute an armed

---

[64] ICJ, *Nicaragua* case (Merits), § 191. [65] GA Res. 2625 (XXV) of 24 October 1970.
[66] ICJ, *Nicaragua* case (Merits), § 191. [67] Ibid., § 195 (emphasis added).
[68] E.g., D. Raab, '"Armed attack" after the *Oil Platforms* case', (2004) 17 Leiden JIL 719–35, at 724–5; W. H. Taft IV, 'Self-defence and the *Oil Platforms* decision', (2004) 29 YJIL 295–306, at 302.
[69] ICJ, *Nicaragua* case (Merits), § 195: 'Such assistance may be regarded as a threat or use of force, or amount to intervention in the internal or external affairs of other States.'

attack but may nevertheless involve a use of force'.[70] In other words, after determining that an 'armed attack' presupposes certain 'scale and effects', it raises the question whether *forcible* counter-measures may sometimes be undertaken against less grave uses of force. While it is conceded that this constitutes a relevant issue from a theoretical point of view, the possibility for the *direct victim* to undertake forcible counter-measures is deliberately left unanswered. At the same time, forcible reactions by *third States* are firmly excluded: 'States do not have a right of "collective" armed response to acts which do not constitute an "armed attack".'[71]

The contrast between these dicta creates the impression that the ICJ implicitly left open the door for proportionate forcible countermeasures by the direct victim of less grave uses of force.[72] This impression is reinforced by paragraph 249:

> [A] use of force of a lesser degree of gravity cannot, ... produce any entitlement to take collective counter-measures involving the use of force. The acts of which Nicaragua is accused ... could only have justified proportionate counter-measures on the part of the State which had been the victim of these acts ... They could not justify counter-measures taken by a third State ... and in particularly could not justify intervention involving the use of force.[73]

The different treatment of counter-measures by the direct victim and by third States may well have been inspired by a desire to limit third State involvement in order to avoid the escalation and internationalization of certain conflicts.[74] Nonetheless, it is rather flabbergasting that the Court flags a crucial *potential* gap in the rules on the use of force, which would seem to be prima facie incompatible with the comprehensive regime established by Articles 2(4) and 51 of the UN Charter, without providing any further guidance or supporting arguments.

---

[70] *Ibid.*, § 210.
[71] *Ibid.*, § 211: '[F]or one State to use force against another, on the ground that that State has committed a wrongful act against a third State, is regarded as lawful, by way of exception, only when the wrongful act provoking the response was an armed attack. Thus the lawfulness of the use of force by a State in response to a wrongful act of which it has not itself been the victim is not admitted when this wrongful act is not an armed attack. ...'
[72] See, e.g., Y. Dinstein, *War, aggression and self-defence*, 4th edn. (Cambridge University Press, 2005), p. 194; Hargrove, 'The *Nicaragua* judgment', 138; Kritsiotis, 'Topographies of force', pp.72–3.
[73] ICJ, *Nicaragua* case (Merits), § 249. Contra: *ibid.*, Dissenting opinion of Judge Schwebel, §§ 175–7.
[74] See, e.g., *ibid.*, Dissenting opinion of Judge Jennings, 543. See also: Macdonald, 'The *Nicaragua* case', 149.

In the *Oil Platforms* judgment, the Court reiterates the distinction between 'the most grave forms of the use of force' and 'other less grave forms', and reaffirms that only the former qualify as 'armed attacks'.[75] No reference whatsoever is made to the possible lacunae vis-à-vis forcible counter-measures against less grave uses of force. This, however, is much regretted by Judge Simma, who elaborates his views on 'some of the less fortunate statements' in the *Nicaragua* judgment.[76] Relying on the ambiguous position in the latter case regarding counter-measures by victims of less grave uses of force, Simma argues that two possible scenarios ought to be distinguished:

> I would suggest a distinction between (full-scale) self-defence within the meaning of Article 51 against an 'armed attack' . . . on the one hand and, on the other, the case of hostile action, for instance against individual ships, below the level of Article 51, justifying proportionate defensive measures on the part of the victim, equally short of the quality and quantity of action in self-defence expressly reserved in the United Nations Charter.[77]

According to Simma, the former category concerns military attacks 'in the substantial, massive sense of amounting to "*une agression armée*".'[78] Against such acts, a broad variety of defensive action is considered permissible. By contrast, the latter category covers a 'lower level of hostile military action'. These actions warrant a forcible response, 'but only within a more limited range and quality of responses (the main difference being that the possibility of collective self-defence does not arise, cf. *Nicaragua*) and bound to necessity, proportionality and immediacy in time in a particularly strict way'.[79]

With respect, it may strongly be doubted that the dichotomy put forward by Judge Simma was widely shared by his honourable colleagues. Judge Simma, in his own words, '*agreed* with the Court' that the alleged attacks by Iran 'did not *amount* to an "armed attack" under Article 51'.[80] Insofar as this suggests that the Court refrained from labelling these acts as 'armed attacks' because of a lack of 'gravity', this appears to be a

---

[75] ICJ, *Case concerning oil platforms (Islamic Republic of Iran v. United States of America)*, Judgment of 6 November 2003, (2003) ICJ Rep 161–219, §§ 51, 64.

[76] *Ibid.*, Individual opinion of Judge Simma, §§ 12–16. Judge Simma had already expressed his views on this matter much earlier. See: A. Verdross and B. Simma, *Universelles Völkerrecht: Theorie und Praxis*, 3rd edn (Berlin: Dunker un Humblot, 1984), 240.

[77] ICJ, *Oil Platforms* case, Individual opinion of Judge Simma, § 12.   [78] *Ibid.*, § 13.

[79] *Ibid.*   [80] *Ibid.*, § 14 (emphasis added).

misrepresentation of the judgment. Rather, the Court's attitude seemed inspired by other reasons, chief among them the lack of persuasive evidence attributing the alleged attacks to Iran.[81] Furthermore, the Court explicitly stated that it '[did] not exclude the possibility that the mining of a single military vessel might be sufficient to bring into play the "inherent right of self-defence".'[82] The latter consideration may be taken as a concession that the *de minimis* threshold should be interpreted flexibly and that, contrary to Judge Simma's suggestion, the concept of 'armed attack' should not be confined to 'substantial, massive' hostile acts. The reader is left to wonder whether this more liberal construction of 'armed attack' would in the Court's view also remove the need for (and permissibility of) forcible counter-measures against less grave uses of force.

3.2.1.b   Criticism and alternate constructions in legal doctrine

Over the years, the aforementioned dicta from the *Nicaragua* case have elicited a storm of criticism, with several scholars explicitly denouncing the 'otherworldliness'[83] of the distinctions put forward by the Court. Academic attacks have been launched on different fronts. A large share of the negative reaction has targeted the Court's narrow reading of Article 3(g) of the Definition of Aggression, more specifically its finding that the concept of 'armed attack' does not extend to 'assistance to rebels in the form of the provision of weapons or logistical or other support'.[84] This discussion concerns the *ratione personae* aspect of the 'armed attack' requirement and is further explored in Chapter 5.

Scholars have also in more general terms questioned the distinction made between the 'most grave' and 'less grave' forms of the use of force, and the concomitant distinction between self-defence and countermeasures. On the one hand, several authors have expressed concern at the Court's insistence on certain 'scale and effects', and, more specifically, at its exclusion of 'mere frontier incidents.' First, some have pointed out that it would be fallacious to automatically dismiss all frontier incidents from the application of Article 51. In the words of Fitzmaurice: '[T]here are frontier incidents and frontier incidents.

---

[81] ICJ, *Oil Platforms* case, §§ 64, 72.
[82] *Ibid.*, § 72. Cf. By contrast, Judge Simma argues that hostile action against individual ships falls below the level of Article 51 (Individual opinion of Judge Simma, § 12).
[83] E.g., Hargrove, 'The *Nicaragua* judgment', 139.
[84] ICJ, *Nicaragua* case (Merits), § 195.

Some are trivial, some may be extremely grave.'[85] Second, it has been stressed that Article 51 speaks of 'armed attack', without limiting the concept to especially large or important attacks.[86] According to Kunz: 'If "armed attack" means illegal armed attack, it means, on the other hand, any illegal armed attack, even a small border incident.'[87] Several authors have taken this reasoning a step further by suggesting that *any* use of force, regardless of its scale and effects, ought to permit defensive action, provided the defending State strictly abides by the proportionality principle.[88] The result is that these scholars in fact equate the concepts of 'use of force' and 'armed attack'. Dinstein takes a more moderate approach. While admitting that there exists a gap between the two stipulations, he argues that it should be construed quite narrowly. Interestingly, he gives some examples of illegal uses of force which would not qualify as an 'armed attack' and would not justify the exercise of self-defence, such as a situation where 'agents of Arcadia – without inflicting any casualties or much damage – [would] break into a Utopian diplomatic bag or detain a Ruritarian ship in circumstances disallowed by international law'.[89]

The Court's ambiguous stance concerning the possibility of forcible counter-measures by States victim of 'less grave' uses of force has also attracted criticism.[90] Hargrove, for instance, observing that the Court 'strongly suggested' that forcible counter-measures would be available in the latter situation, denounces this as another 'arbitrary

---

[85] G. G. Fitzmaurice, 'The Definition of Aggression', (1952) 1 ICLQ 137–44, at 139 (criticizing the Soviet draft Definition of Aggression). Dinstein agrees that '[m]any frontier incidents comprise fairly large military engagements, and an attempt to dissociate them from other forms of armed attack would be spurious', Dinstein, *War, aggression and self-defence*, p. 195.

[86] E.g., *ibid.*, p. 195 ('There is certainly no cause to remove small-scale armed attacks from the spectrum of armed attacks'); Hargrove, 'The *Nicaragua* judgment', 139; Taft, 'The *Oil Platforms* decision', 300. See also: T. Gazzini, *The changing rules on the use of force in international law* (Manchester University Press, 2005), pp. 133, 138–9.

[87] J. L. Kunz, 'Individual and collective self-defense in Article 51 of the Charter of the United Nations', (1947) 41 AJIL 872–9, at 878. See also: B. Levenfeld, 'Israel's counter-*fedayeen* tactics in Lebanon: self-defense and reprisal under modern international law', (1982) 21 Columbia JTL 1–48, at 20–1.

[88] E.g., Hargrove, 'The *Nicaragua* judgment', 136, 139; R. Higgins, *Problems and process: international law and how we use it* (Oxford: Clarendon Press, 1994), p. 251. Randelzhofer expresses strong sympathy for closing the gap between Articles 2(4) and 51 by permitting proportionate self-defence against any use of armed force, but doubts whether this view is consistent with the Charter framework. Randelzhofer, 'Article 51', pp791–2. Consider also: Brownlie, 'The use of force in self-defence', 245.

[89] Dinstein, *War, aggression and self-defence*, p. 193.   [90] *Ibid.*, p. 194.

announcement'.[91] He accuses the Court of fundamentally weakening the prohibition on the use of force by creating an open-ended and wholly new category of exceptions, of unknown content and limit – a category which seems 'to have been developed on the spot to accommodate the circumstances of the *Nicaragua* case, and is one that is clearly in conflict with the Charter and corrosive of its restraints on the use of force'.[92]

In the end, we are confronted with two crucial questions. The first concerns the actual gravity threshold of Article 51 UN Charter. *Grosso modo*, three main options can be discerned: it might be submitted (1) that a substantial or massive attack is needed to qualify as an 'armed attack' (this is the view advanced by Judge Simma); (2) that a relatively small-scale attack is sufficient; or, finally, (3) that any use of (armed) force qualifies as an 'armed attack'. The second question requires a simple 'yes' or 'no': do violations of the prohibition on the *use* of force[93] not reaching the aforementioned threshold allow for (proportionate) *forcible* counter-measures? The two questions are obviously interlinked. The lower the gravity threshold, the less need, from a policy perspective, to answer the latter question affirmatively. Furthermore, if one would adopt the third option vis-à-vis the gravity threshold – in other words, if one would fully close the gap between Articles 2(4) and 51 – the second question would consequently become moot. The resulting paradigm may be summed up as follows:

– *Option 1: Article 51 requires a 'substantial/massive' attack*
  • 1(a): no forcible counter-measures allowed below this threshold
  • 1(b): proportionate forcible counter-measures by the direct victim permitted against other unlawful uses of force
– *Option 2: a 'small-scale' attack is sufficient to activate Article 51*
  • 2(a): no forcible counter-measures allowed below this threshold
  • 2(b): proportionate forcible counter-measures by the direct victim permitted against other unlawful uses of force
– *Option 3: any unlawful use of force permits a proportionate defensive response*

Starting with the second question regarding the permissibility of forcible counter-measures against unlawful uses of force not qualifying as 'armed attacks', it must be emphasized that States as well as authors generally

---

[91] Hargrove, 'The *Nicaragua* judgment', 141. [92] *Ibid.*, 142.
[93] Remark: possible reactions to the threat of force fall under the scope of Chapter 4.

recognize the Charter framework to be a comprehensive one, allowing unilateral defensive action only in cases of self-defence 'if an armed attack occurs'.[94] In light hereof, it is difficult not to agree with Hargrove that the Court's ambiguous position is prima facie inconsistent with the Charter provision.[95] Any lingering doubts in this respect have arguably been swayed by the ILC Draft Articles on State Responsibility (2001).[96] Indeed, apart from the assertion that counter-measures cannot be invoked to disregard peremptory norms, Article 50(1)(a) explicitly determines that 'counter-measures shall not affect the obligation to refrain from the threat or use of force as embodied in the [UN] Charter'.[97] According to the ILC Commentary, this paragraph excludes forcible measures from the ambit of permissible counter-measures. This rule is considered to be incorporated in the UNGA Declaration on Friendly Relations and is found to be consistent with prevailing doctrine as well as with a number of authoritative pronouncements of international judicial and other bodies (including the ICJ's own *Corfu Channel* case).[98] Ergo, options 1(b) and 2(b) can be ruled out.[99]

Turning back to our first question, it does not seem sensible at this stage to proceed to a definitive answer without first engaging in a closer analysis of relevant customary practice. Still, a number of interim reflections can be put forward:

- Most authors accept that the *Nicaragua* case establishes the broad guidelines for the evaluation of the 'armed attack' requirement and agree that not every use of force warrants the exercise of the right of

---

[94] E.g., J. Mrazek, 'Prohibition on the use and threat of force: self-defence and self-help in international law', (1989) 27 Can YBIL 81–111, at 90; Pompe, *Aggressive war*, p. 97.

[95] See Hargrove, 'The *Nicaragua* judgment', 141–2. Also: Dinstein, *War, aggression and self-defence*, p. 194.

[96] ILC, 'Commentary on the Draft Articles on the Responsibility of States for Internationally Wrongful Acts', (2001-II) YBILC 131–2.

[97] *Ibid.*, 75, 84–5, 131.

[98] *Ibid.*, 132. See also: ICJ, *Corfu Channel* (*United Kingdom* v. *Albania*), Judgment of 9 April 1949, (1949) ICJ Rep 4–38, at 35. In a similar vein: Y. Arai-Takahashi, 'Shifting boundaries of the right of self-defence: appraising the impact of the September 11 attacks on *Jus ad Bellum*', (2002) 36 *International Lawyer* 1081–102, at 1085–6; A. Zimmerman, 'The Second Lebanon War: *Jus ad Bellum, Jus in Bello* and the issue of proportionality', (2007) 11 MPYBUNL 99–141, at 105.

[99] Remark: some authors have occasionally asserted that certain cases of inter-State recourse to force can be justified by reference to alternative legal bases, such as a right of 'hot pursuit' or a 'state of necessity'. These legal grounds are addressed in Section 5.1.1.b.

self-defence.[100] Nonetheless, a considerable group of scholars has expressed strong discomfort with the Court's approach, and has either tried to bend the Court's dicta so as to limit the implications of its reasoning to indirect military aggression or collective self-defence,[101] or has simply rejected the Court's categorization. In recent years, a growing number of scholars flatly repudiates the need for a *de minimis* threshold in relation to attacks by *regular* armed forces.[102] By contrast, many accept that for attacks by *non-State actors* to trigger the right of self-defence, they have to be large-scale.[103]

- Against Option 1, it must be stressed that the Court did not necessarily raise a very high threshold. It did not distinguish the 'most grave (armed) *attacks*' from 'less grave (armed) *attacks*', but discriminated between the 'most grave forms of the *use of force*' and 'less grave' forms. Neither does the Court's assessment of the concrete incidents render support to Option 1. In *Nicaragua*, the Court refrained from shedding further light on the concept of 'frontier incidents', instead noting that '[v]ery little information is however available ... as to the circumstances of [the alleged] incursions or their possible

---

[100] E.g., Constantinou, *The right of self-defence*, pp. 61–4; (implicitly) N. M. Feder, 'Reading the U.N. Charter connotatively: toward a new definition of armed attack', (1987) 19 NYUJILP 395–432, at 418; P. Malanczuk, 'Countermeasures and self-defence as circumstances precluding wrongfulness in the International Law Commission's Draft Articles on State Responsibility', (1983) 43 GYBIL 705–812, at 757; G. Redsell, 'Illegitimate, unnecessary and disproportionate: Israel's use of force in Lebanon', (2007) Cambridge Student L Rev 70–85, at 72–4; J. P. Rowles, '"Secret Wars," self-defense and the Charter – a reply to Professor Moore', (1986) 80 AJIL 568–83, at 572; C. Stahn, 'Terrorist acts as "armed attack": the right to self-defence, Article 51 of the UN Charter, and international terrorism', (2003) 27 *Fletcher Forum of World Affairs* 35–54, at 45.

[101] Remark: Gray, for example, apparently downplays the implications of the gravity threshold in *Nicaragua* by suggesting that the Court's concern was with collective self-defence and the possibility of third-party involvement. Similarly, she questions the precedential value of the distinction between 'armed attacks' and less grave uses of force in *Oil Platforms* by stressing that the context was one of (US) third-State intervention in an international armed conflict (between Iran and Iraq). See: C. Gray, *International law and the use of force*, 3rd edn. (Oxford University Press, 2008), pp. 148–50; C. Gray, 'The Ethiopia/Eritrea Claims Commission oversteps its boundaries: a partial award?', (2006) 17 EJIL 699–721, at 719–20.

[102] See, for instance, the remarks of the various respondents in E. Wilmshurst, 'Principles of international law on the use of force by States in self-defence', Chatham House International Law Working Paper 05/01, October 2005, available at www.chathamhouse.org.uk/files/3278_ilpforce.doc (accessed 4 May 2009). In a similar vein, e.g., Raab, 'Armed attack', 724–5.

[103] Ibid.

motivations, which renders it difficult to decide whether they may be treated ... as amounting, *singly* or collectively, to an "armed attack"'.[104] In *Oil Platforms*, the Court mainly focused on the lack of proof for the alleged attacks (and their attributability to Iran).[105] Furthermore, as was noted earlier, the Court's suggestion that the mining of a single military vessel might trigger Article 51 is hard to fit into Option 1.

- Against Option 3, it must be recalled that the different wording used in Article 2(4) UN Charter and Article 51 strongly suggests that 'armed attack' has a narrower scope than 'use of force'. Furthermore, it seems that authors adhering to this option sometimes fail to envisage the wide variety of acts which may constitute an unlawful use of force under Article 2(4). One may wonder, for instance, how many would be willing to accept Waldock's view that Denmark or Sweden could lawfully use armed force to prevent the illegal arrest of one of their fishing vessels on the high seas in the Baltic.[106] And what would these scholars think about a forcible response to the examples listed by Dinstein, such as breaking into another State's diplomatic bag?[107] Or, what about the following situations: a group of teenagers throwing rocks across a border; a police patrol pursuing a criminal into the territory of a neighbouring country; or a weary border guard practising his shooting skills on cattle grazing on the other side of the border. Can it be said in such cases that an armed attack has taken place in the sense of Article 51 UN Charter, and, if so, does the proportionality standard really provide a suitable tool to regulate the resort to counterforce?

- In the end, the doctrinal debate is by and large inspired by policy considerations.[108] Scholars rejecting a high *de minimis* threshold are markedly motivated by the need for States effectively to protect themselves against unlawful uses of force, regardless of the intensity of the attack(s) concerned. They warn of the danger that such threshold would encourage aggressor States to resort to hit-and-run tactics and to make use of armed bands in order to escape a defensive response. It

---

[104] ICJ, *Nicaragua* case (Merits), § 231.   [105] ICJ, *Oil Platforms* case, §§ 64, 72.
[106] C. H. M. Waldock, 'The regulation of the use of force by individual states in international law', (1952-II) 81 RdC 451–517, at 497. Supported by Schwebel: ICJ, *Nicaragua* case (Merits), Dissenting opinion of Judge Schwebel, § 173.
[107] Dinstein, *War, aggression and self-defence*, p. 193.
[108] See, e.g., Hargrove, 'The *Nicaragua* judgment', 139; Randelzhofer, 'Article 51', pp. 791–2; Gazzini, *The changing rules*, p. 138.

is moreover considered unrealistic to impose a gravity threshold which States most certainly will not feel bound to respect. On the other hand, scholars insisting on a certain scale and intensity often proceed on the basis that a *de minimis* threshold fosters conflict containment and strengthens the stability of the international order by avoiding rapid escalation of conflicts into an unstoppable cycle of force and counter-force. Especially when taking account of the dozens of territorial conflicts and tense border situations between both smaller and larger States worldwide, it is sometimes argued that a mere reliance on the vague and flexible necessity and proportionality thresholds is no sufficient guarantee to prevent these situations from going out of control. There is merit in both views. At the same time, one may wonder whether it is really the scholar's task to determine the right place of the gravity threshold on the continuum between 'apology' and 'utopia'.[109] Rather, as Article 51 UN Charter itself does not specify the precise scope of the concept of 'armed attack', it seems more appropriate to first rely on customary practice in order to judge the existence of the *de minimis* threshold.

3.2.1.c Customary practice

Turning our attention to customary practice, we will first try to distil relevant clues from the Definition of Aggression and its *travaux*. Subsequently, since these sources only provide 'circumstantial' evidence of the scope of permissible self-defence, the latter insights will be tested against their application in concrete instances of recourse to force.

In casu, the relevance of the Definition of Aggression is threefold. First of all, as was noted before, the *travaux* generally support the idea of a cascading relationship between the terms 'use of force', '(act of) aggression' and 'armed attack', whereby the latter concept constitutes the narrowest of the three. Both the Thirteen-Power proposal and the Soviet proposal discussed by the Fourth Special Committee referred to 'armed aggression'/'armed attack' as 'the most serious and dangerous form of aggression'.[110] This provision was eventually replaced by the observation that '*aggression* is the most serious and dangerous form of

---

[109] The notion of 'apology' reflects the idea that when a normative standard is very flexible, it becomes nothing but a fig-leaf, an excuse for states to use at their convenience. Against this, when a normative standard is set too high, it may become a distant and unattainable utopia. Cf. M. Koskenniemi, *From apology to utopia: the structure of international legal argument* (Cambridge University Press, 2005: reissue with new epilogue).

[110] UN Doc. A/AC.134/L.16 (and Corr. 1); UN Doc. A/AC.134/L.12 (and Corr. 1).

the illegal use of force'.[111] Throughout the negotiations, numerous countries stressed that only the 'most serious' uses of force qualified as 'armed attacks'.[112] In this context, the *travaux* support the view that the different phrases used in Articles 2(4) and 51 cannot simply be ignored and that a certain gap indeed exists between the two (contra Option 3).

Second, the *de minimis* issue was brought up during the negotiations on the inclusion in the Definition of various forms of indirect aggression. Again, whereas the Thirteen-Power proposal expressly excluded the exercise of self-defence in such cases, the Six Powers refused to vote for any draft resolution which did not cover some form of indirect aggression.[113] As the different positions began to converge, it became clear that two elements were key to determine the possiblity of self-defence against indirect aggression: on the one hand, the nature of State involvement – whether a State was 'organizing', 'sending', 'instigating' or 'supporting' armed bands (i.e., the *ratione personae* element, cf. *infra*) – and, on the other hand, the *gravity* of the attacks.[114] France, for instance suggested that the Definition 'should perhaps include a clear statement of the idea that serious flagrant cases of subversion should be placed on the same footing as direct armed attack within the meaning of Article 51 of the Charter'.[115] In a similar vein, Indonesia accepted that 'in some cases infiltration was so substantial and posed so great a danger that it was tantamount to an armed attack and justified the exercise of the right of self-defence'.[116] The relevance of a *de minimis* threshold for cases of indirect aggression was made explicit in Article 3(g), which indeed refers to 'acts of armed force ... *of such gravity* as to amount to the acts listed above' (emphasis added).

---

[111] GA Res. 3314 (XXIX) of 14 December 1974 (second preambular paragraph) (emphasis added).

[112] See, e.g., UN Doc. A/AC.134/SR.52–66, 104 (Yugoslavia), 118–19 (Cyprus); UN Doc. A/AC.134/SR.67–78, 5 (UK), 7 (Japan), 112 (Uruguay); UN Doc. A/AC.134/SR.79–91, 35 (USSR), 47 (France), 48 (Colombia); UN Doc. A/AC.134/SR.100–9, 16 (USSR).

[113] Article 7, UN Doc. A/AC.134/L.16 (and Corr. 1). See *infra*, Section 5.1.2.

The United States argued that the proportionality principle would be a sufficient standard to govern recourse to self-defence (UN Doc. A/AC.134/SR.52–66, 116), yet its attempt to convince the Thirteen Powers failed (e.g., UN Doc. A/AC.134/SR.52–66, 119 (Cyprus)).

[114] E.g., Ferencz, *Defining international aggression*. Vol. II, p. 39. See e.g., UN Doc. A/AC.134/SR.52–66, 99 (Ghana), 118 (Cyprus); UN Doc. A/AC.134/SR.67–78, 52 (DRC); UN Doc. A/AC.134/SR.79–91, 60 (Madagascar).

[115] UN Doc. A/AC.134/SR.67–78, 119 (France).

[116] UN Doc. A/AC.134/SR.79–91, 96 (Indonesia).

THE 'ARMED ATTACK' REQUIREMENT *RATIONE MATERIAE* 151

Last but not least, apart from the debate on *indirect* aggression, 'gravity' was also thought to be relevant for the exercise of self-defence in general. Already in 1956, the Netherlands stressed that 'small-scale hostilities connected with border incidents fell outside the scope of [Article 51]'.[117] Before the Fourth Special Committee, several countries referred to the importance of certain scale and effects and excluded 'local disturbances' and 'border incidents' from the scope of 'aggression', sometimes explicitly denouncing the exercise of self-defence in such situations.[118] The Soviet representative, for example, stressed that it was 'essential to introduce the concept of "intensity" of the act, so that a distinction could be drawn between acts of aggression and other forms of the use of force'.[119] Mexico remarked that 'the general definition of aggression would be acceptable if the Special Committee agreed upon a satisfactory formula for the exclusion of minor incidents and the use of force not constituting an act of aggression under the terms of Article 51 of the Charter'.[120] Although the support for a minimal scale and effects was less unequivocal than in relation to cases of 'indirect' aggression, States eventually agreed that 'gravity' generally did play a role for the determination of an 'act of aggression'.[121] This is reflected in Article 2 of the Definition, according to which 'the Security Council may ... conclude that a determination that an act of aggression has been committed would not be justified in the light of other relevant circumstances *including the fact that the acts concerned or their consequences are not of sufficient gravity*' (emphasis added).

In conclusion, the Definition of Aggression and its *travaux* support the view that a gap exists between Articles 2(4) and 51 UN Charter,[122] and that 'gravity' matters to determine whether the use of armed force (especially – but not exclusively – when emanating from irregulars or

---

[117] Report of the 1956 Special Committee on the Question of Defining Aggression, 8 October – 9 November 1956, UN Doc. A/3574, 24.
[118] E.g., UN Doc. A/AC.134/SR.52–66, 27 (Canada: '[The attacks] might be mere localized disturbances, minor border incidents or use of force in a manner so limited in nature and in duration that an allegation of aggression could not but fail to be substantiated.'), 44 (Turkey), 46 (Bulgaria); UN Doc. A/AC.134/SR.67–78, 23 (US), 118 (Romania), 118 (Cyprus), 145 (USSR), 146 (UK); UN Doc. A/AC.134/SR.79–91, 19 (US), 20 (Mexico).
[119] UN Doc. A/AC.134/SR.100–9, 16. See also *ibid.*, 49 (Ghana). [120] *Ibid.*, 29.
[121] E.g., Broms, 'The definition of aggression', 346; Ferencz, *Defining international aggression*. Vol. II, p. 32.
[122] In a similar vein: ICJ, *Oil Platforms* case, Reply and defence to counter-claim submitted by the Islamic Republic of Iran, 10 March 1999, § 7.17.

armed bands) amounts to an 'armed attack'. To what extent is this approach upheld in respect of concrete recourses to self-defence? Of course self-defence has on occasion been invoked against large-scale attacks involving massive territorial incursions, as in the case of the 1950 Korean War, the 1982 Falklands War or the 1990 Iraqi invasion of Kuwait. In such situations, the *de minimis* problem does not arise. On the other hand, these cases are obviously not the only type of attacks warranting a defensive reaction.

When a State's territory or its external manifestations abroad become the target of artillery shelling, air strikes, bombings and the like, there is in principle little doubt that such attacks reach the necessary gravity to qualify as 'armed attacks'. Where such attacks occur, victim States feel little reluctance to invoke the right of self-defence. Third States will generally not question that such acts constitute armed attacks. Rather, when criticism is uttered, it often focuses on the lack of necessity and proportionality, and/or on the proof of the attack (and its attributability to the State concerned) – two aspects that played a significant part in forming the Court's conclusions in *Oil Platforms*. Thus, when in 1998 terrorists bombed the US embassies in Nairobi and Dar Es Salaam, killing hundreds and leaving thousands injured, there was little doubt that the attacks were *sufficiently grave* to constitute 'armed attacks'. Relying on Article 51 UN Charter, the US responded by missile attacks on a terrorist training camp in Afghanistan and a pharmaceutical plant in Sudan.[123] Some Western States expressed sympathy for the US actions; others condemned the air strikes. On the whole, third States remained shrouded in silence, although considerable doubt was expressed in relation to US allegations that the Sudanese pharmaceutical plant was in fact a chemical weapons factory linked to international terrorism.[124]

It does not appear to be necessary for a missile, artillery or bomb attack to have large-scale effects in terms of material damage inflicted or numbers of casualties in order to reach the *de minimis* threshold. What

---

[123] UN Doc. S/1998/780, 20 August 1998 (US). See also: (1998) UNYB 1219–20; SC Res. 1189 (1998) of 13 August 1998. See also: S. L. Myers and T. Weiner, 'After the attack: the chemicals; possible benign use is seen for chemical at factory in Sudan', *NY Times* 27 August 1998.

[124] See T. Franck, *Recourse to force: State action against threats and armed attacks* (Cambridge University Press, 2002), p. 95; Gray, *The use of force*, p. 197. Also *infra* Section 5.2.1.b.

matters is that the attack is *liable to produce* such consequences.[125] It can, for example be inferred from the generally supportive attitude towards the US military raid against the Iraqi intelligence headquarters in 1993 that States implicitly endorsed the US qualification of the failed attempt to assassinate former President Bush as an 'armed attack'.[126] Similarly, although the Security Council condemned the British raid against Harib Fort in 1964[127] – with some Members stressing that the prior attacks by Yemeni aircraft had resulted, not in the loss of lives, 'but the loss of a few precious camels'[128] – a closer look reveals that third States did not deny that some form of defensive response was permitted, but rather believed that the British action was disproportionate and constituted a reprisal rather than lawful self-defence.[129] Thus, Czechoslovakia claimed that '[i]f the alleged ... attacks from Yemen had been carried out by isolated aircraft and helicopters, the only immediate defence should have been directed against those machines."[130]

---

[125] E.g., Dinstein, *War, aggression and self-defence*, p. 193.

The arguments put forward by the United States in the *Oil Platforms* case actually come close to this line of reasoning. According to the US: 'Article 51 of the UN Charter contains no qualifications regarding the size of "armed attacks" ... The scale of the attack is at issue, *in most cases*, not in the legal characterization as an 'armed attack' but rather in an examination of the proportionality of the actions taken in self-defence. ... In any event, Iranian attacks were unquestionably lethal, dangerous and serious, inflicting extremely serious damage to the ships attacked, leaving at least 63 people dead and 99 wounded. Iran contends that only "massive" attacks on a State's marine fleet amount to armed attacks under Article 51. Such a rule has no basis in the law of self-defense. Moreover, its adoption would only lead to confusion in the law. For instance, if "small attacks" are not "armed attacks", at what point along the continuum from small-to-large do attacks merit characterization as "armed" under Article 51? At what point would several small attacks, spread across time, become "armed attacks"? ... Such questions underscore the difficulty of applying a restrictive interpretation to Article 51. Article 51 requires not rigid rules but a contextual, case-by-case approach, examining all of the circumstances surrounding the "armed attack" and the action taken in self-defence.' ICJ, *Oil Platforms* case, Rejoinder submitted by the United States of America, 23 March 2001, §§ 5.16–5.18.

[126] See UN Doc. S/PV.3245, 27 June 1993.   [127] SC Res. 188 (1964) of 9 April 1964.

[128] E.g., UN Doc. S/PV.1106, 2 April 1964, § 67 (Iraq). The UK objected along the following lines: 'Some ... chose to make light of the fact that, as a result of the attack ... two camels were killed and two tents burned. But, in spite of these efforts to gloss it over, this is in fact a serious matter and what the Council must recognize is that no less than three deliberate air attacks took place ... and that these attacks were carried out in spite of protests and warnings and were executed with incendiary bombs and machine-guns.' UN Doc. S/PV.1107, 3 April 1964, § 3.

[129] E.g., UN Doc. S/PV.1108, 6 April 1964, at §§ 32–5 (Morocco), 48–50 (Ivory Coast).

[130] UN Doc. S/PV.1110, 8 April 1964, § 24 (Czechoslovakia). Consider also the Iraqi position: UN Doc. S/PV.1107, 3 April 1964, §§ 15, 17; UN Doc. S/PV.1108, 6 April 1964, § 102; UN Doc. S/PV.1109, 7 April 1964, § 57.

This illustrates that the gravity of the initial attack is not so much crucial to determine whether defensive action is permissible at all, but rather to establish whether it may go beyond immediate and 'spontaneous' on-the-spot-reaction. This was arguably also the crux of the debate regarding the Gulf of Tunkin incident in 1964. *In casu*, the United States claimed that two military vessels had been attacked (on 2 and 4 August) by high-speed North Vietnamese boats with machine guns and torpedos.[131] In response, the US had taken defensive action against the torpedo boats and support facilities – action that received support from the UK and the Republic of China.[132] The Soviet Union and Czechoslovakia disagreed with the US version of the facts and labelled the bombing of targets on the coast of North Vietnam as unlawful retaliation.[133] Both countries implicitly agreed that while the US action *against North Vietnamese territory* exceeded the restraints of necessity, action to repel the alleged attacks by torpedo boats as such fell under the rubric of lawful self-defence. Again, this incident makes clear that the *de minimis* threshold does not per se rule out the exercise of self-defence vis-à-vis hostile encounters between isolated military vessels or aircraft. While these are often not the most widely publicized incidents or the ones that are most lengthily debated within the Security Council, incidents such as these do fall within the purview of Article 51 UN Charter. By way of a final example of this kind, it may be noted that in 1981 the US invoked Article 51 to justify the shooting of two Libyan aircraft in the Gulf of Sidra.[134] According to the US, American aircraft participating in a 'routine' peaceful naval exercise in international waters were subject to an unprovoked attack by Libyan aircraft and had returned fire in self-defence.[135] Libya presented a wholly different account of the facts: it claimed that the naval exercise had taken place in Libyan territorial waters in an attempt to provoke Libya and argued that its aircraft were conducting reconnaissance duties when they were shot down.[136]

---

[131] (1964) UNYB 147–9. See also *infra* Section 4.3.3.b.
[132] UN Doc. S/PV.1140, 5 August 1964, §§ 33–74 (US), 78–81 (UK), 83 (Republic of China).
[133] (1964) UNYB 148; UN Doc. S/PV.1141, 7 August 1964, §§ 24–31 (Czechoslovakia), 76–86 (USSR).
[134] See (1981) UNYB 360–1. For an elaborate account, see S. R. Ratner, 'The Gulf of Sidra incident of 1981: a study of the lawfulness of peacetime aerial engagements', (1984) 10 Y JIL 58–76.
[135] UN Doc. S/14632, 19 August 1981 (US).
[136] UN Doc. S/14636, 20 August 1981 (Libya). See also UN Doc. S/14638/Rev.1, 21 August 1981 (Algeria, on behalf of the Group of Arab States).

In the end, customary practice suggests that, subject to the necessity and proportionality criteria, even small-scale bombings, artillery, naval or aerial attacks qualify as 'armed attacks' activating Article 51 UN Charter, *as long as they result in, or are capable of resulting in destruction of property or loss of lives*. By contrast, the firing of a single missile into some uninhabited wasteland as a mere display of force, in contravention of Article 2(4) UN Charter, would arguably not reach the gravity threshold.

In sum, the following general conclusions can be made: (1) the *travaux* of the Definition of Aggression suggest that a minimal gravity is indeed required and seem to rule out the aforementioned Option 3; (2) 'concrete' customary evidence nonetheless makes clear that the gravity threshold should not be set too high and that even small-scale attacks involving the use of (possibly) lethal force may trigger Article 51.

Between these broad guidelines, a considerable grey area remains. This is especially the case for minor territorial intrusions by infantry units or low-level exchange of fire across national borders, acts that are sometimes labelled as border incidents or skirmishes. Despite all the academic criticism of the Court's reference to 'mere frontier incidents', it has to be conceded that this concept is not a random phantasm of the Hague judges. Indeed, as noted before, the Netherlands in 1956 argued that 'small-scale hostilities connected with border incidents fell outside the scope of [Article 51]'.[137] Likewise, within the Fourth Special Committee, several countries cautioned against the recourse to self-defence in response to 'local disturbances', 'border incidents', or 'minor incidents'.[138] At the same time, customary practice provides no clear guidelines as to the scale and effects required for a 'frontier incident' to qualify as an 'armed attack'. Even if border skirmishes regrettably take place on a regular basis in international relations,[139] these incidents are generally not brought to the attention of the Security Council.[140] Self-defence claims are only rarely brought forward. International reactions,

---

[137] Report of the 1956 Special Committee on the Question of Defining Aggression, 8 October – 9 November 1956, UN Doc. A/3574, 24.
[138] E.g., UN Doc. A/AC.134/SR.52–66, 44 (Turkey), 46 (Bulgaria); UN Doc. A/AC.134/SR.67–78, 118 (Romania), 118 (Cyprus), 145 (USSR), 146 (UK); UN Doc. A/AC.134/SR.79–91, 29 (Mexico).
[139] See, e.g., (1992) 38 *Keesing's* 39165 (border incident between Saudi Arabia and Qatar); (1981) 27 *Keesing's* 31222 (China–Laos); (1984) 30 *Keesing's* 33106 (China–Vietnam); 'Iranian killed in Iran–Afghan border clash', *Radio Free Europe* 23 April 2009.
[140] See, e.g., (1958) UNYB 77–8 (dispute between Tunisia and France); UN Doc. S/2007/69, 8 February 2007 (Israel).

if any are made, will often be confined to calling on States to exercise restraint in their actions.[141] Moreover, a legal evaluation of the incident will frequently be hampered by the difficulty of determining the precise factual circumstances (the different accounts of the States concerned traditionally have a tendency to be diametrically opposed).[142]

This, however, does not mean that such incidents necessarily fall beyond the scope of Article 51 UN Charter. In 1976, for example, China stated that a group of Indian troops had intruded into Tibet.[143] When told to withdraw by the staff of a civilian checkpost, they had opened fire, whereupon the checkpost staff had allegedly fired back in self-defence. In 2000, Pakistan reported to the Security Council that Indian forces had allegedly launched a 'premeditated attack against a small Pakistani post ... on the Pakistani side of the line of control ... It was a company strength attack with mortars and recoilless refile bunker-busting fire. The Indian attack resulted in the death of two Pakistani soldiers while five are still missing.'[144] According to Pakistan's Foreign Minister, '[Pakistani] troops fought gallantly in self-defence and succeeded in repelling the Indian attack.'[145] In February 2007, Israel reported to the Security Council that soldiers operating within Israeli territory had been fired upon by the Lebanese army. According to Israel, returning fire was 'entirely legitimate and in self-defence'.[146] Again, in October 2008, both Cambodia and Thailand invoked Article 51 UN Charter in relation to a gun battle in the disputed border area surrounding the Temple of Preah Vihear.[147]

One of the rare cases of self-defence against a relatively small-scale cross-border attack that was debated at length before the Security Council concerns Israel's intervention in Lebanon in 2006. *In casu*, Hezbollah militants ambushed an Israeli border patrol, capturing two

---

[141] E.g., 'Ban Ki-Moon urges restraint by Ethiopia and Eritrea as tensions rise', *UN News Service* 11 October 2007.
[142] See, e.g., the different accounts provided of the 1960 attack on a Soviet survey ship in the Korean Bay, (1960) 6 *Keesing's* 17229 (USSR–South Korea).
[143] See (1976) 22 *Keesing's* 27548. Remark: India nonetheless claimed that its soldiers were performing routine duties within the Indian side of the border when they were attacked.
[144] UN Doc. S/2000/49, 24 January 2000 (Pakistan).
[145] *Ibid.* (press statement annexed to Pakistan's letter to the UN Secretary-General).
[146] UN Doc. S/2007/69, 8 February 2007 (Israel).
[147] UN Doc. S/2008/653, 15 October 2008 (Cambodia); UN Doc. S/2008/657, 16 October 2008 (Thailand). Shortly following the incident, the two countries agreed to joint border patrols. See 'Thailand–Cambodia agree to joint border patrols', NY Times 16 October 2008.

soldiers and killing three.[148] Simultaneously, Hezbollah launched a diversionary attack, firing Katyusha rockets and mortars at Israeli military positions and border villages, wounding five civilians. Israel responded with artillery fire, air strikes and a naval bombardment, as well as with a ground operation to rescue the captured soldiers. In the following days, the conflict rapidly escalated into an all-out conflict between Israeli forces and Hezbollah fighters. What is important to note is that, even though some States regarded Israel's response as 'aggression', a majority of Security Council members (eleven out of fifteen) and of other States intervening in the Council debates accepted in principle that Israel could exercise its right of self-defence.[149] Admittedly, most condemned Israel's conduct as disproportionate. Still, the fact remains that a majority of States endorsed the view that the relatively small-scale cross-border attack which took place on 12 July 2006 constituted an 'armed attack' in the sense of Article 51 UN Charter. This is all the more remarkable because the attack did not emanate from regular forces, thus casting doubt on the idea that the gravity threshold should necessarily be set much higher for attacks by non-State actors.

In conclusion, small-scale border attacks involving the use of lethal force are not automatically exempt from the notion of 'armed attack' and may sometimes trigger the right of self-defence. Evidently, any defensive response must abide by the standards of necessity and proportionality. The more limited the initial attack, the more the defensive response should be confined to so-called 'on-the-spot-reaction', i.e., action aimed strictly and directly to the repelling of the attack, staying clear of (extensive) cross-border action, and avoiding further escalation of the conflict. The question does remain which small-scale attacks or incidents qualify as 'armed attacks' and which do not. To answer this question, it is not sufficient to merely examine the scale and effects of the attack. Two other factors must be addressed, namely the so-called '*animus aggressionis*' and the repetitive or isolated nature of the attack(s). Especially when uncertainty exists as to the application of the *de minimis* threshold, these factors play an important role to determine whether the use of armed force qualifies as an 'armed attack' *ratione materiae*.

---

[148] For a more elaborate analysis, see *infra* Section 5.2.3.b.
[149] See the verbatim records of the Council debates of 14 and 21 July 2006 (UN Doc. S/PV.5489 and S/PV.5493).

3.2.2 *The 'animus aggressionis' and accumulation of events*

3.2.2.a 'Animus aggressionis'

Even though the concept of 'attack' – as opposed to 'incident' – intuitively seems to presuppose an element of intent, the need for a *'mens rea'* to determine the existence of an armed attack does not go uncontested. Some authors, such as Wilmshurst, accept that the attacker must have the intention to attack in order to trigger the right of self-defence.[150] Others flatly reject the idea that the evaluation of the scale and effects of an armed attack must take account of the *mens rea*, on the grounds that it is impossible to establish the aggressor's precise intention.[151]

The question of the *'animus aggressionis'* first surfaced in the context of the International Law Commission's work on the Definition of Aggression. In 1951, Special Rapporteur Spiropoulos made clear that the mere fact that a State acted first did not, per se, constitute 'aggression' as long as there was no aggressive intention.[152] It followed from the very essence of the notion of aggression as such that this subjective element formed an integral part thereof. Spiropoulos' distinction between an objective and a subjective element was supported by some members of the Commission.[153] Others, however, argued that the act of using force itself revealed the presence of the subjective element. In the words of Alfaro: 'If a town is unexpectedly bombarded or a port is blockaded, there can be no doubt as to the intention accompanying the bombardment or blockade, because force has been used in a manner and for purposes contrary to the present international order.'[154]

In the subsequent debates within the UNGA on the Definition of Aggression, the issue arose again. The Six-Power proposal submitted to the Fourth Committee, for example, linked the concept of 'aggression'

---

[150] Wilmshurst, 'The use of force by States in self-defence', 6.
[151] Constantinou, *The right of self-defence*, p. 62; Feder, 'Reading the U.N. Charter connotatively', 412; J. A. Green, 'Self-defence: a state of mind for States?', (2008) 55 NILR 181–206; Raab, 'Armed attack', 728–9; Zourek, 'La définition de l'agression', 843–4.
[152] Second Report by Mr J. Spiropoulos on the Draft Code of Offences against the peace and security of mankind, 12 April 1951, (1951) YBILC, vol. II, 67–8 (UN Doc. A/CN.4/44).
[153] See: Solera, *Defining the crime of aggression*, pp. 105–7. See also the opinion of G. Scelle in (1951) YBILC, vol. II, 41–2 (UN Doc. A/CN.4/L.19).
[154] See the opinion of R. J. Alfaro in (1951) YBILC, vol. II, 39, § 59 (UN Doc. A/CN.4/L.8): 'On the question of "intention", it cannot be denied, of course, that this is a natural element of aggression. . . . But the point is that the act of using force reveals the intention by itself.'

to a list of five specifically prohibited goals: force had to be used either to (1) diminish the territory or alter the boundaries of another State; (2) alter internationally agreed lines of demarcation; (3) disrupt or interfere with the conduct of the affairs of another State; (4) secure changes in the government of another State; or (5) inflict harm or obtain concessions of any sort.[155] The Soviet proposal, on the other hand, suggested that the State that first used armed force should automatically be regarded as the aggressor (i.e., the principle of priority).[156] Fierce discussions took place as to which principle – priority or intent – should be given preference.[157] Proponents of the former (mainly the USSR as well as various developing countries) maintained that the 'first use' constituted the only objective criterion.[158] It was directly derived from the Charter, and, according to some, rightly proscribed 'preventive' self-defence. The intent criterion would cast an unreasonable burden of proof on the victim and was too susceptible to abuse by aggressors claiming to be acting upon some alleged noble motive. In turn, the Six Powers and several other countries warned *inter alia* that it was fallacious to presume that it would always be easy to determine objectively who was the first to resort to the use force.[159] Furthermore, even if this could be established, an automatic application of the priority principle could lead to manifestly unjust results, for example in cases where force had been used by mistake or by accident.

As the negotiations progressed, States began to recognize that the two criteria were not incompatible.[160] This eventually led to the compromise incorporated in Article 2 of the Definition of Aggression:

---

[155] Article 2(A), UN Doc. A/AC.134/L.17 (and Corr. 1).
[156] Articles 1 and 2 UN Doc. A/AC.134/L.12 (and Corr. 1).
[157] Overviews of the main arguments can be found in: Ferencz, *Defining international aggression*. Vol. II, p. 31; Schwebel, 'Aggression, intervention and self-defence', 468-70; Zourek, 'La définition de l'agression', 843-4.
[158] E.g., UN Doc. A/AC.134/SR.52-66, 36 (France), 46 (Bulgaria), 79 (Iraq), 86 (Mexico), 91 (Cyprus), 136 (UAR); UN Doc. A/AC.134/SR.67-78, 44 (Cyprus); UN Doc. A/AC.134/SR.79-91, 55 (Algeria), 76 (Iraq).
[159] E.g., UN Doc. A/AC.134/SR.52-66, 27 (Canada), 36 (France), 41 (Japan), 132 (Italy), 136 (Ghana); UN Doc. A/AC.134/SR.67-78, 44 (Italy, suggesting that the crossing of a frontier by a police patrol might be considered an intervention or aggression, according to what the purpose had been).
[160] E.g., UN Doc. A/AC.134/SR.52-66, 37 (Norway), 43-4 (Turkey), 79 (Iraq), 114 (Guyana): UN Doc. A/AC.134/SR.79-91, 14 (DRC), 15 (Guyana), 18 (US, noting that the views concerning priority and intent were getting closer and agreeing that priority should be included in any definition of aggression), 27 (Cyprus), 34 (Japan), 36 (USSR), 46 (Czechoslovakia), 48 (France), 50 (UK).

> The first use of armed force ... shall constitute prima facie evidence of an act of aggression although the Security Council may ... conclude that a determination that an act of aggression has been committed would not be justified in the light of other relevant circumstances ...

In light of the preparatory works, a number of comments can *grosso modo* be made in relation to this provision.[161] First, the first use of armed force is indeed considered as a prima facie presumption of aggression. Second, this presumption is rebuttable in light of 'other relevant circumstances'. Such circumstances can consist in a 'lack of sufficient gravity' of the use of force as the last sentence of Article 2 indicates. They can also consist in the lack of an *'animus aggressionis'* or 'aggressive intent'.[162] Third, the concept of 'aggressive intent' does *not* imply an analysis of the *motives* or *purposes* of the State using armed force.[163] The list of intentions originally espoused by the Six Powers was not withheld. Instead, Article 5(1) of the Definition makes clear that 'no consideration of whatever nature, whether political, economic, military or otherwise, may serve as a justification for aggression'. The concept of *'animus aggressionis'* is therefore best construed as requiring the *deliberate* use of armed force against another State or its external manifestations, or, in other words, a *hostile intent*.[164] The same picture emerges from examining the examples put forward throughout the Committee negotiations. Most of these concerned cases where armed force was used by accident or by mistake. Canada referred to the situation where, as a result of an emergency aboard an aircraft, bombs had to be jettisoned over the sea, incidentally damaging a ship on the high seas or an oil installation in a State's territorial waters.[165] States generally agreed that these situations would not fall under the rubric of 'aggression'.[166] Reference was also

---

[161] See especially UN Doc. A/AC.134/SR.67–78, 21–2 (US), 29–31 (USSR), 35–7 (France), 37–9 (Italy).

[162] E.g., Broms, 'The definition of aggression', 364. As Broms explains, it was the intention of the drafters that the phrase 'other relevant circumstances' should include considerations of intent. This was a *quid pro quo* for the inclusion of the principle of priority in Article 2.

[163] E.g., UN Doc. A/AC.134/SR.67–78, 22 (US), 29 (USSR). Also: Report of the UN Secretary-General, 3 October 1952, UN Doc. A/2211, §§ 361–2.

[164] See, e.g., UN Doc. A/AC.134/SR.79–91, 36 (USSR: 'his delegation doubted whether there was any need to refer to motives in a definition of aggression. Aggressive intent would suffice.'), 48 (France: '[I]t would be sufficient ... to speak of deliberate aggression").

[165] UN Doc. A/AC.134/SR.67–78, 20.

[166] UN Doc. A/AC.134/SR.52–66, 27 (Canada), 36 (France), 41 (Japan); UN Doc. A/AC.134/SR.67–78, 20 (Canada: 'Most members of the Committee seemed to agree that an act committed by accident could not constitute aggression').

made to the use of armed force in the context of the hot pursuit of criminals. The United States, suggested that it would be extending the concept too far to regard as an act of aggression shots aimed at a fugitive which struck one or more inhabitants of another country.[167] Likewise, the UK observed that the pursuit of a criminal across a frontier might well be unlawful under international law but would not be aggression.[168] Fourth and last, as can be inferred from the aforementioned examples, the concept of *'animus aggressionis'* is most relevant when dealing with small-scale uses of force, in particular 'border incidents' and the like.[169] When dealing with more large-scale military engagements, such as aerial bombardments, naval blockades or substantial cross-border attacks, it is generally inherent in the act itself.[170] Thus, Cyprus noted that '[a]cts such as invasion and air and naval bombardment of sovereign territory were clearly acts of aggression in which an element of intention was to be assumed until the contrary was proved.'[171] In sum, for more substantive uses of force, the *'animus aggressionis'* can be presumed unless there are clear indications to the contrary.

To what extent can these findings be transplanted to the exercise of self-defence? As mentioned earlier, the ICJ in its appraisal of the facts in *Nicaragua* shed little light on the precise distinction between 'armed attacks' and 'less grave uses of force'. Examining the US' allegations that certain transborder incursions into Honduras and Costa Rica were imputable to Nicaragua,[172] the Court confined itself to the following general observation:

> Very little information is . . . available to the Court as to the *circumstances of these incursions or their possible motivations*, which renders it difficult to decide whether they may be treated for legal purposes as amounting,

---

[167] UN Doc. A/AC.134/SR.67–78, 23.
[168] *Ibid.*, 146. In a similar vein: *ibid.*, 118 (Romania).
[169] E.g., UN Doc. A/AC.134/SR.67–78, 22 (US).
[170] Cf. according to Turkey: '[A]ggression was an illegal act of such gravity that the intention must be presumed. The problem arose in connection with other illegal acts, which, when considered singly, did not constitute aggression, but which, when they were repeated and took on a certain magnitude, became a breach of the peace. It was in respect of such acts that recourse might be had to the notion of aggressive intent. A distinction ought to be made between acts of aggression according to their gravity (. . .)'. UN Doc. A/AC.134/SR.52–66, 44. See also UN Doc. A/AC.134/SR.79–91, 61 (Turkey).
[171] UN Doc. A/AC.134/SR.79–91, 27. See also UN Doc. A/AC.134/SR.52–66, 134 (USSR).
[172] ICJ, *Nicaragua* case (Merits), § 230.

singly or collectively, to an 'armed attack' by Nicaragua on either or both States.[173]

The Court left open the question whether armed attacks had taken place, instead turning to other considerations which indicated that these incursions could not be relied upon as justifying the exercise of self-defence (e.g., the lack of a request by the victim States and the absence of a report to the Security Council).[174] In spite of its brevity, the aforementioned quote carries important implications. First of all, the word 'singly' implicitly leaves open the possibility that a single territorial incursion can qualify as an 'armed attack'. The word 'collectively' furthermore seems to hint at a positive appraisal of the 'accumulation of events' theory, an issue which is addressed in the following section. Third, and most important in the present context, the Court's reference to 'circumstances' and to the controversial (and perhaps ill-chosen) concept of 'possible motivations' suggests that the *'animus aggressionis'* is considered relevant. According to Gray, what the Court seems to say is that episodes where there is no intent to carry out an armed attack, including accidental incursions and incidents where officials disobey orders, would be considered as 'frontier incidents', rather than 'armed attacks'.[175]

In the *Oil Platforms* case, the ICJ again touched upon the issue of aggressive intent when dealing with the attack against the *Sea Isle City*. On 16 October 1987, the latter vessel was hit by a Silkworm missile, causing damage to the ship and injury to six crew members.[176] After dealing extensively with the evidence submitted by both parties, the Court decided that the burden of proof of the existence of an armed attack by Iran on the US had not been discharged.[177] Even in the hypothesis that the attack could have been attributed to Iran, the Court observed that the *Sea Isle City* was in Kuwaiti waters at the time of the attack on it, and that a Silkworm missile allegedly fired from more than 100 km away could not have been aimed at the specific vessel, but simply programmed to hit some target in Kuwaiti waters.[178] In a similar vein, it argued that even if US allegations concerning Iranian mine-laying had been adequately proven (*quod non*), '[t]here is no evidence that the minelaying ... was aimed specifically at the US; and similarly it has not been established that the mine struck by the *Bridgeton* was laid with the specific intention of harming that ship, or other US vessels'.[179] These

---

[173] *Ibid.*, § 231 (emphasis added).   [174] *Ibid.*, §§ 232–8.
[175] Gray, *The use of force*, p. 179.   [176] ICJ, *Oil Platforms* case, §§ 52 et seq.
[177] *Ibid.*, § 61.   [178] *Ibid.*, § 64.   [179] *Ibid.*

dicta appear to be inspired by earlier suggestions by Iran regarding the need for attacks to be somehow 'specifically targeted'.[180] This argument had nonetheless been heavily criticized by the United States. According to the US, it would give carte blanche to States launching missiles from remote locations and subsequently denying repsonsibility. It would also be akin to arguing that an artillery barrage against a city would not constitute an armed attack because it was not aimed at any specific identifiable target.[181] The US's objections are not without foundation. It would indeed be a desecration of existing law to suggest that *indiscriminate* attacks could not trigger the right of self-defence. This would not only lead to manifestly absurd results, but might even encourage States to carry out such attacks. In light of these concerns, it seems more appropriate to construe the Court's somewhat obscure statement as requiring a general intention to attack another State, rather than to attack a specific target.[182] With this reservation in mind, the *Oil Platforms* case appears to render support to the idea that the subjective element is relevant for determining the existence of an armed attack, even for more large-scale attacks.

The relevance of the subjective element is difficult to falsify on the basis of concrete instances of inter-State recourse to force. As mentioned before, small-scale cross-border incidents – i.e., those situations where intent would appear to matter most – have seldom generated public self-defence claims, let alone substantial international reactions. In relation to more large-scale attacks, on the other hand, the element of intent has rarely been brought up, as it has been assumed to be implicit in the act itself. Still, there are some clues that render support to the importance of the '*animus aggressionis*'. In numerous cases, States claiming to be the

---

[180] ICJ, *Oil Platforms* case, Reply and defence to counter-claim submitted by the Islamic Republic of Iran, 10 March 1999, § 7.36.

[181] ICJ, *Oil Platforms* case, Rejoinder submitted by the United States of America, 23 March 2001, § 5.23: 'Applied to a domestic legal setting, it is akin to allowing a criminal to shoot into a crowd, killing and injuring individuals, but elude responsibility because he did not intend to hit a particular victim. ... As a matter of principle, the law does not, and could not, countenance a principle by which indiscriminate attacks were immunized while targeted attacks were the subject of responsibility.'

[182] See, e.g., Dinstein, *War, aggression and self-defence*, p. 209; N. Ochoa-Ruiz and E. Salamanca-Aguado, 'Exploring the limits of international law relating to the use of force in self-defence', (2005) 16 EJIL 499–524, at 514; N. Ronzitti, 'The expanding law of self-defence', (2006) 11 JCSL 343–59, at 350; Taft, 'The *Oil Platforms* decision', 302–3; Wilmshurst, 'The use of force by States in self-defence', 6.

victim of an armed attack in the sense of Article 51 UN Charter have emphasized the 'deliberate' or 'coordinated' nature of the attack(s). In relation to the Gulf of Tunkin incident, for instance, the United States stated that after the (alleged) attack by torpedo boats against a US destroyer, it 'had hoped that the incident was an isolated or uncalculated action'. However, when a new attack took place two days later, 'there could no longer be any shadow of doubt that a planned, deliberate military attack had occurred', leading the US to exercise its right of self-defence.[183] The 'premeditated', 'offensive' or 'deliberate' character of alleged attacks was emphasized on numerous other occasions, including the 1964 Harib Fort raid,[184] the 1967 Six Day War,[185] the 1968 Israeli campaign against Lebanon,[186] border clashes between India and China in 1976[187] or a 1993 Israeli aerial raid in Syrian territory.[188] Furthermore, it is worth noting that while several States branded the intrusion of Soviet airspace by a US military reconnaissance plane in May 1960 (the U-2 incident) as a violation of Article 2(4) UN Charter, others argued that it did not constitute aggression due to a lack of aggressive intent.[189] Explaining why it had shot down the plane, the Soviet Union observed that 'at a time when there can be no guarantee that US aircraft appearing over the territory of the USSR are not carrying a lethal cargo', it might 'find itself faced with the need to take action to repel aggression'.[190] During the *Oil Platforms* case, the US moreover stressed that the alleged attacks by Iran 'were not isolated border incursions by a few soldiers following a confused or rash junior officer, or other matters of limited

---

[183] (1964) UNYB 147. See also UN Doc. S/6174, 7 February 1965 (US).
[184] UN Doc. S/PV.1107, at 2, 3 April 1964, § 3 (UK).
[185] (1967) UNYB 175 (the UAR spoke of 'a treacherous, premeditated aggression' by Israel; Israel accused Egypt of having moved in an 'offensive thrust' against Israel's borders).
[186] (1968) UNYB 191.   [187] (1976) 22 *Keesing's* 27548.
[188] UN Doc. S/PV.4836, 5 October 2003, 17 (Morocco).
[189] See UN Department of Political and Security Council Affairs, *Repertoire of the Practice of the Security Council 1959-1963* (New York, 1965), 281-2; (1960) UNYB 40-1. The USSR, Poland, Argentina, Ceylon, Ecuador and Tunisia regarded the intrusion as a violation of the Charter. The US, UK, France, Italy and the (then) Republic of China objected that the overflight of the U-2 plane did not constitute aggression, because it was carried out for the purpose of reconnaissance against a surprise attack. In the end, no formal condemnation was adopted by the Council, in part because the United States had promised that all such overflights would stop.
[190] UN Doc. S/4315, 19 May 1960 (USSR), 3. This warning again materialized only two months later when the USSR shot down another US RB-48 reconnaissance bomber. UN Doc. S/4385, 13 July 1960 (USSR). See also: (1960) UNYB 41-2.

consequence', but 'deliberate, dangerous military actions that were part of a broad pattern of unlawful use of force by Iran'.[191]

Despite the problematic evidentiary value of omissions in terms of State practice and *opinio iuris*, it is also submitted that several cases can be identified where the use of force against another State was not branded as an 'armed attack' and where no defensive action was undertaken, (in part) due to a lack of hostile intent. This is true both for small-scale uses of force as well as incidents of more substantial gravity. As for the former, one could refer, for example, to the shooting incident which took place in the Suez Canal in March 2008, when a container ship contracted by the US Navy fired warning shots at a number of small boats approaching it, killing an Egyptian cigarette vendor.[192] Following the incident, the US President offered apologies and pledged that the US would cooperate in the investigation of the incident. Despite the strong public outcry in Egypt, nothing indicated that Egyptian officials regarded the incident as an 'armed attack'. As for the latter category, an illustration is provided by the destruction during NATO's Operation 'Allied Force' of the Chinese embassy in Belgrade on 7 May 1999, killing four Chinese nationals and injuring twenty others.[193] NATO immediately issued an apology to China, stressing that the attack – carried out by US stealth bombers – had resulted from an error in the intelligence process. The United States similarly apologised for the incident and declared that 'faulty information had led to a mistake in the initial targeting of this facility'.[194] In China, the attack was greeted with violent mass protests against the UK and US embassies in Beijing. Chinese authorities called on NATO to publish the details of its investigation into the bombing, and to punish those responsible for the mistake. Several elements of China's diplomatic relations with the US were moreover suspended. At no point, however, was there any suggestion that China regarded the incident as an 'armed attack', or that it considered a defensive (or retaliatory) response.

---

[191] ICJ, *Oil Platforms* case, Counter-memorial and counter-claim submitted by the United States of America, 23 June 1997, § 4.11.
[192] E.g., 'US examines Suez Canal shooting', *BBC News*, 25 March 2008; 'Navy says Egyptian dies in Suez clash', *NY Times* 27 March 2008; 'Bush gives apology for Suez shooting', *NY Times* 28 March 2008.
[193] See, e.g., (1999) 45 *Keesing's* 42955.
[194] The US later admitted that the targeting error had resulted from the use of an outdated map. The pilots reportedly believed they had bombed the Yugoslav Federal Directorate of Supply and Procurement, *ibid*.

Finally, despite their generally confidential nature, it is well-known that the concept of 'hostile intent' plays a crucial rule in national Rules of Engagement.[195] The latter documents *inter alia* provide concrete guidelines to a State's military forces, coastguard and border patrols as to *when* and *how* to respond to small-scale territorial incursions and localized encounters between military units. With regard to confrontations between military vessels or aircraft, for example, there are numerous elements, apart from the general geopolitical and security context, that give an indication of the opponent's hostile intent: e.g., the 'locking on' of fire control radars, the opening of bomb bay doors, the acoustic detection of torpedo or missile tube doors, the distance and speed of the opposing unit, the opposing unit's manoeuvring into a weapon launch profile, et cetera.[196] When uncertainty exists as to the opponent's intent, ROE's generally prescribe a number of measures that essentially aim at de-escalating the situation or at forcing the other side to betray its hostile intention in accordance with the so-called theory of graduated force.[197] Such steps may involve verbal warnings, special manoeuvres (for instance a fighter plane wiggling its wings in an international signal to move off), flares, warning shots, et cetera.[198] The role of the *'animus aggressionis'* in localized hostile encounters is explored in greater detail in Section 3.3.

In the end, the Definition of Aggression, the case law of the ICJ and customary practice provide credible indications that hostile intent is a relevant factor for determining whether an 'armed attack' has occurred.[199] The *'animus aggressionis'* is particularly important for

---

[195] E.g., US Department of the Navy and US Department of Homeland Security, *The Commander's Handbook of the Law of Naval Operations*, July 2007, NWP 1-14M, available at www.nwc.navy.mil/cnws/ild/documents/1-14m_(jul_2007)_(nwp).pdf (accessed 4 May 2009), 4-5, 4-6. See also on the 2005 US Standing Rules of Engagement/Standing Rules for the Use of Force (ROE/RUF): S. P. Henseler, 'Self-defense in the maritime environment under the new standing rules of engagement/standing rules for the use of force (SROE/SRUF)', (2006) 53 Naval L Rev 211-28. Also Fleck, 'Rules of engagement of maritime forces', 181-2.

[196] See, e.g., D. Stephens, 'Rules of engagement and the concept of unit self-defense', (1998) 45 Naval L Rev 126-51, at 148.

[197] E.g., D. P. O'Connell, *The influence of law on sea power* (Manchester University Press, 1975), pp. 53 *et seq*.

[198] See, e.g., Henseler, 'Self-defense in the maritime environment', 217-18; Ratner, 'The Gulf of Sidra incident', 69.

[199] Remark: some authors incorporate the subjective element in their conception of the 'necessity' criterion, in the sense that their would be no 'need' to repel an armed attack if the attack resulted from error or accident (e.g., Dinstein, *War, aggression and self-defence*, p. 209). While the practical outcome would arguably be little different, legal

qualifying small-scale uses of force.[200] Thus, the premeditated and well-organized nature of Hezbollah's attack against an Israeli border patrol in July 2006 – illustrated by the simultaneous launch of diversionary rocket attacks against Israeli military posts and border villages as well as the ongoing kidnapping of two Israeli soldiers[201] – helps to explain why, despite the relatively small scale,[202] it was generally considered to constitute an 'armed attack' triggering the right of self-defence.[203] When dealing with larger scale uses of armed force, the subjective element will generally be implicit in the act itself. Nonetheless, if clear indications point to the contrary, then again there is no 'armed attack' in the sense of Article 51 UN Charter. Some situations are relatively straightforward.[204] In a case of massive invasion, aggressive intent can evidently be deduced from the force and eloquence of the ascertained facts. Conversely, when an unarmed missile launched from the territory of State A lands on the territory of a befriended neighbour, there is no armed attack. When dealing with more complex cases, it is important not only to differentiate on the basis of scale and effects, but to take account of the broader context as well.[205] Are relations between the States concerned friendly overall, or is there a hostile environment? Has the State offered an

doctrine and State practice suggest that the subjective element is an integral element of the 'armed attack' criterion, rather than a modality related to the exercise of self-defence. In a similar vein, the ICJ's references to the subjective element were made in the course of its analysis of the 'armed attack' requirement, rather than in its discussion of the necessity criterion. In other words, it would seem more suitable to argue, for instance, that the accidental destruction of the Chinese embassy in Belgrade did not constitute an armed attack in the sense of Article 51 UN Charter, than to suggest that it was an armed attack against which no defensive action was 'necessary'.

[200] E.g., Wilmshurst, 'The use of force by States in self-defence', 6. Also: Brownlie, 'The use of force in self-defence', 258; I. Brownlie, *International law and the use of force by States* (Oxford: Clarendon Press, 1963), p. 366.

[201] After the Israeli intervention, Hezbollah leader Nasrallah publicly apologized on Lebanese television, saying that he 'would not have ordered the operation' if he had known it would lead to a month-long war with Israel. See P. Kruger, 'Nasrallah apologizes for capture of Israeli soldiers', *World Today* 28 August 2006.

[202] Cf. some States used the phrase '(border) incident' to describe the initial events. UN Doc. S/PV.5489, 14 July 2006, 4 (Lebanon), 7 (Russia), 11 (Qatar), 12 (Japan); UN Doc. S/PV.5493 (resumption 1), 21 July 2006, 21 (Algeria), 31 (Iran).

[203] See T. Ruys, 'Crossing the Thin Blue Line: an inquiry into Israel's recourse to self-defense against Hezbollah', (2007) 43 Stanford JIL 265–94, at 268–73. See also: UN Doc. S/PV.5489, 14 July 2006, 10 (US), 14 (Peru), 15 (Denmark); UN Doc. S/PV.5493 (Resumption 1), 21 July 2006, 6 (UK), 45 (Mexico).

[204] Schwebel, 'Aggression, intervention and self-defence', 470.

[205] Consider the following passage from the 1926 de Brouckère Report: 'Every act of violence does not necessarily justify its victim in resorting to war. If a detachment of soldiers goes a few yards over the frontier in a colony remote from any vital centre; if the

apology and/or reparation for its actions? Has it punished those responsible for the incident? Another indicator concerns the question whether the use of force constitutes an isolated event, or whether it forms part of a broader series of similar uses of armed force. This brings us to the so-called 'accumulation of events' theory.

3.2.2.b 'Accumulation of events'

The 'accumulation of events'– or *Nadelstichtaktik* (needle prick) – theory holds that several minor attacks/incidents may be 'accumulated' for the purposes of assessing self-defence claims. It deals with situations where consecutive attacks take place that are linked in time, source and cause, in particular when those attacks are part of a 'continuous, overall plan of attack purposely relying on numerous small raids'.[206] 'Accumulation of events' is important mainly from a twofold perspective. First of all, it suggests that the proportionality analysis of a particular defensive action should not focus strictly on its immediate cause, but also entails a retrospective element (cf. *supra*). In other words, a larger scale response is permitted to a continuous series of attacks of a certain gravity, than to an isolated armed attack of similar gravity. A second aspect concerns the *de minimis* threshold. In this context, it is argued that incidents that would in themselves merely constitute 'less grave uses of force', can, when forming part of a chain of events, qualitatively transform into an 'armed attack' triggering the right of self-defence. Since we have previously argued that the gravity threshold should be set relatively low, the importance of this aspect should not be overestimated.[207] This, however, is not to say that it becomes entirely insignificant. Some authors also fit into this theory a third aspect, namely the prospective element of the necessity and proportionality analysis – more specifically the idea that defensive action may be undertaken after the armed attack is factually over on condition that there exists a strong likelihood that more attacks

circumstances show quite clearly that the aggression was due to an error on the part of some subaltern officer; if the central authorities of the 'aggressor State' reprimand the subordinate concerned as soon as they are apprised of the facts; if they cause the invasion to cease, offer apologies and compensation and take steps to prevent any recurrence of such incidents – then it cannot be maintained that there has been an act of war and that the invaded country has reasonable grounds for mobilizing its army and marching upon the enemy capital.' Quoted in Report of the UN Secretary-General, 3 October 1952, UN Doc. A/2211, § 301.

[206] Formula used by Levenfeld, 'Israel's counter-*fedayeen* tactics', 41.
[207] Gazzini, for example, considers this aspect of 'accumulation' unnecessary. It should be noted, however, that he rejects the existence of any gravity threshold. See Gazzini, *The changing rules*, p. 144.

will imminently follow.[208] The present section, however, focuses on the two former dimensions.

While the doctrine does not go uncontested, 'accumulation of events' enjoys considerable support in legal doctrine, especially in relation to attacks by irregulars and armed bands.[209] The latter groups will virtually always rely on hit-and-run tactics. Hence, if each incident should be considered separately, a cross-border defensive response would in principle be excluded, thus in fact allowing irregular groups to operate with impunity and leaving the victim State without effective protection.[210] At the same time, several authors have cautioned that many occasions where States – first Israel, then others, such as Portugal, the US and South Africa – invoked the doctrine, the Security Council has apparently rejected this.[211] Against this, it is argued that while many of these self-defence claims were indeed formally rejected by the Security Council, a closer look at the debates reveals that States did not reject the application of the 'accumulation of events' theory as such.[212] Rather, their attitude appears to have been inspired by the specific circumstances of the cases at hand. In many of the aforementioned cases, military actions were grossly disproportionate – several of them resulted in large numbers of civilian deaths – and/or punitive in nature. Furthermore, international reactions

---

[208] *Ibid.*, pp. 143–4; Y. Z. Blum, 'State response to acts of terrorism', (1976) 19 GYBIL 223–37, at 233. For a discussion of the prospective element, see Section 2.2.2.b.

[209] E.g., Ago, 'Addendum', 69–70; Blum, 'State response', 233–5; D. W. Bowett, 'Reprisals involving recourse to armed force', (1972) 66 AJIL 1–36, at 9; Brownlie, 'The use of force in self-defence', 245; Constantinou, *The right of self-defence*, p. 64; Dinstein, *War, aggression and self-defence*, pp. 202, 230–1 ('A persuasive argument can be made that, should a distinctive pattern of behaviour emerge, a series of pin-prick assaults might be weighed in its totality and count as an armed attack.'); Feder, 'Reading the U.N. Charter connotatively', 395–432; Gazzini, *The changing rules*, pp. 143–4; R. Higgins, *The development of international law through the political organs of the United Nations* (Oxford University Press, 1963), pp. 201–2; Stahn, 'Terrorist acts as 'armed attack', 46.

[210] Remark: on this view, the victim State would arguably only be able to respond by means of military or police action within the boundaries of its own territory, subject to the rules of international human rights law and/or, when applicable, international humanitarian law.

[211] See, e.g., Bowett, 'Reprisals', 7–8; Feder, 'Reading the U.N. Charter connotatively', 417, 431; Levenfeld, 'Israel's counter-*fedayeen* tactics', 40; F. M. Higginbotham, 'International law, the use of force in self-defense, and the Southern African Conflict', (1987) 25 Columbia JTL 529–92, at 558–9. See also: A. Sicilianos, *Les réactions dé centralisées à l'illicite: des contre-mesures à la légitime défense* (Paris: Librairie générale de droit et de jurisprudence, 1990), 327–9.

[212] See, e.g., T. Gazzini, 'The rules on the use of force at the beginning of the XXI century', (2006) 11 JCSL 319–42, at 331; Gray, *The use of force*, p. 155.

were often strongly influenced by politically laden considerations, such as support for the struggle of national liberation movements, disapproval of apartheid regimes or Cold War divisions, thus making it difficult to identify the applicable legal parameters.

With regard to the 1956 Suez crisis, for example, Israel justified its intervention in Egypt as a necessary exercise of its right to self-defence, aimed at eliminating *fedayeen* bases from which continuous cross-border attacks had been carried out.[213] A large majority of States condemned Israel's military response.[214] However, one should not lose sight of the fact that several States did express some degree of sympathy for Israel's position – France for example observed that *in the face of the recurrence of serious incidents* it was inevitable that Israel should at some given moment feel compelled to react[215] – nor of the fact that Israel had engaged in a massive ground operation and had occupied the whole Sinaï Peninsula.[216] Even 'accumulating' the various *fedayeen* attacks, it is difficult to see how an operation of this size could pass the proportionality threshold. The international reaction therefore does not exclude the possibility that a more limited intervention directed specifically against individual *fedayeen* bases would have been justified.[217]

Similarly, several cases, which according to Bowett illustrate that the Security Council has rejected the 'accumulation of events',[218] are altogether fairly unequivocal examples of punitive and disproportionate expeditions.[219] The 1955 Lake Tiberias incident may serve as an

---

[213] See UN Doc. S/PV.749, 30 October 1956, §§ 33–93 (Israel). According to Israel, in the preceding ten months, *fedayeen* attacks had killed twenty-eight Israelis and wounded 127.

[214] A draft resolution in which Israel was called upon to withdraw immediately received seven votes in favour, two against, with two abstentions, but was not adopted due to the two vetoes cast by the UK and France. (1956) UNYB 26.

[215] UN Doc. S/PV.749, 30 October 1956, §§ 154–73 (France). Also *ibid.*, §§ 132–3 (Republic of China), 179 (Belgium); UN Doc. S/PV.748, 30 October 1956, § 37 (Australia).

[216] See, e.g., UN Doc. S/PV.748, 30 October 1956, § 5 (US); UN Doc. S/PV.749, 30 October 1956, § 33 (Israel).

[217] Higgins, *The development of international law*, p. 202.   [218] See Bowett, 'Reprisals', 7–8.

[219] For instance, as mentioned above, the UK in 1964 justified its raid against Harib Fort as a defensive reaction to a series of Yemeni incursions (by land and air), the latest of which has resulted in the burning of several tents and the killing two camels (the UK did not claim that any of these attacks had actually resulted in loss of life) (see UN Doc. S/PV.1106, 2 April 1964, §§ 39–48; UN Doc. S/PV.1107, 3 April 1964, §§ 3–4). While some States drew attention to the 'culmination of incidents' that had preceded the intervention (UN Doc. S/PV.1111, 9 April 1964, § 5 (US), § 11 (Republic of China)), it is again hard to see how this series of incursions could warrant a planned raid that destroyed a military fort (or police precinct?) and reportedly resulted in twenty-five casualties and many more wounded (UN Doc. S/PV.1106, 2 April 1964, § 15 (Yemen)).

THE 'ARMED ATTACK' REQUIREMENT *RATIONE MATERIAE* 171

example.[220] *In casu*, Israel complained of a 'policy of harassment' of Israeli boats by Syrian artillery posts close to the Lake border. It responded by a pre-planned attack which reportedly left thirty-seven Syrian soldiers and twelve civilians dead. The Council eventually adopted a resolution which, after 'noting' that there had been complaints of 'Syrian interference with Israeli activities on the Lake', 'condemned' the attack.[221]

In several other cases where States claimed to respond to 'continuous provocations' and 'series of incursions', Security Council debates focused virtually exclusively on issues of colonialism and self-determination, without paying much attention to the contours of self-defence.[222] Thus, the condemnation of the Portuguese attack on the Senegalese village of Samine in 1969 was by and large inspired by Portugal's 'aggressive colonial policies' as opposed to Senegal's 'peace-loving' attitude.[223] Similar observations can *mutatis mutandis* be made in relation to other cases, such as the Israeli interventions in Lebanon in 1972,[224] or South African incursions in Angola in 1985.[225]

In all, it is difficult to ignore the many occasions where States invoked the 'accumulation of events' theory in support of their self-defence claims – apart from the aforementioned examples, one might refer to the 1964 Gulf of Tunkin incident,[226] Israel's raid against the PLO headquarters in Tunis (Tunisia) in 1985,[227] US airstrikes against Libya in 1986 in reaction to alleged Libyan involvement in terrorist attacks,[228] or

---

[220] See (1955) UNYB 34–5; (1956) UNYB 3–4.   [221] SC Res. 111 of 19 January 1956.
[222] Remark: Bowett himself admits that the negative attitude among third States towards Israeli incursions was heavily influenced by Israel's military occupation of Arab lands. Bowett, 'Reprisals', 18–9, 23. Also: Dinstein, *War, aggression and self-defence*, pp. 230–1.
[223] See (1969) UNYB 137–40; UN Doc. S/PV.1516–20, 4–9 December 1969; UN Doc. S/PV.1516, §§ 61–6; UN Doc. S/PV.1516, § 73 (Algeria); UN Doc. S/PV.1517, §§ 63–4 (Hungary); S/PV.1518, § 58 (UAR), §§ 105 *et seq.* (USSR); UN Doc. S/PV.1519, §§ 14–15, 17 (Pakistan), 36 (Finland); UN Doc. S/PV.1520, §§ 32–3 (Republic of China). See: SC Res. 273 (1969) of 9 December 1969.
[224] (1972) UNYB 158–71, at 158, 161 (Israel), 163 (France).   [225] (1985) UNYB 180–93.
[226] (1964) UNYB 147.
[227] (1985) UNYB 285–91; UN Doc. S/PV.2610–13, S/PV.2615, 2–4 October 1985. In particular UN Doc. S/PV.2611, §§ 60 *et seq.*
[228] On 14 April 1968, US air forces carried out air strikes against several targets in Libya in a large-scale operation involving over forty aircraft. The US claimed that its action had been undertaken in self-defence in response to 'an ongoing pattern' of attacks by Libya targeting US citizens and installations, most recently the bombing of a Berlin discotheque, killing one US soldier and injuring numerous others. A large majority of States condemned the US actions. Most found that the US had not provided persuasive

to border incidents between China and Vietnam in 1979.[229] States have very rarely argued directly against this line of reasoning.[230] Quite the contrary, several States have expressed support for a more contextual, 'cumulative' approach.[231] In more recent years, the invocation of the doctrine has become rather mainstream. Apart from Israel, which continues to invoke it on a regular basis,[232] different versions of the doctrine have been (explicitly or implicitly) invoked *inter alia* by Russia (in response to 'bandit sorties' from Georgia),[233] Lebanon (in response to Israeli violations of Lebanese airspace),[234] Iran (in response to cross-border attacks by the Mojahedin-e-Khalq Organization from Iraq),[235] Iraq (in response to aerial incursions by the UK and the US),[236] Liberia (against cross-border attacks from Guinea),[237] and Sudan (against Chad).[238]

evidence that Libya was behind the Berlin bombing. Even States inclined to accept that Libya was systematically targeting US overseas personnel considered the air strikes disproportionate to that threat. See (1986) UNYB 252–8; Franck, *Recourse to force*, pp. 89–91. A Security Council resolution condemning the US action obtained nine affirmative votes, but was vetoed by France, the UK and the US. On 20 November 1986, the General Assembly did, however, adopt a formal condemnation (GA Res. 41/38).

[229] See UN Doc. S/13094, 19 February 1979 (PRC).
[230] E.g., UN Doc. S/PV.1648, 23 June 1972, § 121 (Sudan, re Israel's intervention into Lebanon). Implicitly, UN Doc. S/PV.2374, 5 June 1982, 3 (UK, Ireland).
[231] See, e.g., UN Doc. S/PV.748, 30 October 1956, § 37 (Australia); UN Doc. S/PV.749, 30 October 1956, §§ 154–73 (France), §§ 132–3 (Republic of China, re the 1956 Suez crisis); UN Doc. S/PV.1111, 9 April 1964, § 5 (US), § 11 (Republic of China, re the Harib Fort incident); (1964) UNYB 148 (UK re the Gulf of Tunkin incident); UN Doc. S/PV.2615, 4 October 1985, § 252 (US, abstaining in the vote on a resolution condemning Israel for its raid against the PLO headquarters in Tunis: '[W]e recognize and strongly support the principle that a State subjected to continuing terrorist attacks may respond with appropriate use of force to defend itself against further attacks. This is an aspect of the inherent right of self-defence recognized in the Charter . . .'); (1968) UNYB 206 (US: 'The [US] did not condone the major military attack of 4 August by Israel against Jordan, but neither did it condone the terrorism and sabotage which had been launched with increasing frequency from Jordan in the past weeks. Those acts should not be judged as isolated events; they were a concerted effort that could not but have a cumulative impact').
[232] E.g. UN Doc. S/2003/976, 9 October 2003 (Israel).
[233] E.g., UN Doc. S/2002/1012, 11 September 2002 (Russia).
[234] E.g., UN Doc. S/2003/148, 4 February 2003 (Lebanon).
[235] E.g., Letters from the Islamic Republic of Iran: UN Doc. S/2000/216, 13 March 2000; UN Doc. S/2001/271, 22 March 2001; UN Doc. S/2001/381, 18 April 2001.
[236] E.g., UN Doc. S/2001/370, 13 April 2001 (Iraq).
[237] E.g., Letters from Liberia: UN Doc. S/2001/474, 11 May 2001; UN Doc. S/2001/562, 4 June 2001; UN Doc. S/2001/851, 6 September 2001; UN Doc. S/2002/310, 26 March 2002.
[238] E.g., Letters from the Sudan: UN Doc. S/2008/20, 9 January 2008; UN Doc. S/2007/774, 28 December 2007.

Furthermore, the ICJ seems to have implicitly endorsed the doctrine to some extent. In *Nicaragua*, the Court observed that the lack of information in relation to alleged cross-border attacks against Honduras and Costa Rica made it difficult to decide whether they could 'singly *or collectively*' amount to an 'armed attack'.[239] In the *Oil Platforms* case, the Court implicitly followed the US argument that the various alleged attacks should be considered together.[240] In relation to the US raids of 19 October 1987, the Court stated that '[o]n the hypothesis that all the incidents complained of are to be attributed to Iran ... the question is whether that attack, either in itself or in combination with the rest of the "series of ... attacks" cited by the US can be categorized as an "armed attack" on the US justifying self-defence'.[241] It was concluded, however, that '[e]ven taken cumulatively', these incidents did not seem to constitute an armed attack on the US.[242] Finally, the 'accumulation of events' was incidentally brought up in *DRC v. Uganda*.[243] *In casu*, Uganda tried to defend its invasion and occupation of large parts of Congolese

---

[239] ICJ, *Nicaragua* case (Merits), § 231 (emphasis added).

[240] See ICJ, *Oil Platforms* case, Counter-memorial submitted by the United States of America, 23 June 1997, §§ 4.10–4.11, 4.33; ICJ, *Oil Platforms* case, Rejoinder submitted by the United States of America, 23 March 2001, §§ 5.08, 5.22. Contra: ICJ, *Oil Platforms* case, Reply and defence to counter-claim, Islamic Republic of Iran, §§ 7.19–7.27.

[241] ICJ, *Oil Platforms* case, § 64.

[242] *Ibid*. Remark: in relation to the US raid of 18 April 1988, the Court *a contrario* observed that "[n]o attacks on US-flagged vessels ... have been brought to the Court's attention, other than the mining of the USS *Samuel B. Roberts* itself. The question is therefore whether that incident sufficed in itself to justify action in self-defence, as amounting to an "armed attack"' (§ 72).

[243] Remark: Gray notes that in this case the issue was framed in terms of establishing State responsibility for violations of the prohibition on the use of force, instead of being discussed in a self-defence context. Thus, Cameroon argued that cross-border attacks by Nigeria attested to a 'persistent' use of force against the territorial integrity of Cameroon (see ICJ, *Cameroon v. Nigeria*, Mémoire de la République de Cameroun, 16 March 1995, §§ 6.120 *et seq*.). Nigeria objected, however, that Cameroon was obliged to provide evidence of each incident which it alleged constituted a violation of Article 2 (4): 'Treating the incidents "as a whole" rather than as separate, discrete events, does not avoid the need to establish them by proper evidence: and where something is alleged to have been done "persistently" or "regularly", it must be proved to have been done on several occasions, not just once. Incidents cannot simpy be taken "as a whole" without more, on the basis of assertions however often repeated, but must be substantiated one by one.' See ICJ, *Cameroon v. Nigeria*, Rejoinder of the Federal Republic of Nigeria, January 2001, §§ 119.31–34. Also §§ 15.8 *et seq*.; ICJ, *Cameroon v. Nigeria*, Counter-memorial of the Federal Republic of Nigeria, May 1999, §§ 24.41 *et seq*., 24.51, 24.60 *et seq*. In its Réplique, Cameroon seems to endorse this approach: ICJ, *Cameroon v. Nigeria*, Réplique de la République du Cameroun, 4 April 2000, § 10.41. The Court

territory as a response to a series of cross-border attacks by groups of irregulars operating from within the DRC. Both countries appeared to proceed on the basis that these attacks should be considered together, but strongly disagreed on the permissibility of defensive action against indirect military aggression.[244] The ICJ eventually rejected Uganda's self-defence claim, on the grounds that 'even if this series of deplorable attacks could be regarded as cumulative in character, they still remained non-attributable to the DRC'.[245] By way of *obiter dictum* it went on to determine that 'the taking of airports and towns many hundreds of kilometres from Uganda's border would not seem proportionate to *the series of transborder attacks* it claimed had given rise to the right of self-defence, nor to be necessary to that end'.[246]

We may conclude that there is considerable support for the view that the 'accumulation of events' does affect the possibility of exercising the right of self-defence. At the same time, we must concede that the evidence is not entirely unequivocal. This is largely due to the fact that the doctrine has in the past frequently been invoked in attempts to justify manifestly disproportionate interventions and in relation to cross-border actions by oppressive regimes against national liberation movements. These precedents indicate that 'accumulation of events' remains a difficult doctrine and that one should avoid ascribing to it consequences which would not seem warranted. It does not relieve the defending State of its duty to demonstrate that it has actually been the victim of the use of armed force.[247] Merely hiding behind a general hostile environment or behind unsubstantiated assertions of territorial intrusions is certainly insufficient. Furthermore, as noted above, given our finding that a small-scale attack may also constitute an 'armed attack', the impact of the doctrine is limited from a *de minimis* point of view. Still, it may be important in the sense that, in cases of doubt, it can provide evidence of the '*animus aggressionis*'. This purport is illustrated by the following

eventually found that 'neither of the Parties sufficiently proves the facts which it alleges, or their imputability to the other Party.' ICJ, *Case concerning the land and maritime boundary between Cameroon and Nigeria (Cameroon v. Nigeria: Equatorial Guinea intervening)*, Judgment of 10 October 2002, (2002) ICJ Rep 303–458, § 324.

[244] E.g., ICJ, *DRC v. Uganda*, Counter-memorial submitted by the Republic of Uganda, 21 April 2001, 196, 200; ICJ, *DRC v. Uganda*, Réplique de la République Démocratique du Congo, May 2002, §§ 3.84, 3.116 *et seq.*

[245] ICJ, *DRC v. Uganda*, Judgment of 19 December 2005, § 146.

[246] *Ibid.*, § 147 (emphasis added).

[247] In this sense see: ICJ, *Oil Platforms* case, Reply and defence to counter-claim, Islamic Republic of Iran, §§ 7.19–7.27; ICJ, *Cameroon v. Nigeria*, Rejoinder of the Federal Republic of Nigeria, January 2001, §§ 119.31–34.

declaration by the UK representative in relation to the 1964 Gulf of Tunkin incident:

> In the present case, there has not been merely one isolated attack on United States warships in international waters; we have been told that there have been repeated attacks, *the nature of which is such as to indicate that they were deliberately mounted*.[248]

'Accumulation of events' is probably most relevant from a proportionality point of view. In this context, if a State undertakes defensive action against an attack which is only the latest in a series of attacks, it is generally accepted that its response may exceed the scale and effects of the former attack. A more flexible, functional application of the proportionality criterion would thus seem warranted than in case of a single armed attack. This is particularly relevant in relation to attacks by irregulars, terrorists and armed bands, since a single small-scale non-State attack would generally not sanction a cross-border response, but would need to be tackled within the confines of the victim State's territory (see Chapter 5). As some of the cited precedents indicate, even repeated (small-scale) cross-border attacks in principle do not permit the victim State to engage in a large-scale invasion or occupation.[249] Finally, 'accumulation of events' only applies to situations where consecutive attacks are linked in time, cause and source. Previous attacks that are too remote in time are removed from the equation.

3.2.3 Connecting the dots: the panoply of scenarios and the role of context

In the end, the general ingredients of an armed attack are still largely the same as those laid down in the 1952 report of the UN Secretary-General.[250] At least from a *ratione materiae* perspective, no significant trends appear to have occurred in customary practice. The essence of an 'armed attack' remains of course the objective element. In this regard, recourse to self-defence presupposes first of all that armed force has unlawfully been used against a State. Moreover, as the ICJ has made

---

[248] UN Doc. S/PV.1140, 5 August 1964, § 80 (emphasis added). In a similar vein: UN Doc. A/AC.134/SR.52–66, 44 (Turkey).
[249] E.g., in relation to the 1968 Israeli intervention in Lebanon: (1968) UNYB 194 (Brazil, Canada, Denmark), 198 (Pakistan), 208 (Pakistan).
[250] Report of the UN Secretary-General, 3 October 1952, UN Doc. A/2211, §§ 299–304, 361–2.

clear, a certain gap exists between the concepts of 'use of force' and 'armed attack'. Only when the unlawful use of force reaches a minimal gravity will it qualify as an 'armed attack'. An adequate construction of this *de minimis* threshold is provided by Dinstein, who finds that an armed attack requires '*a use of force producing (or liable to produce) serious consequences, epitomized by territorial intrusions, human casualties or considerable destruction of property*. When no such results are engendered by (or reasonably expected from) a recourse to force, Article 51 does not come into play.'[251] On the other hand, our analysis suggests that small-scale attacks are not excluded from the purview of Article 51 UN Charter. Rather, the correct approach seems to be that the lawfulness of defensive action undertaken in response to small-scale attacks should be measured primarily by applying the proportionality and necessity criteria to the particular context. As affirmed in the *Nuclear Weapons* advisory opinion, the type of weapon used in the attack is immaterial.[252] An 'armed attack' can be committed by means of conventional weapons, such as small arms, explosives, artillery or air strikes, but also by unconventional means, whether a so-called 'dirty bomb' or a hijacked plane turned into a weapon. Arguably, the same would be true in the hypothetical case a so-called 'computer network attack' (CNA) were to cause fatalities or large-scale property destruction (for example due to a shutdown of computers controlling waterworks, misinformation fed into aircraft computers or a computer-generated meltdown of a nuclear reactor).[253] It is generally irrelevant *where* the attack takes place.[254] The most obvious case is of course an attack involving territorial intrusions. Yet, an armed attack may also be directed against a State's external

---

[251] Dinstein, *War, aggression and self-defence*, p. 193 (emphasis added).
[252] ICJ, *Legality of the threat or use of nuclear weapons*, Advisory opinion of 8 July 1996, (1996) ICJ Rep 226–67, §§ 38–9.
[253] See Y. Dinstein, 'Computer network attacks and self-defence', (2002) 76 *International Law Studies – Naval War College* 99–119, at 105. If the CNA would merely result in the disruption of communications without causing human casualties or significant destruction of property, or if it would only consist in espionage activities, it would not be deemed an armed attack. See also: M. N. Schmitt, 'Computer network attack and the use of force in international law: thoughts on a normative framework', (1989–99) 37 Columbia JTL 885–937. According to Schmitt, to constitute an 'armed attack', the CNA 'must be intended to directly cause physical damage to tangible objects or injury to human beings' (935). See also the contributions of Silver (85), Robertson Jnr (132–8) and Doyle Jnr (151–4) in (2002) 76 *International Law Studies – Naval War College*. Remark: it is striking that these authors emphasize the importance of the 'hostile intent' in relation to CNAs.
[254] See Dinstein, *War, aggression and self-defence*, pp. 196–9.

manifestations present within the territory of another State (e.g., a military base abroad, see Section 3.4). In other cases, the attack may occur beyond the boundaries of all States, for example when it targets a military vessel on the high seas, or a military satellite orbiting in outer space.[255]

The second constitutive element of an 'armed attack' is the *'animus aggressionis'*. This element does not refer to any particular motives, but presupposes that territorial incursions have been carried out with a general 'hostile intent', and/or that armed force has *deliberately* been used to cause loss of life or property destruction. As a result, self-defence is in principle excluded in cases of error or accident. The subjective element is particularly important when dealing with small-scale attacks or minor territorial intrusions. With regard to more substantial attacks, it is normally implicit in the act itself, unless there are clear indications to the contrary. In any event, the *'animus aggressionis'* must be evaluated in light of the broader context in which force has been used.

Since small-scale attacks are not necessarily excluded from the purview of Article 51 UN Charter, the 'accumulation of events' doctrine seems more relevant for assessing the proportionality of defensive action, rather than to determine the existence of an armed attack *ratione materiae*. Still, in cases of doubt regarding the two constitutive elements, the fact that an attack forms part of a series of interlinked incidents may tilt the balance in favour of permitting proportionate action in self-defence.

It is clear by now that establishing the basic ingredients for the exercise of the right of self-defence is not an effortless enterprise. For evidentiary purposes, we would be best served by a norm which (1) determines the existence of an armed attack purely by the actual facts, namely the incidence of territorial intrusions, human casualties and/or serious destruction of property; (2) excludes any reference to subjective factors; and (3) measures the proportionality of the reponse on a strictly quantitative basis. By contrast, building upon customary practice, the present study has so far spelt out a framework in which (1) the existence of an 'armed attack' is derived from the actual as well as the potential consequences of the attack; (2) a subsidiary, disabling role is awarded to the subjective element; and (3) proportionality is evaluated on a case-by-case basis through a combination of the quantitative and the functional approach. This may not be the easiest framework to apply, but, by taking

---

[255] *Ibid.*, p. 197.

account of the context, it avoids some of the pitfalls that would result from adhering to an artificial, mathematical equation.

These parameters remain particularly difficult to apply in the context of small-scale cross-border incidents, where the facts are often disputed and where the 'aggressive intent' may be uncertain. One cannot overlook the fact that in all three cases brought before the ICJ where a State relied on self-defence against small-scale cross-border attacks, the Court avoided pronouncing on the matter. In *Nicaragua*, the Court found that there was insufficient information to decide whether the alleged incursions could amount (singly or collectively) to an 'armed attack',[256] and instead turned to consider compliance with other requirements.[257] In *Cameroon v. Nigeria*, the Court simply declared that 'neither of the Parties sufficiently proves the facts which it alleges, or their imputability to the other Party'.[258] Finally, in *DRC v. Uganda*, Uganda's self-defence claim was rejected on the grounds that 'even if this series of deplorable attacks could be regarded as cumulative in character, they still remained non-attributable to the DRC'.[259] In both *Nicaragua* and *DRC v. Uganda*, the Court stressed the lack of proportionality and necessity as an additional ground of wrongfulness.[260]

The Court's ambiguous, yet at the same time cautious approach stands in marked contrast to the bold declaration in the Ethiopia–Eritrea Claims Commission's Partial Award on the *Jus ad Bellum* (delivered on the same day as the *DRC v. Uganda* judgment) that '[l]ocalized border encounters between small infantry units, even those involving the loss of life, do not constitute an armed attack for purposes of the Charter'.[261] *In casu*, Ethiopia asked the Commission to decide that Eritrea had started the conflict between the two countries in 1998, by means of a programme of pre-planned and coordinated attacks in violation of the prohibition on the use of force.[262] In a remarkably brief manner – the findings on self-defence take up less than two pages of the seven-page Partial Award – the Commission does away with Eritrea's claim that it had acted in self-defence against incursions by Ethiopian troops. In relation to the low-intensity fighting that took place between 6 and 12 May 1998, the Commission '[was] satisfied that these relatively minor incidents were

---

[256] ICJ, *Nicaragua* case (Merits), § 231. [257] *Ibid.*, §§ 232–8.
[258] ICJ, *Cameroon v. Nigeria*, §§ 322–4. [259] ICJ, *DRC v. Uganda*, § 146.
[260] ICJ, *Nicaragua* case (Merits), § 237; ICJ, *DRC v. Uganda*, § 147.
[261] Ethiopia–Eritrea Claims Commission, Partial Award *Jus ad Bellum*, Ethiopia Claims 1–8, 19 December 2005, reprinted in (2006) 45 ILM 430, § 11.
[262] *Ibid.*, § 10.

not of a magnitude to constitute an armed attack by either State against the other within the meaning of Article 51 of the UN Charter'.[263] Ergo, the attack against and subsequent occupation of the town of Badme on 12 May could not be justified as an exercise of self-defence.[264]

While the final conclusion of the Commission may well be correct, the cursory way in which it dealt with the difficult issue of self-defence against cross-border attacks stands open to serious criticism. As Gray finds, the Commission not only failed to provide any explanation of its approach to the evidence in the case, but also ignored the context in which the 'minor incidents' under consideration took place as well as the possibility that they might 'cumulatively' amount to an 'armed attack'.[265] A more appropriate mode of operation might have been to hold – by analogy with the cited ICJ cases – that there was insufficient evidence to decide whether the alleged incursions could singly or collectively amount to an 'armed attack', while stressing that the Eritrean attack of 12 May 1998 – which comprised at least two brigades of regular soldiers, supported by tanks and artillery – was in any event a disproportionate and unnecessary response to the alleged incursions. By contrast, a categorical rejection of proportionate on-the-spot defensive action to ward off a small-scale cross-border attack does not accurately reflect the customary law on the use of force.

The Commission's bold statement is illustrative of a deeper dichotomy in the framework used by international lawyers and people in the military respectively. International lawyers, on the one hand, seem to focus on those large-scale interventions that generate important shockwaves within the international community – e.g., the US-led intervention in Afghanistan of 2001 or the Israeli intervention in Lebanon of 2006 – but tend to ignore less 'high-profile' instances of inter-State recourse to force that do not result in public legal claims and often take place in unclear circumstances. The individual military commander, on the other hand, is

---

[263] *Ibid.*, § 12. '[T]he Commission takes note of the sharply different accounts offered by the Parties as to the precise location of the incidents ... and of the numbers and types of forces involved. It need not resolve these differences, because it is clear from the evidence that these incidents involved geographically limited clashes between small Eritrean and Ethiopian patrols along a remote, unmarked, and disputed border.'
[264] *Ibid.*, §§ 12–16.
[265] See Gray, 'The Ethiopia/Eritrea Claims Commission', 714–20. 'It seems almost unbelievable that such an important issue as the illegal use of force, in a case where the facts were contested, and potentially involving extensive liability, could be disposed of in this apparently cursory way. Many extremely controversial legal issues were inevitably glossed over.' (714–15).

more interested in knowing when he is permitted to open fire against an incoming aircraft or a trespassing border patrol. These different mindsets, one inspired by the Charter provisions as interpreted by the ICJ, the other by national rules of engagement, partially explain how members on both sides often hold different views on, say, the *de minimis* threshold or the *ratione temporis* dimension of the armed attack requirement. Some have attempted to bridge this schism by distinguishing between different scenarios of defensive action, each subject to a different legal framework. Thus, in his individual opinion in *Oil Platforms*, Judge Simma drew a distinction between 'full-scale self-defence' and 'proportionate defensive measures' (cf. *supra*).[266] A different distinction, which sometimes figures in ROEs and the like, is that between 'national self-defence' and 'unit self-defence'.[267]

Distinctions between different scenarios of defensive action, elaborating on the differentiated application of the main parameters, may well offer a useful instrument to convey these rules in a practical terms to military commanders and decision-makers. For instance, the need for self-defence to be a 'last resort' obviously has a different meaning with regard to the UK's decision to deploy troops to the Falklands than with regard to the decision of the individual fighter pilot in the Gulf of Sidra whether or not to open fire on his opponent. At the same time, it is imperative to recognize that the entire panoply of scenarios in which State A may use armed force against State B potentially falls within the ambit of the Charter rules on the use of force. Hence, except when authorized by the Security Council, the recourse to force by State A must abide by the legal parameters of the right of self-defence. Unlike Judge Simma, the present author believes that suggestions to split up *the legal basis* for self-defence go against the comprehensive nature of the Charter provisions on the use of force. They also seem incompatible with States' conception of self-defence in customary practice. It may be recalled for instance that the US justified the resort to force in relation to hostile encounters with North Vietnamese and Libyan military units

---

[266] ICJ, *Oil Platforms* case, Individual opinion of Judge Simma, §§ 12–16.
[267] The 2005 US Standing Rules of Engagement and Rules for the Use of Force, for example, distinguish between national self-defence, collective self-defence and unit self-defence. See Henseler, 'Self-defense in the maritime environment', 211–12. According to Stephens, 'national self-defence' is governed by the UN Charter, whereas 'unit self-defence' constitutes a *sui generis* right that 'draws its jurisprudential authority directly from the "Caroline" prescription.' See Stephens, 'The concept of unit self-defense'.

in the Gulf of Tunkin (1964) and the Gulf of Sidra (1981) precisely by reference to Article 51 UN Charter.[268]

The most convincing classification of scenarios of defensive action, which may appeal to military commanders and international lawyers alike, is arguably the one put forward in Dinstein's *War, aggression and self-defence*.[269] In this work, Dinstein distinguishes between three main 'modalities' of self-defence: on-the-spot reaction, defensive armed reprisals and 'war'.[270] At the same time he stresses that there is a quantitative but no qualitative difference between a single unit responding to an armed attack and the entire military structure doing so: 'Once counter-force of whatever scale is employed by military units of whatever size – in response to an armed attack by another State – this is a manifestation of . . . self-defence', and the legality of the action is determined by Article 51 UN Charter as supplemented by customary international law.

'On-the-spot-reaction' refers to 'the case in which a small-scale armed attack elicits at once, and *in situ*, the employment of counter-force by those under attack or present nearby', for example, when a border patrol is ambushed or when a hostile confrontation takes place on the high seas between a destroyer of State A and a submarine of State B.[271] For defensive action to be lawful in this scenario, it is crucial that it be 'immediate': the counter-force must be 'temporally interwoven' with the armed attack triggering it.[272] Furthermore, whether or not self-defence is used as a last resort must be assessed on the tactical level, i.e., from the point of view of the individual military commander. Finally, the proportionality criterion requires force and counter-force to be similar in 'scale and effects'.

The second 'modality' is 'defensive armed reprisals'.[273] In this situation, the defensive action is undertaken at a time and place different from the original armed attack, and pursuant to a decision at the political/strategic level, rather than at the tactical level. 'Defensive armed reprisals' must not only abide by the rules of IHL, they must above all be *quantitatively* proportionate to the 'scale and effects' of the initial attack (exact

---

[268] See (1964) UNYB 147–9; (1981) UNYB 360–1.
[269] Dinstein, *War, aggression and self-defence*, pp. 219–43.
[270] *Ibid.* The two former categories fall under the category of 'measures short of war' as opposed to the third category. Dinstein also discusses a third modality of 'measures short of war', namely 'protection of nationals abroad' (231–4), but this is altogether a category of a special nature (and of controversial legality). The lawfulness of the latter category is addressed in greater detail in Section 4.4.
[271] *Ibid.*   [272] *Ibid.*, p. 221.   [273] See *ibid.*, pp. 221–31.

symmetry is not required). The necessity principle moreover requires that the victim first attempts to resolve the dispute through peaceful means, and that, while reaction does not have to be strictly 'immediate,' the time lapse between force and counter-force be reasonably short.[274] Last but not least, for such actions to qualify as lawful self-defence rather than as unlawful reprisals, they should not purely aim at punishing past transgressions. Rather, they should be future-oriented, aimed at deterring future attacks by the delinquent State.[275]

Finally, when the original armed attack is 'critical' enough, the right to self-defence may actually transform into a right to resort to 'war'.[276] Again, the time lapse between force and counter-force should be reasonably short, although the need to make appropriate preparations or other circumstances may justify a certain delay.[277] Before resorting to 'war', the victim State should verify that a peaceful settlement is not reasonably attainable. However, once this is done, Dinstein finds that the exercise of self-defence may bring about the destruction of the enemy's army, regardless of the condition of proportionality:[278] 'Once a war of self-defence is justified by the merits of the case, only the Security Council can contain hostilities.'[279]

There is certainly great value in the classification used by Dinstein. At the same time, a number of reservations could arguably be made. First, whereas Dinstein rightly argues that the principles of necessity and proportionality apply differently depending on the 'scale and effects' of the initial attack, one might stress the relevance of the two other elements discussed in the present section, namely 'hostile intent' and 'accumulation of events'. The former is especially relevant in the context of 'on-the-spot-reactions'. In cases of doubt, the individual commander should take graduated measures to verify the hostile intent of the opponent and/or de-escalate the situation. The latter factor is of particular importance for what Dinstein calls 'defensive armed reprisals'. On the one hand, the repeated nature of small-scale attacks will determine whether or not defensive action is at all permitted after the initial attack is 'terminated' (this will generally not be the case when confronted with a single isolated attack). On the other hand, the accumulated nature of the attacks may warrant a more flexible, functional application of the proportionality criterion to the defensive action undertaken.[280]

---

[274] *Ibid.*, p. 225. [275] *Ibid.*, p. 227. [276] *Ibid.*, pp. 235–43. [277] *Ibid.*, p. 242–3.
[278] *Ibid.*, p. 238. [279] *Ibid.*, p. 240.
[280] Dinstein also seems to recognize this possibility. See *ibid.*, pp. 230–1.

Second, as we have seen before,[281] there is considerable support for the distinction between lawful self-defence and unlawful armed reprisals, and States themselves are keen to uphold the different terminology in order to limit possible abuse.[282] While the distinction may not always be easy to make, a recognition of the legality of certain 'reprisals',[283] risks generating a slippery slope, triggering forcible responses that are irreconcilable with the necessity and proportionality criteria. Paradoxically enough, Dinstein admits that the legal analysis might benefit 'if the nomenclature of "armed reprisals" were simply abandoned'.[284] It is therefore somewhat puzzling why he does not use a more neutral denominator, such as, for example, 'restricted *post facto* self-defence'. In this regard, it should also be noted that he apparently sets the necessity threshold too low. The mere fact that a forcible response may have a general deterrent effect on the aggressor cannot suffice. Instead, there must be an element of 'prevention': post-attack self-defence can only be permitted when there is compelling evidence that more attacks will imminently follow.

Similarly, as for the final category, there is again a terminological impediment and a substantial one. On the one hand, the category of 'war' (and the concomitant 'right to war') seems an anachronistic and undesirable reference to the long rejected *compétence de guerre*, and goes against the trend of replacing the vocabulary of 'war' by the vocabulary of 'armed conflict'.[285] More fundamentally, even if one were to use the concept of 'unrestricted self-defence', the suggestion that the necessity and proportionality criteria by and large become moot in such scenarios goes against the universal applicability of these standards as recognized by customary practice.[286] Indeed, even when confronted with a large-scale attack (such as an invasion of part of a State's territory), the necessity and proportionality criteria still apply, be it in a more flexible manner. For instance, especially if there is a certain delay between force and counter-force, the victim State must engage in bona fide efforts to resolve the dispute by peaceful means.[287] Furthermore, as illustrated by

---

[281] See *supra* Section 2.2.2.b.ii.
[282] Cf. letter by US Secretary of State Rush, reproduced in (1974) 68 AJIL 736.
[283] Cf. O. Schachter, *International law in theory and practice* (Dordrecht: Martinus Nijhoff, 1991), p. 154.
[284] Dinstein, *War, aggression and self-defence*, p. 226.
[285] See Kritsiotis, 'Topographies of force', p. 35.   [286] See also *ibid.*, pp. 40–5.
[287] J. Gardam, *Necessity, proportionality and the use of force by States* (Cambridge University Press, 2004), pp. 150–1.

the Falklands War, proportionality may require a certain geographical limitation of the defensive response.[288]

Fourth and last, while the aforementioned typology of defensive responses may have practical value for assessing the legal parameters in concrete scenarios, a rigid separation must be rejected. Depending on gravity and/or repetition, an armed attack may justify both an on-the-spot-reaction and certain restricted post-attack measures. It is equally possible that limited counter-force results in a reciprocal escalation of the conflict and develops into an international armed conflict. In this regard, a fundamental weakness of Dinstein's classification is that his distinction between 'measures short of war' and 'war' depends entirely on the 'critical character' of the attack. Given the far-reaching consequences – recall that 'measures short of war' have to be quantitatively proportionate to the initial attack, whereas 'wars of self-defence' can only be contained by the Security Council – it is slightly disconcerting that the author refrains from giving any indications on how to establish this threshold. The present author is not convinced that a rigid separation of these models of defensive action corresponds to the realities of inter-State use of force. Instead, it would seem more realistic to frame the differentiated application of the necessity and proportionality criteria in terms of a continuum, as considered above. In the end, faced with the panoply of possible scenarios, context is everything.

3.3 Small-scale incursions by land, sea or air

The variables spelt out in the previous Section enable us to determine when attacks on a State's territory allow it to exercise its right of self-defence by means of on-the-spot reaction and/or *post facto* defensive measures. In order to illustrate how the general ingredients of the armed attack requirement apply and interact, the present section examines a particularly complex topic, which to a large extent forms the 'missing link' between Articles 2(4) and 51 UN Charter, namely small-scale territorial incursions by foreign military units by land, sea or air. More precisely we will examine to what extent a State can respond to such incursions by means of on-the-spot defensive measures *within its own territory*.

At the outset it should be noted that there is a considerable degree of confusion as to whether and when such incursions fall within the ambit

---

[288] See *supra* Section 2.2.2.c.ii.

of the Charter provisions on the use of force. This uncertainty partially flows from the fact that incidents of this type have seldom generated substantial exchanges of legal claims and counter-claims, let alone debates within the UN political bodies. On some occasions, victim States have – for diplomatic reasons or because of a manifest lack of gravity – refrained from labelling such incursions as violations of Article 2(4), but instead complained of violations of their sovereignty.[289] In light thereof, several authors frame these incursions and possible reactions thereto in terms of 'enforcement of sovereign rights' and police operations, governed by a specific customary practice, which is especially well-developed in the realm of aerial incursions, and which operates separately from the Charter rules on the use of force.[290] While it is not the present author's aim to determine from what point small-scale territorial incursions qualify as a 'use of force' in the sense of Article 2(4),[291] we nonetheless agree with Dinstein that whenever State A

---

[289] See on this O. Corten, *Le droit contre la guerre; l'interdiction du recours à la force en droit international contemporain* (Paris: Pedone, 2008), pp. 63–121. In the *Nicaragua* case, for example, the ICJ found that the unauthorized overflight of a State's territory by aircraft belonging to or under the control of the government of another State infringed the principle of respect for territorial sovereignty. ICJ, *Nicaragua* case (Merits), § 251 (Remark: in the present author's view, however, this should not be taken as implying that the Court ruled out that unauthorized overflight can also qualify as a breach of Article 2(4). By analogy, it may be noted that in its dispositif, the Court qualifies the US support for the Contras 'only' as a violation of the customary norm of non-intervention (§ 292), even if earlier paragraphs of the judgment clearly indicate that some forms of support violated the prohibition on the use of force (§ 228)). Also Brownlie, 'The use of force in self-defence', 256 (observing that violations of airspace by military aircraft generally do not lead to specific charges of violations of Article 2(4) UN Charter, but adding that there have been particular cases where violations have been labelled 'act of aggression').

[290] Corten, *Le droit contre la guerre*, pp. 65–85. Also taking the view that the use of force within a State's own territory against intruding persons, vessels or aircraft falls beyond the scope of Article 2(4) UN Charter: D. Schindler, 'Die Grenzen des völkerrechtlichen Gewaltverbots', in D. Schindler and K. Hailbronner (eds.), *Die Grenzen des völkerrechtlichen Gewaltverbots* (Heidelberg: Müller Juristischer Verlag, 1986), pp. 11–44, at 14–15, 45; Fleck, 'Rules of engagement of maritime forces', 179–80; O. Schachter, 'The right of States to use armed force', (1983–4) 82 Michigan L Rev 1620–46, at 1626; Verdross and Simma, *Universelles Völkerrecht*, § 472. See also: ICJ, *Oil Platforms* case, Reply and defence to counter-claim submitted by the Islamic Republic of Iran, 10 March 1999, § 7.41. Brownlie deals with trespassing ships and vessels under the heading 'problems relating to self-defence' but nonetheless remains vague as to the legal basis for action against such incursions. See Brownlie, *The use of force by States*, p. 373.

[291] Randelzhofer, for example, states that: '[A]n incursion into the territory of another State constitutes an infringement of Art. 2(4), even if it is not intended to deprive that State of

deliberately uses (potentially) lethal force within its own territory – including its territorial sea and its airspace – against military or police units acting in their official capacity in State B, this amounts to inter-State recourse to force, which must be justified on the basis of self-defence (except when authorized by the UN Security Council).[292] This view is supported by the fact that – even if it is sometimes difficult to envisage them as 'attacks' in the literal sense – the parameters established in customary practice governing forcible responses to such incursions are essentially the same as those set out in the previous section. Moreover, while the Charter language and the right of self-defence

part of its territory and if the invading troops are meant to withdraw immediately after completing a temporary and limited operation ("in-and-out operations").' A. Randelzhofer, 'Article 2(4)', in Simma et al. (eds.), *The Charter of the United Nations*, pp. 114–37, at 123. By contrast, Corten defines Article 2(4) in much narrower terms, and identifies six criteria: the *locus* of the action; the political context; the level at which actions were authorized; the target of the incursion; whether the incursion has resulted in actual confrontations between forces of the States concerned; and the gravity and means used. See Corten, *Le droit contre la guerre*, pp. 63 *et seq.*, especially pp. 120–1. While Corten certainly deserves credit for his elaborate analysis of the scope of the prohibition on the use of force, several reservations can be made. In his analysis of invocations of Articles 2(4) and 51 in concrete precedents, for instance, he makes no distinction between incursions by military and police units of a foreign State and other non-State incursions. Furthermore, with respect to some precedents, he finds that the lack of express reference to Articles 2(4) and/or 51 is probably due to diplomatic considerations (e.g., *ibid.*, p. 114), whereas in other cases he finds such omission to be 'highly significant'. No indication is given as to why such omission is significant in one case, while it is not in others. Finally, in some respects, the analysis puts the cart before the horse. For example, one of the factors which is considered relevant to establish whether an incursion constitutes a 'use of force' is whether there have been actual confrontations between the troops of the States concerned. Yet, this criterion is self-defeating, since it passes over the underlying question whether the State whose territory is violated would be allowed to take action against it in the first place. In the end, Corten's analysis is somewhat circular (perhaps inevitably?), in that it eventually finds that there is a 'use of force' when the victim State decides to label it as such.

[292] Dinstein, *War, aggression and self-defence*, p. 198, footnote 117. In a similar vein: P. Jimenez Kwast, 'Maritime law enforcement and the use of force: reflections on the categorization of forcible action at sea in the light of the *Guyana/Suriname* Award', (2008) 13 JCSL 49–91, at 84–5; J. Kammerhofer, 'The *Armed Activities* case and non-State actors in self-defence law', (2007) 20 Leiden JIL 89–113, at 105; UN Doc. A/AC.125/SR.110–14, 43 (Italy).

Remark: for present purposes, the notion of military and police personnel acting in their official capacity probably does not include the clandestine presence of ununiformed agents of State A on the territory of State B, for example, for the purpose of collecting intelligence or abducting a suspected terrorist or war criminal (cf. the Eichmann incident). When State B decides to apprehend or otherwise take action against these agents, this is a matter of law enforcement, which is not governed by Article 51 UN Charter.

THE 'ARMED ATTACK' REQUIREMENT *RATIONE MATERIAE* 187

have often not been invoked, there are numerous incidents where this has been the case. Examples are:

- the sinking by the United Arab Republic of the Israeli destroyer *Eilat* in UAR territorial waters in 1967;[293]
- the use of depth charges against a foreign submarine in Swedish territorial waters in 1982;[294]
- the seizure by the North Korean Navy of the USS *Pueblo* in 1968;[295]
- the downing of an American military air transport in Yugoslav airspace;[296]
- letters to the Security Council from *inter alia* Libya, Lebanon and Iraq, complaining of repeated incursions of their airspace and asserting the concerned States' right of self-defence;[297]
- the reference to self-defence as a legal basis for the interception of intruding vessels in national military manuals such as the US Commander's Handbook on the Law of Naval Operations.[298]

The crucial question of course is what factors turn a mere small-scale incursion into an actual or impending 'armed attack' in the sense of Article 51 UN Charter.

In accordance with our conclusion in the previous Section, a first prerequisite is of course that the territorial incursions concerned be *unlawful*. This will not be the case if the action is sanctioned by a so-called 'hot pursuit agreement'. Such agreements are indeed regularly concluded on a bilateral (and sometimes multilateral) basis to facilitate police enforcement and to bring escaping wrongdoers before the

---

[293] Justified on the basis of self-defence, *infra*, note 328.   [294] *Idem, infra*, note 335.
[295] Again, North Korea centered its justification on self-defence and security necessity claims rather than on a law enforcement basis (Jimenez Kwast, 'Maritime law enforcement', 84). See: UN Doc. S/PV.1389, 27 January 1968, §§ 64 *et seq.* (USSR, reiterating the arguments raised by North Korea and agreeing that measures were taken in self-defence and did not violate international law). Remark: according to North Korea and the Soviet bloc, the USS *Pueblo* had been spying in North Korea's territorial waters. The United States and other Western States objected that the vessel was engaged in peaceful activities in international waters. See (1968) UNYB 168–73.
[296] *In casu*, the United States argued that, since the plane in no way constituted a threat to the sovereignty of Yugoslavia, the Yugoslav actions were a plain violation of the obligation under the UN Charter not to use force except in self-defence. See quote in: O.J. Lissitzyn, 'The treatment of aerial intruders in recent practice and international law', (1953) 47 AJIL 559–89, at 571.
[297] *Infra*, note 322; UN Doc. S/14094, 6 August 1980, (Libya), Annex, 2–3.
[298] *Infra*, note 317.

jurisdictions of the injured State.[299] Another possibility is that the States concerned have adopted an agreement providing for the creation of a military base by State A in the territory of State B, and allowing for certain troop movements to take place, or that State B has otherwise consented to the presence of foreign troops on its soil. In April 2008, for example, Somali authorities authorized French forces to pursue within its borders a gang of pirates that had temporarily held a French tourist yacht for ransom.[300] While ground and aerial incursions presuppose the agreement of the territorial State, the situation is more complex when dealing with naval incursions. Indeed, entry of the territorial sea by foreign warships is in principle permitted by the 1982 United Nations Convention on the Law of the Sea (UNCLOS), provided that it qualifies as 'innocent passage', or, in other words, 'as long as it is not prejudicial to the peace, good order or security of the coastal State' (Articles 18–19 (1)).[301] Article 19(2) makes clear that this will not be the case if the ship engages in a number of unpermitted activities, such as military exercises, threats or uses of force in violation of the UN Charter, willful and serious pollution, survey activities, et cetera. Article 21 furthermore recognizes that the coastal State may adopt additional regulations, for instance to guarantee the safety of navigation or for the preservation of the environment. In order to be able to verify innocent passage, submarines are required to navigate on the surface and show their flag (Article 20). Article 30 moreover states that if a warship does not abide by the aforementioned regulations and disregards a request for compliance, the coastal State may require it to leave the territorial sea immediately. Special regimes apply for instance vis-à-vis international straits or neutral shipping in times of armed conflict. It should finally be noted that

---

[299] See on this: N. M. Poulantzas, *The right of hot pursuit in international law*, 2nd edn (Dordrecht: Martinus Nijhoff, 2002), pp. 11–35. E.g., Article 41 of the Convention implementing the Schengen Agreement, 19 June 1990, OJ 22 September 2000, L-239, 19–62. Agreements of this type are not necessarily limited to the cross-border pursuit of criminals by police forces, they may also relate to more large-scale military operations against armed groups in border regions. In 1983, for example, Turkey and Iraq signed a Frontier Security and Cooperation Agreement, which gave both States the right to carry out hot-pursuit operations against armed groups in the other's territory. See W. Hale, *Turkey, the US and Iraq* (London: Saqi, 2007), pp. 32–7.

[300] (2008) 54 *Keesing's* 48505.

[301] UN Convention on the Law of the Sea, Montego Bay, 10 December 1982, 1833 UNTS 31363. See also M. H. Nordquist (ed.), *United Nations Convention on the Law of the Sea: a commentary*. Vol. II (Dordrecht: Martinus Nijhoff, 1985), pp. 164–203, 253–5. See F. D. Froman, 'Uncharted waters: non-innocent passage of warships in the territorial sea', (1983–4) 21 San Diego L Rev 625–89, at 625–64.

the right of hot pursuit at sea ceases as soon as the fleeing ship concerned enters the territorial sea of its own State or of a third State (Article 111(3)).

Once it is established that an intrusion is unlawful, one must examine its gravity, as well as the hostile intent (or lack thereof). In case of a large-scale operation, the latter issue generally becomes moot. Thus, it is uncontroversial that the trespassing into Hawaian airspace by the Japanese airforce, the crossing of the Polish border by entire brigades of German panzers or the entering of British waters by the Spanish Armada would all have qualified as armed attacks under Article 51 UN Charter, even if no single shot had as yet been fired.[302] By contrast, while small-scale incursions are not automatically excluded from the notion of 'armed attack', it is important in these situations to verify the intention of the intruder. It may occur, for instance, that a border patrol of State A has by error crossed into State B's territory. Or it could be that a State A police unit knowingly entered State B's territory to pursue a group of criminals, even if no hot pursuit agreement exists.[303] Neither of these cases would as such warrant State B to actively use lethal force in self-defence. In a similar vein, it must be stressed that a 'non-innocent' entry of the territorial sea by a foreign warship does not necessarily imply an *animus aggressionis*. Thus, if a State A warship takes on board a civilian aircraft, dumps large quantities of worn-out military equipment in State B's territorial sea, or if its entire crew pulls out their fishing gear, there may be a violation of Article 19 UNCLOS, but this unlawful behaviour would clearly not amount to an 'armed attack' in the sense of Article 51 UN Charter. Neither will the unlawful ignoring of coast State regulations imposed in accordance with Article 21 UNCLOS automatically constitute an 'armed attack'. In August 1980, for example, after a nuclear-powered Soviet submarine had been heavily damaged by a fire, the Soviet Union asked Japan for permission to tow the submarine through its territorial waters towards the port of Vladivostok. Japan agreed in principle, but conditioned its approval upon a satisfactory response to two questions: was there any danger of radioactive pollution from the submarine?; and were there nuclear weapons on board?[304] The Soviet Union

---

[302] Remark: whether such attacks may be 'pre-empted' or 'prevented' is examined in Chapter 4.
[303] Remark: hot pursuit on land is only lawful when the 'receiving' State consents to it. See Poulantzas, *The right of hot pursuit*, p. 346; I. Brownlie, 'International law and the activities of armed bands', (1958) 7 ICLQ 712–35, at 734. See also *infra*, Section 5.1.1.b.
[304] For an elaborate analysis, see R. J. Grammig, 'The Yoron Jima submarine incident of August 1980: a Soviet violation of the law of the sea', (1981) 22 HILJ 331–54.

only provided an answer to the first question. Despite Japanese orders to stay outside its territorial waters until a response to the second question was given, the Soviets towed the submarine through the strait between Yoron Jima and Okino Erabu Shima. Japan subsequently announced that it 'deeply deplored the Soviet Union's violation of its territorial waters,' but undertook no further action against the rescue operation.[305] *In casu*, the unlawful passage through Japan's territorial waters clearly lacked the necessary *'animus aggressionis'* to be qualified as an 'armed attack'. Finally, aerial incursions may similarly be inspired by a wide variety of essentially harmless intentions, such as the desire to shorten a flight or avoid bad weather, or may result from distress or navigation errors.[306]

When the subjective element of the 'armed attack' requirement is absent or uncertain, the State whose territory is violated may essentially engage in a number of graduated measures that shift the onus onto the trespassing unit(s) and force it either to terminate its unlawful behaviour or to reveal a hostile intent. These measures constitute the prelude to the actual exercise of the right of self-defence and form the crucial discerning factor on the slope between police action and actual recourse to force. Even if the intruder persists in its course of action, it is imperative that any forcible response be reasonably proportionate to the gravity of the abuse and/or the threat posed.[307] National Rules of Engagement and comparable instructions to police personnel, coastguards, et cetera may vary considerably, yet their application must always be assessed on a case-by-case basis by reference to the necessity and proportionality criteria.

In relation to small-scale land incursions, for instance, the appropriate reaction vis-à-vis a trespassing border patrol would generally be to issue a warning and call on the intruders to withdraw; to fire warning shots if the call went unheeded;[308] and to submit diplomatic protests after the incident. Only if the intruders were to persist in their course of action and come to pose a threat to the territorial State would limited recourse to force be permissible. Furthermore, if a State A police unit would unlawfully engage in the hot pursuit of a criminal on the territory of State B, the latter State could undertake a number of gradual measures to enforce its jurisdiction. This could involve the use of verbal warnings or visual

---

[305] *Washington Post* 24 August 1980, A 18.
[306] E.g., Lissitzyn, 'The treatment of aerial intruders', 559–60.
[307] E.g., K.-G. Park, *La protection de la souveraineté aérienne* (Paris: Pedone, 1991), p. 319.
[308] Cf. (1976) 22 *Keesing's* 27548 (re a border incident between China and India).

signs urging the intruders to break off the pursuit, as well as the use of warning shots or roadblocks in order to halt and/or arrest the intruders.[309] It is, however, hardly conceivable that such unlawful action would warrant the active use of lethal force pursuant to Article 51 UN Charter.

Analogous principles are applicable to forcible action against trespassing military aircraft. While national ROEs may differ, it is generally accepted that the 'victim' State may lawfully take measures to intercept a foreign military aircraft which makes an unauthorized passage through its territorial airspace and force it to land.[310] Intruding aircraft must obey all resonable orders of the territorial sovereign, including orders to land, to turn back, or to fly on a certain course.[311] A special regime applies to military aircraft in distress: although it is not clear whether such planes have a right of passage over foreign airspace or not,[312] they cannot lawfully be forced to land or be shot down if they fail to heed an order of the territorial sovereign.[313] In other cases, a number of key principles can be discerned (States concerned generally agree on the principles, but present different factual accounts of the incidents). If a military aircraft ignores orders to land, forcible measures may be undertaken. *In extremis*, the territorial State is allowed to shoot the aerial intruder, provided this action meets the requirements of necessity and proportionality. Still, intruding aircraft whose intentions are known to be harmless must not be attacked even if they disobey orders to land.[314] In principle, no aircraft may be shot down unless prior warning has been given and/or warning

---

[309] In this context, Poulantzas refers to an incident which took place at the French–German border in 1966: German policemen pursued an Australian offender into French territory. The policemen, who penetrated sixty metres into French soil and shot and wounded the fugitive, were in their turn pursued and arrested by French policemen. See Poulantzas, *The right of hot pursuit*, p. 11, footnote 6.

[310] See Lissitzyn, 'The treatment of aerial intruders'; Park, *La souveraineté aérienne*, pp. 291–320; J. Sundberg, 'Legitimate responses to aerial intruders: the view from a neutral State', (1985) 10 AASL 251–73.

[311] Lissitzyn, 'The treatment of aerial intruders', 586.

[312] Some argue this right flows from Articles 4 and 22 of the 1919 Paris Convention for the Regulation of Air Navigation or from application by analogy of Article 25 of the Chicago Convention (e.g., T. A. Geraci, 'Overflight, landing rights, customs and clearances', (1994) 37 Air Force L Rev 155–89, at 158; Lissitzyn, 'The treatment of aerial intruders', 564). The issue nonetheless remains controversial. See Park, *La souveraineté aérienne*, pp. 219–23.

[313] Remark: the problem herewith is that foreign aircraft may feign distress to evade interception. See Lissitzyn, 'The treatment of aerial intruders', 587, 589.

[314] *Ibid.*, 587.

shots have been fired.[315] Two important exceptions exist. When the aerial intruder is the first to open fire, the issuing of a warning may obviously be skipped. Second, in cases of urgency, when there are strong indications that the intruder is on the verge of attacking one or more targets, the territorial State can resort to defensive action even if no warning has been communicated.[316]

It follows from these guidelines that the permissibility of defensive action by the territorial sovereign is heavily influenced by the *'animus aggressionis'* of the intruder.[317] In certain situations the subjective element may be difficult to determine. Still, there are a number of elements that assist in establishing whether the intruder poses a threat to the security of the territorial sovereign.[318] A first indicator is the political context, more precisely the friendly or hostile nature of the relationships between the territorial sovereign and the intruder State. A second element which may reveal the hostile intention of the incursion is its accumulated or repeated nature. Thus, in 1946 the United States protested against the downing of a US plane by Yugoslavia, on the grounds

---

[315] See, e.g., UN Doc. S/4385, 13 July 1960 (USSR), at 2 ('Notwithstanding the signals given by a Soviet fighter aircraft to follow it down and make a landing, the violating aircraft penetrated further into the airspace of the Soviet Union. Consequently, it was shot down over Soviet territorial waters ...').

[316] Brownlie, *The use of force by States*, p. 373; Lissitzyn, 'The treatment of aerial intruders', 579 (referring to the relevant US ROE); Park, *La souveraineté aérienne*, p. 318; Sundberg, 'Legitimate responses to aerial intruders', 259, 266–8 (referring to the instructions to the Swedish armed forces).

[317] According to the US Commander's Handbook on the Law of Naval Operations: 'A state's right to use force against an aircraft in flight during peacetime is based on the degree to which that aircraft poses a threat to the vital interests of the state using force and the availability and effectiveness of lesser measures. Military aircraft intruding into foreign airspace on a military mission may constitute a sufficient threat to justify the use of force in self-defense. This appears true both for tactical military aircraft capable of directly attacking the overflown state and for unarmed military aircraft capable of being used for intelligence-gathering purposes. State practice also suggests that an aircraft with military markings may be presumed to be on a military mission unless evidence is produced to the contrary by its state of registry.' The Handbook in principle rules out the recourse to force 'against military aircraft that stray into national airspace through navigational error or that are in distress.' See US Department of the Navy and Department of Homeland Security, *The Commander's Handbook of the Law of Naval Operations*, 4–4.

[318] In this regard, it is interesting to look at the considerations that led US personnel in the Gulf in 1988 to conclude that the aircraft which was later identified as Iran Air flight 655 had hostile intentions. See: Report of the ICAO Fact-finding Investigation on the destruction of Iran Airbus A300, November 1988, (1989) 28 ILM 900–43, at 913, 923–4. Also *infra* Section 4.3.3.b.

that the plane had no hostile intentions, but had instead been forced to fly over Yugoslav territory due to bad weather.[319] The Yugoslav government responded by observing that: 'From the number of planes which daily and repeatedly fly over Yugoslav territory, it is clear that in all cases this is not done owing to necessity or to bad weather, but that in a majority of cases our territory was again deliberately crossed'.[320] Likewise, when justifying the downing of two US reconnaissance planes in 1960, the Soviet Union laid much emphasis on the repeated nature of the violations of Soviet airspace.[321] In general, when confronted with repeated incursions by *fighter* planes from enemy nations, States seem to feel little reluctance to exercise or at least invoke the right of self-defence.[322] Other relevant indicia include the speed and flying altitude of the intruder; the opening of bomb bay doors; the locking of missile radars; or the plane's engaging in a bombing run.

In any event, while the concept of hostile intent of aerial incursions is broader than the intent to engage in actual combat and may for instance cover reconnaissance and surveillance flights, defensive action must always abide by the rule of proportionality.[323] Again, the repeated or isolated nature of, for example, an unauthorized surveillance flight may be relevant to assess what action is permitted. Other factors include the specific features of the intruder plane – is it armed or not? is it a transport plane or a reconnaissance plane? – as well as the means used to intercept the plane (cf. a few rounds of machine gun fire aimed at the plane's engines compared to the launching of a anti-aircraft missile). It is interesting to note, for instance, that following US complaints in 1946 that the shooting without prior warning of an unarmed American military air transport over Yugoslav territory violated the Charter prohibition on the use of force, Marshal Tito forwarded the following notice to the US Ambassador:

> I have issued orders to our military authorities to the effect that no transport planes must be fired at any more, even if they intentionally fly over our territory without proper clearance, but that in such cases they

---

[319] See Lissitzyn, 'The treatment of aerial intruders', 570–2.   [320] Quoted in *ibid.*, 572.
[321] See (1960) UNYB 40–2; UN Doc. S/4315, 19 May 1960 (USSR); UN Doc. S/4385, 13 July 1960 (USSR).
[322] See, e.g., UN Doc. S/2003/148, 4 February 2003 (Lebanon re Israeli violations of Lebanese airspace); UN Doc. S/2001/370, 13 April 2001 (Iraq re US and UK violations of Iraqi airspace).
[323] Park, *La souveraineté aérienne*, p. 319; Sundberg, 'Legitimate responses to aerial intruders', 260.

should be invited to land; if they refused to do so their identity should be taken and the Yugoslav government informed hereof so that any necessary steps could be undertaken through appropriate channels.[324]

In sum, while defensive action against aerial intrusion is regulated by a number of relatively clear guidelines, the latter must always be applied by reference to the concrete factual circumstances of the case at hand.

Finally, as far as unlawful intrusions of the territorial sea by foreign military vessels are concerned, reference must be made to the relevant provisions of the 1982 Law of the Sea Convention. According to Article 30 UNCLOS, a vessel that violates coastal State regulations will be requested to comply therewith. If the request is ignored or if the vessel engages in 'non-innocent' passage, the coast State 'may require it to leave the territorial sea immediately'. If the call is heeded, this concludes the incident. If not, the coastal State may take graduated and proportionate measures to compel the vessel to change its course or display a hostile intent. Although relevant practice is limited, an appropriate response, short of the actual recourse to force, would consist in the use of an escort ship or aircraft to accompany the ship outside territorial waters, or, possibly, the firing of warning shots.[325] Thus, Ratner cites an incident whereby Algeria escorted US warships out of claimed Algerian waters without resistance by the United States.[326]

In principle, the actual resort to proportionate lethal force against the intruder should be confined to situations where the foreign ship would wilfully ignore orders to leave the territorial sea and would show a hostile intent – for example if the coastal State were to accoustically detect the opening of missile tube doors. Nonetheless, exceptions may be made when there are strong indications that an intruding vessel is on the verge of launching an attack. Thus, in a letter dated 22 October 1967, the United Arab Republic informed the Security Council that it had spotted the Israeli destroyer *Eilat* speeding in its territorial waters off Port Said in contravention of the ceasefire. Since the destroyer had earlier been involved in the sinking of two UAR boats in territorial waters, the UAR

---

[324] Quoted in Lissitzyn, 'The treatment of aerial intruders', 572–3.
[325] E.g., Froman, 'Uncharted waters', 674 (footnote 230); Ratner, 'The Gulf of Sidra incident', 71 (With regard to the Gulf of Sidra incident, Ratner notes that '[a]ccording to an American military authority, however, Libya had no right under international law to use force [against the alleged intrusion of its territorial waters by US military vessels] without first attempting to escort the intruding forces from claimed territory or requestion the United Nations Security Council to effect such removal').
[326] Ratner, 'The Gulf of Sidra incident', 71, footnote 58.

had seen no alternative but to use force in self-defence.[327] The resulting exchange of fire ultimately had led to the sinking of the *Eilat*. In the subsequent Security Council debates, several States expressed support for the UAR's self-defence claim, while others confined themselves to urging both parties to show restraint.[328] Israel strongly objected that the *Eilat* was on a routine patrol on the high seas,[329] but the report of the UN Secretary-General found that the vessel 'was eleven nautical miles in north-eastern direction from Port Said', or, in other words, within UAR territorial waters.[330]

Additional dilemmas arise with regard to unlawful intrusions by foreign submarines. As mentioned earlier, submarines passing through another State's territorial sea are required to navigate on the surface and to show their flag (Article 20 UNCLOS). Yet, what action is available to the coastal State when it detects a submerged submarine? In such situations, it is impossible to verify objectively whether the intrusion is caused by a navigation error or distress, or is undertaken deliberately, for example, for purposes of surveillance. Furthermore, it is impossible for anyone outside a submarine to assess its state of readiness.[331] For this reason, Dinstein argues that the intrusion by a submerged submarine may be regarded as an incipient armed attack and allows the coastal State to employ forcible measures of self-defence.[332] This argument finds support in a number of instances whereby States have in fact exercised forcible measures against submerged submarines, or have asserted the permissibility thereof. In 1982, for example, Swedish naval units spotted a foreign submarine in Harsfjarden, near a top-secret Swedish naval base.[333] In the following days, search units made sonor contacts with a submarine and responded by dropping depth charges as well as by

---

[327] UN Doc. S/8205, 22 October 1967 (UAR). See also: Fleck, 'Rules of engagement of maritime forces', 171–2. Remark: a similar line of reasoning was apparently used by Libya in relation to the 1981 Gulf of Sidra incident. According to Ratner, Libya not only regarded the US naval exercises in the Gulf of Sidra as taking place in its territorial waters, it also believed that the US fleet and planes were in position for an imminent raid upon the northern parts of the country. See Ratner, 'The Gulf of Sidra incident', 71.

[328] See in particular: UN Doc. S/PV.1369, 24 October 1967, §§ 16–20 (UAR), § 57 (USSR), § 105 (Bulgaria); UN Doc. S/PV. 1371, 25 October 1967, § 25 (Syria), §§ 33–6 (USSR).

[329] UN Doc. S/PV.1369, § 27; UN Doc. S/PV. 1371, § 55.

[330] Report of the UN Secretary-General, UN Doc. S/7930/Add.49.

[331] See D. P. O'Connell, *The influence of law on sea power*, p. 78.

[332] Dinstein, *War, aggression and self-defence*, p. 198.

[333] See on this: R. Sadurska, 'Foreign submarines in Swedish waters: the erosion of an international norm', (1984) 10 YJIL 34–57, at 37 *et seq.*; (1982) 28 *Keesing's* 31512.

detonating mines. The submarine, thought to be of Soviet origin, eventually managed to escape. The Soviet government dismissed all accusations. Following the incident, the Swedish Submarine Defence Commission issued a report in which it was argued that the Swedish actions constituted lawful self-defence under Article 51 UN Charter.[334] Furthermore, Sweden changed the instructions to its armed forces for dealing with submerged submarines.[335] In accordance with the new Ordinance, a submarine found submerged in Swedish territorial waters was to be turned back to the high seas, by armed force if necessary. An intruding submarine found submerged was to be forced to the surface. No prior warning was considered necessary for the use of force in the latter situation. The promulgation of the new Swedish policy was apparently approved by Norway and Denmark and tolerated by other members of the international community.[336] One year later, a similar incident took place when Norway used missiles and depth charges against a number of submarines that had been detected in its territorial waters.[337] Although the measures were to no avail, several days after the events the Norwegian government issued the following guidelines:

> If new contact is made with a possible submarine, weapons are to be used for the purpose of forcing it up to the surface regardless of the potential danger of losing the submarine ... If it may be assumed that a possible submarine can no longer escape, one should avoid using such powerful weapons as will entail imminent risk of the submarine being lost. If a possible submarine tries to escape and it is not otherwise possible to prevent the escape, Norwegian authorities will, as a last resort, permit the use of all available weapons.[338]

Furthermore, it can be noted that Argentina has on a number of occasions used depth charges in similar situations[339] and that a number of States, including the Soviet Union, have asserted that they would attack submerged submarines in their territorial waters.[340] On the other hand, it is probably true that many national regulations do not go as far as the quoted instructions to the Swedish and Norwegian armed forces and that most incidents involving submerged submarines do not generally involve a recourse to force. Thus, when in November 2004 Japan engaged

---

[334] See Sadurska, 'Foreign submarines in Swedish waters', 47–8. [335] See *ibid.*, 34, 48–9.
[336] *Ibid.*, 34, 52. [337] See Froman, 'Uncharted waters', 684–8.
[338] Quoted in *ibid.*, 685. [339] It did so in 1958 and in 1960. See (1960) 6 *Keesing's* 17354.
[340] See D. P. O'Connell, *The international law of the sea*. Vol. II (Oxford: Clarendon Press, 1984), p. 297 (footnote 231).

in a so-called 'maritime security operation' against a submerged Chinese submarine, it did not employ depth charges or mines, but instead dispatched anti-submarine patrol planes to track the vessel.[341] According to the Japanese Prime Minister, the demand would be made 'to surface and to show the flag'. If the vessel did not respond, the demand would be made to leave the territorial sea.[342] The incident eventually ended without further sabre-rattling. Japan issued a protest against China and insisted that the incident would not be repeated. China suggested that the submarine had entered Japanese territorial waters by mistake and apologized for the events.

In the end, upon closer examination, whether or not force can lawfully be used against a submerged submarine must be assessed on a case-by-case basis, taking account of the political and security context, as well as other factors that may or may not indicate the existence of a hostile intent. Submerged transit may, for instance, be inspired by the desire to avoid damage resulting from heavy weather conditions. It is therefore important to look at factors such as the extent of the territorial sea, the weather conditions at the time of passage and the track taken by the submarine.[343] What seems to have been a critical factor in the Swedish and Norwegian cases was the repeated nature of the incursions, which made clear that they could not be attributed to distress or navigational errors. In 1982, for instance, Sweden reported no less than forty violations of its territorial waters by foreign submarines.[344] As in the case of the Harsfjarden incident, the submarine's proximity to military installations may moreover indicate that its passage is not innocent, but is aimed at gathering military intelligence. Other factors may be more country-specific.[345] If, taking into account these different elements, no hostile intent can be established, the coastal State should arguably confine itself to demanding the submarine to withdraw and lodging a diplomatic protest against the presumed State of origin. Otherwise, weapons may indeed be used to force the submarine to emerge, and, exceptionally, to destroy it. Even then, however, as is illustrated by the Swedish practice[346]

---

[341] See Y. Hamamoto, 'The incident of a submarine navigating underwater in Japan's territorial sea', (2005) 48 Japanese Annual IL 123–9.
[342] See *ibid.*, 124.   [343] D. P. O'Connell, *The international law of the sea*, p. 296.
[344] See Froman, 'Uncharted waters', 680.
[345] See *ibid.*, 686 (referring to the impracticability for Norway, due to the numerous fjords, to patrol its entire coastline); Sadurska, 'Foreign submarines in Swedish waters', 42 (referring to Sweden's desire to assert and uphold its neutral status).
[346] See Froman, 'Uncharted waters', 683.

and by the cited guidelines of the Norwegian government, defensive measures must be proportionate. The implication is that, except in special circumstances, a warning should first be given, for example by dropping hand grenades at certain intervals to make underwater sound signals.[347] Furthermore, in light of the high probability of casualties, the coastal State should normally first have recourse to weapons that would immobilize or damage the vessel without actually destraying.[348]

So far, we have attempted to summarily sketch the permissibility of defensive measures within a State's own territory in response to small-scale incursions by foreign military or police units by sea, land or air. While the overview may not fully do justice to the complexities of concrete incidents – it does not go into issues of neutrality, the creation of Air Defence Identification Zones or the difficulties arising from competing territorial claims – it nonetheless illustrates that, even though contexts may differ, the applicable legal parameters are essentially the same.

On a concluding note, it must be stressed that forcible action within the State's territory against incursions by *non-State actors* generally does not bring into play the *Ius ad Bellum* framework. Indeed, when, for instance, criminals or armed bands cross their borders, States may take appropriate measures of law enforcement. *In casu*, the possibility for police and the military to use lethal force is governed primarily by human rights law, and possibly – if the situation amounts to an armed conflict – by international humanitarian law. Forcible action against private ships is governed *inter alia* by the relevant provisions on jurisdiction of the 1982 Convention on the Law of the Sea, and the 1952 and 1999 Arrest Conventions,[349] and, in times of armed conflict, by the applicable rules of naval warfare. It is well established in international case law that these rules not only permit the coastal State to engage in the boarding, searching or arresting of a ship, but also entitle it to use such reasonable force as is necessary for securing this objective, even if incidental sinking results.[350] As for aerial incursions (for drug transports for example),

---

[347] E.g. D. P. O'Connell, *The influence of law on sea power*, p. 144.

[348] E.g., Sadurska, 'Foreign submarines in Swedish waters', 50.

[349] See on this: F. Berlingieri, *Arrest of ships: a commentary on the 1952 and 1999 Arrest Conventions*, 3rd edn (London: Informa Publishing, 2000).

[350] Leading cases in this regard are the *I'm Alone* case (*Canada v. United States* of America, (1935) III RIAA 1609) and the *Red Crusader* case (Commission of Enquiry, *Denmark v. United Kingdom*, (1962) 35 ILR 485). In the *M/V 'Saiga'* case, the International Tribunal for the Law of the Sea stated that 'international law ... requires that the use of force must be avoided as far as possible and, where force is unavoidable, it must not go beyond what is

reference must be made to the relevant ICAO regulations on the interception of civil aircraft,[351] as well as to Article 3 *bis* of the Chicago Convention on International Civil Aviation, incorporated after the downing by a Soviet fighter of Korean Airlines Flight 007 in 1983.[352] Article 3 *bis*(a) now provides that:

> every State must refrain from resorting to the use of weapons against civil aircraft in flight and that, in case of interception, the lives of persons on board and the safety of aircraft must not be endangered. This provision shall not be interpreted as modifying in any way the rights and obligations of States set forth in the Charter of the United Nations.

This does not mean that the issue of self-defence may never arise. Indeed, in order to ascertain whether forcible action against incursions by non-State actors may *extend to another State's territory*, one must verify whether such incursions can amount to an armed attack in the sense of Article 51 UN Charter. This is the main question addressed in Chapter 5.[353]

3.4 Attacks against external manifestations of the State

3.4.1 Military units and military installations abroad

The previous Section has attempted to shed some light on the application of the parameters of self-defence in relation to incursions on a State's

---

reasonable and necessary in the circumstances. . . . The normal practice used to stop a ship at sea is first to give an auditory or visual signal to stop, using internationally recognized signals. Where this does not succeed, a variety of actions may be taken, including the firing of shots across the bows of the ship. It is only after the appropriate actions fail that the pursuing vessel may, as a last resort, use force. Even then, an appropriate warning must be issued to the ship and all efforts should be made to ensure that life is not endangered.' ITLOS, *The M/V 'Saiga' case (No.2) (Saint Vincent and the Grenadines* v. *Guinea)*, Judgment of 1 July 1999, (1999) 38 ILM 1323-64, at 1355-6. For an overview of relevant cases, see, e.g., W. J. Fenrick, 'Legal limits on the use of force by Canadian warships engaged in law enforcement', (1980) 18 Can YBIL 113-45, at 129 *et seq.*

[351] ICAO, *Manual concerning interception of civil aircraft*, 1990 (2nd edn), Doc. 9433-AN/926. See on this Park, *La souveraineté aérienne*, pp. 298-307.

[352] See G. F. Fitzgerald, 'The use of force against civil aircraft: the aftermath of the KAL flight 007 incident', (1984) 22 Can YBIL 291-311.

[353] Furthermore, in the wake of the 9/11 attacks it has been suggested that the concept of 'armed attack' could also cover the use of a (possibly hijacked) civil aircraft as a weapon. On whether such a 'renegade' aircraft can be shot down in the exercise of self-defence (in accordance with Article 3 bis(a) Chicago Convention *in fine*), see, e.g.: B. E. Foont, 'Shooting down civilian aircraft: is there an international law?', (2007) 72 JALC 695-725 (especially at 724-5); R. Geiß, 'Civil aircraft as weapons of large-scale destruction: countermeasures, Article 3 bis of the Chicago Convention, and the newly adopted German "Luftsicherheitsgesetz"', (2005) 27 Michigan JIL 227-56.

territory. In relation to attacks against other targets, outside the State's territory, an additional question needs to be addressed, namely, to what extent does the target qualify as an 'external manifestation of the State' for the purpose of Article 51 UN Charter? In order to answer this question, the present Section distinguishes between four different types of possible targets. The categories are dealt with in order of increasing controversiality.

First of all, it is undisputed that military units and military installations abroad can be regarded as 'external manifestations of the State' for the purpose of triggering the right of self-defence.[354] Support for this can be drawn from Article 3(d) of the Definition of Aggression, according to which '[a]n attack by the armed forces of a State on the land, sea or air forces ... of another State' shall constitute aggression. Article 6 of the North Atlantic Treaty moreover provides for collective self-defence against 'an armed attack on the territory ... or on the forces ... of any of the parties'.[355] Furthermore, as is illustrated by the Gulf of Tunkin[356] and the Gulf of Sirte[357] incidents (and, ironically, by the US invocation of self-defence in relation to the shooting by the USS *Vincennes* of an Airbus of Iran Air in 1988),[358] States agree in principle that a military aircraft or vessel which is unlawfully attacked may exercise its right of self-defence.[359] It may also be recalled that in the *Oil Platforms* case, the Court did 'not exclude the possibility that the mining of a single military vessel might be sufficient to bring into play the "inherent right of self-defence"'.[360]

---

[354] E.g., Brownlie, *The use of force by States*, p. 305; Corten, *Le droit contre la guerre*, p. 614, footnote 21; Dinstein, *War, aggression and self-defence*, p. 200; Gazzini, *The changing rules*, p. 136; M. Hakenberg, *Die Iran-Sanktionen der USA während der Teheraner Geiselaffäre aus völkerrechtlicher Sicht* (Frankfurt am Main: Verlag Peter Lang, 1988), p. 226 (stressing the territorial nexus of military vessels and aircraft abroad); P. Malanczuk and M. Akehurst, *Akehurst's modern introduction to international law*, 7th edn (London: Routledge, 1997), p. 315; Randelzhofer, 'Article 51', p. 797; C. Westerdiek, 'Humanitäre Intervention und Maβnahmen zum Schutz eigener Staasangehöriger im Ausland', (1983) 21 AdV 383–401, at 396.
[355] Article 6, North Atlantic Treaty, Washington DC, 4 April 1949, 34 UNTS 243.
[356] See (1964) UNYB 147–9; UN Doc. S/PV.1140, 5 August 1964, §§ 33–74 (US), §§ 78–81 (UK), § 83 (Republic of China).
[357] See (1981) UNYB 360–1; UN Doc. S/14632, 19 August 1981 (US); UN Doc. S/14636, 20 August 1981 (Libya).
[358] UN Doc. S/19989 and UN Doc. S/20005, 6 and 11 July 1988. See *infra* Section 4.3.3.b.
[359] See, e.g., UN Doc. S/PV.1140, 5 August 1964; UN Doc. S/PV.114, 17 August 1964; UN Doc. S/14632, 19 August 1981 (US).
[360] ICJ, *Oil Platforms* case, § 72.

3.4.2 Embassies and diplomatic envoys

Does Article 51 UN Charter extend to attacks against a State's embassies abroad? Several scholars answer in the negative on the grounds that an embassy lacks the quasi-territorial connection to the sending State which military units abroad are endowed with.[361] However, it should be noted that in the *Tehran Embassy* case, the ICJ repeatedly used the phrase 'armed attack' to label the seizure by Islamic militants of the US embassy in Tehran and the hostage-taking of its staff (with the approval of the Iranian government).[362] The Court 'took note'[363] of the fact that the United States had justified its failed attempt to liberate the embassy staff[364] on the basis of Article 51 UN Charter.[365] It expressed understanding for the US', preoccupation with respect to the well-being of its nationals, but at the same time stressed that the conducting of such an operation at a time when the Court was preparing its judgment tended to undermine respect for the judicial process in international relations.[366] If the Court refrained from explicitly ruling on the legality of the rescue attempt, these dicta, when taken together, may suggest that it would have rejected the US's self-defence claim, not because of a lack of an 'armed attack', but because of a failure to exhaust peaceful means.[367]

---

[361] Hakenberg, *Die Iran-Sanktionen*, p. 226; Randelzhofer, 'Article 51', p. 798; T. Schweisfurth, 'Operations to rescue nationals in third States involving the use of force in relation to the protection of human rights', (1980) 23 GYBIL 159–80, at 164.

[362] ICJ, *Case concerning United States diplomatic and consular staff in Tehran (United States of America v. Islamic Republic of Iran)*, Judgment of 24 May 1980, (1980) ICJ Rep 3–46, §§ 57, 64, 91. See: T. L. Stein, 'Contempt, crisis, and the Court: the World Court and the hostage rescue attempt', (1982) 76 AJIL 499–531, at 500–1.

[363] ICJ, *Tehran Embassy* case, § 32.

[364] Remark: the rescue attempt was aborted after a US helicopter collided with a US C-130 transport aircraft over Iranian territory. See: (1980) 26 *Keesing's* 30531.

[365] See UN Doc. S/13908, 25 April 1980 (US). According to the letter, the rescue mission 'was carried out by the United States in exercise of its inherent right of self-defence, with the aim of extricating American nationals who have been and remain the victims of the Iranian armed attack on our embassy'. Compare: UN Doc. S/1395, 28 April 1980 (Iran).

[366] ICJ, *Tehran Embassy* case, §§ 93–4. See on this: Stein, 'Contempt, crisis, and the Court'; O. Schachter, 'International law in the hostage crisis: implications for future cases', in W. Christopher, H. H. Saunders, G. Sick and P. H. Creisberg (eds.), *American hostages in Iran: the conduct of a crisis* (New Haven, CT: Yale University Press, 1985), pp. 325–73, at 339–45.

[367] Also G. Arangio-Ruiz, 'Fourth Report on State Responsibility', (1992-II) YBILC, Part One, 27. Remark: Judges Morozov and Tarazi nonetheless rejected the idea that the United States had suffered an 'armed attack'. ICJ, *Tehran Embassy* case, Dissenting opinion of Judge Morozov, 57; Dissenting opinion of Judge Tarazi, 64–5. By contrast, in his Dissenting opinion in the *Nicaragua* case, Judge Schwebel asserted that the US

In 1998, in response to the terrorist bombings of the US embassies in Nairobi and Dar Es Salaam – which resulted in the deaths of twelve American nationals and over 250 other persons –[368] the United States relied on Article 51 UN Charter to justify aerial strikes against alleged Al Qaeda targets in Sudan and Afghanistan.[369] International reaction was generally mixed and muted.[370] However, those States that did express criticism at the strikes seemed to focus mainly on the *ratione personae* aspect – viz. the lack of involvement of Afghanistan and Sudan in the attacks – and the choice of targets (in particular the targeting of a pharmaceutical plant in Sudan).[371] No State suggested that the embassy bombings could not as such constitute an armed attack. In light thereof, it seems plausible that at least *large-scale* attacks against embassies could be considered as 'armed attacks' in the sense of Article 51.[372]

Several authors suggest that high-level State officials and diplomatic envoys themselves may also be regarded as 'external manifestations' of the State for the purpose of Article 51 UN Charter.[373] In this regard, it may be observed that in 1993, the United States justified its military strikes against the Iraqi intelligence headquarters in Baghdad on the grounds that the attempt to assassinate former President Bush Snr on a

---

self-defence claim constituted 'a sound legal evaluation of the rescue attempt'. ICJ, *Nicaragua* case (Merits), Dissenting opinion of Judge Schwebel, § 65.

[368] The Security Council strongly condemned the terrorist attacks, but refrained from making reference to the concept of 'armed attack' or to the right of self-defence. SC Res. 1189 (1998) of 13 August 1998.

[369] UN Doc. S/1998/780, 20 August 1998 (US).

[370] See Corten, *Le droit contre la guerre*, p. 692; Franck, *Recourse to force*, 94–6; J. Lobel, 'The use of force to respond to terrorist attacks: the bombing of Sudan and Afghanistan', (1999) 24 YJIL 537–57; R. Wedgwood, 'Responding to terrorism: the strikes against bin Laden', (1999) 24 YJIL 559–76. See also *infra* Section 5.2.1.b.

[371] See e.g., (1998) UNYB 185, 1219–20.

[372] Accepting that attacks against a State's embassy can trigger the right of self-defence: e.g., Dinstein, *War, aggression and self-defence*, pp. 197–8; Gazzini, *The changing rules*, p. 137; Schachter, 'International law in the hostage crisis', p. 328; I. Seidl-Hohenveldern, *Völkerrecht*, 5th edn (Cologne: Carl Heymans Verlag, 1984), § 717; T. C. Wingfield and J. E. Meyen, 'Lillich on the forcible protection of nationals abroad', (2002) 77 *Naval War College – Int'l Law Studies* 73. See also G. Arangio-Ruiz, *The UN Declaration on Friendly Relations and the system of the sources of international law* (Alphen aan de Rijn: Sijthoff, 1979), p. 105.

[373] E.g., Dinstein, *War, aggression and self-defence*, p. 200 (referring to diplomatic envoys and visiting dignitaries); Gazzini, *The changing rules*, p. 137. See also Arangio-Ruiz, *The UN Declaration on Friendly Relations*, p. 105. However, expressing doubts: L. Condorelli, 'A propos de l'attaque américaine contre l'Irak du 26 juin 1993: letter d'un professeur désemparé aux lecteurs du JEDI', (1994) 5 EJIL 134–44, at 136. Against: see footnote 361.

State visit to Kuwait City constituted a 'direct attack on the United States'.[374] In the subsequent Security Council debate, a majority of Council Members expressed their approval of the US actions. The representative of New Zealand explicitly stated that '[a]ny nation that seeks to assassinate the Head of State or a member of the senior political leadership of another State commits an act of aggression. Such actions are at the most serious end of the scale because Heads of States symbolize the sovereignty and integrity of their country.'[375] Still, it is difficult to find other examples of forcible responses to attacks against political leaders or diplomatic envoys abroad. In 1983, four South Korean ministers as well as several other officials were killed in a bomb explosion during a visit to Rangoon, in what appeared to be an attempt by North Korea to assassinate the South Korean President. South Korea openly blamed the North for the attack and initially made vague threats of a military response, yet it eventually refrained from engaging in the use of force.[376] Furthermore, while terrorist attacks against individual diplomats have regrettably taken place on numerous occasions,[377] these acts have generally been framed in terms of 'crimes' punishable before a court of law, rather than as 'armed attacks', warranting the exercise of self-defence.[378] In 1982, Israel did draw attention to a number of attacks against its diplomats to justify its intervention in Lebanon.[379] At the same time, it has to be conceded that these attacks formed part of a larger list of alleged terrorist attacks which Israel relied on,[380] and that several States explicitly noted that the murder of a single ambassador, however despicable, could not justify the invasion of Lebanese territory.[381] The precedential significance of the incidents concerned is difficult to evaluate, since in virtually all cases, attacks against diplomats have been carried out by non-State groups, thus inevitably bringing into play the *ratione personae*

---

[374] UN Doc. S/PV.3245, 27 June 1993, 6.
[375] *Ibid.*, 23. See also: D. Kristiotis, 'The legality of the 1993 US missile strike on Iraq and the right of self-defence in international law', (1996) 45 ICLQ 162-77, at 173.
[376] (1983) 29 *Keesing's* 32566; A. D. Surchin, 'Terror and the law: the unilateral use of force and the June 1993 bombing of Baghdad', (1994–5) 5 Duke JCIL 457-97, at 470-1.
[377] Remark: relevant incidents are listed in the United Nations Yearbooks under the heading 'protection of diplomats'. See, e.g., (1983) UNYB 1116-17; (1985) UNYB 1172-3; (1986) UNYB 993-4.
[378] E.g., UN Doc. S/14951, 3 April 1982 (Israel re the shooting of an Israeli diplomat in Paris); UN Doc. S/15158, 4 June 1982 (Israel re the shooting of the Israeli ambassador in London).
[379] UN Doc. S/PV.3275, 6 June 1982, 3.   [380] *Ibid.*
[381] E.g., UN Doc. S/PV.3274, 5 June 1982, 3 (UK as well as Ireland).

controversy (cf. *infra*). Still, an argument could be made that an isolated attack against a diplomat – as opposed to an attack against a head of State or a former head of State? – is as such of insufficient gravity to permit a *post facto* defensive response.

3.4.3 Civilian aircraft and merchant vessels

This brings us to a third category of possible targets of attacks, namely civilian aircraft and merchant vessels. Contrary to their military counterparts, they do not constitute quasi-territorial extensions of their respective home States. Nor do they in any way officially represent their State abroad as embassies and diplomatic envoys do. Instead they are mere private chattels, often located hundreds or thousands of miles from the flag State or State of registration, and having little connection with the latter.[382] How then can they be regarded as 'external manifestations' of the State for present purposes?

The question has mainly come up in relation to attacks against fishing and other merchant vessels, because of their vital economic interest for many States. Thus, throughout the negotiations on the Definition of Aggression, Japan noted that its marine transport was vital to its existence, and that an attack against its maritime fleet would be just as devastating as an invasion or a blockade.[383] For this reason, Japan, supported by other States with comparable fishing interests (as well as by the USSR and the US), insisted on the inclusion in the Definition of Aggression of such attacks. On the other hand, Indonesia, Ecuador, Syria and other coastal States feared that this proposal might inspire retaliatory action in the name of self-defence against a State that simply took action against vessels fishing illegally within their territorial waters, and emphasized that there should be no restraint on the right to use force if necessary to preserve their coastal resources from illegal exploitation.[384] In the end, a compromise solution was found through the reference in Article 3(d) of the Definition to an attack on the 'marine and air fleets of another State.' According to Broms, this phrase was carefully chosen to indicate that it did not apply to cases where naval or police action was

---

[382] A. V. Lowe, 'Self-defence at sea', in W. E. Butler (ed.), *The non-use of force in international law* (Dordrecht: Kluwer) (1989), pp. 185–202, at 188–9.
[383] Broms, 'The definition of aggression', 350; Ferencz, *Defining international aggression*. Vol. II, p. 36. E.g., UN Doc. A/AC.134/SR.106, 30.
[384] Ferencz, *Defining international aggression*. Vol. II, p. 36.

directed against one or a few vessels fishing within the territorial sea of another State nor to a case arising from a less important incident.[385] The same was to apply *mutatis mutandis* to civilian aircraft.[386] As part of the compromise, an explanatory (foot)note was added to the report of the Special Committee, confirming that 'nothing in the Definition, and in particular Article 3(d), shall be construed as in any way prejudicing the authority of a State to exercise its rights within its national jurisdiction, provided such exercise is not inconsistent with the Charter of the United Nations'.[387]

The wording of Article 3(d) of the Definition of Aggression has given rise to two juxtaposed strands in legal doctrine. On the one hand, a number of authors interpret the reference to *fleets* as implying that only a massive attack directed against a State's entire merchant fleet will qualify as an 'armed attack', and then only if the State's economy depends on its marine commerce or fisheries.[388] On the other hand, many scholars reject this restrictive approach as incompatible with customary practice.[389] According to Brownlie, 'there can be no doubt' that the armed forces of the flag State may use reasonable force to defend vessels on the high seas from attack whether by pirates or forces acting with or without the authority of any State.[390] Lowe and Gray find that the use of force by a

---

[385] Broms, 'The definition of aggression', 351.   [386] Ibid.
[387] Remark: Japan again asserted that paragraph 3(d) was not intended to cover minor incidents or isolated cases, *ibid.*, at 365. See also: UN Doc. A/AC.134/SR.106, at 24 (Indonesia). Throughout the final debates within the UNGA 6th Committee in October 1974, numerous countries emphasized that Article 3(d) left intact the coastal State's right to exercise its jurisdiction vis-à-vis foreign vessels engaged in unlawful activities within the oceanic areas under its jurisdiction. See, e.g., UN Doc. A/C.6/SR.1473, § 12 (Canada); UN Doc. A/C.6/SR.1474, § 8 (Peru); § 20 (Chile); § 35 (Madagascar); § 50 (Brazil); § 58 (Colombia); UN Doc. A/C.6/SR.1475, § 15 (PRC); § 20 (Syria); UN Doc. A/C.6/SR.1476, § 3 (Ecuador); UN Doc. A/C.6/SR.1477, § 2 (Pakistan); § 15 (Libya); § 21 (UK); UN Doc. A/C.6/SR.1478, § 3 (Bangladesh); § 12 (Iraq); § 30 (Australia); UN Doc. A/C.6/SR.1479, § 27 (Yemen).
[388] E.g., Constantinou, *The right of self-defence*, p. 82 (Constantinou does add that the attacked ship may be entitled to take proportionate counter-measures to repel the use of force against it). Also, more moderately: Dinstein, *War, aggression and self-defence*, p. 200.
[389] See, e.g., C. Greenwood, 'Comments', in I. F. Dekker and H. H. G. Post (eds.), *The Gulf War of 1980–1988: the Iran–Iraq War in legal perspective* (Dordrecht: Martinus Nijhoff, 1992), pp. 212–16, at 213–14. Also Raab, 'Armed attack', 726–7; N. Ronzitti, *Rescuing nationals abroad through military coercion and intervention on grounds of humanity* (Dordrecht: Martinus Nijhoff, 1985), p. 148.
[390] Brownlie, *The use of force by States*, p. 305.

State to protect its flag vessels if they have come under attack is 'generally acknowledged' and 'uncontroversial'.[391]

The latter view appears to be more convincing. Customary practice offers a good deal of evidence supporting the view that flag States may sometimes intervene when one or more merchant vessels are under attack. In early 1959, for example, Mexico broke off diplomatic relations with Guatemala following an incident in which planes of the Guatemalan Air Force machine-gunned three Mexican shrimp boats that, according to Guatemala, were illegally fishing in its territorial waters, killing three fishermen and wounding fourteen others.[392] The Mexican President publicly stated that the use of force to repel force would have been authorized by Article 51 of the Charter.[393] Furthermore, the US Commander's Handbook on the Law of Naval Operations asserts in general terms that although 'US armed forces should not interfere in the legitimate law enforcement actions of foreign authorities, even when directed against US vessel [or] aircraft', '[i]nternational law, embodied in the doctrines of self-defense and protection of nationals, provides the authority for the use of proportionate force by US warships and military aircraft when necessary for the protection of US flag vessels and aircraft ... against unlawful violence in and over international waters'.[394] Article 6(1) of the North Atlantic Treaty provides for collective self-defence against 'an armed attack on the territory of any of the parties ... or on the forces, *vessels or aircraft* in this area of any of the parties'. Most importantly, supporting evidence can be derived from the practice of States during the 1980–88 'Tanker War' in the Persian Gulf. Despite repeated calls from the Security Council to respect the freedom of navigation,[395] both Iran and Iraq repeatedly engaged in attacks on merchant vessels of neutral States. Although third States generally did not contest the right of belligerents to search and visit of merchant vessels, several Western naval powers (mainly the US, UK, France and Italy) sent warships to the Gulf in order to act as 'escorts' of their merchant vessels.[396] In doing so, these States clearly acted upon the assumption that

---

[391] C. Gray, 'The British position with regard to the Gulf conflict (Iran–Iraq): Part 2', (1991) 40 ICLQ 464–73, at 469; Lowe, 'Self-defence at sea', p. 188.

[392] See (1959) 12 *Keesing's* 16690. [393] See Brownlie, *The use of force by States*, p. 305.

[394] US Department of the Navy and US Department of Homeland Security, *The Commander's Handbook of the Law of Naval Operations*, pp. 3–7.

[395] E.g., SC Res. 540 (1983) of 31 October 1983; SC Res. 552 (1984) of 1 June 1984.

[396] A. de Guttry and N. Ronzitti, 'Introduction', in A. de Guttry and N. Ronzitti (eds.), *The Iran–Iraq War (1980–1988) and the law of naval warfare* (Cambridge: Grotius Publications, 1993), pp. 3–15, at 5–7.

it was lawful to use force to protect their merchant ships from unlawful attacks.[397] This reasoning explains why numerous (Kuwaiti and other) merchant vessels were re-flagged to the flag of one of these naval powers.

In the *Oil Platforms* case, which resulted from a number of armed incidents between the US and Iran in the Persian Gulf, the two different views surfaced in the respective memorials submitted by the two parties. In relation to the missile attack against the *Sea Isle City*, a US-reflagged Kuwaiti tanker, Iran contended that there was no 'armed attack', 'because a single merchant ship does not belong to those external manifestations of a State which are protected under . . . Article 2(4) of the Charter . . .'.[398] Relying on the reference to 'marine and air fleets' in the Definition of Aggression, Iran argued that 'military action against an individual merchant ship may be an infringement of the rights of the flag State, but it does not constitute an armed attack triggering that State's right of self-defence'.[399] Hence, according to Iran, only massive acts of violence against the merchant shipping of a State, attacking whole fleets, would permit a recourse to self-defence.[400] By contrast, the US stressed that nothing in the *Nicaragua* judgment suggested that mine and missile attacks on naval and commercial vessels were anything less than an armed attack,[401] and that, in any case, the Definition of Aggression did not attempt to define 'armed attacks' as such.[402] The US warned that if the Iranian view were adopted, this would license any attacking State to freely conduct sneak attacks beyond the reach of any viable legal regime of self-defence.[403]

While these two positions seem at first sight diametrically opposed, it is important to add that Iran not only recognized that 'an armed attack against an individual merchant ship constitutes an illegal infringement of the sovereignty of the flag State', but also accepted that a State has the

---

[397] Greenwood, 'Comments', p. 214. For relevant official documents, see de Guttry and Ronzitti (eds.), *The Iran–Iraq War (1980–1988)*.
[398] ICJ, *Oil Platforms* case, Reply and defence to counter-claim submitted by the Islamic Republic of Iran, 10 March 1999, § 7.13(4).
[399] *Ibid.*, §§ 7.36–38.   [400] *Ibid.*, § 7.38.
[401] ICJ, *Oil Platforms* case, Counter-memorial and counter-claim submitted by the United States of America, 23 June 1997, § 4.19.
[402] ICJ, *Oil Platforms* case, Rejoinder submitted by the United States of America, 23 March 2001, §§ 5.16–5.20.
[403] *Ibid.*, § 5.19. The US moreover argued that the attack against the *Sea Isle City* formed part of a 'widespread, deliberate effort to undermine the security of US shipping in the Gulf through the use of armed force' (§§ 5.21–5.22).

right 'to protect itself against such infringements'.[404] More concretely, Iran accepted that 'a flag State can use force against a foreign vessel or aircraft actually attacking a merchant ship under its flag. It need not stand idle and let the ship be destroyed'.[405] In other words, even if it did not formally regard this as an exercise of the right of self-defence, Iran agreed that some degree of counter-force by the flag State was permitted. This illustrates that the right of the flag State to use force in order to protect a merchant vessel against unlawful attack was as such not contested. Rather, the disagreement between the US and Iran – and, for that matter, between the two strands in legal doctrine – hinges mainly on (1) the legal basis of that right, and (2) on the question whether an attack against one or more merchant vessels warrants not only on-the-spot reaction, but may sanction the use of force by the flag State *after* the attack itself has ended (as in the *Oil Platforms* case).

As regards the first issue, writers have generally avoided explaining the legal basis of the right of flag States to protect their merchant ships against attack.[406] In light of the comprehensive character of the Charter rules on inter-State use of force, however, it may be presumed that this right can only be a special application of the right of self-defence, inspired by the ships' economic interest for the flag State.[407] This seems to correspond to the way States have generally framed it: Mexico in 1959 did invoke the language of Article 51 UN Charter, and the US Commander's Handbook on the Law of Naval Operations similarly refers to the international legal doctrine of self-defence (cf. *supra*). Significantly, several statements of the ICJ in the *Oil Platforms* case implicitly confirm the possibility that deliberate unlawful attacks against merchant vessels may sometimes be equated with an 'armed attack' against the State.[408] In paragraph 64, after finding that the Silkworm missile could not have been aimed specifically at the *Sea Isle City*, the Court noted that the *Texaco Caribbean* was not flying a US flag, 'so that an attack on the vessel is not in itself to be equated with an attack on that State'.[409] Subsequently, in relation to the US attacks against the Salman

---

[404] ICJ, *Oil Platforms* case, Reply and defence to counter-claim submitted by the Islamic Republic of Iran, 10 March 1999, § 7.41.
[405] *Ibid.* [406] Lowe, 'Self-defence at sea', p. 188.
[407] See, e.g., *ibid.*; Gray, 'The British position', 469; Ronzitti, 'The expanding law of self-defence', 350. But see M. Bothe, 'Neutrality at sea', in I. F. Dekker and H. H. G. Post (eds.), *The Gulf War of 1980–1988*, pp. 205–11, at 209–10.
[408] Several authors come to this conclusion: e.g., Jimenez Kwast, 'Maritime law enforcement', 58–9, 85; Ochoa-Ruiz and Salamanca-Aguado, 'Exploring the limits of international law', 513; Ronzitti, *Rescuing nationals abroad*, p. 148.
[409] ICJ, *Oil Platforms* case, § 64.

and Nasr complexes, the Court declared that: 'No attacks on United States-flagged vessels ... have been brought to the Court's attention, other than the mining of the USS *Samuel B. Roberts* [(a US warship)] itself. The question is therefore whether that incident sufficed in itself to justify action in self-defence, as amounting to an "armed attack".'[410]

In light thereof, we may provisionally conclude that Article 51 UN Charter permits *on-the-spot* defensive measures by the flag State to protect merchant vessels from unlawful attacks. At the same time, as the preparatory works of the Definition of Aggression make clear, forcible measures by the flag State may not interfere with the exercise of the right to board, search and arrest by another State as governed by the applicable rules of the law of the sea (and international law on naval warfare), nor with the use of (reasonable) force to this end, as recognized in the *I'm Alone* and other cases.[411] For this reason, the flag State in principle cannot intervene in the territorial waters of another State nor in the adjacent fishery zones in order to protect its vessels.[412] Furthermore, the use of force to protect merchant vessels must at all times meet the necessity and proportionality standards. The implication is that mere interposition of warships, without actual recourse to force – as applied for example by the United Kingdom in the *Red Crusader* incident[413] – will probably suffice in the majority of cases.

---

[410] *Ibid.*, § 72.
[411] See *supra* note 350. Remark: as Jimenez Kwast observes, there is a difficult yet significant distinction between naval law enforcement and the use of force in the sense of Article 2 (4). Both categories of 'force' at sea can be lawful or unlawful: '[U]nlawful forcible law enforcement will not necessarily constitute the use of force in the sense of Article 2(4) anymore than that lawful use of force will automatically qualify as law enforcement' (62–3). The author tentatively identifies three factors which may serve to conceptualize the international legal classification of forcible action at sea: (1) the functional object (especially whether force was used by police forces or military units); (2) the status of the subjected vessel (here the implication is that forcible action against foreign vessels with 'sovereign status' falls within the Charter framework); and (3) the location of the actions (was this an area over which the State had jurisdiction?). Jimenez Kwast, 'Maritime law enforcement', 72 *et seq.*
[412] See Ronzitti, *Rescuing nationals abroad*, pp. 144–8. According to Ronzitti, the flag State is not entitled to intervene in the territorial waters or fishery zones of another State, even if the measures taken by the coastal State against the intruding foreign vessel are excessive and out of proportion. On the other hand, the flag State may intervene when, outside the aforementioned areas, the vessel of another State, exercising the right of hot pursuit, opens fire and endangers the lives of the crew of the pursued vessel.
[413] *In casu*, a UK warship, the HMS *Troubridge*, interposed between a Danish warship, the *Niels Ebbesen*, and a UK fishing boat, the *Red Crusader*. The latter vessel had escaped arrest and was being pursued by the *Niels Ebbesen*, which, according to the Commission

As regards our second issue, the aforementioned excerpts from the *Oil Platforms* case also indicate that the Court to some extent followed the US line of reasoning according to which attacks against merchant vessels could be taken into consideration to examine whether a *post facto* defensive response, aimed at the prevention of future attacks, meets the necessity and proportionality thresholds. Put more plainly, an attack against a merchant vessel, when repeated or combined with other attacks, can possibly justify a proportionate *post facto* defensive response. On the other hand, a single attack against a merchant vessel is probably insufficient to justify anything beyond on-the-spot-reaction.[414] The lack in customary practice of public invocations of self-defence in response to the unlawful sinking or arrest of a merchant vessel points in the same direction. Indeed, flag States challenging the legality of the seizure of their merchant vessels or claiming the use of excessive force during arrest, have generally presented their challenges through peaceful settlement processes; either by diplomatic process (as in the *Virginius* case), or international adjudication (as in the *I'm Alone*, *Corfu Channel* and *M/V 'Saiga'* cases).[415] In those cases where the concerned international tribunals or commissions of inquiry found that seizure had been unlawful or that excessive force had been used, this conduct was labeled a 'violation of the rights of the flag State', but not an 'armed attack'.[416] Even in those cases where merchant vessels were deliberately attacked in situations unrelated to naval law enforcement – and where the label of 'armed attack' would appear more appropriate – flag States have generally not engaged in defensive measures after the completion of the attack. Thus, returning to the 1959 incident between Mexico and Guatemala, the Mexican President

---

of Inquiry, had used excessive force to halt the escaping vessel. The Commission found that the British commanders 'made every effort to avoid any recourse to violence between *Niels Ebbesen* and *Red Crusader*. Such an attitude and conduct were impeccable.' Commission of Enquiry, *Red Crusader* case, 500.

[414] See also Bothe, 'Neutrality at sea', p. 209; Brownlie, *The use of force by States*, p. 305.

[415] See J. J. Paust, 'The seizure and recovery of the *Mayaguez*', (1975–6) 85 Yale LJ 774–806, at 796–7. See also: Fenrick, 'Legal limits on the use of force', 139 *et seq.*

[416] E.g., ITLOS, *The M/V 'Saiga'* case (No.2), § 159. Remark: interestingly, in *Guyana v. Suriname*, the Arbitral Tribunal found that 'the expulsion from the disputed area of the CGX oil rig and drill ship *C.E. Thornton* by Suriname on 3 June 2000 constituted a threat of the use of force in breach of ... the UN Charter ...'. *Guyana and Suriname*, Arbitral Award of 17 September 2007, available at www.pca-cpa.org/upload/files/Guyana-Suriname%20Award.pdf (accessed 4 May 2009).

claimed that he could have used force under Article 51 UN Charter to *repel* the attacks by the Guatemalan Air Force against Mexican fishing boats. Mexico did not assert, let alone exercise, a right to use force after these attacks had taken place, instead confining itself to diplomatic measures.[417] A notable exception in customary practice concerns the 1975 US commando operation organized to achieve the release of the *Mayaguez* and its crew after arrest by Cambodian forces, which was reported to the Security Council as an exercise of the right of self-defence in accordance with Article 51 of the UN Charter.[418] However, even if one were to agree with the US view that the seizure of the *Mayaguez* had been unlawful, in light of the foregoing, it can hardly be maintained that this in itself amounted to an armed attack justifying a recourse to self-defence.[419]

It should finally be noted that by the late 1980s some of the States that deployed warships to the Gulf during the Iran–Iraq War to protect merchant shipping made suggestions that they would also intervene to protect neutral merchant ships of other States against unlawful attack. The Commander of the French naval forces, for instance, stated that his warships would fire on Iranian gunboats that refused to break off attack on neutral merchant ships.[420] Likewise, while the US had earlier confined itself to the rescuing of crew members from damaged vessels, in 1988 it announced that it extended naval protection to cover 'friendly innocent neutral vessels flying a non-belligerent flag outside declared war/exclusion zones, that [were] not carrying contraband or

---

[417] See (1959) 12 *Keesing's* 16690; See Brownlie, *The use of force by States*, p. 305.
[418] See UN Doc. S/11689, 14 May 1975 (US). According to the US, the 'seizure was unlawful and involved a clear-cut illegal use of force'. Therefore the US had taken 'appropriate measures under Article 51 of the United Nations Charter . . .'.
[419] Also Dinstein, *War, aggression and self-defence*, p. 200 (quoted with approval by Iran: ICJ, *Oil Platforms* case, Reply and defence to counter-claim submitted by the Islamic Republic of Iran, 10 March 1999, § 7.37); U. Beyerlin, '*Mayaguez* incident', in EPIL *Vol. 3*, 333–5. For an extensive analysis of the case, see Paust, 'The seizure and recovery of the *Mayaguez*', 800–3; J. J. Paust, 'More revelations about *Mayaguez* (and its secret cargo)', (1981) 4 Boston College ICLRev 61–76. According to Paust, the operation was mainly justified as an operation to protect the lives of American nationals. It therefore appears to be more relevant for our analysis on the controversial issue of 'protection of nationals abroad' (cf. *infra*). Furthermore, the US operation probably violated the necessity and proportionality standards, since diplomatic negotiations were going on and Cambodia had declared that it would soon release the crew. See Paust, 'The seizure and recovery of the *Mayaguez*', 800–3.
[420] See Fleck, 'Rules of engagement of maritime forces', 173.

resisting legitimate visit and search by a Persian Gulf belligerent'.[421] The US Navy intervened at least twice to attacks against neutral ships by Iranian gunboats (to protect a Danish and a Panamanian tanker).[422]

However, while Lowe argues that there are good policy reasons for permitting third States to intervene for the protection of merchant ships that represent an economic interest for them and sees an 'emerging train of thought', he admits that there is insufficient evidence in customary practice to elevate this argument to the status of a rule of law.[423] Significantly, in the *Oil Platforms* case, Iran argued that attacks against non-US flagged merchant vessels could not be of any relevance for the question of self-defence.[424] While the United States claimed that the attack against the US-flagged *Sea Isle City* should be regarded as an 'armed attack' against the US, it did not make similar assertions in relation to attacks against merchant vessels of other States, but merely made a general reference to the widespread attacks against neutral shipping, in violation of the freedom of navigation.[425] In the end, as noted *supra*, the Court unequivocally stated that 'the *Texaco Caribbean*, whatever its ownership, was not flying a United States flag, so that an attack on the vessel is not in itself to be equated with an attack on that State'.[426] Our conclusion must therefore be that the use of force to protect third-State merchant vessels from unlawful attacks is excluded, unless (1) the flag State consents or has done so in a prior

---

[421] See Gray, 'The British position', 468; Lowe, 'Self-defence at sea', p. 185; (1988) 31 *Keesing's*, at 36169. Remark: the US *Commanders' Handbook on the Law of Naval Operations* provides that: 'International law, embodied in the concept of collective self-defense, provides authority for the use of proportionate force necessary for the protection of foreign flag vessels and aircraft and foreign nationals and their property from *unlawful* violence, including terrorist or piratical attacks, at sea. In such instances, consent of the flag nation should first be obtained unless prior arrangements are already in place or the necessity to act immediately to save human life does not permit obtaining such consent.' US Department of the Navy and US Department of Homeland Security, *The Commander's Handbook of the Law of Naval Operations*, pp. 3–8.

[422] See Gray, 'The British position', 469. Remark: the UK expressed sympathy for this policy, but continued to adopt a more restrictive policy (see *ibid.*; Lowe, 'Self-defence at sea', pp. 186–7).

[423] *Ibid.*, 198.

[424] ICJ, *Oil Platforms* case, Memorial submitted by the Islamic Republic of Iran, 8 June 1993, § 4.52.

[425] ICJ, *Oil Platforms* case, Rejoinder submitted by the United States of America, 23 March 2001, § 5.22.

[426] ICJ, *Oil Platforms* case, § 64. Also Raab, 'Armed attack', 729.

arrangement, so that protective action would qualify as collective self-defence, or (2) if a warship is interposed between victim and attacker, so that an attack against the merchant vessel could also be regarded, because of the particular context, as an armed attack against the warship itself.

3.4.4 Protection of nationals[427]

3.4.4.a The doctrinal debate

The last and most contentious aspect regarding the extra-territorial scope of the 'armed attack' concept concerns the permissibility of military intervention in the territory of a third State aimed at the protection and/or rescuing of threatened nationals of the intervening State.[428] States and scholars tend to define the so-called 'protection of nationals' doctrine in terms of the three cumulative conditions spelled out by Waldock. According to the latter: (1) there must be an imminent threat of injury to nationals; (2) a failure or inability on the part of the territorial sovereign to protect them; and (3) the action of the intervening State must be strictly confined to the object of protecting its nationals against injury.[429] There is little doubt that before 1945 interventions of this type were permitted.[430] Similarly, it is accepted in the Charter era that rescue or evacuation can lawfully be undertaken when the territorial State consents. Problems arise, however, when no such approval is given, or when the approval is of questionable validity (e.g., when the territorial State is plagued by civil strife or anarchy). Indeed, whether or not *forcible*

---

[427] The present section is based on an article previously published in the Journal of Conflict and Security Law: T. Ruys, 'The "protection of nationals" doctrine revisited', (2008) 13 JCSL 233–71.

[428] Remark: 'protection of nationals' bears some resemblance to so-called 'humanitarian intervention' in the sense that both involve the use of force to prevent harm or additional harm to individuals or groups in the territory of another State. On the other hand, it is generally agreed that, from a legal perspective, the two must be kept separate. The primary reason is that humanitarian intervention essentially aims at protecting the territorial State's population against massive human rights abuses, whereas protection of nationals is (primarily) geared towards the well-being of the intervening State's own nationals. See, e.g., K. E. Eichensehr, 'Defending nationals abroad: assessing the lawfulness of forcible hostage rescues', (2007–08) 48 Virginia JIL 451–84, at 461–3.

[429] Waldock, 'The regulation of the use of force', 467.

[430] See *ibid.*, 467; Brownlie, *The use of force by States*, pp. 289 *et seq.*

protection of nationals is compatible with the Charter provisions on the recourse to force is one of the most hotly debated issues of the *Ius ad Bellum*. Both legality and legal basis are contested.

Scholars supporting the doctrine invoke a wide variety of legal bases.[431] A first group contends that forcible intervention for the protection of nationals does not infringe Article 2(4) UN Charter, since such action does not impair the 'territorial integrity or political independence' of a State; it merely rescues nationals from a danger which the territorial State cannot or will not prevent.[432] A second and more widespread approach holds that it constitutes an exercise of the right of self-defence.[433] Under this heading, a twofold argument is put forward. First, Bowett and others claim that the doctrine forms part of pre-existing custom, which was left unabridged by the inclusion in the Charter of the *inherent* right of self-defence. Second, it is argued that nationals abroad form part of a State's population and are therefore one of its essential attributes, implying that an attack against nationals abroad can be equated to an attack against the State itself. Other justifications which have on occasion been raised but which have generated little imitation include the state of 'necessity'[434] or the growing importance attached to humanitarian considerations and human rights

---

[431] For a discussion hereof see: Ronzitti, *Rescuing nationals abroad*, pp. 1–23; R. J. Zedalis, 'Protection of nationals abroad: is consent the basis of legal obligation?', (1990) 25 Texas JIL 209–70, at 221–44.

[432] E.g., L. Henkin, *How nations behave. Law and foreign policy*, 2nd edn (New York: Columbia University Press, 1979), p. 145; R. Higgins, *The development of international law*, pp. 220–1; R. B. Lillich, 'Forcible self-help to protect human rights', (1967) 53 Iowa LRev 325–51, at 336–7; J. J. Paust, 'Entebbe and self-help: the Israeli response to terrorism', (1978) 2 *Fletcher Forum* 86–91, at 89–90.

[433] E.g., Bowett, *Self-defence in international law*, pp. 87–105; L. Doswald-Beck, 'The legality of the United States intervention in Grenada', (1984) 31 NILR 335–77, at 360; G. Fitzmaurice, 'The general principles of international law considered from the standpoint of the rule of law', (1957-II) 92 RdC 1–227, at 172–3; A. Gerard, 'L'Opération Stanleyville-Paulis devant le Parlement belge et les Nations Unies', (1967) 3 RBDI 242–69, at 254–5; C. Greenwood, 'International law and the United States air operation against Libya', (1986–7) 89 West Virginia LRev 933–60, at 941; R. B. Lillich, 'Forcible protection of nationals abroad: the Liberian "incident" of 1990', (1993) 35 GYBIL 205–23, at 216; O. Schachter, 'In defense of international rules on the use of force', (1986) 53 Un Chicago LRev 113–46, at 139; O. Schachter, 'The right of States to use armed force', (1983–4) 82 Michigan L Rev 1620–46, at 1632; T. C. Wingfield, 'Forcible protection of nationals abroad', (1999–2000) 104 Dickinson L Rev 439–69, at 468.

[434] E.g., J. Raby, 'The state of necessity and the use of force to protect nationals', (1988) 26 Can YBIL 253–72.

norms.[435] Last but not least, several authors, observing that protection of nationals is difficult to fit into predetermined legal categories, have argued that it constitutes an autonomous exception to Article 2(4), separate from Article 51 UN Charter, and grown out of customary practice.[436]

Against this, however, a considerable group of scholars regard 'protection of nationals' as such as incompatible with Articles 2(4) and 51 UN Charter, and therefore unlawful.[437] Both opposing tendencies include prominent authorities. Various scholars have on occasion claimed to belong to the majority group, but it appears difficult to determine which side holds the upper hand numerically.[438]

A number of arguments invoked to support the interventions under consideration have been discarded in previous chapters. Thus, the suggestion that forcible rescue operations fall outside the scope of Article 2(4) UN Charter is incompatible with that provision's comprehensive nature, as supported by the Charter's *travaux* and customary practice.[439] The idea that Article 51 UN Charter left unaffected pre-existing custom was rejected in our opening chapter. It is submitted the 'state of necessity' cannot provide a satisfactory legal basis either.[440] Still, if some consider it wholly artificial to expand the concept of 'armed attack' of Article 51 to cover attacks against nationals abroad,[441] the present author does not believe that this interpretation can be ruled out per se. Several scholars

---

[435] E.g., D.J. Gordon, 'Use of force for the protection of nationals abroad: the Entebbe incident', (1977) 9 Case Western Res JIL 117–34, at 132; Schweisfurth, 'Operations to rescue nationals', 161 *et seq.*

[436] E.g., Gazzini, *The changing rules*, p. 173; Ronzitti, 'The expanding law of self-defence', 354. Consider also E. Giraud, 'La théorie de la légitime défense', (1934-III) 49 RdC 687–868, at 738.

[437] Regarding protection of nationals as unlawful: e.g., U. Beyerlin, 'Die israelische Befreiungsaktion von Entebbe in völkerrechtlicher Sicht', (1977) 37 ZaöRV 213–43; M. Bothe, 'Friedenssicherung und Kriegsrecht', in W. Graf Vitzthum (ed.), *Völkerrecht*, 4th edn (Berlin: de Gruyter, 2007), pp. 637–725, at 656; I. Brownlie, 'The principle of non-use of force in contemporary international law', in W. E. Butler (ed.), *The non-use of force*, pp. 17–27, at 23; Mrazek, 'Prohibition on the use and threat of force', 97; J. Quigley, 'The legality of the United States invasion of Panama', (1990) 15 YJIL 276–315, at 287, 292–4; Randelzhofer, 'Article 51', pp. 798–9; Randelzhofer, 'Article 2 (4)', pp. 132–3; Verdross and Simma, *Universelles Völkerrecht*, § 1338; H. Wehberg, 'L'interdiction du recours à la force. Le principe et les problèmes qui se posent', (1951-I) 78 RdC 1–121, at 71.

[438] However: cf. *infra* for the views of the Members of the International Law Commission.

[439] See *supra*, Section 2.1.2.   [440] See on this: *infra*, Section 5.1.1.b.

[441] J. E. S. Fawcett, 'Intervention in international law: a study of some recent cases', (1961-II) 103 RdC 343–423, at 404; Zedalis, 'Protection of nationals abroad', 236–7.

have emphasized the omission in the UNGA Definition of Aggression of a reference to 'attacks against nationals abroad'. Contrasting this lacunae with the inclusion of attacks against 'marine and air fleets of another State' (Article 3(d)), these authors conclude that the Definition prohibits forcible action in the former case.[442] Against this, it can be argued that the list of Article 3 is not exhaustive, and that paragraph (d) illustrates that the 'armed attack' concept is not strictly confined to attacks against a State's territory.[443] Furthermore, it must be recalled that the Definition can only provide circumstantial evidence vis-à-vis the scope of self-defence, evidence which must at all times be tested against the resolution's *travaux* (cf. *infra*). In the end, the Charter provisions neither authorize nor definitively rule out protection of nationals per se. As a result, we must look to customary practice for answers.

3.4.4.b Overview of concrete invocations of the doctrine after 1945

Although cases whereby States have relied on the 'protection of nationals' doctrine have become less frequent after 1945, a good deal of relevant practice can still be found.[444] For present purposes, we will confine ourselves to a synopsis of several cases, with an emphasis on those which have resulted in an exchange of explicit claims and counter-claims. At the outset, it should be noted that purely *consensual* operations are excluded from the analysis. By contrast, interventions where the validity of the consent was contested and where 'protection of nationals' was invoked as a supplementary legal justification do merit closer scrutiny.

3.4.4.b.i Early Cases: the Suez Canal (1956), Lebanon (1958) and the Congo (1960 and 1964)

The first country to rely on the 'protection of nationals' doctrine after 1945 was the United Kingdom,[445] which invoked it to justify the Anglo-French intervention during the 1956 Suez crisis. British authorities pointed to the need to safeguard British lives, arguing that 'self-defence undoubtedly includes a situation in

---

[442] See Ronzitti, *Rescuing nationals abroad*, p. 11.
[443] See, e.g., Corten, *Le droit contre la guerre*, pp. 614–15 (footnotes 20 and 24).
[444] For relevant overviews of these interventions, see: Ronzitti, *Rescuing nationals abroad*, pp. 26–49; Wingfield and Meyen, 'Lillich on the forcible protection of nationals abroad'.
[445] Remark: already in 1946, 1951 and 1952, the UK had hinted at the possibility of interventions to protect British residents in Iran and Egypt. See Brownlie, *The use of force by States*, pp. 296–7; Ronzitti, *Rescuing nationals abroad*, pp. 26–8.

which the lives of a State's nationals abroad are threatened and it is necessary to intervene on that territory for their protection'.[446] Interestingly, Foreign Secretary Selwyn Lloyd expressly claimed that protection of nationals constituted an exercise of self-defence under Article 51 UN Charter, and defined this concept by reference to the three criteria spelt out by Waldock.[447] On the other hand, while the doctrine was staunchly defended at the domestic level, it was raised only once in the margin of the Security Council debate.[448] The UK consistently maintained that its core objectives concerned the safeguarding of the freedom of navigation in the Suez Canal and the restoration of peace between Egypt and Israel.[449] France did not make any reference to the doctrine whatsoever. A considerable number of States took a negative stance against the intervention.[450] It was also generally agreed that the British justification lacked any foundation in fact:[451] British lives were not imminently threatened, and, even if one would hold otherwise, the bombing of Egyptian airports and the continued occupation of key positions along the Canal clearly went beyond what was necessary for the protection of British residents. It is unsurprising then that the British justification was 'dismissed by almost all commentators as utterly without merit and illustrative of how the right of forcible protection may be open to abuse'.[452]

When, two years later, around 10,000 US servicemen landed in Lebanon, President Eisenhower also made cursory reference to the need to protect US citizens.[453] However, after some initial press releases, this rationale was abandoned. Instead, the United States declared that its forces were in Lebanon 'for the sole purpose of helping the government of Lebanon, *at its request*, in its efforts to stabilize the situation brought on by threats from the outside ...'.[454] The subsequent Security Council debates focused mainly on whether or not the intervention constituted a proper exercise of collective self-defence.[455] Nonetheless, some States

---

[446] Quoted in Ronzitti, *Rescuing nationals abroad*, p. 29.
[447] Text reproduced in G. Marston, 'Armed intervention in the 1956 Suez crisis: the legal advice tendered to the British government', (1988) 37 ICLQ 773–817, at 800–1.
[448] UN Doc. S/PV.749, 30 October 1956, § 141.
[449] *Ibid.*, § 139; UN Doc. S/PV.750, 30 October 1956, §§ 64–7; UN Doc. S/PV.751, 31 October 1956, §§ 45–50.
[450] See the opinions expressed by the USSR, Egypt, Iran, Yugoslavia and others in UN Doc. S/PV.751.
[451] E.g., Brownlie, *The use of force by States*, p. 297.
[452] Wingfield and Meyen, 'Lillich on the forcible protection of nationals abroad', 98.
[453] See *ibid.*, 42–7.   [454] (1958) UNYB, 38.   [455] See *ibid.*, 38–40.

apparently took a negative stance vis-à-vis the 'protection of nationals' rationale before the Security Council[456] and the General Assembly.[457] Ethiopia, for example, accepted that the US intervention was validly requested by the Lebanese government, but added that it strongly opposed 'any introduction or maintenance of troops by one territory within the territory of another country under the pretext of ... protection of lives of citizens or any other excuses'.[458]

A more significant precedent concerns the Belgian intervention following Congolese independence in 1960. *In casu*, mutinying Congolese troops committed atrocities on Belgian residents and other European nationals. In response, Belgian paratroopers entered the country to protect and evacuate Belgian nationals and other foreigners. Foreign Minister Wigny declared that Belgium 'had a right to intervene when it was a question of protecting our compatriots, our women, against such excesses'.[459] He explained that the operation was strictly proportionate and that troops would be withdrawn as soon as the UN effectively ensured the safety of all foreigners.[460] France, Italy and the UK all expressed sympathy for what the French representative labeled 'an intervention on humanitarian grounds'.[461] The Argentinian representative declared that: '[T]he protection of the life and honour of individuals is a sacred duty to which all other considerations must yield ... Any other State would have done the same.'[462] On the other hand, the Soviet Union and several other States, including Tunisia and Poland, condemned the intervention as an outright 'aggression'.[463] According to these States, the protection of nationals was a mere pretext to mask an illegal intervention aimed at influencing Congolese domestic affairs. Ultimately, the Security Council adopted a number of resolutions which called upon Belgium to

---

[456] UN Doc. S/PV.830, 16 July 1958, § 16 (USSR: 'As to the "concern" for the safety of United States citizens, it may be asked what rules of international law permit foreign Powers to send their armed forces into the territory of other States for such purposes. There are no such rules of international law.'); UN Doc. S/PV.831, 17 July 1958, § 79 (USSR), § 110 (UAR).
[457] UN Docs. A/PV.738-40, 18–19 August 1958: UN Doc. A/PV.738, § 116 (India); UN Doc. A/PV.739, § 76 (Albania); UN Doc. A/PV.740, § 84 (Poland).
[458] UN Doc. A/PV.742, 20 August 1958, § 75.
[459] UN Doc. S/PV.877, 20–21 July 1960, 18.
[460] *Ibid.*, 29–30; UN Doc. S/PV.879, 21 July 1960, § 149.
[461] UN Doc. S/PV.873, 13–14 July 1960, 22–28 (esp. § 121 (Italy, speaking of a 'temporary security action'); § 130 (UK, 'Belgian troops have performed a humanitarian task for which my Government is grateful'); § 144 (France)). Also UN Doc. S/PV.879, 21 July 1960, §§ 10–2 (Italy), § 26 (UK), § 31 (Republic of China), §§ 52–60 (France).
[462] Quoted in Ronzitti, *Rescuing nationals abroad*, p. 32.   [463] (1960) UNYB 63 *et seq.*

THE 'ARMED ATTACK' REQUIREMENT *RATIONE MATERIAE* 219

withdraw its troops and requested that all States refrain from actions that might undermine the Congo's territorial integrity and political independence.[464]

Four years later, Belgium and the United States launched another intervention in the Congo, after rebel forces fighting the Tshombe government seized control of the cities of Stanleyville and Paulis.[465] In a few weeks, thirty-five foreign residents were killed, including nineteen Belgians and two Americans.[466] Against this backdrop, the two countries initiated a large-scale evacuation operation, which was explicitly authorized by the Congolese government. Belgium and the United States both justified their actions on a twofold basis, i.e., on the one hand, the consent of the legitimate Congolese authorities, and, on the other hand, the responsibility to protect their nationals abroad.[467]

A number of States, including the UK, France, Bolivia, Nigeria, Brazil and (the Republic of) China expressed cautious support for the operation, accepting that the intervention aimed solely at saving lives and/or recognizing that consent had been given by the Congolese government.[468] However, despite the relatively limited nature of the operation, the Soviet Union, Yugoslavia and twenty-one African and Asian States accused Belgium and the US of 'premeditated aggression'.[469] Many States argued that the Tshombe government was not the 'legal' government of the Congo, but a mere puppet regime imposed by force. The so-called 'rescue operation' was considered a pretext for intervening in Congolese politics. In addition, numerous delegations criticized the 'racist' nature of the mission, which had only aimed at saving white hostages, as well the lack of respect for ongoing mediation efforts by the OAU.[470] In the end,

---

[464] SC Res. 143 (1960) of 13 July 1960; SC Res. 145 (1960) of 22 July 1960.
[465] For an analysis of the legality of the intervention, see Gerard, 'L'Opération Stanleyville-Paulis'.
[466] See Wingfield and Meyen, 'Lillich on the forcible protection of nationals abroad', 50–1.
[467] UN Doc. S/6062, 24 November 1964 (US); UN Doc. S/PV.1174, 13; UN Doc. S/6063, 24 November 1964 (Belgium). See also Gerard, 'L'Opération Stanleyville-Paulis', 243–5.
[468] UN Docs. S/PV.1175–77, 15–16 December 1964; UN Doc. S/PV.1175, 4 (UK); UN Doc. S/PV.1176, 3 (Nigeria), 15 (France); UN Doc. S/PV.1177, 19 (Brazil), 26 (Republic of China); UN Doc. S/PV.1183, 22 December 1964, 10 (Norway); 14 (Bolivia).
[469] (1964) UNYB 95 *et seq.* (the twenty-two States requesting that the Council denounce the operation as a 'flagrant violation of the UN Charter' were: Afghanistan, Algeria, Burundi, Cambodia, the Central African Republic, the Congo (Brazzaville), Dahomey, Ethiopia, Ghana, Guinea, Indonesia, Kenya, Malawi, Mali, Mauritania, Somalia, Sudan, Uganda, the UAR, Tanzania, Yugoslavia and Zambia).
[470] See Wingfield and Meyen, 'Lillich on the forcible protection of nationals abroad', 53–7; Gerard, 'L'Opération Stanleyville-Paulis', 249–51, 258–9, 261.

the Council, '[deplored] the recent events in [the Congo]', and [requested] all States to refrain or desist from intervening in its domestic affairs.[471]

Leaving aside the mixed international reactions, Belgium's invocation of the 'protection of nationals' doctrine (once as a principal and once as a supplementary justification) would seem to indicate that it regards such forcible interventions as lawful. Nonetheless, when, upon the request of the Zairian authorities, France and Belgium in 1978 launched a comparable evacuation operation in the Katanga province, Belgium apparently regarded the territorial State's authorization as a legal prerequisite.[472] Indeed, speaking before the Belgian Parliament, Prime Minister Tindemans posed the following rhetorical question:

> Must one add that Zaire is a sovereign country where Belgium cannot simply intervene and that, consequently, an authorization of the Zairian authorities was required to conduct a rescue operation...[473]

3.4.4.b.ii The US interventions in the Dominican Republic (1965), Grenada (1983) and Panama (1989)

The latter statement casts doubt upon the consistency of Belgium's practice. The United States, on the other hand, has relied on the 'protection of nationals' doctrine on several occasions after the Stanleyville operation. The legal significance of the cases concerned nonetheless varies strongly. In 1965, when fighting between rival factions in the Dominican Republic plunged the country into anarchy, the US sent in some 1,700 troops. According to a statement submitted to the Security Council, '[t]he [US] Government have been informed by military authorities ... that American lives are in danger. These authorities are no longer able to guarantee their safety and have reported that the assistance of military personnel is now needed ...'.[474] In the absence of governmental authority, American troops had gone ashore 'to give protection to hundreds of Americans who are still in the Dominican Republic and to escort them safely back [to the US]'.[475] After the adoption of an OAS resolution creating an Inter-American force, the

---

[471] SC Res. 199 (1964) of 30 December 1964.
[472] See Wingfield and Meyen, 'Lillich on the forcible protection of nationals abroad', 101.
[473] Quoted in (1980) 15 RBDI 632.
[474] Presidential Statement, Annex to UN Doc. S/6310, 29 April 1965 (US) (author's translation).
[475] See UN Doc. S/PV.1196, 3 May 1965, §§ 67–71 (remark: while the US did not claim that this was a 'consensual' intervention, it did mention that there had been 'a request for assistance from those Dominican authorities still struggling to maintain order'.

US expanded its military presence on the island to around 22,000 forces and put increasing emphasis on the OAS legal umbrella as justification for its continued presence.[476] Ultimately, the precedential value of the US plea is difficult to evaluate. First, the 'protection of nationals' rationale was not used as an exclusive legal argument, but was combined with the idea of 'regional peace-keeping' under the auspices of the OAS, which gradually became the principal justification. The appraisal of third States was mixed. A number of Security Council members expressed understanding for the operation, with the UK and the Netherlands conveying their gratitude for the saving of their nationals.[477] France in principle accepted that States concerned with the safety of their nationals abroad could organize their evacuation, but insisted that such operations should be limited in their objective, duration and scope.[478] Although it refrained from condemning the operation, France implied that, taking into account the 'considerable number of US troops', the operation exceeded these parameters and constituted a 'genuine armed intervention the necessity of which is not apparent'. Several Latin-American and other States explicitly denounced the operation as a violation of the UN Charter.[479] The Soviet Union and Cuba in particular spared no effort to clarify that the 'protection of nationals' was nothing but a false pretext for intervention.[480] As both countries pointed out, the duration and size of the operation clearly exceeded what was needed for a quick evacuation mission. Moreover, despite US claims that it was not taking sides in the Dominican conflict,[481] many indications pointed to the contrary. President Johnson partially justified the expansion of the US force by asserting that the Dominican revolution had been 'seized and placed in

---

However: Corten, *Le droit contre la guerre*, p. 789); UN Doc. S/PV.1200, 5 May 1965, § 16; UN Doc. S/PV.1212, 19 May 1965, § 149.

[476] Wingfield and Meyen, 'Lillich on the forcible protection of nationals abroad', 62.
[477] UN Doc. S/PV.1198, 4 May 1965, § 57 (UK); UN Doc. S/PV.1202, 6 May 1965, § 19 (Republic of China); UN Doc. S/PV.1203, 7 May 1965, § 4 (Netherlands).
[478] UN Doc. S/PV.1198, §§ 111–12.
[479] See UN Doc. S/PV.1196, §§ 47–50 (USSR, referring to denunciations of the operation by Peru, Venezuela, Chile and Colombia); UN Doc. S/PV.1198, § 8 (Uruguay); UN Doc. S/PV.1202, § 7 (Malaysia, but very cautious); UN Doc. S/PV.1214, 21 May 1965, § 116 (Jordan).
[480] See, e.g., UN Doc. S/PV.1196, §§ 15 *et seq.*, §§ 191–3 (USSR), §§ 100 *et seq.* (Cuba); UN Doc. S/PV.1203, § 51 (Cuba); UN Doc. S/PV.1212, 19 May 1965, §§ 94 *et seq.* (USSR). Remark: a Soviet draft resolution which condemned the intervention was defeated by a majority of Security Council members.
[481] See, e.g., UN Doc. S/PV.1196, § 89; UN Doc. S/PV.1200, § 53; UN Doc. S/PV.1212, § 144.

the hands of a band of Communist conspirators ...'.[482] The US openly declared before the Security Council that it could not permit 'the establishment of another communist government in the western hemisphere'.[483] Most scholars[484] agreed with Senator Fullbright that the 'danger to American lives was more a pretext than a reason for the massive US intervention'.[485] The reverse side is that it is difficult to determine whether States denouncing the action were opposed to 'protection of nationals' per se or saw the intervention as an abusive application thereof.[486]

For broadly analogous reasons, it is difficult to deduce convincing evidence from the US interventions in Grenada in 1983 and in Panama in 1989. First, in both cases, multiple justifications were put forward. In the former, the US held, on the one hand, that those responsible for the military coup 'might decide at any moment to hold hostage the 1,000 American citizens on [the] island',[487] and, on the other hand, contended that the presence of the 8,000 US troops had been requested by the Organization of Eastern Caribbean States (OECS).[488] In addition, the US emphasized that the OECS action had actually been invited by the Governor-General of Grenada, 'the sole remaining symbol of governmental authority on the island'.[489] Following General Noriega's refusal to accept his electoral defeat in 1989, the United States explicitly relied on Article 51 UN Charter to justify its intervention in Panama. In essence, the actions were presented as an exercise of self-defence designed to protect the lives of around 35,000 US citizens in Panama and to defend the integrity of the Panama Canal Treaties.[490] Several other arguments were raised, including the need to tackle drug-trafficking, as well as the fact that actions were approved by the new democratically elected leaders.[491]

---

[482] Quoted in Wingfield and Meyen, 'Lillich on the forcible protection of nationals abroad', 62.
[483] UN Doc. S/PV.1196, § 81.
[484] E.g., W. Friedman, 'United States policy and the crisis of international law', (1965) 59 AJIL 857–71, at 867; V. P. Nanda, 'The United States' action in the 1965 Dominican crisis: impact on world order – Part I', (1966) 43 Denver LJ 439–79, at 464–72.
[485] Quoted in Wingfield and Meyen, 'Lillich on the forcible protection of nationals abroad', 63.
[486] Only Cuba explicitly rejected the doctrine as such: UN Doc. S/PV.1200, §§ 79–83.
[487] UN Doc. S/PV.2491, 27 October 1983, §§ 66–8.
[488] Ibid., §§ 69–75. Also: UN Doc. S/16076, 25 October 1983 (US).
[489] UN Doc. S/PV.2491, § 74. [490] UN Doc. S/PV.2899, 20 December 1989, 31–6.
[491] Ibid.

A second binding factor is the incompatibility of both interventions with the basic tenets of 'protection of nationals'. As for Grenada, dozens of States pointed out that the Revolutionary Military Council of Grenada had assured that US citizens would not be harmed and were free to leave the country; that the Vice Chancellor of the Medical School where most US nationals were based had stressed that they were not in danger; and that there was not a single press report that suggested otherwise.[492] In relation to Panama, there had been actual violence against US nationals, including the killing of an unarmed US serviceman and the mistreating of another.[493] The result was that *in casu* the 'protection of nationals' argument met with greater understanding.[494] Still, as in 1983, the large-scale and prolonged intervention undoubtedly exceeded the objective of protecting US citizens.[495] Consequently, both operations were generally condemned by the international community.[496] While scholars generally agree that the interventions went beyond what is envisaged under the 'protection of nationals' doctrine,[497] the problem remains that an

---

[492] E.g., UN Doc. S/PV.2487, 25 October 1983, §§ 74–5 (Guyana); §§ 90–3 (Grenada); § 118 (Cuba), § 146 (Libya), § 160 (USSR); UN Doc. S/PV.2489, 26 October 1983, at § 36 (Poland), § 170 (Laos); UN Doc. S/PV.2491, § 38 (Zimbabwe), § 256 (Afghanistan), § 340 (Mongolia), § 356 (Mozambique).

[493] UN Doc. S/PV.2902, 23 December 1989, 13.

[494] Cf. compare for instance the reaction of France vis-à-vis Grenada (UN Doc. S/PV.2489, § 146) and Panama (UN Doc. S/PV.2899, 22–3). Compare also the UK reaction vis-à-vis Grenada (UN Doc. S/PV.2491, §§ 205–6) and Panama (UN Doc. S/PV.2899, 26–7).

[495] As a result of the intervention in Panama, for example, several hundred Panamanians were killed, 3,000 civilians were wounded, and approximately 18,000 lost their homes (see R. Wedgwood, 'The use of armed force in international affairs: self-defense and the Panama invasion', (1991) 29 Columbia JTL 609–28, at 621–2). See, e.g., UN Doc. S/PV.2900, 21 December 1989, 14–5 (Finland), 22–3 (Malaysia).

[496] For Grenada, see UN Doc. S/PV.2487, UN Doc. S/PV.2489; UN Doc. S/PV.2491 A draft resolution 'deploring' the intervention as a 'flagrant violation of international law' gained eleven votes, but was vetoed by the United States (Togo and Zaire abstained because the proposed condemnation did not go far enough. See UN Doc. S/PV. 2491, §§ 431 *et seq.*). A comparable resolution was adopted by the UN General Assembly with 108 votes against nine, and twenty-seven abstentions. GA Res. 38/7 of 31 October 1983.

For Panama, see UN Doc. S/PV.2899, UN Doc. S/PV.2900 and UN Doc. S/PV.2902. A draft resolution 'deploring' the intervention as a 'flagrant violation of international law' gained ten votes, but was vetoed by the US, the UK and France (See UN Doc. S/PV. 2902, 18–20). A largely identical resolution was adopted by the UN General Assembly with seventy-five votes against twenty, and forty abstentions. GA Res. 44/240 of 29 December 1989.

[497] See, e.g., on Grenada: F. A. Boyle, A. Chayes, I. Dove, R. Falk, M. Feinrider, C. C. Ferguson Jnr, J.D. Fine, K. Nunes and B. Weston 'International lawlessness in Grenada', (1984) 78 AJIL 172–5, at 172; Doswald-Beck, 'The United States intervention in

analysis of the Security Council debates yields little in terms of explicit *opinio iuris* relating to the lawfulness of 'protection of nationals' as such.

3.4.4.b.iii More limited US operations: *Mayaguez* (1975), Tehran (1980), Libya (1986) and Sudan/Afghanistan (1998)

The 'protection of nationals' rationale also surfaces in relation to a number of more limited US incursions, such as the 1975 *Mayaguez* incident, the 1980 Tehran hostage situation, the 1986 air strikes against several Libyan targets and the 1998 air strikes in Sudan and Afghanistan. In each case, the US invoked Article 51 UN Charter to 'protect American lives'.[498] The incidents reaffirm the US's broad interpretation of the 'armed attack' concept and its support for the 'protection of nationals' doctrine. At the same time, several factors mitigate their potential impact. A first element is the different nature of the operations. The two former incidents concerned rescue/recovery operations: the first secured the recovery of the *Mayaguez* – a US-flagged vessel which, according to the US, had been unlawfully seized by Cambodian authorities in the high seas – and the liberation of its crew; the second failed to free the hostages in the US embassy in Tehran. The two other operations, on the other hand, did not aim at the rescuing and/or evacuating of nationals abroad, but at the preventing/deterring of future terrorist attacks following the bombing of a discotheque in West Berlin frequented by US servicemen (1986) and

Grenada', 362, 373–4; C. Joyner, 'Reflections on the lawfulness of invasion', (1984) 78 AJIL 131–44, at 134–5; V. P. Nanda, 'The United States armed intervention in Grenada – impact on world order', (1984) 14 California Western ILJ 395–424, at 410–1; D. F. Vagts, 'International law under time pressue: grading the Grenada take-home examination', (1984) 78 AJIL 169–72, at 170.

See, e.g., on Panama: T. J. Farer, 'Panama: beyond the Charter paradigm', (1990) 84 AJIL 503–15, at 506, 513; L. Henkin, 'The invasion of Panama under international law: a gross violation', (1991) 29 Columbia JTL 293–317, at 296–7, 308; V. P. Nanda, 'The validity of United States intervention in Panama under international law', (1990) 84 AJIL 494–503, at 497; Quigley, 'The United States invasion of Panama', 294–7.

[498] See the following reports by the American representative to the Security Council: Letter of 15 May 1975, UN Doc. S/11689 ('In the circumstances the [US] has taken certain appropriate measures under Article 51 [UN] Charter whose purpose is to achieve the release of the vessel and its crew'.); Letter of 25 April 1980, UN Doc. S/13908 ('That mission was carried out by the United States in the exercise of its inherent right of self-defence, with the aim of extricating American nationals who have been and remain the victims of the Iranian armed attack on our embassy.'); Letter of 14 April 1986, UN Doc. S/17990; Letter of 20 August 1998, UN Doc. S/1998/780 ('In accordance with Article 51 ... [the US] has exercised its right of self-defence in responding to a series of armed attacks against United States embassies and United States nationals'). Remark: Franck also includes the interception by the United States of a flight carrying the hijackers of the *Achille Lauro* (1985–6). See Franck, *Recourse to force*, pp. 88–9.

the attacks against the US embassies of Nairobi and Dar Es Salaam (1998), respectively. It must also be emphasized that we are not dealing with attacks against US nationals *simpliciter*. Rather, the incidents involved alleged attacks against US embassies, US servicemen and a US-flagged vessel, i.e. units that could otherwise be qualified as external manifestations of the State for purposes of Article 51 UN Charter (cf. *supra*), without need for recourse to the controversial protection of nationals doctrine.[499] Furthermore, the exchange of views following the various interventions (again) sheds little light on State's positions regarding the inclusion of attacks against nationals abroad within the scope of Article 51 UN Charter. In relation to the 1986 air strikes against Libya, third State reactions mainly focused on the lack of evidence of Libyan involvement in attacks against US targets abroad, on the punitive character of the expedition, as well as its disproportionate nature.[500] For our purposes, the only explicit fragment of *opinio iuris* concerns the claim of Ghana that 'the fact that a national or nationals of [a] State became victims of the incidents could ... not be sufficient to trigger the use of force in the name of self-defence'.[501]

The Tehran rescue operation, the 1998 air strikes in Sudan and Afghanistan, and the *Mayaguez* incident were not discussed in the Security Council. A number of States labelled the forcible recovery of the *Mayaguez* as an armed aggression, since the vessel had been seized in Cambodia's territorial waters and because Cambodia had already begun preparations for the release of the vessel and its crew.[502] As for the 1998

---

[499] E.g., Greenwood, 'The United States air operation against Libya', 941–2 (re the US strikes against Libya in 1986).
[500] See UN Docs. S/PV.2674–83, 15–24 April 1986. A draft resolution condemning the operation obtained nine votes in favour, but was vetoed by France, the UK and the US. A comparable resolution was subsequently adopted by the UN General Assembly by seventy-nine votes against twenty-eight, with thirty-three abstentions (GA Res. 41/38 of 20 November 1986).
[501] UN Doc. S/PV.2680, 32.
[502] See Ronzitti, *Rescuing nationals abroad*, p. 36 (in particular the statements of China and Cambodia itself). Also: UN Security Council, 1941st meeting, 12 July 1976, UN Doc. S/PV.1941, § 39 (Somalia). Remark: Paust takes the view that the operation did not in any event meet the criteria of the 'protection of nationals' doctrine. In his view, 'there was never any showing that the lives of the crew were in danger' and '[t]he bombing of the Cambodian mainland and the landing of Marines on a Cambodian island were completely disproportionate responses to a dispute concerning the seizure of a merchant vessel and the detention of her crew'. Paust moreover finds that the US failed to exhaust peaceful means, since negotiations on the crew's release were ongoing. See Paust, 'The seizure and recovery of the *Mayaguez*', 800–2.

strikes in Sudan and Afghanistan, we previously noted that, on the one hand, international reaction was generally muted,[503] while, on the other hand, criticism focused on the lack of involvement of Afghanistan and Sudan in the embassy bombings, and on the targeting of a pharmaceutical plant in Sudan.[504] Finally, the Tehran rescue attempt similarly met with mixed reactions. Many European States as well as Australia, Israel, Japan, Canada and Egypt expressed understanding and/or approval.[505] On the other hand, the Soviet Union, China, Saudi Arabia, Pakistan, India and Cuba labelled it as unwarranted military adventurism and/or as a violation of international law.[506]

3.4.4.b.iv Entebbe (1976) and Larnaca (1978) A particularly interesting incident, which scholars have often identified as the clearest example of the doctrine under discussion,[507] concerns the Israeli Entebbe raid of 1976. *In casu*, terrorists had hijacked a French aircraft and diverted it to the Ugandan airport of Entebbe, where non-Israeli passengers were released. It was threatened that the remaining hostages would be killed if Israel refused to comply with the hijackers' demands. Without authorization by Uganda, an Israeli aerial commando stormed the plane, resulting in the killing of the hijackers as well as a small number of hostages. Several Ugandan soldiers were also wounded and about ten Ugandan aircraft were destroyed. Before the Security Council, Israel relied on 'the right of a State to take military action to protect its nationals in mortal danger'.[508] This right was allegedly recognized 'by

---

[503] See references *supra* note 370.
[504] See, e.g., (1998) UNYB 185, 1219–20. Also: UN Doc. S/1998/786, 21 August 1998 (Sudan)
[505] See Ronzitti, *Rescuing nationals abroad*, pp. 44–7.
[506] See *ibid*. pp. 47–8. Remark: as mentioned earlier, the ICJ in the *Tehran Embassy* case refrained from explicitly ruling on the legality of the operation. See *supra* Section 3.4.2. Depending on their diverging views vis-à-vis the protection of nationals doctrine, scholars have come to different conclusions regarding the legality of the rescue attempt. Different opinions have moreover been expressed as to whether the lives of the US hostages were in 'imminent danger'. See the authors cited in Wingfield and Meyen, 'Lillich on the forcible protection of nationals abroad', 67–73. Also Eichensehr, 'Defending nationals abroad', 470 *et seq*.; Schachter, 'The right of States to use armed force', 1631.
[507] E.g., Dinstein, *War, aggression and self-defence*, p. 233; Schachter, 'The right of States to use armed force', 1630. Also Eichensehr, 'Defending nationals abroad', 478; Gordon, 'The Entebbe incident', 133; Paust, 'Entebbe and self-help: the Israeli response to terrorism', 90.
[508] See UN Doc. S/PV.1939, 9 July 1976, §§ 105–21.

all legal authorities in international law', and was regulated by the criteria of the *Caroline* case:[509]

> What mattered to [Israel] ... was the lives of the hostages, in danger of their very lives. No consideration other than this ... motivated the government of Israel. Israel's rescue operation was not directed against Uganda ... They were rescuing nationals from a band of terrorists and kidnappers who were being aided and abetted by the Ugandan authorities.[510]

Israel's reasoning was accepted and copied by the United States, which argued that:

> there is a well established right to use limited force for the protection of one's own nationals from an imminent threat of injury or death in a situation where the State in whose territory they are located is either unwilling or unable to protect them. This right, flowing from the right of self-defence, is limited to such use of force as is necessary and appropriate to protect threatened nationals from injury.[511]

In light of the 'unusual circumstances of this specific case', including the reproachable attitude of the Ugandan authorities, the US concluded that 'the requirements of this right ... were clearly met'.[512]

Despite the fact that at least two of Waldock's criteria – namely the imminent threat to the lives of nationals and the limited nature of the operation – would prima facie seem to be complied with, it is striking that the US was the only country explicitly to support Israel's legal case. A number of countries adopted an ambiguous position. Sweden for instance, 'while unable to reconcile the Israel action with the strict rules of the Charter, [did] not find it possible to join in a condemnation'.[513] Japan found that the actions violated the sovereignty of Uganda, but 'reserved' its opinion as to whether the situation met the conditions required for the exercise of self-defence.[514] France noted that 'if there was a violation of the sovereignty of Uganda, it was not in order to infringe the territorial integrity or the independence of that country but exclusively to save endangered human lives, and this in an extremely particular and special situation'.[515] Germany and the UK simply expressed

---

[509] *Ibid.* Reference was *inter alia* made to the *Mayaguez* incident (§§ 116–18).
[510] *Ibid.*, § 121.   [511] UN Doc. S/PV.1941, 12 July 1976, §§ 77–81.   [512] *Ibid.*
[513] UN Doc. S/PV.1940, 12 July 1976, §§ 122–3.
[514] UN Doc. S/PV.1942, 13 July 1976, §§ 57–8.
[515] UN Doc. S/PV.1943, 14 July 1976, § 45.

relief at the successful ending of the rescue attempt.[516] A broad majority of States denounced the operation as a violation of international law.[517] Many were convinced that Uganda had in fact played a positive role in negotiating with the hijackers (*inter alia* by securing the release of a number of passengers).[518] This may imply that those countries did not consider the third of Waldock's prerequisites – viz. the inability or unwillingness of the territorial State to protect foreign nationals – to be fulfilled. On the other hand, many of those condemning the raid relied on more principled arguments to do so. Thus, it was claimed that (1) Israel had not been the subject of an armed attack; (2) that terrorist kidnappings and hijackings, reprehensible as they were, had to be tackled through negotiations; (3) that operations such as the Entebbe raid irresponsibly jeopardized the lives of innocent passengers; and (4) that 'protection of nationals' was nothing but an excuse for powerful States to engage in 'gunboat diplomacy'.[519] These statements suggest that many States reject the admissibility of forcible 'protection of nationals' abroad in response to terrorist kidnappings, hijackings and the like, irrespective of the precise factual circumstances. Interestingly, Italy recognized that States held different views in respect of the use of limited force to protect endangered nationals abroad.[520] Each view was supported 'by the citation of prominent jurists or of the [UN] Charter'. Given this lack of agreement, Italy wondered if it might not be more appropriate to refer the issue to the ILC 'in order to lay the groundwork for the adoption of a universally accepted doctrine on the matter and avoid . . . a repetition of

---

[516] UN Doc. S/PV.190, § 92 (UK); UN Doc. S/PV.1941, §§ 51–4 (Federal Republic of Germany). Also: UN Doc. S/PV.1943, § 174 (UK).

[517] See UN Doc. S/PV.1939–1943 (including China, USSR, Pakistan, India, Yugoslavia, Kenya, et cetera).

[518] E.g., UN Doc. S/PV.1939, § 34 (Uganda), § 44 (Mauritania), § 170 (Qatar), § 185 (France), § 215 (Cameroon); UN Doc. S/PV.1940, §§ 33–5 (Guinea), § 57 (Mauritius); UN Doc. S/PV.1941, §§ 127–30 (Pakistan); UN Doc. S/PV.1943, § 85 (Cuba). Remark: several countries also considered the wounding of Ugandan troops and the destruction of Ugandan aircraft as an aggravating factor: e.g., UN Doc. S/PV.1939, § 43 (Mauritania), § 210 (Cameroon), § 224 (PRC); UN Doc. S/PV.1940, § 65 (Mauritius), § 77 (Guyana); UN Doc. S/PV. 1941, § 132 (Pakistan), § 152 (USSR).

[519] E.g., UN Doc. S/PV.1939, § 49 (Mauritania), § 148 (Kenya), § 225 (PRC); UN Doc. S/PV.1941, § 67 (Yugoslavia), §§ 102, 109 (Tanzania); UN Doc. S/PV. 1942, § 27 (Panama), § 39 (Romania), §§ 145–6 (India: 'The fact that the . . . operation was limited to rescuing hostages should not hide the more important fact that it did involve . . . a breach of Uganda's sovereignty and territorial integrity'); UN Doc. S/PV.1943, § 87 (Cuba).

[520] UN Doc. S/PV.1943, § 56.

the differences which have emerged in this debate'. As a result of the conflicting views of the Security Council members, no resolution was adopted.[521]

In 1978, two years after the Israeli operation, Egyptian forces carried out a similar commando raid at the Cypriot airport of Nicosia.[522] *In casu*, Palestinian terrorists had taken several hostages, including a number of Egyptian nationals. Fearing that the Cypriot authorities would let the terrorists go in return for the release of the hostages, Egypt flew an aircraft carrying a seventy-five-man commando unit to Nicosia.[523] When Egyptian soldiers suddenly emerged from the plane and started firing, the Cypriot national guard intervened, killing several Egyptian commandos and taking others prisoner. During the fighting, the Cypriots arrested the terrorists while the hostages managed to escape. The incident at Larnaca airport resulted in a significant deterioration of diplomatic relations between the two countries. Cyprus described the Egyptian intervention as a violation of its sovereignty. Egypt, on the other hand, claimed to have acted lawfully, and demanded the repatriation of the Egyptian prisoners and the extradition of the two terrorists. While the characteristics of the incident are reminiscent of the Entebbe raid, it must be noted that Egypt did not invoke the 'protection of nationals' doctrine, but merely referred to its commitment 'to fight terrorism and to bring all those who used such methods to justice'.[524]

3.4.4.b.v A new element in State practice?

Apart from the aforementioned cases, reference must briefly be made to a number of invocations/applications of the 'protection of nationals' doctrine which have not been reported to the Security Council, and which by and large escaped international scrutiny. A majority of these concern French military operations in various African countries, namely the operations in Mauritania in 1977–9; in Chad in 1978, 1979 and 1990; in Gabon in 1990 and 2007; in Rwanda in 1990–4; in the Central African Republic in 1996 and 2003; in the Ivory Coast in 2002–3; in Liberia in 2003, and the operations conducted together with Belgium in (then) Zaire in 1978, 1991 and

---

[521] (1976) UNYB 319–20.
[522] See Ronzitti, *Rescuing nationals abroad*, pp. 40–1; (1978) *Keesing's* 29305; 'Murder and Massacre on Cyprus', *Time Magazine* 6 March 1978.
[523] Cyprus was told that the plane carried officials which would participate in the hostage negotiations, and authorized its landing.
[524] See Ronzitti, *Rescuing nationals abroad*, p. 41.

1993.[525] On several occasions the 'protection of nationals' rationale was primarily used as a pretext to use force in support and at the request of the territorial State against rebel groups.[526] As for those interventions that were actually confined to the evacuation of French nationals, it appears that these too were in general approved or even requested by the territorial State.[527] Of greater interest, however, are the handful of evacuation operations which were launched throughout the 1990s and beyond, and which were carried out without apparent approval. Thus, when in 1990, President Habré was overthrown by Idriss Déby, France flew in troops to Chad to ensure the security of French citizens and to organize their repatriation.[528] No attempt was made to oppose Déby or to otherwise intervene in internal Chadian matters. In a similar vein, following the overthrowal of President Patasse by General Bozzize in 2003, France deployed some 300 soldiers to the Central African Republic to evacuate foreign nationals.[529]

Apart from France, numerous other countries have organized the evacuation of nationals from countries plagued by violent unrest, or by internal or international conflicts. These operations have often assumed large-scale dimensions involving a considerable number of States.[530]

---

[525] *Ibid.*, p. 40; Wingfield and Meyen, 'Lillich on the forcible protection of nationals abroad', 99–108; Also (1990) *Keesing's* 37765-6; (1990) 94 RGDIP 1071; (1991) 95 RGDIP 746; (1993) *Keesing's* 39305; (1994) *Keesing's* 39443-4; (1996) *Keesing's* 41080-1; (2002) *Keesing's* 44968, 45026, 45131; (2003) *Keesing's* 45276, 45230-1, 45452; (2007) *Keesing's* 47793.

[526] This appears to have been the case *inter alia* with regard to the French operations against the Polisario Front in Mauritania in 1977-9. Similarly, in 1978, France helped the Chadian army against the Frolinat rebels by means of air cover, without making an effort to evacuate French nationals. See: Wingfield and Meyen, 'Lillich on the forcible protection of nationals abroad', 100-2. Similar indications exist with regard to the interventions in the Central African Republic in 1996 ((1996) *Keesing's* 41081), and Ivory Coast in 2002 ((2002) *Keesing's* 44968, 45026, 45131).

[527] Examples are: the French–Belgian intervention in Zaire in 1978 and the French evacuation operation in Gabon in 1990. See: Wingfield and Meyen, 'Lillich on the forcible protection of nationals abroad', 101, 103-4.

[528] *Ibid.*, 105. See also on the French operation in Zaire in 1993, *ibid.*, 106-7.

[529] (2003) *Keesing's* 45276. See also 'CAR coup strongly condemned', *BBC News* 17 March 2003.

[530] Examples are the multinational evacuation operation in Rwanda in 1994 (see: Wingfield and Meyen, 'Lillich on the forcible protection of nationals abroad', 107), the evacuation of foreign nationals from Lebanon during the Israeli–Lebanese conflict in the summer of 2006 ('At a glance: Lebanon evacuations', *BBC News* 30 January 2003), or the evacuation of foreign nationals from Indonesia in 1998 ('Foreign exodus under way', *BBC News* 15 May 1998; 'Foreign countries evacuate citizens from Indonesia', *BBC News* 15 May 1998).

While reliable information is often difficult to obtain, evacuations have frequently met with the approval of the territorial State. On the other hand, some operations were probably carried out without such approval – sometimes due the complete breakdown of governmental authority. Where such actions have been confined to the actual protection and repatriation of nationals, without engaging in active combat on either side of the conflict, they have not been the subject of international criticism. Examples are the evacuation of US nationals during the civil war in Lebanon in 1976[531] and in Liberia in 1990.[532] The latter operation was undertaken in response to threats by one rebel leader to arrest US nationals, as well as the general deterioration of security in Liberia. As Lillich observes, there was a 'near-complete absence of legal or other criticism' of the operation.[533] The evacuation operations by several Western States in Albania in March 1997 – in particular the German Operation 'Libelle' – could possibly be cited as another example.[534] These operations were launched after the collapse of a fraudulent pyramid

---

[531] On 28 June 1978, the US evacuated several nationals by means of a warship, seemingly without requesting the permission of the Lebanese authorities. As for a later evacuation operation on 27 July, the US government did not contact the Lebanese authorities, but rather the Palestinian organizations in control of the area where the evacuation took place. See Ronzitti, *Rescuing nationals abroad*, p. 36-7.

[532] *In casu*, the US landed 255 marines in Monrovia to evacuate US and other nationals desiring to leave the country without seeking or receiving permission from President Doe or either of the rival rebel faction leaders. Wingfield, 'Forcible protection of nationals abroad', 460.

[533] See Lillich, 'The Liberian "incident" of 1990', especially 208-13, 221-3.

[534] See (1997) *Keesing's* 41556-8; J. Perlez, 'Albania Chief's Associates Flee; gunfire halts evacuation by U.S.', *NY Times* 15 March 1997; F. Schorkopf, *Grundgesetz und überstaatlichkeit: Konflikt und Harmonie in den Auswärtigen Beziehungen Deutschlands* (Tübingen: Mohr Siebeck), pp. 129-33. See in particular: C. Kreß, 'Die Rettungsoperation der Bundeswehr in Albanien am 14. März 1997 aus völker- un verfassungsrechtlicher Sicht', (1997) 57 ZaöRV 329-62; S. Talmon, 'Changing views on the use of force: the German position', (2005) 5 Baltic YBIL 41-76. Bundestagdrücksache 13/7233, 18 March 1997, 1-2; Plenarprotokoll Bundestag, 13/166, 20 March 1997, 1496-7. It remains unclear whether or not there was a valid consent for the evacuation operations. Apparently, the Albanian President called upon European States to intervene 'to restore law and order' in his country. It is also suggested that the Italian evacuation operation was approved by the (remaining) Albanian authorities. In the case of Operation 'Libelle', however, it appears that the Albanian Government could not be reached in time to ask for its consent. Kreß suggests that the operation was lawful on the basis of the implied consent of the Albanian government (which 'was not given in an entirely unambiguous manner'), yet at the same time suggests that it adds to State practice in support of the exercise of self-defence for the protection of nationals abroad (337-9, 347-9, 361).

finance scheme caused large numbers of Albanians to lose their life savings, spurring an armed rebellion in large parts of the country and resulting in a complete breakdown of governmental authority. Furthermore, when Thai nationals were attacked by angry crowds in Cambodia following heightened political tension between the two countries in 2003, Thailand sent military transport planes to Phnom Penh to evacuate several hundreds of Thai citizens. Even if the operation was carried out with cooperation from the Cambodian army, it is worth noting that the Thai Prime Minister had earlier threatened to send in troops to protect its citizens.[535]

Following clashes between Georgian troops and separatist militants in South Ossetia in August 2008, Russia also made cursory reference to the 'protection of nationals' rationale in order to justify its intervention in Georgia.[536] Russia argued that it was responsible for protecting the numerous Russian citizens in the separatist region, albeit that it is difficult to detect a coherent legal argument in its statements before the Security Council (Russia seemingly alluded to a mixture of legal bases, including self-defence, humanitarian intervention and regional peace-keeping).[537] In contrast to the aforementioned operations, however, the Russian operation was not aimed at the evacuation of a small group of threatened nationals, but instead took the form of a large-scale military offensive, resulting in the occupation of a substantial part of Georgian territory.[538] In addition, the questionable legality of Russia's passport policy – Russia had been handing out passports to thousands of inhabitants of the breakaway regions of Abchazia and South Ossetia – indicates that the intervention hardly qualifies as an orthodox application of the 'protection of nationals' doctrine.[539] Many States were highly

---

[535] See (2003) *Keesing's* 45196; 'Panicked Thais flee Cambodia', *BBC News* 30 January 2003.

[536] See, e.g., P. Roudik, 'Russian Federation – Legal Aspects of War in Georgia', September 2008, available at www.loc.gov/law/help/russian-georgia-war.pdf (accessed 4 May 2009), 9–11 (referring to statements by the Chief Justice of the Russian Constitutional Court); International Crisis Group, '*Russia* vs *Georgia*: the fallout', 22 August 2008, available at www.crisisgroup.org/home/index.cfm?id=5636 (accessed 4 May 2009), 28 (referring to a Statement by Foreign Minister Lavrov).

[537] See UN Docs. S/PV.5951-3, 8–10 August 2008.

[538] Also O. Luchterhandt, 'Völkerrechtliche Aspekte des Georgien-Krieges', (2008) 46 AdV 435–80, at 469; J. Kranz, 'Der Kampf um den Frieden und sein besonderer Facilitator', (2008) 46 AdV 481–501, at 492.

[539] See *ibid.*; Roudik, 'Legal Aspects of War in Georgia', 9–11; International Crisis Group, '*Russia* vs *Georgia*: the fallout', 28. Remark: while the granting of nationality is in principle a purely domestic matter, Article 1 of the 1930 Hague Convention on

critical of Russia's conduct, yet for various reasons – e.g., Russia's diffuse legal justification, the contested status of South Ossetia or the confusion as to which side had actually opened hostilities[540] – no discussion took place in relation to the legality of 'protection of nationals'.

3.4.4.c Customary evidence *in abstracto*

3.4.4.c.i The Definition of Aggression and the 1979 Hostage Convention
Before attempting to draw conclusions, it is worth looking at relevant UNGA debates for abstract statements indicating States' approval or denunciation of the protection of nationals doctrine. At the outset, it must be noted that there has been no direct attempt to adopt 'a universally accepted doctrine' on the matter, as was suggested by the Italian representative during the Entebbe debate.[541] However, the issue was raised on several occasions,[542] in particular during the *travaux* of the Definition of Aggression, the 1979 International Convention against the Taking of Hostages,[543] and, most recently, the 2006 ILC Draft Articles on Diplomatic Protection.[544] Each will be addressed in turn.

As far as the negotiations on the Definition of Aggression are concerned, the Soviet Union in its 1950 draft provided both a list of acts of aggression, as well as a series of motives which could not be considered as a valid excuse for launching an attack. One such inadmissible 'excuse' concerned 'any danger which may threaten the life or property of aliens'.[545] Belgium objected that '[this] meant that a State might, with

Certain Questions Relating to the Conflict of Nationality Laws stresses that national policies must be 'consistent with international conventions, international custom and the principles of law generally recognized with regard to nationality'. *In casu*, it might be argued that Russia's passport policy amounted to intervention in Georgia's domestic affairs and impaired its sovereignty. Moreover, as States cannot exercise diplomatic protection vis-à-vis nationals that are also nationals of the territorial State, one might wonder, whether, by analogy, forcible 'protection of nationals' is also excluded in relation to persons with double nationality. See, generally: ILC, Draft Articles on Diplomatic Protection with Commentaries, 2006, http://untreaty.un.org/ilc/texts/instruments/english/commentaries/9_8_2006.pdf (accessed 4 May 2009), 30–47.

[540] This issue was eventually clarified in the report of the EU-backed Independent International Fact-Finding Commission on the Conflict in Georgia, September 2009, available at www.ceiig.ch/Report.html (accessed 30 January 2010).
[541] UN Doc. S/PV.1943, § 56.
[542] See, e.g., UN Doc. A/C.1/20/1396, § 23 (Cuba); UN Doc. A/C.6/35/SR.50, § 3 (Romania).
[543] International Convention against the Taking of Hostages, 17 December 1979, GA Res. 34/146 (adopted by consensus), 1316 UNTS 205.
[544] ILC, Draft Articles on Diplomatic Protection with Commentaries.
[545] USSR Draft Resolution on the Definition of Aggression, 4 November 1950, UN Doc. A/C.1/608, reprinted in Ferencz, *Defining international aggression*. Vol. II, p. 79.

impunity, threaten the life and property of another State ...'.[546] UK representative Fitzmaurice declared that:

> by mistreating foreigners on its own territory, a State committed an act of aggression against the country of which the foreigners were nationals: and in defending itself, the State concerned was exercising its right of self-defence.[547]

Recourse to force was not always justified in such cases, the UK admitted, yet, it could certainly not be ruled out *ex ante*.[548] Greece and the Netherlands took the view that a State could lawfully use force to protect its nationals abroad from 'genocide' or 'massacres'.[549] On the other hand, a number of non-Western countries concurred with the Soviet Union. Egypt, for instance, found that the ill-treatment of a country's nationals by a foreign State should be dealt with by arbitration or by the ICJ, and could not, in any event, justify the use of force.[550] Iran also expressed its 'warm support' for the Soviet draft[551] and emphasized that Fitzmaurice's argument was 'erroneous both in fact and law'.[552]

After the establishment of the Fourth Special Committee, some countries again stressed that the use of force to protect nationals abroad was unlawful.[553] Mexico, for one, affirmed that the 'excuse of self-defence' could not be invoked in the case of 'danger to life or property' of nationals abroad.[554] At the same time, contrary to the 1950 Soviet draft, none of the proposals pending before the Special Committee made express mention of the issue,[555] and most participants refrained from explicitly pronouncing on the matter. In sum, States simply agreed to disagree.

Shortly after the adoption of the Definition of Aggression, the controversy was again raised during the negotiations on an International Convention against the Taking of Hostages. Inspired by the Entebbe raid, Algeria and Tanzania submitted a draft amendment according to which 'States shall not resort to the threat or use of force against the sovereignty, territorial integrity or independence of other States as a means of

---

[546] UN Doc. A/C.6/6/SR.287, § 43.   [547] UN Doc. A/C.6/6/SR.292, § 38.
[548] Ibid.   [549] Quoted in Ronzitti, *Rescuing nationals abroad*, p. 50.
[550] UN Doc. A/C.6/6/SR.293, § 12.
[551] UN Doc. A/C.6/6/SR.293, §§ 19–20.   [552] Ibid. See also UN Doc. A/C.6/7/SR.330, § 50.
[553] E.g., UN Doc. A/AC.134/SR.46, 208, 211 (Cyprus).
[554] UN Doc. A/AC.134/SR.15, 146. See also UN Doc. A/C.6/18/SR.806, § 12 (Mexico).
[555] N. Ronzitti, *Rescuing nationals abroad*, p. 50.

rescuing hostages'.[556] Some States expressed sympathy for the proposal, while others considered it as irrelevant or superfluous.[557] Syria submitted a slightly different version, which provided that '[n]othing in this Convention can be construed as justifying in any manner the threat or use of force or any interference whatsoever against the sovereignty, independence or territorial integrity of peoples and States, under the pretext of rescuing or freeing hostages'.[558] In the end, a much more neutral provision was used in the final text. Article 14 simply states that '[n]othing in this Convention shall be construed as justifying the violation of the territorial integrity or political independence of a State in contravention of the [UN] Charter'. By neither authorizing nor specifically prohibiting the recourse to force to secure the release of nationals that are taken hostage abroad, the Convention left the conundrum exactly where it was before its adoption.[559] No conclusive solution is therefore to be found in the Convention or its *travaux*.[560]

3.4.4.c.ii The ILC Draft Articles on Diplomatic Protection

The most recent and arguably most interesting exchange of views vis-à-vis forcible protection of nationals concerns the negotiation process within the ILC and within the UNGA Sixth Committee on the issue of diplomatic protection. The immediate cause was the proposal of Special Rapporteur Dugard to include a specific provision on the matter in the ILC draft Articles.[561] Dugard disagreed with his predecessors García Amador and

---

[556] Working Paper submitted by Algeria and Tanzania to the Ad Hoc Committee on the drafting of an International Convention against the Taking of Hostages, 12 August 1977, UN Doc. A/AC.188/L.7.

[557] E.g., Ad Hoc Committee on the Drafting of an International Convention against the Taking of Hostages, 12th meeting, 16 August 1977, UN Doc. A/AC.188/SR.12, § 14 (US), § 15 (Federal Republic of Germany); 13th meeting, 17 August 1977, UN Doc. A/AC.188/SR.13, § 11 (Federal Republic of Germany), § 12 (Sweden, regarding it as superfluous); 15th meeting, 18 August 1977, UN Doc. A/AC.188/SR.15, § 7 (US, regarding it as irrelevant), § 14 (Mexico, expressing support).

[558] Working Paper submitted by Syria to the Ad Hoc Committee on the drafting of an International Convention against the Taking of Hostages, 16 August 1977, UN Doc. A/AC.188/L.11.

[559] E.g., R. Rosenstock, 'International Convention against the taking of hostages: another international community step against terrorism', (1980) 9 Denver JILP 169–95, at 186; F. A. Boyle, 'International law in the time of crisis: from the Entebbe raid to the hostages convention', (1980) 75 Northwestern Un L Rev 768–856, at 846.

[560] E.g., N. Ronzitti, *Rescuing nationals abroad*, pp. 51–2.

[561] See Special Rapporteur Dugard, 'First Report on Diplomatic Protection', 7 March 2000, UN Doc. A/CN.4/506, §§ 46–60; statement by Dugard during the 2617th meeting of the ILC, 9 May 2000, (2000-I) YBILC, Part I, 39–40.

Bennouna, who had wished explicitly to assert that the use of force is prohibited as a means of diplomatic protection.[562] In his view, this approach took little account of contemporary practice, which allowed for the recourse to force in exceptional circumstances.[563] Dugard sympathized with the idea that Article 51 preserved pre-existing custom and drew attention to the 'amount of State practice since 1945 in support of military intervention to protect nationals abroad in time of emergency and the failure of courts and political organs of the United Nations to condemn such action'. While conceding that the doctrine had been greatly abused in the past, he did not regard this as a reason to ignore its existence. Rather, he considered it wiser to recognize the right, but to prescribe severe limits. Founding his arguments mainly on the parameters of the Entebbe precedent, Dugard identified several criteria closely ressembling those listed earlier by Waldock. His draft Article 2 read as follows:

> The threat or use of force is prohibited as a means of diplomatic protection, except in the case of rescue of nationals where:
> (a) The protecting State has failed to secure the safety of its nationals by peaceful means;
> (b) The injuring State is unwilling or unable to secure the safety of the nationals of the protecting State;
> (c) The nationals of the protecting State are exposed to immediate danger to their persons;
> (d) The use of force is proportionate in the circumstances of the situation;
> (e) The use of force is terminated, and the protecting State withdraws its forces, as soon as the nationals are rescued.[564]

As Dugard expected,[565] support for his proposal was extremely scarce. Within the ILC, only two delegates accepted in principle that the use of force in the exercise of diplomatic protection could constitute a form of self-defence. According to Lukashuk, the concept of 'armed attack' encompassed not only the State's territory, but also its population. He therefore agreed that the draft provision should reflect the practice of States, be it that 'protection of nationals should be restricted to extreme cases'.[566] Rosenstock believed that the Special Rapporteur 'was correct both in law and in terms of the view that States would take if their

---

[562] UN Doc. A/CN.4/506, §§ 49–51.   [563] *Ibid.*, §§ 57–8.   [564] *Ibid.*, § 46.
[565] See (2000-I) YBILC, Part I, 39, § 23.
[566] 2618th meeting of the ILC, 10 May 2000, (2000-I) YBILC, Part I, 53, §§ 54–5.

THE 'ARMED ATTACK' REQUIREMENT *RATIONE MATERIAE* 237

nationals' lives were at stake'.[567] All other delegates opposed draft Article 2.

Numerous delegates strongly denounced the proposal on the grounds that the doctrine had often been used as a pretext for intervention in another State's domestic affairs, and asserting that the exception of Draft Article 2 constituted a dangerous expansion of the rules on the use of force, incompatible with the provisions of the UN Charter.[568] Several ILC Members even called for an express provision prohibiting the use of force as a means of diplomatic protection.[569] According to Economides: 'A small minority of writers maintained that force might be permissible to rescue nationals in danger. It was time to put an end to that theory.'[570]

At the same time, not all Members necessarily agreed that 'it was time to put an end' once and for all to the protection of nationals doctrine. Several delegates rejected the draft Article while seemingly reserving their opinion on the doctrine per se.[571] Some thought it unwise from a policy perspective to explicitly 'legalize' the doctrine.[572] Others merely observed that the topic lay outside the Commission's mandate.[573] Distinguished members such as Brownlie, Pellet and Simma opposed the insertion of an express prohibition of the use of force as a means of diplomatic protection, instead preferring to avoid the issue altogether.[574]

The debates within the UNGA Sixth Committee show a broadly similar picture.[575] Only one State implicitly supported the legality of forcible protection of nationals: Italy stressed that Article 2 should state explicitly that the use of force by a State in the protection of nationals abroad should be limited to highly exceptional circumstances in which

---

[567] 2619th meeting of the ILC, 11 May 2000, (2000-I) YBILC, Part I, 57, § 8.
[568] 2617th-26220th meetings of the ILC, 9–12 May 2000, (2000-I) YBILC, Part I, 42 *et seq.*: E.g., *ibid.*: Baena Soares (43, § 58); Economides (44, § 65); Illueca (47–8); Kabatsi (48; § 17); Pellet (50, § 25); Idris (51, § 32); Rodriguez Cedeno (53, § 61); Kateka (54, § 68); Hafner (55, 75); Galicki (56, § 3); He (58, § 23); Pambou-Tchivounda (59, § 33); Candioti (59, § 40).
[569] E.g., *ibid.*: Economides (44, § 65); Candioti (59–60); Opertti Badan (64, § 2); Goco (65, § 11).
[570] *Ibid.*, 60, § 53. See also the statement of Kabatsi, 48, § 17.
[571] *Ibid.*, 45, § 73 (Tomka); 61, § 62 (Kamto); 68, § 29 (Momtaz).
[572] *Ibid.*, Kateka (54, § 68).
[573] *Ibid.*, Gaja (44, § 62); Goko (45, § 73); Addo (57, § 11); Simma (66–7, § 22). Also, combining this with other arguments: Brownlie (42, § 49); Idriss (51, § 32); Rodriguez Cedeno (54; § 61); Rosenstock (57, § 8); He (58, § 23); Pambou-Tchivounda (59, § 33).
[574] *Ibid.*, Pellet (60, § 49); Brownlie (60, § 51); Lukashuk (61, § 56); Simma (66, § 22).
[575] See UNGA, 55th Session, 6th Committee, 15th to 24th meetings, 24 October – 3 November 2000, UN Docs. A/C.6/55/SR.15-A/C.6/55/SR.24.

their lives were in imminent danger.[576] Against this, numerous States in general terms rejected the legality of the use of force as a means of diplomatic protection. China declared that '[i]n order to prevent power politics ... the use or threat of force in exercising [the right to diplomatic protection] should be prohibited'.[577] Recalling 'past abuses', Slovenia denounced that Article 51 UN Charter could be used 'as a legal basis for armed intervention to protect nationals'.[578] Other countries that expressed themselves negatively on the protection of nationals and/or called for an express prohibition on the threat or use of force as an instrument of diplomatic protection were Poland, Mexico, Argentina, Venezuela, Iran, Iraq, Jordan, Libya, Colombia, Burkina Faso and Cuba.[579]

As with the ILC debate, however, many States refrained from taking sides. South Africa, Indonesia, France, the UK, Bosnia-Herzegovina, Cyprus, Japan and Portugal simply claimed that the issue fell outside the scope of the topic, which was concerned only with peaceful procedures of diplomatic protection.[580] According to Switzerland, '[i]t was open to question whether the use of force was legitimate even in the cases provided for in draft Article 2. However, the issue was irrelevant, since the threat or use of force was not an instrument of diplomatic protection...'.[581] Likewise, the German representative, '[w]ithout ruling out any use of force in the context of diplomatic protection, [doubted] whether a discussion of the use of force was warranted in [this] context'.[582]

It was eventually agreed to abandon draft Article 2 and to stress instead that diplomatic protection concerns the invocation of State responsibility 'through a diplomatic action or other means of peaceful

---

[576] UN Doc. A/C.6/55/SR.19, § 15.   [577] UN Doc. A/C.6/55/SR.19, § 30.
[578] UN Doc. A/C.6/SR.20, § 16.
[579] UN Doc. A/C.6/55/SR.19, § 56 (Poland); UN Doc. A/C.6/SR.20, § 47 (Mexico), § 52 (Argentina), § 78 (Venezuela), § 85 (Iran), §§ 90–1 (Iraq); UN Doc. A/C.6/55/SR.21, § 7 (Jordan), § 55 (Libya); UN Doc. A/C.6/55/SR.23, § 5 (Colombia, on behalf of the Rio Group); UN Doc. A/C.6/55/SR.24, § 55 (Burkina Faso), § 71 (Cuba). More ambiguously: UN Doc. A/C.6/55/SR.19, § 5 (Spain), §§ 38–9 (India); UN Doc. A/C.6/55/SR.23, § 69 (Romania).
[580] UN Doc. A/C.6/SR.15, § 68 (South Africa); UN Doc. A/C.6/SR.18, § 39 (Indonesia), § 108 (France); UN Doc. A/C.6/55/SR.19, § 23 (UK), § 48 (Nordic countries), § 51 (Bosnia-Herzegovina); UN Doc. A/C.6/55/SR.21, § 2; UN Doc. A/C.6/55/SR.23, § 80 (Japan); UN Doc. A/C.6/55/SR.24, § 22 (Portugal).
[581] UN Doc. A/C.6/55/SR.21, § 20.   [582] Ibid., § 64.

settlement' (Article 1).[583] The negative attitude and/or suspicion of many States and ILC delegates is reflected in the ILC Commentary, which states (somewhat circularly) that '[t]he use of force, prohibited by [Article 2(4) UN Charter], is not a permissible method for the enforcement of the right of diplomatic protection'.[584]

3.4.4.d   Evaluation *de lege lata*: running around in circles?

What can be concluded from this overview of (abstract and concrete) customary evidence? Those scholars who support the legality of forcible protection of nationals in exceptional circumstances, primarily point to the considerable number of interventions which were (partially) justified by reference to this doctrine and which escaped condemnation by the Security Council. The cases mentioned indeed leave little doubt that the US, the UK, France and Israel regard military action as a permissible means to protect nationals abroad. Between these countries there appears to be agreement that forcible intervention is governed by the three cumulative preconditions cited earlier.[585] On most occasions, the alleged right has been framed as an application of the right of self-defence, enshrined in Article 51 UN Charter,[586] even if it was sometimes argued that protection of nationals, because of its 'humanitarian' nature, does not violate the territorial State's integrity or political independence and therefore falls beyond the scope of Article 2(4) UN Charter.[587] The

---

[583] See ILC, Draft Articles on Diplomatic Protection with Commentaries, 24: 'diplomatic protection consists of the invocation by a State, through a diplomatic action or other means of peaceful settlement, of the responsibility of another State for an injury caused by an internationally wrongful act of that State to a natural or legal person that is a national of the former State ...'.
[584] *Ibid.*, § 8.   [585] See Waldock, 'The regulation of the use of force', 467.
[586] This argument was *inter alia* used by the UK in relation to the Suez crisis, by Israel vis-à-vis the Entebbe raid, and by the US in relation to the intervention in Panama, the Entebbe raid, the *Mayaguez* incident, the Tehran rescue operation, the 1986 strikes against Libya and the 1998 strikes against Sudan and Afghanistan. See: *supra* notes 447, 490, 498, 510, 511. Cf. Lillich notes 'an almost uniform reliance on the self-defence argument'. Lillich, 'The Liberian "incident" of 1990', esp. at 217.
[587] This line of reasoning was mainly followed by France: e.g., *supra* notes 461 (the Belgian intervention in the Congo in 1960), 515 (Entebbe). However, the argument also surfaced in the US justification for the intervention in the Dominican Republic: UN Doc. S/PV.1198, §§ 155–6. Remark: the 'Handbook for Operations and Deployment of the German Armed Forces outside the Territory of the Federal Republic of Germany in Peacetime' finds that there is neither settled State practice nor a uniform view in the literature with regard to protection of nationals. It adds that: 'The main argument in favour of its permissibility is the justification as a customary international law exception to the prohibition of the use of force in Article 2(4) of the UN Charter. Self-defence and

doctrine under discussion has also on occasion met with the support or at least understanding of a handful of other States, such as Belgium, Italy and, more recently, Russia, be it that these States' attitude have often been inconsistent and ambiguous.[588]

Is this evidence sufficient to attest to the existence in customary law of a (limited) right of forcible protection of nationals? On closer examination, this would not appear to be the case. The suggestion of Dugard and others that the simple lack of condemnation by the UN's political bodies transmutes these incidents into norm-changing precedents cannot be upheld. First, while Dugard observes that '[i]n all instances in which force has been used to rescue or protect nationals the Security Council has been unable to reach a decision',[589] he forgets to add for instance that the US interventions in Grenada and Panama were nonetheless condemned by the General Assembly.[590] Furthermore, even assuming that the intervention would have evaded a General Assembly reprimand, the vetoing by the US of a Security Council resolution which 'deplored' the intervention in Grenada in 1983 (and which gained eleven positive votes and three abstentions), for example, certainly did not mean that its actions were somehow cloaked in legitimacy. Such an approach is short-sighted, since it completely passes over the positions taken during the debates within the UN political bodies vis-à-vis the alleged precedents, and which, as we have seen, have been predominantly negative.

Still, it could be objected that third States' criticism of the various interventions was directed against the abusive application of the 'protection

---

necessity on the other hand are controversial as justifications.' Quoted in Talmon, 'The German position', 72.

[588] These States are: Belgium (*supra* note 459 (the Congo 1960), note 546 (Definition of Aggression)); however: *supra* note 473 (1978 French–Belgian intervention in the Congo)); Argentina (*supra* note 462 (the Congo 1960); however: note 579 (diplomatic protection)); Italy (*supra* note 461 (the Congo 1960), note 577 (diplomatic protection)); Greece (*supra* note 549 (Definition of Aggression)); the Netherlands (*supra* note 477 (Dominican Republic 1965), *supra* note 549 (Definition of Aggression)). See also below for Canada's position on evacuation operations. Russia was once a staunch opponent of the doctrine, but seems to have included the 'protection of nationals' in its military doctrine. See N. Ronzitti, 'The current status of legal principles prohibiting the use of force and legal justifications of the use of force', in M. Bothe, M. E. O'Connell and N. Ronzitti (eds.), *Redefining sovereignty: the use of force after the Cold War* (Ardsley: Transnational Publishers, 2005), pp. 91–122, at 101. See also *supra*, on Russia's justification for the intervention in Georgia in 2008.

[589] UN Doc. A/CN.4/506, § 58, footnote 90.

[590] See GA Res. 38/7 of 31 October 1983; GA Res. 44/240 of 29 December 1989. Also (2000-I) YBILC, Part I, 42, § 50 (remarks of Brownlie).

of nationals' doctrine, rather than against its admissibility *as such*.[591] There is some value in this, in the sense that the British intervention in the Suez crisis and the US interventions in Grenada and Panama in all likelihood went beyond a limited operation aimed at the rescuing of nationals in mortal danger. Similarly, negative reactions to the Belgian operations in the Congo in 1960 and 1964 were to a large degree inspired by the conviction that Belgium was merely using the opportunity to meddle in the Congo's domestic affairs. However, even if the opposition of many developing countries to the doctrine results from their fear that it constitutes a facile pretext for powerful States to promote their political and economic interests abroad, or a more politically correct packaging of the nineteenth century 'gunboat diplomacy', the following considerations must be kept in mind:

- In the course of UN debates dealing with concrete interventions, several non-Western States *in general terms* rejected the 'protection of nationals doctrine'.[592]
- Even with regard to the Entebbe raid, i.e., the only relevant intervention addressed by the Security Council where there was no suspicion of a 'hidden agenda', a majority of States still took the view that Israel's actions violated international law.[593] Instead of agreeing with Dugard and others that the Entebbe operation serves as a model for the doctrine under consideration,[594] the present author is therefore more inclined to concur with Brownlie that the international community did not 'positively approve of the action as being lawful'.[595] At best, the slow and unequivocal condemnation by third States signals a tendency to 'waive illegality' in the case at hand.[596]

---

[591] See, e.g., on Grenada: Doswald-Beck, 'The United States intervention in Grenada', 361: 'It is significant that generally speaking the States which condemned the US intervention in the debates of the Security Council did not appear to doubt the legal validity of this legal defence as such, but instead went into detail as to why they thought it manifest that the [US] students were not in danger.' Also: Eichensehr, 'Defending nationals abroad', 478; Schachter, 'The right of States to use armed force', 1632; Zedalis, 'Protection of nationals abroad', 245.

[592] E.g., UN Doc. A/PV.742, § 75 (Ethiopia, vis-à-vis the Suez crisis); UN Doc. S/PV.1200, §§ 79–83 (Cuba, vis-à-vis the Dominican Republic); UN Doc. S/PV.2680, 32 (Ghana, vis-à-vis the strikes against Libya in 1986); UN Doc. S/PV.1943, § 87 (Cuba vis-à-vis Entebbe).

[593] See reference *supra* note 519.   [594] E.g., UN Doc. A/CN.4/506, § 59.

[595] (2000-I) YBILC, Part I, 42, § 50 (Brownlie). Also at 49, § 18 (Kabatsi).

[596] *Ibid.*, § 50 (Brownlie).

– Finally, during the debate within the UNGA Sixth Committee on the issue of diplomatic protection in 2000, a considerable group of States again took an explicitly negative stance vis-à-vis forcible protection of nationals.[597]

The various findings pro and contra leave us with, on the one side, a small group of States which have occasionally applied and/or supported the protection of nationals doctrine, and, on the other side, a somewhat broader group of States which appear to reject it. The former group is made up virtually exclusively of Western States; the latter of developing countries. A third group – probably the largest one – consists of those States that have refrained from directly pronouncing on the matter.

While recognizing the long-standing disagreement between States and scholars, Gazzini and Gray find that 'recent' State practice, such as the US intervention in Liberia in 1990 or the French intervention in Chad the same year, offers a 'significant quantity of cases of military interventions aimed at rescuing foreigners abroad'.[598] 'In contrast with the past', Gazzini continues, 'these interventions have gone entirely unchallenged'.[599] He concludes that '[a]fter decades of opposition by the majority of the international community, the claim seems to have eventually overcome any resistance', and subsequently spells out a list of conditions drawing on those advanced by Waldock.[600] Gray proceeds more cautiously. Finding that issues of legality were not raised in relation to these episodes and acknowledging that many of these cases occurred when there was no effective government in place, she notes a certain willingness of third States to 'acquiesce in the forcible evacuation of nationals' in such situations.[601]

Although both authors are right to draw attention to this alleged new element in State practice, its importance should probably not be overstated. First, as Gray admits, none of the episodes was addressed by the Security Council or General Assembly, or otherwise sparked an exchange of legal claims, implying that it is difficult to distil relevant *opinio iuris*. Second, several of the operations listed were actually approved by the

---

[597] See *supra* notes 577, 578, 579.
[598] Gray, *The use of force*, pp. 159–60; Gazzini, *The changing rules*, pp. 170–1.
[599] *Ibid.*, pp. 170–1.   [600] *Ibid.*, pp. 171–2.
[601] Gray, *The use of force*, pp. 159–60: '[Third States'] concern is roused only with regard to those rescue missions where the territorial State objects to the intervention or where the protection of the nationals was just a pretext for an invasion with wider objectives.' In a similar vein Verdross and Simma, *Universelles Völkerrecht*, p. 906, § 1338.

territorial State and can therefore not be regarded as genuine examples of forcible protection of nationals.[602] In other cases, it remains unclear whether consent was given or not. Third, most of the precedents cited actually pre-date the UNGA debate on diplomatic protection, during which many States denounced the protection of nationals doctrine, so that it is hard to regard these cases as the dominant trend in customary practice.

In light of the foregoing, the present author finds it impossible to assert that there exists *de lege lata* a customary right of forcible protection of nationals.[603] More generally, if the idea that attacks against nationals abroad can never trigger the right of self-defence seems counter-intuitive, customary practice as it stands fails to clarify in what exceptional circumstances recourse to force would be permitted.

3.4.4.e   *De lege ferenda*: Time for a change of discourse?

De lege ferenda, a way out of this impasse may begin with the identification of a number of agreed 'baselines' and the acceptance that 'protection of nationals' is not a 'one size fits all' doctrine.[604] Three basic propositions provide a valuable point of departure for a more neutral debate.

---

[602] See *supra* note 527. See also: Wingfield and Meyen, 'Lillich on the forcible protection of nationals abroad', 103–4 (vis-à-vis the French intervention in Gabon), 104–5 (vis-à-vis the French-Belgian intervention in Rwanda in 1990), 108 (vis-à-vis the French intervention in the Central African Republic in 1996).

[603] Randelzhofer observes that there is a 'considerable reluctance to qualify rescue operations involving the use of force as in any case unlawful'. While conceding that this may possibly give rise to 'a corresponding rule of customary international law *in statu nascendi*', he concludes that 'as the law stands at present, ... no rule of international law allows rescue operations for the protection of a State's own nationals'. Randelzhofer, 'Article 2(4)', p. 133. Fleck finds that protection of nationals might become legitimate *de lege ferenda*. Fleck, 'Rules of engagement of maritime forces', 177–8. Cassese agrees that there is no support in customary practice, but nonetheless argues that it is desirable to accept 'protection of nationals' under certain strict conditions. See A. Cassese 'Article 51' pp. 1349–50.

[604] Beyerlin suggests that the exceptional tolerance by the international community of limited interventions is preferable 'to a solution which generally permits this forcible intervention practice, risking thereby its misuse especially by powerful States and undermining the strict regime of the prohibition of the use of force' (e.g., Beyerlin, 'Die israelische Befreiungsaktion', 243). Others object that the bona fide exercise cannot be ruled out, and insist that the necessity and proportionality criteria provide sufficient protection against abuse (e.g., Fitzmaurice, 'The general principles of international law', 173; Greenwood, 'The United States air operation against Libya', 941). The present author finds that the continuing legal uncertainty is hardly satisfactory and therefore agrees with Lillich that the increased political tolerance of evacuation operations should lead to renewed efforts to develop and refine the various criteria by which a State's

First, as a matter of principle, armed force cannot be employed for the protection of public or private property abroad.[605] The axiom that Article 51 in general does not extend to the protection of property is accepted by the overwhelming majority of legal doctrine, and there appears to be no credible contradictory evidence in customary practice after 1945.[606] Second, the debates in the Security Council unequivocally certify that, unless the host State consents or the Security Council authorizes the operation, attacks against nationals abroad or threats thereof can never justify a prolonged or very large-scale military presence. Third and last, in accordance with the ILC Draft Articles, diplomatic protection in essence involves the use of *peaceful* means to halt or remedy alleged wrongful conduct against a State's national abroad. This is true, for example, both with regard to the seizure of a ship carrying the State's flag – even if the legality of the seizure is contested – as well as when, for example, a national abroad is mistreated and/or arrested.

Having spelt out these parameters, what room could possibly be left for the recourse to force? Given the current impasse, it seems useful to differentiate between different factual contexts. Two main types of situations can be identified. First, the context in which the doctrine is most frequently invoked arguably relates to situations where foreigners are threatened by internal unrest, or by an actual (generally non-international) armed conflict in the territorial State. Relevant examples are the Belgian operations in the Congo in 1960 and 1964, the US intervention in Liberia in 1990, the German evacuation from Albania in 1997, and the French interventions in Chad and in the Central African Republic in 1990 and 2003 respectively. Again, several authors have observed that there is a tendency to tolerate interventions in such situations in recent decades, *if and to the extent that* they are limited to the actual evacuation of nationals (and possibly also other foreigners)

---

forcible protection claim may be judged. See Lillich, 'The Liberian "incident" of 1990', 220.

[605] Admittedly, certain limited exceptions exist: subject to the criteria of necessity and proportionality, recourse to self-defence is arguably permitted in response to (1) attacks against military installations and military equipment abroad, (2) large-scale attacks against embassies, and, finally, (3) deliberate, unlawful, and ongoing attacks against civilian aircraft and merchant vessels of the flag State. See *supra* Sections 3.4.1–3.

[606] E.g., J. Dugard, *International Law: a South African perspective*, 2nd edn (Cape Town: Juta, 2001), p. 422; M. Shaw, *International Law*, 5th edn (Cambridge University Press, 2003), p. 1034. Shaw regards this principle as 'universally accepted'.

without active combat engagement.[607] Thus, while the Belgian operations in 1960 and 1964 met with strong international censure, there has been a 'near-complete absence of legal or other criticism'[608] with regard to more recent incidents. Moreover, even with regard to the contested Stanleyville operation of 1964, third States did not denounce the evacuation of foreign nationals as such, but rather what they saw as an attempt to intervene in Congolese domestic affairs.

Interestingly, a number of countries such as Canada, the US, the UK and Australia have adopted technical guidelines to regulate so-called 'Non-Combatant Evacuation Operations' (NEOs).[609] According to the Canadian NEO doctrine, these operations are 'fundamentally defensive in nature. They are conducted to reduce to a minimum the number of [nationals] at risk and to protect them during the evacuation process. They are not an intervention in the issues in the host nation.'[610] NEOs are launched in a variety of life-threatening circumstances, ranging from natural disasters to internal unrest or even all-out war. The various NEO doctrines distinguish between three types of threat environments: 'permissive', 'uncertain' and 'hostile'.[611] Host State consent is not always considered a *sine que non*. Indeed, although the regulations commend

---

[607] Gazzini, *The changing rules*, pp. 170–1; Gray, *The use of force*, pp. 159–60.
[608] See Lillich, 'The Liberian "incident" of 1990', 208–13, 221–3.
[609] US Department of the Army, Field Manual FM 90-29, 17 October 1994, available at www.globalsecurity.org/military/library/policy/army/fm/90-29/index.html; US Joint Chiefs of Staff, Joint Publication JP 3-68 on Noncombatant Evacuation Operations, 22 January 2007, available at www.fas.org/irp/doddir/dod/jp3-68.pdf; Canadian Joint Doctrine Manual on Non-Combatant Evacuation Operations, B-GJ-005-307/FP-050, 16 October 2003; UK Ministry of Defence, Joint Warfare Publication 3-51, August 2000, available at www.mod.uk/NR/rdonlyres/D0302742-2103-4C9D-9CE8-D6F2E6B1860F/0/20071218_jwp3_51_U_DCDCIMAPPS.pdf; Australian Defence Doctrine Publication ADDP 3.10, Evacuation Operations, April 2004. The French Manual on the Law of Armed Conflict also refers to 'évacuation de ressortissants': French Ministry of Defense, Secrétariat Général pour l'administration, Manuel de droit des conflits armés, available at www.defense.gouv.fr/defense/enjeux_defense/defense_et_droit/droit_des_conflits_armes/manuel_de_droit_des_conflits_armes. (websites accessed 4 May 2009). See also: F. Naert, 'Juridische aspecten van non-combatant evacuation operations (NEOs)', paper presented during a conference of the Koninklijk Hoger Instituut voor Defensie, Brussels, 29 April 2005, 11 pages (sanitized version on file with the author).
[610] Canadian Joint Doctrine Manual on Non-Combatant Evacuation Operations, § 101(4).
[611] (1) In a 'permissive' environment, the host nation has control such that law and order are upheld in the intended area of operations, and the government has both the intent and the capability to assist the NEO. (2) In an 'uncertain' environment, the host nation, whether opposed to or supportive of the NEO, does not have total effective control of the territory and population in the intended area of operations. Host nation

the possible contribution of host State support in logistical and security terms, they also envisage exceptional situations where no consent is given. US JP 3-68, for example, states that a NEO must 'not violate the sovereignty of any nation *other than* the host nation'.[612] The Canadian doctrine provides that '*whenever possible* it will be the Canadian Government's intention to conduct evacuations with the agreement and assistance of the host nation government'.[613]

Interestingly, the UK doctrine finds that legal justification may arise in different ways:

(a) Explicit permission to enter for extraction purposes may be given by the receiving State authorities . . .
(b) Where there has been a breakdown in law and order and there no longer exists a coherent government, or where such government exists but it is unable or unwilling to protect UK nationals, intervention to protect UK nationals may be justified on grounds of self-defence (Article 51 of the UN Charter).[614]

The Australian doctrine identifies three possible legal bases, namely:

(a) the consent of the foreign nation;
(b) the exercise of Australia's inherent right of self-defense to protect its nationals (Australia may agree to the rescue of nationals of other countries in certain circumstances); or
(c) in accordance with a resolution of the [UN] Security Council.[615]

---

governmental cooperation and host nation support may be limited or non-existent. Further escalation is possible. (3) In a 'hostile' environment, the host nation's civil and military authorities have lost control or have ceased to function altogether and there is a general breakdown in law and order. Potential evacuees may be directly targeted and their lives increasingly threatened. The host nation's security forces cannot be expected to support, and may even obstruct, the operation. See: *ibid.*, § 102 (1). See also: UK Joint Warfare Publication 3-51, §§ 105-7; US Department of the Army, Field Manual FM 90-29, section on 'NEO Environments'; US Joint Chiefs of Staff, Joint Publication JP 3-68 on Noncombatant Evacuation Operations, I-3; Australian Defence Doctrine Publication ADDP 3.10, Evacuation Operations, 1/2-1/4.

[612] US Joint Chiefs of Staff, Joint Publication JP 3-68 on Noncombatant Evacuation Operations, I-3, Appendix 2 'Legal Considerations', B-3 (emphasis added).

[613] Canadian Joint Doctrine Manual on Non-Combatant Evacuation Operations, § 403 (1)(a).

The French Manual on the Law of Armed Conflict moreover observes that evacuation operations may constitute an infringement of the host State's sovereignty and should therefore be strictly limited in objective, time and means. French Ministry of Defense, Manuel de droit des conflits armés (see under 'Evacuation de ressortissants').

[614] UK Joint Warfare Publication 3-51, Annex 4A 'Legal issues and Rules of Engagement', at 4A2.

[615] Australian Defence Doctrine Publication ADDP 3.10, Evacuation Operations, Annex B to Chapter 5, 'legal considerations', at 5B/1: 'The preferable basis . . . to enter a foreign

Taking account of recent evacuation operations that have not met with apparent criticism, as well as the fact that opponents of the 'protection of nationals' doctrine are mainly concerned with avoiding interference with the host State's domestic affairs, one may wonder whether it would not be possible to overcome the current legal impasse by abandoning the discredited 'protection of nationals' discourse and replacing it by the language of 'non-combatant evacuation'. This suggestion is more than an exercise in semantics. Indeed, by explicitly tying the recourse to force to *evacuation* purposes, this concept seems less prone to abuse than the much more indeterminate 'protection of nationals' language, thus mitigating the major concern of those States that have traditionally rejected the latter doctrine.

A possible compromise would start from the premise that NEOs in principle require the approval of the host State and that reasonable demands of that State vis-à-vis the implementation of the operation must be complied with.[616] This premise is not only inspired by the imperative of respecting the host State's sovereignty, but also by the fact that such consent will generally facilitate an efficient evacuation. In legal terms, operations of the former type qualify as 'intervention by invitation'. If the consent is valid, there will be no breach of Article 2(4) UN Charter. On the other hand, as the quote from the UK guidelines suggests, there will be situations where there has been a breakdown of law and order, and where governmental authorities have collapsed, or are unable or unwilling to protect foreign nationals. In such situations, NEOs may exceptionally be carried out without host State approval to guarantee the safety of threatened nationals. They could then be regarded as a special application of Article 51 UN Charter. In order to be lawful, the operations should in principle be limited to the evacuation of nationals abroad, to be followed by a swift withdrawal.[617] As practice indicates,[618] they may extend to the evacuation of other threatened

---

nation to conduct [a NEO] is either with the consent of the [host nation] or with the authority of the UN. Military deployments into foreign nations to conduct evacuation operations without such consent or authority have varying degrees of international acceptance.'

[616] See on this: US Joint Chiefs of Staff, Joint Publication JP 3-68 on Noncombatant Evacuation Operations, II-9.

[617] E.g., S. F. Day, 'Legal considerations in noncombatant evacuation operations', (1992) 40 Naval L Rev 45–64, at 57.

[618] See, e.g., Wingfield and Meyen, 'Lillich on the forcible protection of nationals abroad', 105 (the French intervention in Gabon (1990)), 108 (the French intervention in the Central African Republic (1996)).

foreigners, as long as the preponderance of threatened persons are nationals of the intervening State.[619] A second limitation, which is duly reflected in the aforementioned guidelines, holds that reasonable force may be used only when necessary to protect the lives of persons entitled to evacuation as well as the personnel involved in the operation. Whenever possible, the operation should be completed without any bullet being fired.[620] Nonetheless, when persons awaiting evacuation are being attacked, the use of lethal force may be justified.[621] Finally, even if this requirement has not been implemented in recent practice,[622] it must be recalled that NEOs conducted without host State approval, like other applications of the right of self-defence, must be reported to the Security Council.[623] In general, the submission of a report to the Security Council may render credibility to the claim of the intervening State that it has no other objectives than the evacuation of the threatened nationals. Additionally, it enables a review by the UN Security Council when there are indications to the contrary.

The second type of situation that surfaces in customary practice concerns operations aimed at the rescuing of hostages within the territory of another State. Examples are the Israeli raid at Entebbe (1976) and the Egyptian raid at Larnaca (1978). The different factual circumstances that may arise make it difficult to pronounce in a general way on the legality of these operations. On the whole, however, terrorist hijackings, contested seizures of merchant vessels and contested detentions of nationals abroad are virtually always dealt with through negotiations and other peaceful means of diplomatic protection. A considerable group

---

[619] This is the formula used by Special Rapporteur Dugard, UN Doc. A/CN.4/506, § 60. Also: Gazzini, *The changing rules*, p. 174. Remark: insofar as sizeable numbers of nationals of third States are evacuated, and certainly when non-nationals constitute the majority of the evacuees (as during Operation 'Libelle': Kreß, , 'Die Rettungsoperation der Bundeswehr in Albanien', 331), the evacuation arguably constitutes an application of the right of *collective* self-defence. The implication is that, in accordance with the ICJ *Nicaragua* judgment, a formal request from the third State would normally be required. See *supra* Section 2.2.1.c.

[620] See, e.g., A. B. Siegel, 'Eastern exit: the Noncombatant Evacuation Operation (NEO) from Mogadishu, Somalia, in January 1991', October 1991, at www.cna.org/documents/2791021100.pdf (accessed 4 May 2009).

[621] E.g., Gazzini, *The changing rules*, p. 174.

[622] The US operation in Liberia in 1990, the French operation in Gabon in 1990 and the French operation in the Central African Republic in 2003, for example, were not reported to the Council.

[623] Also T. Farer, 'The regulation of foreign intervention in civil armed conflict', (1974-II) 142 RdC 291–406, at 394; Gazzini, *The changing rules*, p. 174.

of States stressed during the UNGA debate on diplomatic protection that recourse to force is not an option. Similarly, during the Security Council discussion on the Entebbe raid a majority of States condemned Israel's intervention. In the former debate, only one State (Italy) supported the protection of nationals doctrine as defined by Special Rapporteur Dugard;[624] in the latter, only one State (the US) explicitly supported Israel's legal case.[625] In light thereof, and even though proposals to include an express prohibition in the 1979 Hostage Convention were not upheld, it cannot be argued that there exists a legal right permitting States to rescue nationals taken hostage abroad.[626] The Entebbe debate and the Larnaca case suggest that there are good policy reasons not to recognize such a right: rescue operations unapproved by the host State may result in significant loss of life; they may make it more difficult to find a negotiated solution in future cases; and they may lead to a marked deterioration of diplomatic relations between the territorial State and the intervening State. The Egyptian raid in Cyprus (1978), through which Egypt wanted to prevent the hijackers from being released, cannot honestly be regarded as a lawful use of force. No Western or other State is likely to condone a similar, unapproved operation within its territory. The starting point is that it falls within the competence of the territorial State to deal with hostage-takings on its soil,[627] in accordance with international obligations enshrined in the 1970 Convention for the Suppression of Unlawful Seizure of Aircraft, the 1979 International Convention against the Taking of Hostages, et cetera. A rescue operation by the State whose nationals are held hostage is only admissible when the territorial State consents – as was the case with the German raid on a hijacked plane in Mogadishu in 1977 and the Indonesian raid against a hijacked plane in Bangkok in 1981[628] – or when authorized by the UN Security Council.[629] The Entebbe incident illustrates that hard cases can and do occur, yet hard cases eventually make bad law. To sum up, while there may be unique factual circumstances that would exceptionally favour a waiver of illegality, it seems unwise to turn the exception into a rule.

---

[624] UN Doc. A/C.6/55/SR.19, § 15.   [625] UN Doc. S/PV.1941, §§ 77–81.
[626] Contra, e.g., Eichensehr, 'Defending nationals abroad' (comparing the Tehran hostage situation and the capture by Iran of a group of British sailors in 2007).
[627] Remark: Article 3 of the 1979 Hostage Convention provides that 'the State Party in the territory of which the hostage is held by the offender shall take all measures it considers appropriate to ease the situation of the hostage, in particular, to secure his release and, after his release, to facilitate, when relevant, his departure'. 1316 UNTS 205.
[628] See Ronzitti, *Rescuing nationals abroad*, pp. 79–81.
[629] A possible example is SC Res. 1816 (2008) of 2 June 2008, dealing with acts of piracy and armed robbery against merchant vessels off the coast of Somalia.

4

The 'armed attack' requirement
ratione temporis

Alas, the controversy continues. Indeed, although Article 51 UN Charter permits the exercise of self-defence 'if an armed attack occurs', a number of authors were quick to point out that the provision did not abrogate the pre-existing customary right of anticipatory self-defence. In addition, they stressed that, in a world gone nuclear, it would be absurd to expect States to await the first – and potentially devastating – blow. In accordance with the famous Webster formula, legacy of the 1837 *Caroline* incident, States should be allowed to resort to armed force when faced with an imminent threat of attack giving rise to a 'necessity of self-defence, instant, overwhelming, leaving no choice of means, and no moment for deliberation'.[1] For most of the Charter era, however, a majority of legal doctrine has cautioned against such broad reading of self-defence, allegedly incompatible with the text and aim of Article 51. More importantly, absent an unequivocal precedent receiving broad international support, it arguably did not experience a breakthrough of any sort. Rather, it kept a slumbering existence, fuelling a never-ending doctrinal debate, and dangling over the *Ius ad Bellum* like the Sword of Damocles.

After the 9/11 terrorist attacks the Sword of Damocles came down hard and unexpectedly. The unprecedented attacks against United States territory[2] led US officials and policy-makers to engage in a fundamental reappraisal of the global security environment, culminating in the adoption

---

[1] R. Jennings, 'The *Caroline* and *McLeod* cases', (1938) 32 AJIL 82–99, at 85; 29 BFSP 1137; 30 BFSP 195–6.

[2] This was the first large-scale attack against US territory since the Japanese attack against Pearl Harbour in December 1941. It is estimated that the latter attack killed over 2,400 Americans, with another 1,200 injured (See: B. Robinson, 'Pearl Harbor: a rude awakening', available at www.bbc.co.uk/history/worldwars/wwtwo/pearl_harbour_01.shtml (accessed 11 May 2009). The 9/11 attacks killed almost 3,000 Americans and foreign nationals ('U.S. deaths in Iraq, war on terror surpass 9/11 toll', *CNN* 3 September 2006).

by the Bush administration of the US National Security Strategy (NSS) in September 2002.[3] In light of the emergence of various 'new' security threats, this influential document strongly advocated the lawfulness of self-defence against imminent threats of attack.[4] What is more, the document openly claimed a right of anticipatory self-defence that is substantially broader than under the traditional Webster formula.[5]

The US NSS sent a shockwave throughout the international community. By analogy with the US, a number of States professed their support for some form of anticipatory self-defence.[6] Many scholars, on either side of the Atlantic, have followed suit. On the other hand, if support for self-defence against *imminent* attacks arguably increased, the discourse surrounding the intervention in Iraq illustrates that the US attempt to broaden self-defence beyond the parameters of the Webster formula was unsuccessful.

Against this background, the present chapter scrutinizes customary practice in order to find an answer to two related questions: (1) are there situations where self-defence can be exercised prior to the occurrence of an armed attack?; and (2) at what moment does an armed attack begin to take place? Section 4.1 looks at the evolution of the debate during the second half of the twentieth century. To this end, it examines the legal arguments raised by opponents and proponents of anticipatory self-defence, the treatment of relevant precedents before the Security Council, as well as the views expressed during UNGA debates. Section 4.2 analyses the extent to which support for, or opposition to, various forms of anticipatory self-defence has altered in the aftermath of the 9/11 attacks and the 2003 Iraq intervention. Finally, section 4.3 identifies a number of borderline cases that contribute to the *ratione temporis* analysis.

Before setting about our task, however, some terminological considerations are indispensable. In the endless literature dealing with the topic under consideration, a multitude of labels surface. First, a distinction is often made between 'reactive' self-defence in response to an actual armed attack, on the one hand, and 'anticipatory' self-defence, which aims

---

[3] White House, The National Security Strategy of the United States of America, September 2002, available at http://georgewbush-whitehouse.archives.gov/nsc/nss/2002/index.html (accessed 11 May 2009).
[4] See *ibid.*, 13–16.   [5] *Ibid.*, 15.
[6] See, e.g., W.M. Reisman and A. Armstrong, 'The past and future of the claim of preemptive self-defense', (2006) 100 AJIL 525–50.

at anticipating a future attack, on the other hand. Second, the latter category is often subdivided in two separate categories, namely self-defence against 'imminent' attacks (in accordance with the Webster formula) and self-defence against 'non-imminent' attacks (as is apparently envisaged by the US National Security Strategy). However, the labels used to define these subcategories vary considerably.[7] Some authors define the former as 'pre-emptive' and the latter as 'preventive' self-defence.[8] 'Anticipatory' self-defence is sometimes taken to refer to the former subcategory alone, and sometimes as including both. Other authors interpret 'pre-emptive' and 'preventive' self-defence the other way round, with the former referring to non-imminent attacks, and the latter to 'imminent' attacks.[9] Another distinction speaks of 'pre-emptive/preventive *war*' versus 'pre-emptive/ preventive self-defence'.[10] In recent years, however, it has become more common to reserve the concept of 'pre-emptive self-defence' for military action against an imminent or proximate threat of attack and to reserve 'preventive self-defence' for non-imminent or non-proximate threats. 'Anticipatory' self-defence is thereby regarded as the overlapping denominator. This is the way in which both terms were coined *inter alia* in the 2004 Report of the UN High-Level Panel on Threats Challenges and

---

[7] See in particular the scenarios spelled out by Kolb: R. Kolb, 'Self-defence and preventive war at the beginning of the millennium', (2004) 59 ZÖR 111–34, at 122–4. Also T. Christakis, 'Vers une reconnaissance de la notion de guerre préventive?', in K. Bannelier, T. Christakis, O. Corten and P. Klein (eds.), *L'intervention en Irak et le droit international* (Paris: Pedone, 2004), pp. 9–45, at 11 (footnote 6); C. Greenwood, 'International law and the pre-emptive use of force: Afghanistan, Al-Qaida, and Iraq', (2003) 4 San Diego ILJ 7–37, at 9.

[8] E.g., (Dutch) Advisory Council on International Affairs (AIV), 'Pre-emptive Action', Advisory Report No. 36, July 2004, available at www.aiv-advies.nl/ContentSuite/upload/ aiv/doc/nr36eng(1).pdf (accessed 11 May 2009), 5; T. D. Gill, 'The temporal dimension of self-defense: anticipation, pre-emption, prevention and immediacy', in M. N. Schmitt and J. Pejic (eds.), *International law and armed conflict: exploring the faultlines: essays in honour of Yoram Dinstein* (Leiden: Martinus Nijhoff) (2007), pp. 113–55, at 115; J. Schwehm, 'Präventive Selbstverteidigung: eine vergleichende Analyse der völkerrechtlichen Debatte', (2008) 46 AdV 368–406, at 369–72.

[9] See, e.g., P. Cahier, 'Changements et continuité du droit international', (1985-VI) 195 RdC 9–374, at 73; Reisman and Armstrong, 'The claim of preemptive self-defense', 526 (using 'anticipatory self-defence' for imminent threats, and 'pre-emptive' self-defence for non-imminent threats); O. Schachter, 'The lawful resort to unilateral use of force', (1985) 10 YJIL 291–4, at 293.

[10] See, e.g., J. Combacceau and S. Sur, *Droit international public*, 6th edn. (Paris: Montchrestien, 2004), p. 628 (referring to '*légitime défense préventive*' and '*guerre pré ventive*'); A. Verdross and B. Simma, *Universelles Völkerrecht: Theorie und Praxis*, 3rd edn. (Berlin: Dunker un Humblot, 1984), p. 288 (distinguishing between '*Präventivkrieg*' and '*präventiven Verteidigung*').

Change[11] and in the 2005 follow-up report of the UN Secretary-General.[12] It is also the way in which they are used in the present study.[13] Third, a number of authors have introduced the additional category of 'interceptive' or 'interceptory' self-defence to define cases where force is used against an attack which 'is being launched', even if it has not yet crossed the border.[14] In such situations, the attack is in a way no longer imminent, but has already begun to take place, albeit that the dividing line between that and pre-emptive self-defence is a very thin one.

The resulting terminological time frame is schematized in Figure 1. Four main categories can be discerned:[15]

- Reactive self-defence stands opposite to anticipatory self-defence. Strictly *reactive* self-defence (excluding interceptive action) follows when an armed attack has struck the territory of the defending State, or its external manifestations abroad. The attack may be completed or may still be ongoing, but its material nature is to some extent an observable fact of reality.
- Interceptive self-defence covers the situation where an attack has been launched, but has not yet struck the 'defending' State. *In casu*, there must be clear and compelling evidence that the opponent has embarked upon an apparently irreversible course of action, thereby 'crossing the legal Rubicon'.[16] This category is located on the fault line between reactive and anticipatory self-defence. The clearest example is the scenario whereby a missile has been launched, but is still in the air.
- Anticipatory action covers both pre-emptive and preventive self-defence. *Pre-emptive* self-defence is directed against an attack which has not yet been launched, but which is 'imminent'. This presupposes

---

[11] Report of the Secretary-General's High-level Panel on Threats, Challenges and Change 'A More Secure World: Our Shared Responsibility', 2 December 2004, UN Doc. A/59/565, § 189.

[12] UN Secretary-General Kofi Annan, 'In Larger Freedom: Towards Development, Security and Human Rights for All', 21 March 2005, UN Doc. A/59/2005, § 122.

[13] Also, e.g., S. Talmon, 'Changing views on the use of force: the German position', (2005) 5 Baltic YBIL 41–76, at 61. Also *supra*, note 8.

[14] E.g., Y. Dinstein, *War, aggression and self-defence*, 4th edn. (Cambridge University Press, 2005), p. 190; O. Corten, *Le droit contre la guerre; l'interdiction du recours à la force en droit international contemporain* (Paris: Pedone, 2008), p. 626; A. Constantinou, *The right of self-defence under customary international law and Article 51 of the UN Charter* (Brussels: Bruylant, 2000), p. 125; T. Gazzini, *The changing rules on the use of force in international law* (Manchester University Press, 2005), p. 151.

[15] See Kolb, 'Self-defence and preventive war', 122–4.

[16] Dinstein, *War, aggression and self-defence*, 4th edn., p. 191.

that there have been certain preparations for attack, such as the mobilization of conventional forces.
- Preventive self-defence, on the other hand, seeks to counter diverse future threats, which have not yet fully materialized.[17] There are no concrete indications that an attack will be launched in the near future, yet action is allegedly undertaken to 'prevent' the threat from becoming imminent.

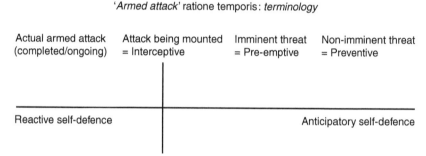

Figure 1

The importance of the different labels and the way in which they are applied should not be understated. Indeed, the confusion regarding the appropriate terms easily leads one to misinterpret the position of those using them as well as to misjudge the impact of customary practice. For this reason, one must avoid taking the terms at face value. Instead, one must not only ascertain which categorization States and authors subscribe to, but also, and more importantly, examine how the precise content of the relevant category is construed. What scenarios are believed to constitute an 'imminent' or a 'non-imminent' threat? When is an attack considered to have been launched? The complexity of these questions soon becomes clear when applied to a concrete incident, such as the Japanese attack on Pearl Harbour. *In casu*, one might wonder at what moment the United States could have initiated forcible 'defensive' measures: when US forces detected the incoming Japanese aircraft?; prior to the launching of the aircraft, when it discovered that the Japanese fleet was sailing in the direction of Hawaii?; or when Japan was making preparations for the attack by drafting attack scenarios and conducting naval exercises?[18] In short, the devil is in the detail.

---

[17] Kolb, 'Self-defence and preventive war', 124.
[18] See Dinstein, *War, aggression and self-defence*, 4th edn., pp. 190–1.

4.1 Anticipatory self-defence: the never-ending saga (1945–2001)

4.1.1 The doctrinal debate – a brief appraisal

4.1.1.a Arguments in favour of anticipatory self-defence

Even if the pros and cons have been elaborated in numerous writings,[19] an analysis of the legality of anticipatory self-defence must inevitably begin with an appraisal of the arguments employed by both camps. As several were already addressed in previous sections, however, we will not overly recapitulate the academic debate, but instead focus on identifying the Charter 'baseline', against which the interpretative or modificatory value of customary practice must be tested.

Starting with those scholars who believe that States need not necessarily await the occurrence of an armed attack,[20] the principal legal argument holds that Article 51 UN Charter failed to abrogate the broader pre-existing customary right of self-defence, which allowed

---

[19] See, e.g., the following overviews: Christakis, 'La notion de guerre préventive', pp. 16–22; S. M. Schwebel, 'Aggression, intervention and self-defence in modern international law', (1972-II) 136 RdC 411–97, at 479–82; L. Van den Hole, 'Anticipatory self-defence under international law', (2003) 19 American Un ILRev 69–106.

[20] E.g. (in order of publication, prior to 2001) C.H.M. Waldock, 'The regulation of the use of force by individual states in international law', (1952-II) 81 RdC 451–517, at 496–9; D.W. Bowett, *Self-defence in international law* (Manchester University Press, 1958), pp. 178–93; M. S. McDougal, 'The Soviet–Cuban quarantine and self-defense', (1963) 57 AJIL 597–604, at 597–601; P. Malanczuk, 'Countermeasures and self-defence as circumstances precluding wrongfulness in the International Law Commission's Draft Articles on State Responsibility', (1983) 43 GYBIL 705–812, at 764; Verdross and Simma, *Universelles Völkerrecht*, p. 288; Schachter, 'Unilateral use of force', 293; ICJ, *Case concerning military and paramilitary activities in and against Nicaragua (Nicaragua v. United States of America)* (Merits), Judgment of 27 June 1986, (1986) ICJ Rep 14–150, Dissenting opinion of Judge Schwebel, § 173 (compare to Schwebel's contribution in the Recueil des Cours some fifteen years earlier (Schwebel, 'Aggression, intervention and self-defence', 479–82), where the author concludes that: '[The] conflicting views are substantial; there is weight on both sides'); D. Fleck, 'Rules of engagement of maritime forces and the limitation of the use of force under the UN Charter', (1989) 31 GYBIL 165–86, at 176; R. Higgins, *Problems and process: international law and how we use it* (Oxford: Clarendon Press, 1994), pp. 242–3. Also: J. N. Moore, 'The secret war in Central America and the future world order', (1986) 80 AJIL 43–127, at 83.

See also the authors cited in: A. Cassese, 'Article 51', in J.-P. Cot and A. Pellet, *La Charte des Nations Unies*, 3rd edn. (Paris: Economica, 2005), pp. 1329–61, at 1336, footnote 3; Constantinou, *The right of self-defence*, p. 112, footnotes 7–14; A. Randelzhofer, 'Article 51', in B. Simma in collaboration with H. Mosler, A. Randelzhofer, C. Tomuschat and R. Wolfrüm (eds.), *The Charter of the United Nations: a commentary. Vol. I* (Oxford University Press, 2002), pp. 788–806, at 803, footnote 138.

for anticipatory action. Most of these authors agree that this right was limited to 'imminent' threats of armed attack, and that the conditions governing its exercise were framed in the aftermath of the '*Caroline* incident'.[21] *In casu*, British troops conducted an attack in American territorial waters against a merchant vessel used by Canadian rebels and their American supporters in attacks against Canada.[22] The sinking of the ship led to a furious reaction by the US, which demanded that Britain showed a 'necessity of self-defence, instant, overwhelming, leaving no choice of means, and no moment for deliberation'. This formula, also known as the 'Webster formula' (after the US Secretary of State), was subsequently accepted by the UK Foreign Minister as the appropriate standard to test the lawfulness of the incursion.[23] The proponents of anticipatory self-defence furthermore claim that the drafters of the UN Charter did not have the intention to restrict self-defence to 'actual' (instead of 'imminent') armed attacks. Instead, as explained earlier, the *travaux* and the reference to the 'inherent' character of the right of self-defence allegedly indicate that Article 51 was only intended to give particular emphasis in a declaratory manner for self-defence in the case of an armed attack.

Apart from the 'pre-existing custom' argument, the 'expansionists' or 'counter-restrictionists' have invoked a number of subsidiary grounds to state their case. From the perspective of textual exegesis, it is sometimes claimed that the phrase 'if an armed attack occurs' is not the same as 'if, and only if, an armed attack occurs'. McDougal and Feliciano, for example, argue that 'a proposition that "if A, then B" is *not* equivalent to, and does not necessarily imply, the proposition that "if, and only if, A, then B"'.[24] According to these scholars, such identification or implication is 'assuredly not a compulsion of logic', but instead reflects a policy choice.[25] Furthermore, it is argued that the Nuremberg and Tokyo Military Tribunals implicitly accepted the legality of anticipatory self-defence.[26] In relation to the invasion of Denmark and Norway, the

---

[21] E.g., Higgins, *Problems and process*, pp. 242–3; Schachter, 'Unilateral use of force', 293; Waldock, 'The regulation of the use of force', 498.
[22] See Jennings, 'The *Caroline* and *McLeod* cases'.
[23] *Ibid.*, 89; 29 BFSP 1137; 30 BFSP 195–6.
[24] M.S. McDougal and F.P. Feliciano, *Law and minimum world public order: the legal regulation of international coercion* (New Haven, CT: Yale University Press, 1961), p. 237, note 261.
[25] *Ibid.*
[26] See, e.g., G.K. Walker, 'Anticipatory collective self-defense in the Charter era: what the treaties have said', (1998) 31 Cornell ILJ 321–76, at 357–9.

former Tribunal held that: 'It must be remembered that preventive action in foreign territory is justified only in case of "an instant and overwhelming necessity for self-defense, leaving no choice of means, and no moment of deliberation" (The Caroline case ...)'.[27] A similar argument was considered by the Tokyo Tribunal in relation to the Japanese attack against the Netherlands East Indies.[28]

Last but not least, from a policy perspective, the supporters of anticipatory self-defence stress time and again that the increasing speed and destructive potential of modern weaponry necessitates a construction of self-defence that is not strictly reactive in nature. Especially in light of the development and proliferation of nuclear weapons, they argue that it would be utterly unrealistic to expect States to suffer the first, and possibly devastating/annihilating, strike. In this regard, it is considered highly significant that the UN Atomic Energy Commission in its First Report to the Security Council declared that 'a violation [of a treaty or convention on atomic energy matters] might be of so grave a character as to give rise to the inherent right of self-defence recognized in Article 51 of the Charter of the United Nations'.[29]

---

[27] Judgment of the International Military Tribunal (Nuremberg), 1 October 1946, reproduced in (1947) 41 AJIL 172–333, at 205. Moreover, when the German defence counsel suggested that the German attack on the Soviet Union had merely anticipated a Soviet attack, this plea was dismissed in relation to the facts, rather than on the merits: 'It was contended for the defendants that the attack upon the U.S.S.R. was justified because the Soviet Union was contemplating an attack upon Germany, and making preparations to that end. It is impossible to believe that this view was ever honestly entertained', *ibid.*, 213.

[28] While Japan claimed that its actions were lawful by virtue of the Netherlands' declaration of war, the Tribunal begged to differ: 'The fact that the Netherlands, being fully apprised of the imminence of the attack, in self-defence declared war ... and thus officially recognized the existence of a state of war which had been begun by Japan cannot change that war from a war of aggression on the part of Japan into something other than that.' Judgment, Cmd. 6964, at 35. Cited in I. Brownlie, *International law and the use of force by states* (Oxford: Clarendon Press, 1963), p. 258.

[29] UN Doc. AEC/18/Rev.1, at 24. See UN Repertory of Practice (1945–54), Vol. 2, available at www.un.org/law/repertory/ (accessed 11 May 2009), 434–5. Remark: the recommendation was adopted following the discussion within the Commission of a US memorandum which called for a more flexible interpretation of self-defence in the following terms: 'It is ... clear that an "armed attack" is now something entirely different from what it was prior to the discovery of atomic weapons. It would therefore seem to be both important and appropriate under present conditions that the treaty define "armed attack" in a manner appropriate to atomic weapons and include in the definition not simply the actual dropping of an atomic bomb, but also certain steps in themselves preliminary to such action.' Cited in UN Repertory of Practice (1945–54), Vol. 2, 434.

4.1.1.b Arguments against anticipatory self-defence

The aforementioned arguments are, however, refuted by a considerable group of international lawyers (sometimes dubbed the 'restrictionists'), who have consistently interpreted the Charter provisions as proscribing recourse to military force against 'imminent' – and *a fortiori* against 'non-imminent' – threats of attack.[30] These scholars denounce the reliance by the previous group on a pre-existing customary right of anticipatory self-defence. On the one hand, it is called into question whether customary law in the first half of the twentieth century really supported such right. The 'episodic reference' to the 1837 *Caroline* incident is considered anachronistic and misguided. Indeed, instead of relying on customary practice from the decades immediately preceding the UN Charter, the 'expansionists' invoke a precedent which dates from an age where States were essentially free to resort to war against one another and lacking a legal regime of self-defence.[31] A number of authors have moreover stressed that the sinking of the *Caroline* can hardly be regarded

---

[30] E.g., (in order of publication, prior to 2001) J.L. Kunz, 'Individuals and collective self-defense in Article 51 of the Charter of the United Nations', (1947) 41 AJIL 872–9, at 878; P. C. Jessup, *A modern law of nations: an introduction* (New York: MacMillan, 1948), p. 166; H. Kelsen, *The Law of the United Nations: a critical analysis of its fundamental problems* (London: Stevens, 1950), pp. 797–8; H. Wehberg, 'L'interdiction du recours à la force. Le principe et les problèmes qui se posent', (1951-I) 78 RdC 1–121, at 81–2; Brownlie, *The use of force by states*, pp. 257–60, 275–8; Q. Wright, 'The Cuban quarantine', (1963) 57 AJIL 546–65, at 560–1; J. de Arechaga, 'International law in the past third of a century', (1978-I) 159 RdC 1–344, at 95–7; L. Henkin, *How nations behave. Law and foreign policy*, 2nd edn. (New York: Columbia University Press, 1979), pp. 140–4. (Henkin does, however, accept a 'small and special exception for the special case of the surprise nuclear attack'); M. Lachs, 'The development and general trends of international law in our time', (1980-IV) 169 RdC 9–377, at 164; A. D'Amato, 'Israel's strike upon the Iraqi nuclear reactor', (1983) 77 AJIL 584–8, at 588; Cahier, 'Changements et continuité', 73; H. Bokor-Szegö, 'The attitude of socialist States towards the international regulation of the use of force', in A. Cassese (ed.), *The current legal regulation of the use of force* (Dordrecht: Martinus Nijhoff, 1986), pp. 453–77, at 465; G. Abi-Saab, 'Cours général de droit international public', (1987-III) 207 RdC 9–463, at 371; D. N. Kolesnik, 'The development of the right to self-defence', in W. E. Butler (ed.), *The non-use of force in international law* (Dordrecht: Martinus Nijhoff, 1989), pp. 153–9, at 154–5; L.-A. Sicilianos, *Les réactions décentralisées à l'illicité: des contre-mesures à la légitime défense* (Paris: Librairie générale de droit et de jurisprudence, 1990), pp. 395 *et seq.*; Constantinou, *The right of self-defence*, pp. 111–27; Randelzhofer, 'Article 51', p. 803.

See also the authors cited by cited in: Cassese, 'Article 51', p. 1336, footnote 4; Constantinou, *The right of self-defence*, pp. 114–15, footnotes 25–35; Randelzhofer, 'Article 51', p. 803, footnote 142.

[31] E.g., I. Brownlie, 'The principle of non-use of force in contemporary international law', in Butler, *The non-use of force*, pp. 17–27, at 18–19.

as an example of *anticipatory* action, since the vessel had already been involved in multiple military actions against Canadian territory.[32]

Second and more convincing, the 'restrictionists' argue that, even if anticipatory self-defence was permitted in the years prior to the adoption of the Charter, pre-existing custom was nonetheless modified by Article 51 UN Charter. This argument, which the present author subscribes to, was extensively discussed in previous chapters and will therefore not be restated in full. In essence, it can be broken down into two parts.[33] First, in light of the equal normative position of customary and conventional law, and in accordance with the *lex posterior* principle, the introduction of the Charter rules on the use of force has removed *incompatible* pre-existing custom. Second, each of the primary elements of interpretation supports the view that the occurrence of an 'armed attack' is a *sine qua non* under Article 51 UN Charter. In accordance with the principle of effectiveness it is hard to give a different twist to the clear wording of the phrase 'if an armed attack occurs'. If the drafters did not intend this phrase to be regulatory, one might have expected them to use a different wording (*'for example*, if an armed attack occurs'), or to have omitted the phrase altogether (*expressio unius est exclusio alterius*). McDougal's objection that 'if A, then B' does not equal 'if, and only if, A, then B' cannot be upheld if one looks at the Charter context. Article 51 constitutes an exception to (or better, qualification of) the comprehensive prohibition on the use of force, and must accordingly be interpreted restrictively.[34] The fact that 'the threat of force' and 'threats to the peace' are mentioned in Articles 2(4) and 39 proves that the drafters were aware of such situations and chose to submit incidents concerned to the Security Council.[35] The 'objects and purpose' of the UN Charter only confirm this reading, since its goal was precisely to limit the unilateral use of force as much as possible and to subject it to the control of the Security Council.

---

[32] E.g., Corten, *Le droit contre la guerre*, p. 622; Dinstein, *War, aggression and self-defence*, 4th edn., p. 184.

[33] See *supra*, Sections 1.1 and 2.1.

[34] See, e.g., Abi-Saab, 'Cours général', 369–71; Christakis, 'La notion de guerre préventive', pp. 19–20.

[35] In a similar vein: UNCIO, Vol. 11, 58 (France, noting that Article 51 makes a 'clear distinction between the prevention and the repression of aggression'. 'As far as prevention of aggression is concerned, it vests in the Security Council the task of ... taking whatever measures are necessary ... But as far as repression of aggression is concerned, and that is a form of legitimate individual or collective self-defence, the text indicates the right ... to act immediately ...').

While the present author believes that the primary elements of interpretation settle the matter conclusively, one might, for argument's sake, object that a literal reading of Article 51 leads to manifestly absurd results and therefore warrants a recourse to the Charter's *travaux* by way of supplementary means of interpretation. Again, however, nothing in the records of the San Francisco Conference suggests that the phrase 'if an armed attack occurs' was intended to be declaratory instead of regulatory. The word 'inherent' was included without any debate taking place as to its meaning.[36] US Governor Stassen emphasized that 'we did not want exercised the right of self-defence before an armed attack had occurred'.[37] When asked what action could be undertaken against a fleet that 'had started from abroad against an American republic but had not yet attacked,' Stassen responded that 'we could not under this provision attack the fleet but we could send a fleet of our own and be ready in case an attack came'.[38]

When taken together, these arguments make clear that the 'pre-existing custom' paradigm is not only artificial, but fundamentally flawed. This view is shared by a considerable majority of legal doctrine.[39] Even among proponents of anticipatory self-defence, many concede that legal support must be sought elsewhere,[40] primarily in post-Charter customary practice. Franck, for instance, claiming that a purely reactive posture has become 'logically indefensible by the advent of a new age of nuclear warheads and long-range rocketry', nonetheless admits that 'it is beyond dispute that the negotiations [at San Francisco] deliberately closed the door on any claim of "anticipatory self-defence"'.[41] In a similar vein, it may be recalled that the United States argued during the *Nicaragua* proceedings that the Charter provisions on the use of force and the customary rules '[were] in

---

[36] See *supra*, Section 3.1.2.b; US Department of State, *Foreign Relations of the United States, Diplomatic Papers. (1945) General: the United Nations* (1967), p. 670.

[37] *Ibid.*, p. 818.   [38] *Ibid.*

[39] See, e.g., R. Ago, 'Addendum to the 8th Report on State Responsibility', (1980-II) 32 YBILC, Part One, 65–6, and the authors cited under note 261; Sicilianos, *Des contre-mesures à la légitime défense*, pp. 296–300, and the authors cited under note 286. See also *supra*, Section 1.1.1.

[40] E.g., *in fine*, M. Bothe, 'Terrorism and the legality of pre-emptive force', (2003) 14 EJIL 227–40, at 229 *et seq.*; M. E. O'Connell, 'The myth of preemptive self-defense', August 2002, available at www.asil.org/taskforce/oconnell.pdf (accessed 11 May 2009), 13; A. Shapira, 'The Six-Day War and the right of self-defence', (1971) 6 *Israeli LRev* 65–80, at 71.

[41] T. M. Franck, *Recourse to force: State action against threats and armed attacks* (Cambridge University Press, 2002), p. 50.

fact identical', leaving no room 'for other customary and general international law'.[42]

If the expansionsists' principal legal argument must be discarded, what about their subsidiary arguments? First, a number of restrictionists downplay the impact of the aforementioned report of the Atomic Energy Commission, as well as the judgments of the Nuremberg and Tokyo Tribunals. As regards the former, Brownlie objects that the cited passage merely constitutes 'the incident expression of views by a subsidiary organ of the Security Council', forming part of a report with 'no direct bearing on self-defence'.[43] As regards the latter, it is noted that: (1) both Tribunals were dealing with the law as it stood before the UN Charter, implying that the cited passages can at best provide guidance vis-à-vis the interpretation of pre-existing custom; and (2) that both were pronouncing on the individual criminal responsibility of the accused, rather than on matters of State responsibility.[44] 'Restrictionists' have also submitted that the North Atlantic Treaty and similar treaties based on Article 51 provide only for defence against 'armed attacks', and not for defence against 'imminent threats'.[45]

Last but not least, 'restrictionists' have invoked various reasons to question the *desirability* of 'anticipatory' self-defence, thereby counterbalancing the policy arguments of Bowett, Schwebel and others. First, they point at the difficulty of assessing claims of anticipatory self-defence.[46] If the analysis of the proportionality of reactive self-defence is already a complex undertaking, how much more difficult is it not to ascertain whether a State has responded proportionally to a threatened attack that has not generated any material effects? Also, the admissibility of anticipatory action would largely hinge upon the intention of the opponent, i.e., a subjective element which may be difficult to substantiate by means of convincing evidence, and which may alter in the course of time. Clear and objective criteria are largely lacking. Second, it is submitted that States can lawfully undertake a number of precautionary

---

[42] ICJ, *Nicaragua* case (Merits), §§ 174, 187.
[43] Brownlie, *The use of force by states*, pp. 276–7. See also: Corten, *Le droit contre la guerre*, pp. 633–4; Sicilianos, *Des contre-mesures à la légitime défense*, p. 397.
[44] E.g., Brownlie, *The use of force by States*, p. 258; Corten, *Le droit contre la guerre*, pp. 631–2.
[45] E.g., ibid.; P. Malanczuk and M. Akehurst, *Akehurst's modern introduction to international law*, 7th edn. (London: Routledge, 1997), p. 312. See however: Walker, 'Anticipatory collective self-defense', 359 *et seq.*
[46] See, e.g., Brownlie, *The use of force by States*, pp. 259–60; Constantinou, *The right of self-defence*, pp. 115 *et seq.*; Randelzhofer, 'Article 51', p. 803.

measures when a threat to their security is emerging.[47] They can engage in military preparations of their own in order to 'be ready in case an attack comes', as US Governor Stassen observed in 1945. In accordance with the ILC DASR,[48] they may adopt non-forcible countermeasures. Another option consists in submitting a complaint to the UN Security Council.[49] True, such démarche will not always/often result in the adoption of concrete measures, yet it may at least have the benefit of exposing the opponent's aggressive posture. Third, while 'expansionists' draw attention to the speed and destructive potential of modern weaponry, 'restrictionists' object that, especially in the nuclear era, military escalation must be avoided, since false alerts may lead to disaster.[50] In the words of Henkin: 'It is precisely in the age of the major deterrent that nations should not be encouraged to strike first under pretext of prevention or pre-emption.'[51]

4.1.1.c The ICJ's non-position

Both opponents and proponents of anticipatory self-defence have occasionally cited the case law of the ICJ to support their respective points of view. Waldock, for instance, finds that in the *Corfu Channel* case[52] the Court deemed 'a strong probability of armed attack' sufficient to trigger the right of self-defence.[53] Despite his support for the legality of anticipatory action, Bowett nonetheless concludes that 'it is difficult to deduce from the judgement anything quite so definite'.[54] Indeed, neither the UK argument, not the Court's judgment, expressly rested on the basis of self-defence. Rather, the action concerned was based on the right of innocent passage, 'a right not invalidated by the fact that it was

---

[47] See Constantinou, *The right of self-defence*, pp. 122–4; Dinstein, *War, aggression and self-defence*, 4th edn., p. 187.

[48] ILC, 'Commentary on the Draft Articles on the Responsibility of States for Internationally Wrongful Acts', (2001-II) YBILC 128 *et seq*.

[49] E.g., Jessup, *A modern law of nations*, p. 166 ('Under the Charter, alarming military preparations by a neighboring state would justify a resort to the Security Council, but would not justify resort to anticipatory force by the state which believed itself threatened').

[50] E.g., Lachs, 'General trends of international law', 164.

[51] Henkin, *How nations behave*, p. 142. Also D'Amato, 'Israel's strike upon the Iraqi nuclear reactor', 588.

[52] ICJ, *Corfu Channel (United Kingdom v. Albania)*, Judgment of 9 April 1949, (1949) ICJ Rep 4–38, at 30–1. The passage concerned deals with the unauthorized passage of British warships through the Corfu channel.

[53] See Waldock, 'The regulation of the use of force', 498–501.

[54] Bowett, *Self-defence in international law*, p. 190.

accompanied by preparations for self-defence should the need arise'.[55] Furthermore, some have deduced support for anticipatory self-defence from the ICJ's construction of the relationship between the Charter rules and customary law in *Nicaragua*.[56] In turn, some 'restrictionists' have emphasized that the Court implicitly excluded anticipatory action by subjecting self-defence to the occurrence of an armed attack.[57] In the end, both interpretations seem oblivious to the Court's explicit declaration in *Nicaragua* and *DRC* v. *Uganda* that: '[T]he issue of the lawfulness of a response to the imminent threat of armed attack has not been raised. Accordingly, the Court expresses no view on that issue.'[58] In the end, the better view is that the Court has indeed refrained from taking sides in the long-standing academic row regarding pre-emptive action (even if a number of individual judges have been more outspoken).[59]

4.1.1.d A doctrinal divide greatly exaggerated?

Turning back to the four temporal phases spelled out in the introduction (strictly reactive, interceptive, pre-emptive, preventive), what can be concluded in terms of academic support and compatibility with the Charter rules? First, as far as academic support is concerned, we have seen that there has long been a doctrinal divide between those supporting a right of anticipatory self-defence, and those rejecting such option. At least prior to 2001, it is submitted that the so-called 'restrictionist' group held the upper hand[60] (even if its preponderance was not as

---

[55] Ibid. Also: Sicilianos, *Des contre-mesures à la légitime défense*, pp. 397–8.
[56] E.g., J. Dugard, *International law: a South African perspective*, 3rd edn. (Cape Town: Juta, 2005), p. 508. Remark: see also Franck, *Recourse to force*, p. 98.
[57] E.g., G.M. Danilenko, 'The principle of non-use of force in the practice of the International Court of Justice', in Butler, *The non-use of force*, pp. 101–10, at 105–6; R.S.J. Macdonald, 'The *Nicaragua* case: new answers to old question?', (1986) 24 Can YBIL 127–60, at 154; E. Zoller, 'The law applicable to the preemption doctrine', (2004) 98 ASIL Proc 333–7, at 335.
[58] ICJ, *Nicaragua* case (Merits), § 194; ICJ, *Case concerning armed activities on the territory of the Congo (Democratic Republic of the Congo v. Uganda)*, Judgment of 19 December 2005, (2005) ICJ Rep 116–220, § 143.
[59] See, e.g., ICJ, *Nicaragua* case (Merits), Dissenting opinion of Judge Schwebel, § 173; ICJ, *Legal consequences of the construction of a wall in the Occupied Palestinian Territory*, Advisory opinion of 9 July 2004, (2004) ICJ Rep 136–203, Separate opinion of Judge Higgins, § 33; Separate opinion of Judge Kooijmans, § 35. Also Randelzhofer, 'Article 51', p. 804. However, on the ICJ's position on *preventive* self-defence in *DRC* v. *Uganda*, See *infra*, note 438.
[60] E.g., Brownlie, 'The principle of non-use of force', p. 24; Dinstein, *War, aggression and self-defence*, 4th edn., p. 185.

overwhelming as some have suggested). At the same time, upon closer reading, the infamous doctrinal divide must be put into perspective. On the one hand, the broad majority of those adhering to the view expounded by Waldock and Schwebel have strictly limited anticipatory self-defence to a form of 'pre-emptive' action against 'imminent' threats of armed attack, governed by the *Caroline* parameters.[61] Only very rarely has a more flexible reading of anticipatory self-defence been put forward.[62]

Conversely, one should not overlook the fact that numerous 'restrictionists' have implicitly[63] or explicitly[64] accepted the admissibility of 'interceptive' self-defence, following the commencement/launch of an armed attack. Scholarly writings which consciously confine Article 51 UN Charter to *strictly reactive* forms of self-defence, excluding 'interceptive' action, are hard to find. At best, it has been objected that the concept of 'interceptive' self-defence is 'ingenious but rather casuistic'.[65] In sum, throughout most of the Charter era, the two extreme forms of the *ratione temporis* conundrum have received scarce academic approbation. Hence, the doctrinal controversy essentially boils down to a preference for either interceptive or pre-emptive self-defence.

---

[61] E.g., Higgins, *Problems and process*, p. 242; Malanczuk, 'Countermeasures and self-defence', 761, 764; Schachter, 'Unilateral use of force', 293; Waldock, 'The regulation of the use of force', 498.

[62] E.g., McDougal, 'The Soviet–Cuban quarantine', 598: 'Even the highly restrictive language of Secretary of State Webster in the *Caroline* case ... did not require "actual armed attack", and the understanding is now widespread that a test formulated in the previous century for a controversy between two friendly States is hardly relevant to contemporary controversies, involving high expectations of violence, between nuclear-armed protagonists.'

However, on support for preventive self-defence after 2001, See *infra*, Section 4.2.

[63] Apparently supporting 'interceptive' self-defence without explicitly using the label: e.g., Abi-Saab, 'Cours général', 371 ('La légitime défense est ainsi une réaction ou une riposte à une action matérialisée, en cours ou du moins à un début d'exécution; mais pas avant'); Brownlie, *The use of force by States*, pp. 276, 367–8;); Cahier, 'Changements et continuité du droit international', 73 (arguing that the US could lawfully have attacked Japanese forces on their way to the Pearl Harbour naval base); Lachs, 'General trends of international law', 164 ('"Armed attack" must be ascertained; it must be clear that it was launched'; Randelzhofer, 'Article 51', p. 803.

[64] Explicitly supporting 'interceptive' self-defence: Christakis, 'La notion de guerre préventive', p. 21; Constantinou, *The right of self-defence*, pp. 125–7; Corten, *Le droit contre la guerre*, pp. 626–7; Y. Dinstein, *War, aggression and self-defence*, 3rd edn. (Cambridge University Press, 2001), p. 172; Gazzini, *The changing rules*, pp. 151–3; Kolb, 'Self-defence and preventive war', 123–5; M.N. Shaw, *International law*, 5th edn (Cambridge University Press, 2003), p. 1030; Sicilianos, *Des contre-mesures à la légitime défense*, pp. 403–5.

[65] Brownlie, *The use of force by States*, p. 276. Also: Corten, *Le droit contre la guerre*, p. 627 ('ce cas de figure reste à ce jour purement théorique.')

Furthermore, the dividing line between 'interceptive' and 'pre-emptive' self-defence is fairly thin. Interestingly, a number of authorities tend to confuse the two concepts. Waldock, one of the leading supporters of pre-emptive action, coined the *Caroline* doctrine in the following terms:

> [It] allows and only allows a right of defence in face of imminent threat of attack – in face of an attack already impending over the defending State. Where there is convincing evidence not merely of threats and potential danger but of an attack being actually mounted, then an armed attack may be said to have begun to occur, though it has not passed the frontier.[66]

This approach does not appear to be all that different from the view adopted by Dinstein, who is frequently cited as a champion of 'interceptive' self-defence:'[T]he imminence of an armed attack (provided that it is no longer a mere threat) does indeed justify an early response by way of interceptive self-defence.'[67]

Last but not least, upon examining the 'commencement' of armed attacks, Brownlie proclaims that, in light of the existence of long-range missiles, 'the difference between attack and imminent attack may now be negligible'.[68]

Does this mean that the doctrinal divide is no more than a chimera, a merely theoretical conundrum for overzealous lawyers? It appears not. The fundamental distinction between the notions of 'interceptive' and 'pre-emptive' self-defence is that the former broadens the 'armed attack requirement' to include actions which have commenced but which have not yet crossed the border, whereas the latter abandons it altogether, instead relying on the overarching criteria of proportionality and necessity/imminence. This has implications both in terms of the categorization of concrete recourses to force and in terms of compatibility with the Charter baseline. First, although both concepts may produce similar outcomes in a number of cases, in general, interceptive self-defence imposes a narrower timeframe and a heavier burden of evidence than its 'pre-emptive' counterpart. On the ground of the information available (and reasonably interpreted) at the moment of action,[69] there must

---

[66] Waldock, 'The regulation of the use of force', 498.
[67] Dinstein, *War, aggression and self-defence*, 4th edn., p. 182. Later on, Dinstein explicitly relies on the view of Waldock (p. 191).
[68] Brownlie, *The use of force by States*, p. 368.
[69] Dinstein, *War, aggression and self-defence*, 4th edn, p. 192; Shapira, 'The Six-Day War', 76.

be compelling proof that a *concrete* attack is being launched. Military exercises, the drafting of attack schemes and other preparatory steps are insufficient by themselves. In short, 'interceptive' self-defence does not settle with the *capacity* and professed *intention* to initiate an armed attack, but presupposes that these elements are accompanied by actual measures of implementation.[70] Hence, restrictionists argue, the concept is less prone to subjectivity and abuse.

Second, as far as the Charter 'baseline' is concerned, it must be recalled that rules are subject to an interpretative continuum, whereby parties may gradually wander from the original text and intention towards adjusting or updating the content, and, ultimately, to the creation of a new rule through modification (see *supra*, Sections 2.1.3–4). But how do the four *ratione temporis* phases fit into this continuum? It does not require further explanation to attest that 'strictly reactive' self-defence is fully covered by the text of Article 51. In addition, 'interceptive' self-defence is not necessarily excluded by the phrase 'if an armed attack occurs', or the (slightly broader) French version 'dans le cas où un Membre des Nations Unies est l'objet d'une agression armée', and moreover appears to be compatible with the provision's spirit:[71] the Charter's aim is obviously not to favour the aggressor by forcing the defending State to wait until the armed attack has actually achieved its objective. Still, apart from the obvious and often-quoted example of the interception of an incoming missile, it remains to be analysed at what time an armed attack is considered to be launched in customary practice. With regard to 'pre-emptive' self-defence, the present author believes that this doctrine is not covered by the plain meaning of Article 51 and also over-steps the spirit of the Charter rules.[72] Indeed, self-defence is applicable only in relation to armed attacks; threats, even imminent ones, must in principle be submitted to the Security Council for consideration. On the other hand, it could be argued that the realities of modern warfare necessitate an evolutive interpretation of Article 51, allowing for recourse to force when the threat of attack is 'imminent'. This possibility must not be ruled out *a priori*, yet the *onus probandi* falls on those supporting pre-emptive action. Indeed, it remains to be

---

[70] E.g., Corten, *Le droit contre la guerre*, p. 627; Gazzini, *The changing rules*, p. 151; Kolb, 'Self-defence and preventive war', 123.

[71] In a similar vein: Christakis, 'La notion de guerre préventive', p. 21; Dinstein, *War, aggression and self-defence*, 4th edn, p. 191; Kolb, 'Self-defence and preventive war', 125; Sicilianos, *Des contre-mesures à la légitime défense*, p. 405.

[72] Also Kolb, 'Self-defence and preventive war', 125.

demonstrated that this evolutive reading of Article 51 has gained acceptance in customary practice *after* 1945. If the burden of proof is not discharged, only 'interceptive' action remains warranted. Finally, there can be no doubt that the concept of 'preventive' self-defence ignores the text of Article 51 and defeats the object of the UN Charter. If accepted, this notion would preclude any attempt to assess self-defence claims objectively, instead attributing to States the discretionary power to decide for themselves whether a future and potential threat to their security justifies a recourse to force. Only an actual modification of the applicable rules could effect such change. However, given the peremptory character of Articles 2(4) and 51 UN Charter, the threshold for such modification is set very high: apart from a formal amendment of the UN Charter, or the adoption by consensus of a General Assembly resolution, it is unclear how such a broadening of the right of self-defence could materialize (see *supra* Section 2.1.3).

In sum, while the doctrinal divide must not be exaggerated, there is nonetheless a significant discrepancy between the different views expounded.

4.1.2 Customary precedents: evidence in concreto

4.1.2.a The Cuban missile crisis (1962)

As far as concrete recourses to force are concerned, three incidents are consistently cited in legal literature, namely the 1962 Cuban missile crisis, the 1967 Six Day War and the 1981 Israeli strike against the Iraqi nuclear reactor at Osiraq.[73] We will commence our overview with these cases, before glossing over some less well-known instances of State practice.

Our first incident dates back to the clandestine instalment of Soviet missiles in Cuba in 1962, which triggered one of the most tense confrontations of the Cold War era. Upon discovering the disturbing developments, US President Kennedy proclaimed on 23 October that the 'establishment by the Sino-Soviet powers of an offensive military capability in Cuba, including bases for ballistic missiles with a potential range covering most of North and South America' constituted a serious threat to 'the peace of the world and the security of the United States and of all American States'.[74] For this reason, he had decided to impose

---

[73] See, e.g., Franck, *Recourse to force*, pp. 99–107.
[74] US President, Proclamation 3504, Interdiction of the delivery of offensive weapons to Cuba, 23 October 1962, reprinted in (1963) 57 AJIL 512–13.

a naval quarantine on Cuba, aimed at the impeding of the delivery of offensive weapons and associated material. US forces were authorized to intercept, visit and search any vessel or craft proceeding towards Cuba, if necessary by the use of force. Although the Presidential Proclamation did not explicitly couch the operation in legal terms, it did refer to two legal instruments, one domestic and one regional. The former was a Joint Resolution of the US Congress of 3 October 1962, which stressed the US determination 'to prevent by whatever means may be necessary, including the use of arms, ... the creation or use [in Cuba] of an externally supported military capability endangering the security of the United States'.[75] The latter document was a decision of the OAS Council of 23 October 1962, which:

> recommended that the Member States, in accordance with Articles 6 and 8 of the Inter-American Treaty of Reciprocal Assistance, take all measures, individual and collectively, including the use of armed force, which they may deem necessary to ensure that the Government of Cuba cannot continue to receive from the Sino-Soviet powers military materiel ... which may threaten the peace and security of the Continent and to prevent the missiles in Cuba with an offensive capability from ever becoming an active threat to the peace and security of the Continent.[76]

Upon the simultaneous request of the United States, Cuba and the Soviet Union,[77] the matter was brought before the Security Council.[78] Predictably, States' reactions were split along Cold War lines. The UK, France, the Republic of China, Venezuela and Chile all pronounced in favour of the US actions and supported a US-sponsored draft resolution which called for a UN-supervised withdrawal of the missiles.[79] Romania wholeheartedly agreed with Cuba and the Soviet Union that the quarantine breached Article 2(4) UN Charter.[80] Slightly more cautiously, Ghana and the United Arab Republic found the operation contrary to

---

[75] *Ibid.*, § 2.
[76] *Ibid.*,§ 3; OAS Council, Resolution on the adoption of necessary measures to prevent Cuba from threatening the peace and security of the Continent, 23 October 1962, Annex A, Doc. OEA/Ser.G/V/C-d-1024 Rev.2.
[77] UN Doc. S/5181, 22 October 1962 (US); UN Doc. S/5183, 22 October 1962 (Cuba); UN Doc. S/5186, 23 October 1962 (USSR).
[78] See UN Docs. S/PV.1022–5, 23–25 October 1962.
[79] UN Doc. S/PV.1023, §§ 4–5 (Venezuela), §§ 16, 38, 41 (UK); UN Doc. S/PV.1024, at §§ 3–5, 11 (France), §§ 23–4 (Republic of China), §§ 47–8, 52 (Chile).
[80] UN Doc. S/PV.1022, §§ 110, 123–4 (Cuba); §§ 156–8 (USSR); UN Doc. S/PV.1023, §§ 42, 58 (Romania).

international law.[81] It must be admitted, however, that the debate was by and large framed in terms of political and strategic interests, with little attention to the legal implications. Those in favour of the quarantine agreed with the US's and OAS's contention that the missiles were 'offensive' in nature and constituted a serious threat to the Western hemisphere.[82] The opponents, on the other hand, objected that the missiles were defensive in nature and were aimed at the protection of Cuban integrity and independence (especially when considering the 1961 US-sponsored invasion by Cuban exiles at the Bay of Pigs).[83] According to this view, 'the measures which any State takes to preserve its own security are entirely a matter for its judgement'.[84] Ireland, one of the more 'detached' Council members, expressed understanding for Cuba's security concerns, but nonetheless argued that the instalment of long-range ballistic missiles went much further than a mere strengthening of Cuba's defences against invasion, instead upsetting 'the existing delicate balance of world security'.[85] Apart from a few references to the OAS Resolution and its invocation of Articles 6 and 8 of the Inter-American Treaty, the US also provided little by way of legal justification. Instead, the American UN ambassador stated that, although he would 'gladly expand on our position on [the legal basis], ... this is a matter for discussion which, in view of its complexity and length, could be more fruitfully delayed to a later time'.[86] In the end, none of the various draft resolutions being proposed[87] was put to the vote. Rather, the crisis was defused through secret negotiations between the United States and the Soviet Union (involving the removal of Soviet missiles from Cuba in

---

[81] UN Doc. S/PV.1024, § 74 (UAR); §§ 92, 102–10 (Ghana).
[82] E.g., UN Doc. S/PV.1022, §§ 12–13, 59–62 (US, *inter alia* trying to clarify the difference between the 'defensive' missile sites in NATO member countries and the 'offensive' missiles in Cuba); UN Doc. S/PV.1023, § 4 (Venezuela), § 16 (UK); UN Doc. S/PV.1024, § 3 (France), § 23 (Republic of China).
[83] E.g., UN Doc. S/PV.1022, §§ 90, 100–3, 123–4 (Cuba); §§ 146, 155–8, 178 (USSR); UN Doc. S/PV.1023, §§ 43 *et seq.* (Romania). Also: UN Doc. S/PV.1023, § 85 (Ireland). See also Franck, *Recourse to force*, p. 100.
[84] UN Doc. S/PV.1024, § 102 (Ghana).
[85] UN Doc. S/PV.1023, §§ 85–9. See also: UN Doc. S/PV.1023, § 5 (Venezuela: 'Up to now, the more or less precarious balance between the two great blocs has been maintained; but the Soviet action in Cuba has modified it').
[86] UN Doc. S/PV.1024, § 20.
[87] See UN Doc. S/5182, 22 October 1962 (US draft); UN Doc. S/5187, 23 October 1962 (compromise draft from Ghana and the UAR); UN Doc. S/5190, 24 October 1962 (USSR draft).

return for the removal of US missiles from Turkey), without a single shot being fired.[88]

Can it be maintained, as some authors have argued,[89] that the Cuban quarantine, which – despite the deliberate use of the word 'quarantine', instead of the more 'belligerent' 'blockade'[90] – undoubtedly constituted a recourse to force, provides a precedent in favour of anticipatory self-defence? On the one hand, it must be conceded that the political motivation behind the operation consisted in the perception that the instalment of the missiles posed a serious threat to American security, and that many Western and Latin-American States supported the US response. On the other hand, no attempt was made to justify the operation as an exercise of self-defence.[91] The OAS resolution relied on Article 6 of the Inter-American Treaty, which deals with 'aggression which is not an armed attack', rather than on Article 3, which deals with collective and individual self-defence. The same Article 6 was referred to both in the Presidential Proclamation and in the US communication to the Security Council.[92] 'Self-defence' and/or 'Article 51 UN Charter' were never mentioned. This was no coincidence. Indeed, according to US Legal Adviser Chayes, the operation did not fall

---

[88] E.g., Franck, *Recourse to force*, p. 99 ('Since no ship had actually tried to run its blockade, none had been seized'). See also the letter from the Permanent Representatives of the United States and the Soviet Union to the UN Secretary-General of 7 January 1963, thanking him for his mediation efforts (UN Doc. S/5227).

[89] Authors regarding the Cuban quarantine as lawful self-defence: e.g., C.Q. Christol and C.R. Davis, 'Maritime quarantine: the naval interdiction of offensive weapons and associated materiel to Cuba, 1962', (1963) 57 AJIL 525–43, at 543; G.G. Fenwick, 'The quarantine against Cuba: legal or illegal?', (1963) 57 AJIL 588–92, at 592; B. McChesney, 'Some comments on the "Quarantine of Cuba"', (1963) 57 AJIL 592–7; McDougal, 'The Soviet–Cuban quarantine', 601–3. See also the authors cited in *ibid.* -, 603, footnote 14. Contra: e.g., Dinstein, *War, aggression and self-defence*, 4th edn., p. 186; Wright, 'The Cuban quarantine', 559–62.

[90] See, e.g., Franck, *Recourse to force*, p. 99; Wright, 'The Cuban quarantine', 553 (footnote 32), 554–6.

[91] See e.g., Henkin, *How nations behave*, p. 294: 'Although the President and others invoked the needs of American defense and security in political justifications, no responsible spokesman mentioned Article 51, even as possible alternative legal support for the quarantine. Repeatedly, the Legal Adviser and the Deputy Legal Adviser stressed that the United States "did not rest its case" on that ground. Report has it that reference to Article 51 was several times proposed for insertion in statements by the President and others, and every time alert and insistent lawyers succeeded in eliminating it. . . . [S]pokesmen for the United States apparently recognized the dangers which the argument entailed.'

[92] US Proclamation 3504, 'Interdiction of the delivery of offensive weapons to Cuba'; UN Doc. S/5181; UN Doc. S/PV.1022, § 79.

within the purview of Article 51, but 'within a third category: action by regional organizations to preserve the peace', pursuant to Article 52 of the Charter.[93]

It should also be observed that *in casu* it was never suggested that the Soviet Union (and Cuba) were planning to launch an actual attack against the US or any other American State. The OAS resolution, for example, stressed the need to '*prevent the missiles ... from becoming an active threat* to the peace and security of the Continent'.[94] In other words, there was no indication that the US was confronted by an 'imminent threat of armed attack', implying that the action undertaken, if regarded as a case of self-defence, would fall within the category of 'preventive', rather than 'pre-emptive' self-defence. This appears to have had a decisive impact on the US's justificatory discourse. Indeed, as Chayes wrote several years later:

> No doubt the phrase 'armed attack' must be construed broadly enough to permit some anticipatory response. But it is a very different matter to expand it to include threatening deployments or demonstrations that do not have imminent attack as their purpose or probable outcome. To accept that reading is to make the occasion for forceful response essentially a question for unilateral national decision that would not only be formally unreviewable, but not subject to intelligent criticism either ... In this sense, I believe an Article 51 defence would have signalled that the United States did not take the legal issues very seriously, that in its view the situation was to be governed by national discretion, not international law.[95]

In the end, most scholars agree that the quarantine does not offer a valid precedent in support of anticipatory self-defence.[96] The US's reluctance

---

[93] See A. Chayes, 'Law and the quarantine of Cuba', (1962-3) 41 *Foreign Affairs* 550-7, at 554-8. After recalling that 'neither the President in his speech nor the OAS in its resolution invoked Article 51', Chayes attempts to explain why the regional action under the auspices of the OAS would not have violated the requirement of Article 53 UN Charter (which requires that all regional enforcement action be authorized by the Security Council).

[94] UN Doc. S/5193, § 2 (emphasis added).

[95] A. Chayes, *The Cuban missile crisis* (Oxford University Press, 1974), 65-6. Elsewhere, Chayes has written that: 'The commonly held view was that such a claim would set a dangerous precedent.' Cited in Christakis, 'La notion de guerre préventive', p. 27, footnote 52.

[96] E.g., *ibid.* 27; Corten, *Le droit contre la guerre*, pp. 659-60; Gazzini, *The changing rules*, pp. 149-50 ; C. Gray, *International law and the use of force*, 2nd edn (Oxford University Press, 2004), p. 161; Henkin, *How nations behave*, pp. 290-6; Sicilianos, *Des contre-mesures à la légitime défense*, pp. 398-9.

to rely on self-defence may even be seen as an implicit confirmation that States regard *preventive* self-defence (against non-imminent threats) as unlawful. On the other hand, it must be conceded that, apart from a Ghanaian statement that the action could not be reconciled with the Webster formula,[97] the Cuban missile crisis offers virtually no evidence of States' *opinio iuris* – positive or negative – vis-à-vis the legality of *'pre-emptive'* action.

4.1.2.b The Six Day War (1967)

If the Israeli commando raid at Entebbe airport is often cited as the 'textbook example' for the 'protection of nationals' doctrine, the favourite precedent of those supporting anticipatory self-defence is undeniably the 1967 Six Day War.[98] However, even if the degree of 'imminence' was arguably greater than in the Cuban missile crisis, the alleged precedential value is confused by two factors, namely the divergent appraisal of the factual context and the justificatory discourse of States in UN fora.

In the course of 1967, tension between Israel and its Arab neighbours mounted rapidly.[99] In the first few months, Israel was confronted by an upsurge of incidents and *fedayeen* infiltrations along the Syrian border. In addition, Egyptian President Nasser adopted an increasingly hostile posture vis-à-vis Israel. On 14 May, Egyptian troops were sent to the Sinaï border with Israel; Israel responded by ordering a partial mobilization of its reserves.[100] On 16 May, Nasser requested the immediate withdrawal of the UNEF Peace-keeping Force from its base at

---

[97] UN Doc. S/PV.1024, § 110: '[A]re there grounds for the argument that such action is justified in exercise of the inherent right of self-defence? Can it be contended that there was, in the words of a former American Secretary of State … "a necessity of self-defence, instant, overwhelming, leaving no choice of means, and no moment for deliberation"? My delegation does not think so, for … incontrovertible proof is not yet available as to the offensive character of military developments in Cuba.' This statement can be read as an implicit endorsement of the legality of pre-emptive self-defence, within the confines of the Webster formula.

[98] E.g., W.V. O'Brien, *The conduct of just and limited war* (New York: Praeger, 1981), p. 133.

[99] On the run-up to the Six Day War, see, e.g., R. Lapidoth, 'The Security Council in the May 1967 crisis: a study in frustration', (1969) 4 Israeli LRev 534–50; J. Quigley, 'The United Nations action against Iraq: a precedent for Israel's Arab territories?', (1992) 2 Duke JCIL 195–228, at 203–13; Shapira, 'The Six-Day War', 65–8; C. W. Yost, 'How it began', (1967–8) 46 *Foreign Affairs* 304–20.

[100] Shapira, 'The Six-Day War', 66–7.

Sharm El Sheikh. Six days later, he officially announced the closure of the Straits of Tiran for Israeli shipping, thus in fact blocking the port of Eilat. The Egyptian military presence in the Sinaï was further augmented to almost four divisions.[101] Egypt's military build-up was accompanied by two other disturbing elements. First, the signing of a mutual defence pact between Egypt and Jordan and the formation of a joint military command by Egypt and Syria led to a complete encirclement of Israel. In addition, there was an intensifying flood of (semi-)official declarations of belligerency and open threats of war. On 26 May, for example, Nasser declared that: 'We intend to open a general assault against Israel. This will be total war. Our basic aim will be to destroy Israel.'[102]

Against this background, on the morning of 5 June 1967, Israel launched a surprise offensive against Egypt, shelling military targets from the Gaza Strip as well as moving land forces and aircraft into the Sinaï. Israel swiftly succeeded in annihilating the main military threat, namely the large-scale Egyptian Air Force.[103] Despite Israeli warnings, Jordan and Syria quickly joined sides with Egypt, resulting in an open war between the various protagonists. However, with the Egyptian Air Force destroyed, it soon became clear that the Arab countries were no match for Israel's military superiority. By 11 June, Israel had obtained a sweeping victory over its opponents, and its forces occupied Gaza, the West Bank, the Sinaï and the Golan Heights.

The Six Day War was extensively discussed within the UN Security Council[104] and, subsequently, within the Fifth Special Emergency Session of the UN General Assembly.[105] While the Security Council repeatedly called for a cessation of hostilities,[106] draft resolutions branding Israel as

---

[101] *Ibid.*, 67.
[102] Cited in UN Doc. S/PV.1348, 6 June 1967, § 150 (statement of the Israeli ambassador, also referring to an order of 2 June by the Egyptian Commander in the Sinaï, calling on his troops to wage a war of destruction against Israel (§ 151)).
[103] Quigley, 'The United Nations action against Iraq', 203. See also on the importance of Israel's air superiority: Gill, 'The temporal dimension of self-defense', pp. 135–6.
[104] See especially: UN Security Council, 22nd session, 1347th–1348th meetings, 5–6 June 1967, UN Doc. S/PV.1347–8.
[105] See UN General Assembly, 5th Special Emergency Session, 1525th–1548th meetings, 17 June–4 July 1967.
[106] E.g., SC Res. 233 (1967) of 6 June 1967; SC Res. 234 (1967) of 7 June 1967; SC Res. 235 (1967) of 9 June 1967; SC Res. 236 (1967) of 11 June 1967.

the aggressor failed to obtain sufficient votes, both in the Council[107] and in the General Assembly.[108]

As suggested earlier, several international lawyers have claimed that the Six Day War provides an important precedent in support of anticipatory self-defence.[109] This interpretation is grounded in the first place on the conviction that Israel's actions constituted a pre-emptive action in response to an imminent attack, i.e., an expected invasion by its Arab neighbours which threatened the very survival of the isolated and numerically weaker Israeli State and which left it with no other alternative but to take the military initiative. The fact that efforts to apportion the blame to Israel were voted down, despite the widespread perception that it had acted pre-emptively, is said to offer convincing evidence that the actions were considered lawful.

However, other authors have – convincingly – questioned the alleged precedential impact of the Six Day War.[110] Indeed, after a closer look, a

---

[107] A Soviet draft resolution (UN Doc. S/7951/Rev.2) was rejected by the Security Council on 14 June 1967. Operative paragraph 1 'vigourously [condemned] Israel's aggressive activities and continued occupation of part of the territory of the United Arab Republic, Syria and Jordan, regarding this as an act of aggression and the grossest violation of the United Nations Charter ...'. Paragraph 2 '[demanded] that Israel should immediately and unconditionally remove all its troops from the territory of those States ...'. The former paragraph only obtained four votes in favour (Bulgaria, India, Mali, USSR). All other States abstained. The latter paragraph obtained six votes in favour (Bulgaria, Ethiopia, India, Mali, Nigeria, USSR), with nine States abstaining. See (1967) UNYB 190.

[108] (1) A Soviet draft resolution (UN Doc. A/L.519), modelled after the draft Council resolution was rejected by separate votes on individual paragraphs. See (1967) UNYB 193, 209. (2) An Albanian draft resolution (UN Doc. A/L.521) was rejected by seventy-one votes to twenty-two, with twenty-seven abstentions. See (1967) UNYB 202, 220. (3) A third draft resolution from the non-aligned bloc (UN Doc. A/L.523/Rev.1) was rejected by fifty-seven votes to forty-three, with twenty abstentions. See (1967) UNYB 208–9, 220.

[109] E.g., AIV, 'Pre-emptive Action', 17; Dugard, *A South African perspective*, p. 508; Franck, *Recourse to force*, pp. 101–5; Gill, 'The temporal dimension of self-defense', p. 138; Greenwood, 'The pre-emptive use of force', 13–14; Malanczuk, 'Countermeasures and self-defence', 762; J. N. Maogoto, 'New frontiers, old problems: the war on terror and the notion of anticipating the enemy', (2004) 51 NILR 1–39, at 31; O'Brien, *Just and limited war*, p. 133; Schwebel, 'Aggression, intervention and self-defence', 481.

[110] E.g., Brownlie, 'The principle of non-use of force', p. 24; Christakis, 'La notion de guerre préventive', pp. 24–5; J. Combacau, 'The exception of self-defence in U.N. practice', in Cassese (ed.), *The use of force* pp. 9–38, at 24; Constantinou, *The right of self-defence*, p. 117; Corten, *Le droit contre la guerre*, pp. 660–2; Gazzini, *The changing rules*, p. 150; Gray, *The use of force*, p. 161; Kolb, 'Self-defence and preventive war', 124; M.E. O'Connell, 'The myth of preemptive self-defense', 9; Quigley, 'The United Nations action against Iraq', 203–13.

number of elements shed new light on our brief account of the prelude to the war. First, the justification used by Israel made no reference whatsoever to anticipatory self-defence. Quite the contrary, Israel expressly argued that it had responded in self-defence to a *prior armed attack*:

> [This] morning Egyptian armoured columns moved in an offensive thrust against Israel's borders. At the same time Egyptian planes took off from airfields in Sinai and struck out towards Israel. Egyptian artillery in the Gaza Strip shelled the Israel villages of Kissufim, Nahal-Oz and Ein Hashelosha. Netania and Kefar Yavetz have also been bombed. ... The Egyptian forces met with the immediate response of the Israeli Defence Forces, acting in self-defence [in] accordance with Article 51 of the Charter ...[111]

Subsequently, in the UN General Assembly, Israel shifted to a somewhat different line of argument. It was argued that the blockade of the Straits of Tiran to Israeli ships constituted an 'act of war', justifying action in self-defence under Article 51.[112] Thus, after elaborating at length on the imminent peril to Israel's existence, Foreign Minister Eban concluded that:

> The blockade is by definition an act of war, imposed and enforced through armed violence. ... From 24 May onward, the question who started the war or who fired the first shot became momentously irrelevant. ... From the moment the blockade was imposed, active hostilities had commenced and Israel owed Egypt nothing of her Charter rights.[113]

Both justifications are controversial. Even if the UN Secretary-General admitted that the United Nations had no means of ascertaining how the hostilities were initiated,[114] it is widely believed that Israel was the first to (literally) open fire.[115] The fact that Israel abandoned this argument before the General Assembly implicitly affirms this view. Furthermore, in a number of official statements Israel apparently admitted having

---

[111] UN Doc. S/PV.1347, §§ 30–2. Also UN Doc. S/PV.1348, § 155: 'Thus, on the morning of 5 June, when Egyptian forces engaged us by air and land, bombarding the villages of Kissufim, Nahal-Oz and Ein Hashelosha, we knew that our limit of safety had been reached, and perhaps passed. In accordance with its inherent right of self-defence as formulated in Article 51 of the United Nations Chater, Israel responded defensively in full strength.'
[112] (1967) UNYB 195–6.   [113] UN Doc. A/PV.1526, §§ 132–3.
[114] UN Doc. S/PV.1347, § 10.
[115] E.g., Quigley, 'The United Nations action against Iraq', 204–5; Shapira, 'The Six-Day War', 68, footnote 11.

initiated military action.[116] Did the closure of the Straits of Tiran to Israeli shipping in itself amount to an 'armed attack'? While legal opinion is divided,[117] the Definition of Aggression[118] is seen as an indication that proportionate measures of self-defence may be justified if there is an *unlawful* blockade, which is actually being *enforced*, and which has a *strong negative impact on the economy* of the victim State (i.e., if the ports or coasts blocked are the basis of the defending State's economy and thus its main source of income).[119] *In casu*, however, it was disputed whether the closure of the Straits of Tiran constituted an unlawful

---

[116] See Quigley, 'The United Nations action against Iraq', 204–5.

[117] Answering in the affirmative: E. Miller, 'Self-defence, international law, and the Six Day War', (1985) 20 Israeli L Rev 49–73, at 61–5; Shaw, *International law*, p. 1029. Contra: Dinstein, *War, aggression and self-defence*, 4th edn, p. 192; Quigley, 'The United Nations action against Iraq', 210–13.

[118] Article 3(c) of the Definition of Aggression refers to 'the blockade of the ports or coasts of a State by the armed forces of another State.' A note was added in the Report of the Sixth Committee in order to emphasize that 'nothing in the Definition, and in particular 3(c), shall be construed as a justification for a State to block, *contrary to international law*, the routes of free access of a landlocked country to and from the sea' (cited in B. B. Ferencz, *Defining international aggression. The search for world peace: a documentary history and analysis*. Vol. II (Dobbs Ferry, NY: Oceana, 1975), p. 35. See also: B. Broms, 'The definition of aggression', (1977-I) 154 RdC 299–400, at 349–50; J. Zourek, 'La définition de l'agression et le droit international: développements récents de la question', (1958) 92 RdC 755–855, at 826–7). While the Definition itself was only adopted several years after the Six Day War, it is worth noting that Israel referred to a similar provision in the Soviet Draft Definition (UN Doc. A/PV.1526, § 133).

[119] See Constantinou, *The right of self-defence*, pp. 77–81. Constantinou *inter alia* notes that: (1) while Israel regarded the restriction of passage to Israeli shipping through the Suez Canal in 1956 as a 'blockade', it justified its military intervention as an exercise of self-defence against cross-border attacks by *fedayeen* operating from the Sinaï (and not against the alleged blockade); and that (2) in the debates regarding the Six Day War, Israel stressed the importance of the Gulf of Aqaba as a trade route from and to the outside world and the effects it had on the Israeli economy as a whole (at 80). She concludes that 'any interference with the rights of States to free passage through Canals will give rise to a dispute concerning the legal rights and duties of the disputants under the relevant Convention and will constitute a violation of the Convention itself rather than a case of a use of force or an armed attack'. See also Gill, 'The temporal dimension of self-defense', p. 138.

In principle, so-called 'pacific blockades', whereby ships are unlawfully prohibited from entering ports and harbours of third States, are inconsistent with the obligations of Articles 2(3) and 2(4) of the UN Charter and with the Convention on the Law of the Sea. In the course of an actual armed conflict, the parties to the conflict can nonetheless impose a blockade against their opponent, provided that a series of preconditions are met. See, e.g., San Remo Manual on International Law Applicable to Armed Conflicts at Sea, 12 June 1994, reproduced in A. Roberts and R. Guelff (eds.), *Documents on the laws of war*, 3rd edn (Oxford University Press, 2000), pp. 573–606, articles 93–104.

blockade, *inter alia* because some Arab States did not regard it as an international strait through which Israel had a right of innocent passage and because the alleged blockade was confined to Egypt's territorial waters.[120] Moreover, whereas some have pointed to the strategic importance of the port of Eilat for the Israeli economy,[121] others have questioned the alleged 'economic strangulation', on the grounds that Israel had barely used the Gulf of Aqaba – at the end of which sit the Straits of Tiran – for commercial transportation in preceding years.[122] Pakistan, for instance, objected that '[t]he denial of a right of passage through the Strait of Tiran was not tantamount to a blockade of Israel whose trade with the world still remained unhampered along the Mediterranean Coast'.[123] In any event, regardless of the merit of the two arguments, what is crucial for present purposes is that while Israel elaborated at

> Remark: as several UN Members affirmed throughout the debates within the Fifth Special Emergency Session of the UNGA, the mere declaration of a blockade in itself is insufficient to amount to a *casus belli*. E.g., UN Doc. A/PV.1530, §§ 53–7 (Sudan: 'within the meaning of the [UN] Charter a blockade ... is not *ipso facto* an act of war'); UN Doc. A/PV.1531, §§ 122–4 (Pakistan); UN Doc. A/PV.1538, § 5 (Somalia).

[120] See Quigley, 'The United Nations action against Iraq', 210–13; Miller, 'The Six Day War', 61–5.

> See, for instance: UN Doc. A/PV.1530, 43–58 (Sudan), 161–8 (India: 'The [UAR] has always maintained that the Strait of Tiran is part of its territorial waters. India, along with a number of other countries, has supported this position for a decade and more.... [It] is not established that under international law there is a right of free passage through the Strait of Tiran'); UN Doc. A/PV.1531, §§ 117–24 (Pakistan); UN Doc. A/PV.1536, § 11 (Jordan); UN Doc. A/PV.1537, §§ 13–16 (Morocco: '[The] action taken by the [UAR] with regard to the Strait of Tiran and the Gulf of Aqaba was fully within its sovereign rights. ... Moreover, the port of Elath ... was occupied ... in violation of the Armistice Agreements'); UN Doc. A/PV.1538, § 5 (Somalia); UN Doc. A/PV.1543, § 12 (Libya).
>
> More neutral: UN Doc. A/PV.1531, § 96 (France: 'the passage through the Strait of Tiran ... has never been the subject of anything more than a de facto settlement imposed by one of the adversaries on the other'); UN Doc. A/PV.1541, § 73 (Cyprus).
>
> Defending Israel's right of passage: UN Doc. A/PV.1527, § 23 (US); UN Doc. S/PV.1526, § 129 (Israel itself).

[121] E.g., Miller, 'The Six Day War', 64. See the Israeli statements at: UN Doc. S/PV.1526, §§ 129–32; UN Doc. S/PV.1348, §§ 171–5.

[122] E.g., Quigley, 'The United Nations action against Iraq', 211. See also Gill, 'The temporal dimension of self-defense', p. 138. (Gill argues that if Egypt had attempted to cut Israel's sea and air communications completely, the situation would have been different).

[123] UN Doc. S/PV.1360, 14 June 1967, § 52. Also: UN Doc. A/PV.1531, § 119 (Pakistan); UN Doc. A/PV.1536, § 11 (Jordan: 'The Strait of Tiran was never opened to Israel until the aggression of 1956. No vital interests suffered. There has not been an Israeli ship through this strait for the last two and a half years. This is clearly not a question of vital interest. It provides no justification for armed aggression ...'); UN Doc. A/PV.1538, § 5 (Somalia).

length on the security threat emanating from its Arab neighbours, it did not use this as a *legal* justification for its actions.

A second factor that undermines the alleged precedential value of the Six Day War concerns the reactions of third States in the UN fora. Indeed, an analysis of the debates reveals that not a single UN Member explicity subscribed to the lawfulness of Israel's actions.[124] A considerable number of States, including Canada, Denmark, Belgium, Norway, New Zealand, the Ivory Coast and Uruguay, argued that it would be useless to try to apportion blame to one party or the other, and instead preferred to focus on finding a peaceful solution for the conflict.[125] The US and the UK followed a similar point of view, and were particularly keen on denying involvement in the Israeli operations.[126] It may also be recalled that when the Soviet draft resolution was voted down in the Security Council, no-one voted against the operative paragraph which 'condemned Israel's aggressive activities': eleven States abstained; four States supported the provision.[127] This muted stance may indicate a degree of sympathy with the Israeli position, yet it seems difficult to deduce a willingness to establish a precedent in support of pre-emptive self-defence, certainly if one takes into account that a second group of States did condemn outright Israel's actions as a violation of the UN Charter. Apart from the Arab States, the latter group included the Soviet Union, India, Spain, Pakistan, Indonesia, Albania, Bulgaria, Burundi, Belorussia, Czechoslovakia, Guinea, Hungary, Mali, Mongolia, Somalia, Sudan, Ukraine, Tanzania and Zambia.[128] Several of these UN Members publicly fulminated against the possibility of anticipatory self-defence.[129] India, for example, added that the concept of a pre-emptive strike or a

---

[124] Contra: Gill argues that 'the overwhelming majority' supported the Israeli action 'as a reasonable and lawful exercise of anticipatory self-defence'. No evidence is provided, apart from a general reference to the failed attempts formally to condemn Israel. See Gill, 'The temporal dimension of self-defense', p. 136.
[125] (1967) UNYB 199.
[126] E.g., UN Doc. S/PV.1348, §§ 14 *et seq.* (US), 34 (UK); (1967) UNYB 194 (UK).
[127] See (1967) UNYB 190.
[128] See (1967) UNYB 192–3, 197, 199 *et seq.* As the UAR keenly observed (UN Doc. S/PV.1529, § 62), French President de Gaulle initially 'condemned the opening of hostilities by Israel' ((1967) AFDI 895-6). In the course of the UN debates, however, France reverted to a more muted stance.
[129] E.g., UN Doc. A/PV.1527, §§ 94–5 (Czechoslovakia); UN Doc. A/PV.1546, § 59 (USSR: 'Elementary logic suggests that, if the first shot is justified and if we are guided by such a theory, it will be easy enough to drop the first nuclear bomb, to launch the first rocket. And then, for a certainty, nothing will save mankind from catastrophe').

preventive war was contrary to the letter and spirit of the UN Charter.[130] According to the Yugoslav delegate:

> Attempts are being made here to show that the question as to who started the war – that is, who fired the first shot – is irrelevant. My delegation considers, however, that the very act of armed attack is precisely the unassailable criterion for ascertaining aggression and determining the responsibilities of those involved.[131]

Sudan argued that:

> The massing of troops and the supposedly menacing declarations on the part of the Arab leaders could not be regarded as equivalent to an armed attack justifying armed retaliation in self-defence in accordance with Article 51. ... The action taken by Israel was not legitimate self-defence... because no armed attack on her territory had occurred.[132]

Zambia also discarded the view that a threat constitutes an armed attack:

> Even if we accept, for the sake of argument, that there was a threat to the State of Israel, the right course would have been for Israel to bring its complaint to the United Nations ... The mere existence of a threat does not constitute 'an armed attack' requiring 'self-defence' within the terms of Article 51 of the Charter.[133]

Cyprus admitted that '[in] a heavily laden atmosphere, bellicose statements were indeed made and military preparations were mounting,' yet, it insisted that:

> Threats and provocations would give a right of recourse to the United Nations but not a right to self-defence by the use of force. For whatever the provocation, without the actual occurrence of an 'armed attack', as provided in Article 51, the right of the use of force in self-defence does not arise. All legal authorities on the Charter make it abundantly clear that 'no degree of military preparation by a neighbouring State, however alarming, can afford justification for the use of "anticipatory force".' Pre-emptive strike is not recognized by the Charter; for otherwise, the excuses for resorting to war would soon multiply and the very purpose of the Charter would be nullified.[134]

Last but not least, the Six Day War not only fails to provide a valid precedent in support of anticipatory self-defence, it also signals the difficulty of assessing the necessity and proportionality of potential anticipatory action, and, consequently, the susceptibility to abuse. Indeed, while the combination

---

[130] UN Doc. A/PV.1530, § 153.   [131] UN Doc. A/PV.1529, § 93.
[132] UN Doc. A/PV.1530, §§ 57–8.   [133] UN Doc. A/PV.1538, § 84.
[134] UN Doc. A/PV.1541, § 72.

of bellicose statements and military preparations on the part of Egypt and other Arab countries could be regarded as an 'imminent threat', the credibility of this threat was and remains the subject of debate.[135] It has been observed that several official Israeli sources admitted after the war that Egypt did not have the intention of attacking Israel.[136] General Rabin, for example, stated: 'I do not believe that Nasser wanted war. The two divisions he sent into Sinai on May 14 would not have been enough to unleash an offensive against Israel. He knew it and we knew it'.[137] Quigley moreover makes the case that the various steps undertaken by the Arab States were inspired by the concern for an Israeli attack on Syria,[138] thus suggesting that Egypt's actions were not offensive in nature, but defensive. In this context, it is worth noting that during the debates on the Six Day War several UN Members mentioned Israeli threats to 'invade' Syria.[139]

4.1.2.c The Osiraq strike (1981)

The reluctance of Israel to rely on anticipatory defence in 1967 stands in stark contrast to the invocation of this doctrine, in a very broad sense, in relation to the Israeli strike against Iraq in 1981.[140] *In casu*, nine aircraft destroyed the 'Osiraq' nuclear reactor at the Tuwaitha research center

---

[135] See, e.g., Christakis, 'La notion de guerre préventive', p. 25; M E. O'Connell, 'The myth of preemptive self-defense', 9; Quigley, 'The United Nations action against Iraq', 203-13; C. W. Yost, 'How it began', 319-20 ('no government plotted or intended to start a war in the Middle East in the spring of 1967'). See also: Brownlie, 'The principle of non-use of force', 24 (Brownlie suggests that 'if, as may have been the case, Egypt was warned that any attack on Israel would lead to immediate [US] intervention, the need for Israeli action would be difficult to justify'). Contra: Dinstein, *War, aggression and self-defence*, 4th edn, p. 192 ('It seemed to be crystal-clear that Egypt was bent on an armed attack, and the sole question was not whether war would materialize but when'); Gill, 'The temporal dimension of self-defense', pp. 138-9.

[136] See the statements cited in Quigley, 'The United Nations action against Iraq', 206-7: 'General Matitiahu Peled, a member of Israel's general staff in 1967, declared that the thesis according to which Israel struggled for its physical existence was only a bluff born and developed after the war. According to Peled, the General Staff never told the government that the Egyptian military threat represented any danger to Israel or that Israel was unable to crush Nasser's army ...'. In a similar vein former PM Menachem Begin stated that: 'The Egyptian Army concentrations in the Sinai approaches do not prove that Nasser was really about to attack us. We must be honest with ourselves. We decided to attack him'. Also J. J. Mearsheimer and S. M. Walt, *The Israel lobby and US foreign policy* (London: Penguin Books, 2007), p. 85.

[137] 'Le général Rabin ne pense pas que Nasser voulait la guerre', *Le Monde* 19 February 1968.

[138] See Quigley, 'The United Nations action against Iraq', 208-11.

[139] E.g., UN Doc. A/PV.1530, § 49 (Sudan); UN Doc. A/PV.1536, § 56 (Yemen).

[140] See, e.g., G. Fischer, 'Le bombardement par Israël d'un réacteur nucléaire irakien', (1981) 27 AFDI 147-67; W. T. Mallison and S. V. Mallison, 'The Israeli attack on

near Baghdad.[141] The following day, Israel reported to the Security Council that the reactor was designed to produce atomic bombs, the target for which would have been Israel.[142] In a short time, it was argued, the reactor would have been operational and 'hot'. Due to the risk of radioactive fall-out over the city of Baghdad, an attack would have become impossible upon completion of the reactor. For this reason, Israel had decided to forestall this event while minimizing the risk of casualties.[143] Israel explained that it had exercised 'its inherent right of self-defence *as understood in general international law and as preserved in Article 51 [UN Charter]*'.[144] Faced with the threat of nuclear obliteration, demonstrated by Baghdad's emerging nuclear capability combined with the bellicose statements of several Iraqi officials, it had vainly exhausted diplomatic means and was left with no choice but to remove the 'mortal danger'.[145]

Throughout a series of debates within the Security Council[146] and the General Assembly,[147] however, third States levelled the Israeli arguments to the ground. One after the other, Member States pointed out that the target being attacked was a peaceful research facility; that, contrary to Israel itself – which was widely believed to have clandestinely acquired nuclear weapons – Iraq was a party to the Non-Proliferation Treaty; and that Iraq had always complied with the IAEA inspection regime.[148] Many developing countries stressed that all States had the right to develop nuclear technology for peaceful

June 7, 1981, upon the Iraqi nuclear reactor: aggression or self-defense?', (1982) 15 Vanderbilt JTL 417–46; M. S. Nydell, 'Tensions between international law and strategic security: implications of Israel's preemptive raid on Iraq's nuclear reactor', (1983-4) 24 Virginia JIL 459–92.

[141] Franck, *Recourse to force*, p. 105.   [142] UN Doc. S/14510, 8 June 1981 (Israel).
[143] *Ibid*. Israel stated that the operation was carried out on a Sunday so as to minimize the loss of life.
[144] UN Doc. S/PV.2280, 12 June 1981, §§ 58–9 (emphasis added).
[145] *Ibid.*, §§ 58–102. See also: UN Doc. S/PV.2288, §§ 42–74; UN Doc. A/36/PV.52, §§ 30–2.
[146] UN Docs. S/PV.2280-8, 12–19 June 1981.
[147] UN Docs. A/36/PV.52-5, 11–13 November 1981.
[148] E.g., UN Doc. S/PV.2280, §§ 25–44 (Iraq), § 133 (Tunisia), §§ 147, 167 (Algeria), § 177 (Sudan), §§ 195–9 (Jordan); UN Doc. S/PV.2281, § 9 (Kuwait), § 33 (India), §§ 48–9 (Cuba), § 69 (Pakistan), § 82 (Bulgaria); UN Doc. S/PV.2282, § 24 (Uganda), §§ 45–54 (France), §§ 65–7 (German Democratic Republic), §§ 82–3 (Spain), § 95 (Japan); UN Doc. S/PV.2283, § 66 (USSR), §§ 82–5 (Egypt), § 136 (Vietnam), §§ 147, 154 (Sierra Leone), § 169 (Mongolia); UN Doc. S/PV.2284, § 76 (Syria); UN Doc. S/PV.2285, §§ 10–13 (Morocco), § 29 (Cuba), § 101 (Czechoslovakia), §§ 117–23 (Bangladesh); UN Doc. S/PV.2286, §§ 12–13 (Guyana), § 33 (Somalia), § 48 (Turkey), § 60 (Hungary), § 71 (Italy); UN Doc. S/PV.2287, § 9 (Nicaragua), §§ 20–1 (Indonesia), § 32 (Malaysia), § 41 (Sri Lanka); UN Doc. S/PV.2288, § 113 (Mexico).

purposes.[149] Frequent reference was moreover made to the fact that the IAEA[150] and France[151] – which had cooperated with Iraq in the construction of the reactor – had decried the Israeli allegations as false and had denounced the attack.[152] On 19 June, the Security Council unanimously adopted resolution 487 (1981), which gave full credit to the aforementioned considerations.[153] In remarkably strong language, the resolution 'strongly condemn[ed] the military attack by Israel in clear violation of the Charter'; 'call[ed] upon Israel to refrain in the future from any such acts or threats thereof'; labelled the attack 'a serious threat to the entire safeguards regime of the [IAEA]', and; 'fully recognize[d] the inalienable sovereign right of … all States … to develop their economy and industry for peaceful purposes'. On 13 November 1981, the General Assembly, by 109 votes against two (Israel and the United States), and thirty-four abstentions, adopted a resolution which not only copied the aforementioned findings of Security Council resolution, but also added an explicit condemnation of the Israeli *aggression*.[154]

Does this universal[155] condemnation amount to an unequivocal rejection of the legality of anticipatory self-defence? Upon careful analysis,

---

[149] E.g., UN Doc. S/PV.2280, § 38 (Iraq); UN Doc. S/PV.2281, § 33 (India); UN Doc. S/PV.2283, § 47 (Yugoslavia), § 122 (Romania); UN Doc. S/PV.2284, § 29 (Philippines), § 38 (Panama); UN Doc. S/PV.2286, § 14 (Guyana), §§ 30, 39 (Somalia); UN Doc. S/PV.2287, § 9 (Nicaragua), § 43 (Sri Lanka).

[150] See Telegram from the Director-General of the IAEA to the Security Council, 15 June 1981, UN Doc. S/14532 (the IAEA Board of Governors 'strongly condemns Israel for this premeditated and unjustified attack on the Iraqi nuclear research centre, which is covered by Agency safeguards'); UN Doc. S/PV.2288, §§ 16–19 (IAEA Director-General Eklund).

[151] See UN Doc. S/PV.2282, §§ 44–56.

[152] UN Doc. S/PV.2280, §§ 41–9 (Iraq), § 131 (Tunisia); UN Doc. S/PV.2281, § 9 (Kuwait), § 49 (Cuba), § 69 (Pakistan); UN Doc. S/PV.2282, §§ 82–3 (Spain); UN Doc. S/PV.2283, § 47 (Yugoslavia), § 66 (USSR), § 85 (Egypt), § 169 (Mongolia); UN Doc. S/PV.2285, §§ 10–13 (Morocco), § 102 (Czechoslovakia); UN Doc. S/PV.2286, § 71 (Italy); UN Doc. S/PV.2287, § 22 (Indonesia), § 32 (Malaysia), § 41 (Sri Lanka).

[153] SC Res. 487 (1981) of 19 June 1981. In its Preamble, the resolution makes reference to the documents adopted by the IAEA. It also notes that, contrary to Israel, Iraq has been a party to the Non-Proliferation Treaty, and that the IAEA has testified that the safeguards on nuclear activity 'have been satisfactorily applied to date'.

[154] GA Res. 36/27 of 13 November 1981. The resolution also called on all States to cease any provision of arms to Israel, and requested the Security Council to take effective enforcement action against Israel. For voting records, see: (1981) UNYB 282–3.

[155] *All* States intervening in the UN Debates condemned the strike. The United States also 'condemned' the Israeli violation of the UN Charter, yet it resisted attempts to brand the operation as an 'aggression'. E.g., UN Doc. S/PV.2288, §§ 27–33; UN Doc. A/36/PV.54, § 20.

the truth is more complicated. Indeed, Israel never claimed to be threatened with an 'imminent' armed attack; it merely acted to prevent a future threat (namely the development of an Iraqi nuclear arsenal)[156] from arising – this was claimed to be a matter of weeks or months.[157] Admittedly, Israel was well aware that its invocation of anticipatory self-defence went beyond the traditional construction of that right in legal doctrine. In the first instance, citing the writings of Waldock and Bowett, it stated that the right of self-defence, as *preserved* by Article 51, did not require States to suffer the first blow.[158] Subsequently, the Israeli representative declared that:

> [the] concept of a State's right of self-defence has not changed throughout recorded history. Its scope has, however, broadened with the advance of man's ability to wreak havoc on his enemies. Consequently, this concept took on a new and far wider application with the advent of the nuclear era. ... This is particularly true for small States whose vulnerability is great and whose capacity to survive a nuclear strike is very limited. Thus, the concepts of 'armed attack' and the threat of such an attack must be read in conjunction with, and are related to, the present-day criteria of speed and power ...[159]

Turning back to our terminological framework, it is crystal clear that Israel did not rely on 'pre-emptive' self-defence, but rather on 'preventive' self-defence against a 'non-imminent' threat. Given the virtual absence of support for this approach in legal doctrine (cf. *supra*), it is hardly surprising that the great majority of international lawyers refuted Israel's claim[160] (even if a handful of authors have invoked

---

[156] Cf. UN Doc. S/PV.2280, § 96: 'Israel could not possibly stand idly by while an irresponsible, ruthless and bellicose regime, such as that of Iraq, acquired nuclear weapons, thus creating a constant nightmare for Israel.'

[157] See, e.g., the following Israeli statements: UN Doc. S/PV.2280, §§ 92–5; UN Doc. S/14510; UN Doc. S/PV.2288, § 60.

[158] UN Doc. S/PV.2280, §§ 58, 98–100 (Israel was clearly alluding to the idea that Article 51 UN Charter left unaltered pre-existing custom). Remark: Iraq later drew attention to the fact that the quote from Sir Humphrey Waldock by Israel was incomplete and falsely left out the need for an imminent armed attack. See: UN Doc. S/PV.2288, §§ 199–201.

[159] UN Doc. A/36/PV.52, § 63; UN Doc. S/PV.2288, § 85.

[160] E.g., authors rejecting the idea that the strike was a lawful exercise of self-defence: Constantinou, *The right of self-defence*, p. 118; A. D'Amato, 'Israel's air strike against the Osiraq reactor: a retrospective', (1996) 10 Temple ICLJ 259–64, at 261 (but see note 161); Dinstein, *War, aggression and self-defence*, 4th edn, p. 186 (but see note 161); Fischer, 'Le bombardement par Israël', 163–7; Gill, 'The temporal dimension of self-defense', p. 141; W. T. Mallison and S. V. Mallison, 'The Israeli attack on June 7, 1981', 424–32; Nydell, 'Implications of Israel's preemptive raid on Iraq's nuclear reactor',

different legal bases to defend the operation).[161] The real question, however, is to what extent this broad interpretation of self-defence has steered third State reactions in the UN fora. In other words, one must verify whether the condemnations of the Osiraq strike were inspired by the lack of imminence of the alleged threat, or by the conviction that self-defence could only be exercised after an armed attack had been launched.

What answers can be drawn from the UN debates? On the one hand, no doubt exists as to the general and unqualified rejection of the possibility to exercise self-defence 'preventively' against future, non-imminent threats. Dozens of Member States warned that this concept had no basis in international law; that it would leave it up to States themselves to decide at their discretion whether recourse to force

---

471–88; J. Quigley, 'Israel's destruction of Iraq's nuclear reactor: a reply', (1995) 9 Temple ICLJ 441–4, at 441. Contra: supporting the self-defence claim: L R. Beres, 'Preserving the third temple: Israel's right of anticipatory self-defense under international law', (1993–4) 26 Vanderbilt JTL 111–48, at 118–22; L. R. Beres and Y. Tsiddon-Chatto, 'Reconsidering Israel's destruction of Iraq's nuclear reactor', (1995) 9 Temple ICLJ 437–40.

[161] Some authors argued that the Israeli operation could be justified by the technical 'state of war' which characterized the relations between Israel and Iraq (Beres, 'Israel's right of anticipatory self-defense', 118–20; Beres and Tsiddon-Chatto, 'Reconsidering Israel's destruction', 438; Dinstein, *War, aggression and self-defence*, 4th edn, p. 186). However, as D'Amato correctly observes, international law does not recognize this concept and does not entitle States to derive any legal entitlements from it. What matters from the perspective of the *Ius ad Bellum* and *Ius in Bello*, is whether there are actual hostilities/attacks. This is a factual condition. See D'Amato, 'Israel's air strike against the Osiraq reactor', 261–2. Also: Fischer, 'Le bombardement par Israël', 162–3; W. T. Mallison and S. V. Mallison, 'The Israeli attack on June 7, 1981', 432–3; Quigley, 'Israel's destruction of Iraq's nuclear reactor', 444. Thus, before listing possible acts of aggression, Article 3 of the Definition of Aggression clarifies that the provision applies 'regardless of a declaration of war'. It may moreover be noted that Israel did not pay significant attention to this aspect (a brief reference can be found at UN Doc. S/PV.2280, § 74). No State regarded the existence of a 'state of war' as a credible legal basis to justify a recourse to force, and some explicitly denounced it (e.g., UN Doc. S/PV.2282, § 22 (Uganda); UN Doc. A/36/PV.52, § 24 (Iraq); UN Doc. A/36/PV.56, §§ 18–19 (Algeria)). In relation to the 1951 conflict between Egypt and Israel on the right of passage through the Suez Canal, Israel explicitly rejected the possibility of invoking belligerent rights on the basis of a technical state of war, as did most of the UN Security Council members (see *infra*, notes 187, 192).

Finally, D'Amato has suggested that the Osiraq strike did not constitute a use of force 'against either Iraq's territorial integrity or its political independence' and therefore did not violate Article 2(4) UN Charter (D'Amato, 'Israel's air strike against the Osiraq reactor', 584–7). As discussed elsewhere, this reasoning goes against the generally accepted view that the prohibition of Article 2(4) is a comprehensive one. See *supra*, Section 2.1.2.

was suited to tackle a hypothetical security threat; and that it would replace the Charter rules with the 'law of the jungle'.[162] Because of the 'obvious dangers' involved, the European Community, for instance, refused to accept that Article 51 should be interpreted far more widely 'to allow a pre-emptive strike by one State against what it alleges to be the nuclear-weapon development programme of another, potentially hostile, State'.[163] Sweden, like many others, agreed that the proposed interpretation of self-defence meant that the concept could be extended 'almost limitlessly to include all conceivable future dangers, subjectively defined'.[164]

Whether States also considered self-defence against imminent armed attacks to be unlawful is more difficult to tell. In light of the assurances of the IAEA and the lack of compelling proof put forward by Israel, it may well have been that, to paraphrase the ICJ, States found that 'the lawfulness of a response to the imminent threat of armed attack had not been raised', and accordingly 'expressed no view on that issue'. Still, some States did pronounce on pre-emptive self-defence as well. On the one hand, a handful of States rendered implicit support to this concept by emphasizing that Israel had failed to comply with the requirement of imminence. The UK noted that 'there was no instant or overwhelming

---

[162] E.g., UN Doc. S/PV.2280, §§ 157–63 (Algeria), UN Doc. S/PV.2281, § 39 (Brazil), §§ 79–80 (Bulgaria); UN Doc. S/PV.2282, §§ 12–19 (Uganda), §§ 77–8 (Spain: 'Israel seeks to justify this act of aggression by presenting it as preventive action to avert some future, hypothetical threat to its security. That justification is absolutely unacceptable.... The Charter does not allow for ... any right to preventive action by which a Member State could set itself up as judge, party and policeman in respect to another country'), § 89 (PRC); UN Doc. S/PV.2283, §§ 22–31 (Ireland: '[S]uch a definition of self-defence would replace the basic principle of the Charter ... by a virtually unlimited concept of self-defence against all possible future dangers, subjectively assessed'); § 46 (Yugoslavia: 'The absurd and particularly dangerous argumentation concerning the right of preventive attack "in self-defence" must be rejected because not to reject it would be to open the way to lawlessness and to legalize aggression'); § 63 (USSR), § 117 (Romania), §§ 146–9 (Sierra Leone); UN Doc. S/PV.2284, § 28 (Philippines: 'such a dangerous precedent would leave us faced with a situation in which every State, on mere suspicion of bellicose intent, could abrogate unto itself the doubtful right to launch an armed attack against another'), §§ 47–8 (Yemen), §§ 65–6 (Syria); UN Doc. S/PV.2285, §§ 97–9 (Czechoslovakia), § 124 (Bangladesh); UN Doc. S/PV.2286, §§ 15–17 (Guyana), § 31 (Somalia), § 49 (Turkey); UN Doc. S/PV.2287, § 8 (Nicaragua); UN Doc. S/PV.2288, § 115 (Mexico); UN Doc. A/36/PV.53, § 121 (Syria), §§ 131, 142 (PRC), § 152 (Turkey); UN Doc. A/36/PV.54, § 2 (India), § 9 (German Democratic Republic), § 30 (Austria), § 40 (Tunisia), § 65 (Bulgaria), § 79 (USSR), § 104 (Egypt); UN Doc. A/36/PV.55, §§ 24–32 (United Arab Emirates), §§ 39–40 (Oman), § 52 (Romania), § 130 (Poland); UN Doc. A/36/PV.56, § 4 (Guyana), § 26 (Algeria), § 62 (Spain), § 80 (Chile).
[163] UN Doc. A/36/PV.53, § 92.   [164] UN Doc. A/36/PV.56, § 119.

necessity for self-defence'.[165] Sierra Leone similarly declared that 'the plea of self-defence is untenable where no armed attack has taken place *or is imminent*'.[166] Comparable statements were made by the representatives of Niger[167] and Oman.[168] The US condemned the raid only because 'diplomatic means available to Israel had not been exhausted'.[169] While a number of UN Members seemingly left the matter undecided,[170] others voiced their opposition to pre-emptive self-defence by claiming that States that felt threatened should bring the matter before the Security Council,[171] and/or by recalling that Article 51 presupposed the occurrence of an (actual) 'armed attack'.[172] Mexico stressed that 'it is inadmissible to invoke the right to self-defence when no armed attack has taken place'.[173] Chile confirmed that Article 51 only allows for self-defence 'in the case of prior armed aggression'.[174] Pakistan recalled that 'even when Member States are facing a threat, it is imperative that they first resort to the United Nations'.[175]

The implications of the three examples listed so far may be summarized as follows:

(1) The Cuban Missile crisis can be regarded as an implicit rejection (especially on behalf of the US and the OAS) of the admissibility of *preventive* self-defence.

---

[165] UN Doc. S/PV.2282, § 106.
[166] UN Doc. S/PV.2283, § 147–9 (emphasis added). 'As for the principle of self-defence, it has long been accepted that, for it to be invoked or justified, the necessity for action must be instant, overwhelming and leaving no choice of means and no moment for deliberation.'
[167] UN Doc. S/PV.2284, § 11 ('there was aggression, because Israel was in no way facing an *imminent* attack, irrefutably proved and demonstrated' (emphasis added)).
[168] UN Doc. A/36/PV.55, § 39 ('[I]n principle, there can be no talk of self-defence as long as there is no actual or *imminent* armed attack' (emphasis added)). See also: UN Doc. A/36/PV.55, 27 (United Arab Emirates).
[169] UN Doc. S/PV.2288, § 30.
[170] See in particular: UN Doc. S/PV.2283, §§ 22–7 (Ireland); UN Doc. A/36/PV.53, § 92 (European Community).
[171] E.g., UN Doc. S/PV.2284, § 26 (Philippines: 'If Israel was so sure that Iraq was on the verge of manufacturing nuclear weapons, it could have raised the matter before the appropriate international bodies for verification'); UN Doc. A/36/PV.52, § 24 (Iraq). See also: UN Doc. S/PV.2282, § 95 (Japan).
[172] UN Doc. S/PV.2282, § 78 (German Democratic Republic: 'Article 51 . . . limits that right to a case of armed attack . . .'); UN Doc. S/PV.2286, § 15 (Guyana); UN Doc. S/PV.2288, § 141 (Uganda); UN Doc. A/36/PV.53, § 142 (PRC); UN Doc. A/36/PV.54, § 40 (Tunisia); UN Doc. A/36/PV.56, § 4 (Guyana).
[173] UN Doc. S/PV.2288, § 115.   [174] UN Doc. A/36/PV.56, § 80.
[175] UN Doc. S/PV.2281, § 70.

(2) Despite the absence of a formal UN condemnation, the Six Day War reveals the reluctance of a number of States to establish a precedent in favour of *pre-emptive* self-defence as well as the explicit dismissal of such doctrine by several others.

(3) Finally, the international reaction to the 1981 Osiraq strike evidences a broad and categorical denunciation of the concept of 'preventive self-defence'. In spite of the condemnation by the Security Council and the General Assembly, the debates nonetheless reveal a crack in the *opinio iuris* vis-à-vis the legality of pre-emptive action in response to 'imminent' threats. The latter factor is, however, manifestly insufficient to discharge the *onus probandi* required for an evolutive interpretation of the scope of Article 51 extending to threats of attack.[176]

4.1.2.d   Other cases

Do other instances of State practice alter this provisional conclusion? While the aforementioned cases are generally considered the most relevant ones, several 'counter-restrictionists' have cited other alleged precedents. D.P. O'Connell, for example, draws attention to Pakistan's anticipatory action in Kashmir in 1950.[177] *In casu*, Pakistan justified the deployment of troops to Kashmir by reason of its conviction that 'India was mounting an offensive to clear the State of all military resistance'.[178] In response, it had taken action 'to avoid the imminent danger that threatened [its] security and [its] economy'. Contrary to what O'Connell suggests, however, Pakistan did not explicitly frame its actions as a form of (anticipatory) self-defence, nor did it mention Article 51 of the UN Charter. Furthermore, India objected that:

> [Article 51] imposes two limitations upon the right of self-defence: first, there must be an armed attack upon the Member that exercises the right; and, secondly, measures taken ... must be immediately reported to the Security Council. In the present instance there was no armed attack on Pakistan, and admittedly the sending of the army into Kashmir was not reported to the Security Council.[179]

---

[176] Authors questioning/rejecting the precedential value of the Osiraq strike: e.g., Cassese, 'Article 51', p. 1338; Christakis, 'La notion de guerre préventive', p. 26; Corten, *Le droit contre la guerre*, pp. 663–4; Gazzini, *The changing rules*, pp. 150–1; Sicilianos, *Des contre-mesures à la légitime défense*, pp. 401–2;. Contra: e.g., Gill, 'The temporal dimension of self-defense', p. 140; Greenwood, 'The pre-emptive use of force', 14.

[177] D. P. O'Connell, *International law*. Vol. I, 2nd edn (London: Stevens, 1970), p. 317.

[178] UN Doc. S/PV.464, 8 February 1950, 27–30.

[179] UN Doc. S/PV.466, 10 February 1950, 4–5. India reiterated its objections in 1951: UN Doc. S/PV.536, 9 March 1951, § 15.

Apart from India, no other State made any reference to the right of self-defence. This can be explained by the disputed territorial status of Kashmir and the underlying issue of self-determination. Ever since the conclusion of British rule on the subcontinent in 1947 and the partition of the British Indian Empire into the newly independent Union of India and the Dominion of Pakistan, a conflict had been raging as to who should gain sovereignty over the state of Jammu and Kashmir.[180] Since 1948, the Security Council had adopted a variety of resolutions in order to mediate between the two parties and to pave the way for a plebiscite.[181] This uncertainty, Sicilianos suggests, explains why States refrained from testing the protagonists' actions against Articles 2(4) and 51 UN Charter, and consequently reduces the potential precedential impact.[182] It may also be noted that Pakistan has in later years expressly argued against anticipatory self-defence.[183]

A more interesting incident, cited by Bowett,[184] concerns the 1951 conflict between Egypt and Israel as a result of the restriction of Israeli shipping in the Suez Canal. *In casu*, the Chief of Staff of the UN Truce Supervision Organization reported that the Egyptian interference with the passage of goods to Israel through the Suez Canal was an aggressive and hostile act, which contravened and jeopardized the 1949 Armistice Agreement.[185] Shortly hereafter, Israel requested that the Security Council urgently meet to consider the issue.[186]

Egypt invoked a twofold basis to justify its actions. In the first place, it claimed that the 1949 Armistice Agreement had not ended the technical state of war between the two countries, and that, consequently, the visiting and inspecting of ships bound for Israel fell within the ambit of Egypt's belligerent rights.[187] Second, and closely related to this, it relied on its 'right of self-preservation and self-defence, which … transcends all other

---

[180] Pakistan argued that it would be only logical for it to gain control over the area, since Muslims constituted a large majority of the population. Nonetheless, in return for Indian support in combating Pakistani-sponsored irregulars and tribesmen, the Maharaja of Jammu and Kashmir signed a (temporary) accession to India. For a short analysis: V. Schofield, 'Kashmir: the origins of the dispute', *BBC News* 16 January 2002.
[181] SC Res. 38 (1948) of 17 January 1948; SC Res. 39 (1948) of 20 January 1948; SC Res. 47 (1948) of 21 April 1948; SC Res. 51 (1948) of 3 June 1948.
[182] Sicilianos, *Des contre-mesures à la légitime défense*, p. 398.
[183] See *supra*, note 175; *infra*, notes 253, 445.
[184] Bowett, *Self-defence in international law*, p. 191.   [185] See (1951) UNYB 293–4.
[186] UN Doc. S/2241. See following meetings: UN Docs. S/PV.549–53, S/PV.555–6, S/PV.558, 26 July–1 September 1951.
[187] E.g., UN Doc. S/PV.549, §§ 61–8; UN Doc. S/PV.550, §§ 19–32.

rights'.[188] Apparently flirting with the 'pre-existing custom' approach, Egypt quoted the view of Goodrich and Hambro that 'the provisions of Article 51 do not necessarily exclude [the] right of self-defence in situations not covered by this Article'.[189] Both legal bases were strongly opposed by Israel. On the one hand, it argued that: 'The Charter has created a new world of international relations within which the traditional 'rights of war' cannot be enthroned.... There can ... be no room within the regime of the Charter for any generic doctrine of belligerency, since belligerency is nothing but a political and legal formula for regulating the threat or use of force.'[190] On the other hand, it recalled that 'Article 51 allows a nation to undertake action of self-defence only on two conditions ... One of them is that that country shall be the victim of armed attack, and not even the Egyptian himself has invoked such prospect.'[191]

On both accounts, the majority of the Security Council members followed Israel's line of reasoning. By eight votes to none, with three abstentions, the Council adopted a resolution which (1) held that neither party could reasonably assert that it was actively a belligerent, since the armistice regime, which had been in existence for nearly two and a half years, was of a permanent character; (2) found that Egypt's interference could not in the prevailing circumstances be justified on the ground that it was necessary for self-defence; and (3) called upon Egypt to terminate the restrictions on the passage of international commercial shipping and goods through the Suez Canal.[192]

---

[188] E.g., UN Doc. S/PV.549, § 78; UN Doc. S/PV.550, §§ 33 et seq.
[189] UN Doc. S/PV.550, § 39. Also: UN Doc. S/PV.553, § 60: 'neither in Article 51 nor in any other Article does the Charter exclude or even impair the right of self-preservation and self-defence'.
[190] UN Doc. S/PV.549, §§ 11–47, especially at § 32 ('This Armistice Agreement is not a mere suspension of hostilities, leaving belligerent rights intact. This Agreement ... is a permanent and irrevocable renunciation of all hostile acts'), §§ 40–1 ('My Government instructs me to declare that Israel is in no state of war with Egypt and denies that Egypt has the least right to be at war with Israel'). Also: UN Doc. S/PV.551, §§ 30 et seq.
[191] UN Doc. S/PV.551, § 36. The second condition was that the Security Council should not yet have assumed responsibility for the maintenance of international peace and security in the concerned area. Again, this condition was not fulfilled vis-à-vis Egypt's actions.
[192] SC Res. 95 (1951) of 1 September 1951. See also, on the alleged state of war: UN Doc. S/PV.552, §§ 6–7 (UK), §§ 21, 30 (France: 'since the fighting has in effect ceased and an armistice of a specifically permanent character has been concluded, the French Government considers that there is no legal basis upon which one of the parties may exercise in respect of the other the traditional rights of belligerents'), §§ 40–4 (US), § 57 (Brazil); UN Doc. S/PV.553, §§ 8–15 (Netherlands), § 23 (Turkey), § 121 (Ecuador). However: UN Doc. S/PV.553, §§ 28, 37 (Iraq).

According to Bowett, the resolution should not be interpreted as an assertion that the right of self-defence is limited to cases where an actual armed attack occurs, for 'it is conceivable that had large-scale mobilization by Israel threatened an impending breach of the armistice, the prevailing circumstances might have justified the plea of self-defence'.[193] There is a certain merit to this finding insofar as States may well have been guided by the obvious lack of an imminent threat in rejecting Egypt's self-defence claim. Certain statements seem to leave open this possibility.[194] The UK, for instance, stated that 'Egypt is not being attacked and is not under any imminent threat of attack, and we therefore cannot agree that these measures are necessary for the self-defence ... of Egypt'.[195] Brazil similarly stressed that there was 'no imminent danger to the existence of Egypt', nor any evidence that Israel was 'preparing an armed attack'.[196] The Netherlands and Ecuador simply observed that 'there had been no (actual) armed attack' against Egypt.[197] In the end, even if it cannot automatically be concluded from the Security Council's reaction that States – or better all States – opposed pre-emptive self-defence, the converse is no less true: the 1951 Suez crisis certainly does not provide a positive precedent in support of anticipatory action. It may be added that, like Pakistan, Egypt has repeatedly taken a stance against the admissibility of anticipatory self-defence within the UN.[198]

Other incidents that are sometimes alleged – depending on the response of the international community – to prove or disprove the existence of a customary right of anticipatory self-defence include the Israeli intervention in Lebanon in 1975, the South African incursions into Lesotho in 1982, the US strikes against Libya in April 1986 and the 1998 US strikes against Sudan and Afghanistan.[199] On closer inspection, however, these cases do not constitute genuine examples of 'anticipatory self-defence', since the intervening States claimed to be

---

[193] Bowett, *Self-defence in international law*, p. 191.
[194] Israel itself, for example, referred to 'the prospect that a country shall be the victim of an armed attack' (UN Doc. S/PV.551, § 36).
[195] UN Doc. S/PV.552, § 10. Also: UN Doc. S/PV.550, §§ 93–4 (UK).
[196] UN Doc. S/PV.552, § 58.
[197] UN Doc. S/PV.553, § 15 (Netherlands), § 122 (Ecuador).
[198] See *infra*, notes 256, 453.
[199] E.g., Cassese, 'Article 51', pp. 1337–8 (regarding the negative reception of the Israeli intervention in Lebanon in 1975 as a rebuttal of anticipatory self-defence); Christakis, 'La notion de guerre préventive', p. 24 (in relation to the 1982 South African raid against Lesotho (but see note 43)); Malanczuk and Akehurst, *Akehurst's modern introduction to international law*, p. 313 (referring to the April 1986 US raid on Libya).

responding to *prior attacks*, albeit with the (proclaimed) objective of *preventing* the occurrence of *additional attacks*.[200] Hence, we are confronted with a different scenario, which is analytically distinct from actual 'pre-emptive' or 'preventive' self-defence and pertains to the prospective element of the necessity assessment (cf. *infra*, Section 4.3.1). In any event, the reaction of the international community vis-à-vis these interventions does not reveal any State support for such doctrine. Quite the contrary, both in 1982 and 1986, for example, several States challenged the legality of the interventions on the grounds that South Africa and the US had failed to submit convincing proof that prior armed attacks had actually taken place.[201]

As far as the 1986 conflict between the US and Libya is concerned, an additional observation is in place. Two days before the 14 April raid by the US, Libya filed a complaint with the Security Council, informing the body that '[US] aircraft-carriers and other [US] naval units are now proceeding towards the Libyan coast for the purpose of staging military aggression against [Libya]'.[202] In light thereof, Libya considered itself

---

[200] (1) When Israel carried out raids against Palestinian camps in Lebanon in 1975, it claimed that its action was designed to prevent the staging of '*further attacks* on Israel' (emphasis added). See UN Doc. S/PV.1859, 4 December 1975, § 119 (Israeli statement, quoted by Egypt). (2) In 1982, South Africa presented its incursion into Lesotho as a 'pre-emptive action' to '*prevent an escalation* of terrorist activity embracing the perpetration of bombings, sabotage and bloodshed in South Africa ...' (emphasis added). Again, South Africa claimed that it had earlier fallen victim to 'acts of sabotage and violence' by the ANC and 'other terrorist groups' operating from Lesotho. In addition, information at its disposal allegedly indicated that further 'deeds of terror' would be executed during the coming festive season. See: 16 December 1982, UN Doc. S/PV.2409, §§ 137–46. (3) In April 1986, the United States reported to the Security Council that it had exercised the right of self-defence in accordance with Article 51 of the Charter 'by responding to an *ongoing pattern of attacks* by the Government of Libya (emphasis added).' The objective had been 'to destroy facilities used to carry out Libya's hostile policy of international terrorism and to discourage Libyan terrorist attacks in the future'. See: UN Doc. S/17990, 14 April 1986 (US); Doc. S/PV.2674, 15 April 1986, 13–17. (4) Similarly, the 1998 US strikes against Sudan and Afghanistan were reported to the Security Council as an exercise of the right of self-defence in response to 'a series of armed attacks against United States embassies and United States nationals'. In light of 'convincing evidence that further such attacks were in preparation ... [the US] had no choice but to use armed force to prevent [them] from continuing.' See: UN Doc. S/1998/780, 20 August 1998 (US); (1998) UNYB 1219–20.

[201] E.g., UN Doc. S/PV.2407, 15 December 1982, 84–9 (Ireland: '[T]here is no evidence ... of any attack on South Africa from Lesotho, by the ANC or otherwise, in the past'); UN Doc. S/PV.2675, 15 April 1986, §§ 24–5 (Oman); UN Doc. S/PV.2676, 16 April 1986, § 4 (Algeria).

[202] UN Doc; S/17983, 12 April 1986 (Libya).

'as of this moment, in a state of legitimate self-defence under Article 51 of the [UN] Charter'. At face value, this appears to be a clear-cut invocation of anticipatory self-defence. Yet, Libya's self-defence claim was not actually implemented (no military action was undertaken prior to the US raid), nor was it subject to debate within the Security Council.[203] Moreover, the Libyan letter also made reference to a US military aggression against Libya two weeks earlier (viz. the Gulf of Sirte incident).[204] During the Security Council meeting of 14 April – which took place just prior to the US raid – Libya eventually shifted to a more cautious approach. It warned that '*[i]f this American attack were to take place*, Libya would find itself in a state of legitimate self-defence ... under the provisions of Article 51 of the Charter'.[205]

Another case which is rarely cited in legal literature concerns the commencement of the Iran–Iraq war in 1980. *In casu*, Iraq justified the opening of hostilities by a vague reference to 'preventive self-defence'.[206] However, at no time did Iraq elaborate on the existence of a threat of armed attack. A closer look at the Iraqi declarations reveals that its conduct had nothing to do with self-defence, but instead aimed at asserting Iraq's self-proclaimed 'legitimate [territorial] rights and vital interests'.[207] Moreover, as Corten observes, Iraq later shifted to a more orthodox conception of the right of self-defence, claiming that it had been the victim of a prior armed attack by Iran.[208] Last but not least, while third States generally confined themselves to calling on the warring parties to cease hostilities and urging a peaceful resolution of the conflict (without pronouncing on the legal merits),[209] a report of the UN Secretary-General in 1991 concluded that the Iraqi attack

---

[203] See UN Docs. S/PV.2672–2673, 12–14 April 1986. [204] UN Doc. S/17983.
[205] UN Doc. S/PV.2673, 7 (emphasis added).
[206] UN Doc. S/14199, 26 September 1980 (Iraq); UN Doc. S/PV.2250, 15 October 1980, § 40.
[207] See UN Doc. S/14192, 24 September 1980 (Iraq); UN Doc. S/14199; UN Doc. S/PV.2250, §§ 40–1.
[208] See Corten, *Le droit contre la guerre*, p. 662. Already in September–October 1980, claims of 'preventive self-defence' were intermingled with suggestions that Iran had carried out prior attacks. See: UN Doc. S/14199; UN Doc. S/PV.2250, § 40. Also Gray, *The use of force*, p. 162.
[209] See (1980) UNYB 312–18; SC Res. 479 (1980) of 28 September 1980. Remark: it may be recalled that at the time, Iraq still enjoyed considerable political support among Western States. The newly established Islamic Republic of Iran, by contrast, held a pariah status within the international community.

THE 'ARMED ATTACK' REQUIREMENT *RATIONE TEMPORIS* 293

of 22 September 1980 against Iran, could not be justified under the UN Charter.[210]

In order to wind up our overview of concrete customary practice prior to 2001,[211] it may be noted that in 1998 the US and the UK initiated substantial military operations against Iraq in order to degrade the latter country's weapons of mass destruction programmes and its ability to threaten its neighbours (Operation 'Desert Fox'). Instead of relying on a broad doctrine of anticipatory self-defence, both countries claimed to be acting on the basis of an authorization by the Security Council:[212] the repeated 'material breaches' of the conditions laid down in Security Council resolution 687 (1991) which declared the ceasefire at the end of the 1990-1 Gulf War allegedly revived the latter resolution's authorization to use force. This somewhat artificial legal reasoning was criticized by a number of UN Members.[213] The exact same justification was invoked five years later in relation to the controversial intervention in Iraq.[214]

In the end, the lack of a convincing precedent whereby a reliance on anticipatory self-defence received broad international support implies that our provisional conclusion remains standing: concrete customary practice prior to 2001 did not accept the recourse to force in response to threats of armed attacks – whether they be imminent or non-imminent.[215] For the remainder of this section we will turn our attention

---

[210] United Nations Secretary-General, 'Further Report of the Secretary-General on the Implementation of Security Council Resolution 598 (1987)', 9 December 1991, UN Doc. S/23273, §§ 5-7.

[211] Remark: the tragic shooting by the USS *Vincennes* of Iran Air flight 655 in 1988 is discussed below in Section 4.3.3.b. *In casu*, the US did not rely on pre-emptive self-defence, but claimed that the USS *Vincennes* had reacted to what it perceived as an armed attack by Iran (UN Doc. S/19989; UN Doc. S/PV.2818, 56). With the exception of Iran – which stated that 'pre-emptive measures before the occurrence of an armed attack cannot be justified as acts of self-defence' (UN Doc. S/PV.2818, 36-7) – no State made any reference to anticipatory self-defence in the course of the Security Council debates (UN Doc. S/PV.2818-21).

[212] UN Doc. S/1998/1181, 16 December 1998 (US); UN Doc. S/1998/1182, 16 December 1998 (UK).

[213] See UN Doc. S/PV.3955, 16 December 1998 (inter alia Russia (at 4) and PRC (at 5)). See also the communications cited in (1998) UNYB 263.

[214] See Section 4.2.1.b.ii.

[215] Constantinou, *The right of self-defence*, pp. 120-1; Corten, *Le droit contre la guerre*, p. 658; Dugard, A *South African perspective*, p. 508; Gazzini, *The changing rules*, p. 151; Gray, *The use of force*, pp. 160-5; Randelzhofer, 'Article 51', p. 802. Remark: Brownlie gives some examples where States accused their neighbours of planning an attack, without invoking/exercising the right of self-defence: I. Brownlie, 'The use of force in self-defence', (1961) 37 BYBIL 183-268, at 228.

to customary evidence *in abstracto* in order to measure the crack in *opinio iuris* which was identified earlier.

4.1.3 Customary evidence in abstracto

4.1.3.a Early negotiations on a Definition of Aggression

The best abstract evidence in relation to State positions on anticipatory action is found in the negotiations on the Definition of Aggression.[216] Especially in the early stages of the *travaux*, i.e., during the fifties, the issue was addressed head-on. The immediate cause for this was the inclusion in the original Soviet draft of the so-called 'first use' or 'priority' principle.[217] According to this principle, the first State to commit one of a list of acts, such as invasion or bombardment, would be branded the aggressor (Article 1). In addition, Article 3 of the Soviet draft provided that:

> In the event of the mobilization or concentration by another State of considerable armed forces near its frontier, the State which is threatened by such action shall have the right of recourse to diplomatic or other means of securing peaceful settlement of international disputes. It may also in the meantime adopt requisite measures of a military nature ..., without, however, crossing the frontier.[218]

Several countries objected that the first use of force might exceptionally constitute an exercise of self-defence. Greece, for instance, during the 1952 debates within the UNGA Sixth Committee, pointed out that the right to shoot first was recognized in all criminal codes. By analogy, when there was impending aggression a State had the right to attack first to counter the aggressive intention of the other State, even if no actual act of aggression had taken place.[219] Belgium sided with Greece.[220] It drew attention to Article 417 of the Belgian Penal Code, which provided that there was no crime when homicide was committed in repulsing a forced night-time breaking and entering of a house, unless it was proved that the person who used a weapon could not have believed that there was an intention to do grievous bodily harm. By analogy, the US would not have committed aggression if it had anticipated the attack on Pearl

---

[216] For an elaborate analysis, see Corten, *Le droit contre la guerre*, pp. 635–42.
[217] USSR Draft Resolution on the Definition of Aggression, 4 November 1950, UN Doc. A/C.1/608.
[218] *Ibid.* [219] UN Doc. A/C.6/SR.279, 7 January 1952, § 10.
[220] UN Doc. A/C.6/SR.287, 15 January 1952, §§ 27–9.

Harbour and struck at the Japanese naval forces on the high seas. In general, Belgium asserted that a State could act in self-defence not only against an aggression already committed, but also, exceptionally, '*against an imminent aggression, the threat of which had been translated into acts*'.[221] The Soviet Union and Chile, on the other hand, noted that the cited article from the Belgian Penal Code did not conflict with the 'first use' principle. According to the Soviet representative:

> [i]t postulated the commencement of an act, and not a mere supposition that attack was imminent. On the other hand, those who defended the theory of preventive war wished to justify the illegal use of armed force when the victim was merely supposed to have the intention of breaking into their home, even if in reality he was some distance away.[222]

Similarly, Chile reiterated that many national penal codes made self-defence contingent on the existence of an actual or at least inchoate attack.[223] 'None of those codes justified an attack upon an individual merely on the grounds that he was thought to harbor aggressive intentions.' The Belgian Penal Code was no exception in that it presupposed an actual attack. The same principle was valid in international relations: no State could justify recourse to violence against another State by arguing that it had suspected the latter of harbouring aggressive intentions.[224] Still, Belgium insisted that once a direct threat to a State was evident from the signs of an impending attack, the State threatened was in a state of self-defence.[225] In this context, it was important to explain what exactly was meant by the beginning of an attack.[226] China

---

[221] *Ibid.*, § 28 (emphasis added).   [222] UN Doc. A/C.6/SR.288, 16 January 1952, § 34.
[223] UN Doc. A/C.6/SR.290, 18 January 1952, §§ 55–7. Also: UN Doc. A/C.6/SR.281, 9 January 1952, § 28 ('no penal code in any civilized country authorized self-defence of a preventive character': 'a person anticipating an injury could take precautions, but if he killed his opponent before being attacked, he was a criminal.').
[224] UN Doc. A/C.6/SR.290, 18 January 1952, § 57.
[225] *Ibid.*, §§ 60–4. It is not entirely clear whether Belgium was supporting 'pre-emptive' or merely 'interceptory' self-defence. In § 61, for example, Mr Van Glabbeke states that 'as soon as an overt attack occurs, the person has the indisputable right to defend himself.' In § 65, however, Belgium refers to self-defence vis-à-vis an 'impending' attack. In 1954, Belgium reiterated its position in cautiously drafted wording: 'Admittedly, the dividing line between a threat and actual aggression might be hard to draw, and occasions were conceivable in which a State had to act if it wished to avoid being reduced to impotence by the sudden outbreak of hostilities that had been threatening. Nevertheless, it seemed impossible to put aggression and the threat of aggression on the same plane.' UN Doc. A/C.6/SR.410, 28 October 1954, § 15.
[226] UN Doc. A/C.6/SR.290, § 61.

simply observed that 'the question of whether the right of self-defence permitted forestalling armed attack in case of an immediate danger allowing no time for [UN] intervention still required clarification'.[227]

Despite calls for clarification, no genuine attempts were undertaken after 1952 to shed light on the substantial difference between 'imminent', 'impending' or 'actual' attacks. Instead, the debate by and large narrowed down to mere pledges of support for anticipatory self-defence by a small group of States and persistent opposition to this doctrine by a growing majority of UN Members. In 1954 and 1957 it was mainly the Netherlands that urged that the Definition under preparation acknowledged that the concept of armed attack under Article 51 'covered specific cases of threat of force, namely those of imminent threat where a State had no time for any other action than immediate self-defence'.[228] This postulate had been affirmed by the Nuremberg and Tokyo judgments[229] and had acquired particular significance with the dawn of the atomic age. In this context, the Netherlands recalled that the Atomic Energy Commission had recommended that a truly grave violation of a treaty on atomic energy should be regarded as sufficiently serious to give rise to the inherent right of self-defence.[230] The Dutch view was supported by the UK representative, who stressed that the drafters of the Charter had intended to leave the right of self-defence 'admitted and unimpaired',[231] and agreed that the threat of force might in some cases be so imminent and overwhelming as to warrant the threatened State taking such action as was necessary to avert the attack.[232] In a similar vein, Australia found that:

> A flexible interpretation of the Charter provisions would permit a threatened State to use force to ward off a threatened attack, so long as it did not do so against the territorial integrity or political independence of another State.[233]

---

[227] UN Doc. A/C.6/SR.337, 28 November 1952, § 43.
[228] E.g., UN Doc. A/C.6/SR.410, 28 October 1954, § 43; UN Doc. A/C.6/SR.527, 1 November 1957, § 29. But see UN Doc. A/C.6/SR.417, 8 November 1954, § 17 (agreeing to leave the question of an immediate threat undecided, as the definition required was one of aggression and not of self-defence).
[229] UN Doc. A/C.6/SR.410, § 43; UN Doc. A/C.6/SR.417, § 16.
[230] UN Doc. A/C.6/SR.527, § 29; UN Doc. A/C.6/SR.417, § 16; UN Doc. A/C.6/SR.410, § 43. Also: UN Doc. A/C.6/SR.337, 28 November 1952, § 6.
[231] UN Doc. A/C.6/SR.805, 5 November 1963, § 7.
[232] *Ibid.*; UN Doc. A/C.6/SR.412, 1 November 1954, § 10.
[233] UN Doc. A/C.6/SR.817, 21 November 1963, § 23.

While a number of States adopted a more ambiguous position,[234] anticipatory self-defence was denounced by a considerable group of UN members, including the Soviet Union and Chile, but also Ukraine, Egypt, Poland, Iran, Mexico, Belarus, Czechoslovakia, Paraguay, Syria, Romania, Ceylon, Indonesia, Cuba, Cyprus, the Philippines, Mongolia and Ethiopia.[235]

Some delegations simply condemned the attempts to justify 'preventive war' and/or emphasized that self-defence could only be exercised in the event of an armed attack. Others were more specific. Belarus, for instance, claimed that it was not sufficient that an attack was impending.[236] Iran argued that if a State believed itself to be threatened, it

---

[234] E.g., Panama in 1954 declared that 'a State might very well be the first to commit acts regarded as acts of aggression in the exercise of its right of self-defence' (UN Doc. A/C.6/SR.403, 14 October 1954, § 25). In 1963, however, Panama stated that 'the idea of preventive self-defence could easily be used as a cloak for aggression, and nothing in Article 51 could be regarded as authorization for such measures' (UN Doc. A/C.6/SR.824, 3 December 1963, § 8). According to Norway: 'Not all forms of threats should automatically be considered acts of aggression that justified the exercise of the right of self-defence. The gravity of the threat was a question of fact that was better left to the appreciation of the competent United Nations organs' (UN Doc. A/C.6/SR.413, 3 November 1954, §30). See also: UN Doc. A/C.6/SR.417, 8 November 1954, § 30 (PRC); UN Doc. A/C.6/SR.528, 4 November 1957, § 21 (Peru); UN Doc. A/C.6/SR.765, 23 November 1962, § 22 (Peru); UN Doc. A/C.6/SR.997, 14 November 1967, § 25 (Uruguay); UN Doc. A/C.6/SR.520, 22 October 1957, §§ 48–50 (India).

[235] (1) USSR: see *supra*, note 222; UN Doc. A/C.6/SR.341, 4 December 1952, § 14; UN Doc. A/C.6/SR.414, 3 November 1954, § 37; UN Doc. A/C.6/SR.419, 10 November 1954, §§ 2–3; UN Doc. A/C.6/SR.532, 13 November 1957, §§ 28–30; (2) Chile: see *supra*, note, 223; (3) Ukraine: UN Doc. A/C.6/SR.290, 18 January 1952, §§ 2–3; (4) Egypt: UN Doc. A/C.6/SR.291, 19 January 1952, §§ 9–11; (5) Poland: UN Doc. A/C.6/SR.292, 19 January 1952, § 24; UN Doc. A/C.6/SR.406, 20 October 1954, § 39; UN Doc. A/C.6/SR.415, 4 November 1954, §§ 22–4; (6) Iran: UN Doc. A/C.6/SR.405, 18 October 1954, §§ 3–5; UN Doc. A/C.6/SR.416, 5 November 1954, § 32; (7) Mexico: UN Doc. A/C.6/SR.408, 25 October 1954, § 32; UN Doc. A/C.6/SR.415, 4 November 1954, §§ 39–42; (8) Belarus: UN Doc. A/C.6/SR.411, 29 October 1954, §§ 8–15; (9) Czechoslovakia: UN Doc. A/C.6/SR.413, 3 November 1954, §§ 10–11; UN Doc. A/C.6/SR.418, 9 November 1954, §§ 44–6; UN Doc. A/C.6/SR.524, 29 October 1957, §§ 38–43; UN Doc. A/C.6/SR.871, 8 November 1965, § 35; (10) Paraguay: UN Doc. A/C.6/SR.419, 10 November 1954, § 15; (11) Syria: UN Doc. A/C.6/SR.517, 14 October 1957, §§ 4, 7, 21; (12) Romania: UN Doc. A/C.6/SR.520, 22 October 1957, §§ 36, 39, 41; (13) Ceylon: UN Doc. A/C.6/SR.805, 5 November 1963, § 21; (14) Indonesia: UN Doc. A/C.6/SR809, 12 November 1963, § 8; (15) Cuba: 27 UN Doc. A/C.6/SR.820, November 1963, § 22; UN Doc. A/C.6/SR.893, 8 December 1965, § 36; (16) Cyprus: UN Doc. A/C.6/SR.822, 29 November 1963, § 7; (17) Philippines: UN Doc. A/C.6/SR.823, 2 December 1963, § 4; (18) Mongolia: UN Doc. A/C.6/SR.935, 22 November 1966, § 24; (19) Ethiopia: UN Doc. A/C.6/SR.936, 22 November 1966, § 40.

[236] UN Doc. A/C.6/SR.411, § 15.

should bring its case before the Security Council, which was the proper agency to deal with such a situation,[237] a conviction that was shared by several other UN Members.[238] Indonesia noted that according to Jessup, 'under the terms of the Charter alarming military preparations by a neighbouring State justified an appeal to the Security Council, but the threatened State was not entitled to use force in anticipation of an attack'.[239] It was also pointed out that a threatened State should – where appropriate – have recourse to peaceful means of dispute settlement and could in addition take appropriate preparatory measures short of use of force.[240] In order to illustrate the danger of anticipatory self-defence, a number of States recalled that both Japan and Germany had invoked this idea to justify their aggressive conduct in the run-up to the Second World War.[241] Noting that international law required that defensive action be commensurate with the nature of the attack, Czechoslovakia observed that the resort to armed force would be an exaggerated measure of defence to take against a mere threat.[242] Finally, various countries rejected the arguments raised by the Dutch delegation, viz. the recognition of anticipatory self-defence by the Nuremberg and Tokyo Tribunals, and the alleged incompatibility of the requirement of a prior armed attack with the advent of the atomic age.[243]

4.1.3.b   Final negotiations on the Definition of Aggression (1968–74)

After the creation of the Fourth Special Committee on the Question of Defining Aggression in 1968, the debate continued, both within the Special Committee itself and in the UNGA Sixth Committee. As discussed earlier (see *infra* Section 3.2.2.a), the sponsors of the Six-Power draft opposed the automatic application of the 'priority' principle and instead emphasized the relevance of 'intent'. In their view, it was fallacious to presume that it

---

[237] UN Doc. A/C.6/SR.405, § 5.
[238] E.g., UN Doc. A/C.6/SR.517, § 7 (Syria); UN Doc. A/C.6/SR.805 (Ceylon); UN Doc. A/C.6/SR.822 (Cyprus).
[239] UN Doc. A/C.6/SR.809, § 8.
[240] E.g., UN Doc. A/C.6/SR.418, § 44 (Czechoslovakia); UN Doc. A/C.6/SR.419, § 2 (USSR); UN Doc. A/C.6/SR.517, § 21 (Syria); UN Doc. A/C.6/SR.823, § 4 (Philippines).
[241] E.g., UN Doc. A/C.6/SR.405, § 3 (Iran); UN Doc. A/C.6/SR.413, § 10 (Czechoslovakia); UN Doc. A/C.6/SR.415, § 24 (Poland); UN Doc. A/C.6/SR.820, § 22 (Cuba).
[242] UN Doc. A/C.6/SR.413, § 11.
[243] UN Doc. A/C.6/SR.411, § 16 (Belarus); UN Doc. A/C.6/SR.415, §§ 41–2 (Mexico); UN Doc. A/C.6/SR.419, § 3 (USSR); UN Doc. A/C.6/SR.524, §§ 41–2 (Czechoslovakia); UN Doc. A/C.6/SR.528, § 15 (Belarus).

would always be feasible to determine objectively who was the first to resort to force. Furthermore, an automatic application of the priority principle could lead to manifestly unjust results, for example in cases where force had been used by mistake or by accident. Finally, it was suggested that the discretionary power of the Security Council to identify the aggressor should not be diminished. On the other hand, the Soviet Union and several developing countries maintained that the 'first use' constituted the only objective criterion and warned that the intent criterion opened the door to abuse by allowing aggressor States to invoke some alleged noble motive to justify their actions. Eventually, a compromise was reached along the following lines: (1) the first use of force established a prima facie presumption of aggression; (2) exceptionally, this presumption could be rebutted by proving a lack of 'intent' on the part of the alleged aggressor; (3) this situation primarily concerned exceptional cases where force had been used as a result of error or mistake – 'intent' should not be confused with the 'motive' or 'purpose' of the State; and (4) the 'intent' criterion was particularly relevant vis-à-vis small-scale uses of force.[244]

What is remarkable for present purposes is that while several States explicitly praised the 'priority' standard as a safeguard against 'preemptive strikes' and 'preventive war',[245] those opposing it generally refrained from pronouncing on the admissibility of anticipatory action. Indeed, when citing examples of situations where there would be a lack of aggressive intent, they referred *inter alia* to border incidents caused by the unauthorized pursuit of criminals across a frontier,[246] but not to interventions undertaken in response to threats of attack.

Does this mean that support for anticipatory self-defence was non-existent throughout the debates? On the one hand, a number of States recognized the existence of two divergent interpretations of Article 51 UN Charter (viz. the restrictionist and the counter-restrictionist

---

[244] See especially: UN Doc. A/AC.134/SR.67–78, 21–3 (US), 29–31 (USSR), 35–7 (France), 37–9 (Italy), 40 (Cyprus), 41 (UAR), 41 (US); UN Doc. A/AC.134/SR.79–91, 7 June 1971, 14–15 (DRC), 15 (Guyana), 27 (Cyprus), 36 (USSR), 96–8 (Cyprus). Also: *supra*, Section 3.2.2.a.

[245] E.g., UN Doc. A/AC.134/SR.52–66, 46 (Bulgaria: 'The illegality of preventive war could only be postulated on the basis of the principle that an act of self-defence was a reply to an act of armed aggression, that was to say, on the principle of priority. That was the method adopted in Article 51 of the Charter to determine self-defence; the same method should be used in defining aggression.'), 79 (Iraq), 135 (Ghana), 136 (UAR); UN Doc. A/AC.134/SR.67–78, 8 (Iraq), 9 (USSR); UN Doc. A/AC.134/SR.79–91, 39 (Syria), 55–6 (Algeria).

[246] E.g., UN Doc. A/AC.134/SR.67–78, 20–1 (Canada), 21–3 (US), 31 (USSR), 31 (US), 44 (Italy), 118 (Romania).

reading),[247] with some of them actually subscribing to the view that Article 51 does not impair pre-existing custom.[248] On the other hand, explicit support for anticipatory self-defence is remarkably hard to find. Within the Fourth Special Committee, the UK was virtually the only country to hold that self-defence might be exercised in the event of a 'real danger' of armed attack.[249] Similarly, before the Sixth Committee only a handful of States – including Israel,[250] Austria[251] and Guatemala[252] – defended this position. Pakistan in principle ruled out anticipatory action, but conceded by way of exception that, because of their devastating impact, 'the threat of the use of [nuclear] weapons would entitle the intended victim to the full exercise of the right of self-defence'.[253] Several States raised the question, but simply left it unanswered.[254] A broad

---

[247] E.g., UN Doc. A/AC.134/SR.52-66, 167-8 (Norway, observing that two interpretations of Article 51 are possible and that neither the Security Council nor the General Assembly have so far cut the Gordian Knot); UN Doc. A/AC.134/SR.67-78, 19 (France); UN Doc. A/C.6/SR.1077, 22 November 1968, § 4 (Jamaica); UN Doc. A/C.6/SR.1208, 27 October 1970, § 43 (Norway).

[248] E.g., UN Doc. A/AC.134/SR.67-78, 6 (UK), 8-9 (Australia), 14 (Ghana), 116-17 (UK); UN Doc. A/AC.134/SR.79-91, 50-1 (UK). Remark: elsewhere, Ghana seemed to reject anticipatory self-defence. See UN Doc. A/C.6/SR.1169, 3 December 1969, § 52.

[249] UN Doc. A/AC.134/SR.52-66, 167 *juncto* UN Doc. A/AC.134/SR.67-78, 59-60, 116-17.

[250] UN Doc. A/C.6/SR.1170, 4 December 1969, § 2: '[W]hen the territorial integrity or political independence of a State was endangered by threats or acts of aggression, appropriate measures of self-defence were admissible.'

[251] UN Doc. A/C.6/SR.1472, 9 October 1974, § 32: '[T]here might ... be cases where the aggressive intent of a State was manifest. For example, if a State concentrated increasing numbers of troops at the border of another State, the menaced State could, under general international law and under the Charter, exercise its inherent right of individual and collective self-defence. If, in such situation, the menaced State fired the first shot, the Security Council could "in light of other relevant circumstances" qualify the menacing State, on the basis of sufficient evidence, as the aggressor and recognize the right of self-defence of the menaced State.'

[252] UN Doc. A/C.6/SR.1479, 18 October 1974, § 23: '[A] State threatened by aggression could not be asked patiently to await the first blow before reacting, as was its right. Article 51 of the Charter contained rules on that subject, and, since the principle of self-defence was somewhat delicate, it was understandable that it had been difficult to specify the limits of its application in the draft definition.'

[253] UN Doc. A/C.6/SR.1080, 25 November 1968, § 70. See also: UN Doc. A/C.6/SR.1207, 27 October 1970, § 20; UN Doc. A/C.6/SR.1347, 1 November 1972, § 6.

[254] E.g., UN Doc. A/AC.134/SR.52-66, 27 (Canada); UN Doc. A/C.6/SR.1077, § 4 (Jamaica); UN Doc. A/C.6/SR.1208, § 43 (Norway); UN Doc. A/C.6/SR.1351, 6 November 1972, § 1 (Belgium, wondering 'what should be done in a state of extreme emergency, when a State was planning but had not yet committed armed aggression and what the Americans would have done, at the time of the attack on Pearl Harbor, if they had known of the Japanese plans.'). Also UN Doc. A/AC.134/SR.67-78, 55 (US), 59 (Canada).

majority, however, stressed that only an armed attack justified the exercise of the right of self-defence. A provision to this end was incorporated in the Thirteen-Power draft.[255] Express statements were submitted by numerous delegations from the socialist bloc, from developing countries, but also from European States.[256] Sweden, for instance, supported a strict

---

[255] Article 3, UN Doc. A/AC.134/L.16 (and Corr. 1).
[256] Examples are: Algeria (UN Doc. A/AC.134/SR.79-91, 55-6); Bulgaria (UN Doc. A/AC.134/SR.52-66, 46); Chile (UN Doc. A/C.6/SR.1167, 3 December 1969, § 11); the Congo (Brazzaville) (UN Doc. A/C.6/SR.1169, 3 December 1969, § 84); Cuba (UN Doc. A/C.6/SR.1076, 21 November 1968, § 8; UN Doc. A/C.6/SR.1091, 10 December 1968, § 41; UN Doc. A/C.6/SR.1206, 26 October 1970, § 70; UN Doc. A/C.6/SR.1273, 2 November 1971, § 32; UN Doc. A/C.6/SR.1349, 3 November 1972, § 28; UN Doc. A/C.6/SR.1441, 19 November 1973, § 30; UN Doc. A/C.6/SR.1479, 18 October 1974, § 41); Cyprus (UN Doc. A/AC.134/SR.52-66, 90, 118-19; UN Doc. A/AC.134/SR.52-66, 17; UN Doc. A/AC.134/SR.79-91, 12, 27, 71, 82-3); Czechoslovakia (UN Doc. A/C.6/SR.1086, 4 December 1968, § 30); Dahomey (UN Doc. A/C.6/SR.1075, 20 November 1968, § 33); Ecuador (UN Doc. A/AC.134/SR.52-66, 53-5; UN Doc. A/AC.134/SR.52-66, 12); Egypt (UN Doc. A/C.6/SR.1269, 27 October 1971, § 17); Finland (UN Doc. A/AC.134/SR.52-66, 168); France (UN Doc. A/C.6/SR.1166, 2 December 1969, § 3); Gabon (UN Doc. A/AC.134/SR.1205, 22 October 1970, § 36); Ghana (UN Doc. A/C.6/SR.1169, § 52); Guyana (UN Doc. A/AC.134/SR.52-66, 126); Iraq (UN Doc. A/AC.134/SR.52-66, 79; UN Doc. A/AC.134/SR.67-78, 7-8; UN Doc. A/AC.134/SR.79-91, 76; UN Doc. A/C.6/SR.1167, § 16; UN Doc. A/C.6/SR.1202, 16 October 1970, § 19; UN Doc. A/C.6/SR.1271, 1 November 1971, § 22; UN Doc. A/C.6/SR.1348, 2 November 1972, § 12); Italy (UN Doc. A/AC.134/SR.25-51, 27 March 1969, 203; UN Doc. A/AC.134/SR.67-78, 55); Jordan (UN Doc. A/C.6/SR.1271, § 14); Kenya (UN Doc. A/C.6/SR.1350, 3 November 1972, § 32); Lebanon (UN Doc. A/C.6/SR.1212, 30 October 1970, § 28); Mexico (UN Doc. A/C.6/SR.1075, § 24; UN Doc. A/C.6/SR.1095, 13 December 1968, § 36; UN Doc. A/C.6/SR.1165, 2 December 1969, § 35; UN Doc. A/C.6/SR.1276, 4 November 1971, § 34; UN Doc. A/AC.134/SR.100-9, 29); Mongolia (UN Doc. A/C.6/SR.1169, § 4; UN Doc. A/C.6/SR.1274, 3 November 1971, § 37); Nigeria (UN Doc. A/C.6/SR.1351, 6 November 1972, § 20); Romania (UN Doc. A/AC.134/SR.52-66, 146-7; UN Doc. A/AC.134/SR.79-91, 79; UN Doc. A/C.6/SR.1349, § 52; UN Doc. A/C.6/SR.1475, § 5); USSR (UN Doc. A/AC.134/SR.52-66, 134; UN Doc. A/AC.134/SR.52-66, 9 ('The representatives who had sought to justify preventive self-defence had been simply criticizing the Charter, which in no way countenanced such a possibility.... As a major Power, the Soviet Union could with advantage have supported such an interpretation, but it did not want to place its own interests before those of the members of the international community as a whole'; UN Doc. A/AC.134/SR.79-91, 35; UN Doc. A/C.6/SR.1272, 2 November 1971, § 8); Sri Lanka (UN Doc. A/C.6/SR.1478, 16 October 1974, § 56); Sudan (UN Doc. A/AC.134/SR.52-66, 168; UN Doc. A/C.6/SR.1078, 22 November 1968, § 2); Sweden (UN Doc. A/C.6/SR.1079, 25 November 1968, § 6); Syria (UN Doc. A/AC.134/SR.67-78, 57-8; UN Doc. A/AC.134/SR.79-91, 39; UN Doc. A/AC.134/SR.100-9, 37); UAR (UN Doc. A/AC.134/SR.52-66, 110, 136; UN Doc. A/C.6/SR.1164, 1 December 1969, §§ 2-4 (referring to the Six Day War); Uruguay (UN Doc. A/AC.134/SR.52-66, 117; UN Doc. A/AC.134/SR.67-78, 112-13; UN Doc. A/AC.134/SR.79-91, 55; UN Doc. A/AC.134/SR.92-9, 31); Yugoslavia (UN Doc. A/C.6/SR.1167, § 25). See also for Pakistan: *supra* note 253.

interpretation of the right of self-defence and stated that '[a]ggressive attitudes or propensities could not be assimilated to armed attack, and could not give rise to a right of armed self-defence'.[257] Spain agreed that 'only when a country has first been attacked could it exercise its legitimate right of self-defence under Article 51. Any possibility of legalizing preventive war was out of the question'.[258] Mexico keenly pointed out that Article 51 UN Charter had 'completely replaced everything which had existed on the subject ... before the San Francisco Conference',[259] and stressed that: 'If a State was aware of the aggressive intent of another State, it should address itself to the Security Council and refrain from acting on its own behalf'.[260]

In the end, throughout the negotiations on the Definition of Aggression, a clear majority of States voiced its opposition to the doctrine of anticipatory action. While, at the early stages, a number of (Western) delegations tried to convince their colleagues that certain exceptions were needed to protect States from 'imminent' threats, it appears that these calls gradually became rarer and more muted. On the other hand, it is conceded that apart from the debates in the early fifties, no genuine attempt was made to determine at what moment an 'armed attack' could be said to commence or to have an in-depth discussion on the (non)-admissibility of anticipatory self-defence. Instead, as the talks evolved, most States stuck to broad denunciations of 'preventive war' and general assertions that Article 51 presupposed the occurrence of an 'armed attack'. In this context, it may be observed that in 1954, the positions of Belgium, Chile and the Soviet Union (cf. *supra*) were not that far apart. One might therefore wonder whether the picture would have looked different if a more nuanced debate had been attempted within the Fourth Special Committee. Still, considering the fact that the latter Committee was established only six months after the Six Day War, it cannot be assumed that its thirty-five Members were unaware of the dilemma. Rather, the cited positions must be taken to reflect if not the majority's opposition to anticipatory action, then at least a widespread reluctance to establish a new precedent.

As a result, the overall conclusion must be that the Definition of Aggression and its preparatory works do not render support to the legality of anticipatory self-defence.[261] The general definition of Article 1

---

[257] UN Doc. A/C.6/SR.1079, § 6. [258] UN Doc. A/AC.134/SR.1–24, 14 June 1968, 101.
[259] UN Doc. A/C.6/SR.1075, § 24. [260] UN Doc. A/AC.134/SR.100–9, 29.
[261] See e.g., Christakis, 'La notion de guerre préventive', pp. 22–3 ; Corten, *Le droit contre la guerre*, pp. 641–2; Sicilianos, *Des contre-mesures à la légitime défense*, pp. 399–400.

refers to the 'use of armed force' only: a mere threat of force was not considered sufficient.[262] Article 2 creates a presumption that the first use of force shall prima facie be held to constitute aggression. Article 5(1) adds that 'no consideration of whatever nature, whether political, economic, *military* or otherwise, may serve as a justification for aggression'. Moreover, the *travaux* indicate that the disclaimer regarding 'other relevant circumstances' in Article 2 mainly concerned minor incidents, and attacks by error or accident. Concerns that the phrase 'first use of armed force ... *in contravention of the Charter*' (emphasis added) provided a loophole were removed when France declared that States should not be judges in their own cause and that it was solely for the Security Council to apply the proviso.[263]

4.1.3.c Other materials

Apart from the *travaux* of the Definition of Aggression, there is little in terms of abstract customary evidence regarding the *ratione temporis* aspect of the 'armed attack' requirement. Occasionally States have called for clarification of the matter[264] or have insisted that self-defence could be used 'only and exclusively in cases where an armed attack occurred'.[265] By contrast, those States which had earlier expressed sympathy for the doctrine of anticipatory self-defence steered clear from stirring up the debate and carefully refrained from publicly supporting it.[266]

In 1980, the issue was raised, albeit indirectly, in the course of the UNGA debate on the ILC Draft Articles on State Responsibility. *In casu*, Special Rapporteur Ago suggested that a provision be included according to which the international wrongfulness of an act of a State should be precluded 'if the State committed the act in order to defend itself or another State against armed attack as provided for in Article 51 of the [UN] Charter'.[267] Ago recognized that this provision reflected his preference for the 'restictionist' school of thought, which, he asserted,

---

[262] E.g., Broms, 'The definition of aggression', 342; Ferencz, *Defining international aggression*, p. 29.
[263] Broms, 'The definition of aggression', 363–5; Ferencz, *Defining international aggression*, p. 32.
[264] E.g., UN Doc. A/C.6/32/SR.65, 7 December 1977, § 6 (Mexico); UN Doc. A/C.6/34/SR.22, 19 October 1979, § 51 (Lebanon).
[265] E.g., UN Doc. A/C.6/35/SR.30, 27 October 1980, § 72 (Yugoslavia); UN Doc. A/C.6/31/SR.51, 23 November 1976, § 41.
[266] See Corten, *Le droit contre la guerre*, p. 640 ; Gray, *The use of force*, p. 160.
[267] Ago, 'Addendum', 70.

constituted the majority view among international lawyers.[268] According to Ago, adherents of the opposite school of thought were 'misled by an outmoded and incorrect use of the concept of self-defence that involved something more than self-defence'.[269] In the subsequent debate within the ILC, it was decided that the Commission had no mandate to interpret the primary rules relating to self-defence and should make no choice between the two schools of thought.[270] As a result, the specific reference to Article 51 UN Charter was omitted and draft Article 34 was rephrased as follows: 'The wrongfulness of an act of a State not in conformity with an international obligation of that State is precluded if the act constitutes a lawful measure of self-defence taken in conformity with the [UN] Charter.'[271] At the same time, the ILC commentary to the article acknowledges that a majority of writers reject the pre-existing custom paradigm and that a number of ILC members had preferred an explicit reference to Article 51.[272]

Before the UNGA Sixth Committee, many countries expressed satisfaction at the ILC draft article, since the Commission had to refrain from departing from the framework of State responsibility and could therefore not be expected to elaborate primary rules pertaining to self-defence.[273] Others believed that the Commission had better followed the reasoning of the Special Rapporteur and inserted an explicit reference to Article 51.[274] Arguably, the statements of the US and the UK

---

[268] Ibid., 63–8. See also Ago's statement at (1980-I) 32 YBILC 184–8.
[269] (1980-I) 32 YBILC 187.   [270] Ibid., 188–94, 220–3, 227–31, 271–2.
[271] Report of the ILC on the work of its 32nd Session, 5 May–25 July 1980, UN Doc. A/35/10, 52–61. According to the Report, the words 'in conformity with...' 'get round the problems of interpretation that might arise from a reference solely to Article 51 of the Charter and general international law, or to general international law alone'.
[272] Ibid., 60.
[273] E.g., UN Docs. A/C.6/35/SR.44–59, 11–24 November 1980; UN Doc. A/C.6/35/SR.44, § 30 (Netherlands); UN Doc. A/C.6/35/SR.45, § 9 (Federal Republic of Germany); UN Doc. A/C.6/35/SR.48, § 33 (Japan), § 51 (Finland); UN Doc. A/C.6/35/SR.49, §§ 6–9 (Sri Lanka), § 36 (Italy); UN Doc. A/C.6/35/SR.50, § 26 (Argentina: 'The international community should perhaps one day undertake to define the term "self-defence" more clearly. That task was beyond the mandate of the Commission, which had taken a realistic approach to the topic.'); UN Doc. A/C.6/35/SR.51, § 46 (Ethiopia), § 62 (Iraq).
[274] E.g., UN Doc. A/C.6/35/SR.47, § 24–5 (Brazil); UN Doc. A/C.6/35/SR.48, § 23 (Mexico); UN Doc. A/C.6/35/SR.49, § 16 (German Democratic Republic), § 28 (Kuwait); UN Doc. A/C.6/35/SR.50, § 4 (Romania); UN Doc. A/C.6/35/SR.52, § 63 (USSR); UN Doc. A/C.6/35/SR.53, § 51 (Jamaica); UN Doc. A/C.6/35/SR.54, §§ 32–3 (India); UN Doc. A/C.6/35/SR.57, § 42 (Belarus); UN Doc. A/C.6/35/SR.59, § 14 (Bulgaria), § 31 (Yugoslavia). See also (1981) 33 YBILC Vol. II, Part One, 76 (Mongolia); (1982) 34 YBILC Vol. II, Part One, 18 (Belarus), 19 (USSR).

THE 'ARMED ATTACK' REQUIREMENT *RATIONE TEMPORIS* 305

reveal implicit sympathy for the 'pre-existing' custom paradigm.[275] Still, these veiled statements hardly offer convincing evidence in support of anticipatory self-defence.[276] Only Israel claimed that self-defence was not solely linked to cases of armed attack.[277] This position was expressly contradicted by Romania, Mongolia, Trinidad and Tobago, Libya, Poland, Brazil and the German Democratic Republic.[278] In the end, abstract customary evidence generally confirms our conclusion that prior to 2001 customary practice did not accept the admissibility of unilateral use of force in response to threats of armed attack.

4.2 The shockwaves of 9/11

4.2.1 *The 2002 US National Security Strategy and the intervention in Iraq in 2003*

4.2.1.a Back to the drawing board: the 2002 US National Security Strategy

Then came the attacks of 9/11. At 8:46 am on Tuesday, 11 September 2001, a hijacked American Airlines passenger plane crashed into the

---

[275] UN Doc. A/C.6/35/SR.51, § 4 (US: '[D]raft article 34 was properly formulated, so long as it was understood that the words "in conformity" referred to the inherent nature of the right provided for in Article 51 of the Charter.'); § 11 (UK: 'The [UK] delegation had on many occasions made clear its views concerning ... the relationship between Article 51 and customary international law; ... the [ILC] had been well-advised not to seek to define the concept of self-defence'). Also: UN Doc. A/C.6/35/SR.52, § 36 (Greece). Possibly also: (1982) 34 YBILC Vol. II, Part One, 20 (Venezuela); UN Doc. A/CN.4/515, 19 March 2001, 31 (Japan). By contrast: UN Doc. A/C.6/35/SR.50, § 43 (France: '[T]he drafting of the article was acceptable, in that the commentary referred to its conformity not with customary law but with the [UN] Charter ...'). But: UN Doc. A/CN.4/488, 25 March 1998, 89 (France: 'The draft article illustrates a too restrictive approach to self-defence. Instead of "taken in conformity with the [UN] Charter", it would be preferable to say "in conformity with international law"').

[276] Also Cassese, 'Article 51', p. 1339; Gray, *The use of force*, p. 160.

[277] UN Doc. A/C.6/35/SR.50, § 15.

[278] UN Doc. A/C.6/35/SR.50, § 4 (Romania); UN Doc. A/C.6/35/SR.53, § 30 (Mongolia: '[P]reventive self-defence or preventive strike was inadmissible *de lege lata*'); UN Doc. A/C.6/35/SR.56, § 26 (Trinidad and Tobago); UN Doc. A/C.6/35/SR.57, § 35 (Libya); UN Doc. A/C.6/35/SR.58 (Poland); UN Doc. A/C.6/35/SR.47, § 24 (Brazil); UN Doc. A/C.6/35/SR.49, § 16 (German Democratic Republic).

Remark: the final version of the draft articles, adopted in 2001, still refers to 'a lawful measure of self-defence taken in conformity with the Charter of the United Nations.' ILC, *Commentary on the Draft Articles*, p. 74. The first paragraph of the Commentary contains a reference to Article 51 UN Charter.

northern tower of the World Trade Center in New York.[279] Within less than two hours, three other planes crashed: United Airlines Flight 175 hit the southern tower of the World Trade Center; American Airlines Flight 77 hit the Pentagon building in Washington DC, finally, United Airlines Flight 93 went down in a field outside Pittsburgh while passengers undertook an ultimate attempt to overwhelm the hijackers. Almost 3,000 American and foreign nationals lost their lives.[280] As millions around the globe witnessed in horror and disbelief the images of the collapsing towers, it began to dawn that the brief interlude of the post-Cold War period was over and that a new era had started.

In a rare gesture of solidarity, the international community rallied behind the United States as the Bush Administration prepared a military response to the most devastating attack against it since 1941. On 7 October 2001, the US, together with the UK, launched a military intervention against the Al Qaeda terrorist group, as well as the Taleban, the de facto Afghan regime that had cooperated with Al Qaeda and granted it a safe haven. The operation received widespread approval, including from the UN Security Council, the OAS and NATO.[281]

As Operation 'Enduring Freedom' went on, people within the Bush Administration and the Pentagon insisted that the US look beyond the Afghan situation and draw broader lessons from the 9/11 attacks. In their view, what was needed was a fundamental reassessment of the threats facing the US and an adaptation of old security doctrines in order to enable the US effectively to cope with a changed international security environment. The *avant-première* of what would become known as the 'Bush doctrine' was enacted on 1 June 2002, when President Bush gave his famous speech at the West Point Academy in New York.[282] On 17 September 2002, the White House promulgated the 2002 National Security Strategy of the United States of America (hereafter: 'NSS').[283]

---

[279] See: 'The 9/11 Commission Report', 22 July 2004, available at www.9-11commission.gov/report/911Report.pdf (accessed 11 May 2009).
[280] See 'U.S. deaths in Iraq, war on terror surpass 9/11 toll', *CNN* 3 September 2006.
[281] See *inter alia* (2001) UNYB 65-6; Secretary-General Lord Robertson, Statement of 2 October 2001, reprinted in (2001) 41 ILM 1267; Terrorist Threat to the Americas, Res. 1, 24th meeting of Consultation of Ministers of Foreign Affairs, 21 September 2001, OAS Doc. OEA/Ser.F/II.24/RC.24/RES.1/01, reprinted in (2001) 40 ILM 1270.
[282] White House Press Release, 'President Bush delivers graduation speech at West Point', 1 June 2002, available at http://georgewbush-whitehouse.archives.gov/news/releases/2002/06/20020601-3.html (accessed 11 May 2009).
[283] US National Security Strategy.

The covering letter of the NSS already reveals much of what the reader can expect. It finds that government's task of defending the nation against its enemies has changed dramatically: 'Enemies in the past needed great armies and great industrial capabilities to endanger America. Now, shadowy networks of individuals can bring great chaos and suffering to our shores for less than it costs to purchase a single tank. Terrorists ... turn the power of modern technologies against us'.[284] The letter goes on to state that: 'The gravest danger of our Nation lies at the crossroads of radicalism and technology. Our enemies have openly declared that they are seeking weapons of mass destruction, and evidence indicates that they are doing so with determination. The [US] will not allow these efforts to succeed. ... *America will act against such emerging threats before they are fully formed*.'[285]

These brief excerpts illustrate the twofold scope of the NSS as a project to reassess both the threats to US security and the means to tackle them. As regards the first aspect, the doctrine determines that the model of inter-State conventional warfare has become outdated. Instead, 'new' twenty-first century security threats have emerged, most notably trans-national terrorism, proliferation of weapons of mass destruction and 'rogue States'.[286] The ultimate doom scenario would consist in a terrorist group obtaining a nuclear device and smuggling it into US territory. The NSS analysis of the changed international security environment strongly influenced the adoption of related doctrines and declarations in various quarters of the world, such as NATO's Prague Summit Declaration (2002),[287] the OSCE Strategy to Address Threats to Security and Stability in the Twenty-First Century (2003),[288] the European Security Strategy (2003),[289] the African Union's Solemn Declaration on a Common African Defence and Security Policy (2004),[290] as well as the report of the UN High-Level

---

[284] *Ibid.*, covering letter, § 3.   [285] *Ibid.*, covering letter, § 5 (emphasis added).
[286] See *ibid.*, 13–16.
[287] North Atlantic Council, 'Prague Summit Declaration', Prague, 21 November 2002, NATO Press Release (2002) 127, available at www.nato.int/docu/pr/2002/p02-127e.htm (accessed 11 May 2009).
[288] OSCE Ministerial Council, OSCE Strategy to address Threats to Security and Stability in the Twenty-First Century, Maastricht, 1–2 December 2003, available at www.osce.org/documents/mcs/2003/12/4175_en.pdf (accessed 11 May 2009).
[289] European Security Strategy, 'A Secure Europe in a Better World', approved by the European Council on 12 December 2003, available at http://consilium.europa.eu/uedocs/cmsUpload/78367.pdf (accessed 11 May 2009).
[290] 'Solemn Declaration on a Common African Defence and Security Policy', 2nd Extraordinary session of the African Union, Sirte, 28 February 2004, available at www.africa-union.org/News_Events/2ND%20EX%20ASSEMBLY/Declaration%20on%20a%20Comm.Af%20Def%20Sec.pdf (accessed 11 May 2009).

Panel on Threats, Challenges and Change (2004),[291] and the follow-up report 'In Larger Freedom" of UN Secretary-General Kofi Annan (2005).[292] At the same time, substantial divergences exist in the ways the doctrines 'prioritize' the various 'old' and 'new' threats, and in the extent to which they recognize the interrelatedness of security, economic development and respect for human rights.

The second and most interesting aspect of the National Security Strategy concerns the proposed means to tackle the threats identified. Indeed, the Strategy amongst others sets forth a new model of unilateral military action, which directly challenges the Charter rules on the use of force and which constitutes the essence of the 'Bush doctrine.' The NSS finds that because of the motivations of terrorist organizations and rogue States, deterrence is of no avail; that weapons of mass destruction have become 'weapons of choice' rather than 'weapons of last resort', and that modern technology and improved mobility has considerably increased the destructive potential of these actors.[293] In sum, given 'the inability to deter a potential attacker, the immediacy of today's threats, and the magnitude of potential harm', the reactive posture of the past is no longer appropriate. The NSS challenges the *Ius ad Bellum* framework in a twofold manner. A first challenge implicitly flows from the declaration that: 'We make no distinction between terrorists and those who knowingly harbor or provide aid to them.'[294] This statement is more specifically related to the *'ratione personae'* aspect of the 'armed attack' and will be examined in Chapter 5. The NSS also speaks out on the *'ratione temporis'* dimension. The relevant passages merit being restated in full:

> For centuries, international law recognized that nations need not suffer an attack before they can lawfully take action to defend themselves against forces that present an imminent danger of attack. Legal scholars and international jurists often conditioned the legitimacy of preemption on the existence of an imminent threat – most often a visible mobilization of armies, navies, and air forces preparing to attack.
>
> We must adapt the concept of imminent threat to the capabilities and objectives of today's adversaries . . .

---

[291] Report of the Secretary-General's High-Level Panel on Threats, Challenges and Change, 'A More Secure World: Our Shared Responsibility', 1 December 2004, UN Doc. A/59/565.
[292] UN Secretary-General Kofi Annan, 'In Larger Freedom: Towards Development, Security and Human Rights for All', 21 March 2005, UN Doc. A/59/2005.
[293] US National Security Strategy, 15. [294] *Ibid.*, 5.

The United States had long maintained the option of preemptive actions to counter a sufficient threat to our national security. The greater the threat ... the more compelling the case for taking anticipatory action to defend ourselves, even if uncertainty remains as to the time and place of the enemy's attack. To forestall or prevent such hostile acts ..., the United States will, if necessary, act preemptively.

The United States will not use force in all cases to preempt emerging threats, nor should nations use preemption as a pretext for aggression. Yet in an age where the enemies of civilization openly and actively seek the world's most destructive technologies, the United States cannot remain idle while dangers gather.[295]

Two elements are particularly striking. The first is the explicitness of the endorsement of anticipatory self-defence. Even if the NSS itself claims that the US has long supported this doctrine, this is only a half-truth. It is correct that the US has on occasion expressed implicit support for the doctrine within the UN bodies.[296] Similarly, it is true that previous US administrations have occasionally used bold language in past security doctrines.[297] On the other hand, as our overview of customary evidence indicates, the US has traditionally refrained from expressing explicit support for anticipatory self-defence, let alone from attempting to convince other States to endorse the concept. Within UN bodies, the US has shown itself much less of a defender of anticipatory self-defence than, say, the UK, or, in the early days, Belgium and the Netherlands. Furthermore, even if the US has hinted at the possibility of 'pre-emption' (especially in the context of nuclear warfare) in the past, it did so in broad politico-military terms. This contrasts starkly with the NSS's unequivocal attempt to present the admissibility of pre-emptive self-defence as a legal *fait accompli*, which has 'for centuries' been recognized in international law. In doing so, the NSS not only offers an inaccurate depiction of the US's own posture, but also completely disregards the long-standing academic controversy on the matter and the lack of supporting practice.

Yet the most alarming aspect of the NSS is that it broadens the doctrine of anticipatory self-defence beyond the traditional parameters of the Webster formula. It holds that the requirement of an 'imminent

---

[295] *Ibid.*, 15.
[296] E.g., UN Doc. A/C.6/35/SR.51, § 4 (apparently supporting the 'pre-existing custom' paradigm).
[297] White House, 'A National Security Strategy for a New Century', October 1998, available at http://clinton2.nara.gov/WH/EOP/NSC/html/documents/nssr.pdf (accessed 11 May 2009), 2 (stating that the US 'must always be prepared to act alone when that is [its] most advantageous course'). See also *supra* note 29.

threat' must be adapted to the 'capabilities and objectives of today's adversaries', and that anticipatory action may be needed 'even if uncertainty remains as to the time and place of the enemy's attack'. In other words, even if the NSS alludes to 'pre-emptive' self-defence, it could more accurately be described as an endorsement of 'preventive' self-defence vis-à-vis 'non-imminent' threats, which must be prevented from emerging. By so doing, the NSS approves a doctrine which the US deliberately avoided during the 1962 Cuban missile crisis; which has obtained virtually no support among international lawyers in the past; and which was universally rejected after the Osiraq incident in 1981. Despite the hollow reassurance that 'pre-emption should not be used as an excuse for aggression', it is no wonder then that the NSS attracted widespread academic attention.[298] Moreover, soon after the adoption of the NSS, it became clear that the 'Bush doctrine' was not intended to remain a paper tiger. Indeed, the ink had hardly dried when neo-conservatives in the Bush Administration began eyeing Baghdad. In the course of 2002, it grew increasingly probable that Iraq would become the test-case for the US's new doctrine of 'preventive' self-defence.

4.2.1.b The intervention in Iraq

4.2.1.b.i The road to Baghdad Starting in early 2002, US and UK officials began signalling their mounting discontent at Saddam Hussein's consistent failure to abide by the weapons inspections regime imposed in Security Council Resolution 687 (1991)[299] and hinted at the possibility of military action. Political rhetoric in Washington turned

---

[298] See *inter alia:* J.A. Cohan, 'The Bush doctrine and the emerging norm of anticipatory self-defense in customary international law', (2003) 15 Pace ILRev 283–358; C. Gray, 'The US National Security Strategy and the new "Bush doctrine" on preemptive self-defense', (2002) 1 Chinese JIL 437–47; C. Henderson, 'The Bush doctrine: from theory to practice', (2004) 9 *J.C.S.L.* 3–24; B. Langille, 'It's 'instant custom': how the Bush doctrine became law after the terrorist attacks of September 11, 2001', (2003) 26 Boston College ICLRev 145–56; W.P. Nagan and C. Hammer, 'The new Bush National Security doctrine and the rule of law', (2004) 22 Berkeley JIL 375–438; J. R. Paul, 'The Bush doctrine: making or breaking customary international law', (2004) 27 Hastings ICLRev 457–79; M. Pérez Gonzalez, 'La legítima defensa puesta en su sitio: observaciones críticas sobre la doctrina Bush de la acción preventia', (2003) 55 REDI 187–204; D. Rezac, 'President Bush's Security Strategy and its "pre-emptive strikes doctrine": a legal basis for the war in Iraq', (2004) 7 ARIEL 223–42; P. S. Sharma, 'The American doctrine of 'pre-emptive' self-defence', (2003) 43 Indian JIL 215–30.

[299] SC Res. 687 (1991) of 3 April 1991.

increasingly grim. In his State of the Union address, President Bush included Iraq in the so-called 'axis of evil':[300]

> Iraq continues to flaunt its hostility toward America and to support terror. The Iraqi regime has plotted to develop anthrax, and nerve gas, and nuclear weapons for over a decade. This is a regime that has already used poison gas to murder thousands of its own citizens ... This is a regime that agreed to international inspections – then kicked out the inspectors. This is a regime that has something to hide from the civilized world.

On 12 September 2002, President Bush elaborated the case against Iraq before the UN General Assembly. He drew attention to the grave human rights violations committed by the Hussein regime against its own population; claimed that Iraq continued to shelter and support terrorist organizations; and recalled that, despite repeated Security Council condemnations, it had been almost four years since UN inspectors last set foot in Iraq.[301] While stressing his country's willingness to work with the Security Council, the US President unequivocally warned that: 'The Security Council resolutions will be enforced ... or action will be unavoidable.'[302] Unsurprisingly, when five days later, the NSS was adopted (again branding Iraq as a 'rogue State'),[303] the new doctrine of 'preventive' self-defence was widely perceived to have been designed with Iraq in mind.[304]

The repeated warnings did not fall on deaf ears: faced with a build-up of forces in the Gulf, Iraq backed down and notified that it was prepared to allow the UN Monitoring, Verification and Inspections Commission (UNMOVIC) to operate in the country again.[305] Amidst indications that Iraq continued to obstruct the work of the weapons inspectors, the Council

---

[300] President Bush, State of the Union address, Washington, 29 January 2002, available at http://georgewbush-whitehouse.archives.gov/news/releases/2002/01/20020129-11.html (accessed 11 May 2009).
[301] President Bush, Remarks at the UN General Assembly, UN Doc. A/57/PV.2, 12 September 2002, 10.
[302] Ibid.   [303] US National Security Strategy, 14.
[304] Gray, 'The US National Security Strategy', 443.
[305] C. Greenwood, 'Legality of the use of force: Iraq in 2003', in M. Bothe, M. E. O'Connell and N. Ronzitti (eds.), *Redefining sovereignty: the use of force after the Cold War* (Ardsley, NY: Transnational Publishers, 2005), pp. 387–415, at 392. On 16 September, Iraq informed the UN that it had decided to allow the return of UN weapons inspectors (UN Doc. S/2002/1034), a move that was welcomed *inter alia* by the Non-Aligned Movement (S/2002/1108). A first UN team resumed arms inspections on 27 November. See (2002) UNYB 285–90.

on 8 November 2002 adopted reolution 1441.[306] This resolution afforded Iraq 'a final opportunity to comply with its disarmament obligations' (§2). To that end, it was ordered to submit a 'full and complete declaration' of all aspects of its WMD-related programmes, and to allow UNMOVIC and IAEA inspectors unrestricted access (§ 3). Failure to comply would be regarded as a 'material breach of Iraq's obligations' (§ 4) and would entail 'serious consequences' (§13). Upon receipt of a report by UNMOVIC and the IAEA examining Iraq's compliance (§ 11), the Council would immediately convene to consider the situation (§ 12).

In the debate following the adoption of resolution 1441, numerous Council Members stressed that the resolution contained no 'hidden triggers' and no 'automaticity' with respect to the use of force: if UNMOVIC and the IAEA were to find a 'material breach' of the resolution, the matter would again be brought before the Council.[307] The UK and US expressly subscribed to this view,[308] albeit that the US added that:

> If the Security Council fails to act decisively in the event of further Iraqi violations, this resolution does not constrain any Member State from acting to defend itself against the threat posed by Iraq or to enforce relevant United Nations resolutions and protect world peace and security.[309]

Notwithstanding the latter caveat, China, France and Russia issued a joint statement in which they expressed satisfaction with the declarations made by the UK and the US.[310] The League of Arab States asserted that the resolution did not constitute a basis for recourse to the use of military force against Iraq.[311]

Tension continued to mount in the first months of 2003, leading to one of the deepest crises in UN history.[312] Overall, UNMOVIC and the IAEA drew up a positive balance of Iraq's cooperation, although it was at times declared that compliance remained incomplete and that a number of allegations remained unaccounted for.[313] This led the US and the UK to raise the pressure on Iraq and on the Security Council. On 5 February,

---

[306] SC Res. 1441 (2002) of 8 November 2002.
[307] UN Doc. S/PV.1441, 8 November 2002, 7 (Mexico, Ireland), 9 (Bulgaria), 10 (Syria, Norway), 11 (Colombia, Cameroon), 13 (PRC).
[308] Ibid., 3 (US: 'this resolution contains no "hidden triggers" and no "automaticity" with respect to the use of force'), 4–5 (UK: 'There is no "automaticity" in this resolution.').
[309] Ibid., 3.   [310] UN Doc. S/2002/1236, 8 November 2002 (PRC, France, Russia).
[311] UN Doc. S/2002/1238, 11 November 2002 (League of Arab States).
[312] See (2003) UNYB 315–33.
[313] (2002) UNYB 288; (2003) UNYB 317–22, 323–4, 327, 330.

US Secretary of State Powell attended a meeting of the Security Council and presented 'solid intelligence' demonstrating that Iraq continued to defy the Council.[314] In turn, numerous countries insisted that the inspections regime was yielding results and should be pursued. Communiqués to this end were submitted *inter alia* by France, Germany, Russia, China, the African Union, the Non-Aligned Movement, the League of Arab States and the Islamic Conference.[315]

In March 2003, the US – pressured by its British ally – again turned to the Security Council. The result was a dramatic stand-off between the permanent members, with France, Russia and China refusing to adopt a resolution that would authorize the automatic use of force.[316] The UN Secretary-General warned that 'if the US and others were to go outside the Council and take military action it would not be in conformity with the Charter'.[317] Despite strong political protest and massive anti-war demonstrations drawing hundreds of thousands of protesters to the streets in cities around the globe,[318] preparations for a military intervention went ahead. On 18 March, the UN Secretary-General decided to withdraw all UN staff from Iraq in the light of the imminent outbreak of a large-scale military conflict.[319] On 20 March, the US, the UK and Australia informed the Security Council that they had initiated military action against Iraq.[320]

---

[314] UN Doc. S/PV.4701, 5 February 2003, 2–17.
[315] Communiqué of the Seventh Ordinary Session of the Central Organ of the Mechanism for Conflict Prevention, Management and Resolution of the African Union, Addis Ababa, 3 February 2003, Annex to UN Doc. S/2003/142; Letters from France, Germany and Russia, 10 and 24 February 2003, 5 March 2003, UN Doc. S/2003/164, UN Doc. S/2003/214 and UN Doc. S/2003/253; UN Doc. S/2003/238, 28 February 2003 (PRC and Russia); Declaration on the Outcome of the Work of the Fifteenth Regular Session of the Council of the League of Arab States, Sharm el Sheikh, 1 March 2003, Annex to UN Doc. S/2003/247; UN Doc. S/2003/329, 4 March 2003 (Malaysia, on behalf of the Non-Aligned Movement); Communiqué on Iraq adopted at the second emergency session of the Islamic Summit Conference, Doha, Annex to UN Doc. S/2003/288, 5 March 2003.
[316] (2003) UNYB 330–2.
[317] UN Secretary-General's press conference, The Hague, 10 March 2003, available at www.un.org/apps/sg/offthecuff.asp?nid=394 (accessed 11 May 2009).
[318] 'Millions join global anti-war protests', *BBC News* 17 February 2003: 'Between six and 10 million people are thought to have marched in up to 60 countries over the weekend ....'
[319] (2003) UNYB 316.
[320] UN Doc. S/2003/350, 20 March 2003 (UK); UN Doc. S/2003/351, 20 March 2003 (US); UN Doc. S/2003/352, 20 March 2003 (Australia).

4.2.1.b.ii Legal justifications and third-State reactions Does the intervention in Iraq constitute a precedent in favour of anticipatory self-defence? For this to be the case, we need (1) a 'reliance on a novel right' (2) 'shared in principle by other States'.[321] An overview of the relevant materials reveals that both elements are lacking.

First, as far as the justification for the intervention is concerned, a distinction must be made between the political and legal arguments brought forward. From the very beginning, the United States developed a threefold narrative. It relied on the persistent non-compliance with Security Council demands; it presented Iraq's alleged WMD programme and the regime's alleged links with terrorist groups as a threat to the security of the US and of Iraq's neighbours; and it argued that Saddam Hussein's human rights record necessitated a long overdue regime change. These different lines of reasoning can all be discerned in President Bush' address to the General Assembly, in Colin Powell's presentation to the Security Council and in the January 2003 State of the Union message.[322]

However, when we look at the intervening States' communications to the Security Council, only the first element was employed as the legal basis for the operation. More precisely, the US, the UK and Australia invoked the idea that Iraq had again committed a 'material breach' of ceasefire conditions imposed by resolution 687 (1991) in the aftermath of the 1990–1 Gulf War. The alleged implication was a restoration of the authorization to 'use all necessary means' enshrined in resolution 678 (1990)[323] – the same justification was used with regard to Operation 'Desert Fox' in 1998 (cf. *supra*). The letters from the UK and Australian UN representatives simply reiterated this argument without further explanation.[324] The US letter offers a slightly more elaborate restatement of this rationale.[325] Contrary to the UK and Australian letters, however, the final paragraph in general terms adds that:

> [The actions undertaken] are necessary steps to defend the United States and the international community from the threat posed by Iraq and to

---

[321] ICJ, *Nicaragua* case (Merits), § 207.
[322] UN Doc. A/57/PV.2, 10; UN Doc. S/PV.4701, 2–17; President Bush, State of the Union address, Washington, 28 January 2003, available at http://georgewbush-whitehouse.archives.gov/news/releases/2003/01/20030128-19.html (accessed 11 May 2003).
[323] SC Res. 678 (1990) of 29 November 1990.
[324] UN Doc. S/2003/350; UN Doc. S/2003/352.   [325] UN Doc. S/2003/351.

restore international peace and security in the area. Further delay would simply allow Iraq to continue its unlawful and threatening conduct.[326]

Both Australia and the UK developed the legal basis for the operation in a number of documents at the domestic level. The UK did so in a written answer by Attorney-General Lord Goldsmith to a parliamentary question on 17 March 2003, and in a memorandum of the same date to the Foreign Affairs Committee of the House of Commons.[327] The Australian authorities on 18 March issued a Memorandum of Advice on the Use of Force against Iraq.[328] Neither document contained any reference to preemptive or preventive self-defence.[329]

What then about the repeated allusions to the threat to US security, hinted at in the US letter and in other official US statements, such as the October 2002 Congressional authorization?[330] Does this imply a reliance on a separate legal basis, linked to the concept of self-defence? It appears not.[331] Indeed, the absence of an express reference to Article 51 or to the

---

[326] *Ibid.*   [327] Reprinted in (2003) 52 ICLQ 811–14, especially at 812.
[328] Reprinted in (2003) 4 Melbourne JIL 178–82.
[329] Remark: the Australian memorandum stated as follows: 'Given our view that authority for the use of force in Iraq ... is found in existing Security Council resolutions, it is not necessary to consider in this advice self-defence or other possible bases for the use of force', *ibid.*, 178.
[330] See UN Doc. S/2003/351. Also UN Doc. S/PV.1441, 3. On 6 March 2003, President Bush declared that: 'we really don't need the United Nations' approval ... When it comes to our security, we do not need anyone's permission.' See: White House Press Release, 'President George Bush discusses Iraq in national press conference', 6 March 2003, available at http://georgewbush-whitehouse.archives.gov/news/releases/2003/03/20030306-8.html (accessed 11 May 2009). See also the statement of 17 March: White House Press Release, 'President says Saddam Hussein must leave Iraq within 48 hours', 17 March 2003, available at http://georgewbush-whitehouse.archives.gov/news/releases/2003/03/20030317-7.html (accessed 11 May 2009).

Remark: the preamble of the Congressional Joint Resolution of 18 September 2001 authorizing the use of force against Iraq probably contains the most explicit reference to self-defence: 'Whereas Iraq's demonstrated capability and willingness to use weapons of mass destruction, the high risk that the current Iraqi regime will either employ those weapons to launch a surprise attack against the United States or its Armed Forces or provide them to international terrorists who would do so, and the extreme magnitude of harm that would result to the United States and its citizens from such attack, combine to justify action by the United States to defend itself ...'. Reprinted in (2002) 40 ILM 1282.
[331] Most scholars accept that the US chose not to rely on the right of self-defence. E.g., M. Bothe, 'Has Article 2(4) survived the Iraq war?', in Bothe *et al.* (eds.), *Redefining sovereignty*, pp. 417–31, at 422–3; J. Brunnée and S. Toope, 'The use of force: international law after Iraq', (2004) 53 ICLQ 785–806, at 794; O. Corten, 'Opération Iraqi Freedom: peut-on admettre l'argument de "l'autorisation implicite" du Conseil de Sécurité?', (2003) 36 RBDI 205–43, at 207; Dinstein, *War, aggression and self-defence*, 4th edn, p. 183;

right of self-defence in the letter starkly contrasts with previous US communications to the Security Council, such as those concerning the 2001 intervention in Afghanistan, the 1998 strikes against Sudan and Afghanistan, or the 1986 strikes against Libya,[332] as well as with the explicit reliance on a Security Council authorization. In the Council debate of 27 March 2003, the US again claimed that the intervention was 'legitimate and *not unilateral*' on the basis of resolutions 678 (1990), 687 (1991) and 1441 (2002), without adding even the vaguest mention of self-defence.[333] In a similar vein, the US Legal Adviser in an article in the *American Journal of International Law* asserted that the foundation of the intervention lay in its authorization by the Security Council.[334] Our conclusion must therefore be that – at least at the international level – the United States deliberately refrained from presenting the Iraq intervention as an application of the 'Bush doctrine.'

In light of the argumentation of the three protagonists it is obvious that the debate within the Security Council focused on the question whether or not the intervention was (implicitly or explicitly) authorized by the Council, and not on the scope of self-defence. Among the considerable number of States supporting the intervention, several copied the 'material breach' narrative, while others simply asserted that Iraq was to blame for the course of events.[335] Only one delegation justified the intervention by reference to the threat allegedly emanating from Iraq: '[c]onsidering the fact that Saddam Hussein has previously used ... weapons of mass destruction on his own people, Uganda [believed] that the danger of these weapons falling into the hands of terrorist groups [was] real'.[336] Again, the right of self-defence was not explicitly cited. A number of States

---

Greenwood, 'Legality of the use of force', pp. 401–2; S. D. Murphy, 'Assessing the legality of invading Iraq', (2003–04) 92 Georgetown L. J. 173–257, at 174–6.

[332] See UN Doc. S/2001/946; S/1998/780; UN Doc. S/1998/780.

[333] UN Doc. 4726 (Resumption 1), 27 March 2003, 25 (emphasis added).

[334] See W.H. Taft IV and T.F. Buchwald, 'Preemption, Iraq, and international law', (2003) 97 AJIL 557–63. Taft and Buchwald *inter alia* noted that when American, British and French forces used force against Iraq in 1993, UN Secretary-General Boutros-Ghali declared that this action was in conformity with a mandate from the Security Council under SC Res. 678 (1991) (at 559).

[335] E.g., UN Doc. 4721, 19 March 2003, 15 (Spain); UN Doc. S/PV.4726, 15 (Kuwait), 24–5 (Poland), 26 (Singapore), 34–5 (Republic of Korea), 39 (Japan), 39–40 (former Yugoslav Republic of Macedonia), 41 (Georgia), 42 (Latvia), 42–3 (Nicaragua), 45 (Albania), 46 (Iceland), 47 (Mongolia); UN Doc. S/PV.4726 (Resumption 1), at 4 (Marshall Islands), 6 (El Salvador), 8 (Federated States of Micronesia), 29 (Spain), 31 (Bulgaria).

[336] UN Doc. S/PV.4726 (Resumption 1), 13–14. Also: UN Doc. S/2003/373, 24 March 2003 (Uganda).

avoided pronouncing on the legal merits of the intervention, instead urging that attention now focus on the humanitarian aspects of the crisis and that the Security Council members overcome their political differences.[337] A third group of States, arguably the largest one, 'deplored' the intervention and/or labelled it as a violation of the UN Charter.[338] Only a handful of UN Members opposing the intervention dwelled on the admissibility of anticipatory action. Algeria and Iran stressed that, even by any stretch of imagination, there was no imminent threat emanating from Iraq.[339] Lebanon noted that the invocation of self-defence was an invalid argument, 'since Article 51 ... recognizes the right ... only if an armed attack occurs ...'.[340] Malaysia and Yemen rejected the pre-emptive use of force, 'based on mere doubts about the intention of others'.[341]

In the end, the argument that the Iraq intervention constitutes a precedent in favour of anticipatory self-defence is without merit. Those States supporting the operation carefully avoided any justification based on a broad reading of Article 51 UN Charter. Furthermore, a majority of

---

[337] E.g., UN Doc. S/PV.4726, 16 (Chile); UN Doc. S/PV.4726, 36–7 (Argentina), 40 (Colombia), 43 (Norway); UN Doc. S/PV.4726 (Resumption 1), 3 (Canada), 4 (Uruguay), 4–5 (Thailand), 5–6 (Slovakia), 11 (Costa Rica), 19–20 (Angola), 24 (Cameroon), 34 (Guinea).

[338] E.g., UN Doc. S/PV.4726, 6–7 (Malaysia, on behalf of the Non-Aligned Movement, referring to an 'illegitimate act of aggression'), 8 (Malaysia), 8–9 (League of Arab States), 10 (Algeria), 13 (Yemen), 16–17 (Libya), 19–20 (Indonesia), 20–1 (South Africa: 'Some States have come together to invade Iraq without the authorization of the United Nations. This unilateral resort to force is compounded by the fact that progress was being made in dealing with the disarmament of Iraq through inspections authorized by the Security Council'), 21–2 (Cuba), 23 (New Zealand), 23–4 (India: the military campaign was 'unjustified and avoidable'), 27–8 (Brazil), 30 (Switzerland), 31 (Sudan), 31–2 (Vietnam), 32–3 (Jamaica), 33 (Iran), 35 (Lebanon), 37 (Mauritius), 38 (Belarus), 47 (Laos); UN Doc. S/PV.4726 (Resumption 1), at 2 (Liechtenstein), 9 (Tanzania: 'the decision to resort to the use of force against Iraq is null and void, as it goes against United Nations Charter provisions that require the decision to use force against a country threatening international peace and security to be adopted by the Security Council'), 10 (Palestine), 16 (Kyrgyzistan), 20–1 (Pakistan), 26–7 (Russia), 28 (PRC), 28–9 (France), 32 (Syria). See also the Statement by the Troika of the Non-Aligned Movement, Annex to UN Doc. S/2003/357, 19 March 2003.

[339] UN Doc. S/PV.4726, 10 (Algeria), 33 (Iran: 'The unilateral war against Iraq does not meet any standard of international legitimacy. It is not waged in self-defence against any prior armed attack. Nor, even by any stretch of imagination, could Iraq, after 12 years of comprehensive sanctions, be considered an imminent threat against the national security of the belligerent Powers').

[340] *Ibid.*, 35.

[341] *Ibid.*, 8 ('Malaysia: "pre-emptive use of force threatens the very foundation of international law ... It also erroneously asserts the notion that might is right'), 13 (Yemen).

States apparently held the opinion that the operation violated the UN Charter. The combination of both considerations can be regarded as an implicit rebuttal of the 'Bush doctrine' of preventive self-defence against non-imminent threats. On the other hand, as no country seriously contended that there existed *in casu* an *imminent* threat of attack,[342] the lawfulness of 'pre-emptive' self-defence was not at stake. Accordingly, opposition against the intervention should not automatically be qualified as opposition to anticipatory self-defence as such. In this respect, it must be noted that if the Iraq crisis is ultimately of little *direct* relevance to the *ratione temporis* aspect under consideration, the US National Security Strategy (2002) and the Iraq crisis have had an enormous *indirect* effect. Both have acted as a catalyst prompting international lawyers as well as States to reconsider their positions vis-à-vis anticipatory self-defence. Hereafter, we will examine the extent to which this trend has resulted in an evolution of the customary boundaries of self-defence.

4.2.2 Shifting positions of States and scholars: a defeat of preventive *self-defence at the expense of an embrace of* pre-emptive *self-defence?*

4.2.2.a Mapping the academic response

It is likely that no intervention has ever attracted the same amount of attention from international lawyers as the Iraq crisis. Already in the run-up to Operation 'Iraqi Freedom', dozens of diligent scholars were writing op-eds judging the legal merits of a possible intervention. Virtually every self-respecting international law journal included one or several contributions to the legality of the war.

In light of the justifications invoked by the intervening States, the academic debate has focused first and foremost on the question whether Resolutions 678 (1990), 687 (1991) and 1441 (2002) explicitly or implicitly authorized the operation. A considerable number of – mainly American – scholars have answered in the positive and have accepted that Iraq's 'material breach' of the 1991 ceasefire conditions revived the

---

[342] Consider for instance the following statement by President Bush: '[I]n 1 year, or 5 years, the power of Iraq to inflict harm on all free nations would be multiplied many times over ... We choose to meet that threat now, where it arises, before it can appear suddenly in our skies and cities.' White House Press Release, 'President says Saddam Hussein must leave Iraq within 48 hours'.

mandate to use 'all necessary means'.[343] On the other hand, a majority of international lawyers have rejected this thesis as artificial and incompatible with the ordinary meaning and the objectives of the resolutions, in particular when taking account of the numerous statements that resolution 1441 (2002) ruled out any 'automaticity'.[344] While the present author finds the latter approach more credible, an in-depth analysis of the argument falls beyond the scope of our study. Instead, what is more interesting for present purposes is that numerous scholars have used the Iraq war as a test case for the admissibility of anticipatory self-defence.[345]

---

[343] E.g., Y. Dinstein, 'Remarks', (2003) 97 ASIL Proc 147–9, at 147–8; Greenwood, 'Legality of the use of force'; G.B. Roberts, 'The UN Charter paradigm on the brink: the legal and policy predicates for use of force against Iraq', (2003) 42 RDMDG 441–58, at 446–7; R. Wedgwood, 'The military action in Iraq and international law', in M.N. Schmitt and J. Pejic (eds.), *International law and armed conflict: exploring the faultlines: essays in honour of Yoram Dinstein* (Leiden: Brill, 2007), pp. 229–40, at 229–35; R. Wedgwood, 'The fall of Saddam Hussein: Security Council mandates and preemptive self-defense', (2003) 97 AJIL 576–85, at 582; J. Yoo, 'International law and the war in Iraq', (2003) 97 AJIL 563–76, at 567–71.

[344] See A.J. Bellamy, 'International law and the war with Iraq', (2003) 4 Melbourne JIL 497–520, at 501–11; Bothe, 'Has Article 2(4) survived the Iraq war?', pp. 425–8; Corten, 'Opération Iraqi Freedom'; E. de Wet, 'The illegality of the use of force against Iraq subsequent to the adoption of Resolution 687 (1991)', (2003) 16 *Humanitäres Völkerrecht* 125–32; T. M. Franck, 'What happens now? The United Nations after Iraq', (2003) 97 AJIL 607–20, at 611–14; M. Hilaire, 'International law and the United States invasion of Iraq', (2005) 44 RDMDG 85–137, at 114; M. Iovane and F. De Vittor, 'La doctrine européenne et l'intervention en Iraq', (2003) 49 AFDI 17–31, at 24 (arguing that European scholars have 'almost unanimously' rejected the idea that the concerned Security Council resolutions authorized the use of force against Iraq); V. Lowe, 'The Iraq crisis: what now?', (2003) 52 ICLQ 859–71, at 865–6; Murphy, 'Assessing the legality of invading Iraq', 178 *et seq.*; F. Nguyen-Rouault, 'L'intervention armée en Irak et son occupation au regard du droit international', (2003) 107 RGDIP 835–64, at 844–9; M. E. O'Connell, 'La doctrine américaine et l'intervention en Iraq', (2003) 49 AFDI 3–16, at 7–8; Paul, 'The Bush doctrine', 461; C. Schaller, 'Massenvernichtungswaffen und Präventivkrieg – Möglichkeiten der Rechtfertigung einer militärischen Intervention im Irak aus völkerrechtlicher Sicht', (2002) 62 ZaöRV 641–68, at 644–56; Sharma, 'The American doctrine', 226; T. Stein, 'The war against Iraq and the *"Ius ad Bellum"*', (2003) 42 RDMDG 459–65, at 462–3; A. M. Weisburd, 'The war in Iraq and the dilemma of controlling the international use of force', (2004) 39 Texas ILJ 522–60, at 538.
    The same approach was adopted in a series of open letters signed by numerous international law scholars around the globe: 'Military action in Iraq without Security Council authorization would be illegal', reprinted in (2002–03) 34 Ottawa L Rev 1–3, at 1; International Commission of Jurists, 'ICJ deplores moves toward a war of aggression on Iraq', 18 March 2003, reproduced in (2003) 36 RBDI 297–8; 'War would be illegal', *The Guardian* 7 March 2003; 'Statement by Japanese international law scholars on the Iraqi issue', 18 March 2003, reproduced in (2003) 36 RBDI 293–8.

[345] Even if most concede that the argument was not raised by the intervening parties themselves, cf. *supra* note 331.

4.2.2.a.i Going beyond the Webster formula?

First of all, a number of US authors have defended the idea that the threat emanating from the Iraqi regime warranted an exercise of the right of self-defence.[346] These authors depict Saddam Hussein as an 'aggressive, risk-taking miscalculator',[347] and fully subscribe to the picture drawn in the preamble of the US Congressional Joint Resolution: (1) Iraq had a demonstrated capability and willingness to use weapons of mass destruction; (2) there was a high risk that the regime would either employ those weapons to launch a surprise attack against the US or provide them to international terrorists who would do so; (3) the resulting harm would be of such extreme magnitude as to justify anticipatory action by the US.[348]

The scholars belonging to this group generally pay lip-service to the 'imminence' standard that is the traditional hallmark of the 'counter-restrictionist' approach. Nonetheless, upon closer view, it is evident that they support a broader construction of self-defence, encompassing the use of force against threats that lack the temporal imminence of the Webster formula. In other words, they admit to greater or lesser extent the *preventive* recourse to force against *non-imminent* threats, as envisaged by the US National Security Strategy.

A particularly elaborate illustration of this approach can be found in an article by Yoo, who warns that we cannot wait for threats to fully materialize:[349]

> At least in the realm of WMD, rogue nations, and international terrorism ... the test for determining whether a threat is sufficiently 'imminent' to render the use of force necessary ... has become more nuanced than Secretary Webster's nineteenth-century formulation. Factors to be considered should now include the probability of an attack; the likelihood that this probability will increase, and therefore the need to take advantage of a limited window of opportunity; whether diplomatic alternatives are practical; and the magnitude of the harm that could result from the threat. If a State instead were obliged to wait until the threat were truly imminent in the temporal sense envisioned by Secretary

---

[346] M.J. Glennon, 'Preempting terrorism: the case for anticipatory self-defense', *Weekly Standard* 28 January 2002, at 24 (suggesting that 'modern methods of intelligence collection, such as satellite imagery and communications intercepts, now make it unnecessary to sit out an actual armed attack to await convincing proof of a State's hostile intent'); Roberts, 'The UN Charter paradigm on the brink', 450-6; R. F. Turner, 'Military action against Iraq is justified', (2002) 55 *Naval War College Review* 72-5; Yoo, 'The war in Iraq', 571-6.

[347] Roberts, 'The UN Charter paradigm on the brink', 444.

[348] US Congress Joint Resolution. [349] Yoo, 'The war in Iraq', 576.

Webster, there is a substantial danger of missing a limited window of opportunity to prevent widespread harm to civilians. ... Applying the reformulated test ... to ... Iraq reveals that the threat of a WMD attack by Iraq, either directly or through Iraq's support for terrorism, was sufficiently 'imminent' to render the use of force necessary to protect the United States, its citizens, and its allies.[350]

Cohan, while admitting that the 'Bush doctrine' departs from the Charter rules as well as from previous State practice, nonetheless asserts that: '[A]nticipatory offensive intervention has emerged as a valid doctrine. This type of intervention justifies action to literally attack and replace tyrannical regimes that foster international terrorism, endeavour to, or actually develop and maintain biological, chemical, or nuclear weapons.'[351] Pierson claims that the imminence requirement of the *Caroline* doctrine dealt with 'friendly States' and suggests 'a more flexible standard for self-defence in today's struggles with terrorist groups and with rogue regimes'.[352] Other US scholars have openly advocated a 'non-temporal' definition of 'imminent danger'.[353]

Furthermore, some European scholars, while rejecting the broad parameters of the 'Bush doctrine' and regarding the Iraq War as unlawful, have also questioned the requirement of *temporal* imminence.[354] Hofmeister, for example, finds that neither the Webster formula nor the Bush doctrine provide an adequate legal framework: while the former is too restrictive to cope with the emerging threats of the twenty-first century, the latter lacks clear and objective criteria.[355] Instead he puts forward a standard that essentially requires a combination of bellicose

---

[350] Ibid., 574. [351] Cohan, 'The Bush doctrine', 288, 355.
[352] C. Pierson, 'Preemptive self-defense in an age of weapons of mass destruction: Operation Iraqi Freedom', (2004–5) 33 Denver JILP 150–78, at 177.
[353] M. L. Rockefeller, 'The "imminent threat" requirement for the use of preemptive military force: is it time for a non-temporal standard?', (2004–5) 33 Denver JILP 131–49: '[The] temporal standard ... is simply not sufficient to account for the twenty-first century warfare, technologies, and terrorist tactics. A standard forged when the aggressor held a musket is not applicable when an aggressor holds a "dirty bomb"; the consequences are far greater' (at 147, also 144). Also: M. B. Occelli, '"Sinking" the *Caroline*: Why the *Caroline* doctrine's restrictions on self-defense should not be regarded as customary international law', (2003) 4 San Diego ILJ 467–90.
[354] E.g., UK House of Commons, Select Committee on Foreign Affairs, Minutes of Evidence, Written evidence submitted by Daniel Bethlehem QC: 'International Law and the Use of Force: The Law as it is and the Law as it Should Be', 7 June 2004, available at www.publications.parliament.uk/pa/cm200304/cmselect/cmfaff/441/4060808.htm (accessed 11 May 2009), § 35 (suggesting a move away from temporal imminence in relation to 'catastrophic' threats).
[355] H. Hofmeister, 'Preemptive strikes – a new normative framework', (2006) 44 AdV 187–200, at 191–2.

statements and a capacity to mount an attack.[356] Likewise, Gill deems it sufficient that there is evidence of 'a credible threat of probable or, in some cases, even potential attack' in 'the foreseeable future'.[357]

4.2.2.a.ii A firm rebuttal of *preventive* self-defence

The aforementioned attempts to broaden the parameters of self-defence beyond the constraints of the Webster formula starkly contrast with the more cautious approach adopted by counter-restrictionists prior to 2001. At the same time, they remain very much the exception among the college of international lawyers. On the whole, legal scholars have almost *unisono* denounced the doctrine of *preventive* self-defence.

Already in the run-up to the Iraq war, dozens of international lawyers unequivocally rejected the idea that the intervention would be a lawful exercise of self-defence, and *in extenso* rejected the claim that self-defence may be exercised against non-imminent threats.[358] Over thirty Canadian scholars signed a letter according to which '[t]he so-called doctrine of [preventive] self-defence, recently advanced by the U.S. as a justification for the use of force before any attack occurs or is imminent, is contrary to the UN Charter and international law'.[359] Likewise, fifteen prominent UK scholars declared in an op-ed that '[t]he doctrine of [preventive] self-defence against an attack that might arise at some hypothetical future time has no basis in international law'.[360] No less explicit is the following letter, signed by over forty Australian scholars:

> The United States has proposed a doctrine of '[preventive] self-defence' that would allow a country to use force against another country it suspects may attack it at some stage. This doctrine contradicts the . . . prohibition of the unilateral use of force . . . . The weak and ambiguous evidence presented . . . by the US Secretary of State, Colin Powell, to justify a pre-emptive strike underlines the practical danger of a doctrine of [prevention].[361]

---

[356] See *ibid.*, 193–4. [357] Gill, 'The temporal dimension of self-defense', pp. 150–1.
[358] See, e.g., International Commission of Jurists, 'ICJ deplores moves toward a war of aggression on Iraq', 297–8; 'The Australian Section of the ICJ questions the proposed attack on Iraq', reproduced in (2003) 36 RBDI 286–7.
[359] 'Military action in Iraq without Security Council authorization would be illegal', reprinted in (2002–03) 34 Ottawa L Rev 1–3, at 2. Remark: the article uses the term 'pre-emptive', but refers to non-imminent threats.
[360] 'War would be illegal', *The Guardian* 7 March 2003. Remark: the article uses the term 'pre-emptive', but refers to non-imminent threats.
[361] 'Coalition of the willing? Make that war criminals', *The Sydney Morning Herald* 26 February 2003. Remark: the article uses the term 'pre-emptive', but refers to non-imminent threats.

A group of Japanese scholars warned that '[i]f we set a precedent here and now which legitimizes a preemptive self-defence against an armed attack that has not yet occurred, the rules that constrain the exercise of the right of self-defence . . . will be loosened in an unlimited way'.[362] Last but not least, over 300 European lawyers recalled that '[s]elf-defence presupposes the existence of a prior armed attack; consequently, "preventive self-defence" is not admissible under international law'.[363]

Furthermore, in the immense legal literature published in the aftermath of Operation 'Iraqi Freedom', a vast majority of international lawyers, on both sides of the Atlantic, has strongly denounced the admissibility of self-defence against non-imminent threats.[364] In this regard, it is worth observing that even the US Legal Adviser recognized the importance of the imminence requirement. In a series of publications he admitted that '[o]ne may not strike another merely because the second might someday develop an ability and desire to attack it',[365] and insisted that the US 'recognizes the right to use force preemptively only when the traditional tests of necessity and proportionality are met'.[366]

---

[362] 'Statement by Japanese international law scholars on the Iraqi issue', 18 March 2003, reproduced in (2003) 36 RBDI 293–8.
[363] 'Appel de juristes de droit international concernant le recours à la force contre l'Irak', reproduced in (2003) 36 RBDI 266–86 , at 272.
[364] See, e.g., AIV, 'Pre-emptive Action', 20; A. Anghie, 'The Bush administration preemption doctrine and the United Nations', (2004) 98 ASIL Proc 326–9; Bothe, 'Terrorism and the legality of pre-emptive force'; Brunnée and Toope, 'International law after Iraq', 793–4; Christakis, 'La notion de guerre préventive'; Dinstein, 'Remarks', 148; Dinstein, *War, aggression and self-defence*, 4th edn, p. 183; Franck, The United Nations after Iraq', 619–20; Greenwood, 'The pre-emptive use of force'; R. Hofmann, 'International law and the use of military force against Iraq', (2003) 45 GYBIL 9–34, at 31–5; Lowe, 'The Iraq crisis', 865; Murphy, 'Assessing the legality of invading Iraq', 176–7; Nguyen-Rouault, 'L'intervention armée en Irak', 851–3; M.E. O'Connell, 'The myth of preemptive self-defense'; J.A. Ramírez, 'Iraq War: anticipatory self-defense or unlawful unilateralism?', (2003) 34 California Western ILJ 1–27, at 25; M. Sapiro, 'Iraq: the shifting sands of preemptive self-defense', (2003) 97 AJIL 599–607; Schaller, 'Massenvernichtungswaffen und Präventivkrieg', 656 *et seq.*; A.-M. Slaughter, 'The use of force in Iraq: illegal and illegitimate', (2004) 98 ASIL Proc 262–3, at 262; Stein, 'The war against Iraq', 463; Weisburd, 'The war in Iraq', 538–9; R. Wolfrüm, 'The attack of September 11, 2001, the wars against the Taliban and Iraq: is there a need to reconsider international law on the recourse to force and the rules in armed conflict?', (2004) 7 MPYBUNL 1–78, at 30–5.
[365] Taft and Buchwald, 'Preemption, Iraq, and international law', 557.
[366] W.H. Taft IV, 'Preemptive action in self-defense', (2004) 98 ASIL Proc 331–3, at 333. Remark: see also W.H. Taft IV, 'The basis for preemption', 18 November 2002, available at www.cfr.org/publication.html?id=5250 (accessed 11 May 2009).

Put briefly, international lawyers agree virtually unanimously that preventive self-defence patently lacks any basis in international law: it is diametrically opposed to the Charter framework on the use of force and is not supported by any shred of customary evidence in the post-1945 era.[367] In addition, the doctrine is considered highly undesirable from a *de lege ferenda* perspective for a variety of reasons. It would fundamentally undermine the Security Council's responsibility to deal with threats to the peace. It is founded on a vague and subjective threshold which is not suitable to objective verification and would consequently escape international scrutiny. The result would be a return to the pre-Charter era, in the sense that each State would be the judge of its own actions. In other words: right would make might. Despite the NSS's hollow utterance that nations should not use pre-emption as a pretext for aggression,[368] abuse is inevitable: if every State would be allowed to use force in response to what it perceives as a potential threat to its security, this would provide legal justification for Pakistan to attack India, for Russia to attack Georgia, for Azerbaijan to attack Armenia, for North Korea to attack South Korea, and so on.[369] Finally, some authors have warned that preventive self-defence necessarily involves a subjective determination not only of *when*, but also of *how* States may use force. In this context, it is warned that the doctrine could be invoked to justify disproportionate responses seeking regime change abroad.[370]

4.2.2.a.iii All quiet on the academic front?

Must we conclude that the college of international lawyers has resisted the NSS's attempt to broaden the boundaries of self-defence, and that all has remained quiet on the academic front? Yes and no. On the one hand, it is true that the doctrine of preventive self-defence against non-imminent threats has only obtained the support of a handful of scholars, and has conversely been rejected by a near-unanimous academic opinion. At the same time, a growing body of legal scholars has come to accept the admissibility of pre-emptive self-defence along the lines of the Webster formula. Some authors have apparently taken the view – which we rebutted earlier – that customary practice endorsed this approach. Others may well have been

---

[367] E.g., Lowe, 'The Iraq crisis', 865.   [368] US National Security Strategy, 15.
[369] E.g., M. E. O'Connell, 'The myth of preemptive self-defense', 19. Also: Cassese, 'Article 51', p. 1340.
[370] E.g., M. E. O'Connell, 'The myth of preemptive self-defense', 20.

(mis)guided by the NSS's bold declaration that international law has 'for centuries' recognized that the right of self-defence extends to imminent threats of attack. Still others may have found that the changed international security environment, exposed by the 9/11 attacks, warranted the abandoning of the 'restrictionist' interpretation of Article 51 UN Charter.[371] Finally, some may have embraced pre-emptive self-defence as a seemingly inevitable compromise in the confrontation between two extreme views of self-defence; one strictly reactive, the other preventive.

Whatever the motivations, the implication is that the NSS and the Iraq crisis have not left the academic debate unaffected. Indeed, whereas we have earlier established that the 'restrictionist' school of thought traditionally held the upper hand among academics (see Section 4.1.1.d), the balance may well have tilted in favour of the 'counter-restrictionists'. This is certainly the case in the US, the UK and Australia, where a majority of scholars now accept that reliance on self-defence is justified against 'imminent' threats of attack.[372] Yet, beyond the Anglo-Saxon world, support for pre-emptive self-defence also appears to be on the rise.[373] Significantly, the *Institut de Droit International* in October 2007

---

[371] Sapiro, for instance, while critical of preventive self-defence, argues that '[t]he kind of threats the [US] and other countries face today from the lethal combination of new enemies ... and new technologies undermine the idea of waiting for an actual armed attack to occur.' Against this background, she writes, 'the dilemma Iraq posed presents a strong argument for wider acceptance of anticipatory self-defence, but not a more expansive doctrine'. Sapiro, 'Iraq', 604, 607.

[372] E.g., Anghie, 'The Bush Administration preemption doctrine', 326; Bellamy, 'The war with Iraq', 515–17; Greenwood, 'The pre-emptive use of force'; Greenwood, 'Legality of the use of force', p. 400; M. E. O'Connell, 'The myth of preemptive self-defense'; Pierson, 'Preemptive self-defense'; Rockefeller, 'The "imminent threat" requirement'; Sapiro, 'Iraq', 601–4.

[373] See, e.g., (Belgium) J. Verhoeven, *Droit international public* (Brussels: Larcier, 2000), p. 684; J. Wouters, *Internationaal recht in kort bestek* (Antwerp: Intersentia, 2006), p. 209; (France) Combacau and Sur, *Droit international public*, p. 628; Zoller, 'The preemption doctrine', 336–7; (Germany) Bothe, 'Terrorism and the legality of pre-emptive force'; M. Bothe, 'Der Irak-Krieg und das völkerrechtliche Gewaltverbot (2003) 41 AdV 272–94, at 261–2; Hofmeister, 'Preemptive strikes'; Hofmann, 'The use of military force against Iraq', 31; Talmon, 'The German position', 60–3; Stein, 'The war against Iraq', 463–5; Wolfrüm, 'The wars against the Taliban and Iraq', 33; (Italy) Iovane and De Vittor, 'L'intervention en Iraq', 27–9; (Malaysia) Sharma, 'The American doctrine', 220–4; (Netherlands) Gill, 'The temporal dimension of self-defense'; (Spain) A. Remiro Brotons, R. Riquelme Cortado, J. D. Hochleitner, E. O. Calatayud and L. P. Durban, *Derecho internacional* (Valencia: Tirant Lo Blanch, 2007), pp. 1067–9.

adopted a resolution acknowledging amongst other things that the right of self-defence extends to 'manifestly imminent' armed attacks.[374] In short, the present author agrees with Kolb that:

> There is ... a quite astonishing *retour en force* of the concept of anticipatory self-defence. ... [W]e are now confronted with a situation where almost the entirety of US American legal writing considers that such anticipatory self-defence is without any doubt conceded by international law. ... This relaxation of the criteria seems to have also influenced, to some extent, European writers. What is most striking is the way in which all this is taken for granted and the extent to which anticipatory self-defence is allowed as if it had always been undisputedly part and parcel of international law. There is at this juncture an obvious ideological slide towards a position more lenient to the use of force by States in international law.[375]

Two reservations can be made in this context. First of all, while the counter-restrictionist school may be gaining ground, numerous scholars concede that the legality of pre-emptive self-defence is and remains contested.[376] Many prominent authors moreover continue to insist that nothing in State practice supports an extension of the right of self-defence beyond the parameters of Article 51 UN Charter.[377] It may be recalled, for instance, that over 300 European lawyers signed a letter affirming that '[s]elf-defence presupposes the existence of a prior armed attack'.[378] Interestingly, several scholars have drawn attention to the fact that 'interceptory' self-defence forms an integral part of the scope of

---

[374] Institut de Droit International, Tenth Commission – Present Problems of the Use of Armed Force in International Law-self-defence, Resolution of 27 October 2007, Santiago, available at www.idi-iil.org/idiE/resolutionsE/2007_san_02_en.pdf (accessed 11 May 2009). According to paragraph 3, the right of self-defence 'arises for the target State in case of an actual or manifestly imminent armed attack. It may be exercised only when there is no lawful alternative in practice in order to forestall, stop or repel the armed attack ...'. Paragraphs 6 and 7 clarify that '[t]here is no basis in international law for the doctrines of "preventive" self-defence (in the absence of an actual or manifestly imminent armed attack)'.

[375] Kolb, 'Self-defence and preventive war', 125–6.

[376] M. D. Evans, *International Law*, 2nd edn. (Oxford University Press, 2006), p. 601; T. Schweisfurth, *Völkerrecht* (Tübingen: Mohr Siebeck, 2006), 364–5; Schaller, 'Massenvernichtungswaffen und Präventivkrieg', 656 *et seq.*

[377] E.g., Cassese, 'Article 51', p. 1341; Dinstein, 'Remarks', 182–4; J. D. González Campos, L. Sanchez Rodriguez and P. A. Saenz de Santa Maria, *Curso de derecho internacional público*, 3rd ed (Madrid: Thomson, 2003), p. 926.

[378] *Supra*, note 363.

Article 51 UN Charter, and removes the need for any doctrine of pre-emptive self-defence. Gazzini, for example, argues that the interceptive self-defence theory 'permits the striking of a balance between the national security concerns of States and the common interest to outlaw non-defensive use of force'.[379] In Section 4.3.3 we will further analyse the merits of this view. For the moment, it suffices to note that the counter-restrictionists have not (yet) emerged victorious.

Second and more fundamentally, even if the majority and minority are switching sides, scholarly opinion still constitutes a *subsidiary* source of law. In other words, the majority view is not automatically the correct one: the crucial test is whether the customary practice of States confirms one view or the other. Still, it may be suspected that shifting tendencies in the academic debate offer a suitable gauge to measure parallel shifts in States' *opinio*. Two important UN documents seem to confirm this.

4.2.2.b The High-Level Panel Report (2004) and 'In Larger Freedom' (2005)

In his address to the General Assembly on 23 September 2003, UN Secretary-General Annan commented on the political divisions surrounding the Iraq crisis and the resulting paralysis of the Security Council.[380] Observing that the consensus of global solidarity and collective security on which the United Nations was built threatened to unravel, he warned that the UN had reached 'a fork in the road.' The UN Secretary-General announced his intention to establish a High-Level Panel of eminent personalities which was to lay the foundations for a new security consensus, by determining the challenges to international peace and security arising from both 'old' and 'new', 'soft' and 'hard' threats, as well as the need for collective action to best tackle these threats. He also drew attention to the dangers of anticipatory recourse to force:

> Article 51 of the Charter prescribes that all States, if attacked, retain the inherent right of self-defence. But until now it has been understood that when States go beyond that ... they need the unique legitimacy provided by the United Nations. Now, some say this understanding is no longer

---

[379] Gazzini, *The changing rules*, p. 151. See also: Cassese, 'Article 51', p. 1342.
[380] UN Secretary-general Kofi Annan, Address to the General Assembly, New York, 23 September 2003, available at www.un.org/webcast/ga/58/statements/sg2eng030923.htm (accessed 11 May 2009).

tenable, since an 'armed attack' with weapons of mass destruction could be launched at any time, without warning, or by a clandestine group. Rather than wait for that to happen, they argue, States have the right and obligation to use force pre-emptively ... even while weapons systems that might be used to attack them are still being developed. ... This logic represents a fundamental challenge to the principles on which, however imperfectly, world peace and stability have rested for the last fifty-eight years. My concern is that, if it were to be adopted, it could set precedents that resulted in a proliferation of the unilateral and lawless use of force, with or without justification.[381]

In December 2004, the sixteen-Member 'High-Level Panel on Threats, Challenges and Security' presented its *magnum opus*, entitled 'A more secure world: our shared responsibility',[382] and containing an authoritative and comprehensive analysis of the various threats to international security, as well as the numerous concrete proposals regarding counter-proliferation, Security Council reform, et cetera.[383] In paragraphs 188–93, the Panel reflects on Article 51 UN Charter. Despite the observation that the language of this provision is restrictive (§ 188) and despite the Panel's recommendation that Article 51 need not be rewritten or reinterpreted (§ 192), the Report seems to concur with the US National Security Strategy insofar as pre-emptive self-defence is concerned. Indeed, ignoring the long-standing controversy on the matter, the Panel asserts that 'a threatened State, according to long established international law, can take military action as long as the threatened attack is *imminent*, no other means would deflect it and the action is proportionate'.[384] The real problem, the Report argues, relates to preventive action against non-imminent threats, i.e., threats which are not imminent but still claimed to be real, for example the acquisition, with allegedly hostile intent, of nuclear weapons-making capability (§ 188). In this regard, the Report appears to be somewhat ambiguous.[385] It first mentions that non-imminent threats should be submitted to the Security Council for consideration. In cases where the Council chooses not to authorize military

---

[381] *Ibid.*   [382] UN Doc. A/59/565.
[383] For a discussion, see *inter alia* the various contributions in (2007) 38 California Western ILJ 1 *et seq.* and (2005) 7 ILF 1 *et seq.* Also: L. Boisson de Chazournes, 'Rien ne change, tout bouge, ou le dilemme des Nations Unies', (2005) 109 RGDIP 147–61.
[384] UN Doc. A/59/565, § 188.
[385] See T. Ruys, 'Reshaping unilateral and multilateral use of force: the work of the UN High-Level Panel on Threats, Challenges and Change', (2005) 7 ILF 92–100, at 93.

action, it states that 'there will be time to pursue other strategies ... *and to visit again the military option*'(§ 190, emphasis added). The latter phrase could wrongfully be understood as an intentional 'loophole' to allow exceptional recourse to unilateral preventive action. However, when reading the remainder of the section, it becomes clear that the Panel rejects the admissibility thereof. The Report warns that 'allowing one to so act is to allow all' (§ 191) and concludes that the risk to global order and the norm of non-intervention is 'simply too great for the legality of unilateral preventive action' to be accepted.[386]

The Panel Report was a key source of inspiration for 'In Larger Freedom',[387] the report of UN Secretary-General Annan which paved the road for the UNGA 2005 September Summit. Recalling that States have disagreed on the matter, the Report stresses that it is essential that UN Members seek agreement on when and how force can be used (§ 122). Like the NSS and the High-Level Panel, the Report finds that: 'Imminent threats are fully covered by Article 51, which safeguards the inherent right of sovereign States to defend themselves against armed attack. Lawyers have long recognized that this covers an imminent attack as well as one that has already happened.'[388] It moreover stresses that '[w]here threats are not imminent but latent, the Charter gives full authority to the Security Council to use military force, including preventively, to preserve international peace and security' (§ 125). Contrary to the High-Level Panel Report, it does not explicitly rule out preventive self-defence, yet suggests that '[t]he task is not to find alternatives to the Security Council as a source of authority but to make it work better' (§ 126).

In sum, both documents reject the concept of preventive self-defence (one explicitly, the other implicitly) but, at the same time, they take for granted the legality of pre-emptive self-defence. In doing so, both documents show a striking disregard for the long-standing confrontation between the 'restrictionist' and the 'counter-restrictionist' school of thought. Even if the reports were not drafted by international lawyers and do not constitute 'State practice', the symbolic importance can hardly be overstated. Especially when taking account of the high-level

---

[386] Remark: the Panel does emphasize that the Security Council is fully empowered to react to non-imminent threats and is even encouraged to act more proactively than it has done in the past (UN Doc. A/59/565, § 194).
[387] UN Doc. A/59/2005.   [388] *Ibid.*, § 124.

and geographically balanced composition of the Panel,[389] the unequivocal support for self-defence against 'imminent' threats seems to confirm that the tide has turned in favour of the 'counter-restrictionist' view. Ultimately, however, whether this is truly the case must be asserted by reference to the customary practice of States.

4.2.2.c State support for pre-emptive and preventive self-defence after Iraq

After the adoption of the NSS and the launch of Operation 'Iraqi Freedom', several States made claims that sounded remarkably similar to the infamous 'Bush doctrine'. In December 2002, following the Bali bombing, which killed over eighty Australian tourists, the Australian Prime Minister suggested that the Charter provisions on self-defence should be rewritten since international law was no longer adequate to confront the threats to national security.[390] Much to the discontent of other States in the region,[391] he claimed that his country should have the right to attack terrorist groups or bases in neighbouring countries where there was credible evidence that these groups were planning to attack Australia or Australian citizens abroad. In a similar vein, Russia asserted the right to undertake 'pre-emptive strikes' against terrorist bases in neighbouring countries.[392] Threats of anticipatory action were likewise issued *inter alia* by North Korea, Iran and India.[393] Furthermore, several military doctrines and security strategies adopted after 2002 appear to give greater recognition to 'preventive deployment' and the like. The 2003 European Security Strategy notes that '[w]ith the new threats, the first line of defence will often be abroad. . . . [P]reventive engagement can avoid more serious problems in the future.'[394] The Strategic Concept of Italy's Chief of Defence declares that the military 'must develop the

---

[389] The Panel included amongst others three former Prime Ministers as well as former heads of the ILO, the WHO, the OAU and the OAS. For the names and credentials of the fifteen Panel Members, see: www.un.org/secureworld/panelmembers.html (accessed 11 May 2009).

[390] See 'Australia ready to strike abroad', *BBC News* 1 December 2002; J. Shaw, 'Startling his neighbors, Australian leader favors first strikes', *NY Times* 2 December 2002; (2002) *Keesing's* 45147; 'The UN Charter is outdated', IHT 2 December 2002. See also Reisman and Armstrong, 'The claim of preemptive self-defense', 538–40.

[391] E.g., 'Malaysia warns Australia over pre-emptive strike threat', *Beijing Time* 23 September 2004.

[392] E.g., 'Russia targets top Chechen rebels', *BBC News* 8 September 2004; E. Piper, 'Russia set to hit 'terror' worldwide', *Reuters* 8 September 2004.

[393] Cf. *infra*.   [394] European Security Strategy, 11.

capability to dynamically face threats whenever and wherever they occur'.[395] And the French Loi de Programmation 2003–8 states as follows: Outside our borders, ... we must be able to identify and prevent threats as soon as possible. Within this framework, possible preemptive action is not out of the question, where an explicit and confirmed threat has been recognized.[396]

In light of these and other developments, several authors have observed a growing acceptance among States of the admissibility of pre-emptive and even preventive self-defence. Reisman in particular finds that customary law may be in the process of accommodating the US's broad claim to preventive self-defence.[397] Three questions arise. First, has support for the counter-restrictionist approach increased? Second, has there indeed been a growing acceptance of self-defence against non-imminent threats among the adherents of the counter-restrictionist approach? Third and last, to what extent have the majority and minority opinion among States switched sides?

In relation to the first question, the answer is undeniably affirmative. Looking at the rare and often muted support for anticipatory self-defence in olden times (cf. *supra*), there can be no doubt that (declared) support of anticipatory self-defence has increased in recent years.[398] Apart from the 'usual suspects', such as the US,[399] the UK,[400]

---

[395] Chief of the Italian Defence Staff Strategic Concept, April 2005, available at www.difesa.it/NR/rdonlyres/7CF00FEA-D74E-4533-B3ED-9CCCD8B79E89/0/libroconcettostrategico.pdf (accessed 11 May 2009), 10.

[396] French Ministry of Defence, 'Loi de Programmation militaire 2003–2008', Annex, Chapter 3, 6, www.defense.gouv.fr/defense/enjeux_defense/politique_de_defense/programmations/loi_2003_2008/loi_de_programmation_militaire_2003_2008 (accessed 11 May 2009).

[397] See Reisman and Armstrong, 'The claim of preemptive self-defense', 526 *et seq.*

[398] Remark: many relevant statements with regard to the High-Level Panel Report and 'In Larger Freedom' were expressed in the course of a series of plenary meetings of the UN General Assembly: UN Docs. A/59/PV.85–90, 6–8 April 2005. Several declarations made in the course of informal meetings can be consulted at www.reformtheun.org/index.php/government_statements/c303?theme=alt2 (accessed 11 May 2009).

[399] UN Doc. A/59/PV.87, 23; US Statement, UNGA Discussion of Cluster II Issues for the High-Level Event, 22 April 2005: 'The United States has long considered that a State has a right to use force in self-defense in the event of an actual or imminent attack. We welcome that both the Secretary-General's report and the High-Level Panel's report specifically endorsed this principle.'

[400] UN Doc. A/59/PV.85, 26; UK Statement, General Assembly debate on Freedom from Fear, 21 April 2005: 'Some think the High-Level Panel did not interpret Article 51 on

Australia[401] and Israel[402] – all of which expressed satisfaction at the interpretation of Article 51 in the High-Level Panel Report – several other States have joined the counter-restrictionist ranks. Shortly after the promulgation of the NSS, Japan stressed that the Charter allows 'pre-emptive strikes' or 'pre-emptive attacks' when a nation is faced with an imminent threat,[403] a position which was later reiterated in a number of press statements and Defence White Papers.[404] In reaction to parliamentary questions of members of the Reichstag in 2004, the German government acknowledged that Article 51 also applied to an *unmittelbar bevorstehenden Angriff*, in other words, to an imminent attack.[405] Even if the option was strictly confined to the parameters of the Webster formula, this appears to be a departure from the position adopted earlier within the UN.[406] Furthermore, in the run-up to the 2005 World Summit, several UN Members agreed with the construction of Article 51 in the High-Level Panel Report and in 'In Larger Freedom' as encompassing pre-emptive self-defence (against imminent threats).

---

self-defence restrictively enough; others that the Panel were too restrictive. That suggests they got it about right.'

[401] Australian Statement, Plenary Exchange on the Secretary-General's Report 'In Larger Freedom', New York, 7 April 2005.

[402] Israeli Ministry of Foreign Affairs, 'United Nations Reforms – Position Paper of the Government of Israel', 1 July 2005.

[403] Press statement of the Japanese Ministry of Foreign Affairs, Press Conference 27 September 2002, available at www.mofa.go.jp/announce/press/2002/9/0927.html (accessed 11 May 2009).

[404] E.g., Press statement of the Japanese Ministry of Foreign Affairs, Internet Press Chat Conference, 13 July 2006, available at www.mofa.go.jp/announce/press/2006/7/0713.html (accessed 11 May 2009). Referring to the 'possible case in which Japan is already being attacked or about to be attacked by an enemy force clearly intent on attacking Japan. Under such circumstances every nation as part of its natural right is entitled to get rid of the danger.' See also the interpretation of Article 9 of the Japanese Constitution in the Defence White Papers: Japanese Ministry of Defense, Defense of Japan 2008, Part II, Chapter I, at 2–3, available at www.mod.go.jp/e/publ/w_paper/pdf/2008/part2/Chap1.pdf. (accessed 11 May 2009).

[405] Deutscher Bundestag, Antwort der Bundesregierung, 'Umsetzung der Europäischen Sicherheitsstrategie', Drucksache 15/3181, 21 May 2004, 25; Deutscher Bundestag, Antwort der Bundesregierung, 'Bilanz deutscher VN-Politik in der Zeit der Mitgliedschaft Deutschlands im VN-Sicherheitsrat 2003 und 2004', Drucksache 15/3635, 3 August 2004, 17.

[406] See Talmon, 'The German position', 61. Referring to UN Doc. A/C.1/44/PV.47, 47 (statement by the German representative, according to which Article 51 'precludes pre-emptive or preventive warfare on enemy territory').

This approach was adopted by Liechtenstein,[407] Singapore,[408] Uganda,[409] Switzerland[410] and, arguably, the Republic of Korea.[411]

Reisman also draws attention to a series of (quasi-)official declarations, issued after the adoption of the NSS in September 2002, which copy the line of reasoning of the 'Bush doctrine' to argue that State A would be justified to launch a 'pre-emptive strike' against State B.[412] In February 2003, for example, North Korea argued that it was entitled to launch a pre-emptive strike against the US, rather than wait 'until the American military had finished with Iraq'.[413] One month later, the Indian Foreign Minister suggested that India had 'a better case' for a pre-emptive strike against Pakistan than America did against Iraq.[414] In April 2004, the Iranian Defence Minister warned in an interview that preventive operations

---

[407] Statement of Liechtenstein, Informal Meeting of the General Assembly on the Report of the Secretary-General 'In Larger Freedom', Cluster II: 'Freedom from Fear', New York, 21 April 2005: 'It has been long established that the inherent right of self-defense is limited to military action in case of an imminent attack, as a last resort and in a proportionate manner. . . .'.

[408] Statement of Singapore, Informal Meeting of the 59th UNGA Plenary to discuss the High-Level Panel's Report on Threats, Challenges and Change, 27 January 2005: 'On the right to self-defence, the Panel was clearly informed by customary international law in stating . . . that "a threatened State, according to long established international law, can take military action as long as the threatened attack is immminent". Indeed, the reality is that no State, faced with an imminent threat that it realises cannot be averted through diplomatic and other means, will sit and wait to be attacked before exercising its right to self-defence, by which time, there may be nothing left to defend.'

[409] Statement of Uganda, 10th Informal Meeting of the Plenary of the High-Level Plenary Meeting of the General Assembly of September 2005, New York, 1 July 2005: '[A] State is entitled to use force in self-defence in the event of actual or imminent attack. This principle is within the ambit of the Charter of the United Nations and should be clearly reflected in the outcome document.'

[410] See reference cited in Corten, *Le droit contre la guerre*, p. 650, footnote 220. But, more neutral: UN Doc. A/59/PV.86, 22.

[411] Statement of the Republic of Korea, Informal Thematic Consultations at the General Assembly, New York, 21 April 2005. Consider also UN Doc. A/C.6/54/SR.25, 3 November 1999 (statement by Korea in relation to the ILC Draft Articles on State Responsibility, rendering support to the 'pre-existing custom' paradigm).

[412] See Reisman and Armstrong, 'The claim of preemptive self-defense', 538–46.

[413] See J. Watts, 'N. Korea threatens US with first strike', *The Guardian* 6 February 2003. Similar statements were made in subsequent years; e.g., 'N. Korea: U.S. does not have 'monopoly' on pre-emptive strike', *USA Today* 21 March 2006.

[414] See, e.g., A. Waldman, 'India pressed on Kashmir attacks', *NY Times* 9 April 2003. Similar statements were made by the Minister for Civil Aviation (e.g., L. Puri, 'India has right to pre-emptive strike', *The Hindu* 7 April 2003) and by the Indian Finance Minister (S. Krishnaswami, 'Every country has the right to pre-emption: Jaswant', *The Hindu* 1 October 2002). But see: 'US dismisses Iraq Pakistan comparison', *BBC News* 11 April 2003.

were not the monopoly of the US and hinted at the possibility of a pre-emptive strike to prevent an attack on its nuclear facilities.[415]

It would be wrong, however, automatically to equate the latter statements to an actual acceptance of the legality of anticipatory self-defence. Generally, taking account of the language used and the surrounding political context, they can be characterized as political sabre-rattling and muscle-flexing, rather than as reliable manifestations of States' *opinio iuris*. It may be noted that in April 2005, the Iranian UN representative declared that: 'Article 51 in no way covers imminent threats, and international law does not confer any legitimacy on the dangerous doctrine of pre-emption.'[416] Such explicit repudiation of the doctrine of anticipatory self-defence certainly outweighs a vague political threat which was never implemented. By analogy, the Indian intervention in the General Assembly debate in April 2005 appears to reject self-defence against threats, whether they be latent or patent.[417]

Furthermore, it is imperative to look beyond the use of certain labels and examine the precise content of the claims issued. Thus, statements by Russian officials asserting that Russia would launch 'pre-emptive strikes' against terrorists bases 'in any region of the world'[418] at first sight signal its adherence to the doctrine of anticipatory self-defence. Later declarations, however, cast doubt on this interpretation.[419] In a press statement of February 2005, dealing specifically with the possibility of preventive strikes at terrorist bases, the Russian Foreign Ministry clarified that such strikes could be launched '[w]here a country has been subjected to a terrorist attack and there are serious grounds to believe that *a repetition of this attack* from an identified source is inevitable'.[420] In other words, Russia claims that force may be used to

---

[415] See N. Fathi, 'Iran says it may pre-empt attack against its nuclear facilities', *NY Times* 20 August 2004. Remark: on Japanese threats of a first strike against North Korea, see: Christakis, 'La notion de guerre préventive', p. 12, footnote 12.

[416] UN Doc. A/59/PV.87, 17.

[417] UN Doc. A/59/PV.90, 24: '[We] believe that Article 51 is clear enough. The framers of the Charter never intended that article to cover anything beyond its text.... We believe that the Charter gives full authority to the Security Council to preserve international peace and security from threats, whether they be latent or patent.'

[418] E.g., 'Russia targets top Chechen rebels', *BBC News* 8 September 2004; E. Piper, 'Russia set to hit 'terror' worldwide', *Reuters* 8 September 2004.

[419] See Corten, *Le droit contre la guerre*, pp. 650–1.

[420] Russian Foreign Ministry, Information and Press Department Commentary regarding a Russian Media Question concerning Possible Preventive Strikes at Terrorists' Bases, 3 February 2005, available at www.ln.mid.ru/brp_4.nsf/sps/504A679ED357240EC3256F9D 00347AEF (accessed 11 May 2009). See also UN Doc. S/2002/1012.

prevent *further* terrorist attacks. Yet, it does not actually say that it can exercise the right of self-defence before such an attack has already taken place.[421] Similarly, it would be wrong to read the reference to 'preventive engagement'[422] in the 2003 European Security Strategy as an implicit endorsement of a broad right of anticipatory self-defence. It was precisely in order to avoid confusion with this controversial issue that the original reference to 'pre-emptive engagement' was replaced by more neutral wording.[423] In other words, the phrase does not take a stance vis-à-vis unilateral military intervention; it merely emphasizes the need for early and proactive engagement in the realm of conflict prevention and crisis management.[424] What then about the general reference to the possibility of 'pre-emptive action' in the French Loi de Programmation 2003–8?[425] While one might again be inclined to classify this as a mere policy statement, the 2006 White Paper 'La France face au terrorisme'[426] suggests otherwise. Indeed, the latter document cites the reference to 'pre-emptive action' in response to an explicit and confirmed threat, and

---

[421] Remark: in April 2005, Russia affirmed that 'the [UN] Charter remains a reliable and solid legal basis for resolving problems related to the use of force and does not require revision or a new interpretation'. UN Doc. A/59/PV.87, 6. But see UN Doc. A/60/PV.12, 18 September 2005, 11: 'Another equally important topic is that of States, in exercising their Charter right to individual and collective self-defense, to include self-defense in case of an external terrorist attack or the imminent threat of such attack.'

[422] *European Security Strategy*, 11.

[423] See J. Wouters and T. Ruys, 'The legality of anticipatory military action after 9/11: the slippery slope of self-defense', (2006) 59 *Studia Diplomatica* 45–67, at 57.

[424] Remark: because of a lack of agreement among EU Members regarding the admissibility of anticipatory self-defence, the matter was also circumvented in the Paper the EU submitted to the High-Level Panel. See: EU General Affairs and External Relations Council, Paper for the submission to the High-Level Panel on Threats, Challenges and Change, 17–18 May 2004, available at http://consilium.europa.eu/uedocs/cmsUpload/EU%20written%20contribution2.pdf (accessed 11 May 2009), § 37. The Paper asserts that military action going beyond the lawful exercise of the right to self-defence should be taken on the basis of a Security Council decision. Deliberately vague, it fails to say whether lawful self-defence covers military action in the face of imminent or non-imminent threats, but merely warns that the Security Council must be prepared to act quickly and decisively in order to neutralize the various threats. See also EU Presidency Statement – GA Consultations on Cluster II – Freedom from Fear, 21 April 2005, available at www.europa-eu-un.org/articles/en/article_4661_en.htm (accessed 11 May 2009).

[425] French Ministry of Defence, 'Loi de Programmation militaire 2003–2008', 6.

[426] Secrétariat Général de la Défense Nationale, *La France face au terrorisme: Livre Blanc du Gouvernement sur la sécurité intérieure face au terrorisme* (Paris: La Documentation française, 2006).

expressly frames such action as an application of the right of self-defence, enshrined in Article 51.[427]

In all, it can be confirmed that the circle of States accepting the legality of certain forms of anticipatory self-defence has expanded since 2002. At the same time, one must avoid exaggerating this trend by misinterpreting the precedential value of certain political declarations.

As far as our second question is concerned, there can be no doubt that even among States adhering to the 'counter-restrictionist' view, support for self-defence against non-imminent threats is virtually non-existent. Apart from the fact that the sponsors of Operation 'Iraqi Freedom' avoided this justification, it may be observed that many States, such as Germany, Japan, Switzerland, Uganda, Singapore or Liechtenstein, which professed support for anticipatory self-defence after 2002, nonetheless placed great weight on the imminence requirement.[428] Germany, for instance, expressly denounced an erosion of the Charter framework and State practice via the notion of 'preventive self-defence'.[429] Likewise,

---

[427] *Ibid.*, 62. On the other hand, the description of the concept of '*menace imminente*' in the Manuel de droit des conflits armés (only indicative value) seems to reflect support for 'interceptory' self-defence, while excluding self-defence against imminent threats. '*Menace imminente*' is defined as: 'Agression potentielle dont l'accomplissement bien que probable n'est pas encore réalisé. Cette notion correspond à l'expression anglo-saxonne d'intention hostile. Une telle menace, en droit français, ne justifie pas le recours à la légitime défense individuelle, sauf si elle s'est traduite par un début de realisation.' See French Ministry of Defense, Secrétariat Général pour l'Administration *Manuel de droit des conflits armés*, available at www.defense.gouv.fr/defense/enjeux_defense/ defense_et_droit/droit_des_conflits_armes/manuel_de_droit_des_conflits_armes, at 45 (accessed 11 May 2009).

[428] E.g., Statement of Liechtenstein ('It has been long established that the inherent right of self-defense is limited to military action in case of an imminent attack, as a last resort and in a proportionate manner. Threats which do not meet these criteria must be dealt with by the Security Council . . .'); Statement of Singapore, ('Article 51 should neither be rewritten nor reinterpreted, either to extend its long-established scope (for instance, so as to allow preventive measures to non-imminent threats) or to restrict it (such as to allow its application only to actual attacks)'); reference cited in Corten, *Le droit contre la guerre*, p. 650, footnote 220; (Switzerland: 'absolutely imminent'); Statement of Uganda, (referring to an 'actual or imminent attack'); *supra*, notes 403–4 (Japan). Also: Statement of the Republic of Korea.

[429] See Deutscher Bundestag, Drucksache 15/3635, 17; 'Vortrag Bundesjustizministerin Zypries – Friedrich-Ebert-Stiftung', Berlin, 22 September 2003, available at www.bmj. bund.de/enid/0,19eb566d6f6e7468092d093132093a0979656172092d0932303033093a0 9706d635f6964092d09383930/Reden/Brigitte_Zypries_zc.html (accessed 11 May 2009).

the French *politique de défense* unequivocally 'rejects ... the notion of preventive self-defence'.[430]

What is more, even the 'traditional' adherents of the counter-restrictionist interpretation of Article 51 generally appear to uphold the imminence requirement. Despite bold statements by its Prime Minister on the need to adapt the UN Charter,[431] Australia's response to 'In Larger Freedom' was rather cautious: it simply '[supported] reaffirmation by the Secretary-General that Article 51 of the Charter adequately covers the inherent right to self-defence against actual and imminent attack'.[432] Israel called for an explicit recognition in the World Summit Outcome that States may use force in self-defence 'in the event of both actual and imminent attacks'.[433] As far as the British position is concerned, Attorney-General Lord Goldsmith in 2004 declared before the House of Lords that: 'It is ... the Government's view that international law permits the use of force in self-defence against an imminent attack but does not authorize the use of force to mount a pre-emptive strike against a threat that is more remote'.[434]

Even the US position is cloaked in ambiguity. On the one hand, the NSS's successor, the 2006 US National Security Strategy, reiterates that 'under long-standing principles of self-defence, we do not rule out the use of force before attacks occur, even if uncertainty remains as to the time and place of the enemy's attack', and stresses that '[t]he place of preemption in our National Security Strategy remains the same'.[435] On the other hand, it may be recalled that the US Legal Adviser has gone to

---

[430] French Ministry of Defence, 'Politique de défense' (not dated), available at www.defense.gouv.fr/defense/enjeux_defense/politique_de_defense/strategie_de_defense/politique_de_defense (accessed 11 May 2009): '[l]a France ... refuse tout concept de légitime défense preventive ...'. The French White Paper on terrorism similarly makes a distinction between 'pre-emptive' action against imminent threats and 'preventive' action against potential threats, adding that 'preventive recourse to coercive measures, including the use of force, must be authorized by the Security Council' (author's translation). Secrétariat Général de la Défense Nationale, *La France face au terrorisme*, pp. 62 (footnote 3), 63.

[431] *Supra*, note 390.   [432] Statement by Australia.   [433] Israel Ministry of Foreign Affairs.

[434] *Hansard*, House of Lords, 21 April 2004, column 370. Significantly, in an earlier report to Downing Street relating to the legality of an intervention in Iraq, Lord Goldsmith had pleaded against a reliance on Article 51, on the grounds that 'there must be some degree of imminence'. Note by Attorney-General Lord Goldsmith to the Prime Minister, 7 March 2003, made public on 28 April 2005, available at www.number10.gov.uk/Page7445 (accessed 11 May 2009).

[435] White House, National Security Strategy of the United States of America, March 2006, available at http://georgewbush-whitehouse.archives.gov/nsc/nss/2006/ (accessed

great lengths to construe the 'Bush doctrine' in accordance with the requirement of an imminent threat.[436] Furthermore, in a UNGA discussion on 'In Larger Freedom', the US Representative recalled that: 'The United States has long considered that a State has a right to use force in self-defense in the event of an *actual or imminent* attack. We welcome that both the Secretary-General's report and the High-Level Panel's report specifically endorsed this principle.'[437]

In respect of the first two questions, we may therefore conclude that the trend in State practice has been broadly similar to that in legal doctrine: support for anticipatory self-defence has increased, but has by and large restricted this concept to imminent threats. In this context, it is also worth noting that the International Court of Justice seemed to reject self-defence against non-imminent threats in *DRC* v. *Uganda*.[438] While the Court – as in *Nicaragua* – refused to pronounce on the legality of pre-emptive self-defence, 'legitimate security interests' cited by Uganda were dismissed as 'essentially preventative' and were clearly held insufficient to justify the recourse to force. In particular, it was emphasized that '[Article 51] does not allow the use of force by a State to protect perceived security interests beyond these parameters'.[439]

This brings us to the third and last question, regarding the balance of majority and minority opinion among States. Interestingly, Reisman points to a 'significant lack of comment' on the interpretation of self-defence in the Reports of the High-Level Panel and the UN Secretary-General, which, nonetheless constituted 'an attempt at adjustment of the Charter to meet part of the U.S. claim'.[440] In light of this alleged tacit approval, one might be inclined to qualify the extended support for pre-emptive self-defence as a decisive shift in the *opinio iuris* of the

---

11 May 2009), at 18, 23. For a comparison of the 2002 and 2006 versions, see C. Gray, 'The Bush doctrine revisited: the 2006 National Security Strategy of the USA', (2006) 5 Chinese JIL 555–78, at 563–7.

[436] Taft, 'Preemptive action in self-defense'; Taft, 'The basis for preemption', 333.

[437] US Statement, UNGA Discussion of Cluster II Issues for the High-Level Event, 22 April 2005.

[438] ICJ, *DRC* v. *Uganda*, § 143.

[439] *Ibid.*, § 148. Remark: consider also the following paragraph in *Nicaragua*: '[T]he concept of essential security interests certainly extends beyond the concept of an armed attack, and has been subject to very broad interpretations in the past.' ICJ, *Nicaragua* case (Merits), § 224.

Remark: the German Federal Administrative Court voiced a similar position in 2005: Judgment of the Bundesverwaltungsgericht of 21 June 2005, BVerwG, 2 WD 12.04, 79.

[440] Reisman and Armstrong, 'The claim of preemptive self-defense', 532–3.

international community. An analysis of State responses, however, learns that this conclusion is rather precipitate. Indeed, notwithstanding a number of positive (cf. *supra*) and rather vague[441] reactions by several States, numerous UN Members opposed the acceptance of pre-emptive self-defence. Turkey,[442] Argentina[443] and Mexico,[444] for instance, observed that the admissibility of self-defence in response to imminent threats was very controversial and warned that recognition thereof might lead to complications and abuse. Many States went even further and combined a rejection of the interpretation of Article 51 in the two Reports with an explicit affirmation that self-defence could only be exercised in response to an actual armed attack. In the words of Pakistan:

> We certainly do not agree that Article 51 of the Charter provides for the pre-emptive, preventive or protective use of force. In our view, the language of Article 51 is quite explicit and highly limitative. It provides for the use of force in self-defence only in case of an actual attack against a Member State. . . ..[445]

---

[441] E.g., UN Doc. A/59/PV.86, 20 (Chile, rejecting preventive action); UN Doc. A/59/PV.87, 6 (Russia); UN Doc. A/59/PV.89, 4 (Poland), 24 (Venezuela); UN Doc. A/59/PV.90, 3 (Cameroon).

[442] Statement of Turkey, Informal thematic consultations of the General Assembly on 'In Larger Freedom', New York, 22 April 2005: 'The premise that "Article 51 of the UN Charter covers imminent attack and that the right of self-defence can be evoked accordingly" is not a universally accepted interpretation in international law. Therefore, in reaffirming this Article, we should be careful and avoid introducing a new and broad interpretation which might lead to certain complications.'

[443] Statement of Argentina, Informal Thematic Consultations of the General Assembly on 'In Larger Freedom', New York, 22 April 2005: 'What clearly derives from Article 51 is the exercise of a legitimate defense after an armed attack. Neither from the reading of Article 51, nor from the posterior practice of the Security Council can it be affirmed that this norm should include legitimate defense in case of an "imminent" attack. That is still under strong discussion.'

[444] Intervention of Mexico, Informal Thematic Consultations of the General Assembly on 'In Larger Freedom', New York, 22 April 2005, available at www.un.int/mexico/2005/interv_042205.htm (accessed 11 May 2009), §§ 8–20. The Mexican Ambassador dealt with pre-emptive self-defence in a very elaborate manner. He drew attention amongst other things to the clear meaning of Article 51 and the lack of State practice supporting pre-emptive self-defence. Mexico was very critical of the concerned provisions of the UNSG Report: '¿A qué juristas se refiere el Secretario General? Tal apreciación sobre el estado del derecho internacional vigente y de la doctrina jurídica es errónea.' It concluded that: 'No es posible extraer ninguna conclusión definitiva de la práctica de los Estados sobre la existencia del derecho a legitíma defensa ante un ataque inminente . . .'.

[445] Statement of Pakistan, Informal Thematic Consultations on Cluster-II 'Freedom from Fear', New York, 21 April 2005. Also UN Doc. A/59/PV.86, 5 (in relation to 'In Larger Freedom').

Comparable statements were submitted by the representatives of Vietnam,[446] Belarus,[447] Bangladesh,[448] Algeria,[449] Iran,[450] Cuba,[451] Costa Rica[452] and Egypt.[453] Other States that explicitly or implicitly voiced opposition to pre-emptive self-defence include China, India, Syria,[454] Malaysia[455]

---

[446] Statement of Vietnam, Informal Thematic Consultations of the General Assembly on 'In Larger Freedom', New York, 22 April 2005, 3: 'In no way do the spirit and letters of Article 51 provide an expanded scope of permitting States to take military action on the basis of perceived imminent threat.' Also: UN Doc. A/59/PV.89, 22.

[447] Statement of the Republic of Belarus, Informal Thematic Consultations of the General Assembly on 'In Larger Freedom', New York, 22 April 2005, § 4: 'We are especially concerned about the misleading conclusions of the Secretary-General with respect to the application of Article 51. Any interpretation allowing preemptive self-defense actions in response to an imminent threat of armed attack against any State contradicts the literal wording of the Article, the provisions [of] the [UN] Charter as well as the general doctrine of international law.'

[448] Statement of Bangladesh, Informal Thematic Consultations on Cluster-II of 'In Larger Freedom', New York, 21 April 2005.

[449] UN Doc. A/59/PV.86, 9: 'As to the use of force, the Secretary-General clearly endorses the Panel's logic regarding the interpretation of Article 51 on legitimate self-defence. We do not share that reasoning. We believe that the wording of Article 51 is restrictive and that the legitimate right of self-defence can therefore be invoked and applied only in the case of armed aggression. Indeed, doctrine and jurisprudence teach us that Article 51 in no way covers imminent attacks.' Also: Statement of Algeria, Informal Thematic Consultations on Cluster-II 'Freedom from Fear', New York, 21 April 2005, 4.

[450] UN Doc. A/59/PV.87, 17: 'The report argues that "Lawyers have long recognized that [Article 51] covers an imminent attack as well as one that has already happened." ... It is evident that, from a purely legal perspective, nothing can be further from the letter or the spirit of the Charter or the opinion of independent jurists. Various judgments of the [ICJ] in various cases have emphasized that measures in self-defence are legitimate only after an armed attack occurs. Article 51 in no way covers imminent threats, and international law does not confer any legitimacy on the dangerous doctrine of pre-emption.' Also: Statement of Iran, Informal Thematic Consultations on Cluster-II of 'In Larger Freedom', New York, 22 April 2005, § 2.

[451] Statement of Cuba, 18 May 2005: '[W]e reject the attempt to broaden the scope of [Article 51] to include the question of the so-called "imminent threats" (...).' Also: UN Doc. A/59/PV.89, 14.

[452] Statement of Costa Rica, Informal Consultations on the Report of the High-Level Panel, 31 January 2005, available at www2.un.int/Countries/CostaRica/1107238995.pdf (accessed 7 May 2009), 3.

[453] Statement of Egypt, Informal Thematic Consultations on Cluster-II of 'In Larger Freedom', New York, 21 April 2005: 'We emphasize that the right of self-defence under [Article 51] exists only if an armed attack occurs against the State. ... Article 51 has no expanded scope of permitting the threatened States to take military actions as long as threatened attack did not take place factually.' Also UN Doc. A/59/PV.86, 12.

[454] UN Doc. A/59/PV.90, 19.

[455] Statement of Malaysia, Informal Thematic Consultations on Cluster-II of 'In Larger Freedom', New York, 22 April 2005, § 14.

and Indonesia.[456] China, for example, argued that Article 51 needed neither rewriting nor reinterpretation: '[E]xcept in case of self-defence against armed attacks, any use of force must have the authorization of the Security Council. Any "imminent threat" should be carefully judged and handled by the Security Council . . .'.[457] India noted that the framers of the Charter never intended Article 51 to cover anything beyond its text.[458] Significantly, the Non-Aligned Movement in 2005 issued a position paper emphasizing that: 'Article 51 . . . is restrictive and recognizes 'the inherent right of individual or collective self-defence if an armed attack occurs against a Member of the United Nations.' This Article should not be re-written or re-interpreted. This is supported by the practice of the UN . . .'.[459]

In the end, because of the resistance of a considerable number of UN Members to the acceptance of pre-emptive self-defence, the relevant recommendations of the High-Level Panel were not included in the Outcome Document of the 2005 World Summit of the UN General Assembly. No trace of Article 51 can be found in the resolution. Instead, paragraph 79 simply reaffirms 'that the relevant provisions of the Charter are sufficient to address the full range of threats to international peace and security.'[460]

In light of the available evidence, it can be concluded that there has indeed been a shift in States' *opinio iuris* insofar as support for pre-emptive self-defence, fairly rare and muted prior to 2001, has become more widespread and explicit in recent years. At the same time, it seems a bridge too far to claim that there exists today widespread acceptance of the legality of self-defence against so-called 'imminent' threats. Such assertion tends to forego the opposition of a considerable group of mainly Latin-American, north-African and Asian States. In the present

---

[456] UN Doc. A/59/PV.88, 26; Statement of Indonesia, Informal Meeting of the Plenary to Exchange Views on the President's Draft Outcome Document of the High-Level Plenary Meeting of the General Assembly of September 2005, New York, 30 June 2005; Statement of Indonesia, Informal Consultations of the General Assembly, New York, 22 February 2005.

[457] Statement of China, Informal Thematic Consultations on Cluster-II of 'In Larger Freedom', New York, 22 April 2005. Also: Statement of China on the Report of the High-Level Panel, 27 January 2005.

[458] UN Doc. A/59/PV.90, 24.

[459] Comments of the Non-Aligned Movement on the Observations and Recommendations contained in the Report of the High-Level Panel on Threats, Challenges and Change, New York, 28 February 2005, available at www.un.int/malaysia/NAM/Positionpaper280205.doc (accessed 11 May 2009), § 23.

[460] 'World Summit Outcome', GA Res. 60/1, 16 September 2005, UN Doc. A/RES/60/1, § 79.

author's view, it would therefore be more appropriate to argue that the crack in *opinio iuris* among States has widened, without, however, identifying one approach or the other as the majority view. The implication is that, taking account of the Charter 'baseline' and the absence of a concrete precedent in State practice which convincingly demonstrates the international community's support for some form of anticipatory self-defence, it is impossible to identify *de lege lata* a general right of pre-emptive – and *a fortiori* preventive – self-defence.

4.3 Exceptions and borderline cases

At the same time, our examination of the *ratione temporis* dimension cannot end here. A categorical rejection *de lege lata* of pre-emptive self-defence leaves unanswered the question at what precise moment an attack can be said to have commenced in different situations. For this reason, the present section analyses a number of (possible) exceptions and borderline cases. Since most scenarios have already been touched upon in Chapters 2 and 3, we will avoid recapitulating what has been elaborated elsewhere. The section also includes some policy considerations vis-à-vis the desirability of anticipatory self-defence.

4.3.1 The prospective dimension of the necessity standard

At the outset, a recurring misunderstanding should be set straight. On occasion, scholars supporting a broad doctrine of anticipatory self-defence have invoked a series of incidents where States, after suffering an attack, have resorted to the use of force to prevent *further* attacks from being launched.[461] Especially in recent years, these precedents have been cited to demonstrate that the US has always supported the legality of anticipatory self-defence and that it has obtained broad acceptance in customary practice. Yoo, for instance, observes that '[i]n the past two decades, the [US] has used military force in anticipatory self-defence against Libya, ... Iraq, Afghanistan, and the Sudan'.[462] As mentioned before, however,[463] the incidents referred to – the 1986 strikes against Tripoli, the 1993 operation against the Iraqi intelligence headquarters and the 1998 strikes against alleged terrorist infrastructure in Sudan and Afghanistan – are analytically different from pure recourse to force

---

[461] See *inter alia* references under note 199.
[462] Yoo, 'The war in Iraq', 573–4.   [463] *Supra*, Section 4.1.2.d.

against imminent threats. Indeed, in each case, the US claimed that it had been the victim of a prior attack, more precisely 'an ongoing pattern' of Libyan-sponsored terrorist attacks,[464] a series of armed attacks against US embassies and US nationals,[465] and a failed attempt to assassinate former President Bush Snr.[466] For this reason, these cases, as well as other incidents where the intervening State relied on the need to prevent additional attacks – e.g., the 1964 Gulf of Tunkin incident, the 1975 Israeli intervention in Lebanon, the South African incursions into Lesotho in 1982, or the US-led intervention in Afghanistan in 2001 – cannot be regarded as customary evidence in support of anticipatory self-defence.[467] Instead, the better view is that this 'preventive' aspect of the aforementioned interventions pertains to the prospective dimension of the necessity assessment.[468] Indeed, as explained in Section 2.2.2.b.ii, the right of self-defence does not automatically terminate when the armed attack is factually over. Again, customary practice generally supports the view that if a State suffers an attack and there is compelling evidence that further attacks will imminently follow, it is not obliged to confine itself to on-the-spot reaction, but may also engage in *post facto* defensive measures.[469] In the case of an isolated and small-scale attack, *post facto* action will generally be excluded. By contrast, a more flexible assessment is warranted when confronted with consecutive and/or large-scale attacks.

4.3.2. Possible exceptions?

As far as possible exceptions to the general inadmissibility of anticipatory self-defence are concerned, it may be noted that the UNGA Definition of Aggression implicitly identifies one situation where the first use of force can constitute an exercise of self-defence. Indeed, Article 3(e) lists as an example of aggression '[t]he use of armed forces of one State which are within the territory of another State with the agreement of the receiving State, in contravention of the conditions provided for in the agreement *or any extension of their presence in such territory beyond the termination of the agreement*' (emphasis added). In light of this provision, it is accepted

---

[464] UN Doc. S/17990.   [465] UN Doc. S/1998/780.
[466] UN Doc. S/PV.3245, 27 June 1993, 6 (US).
[467] UN Doc. S/PV.1109, 7 April 1964, §§ 17, 29; UN Doc. S/PV.1111, 9 April 1964, § 30; (1964) UNYB 147; UN Doc. S/PV.1859, § 119; UN Doc. S/PV.2409, §§ 137–45; UN Doc. S/2001/946, 7 October 2001 (US); UN Doc. S/2001/947, 7 October 2001(UK).
[468] Also Corten, *Le droit contre la guerre*, p. 659 ; M. E. O'Connell, 'L'intervention en Iraq', 12.
[469] E.g., Ago, 'Addendum', 70; Dinstein, *War, aggression and self-defence*, 4th edn, pp. 227–8.

that if a State no longer consents to the presence of foreign troops on its soil, it may use force in self-defence – even if there has been no 'armed attack' in the literal or military sense – as long as it abides by the necessity and proportionality standards.[470] This means *inter alia* that the victim State should first attempt to resolve the dispute peacefully; that the other State should be given a chance to withdraw; and that it must be made clear that force will be used if withdrawal is refused.

Furthermore, the *travaux* of the Definition of Aggression render some support to the existence of a second exception, viz. the promulgation of a declaration of war. Indeed, throughout the negotiations, there was considerable discussion as to whether such act could in itself activate Article 51 UN Charter. Both the Soviet draft[471] and the Thirteen-Power draft[472] listed it as an example of aggression. However, a number of States objected that a declaration of war was as such a formal act, which was not always followed by an actual recourse to force. In the debate that unfolded, three different interpretations were put forward: some regarded a declaration of war as an 'armed attack' justifying the exercise of self-defence; for others, it was an aggressive act but not equivalent to an 'armed attack'; still others thought it only constituted aggression if accompanied by the actual use of armed force.[473] Canada, France and the US discarded the view that a declaration of war necessarily qualified as aggression.[474] Several other States objected that it did, and a number of them – including Bulgaria, Ghana, Cyprus, the Soviet Union and Greece – asserted that it triggered the right of self-defence.[475] In support of the latter view, it was argued that

---

[470] E.g., Christakis, 'La notion de guerre préventive', p. 23 ; Sicilianos, *Des contre-mesures à la légitime défense*, p. 400. In 1958, for instance, the continued presence of French troops after Tunisia had withdrawn its consent was considered by the latter country as one element of an 'armed aggression' by France, enabling the right of self-defence. See: UN Doc. S/PV.819, 2 June 1958, especially at §§ 45 *et seq.*; (1958) UNYB 77–8. Eventually, the two countries reached a negotiated solution. Remark: Brownlie agrees that the continued presence of foreign forces after the consent of the territorial sovereign has been withdrawn constitutes a use of force if there is armed resistance or threats in answer to attempts by the sovereign to remove such forces. Brownlie, 'The use of force in self-defence', 261.

[471] Article 2(a), UN Doc. A/AC.134/L.12 (and Corr. 1).

[472] Article 5(a), UN Doc. A/AC.134/L.16 (and Corr. 1).

[473] See UN Doc. A/AC.134/SR.67–78, 60 (Italy).

[474] *Ibid.*, 54. According to France, 'a declaration of war, if not accompanied by materially aggressive acts, did not constitute aggression.'

[475] *Ibid.*, 54 (Romania), 56 (Bulgaria), (Ghana: 'When a country declared war, aggressive intent must be presumed against that country. That country was therefore committing an aggressive act and thereby laid itself open to attack . . .'), (Ecuador: '[A] declaration

a declaration of war constituted a clear and unambiguous manifestation of aggressive intent, and was usually accompanied or followed by an actual attack. The Soviet Union, for one, was 'surprised' that the protagonists of the 'intent' criterion refused to recognize it as an act of aggression.[476] On the other hand, Italy, Syria and Uruguay held that a declaration of war, not accompanied by actual use of force, arguably constituted a threat or a breach of the peace, but did not as such give rise to self-defence.[477] According to Uruguay, for instance:

> Only if it was accompanied by the use of armed force could the victim legitimately resort to the use of force in self-defence under Article 51 of the Charter. Where a declaration of war was not accompanied by armed attack, the victim could take any appropriate defensive measures short of armed force.[478]

The UK seemingly adopted a middle road. It claimed that a declaration of war by itself could not be construed as identical with an 'armed attack', and reserved the right of self-defence to cases where the declaration was 'credible', i.e., 'where there was an imminent threat of the use of force'.[479]

In the end, 'declarations of war' were omitted from the (non-exhaustive) list of acts of aggression. The Definition moreover clarifies that the acts listed in Article 3 shall qualify as acts of aggression 'regardless of a declaration of war'. In light of the positions taken in the debate as well as the applicability of the proportionality principle, it can nonetheless be argued that a declaration of war 'patently unaccompanied by deeds' does not sanction an armed response in self-defence.[480] In other

---

of war by a State meant that it was ready to launch an armed attack and that it intended to do so. The declaration of war should therefore be treated as an act of aggression.'), (Cyprus: '[I]t must always be assumed that they would be followed by an armed attack. A declaration of war should therefore be considered as part of an act of aggression, which gave rise to the right of self-defence'), 58–9 (USSR); UN Doc. A/C.6/SR.1208, 27 October 1974, § 6 (Greece).

[476] UN Doc. A/AC.134/SR.67-78, 58–9 ('Since war was unlikely to be declared unless there was an intention to launch an armed attack, the victim should be permitted to take immediate practical measures in self-defence.')

[477] Ibid., 54, 57–8 (Syria: '[A]lthough a declaration of war was a threat to peace, it did not justify the exercise of the right of self-defence under Article 51 of the Charter'), 57 (Uruguay), 55, 60–1 (Italy: 'A declaration of war was merely a formal act expressing the intention to start a war. [Italy] doubted whether such a formal act could, in isolation, be considered as an armed attack within the meaning of Article 51 of the Charter.'). Arguably also Colombia: ibid., 57 juncto 61.

[478] Ibid., 57.   [479] Ibid., 59–60.

[480] Dinstein, War, aggression and self-defence, 4th edn, p. 186, footnote 62; Brownlie, 'The use of force in self-defence', 259.

cases, it is not entirely clear whether Article 51 is activated. Customary practice after 1945 does not provide further clarification. It must be added, however, that if neither State engages in the use of force in the period following the issuing of the declaration of war, the State against which war has been declared cannot at a much later stage rely on the existence of a technical 'state of war' to appeal to Article 51 UN Charter.[481] In any event, the problem is not as acute as it might seem. As many States stressed in the Fourth Special Committee, declarations of war are by and large a thing of the past, and, if adopted, merely tend to formalize hostilities which are already ongoing.[482]

A third possible exception concerns military intervention for the 'protection of nationals'. *If one accepts* that such intervention is a permissible application of the right of self-defence, then it is arguably an exceptional form of pre-emptive self-defence. Indeed, one of the preconditions, as identified by Waldock[483] and restated by supporters of the 'protection of nationals' doctrine,[484] is that a State's nationals abroad must be under an 'imminent threat of injury or death'. In other words, the State must not sit idly and wait until some of its nationals abroad have actually been killed or injured; it is allowed to act when there is a compelling risk that this will be the case in the immediate future.

4.3.3 Interceptive self-defence at the tactical level: on-the-spot reaction

Apart from the aforementioned scenarios, we also need to look into the concept of 'interceptive' self-defence, namely the recourse to force against attacks which have actually 'commenced,' even if they have not yet crossed the border and/or have not yet resulted in actual damage or loss of life. It is as such fairly uncontroversial that Article 51 must inevitably cover some degree of 'interceptive' action: States can hardly be expected to await the *impact* of an armed attack. At the same time, the

---

[481] See *supra* notes 161, 192.
[482] E.g., UN Doc. A/AC.134/SR.67–78, at 56 (Ecuador, Cyprus), 57 (Uruguay, Syria). Also: Broms, 'The definition of aggression', 347.
[483] Waldock, 'The regulation of the use of force', 467.
[484] E.g., Statement of UK Foreign Secretary Selwyn Lloyd, reproduced in G. Marston, 'Armed intervention in the 1956 Suez crisis: the legal advice tendered to the British government', (1988) 37 ICLQ 773–817, at 800–1; UN Doc. S/PV.1939, 9 July 1976, §§ 105–21 (Israel); UN Doc. S/PV.1941, 12 July 1976, §§ 77–81 (US); UN Doc. A/C.6/55/SR.19, § 15 (Italy). Also: See Special Rapporteur John Dugard, 'First Report on Diplomatic Protection', 7 March 2000, UN Doc. A/CN.4/506, §§ 46–60.

exact content of the notion remains unclear. Apart from the obvious example of the interception of an incoming missile, little agreement exists as to what action is envisaged. Furthermore, it appears that authors sometimes fail to distinguish between 'interceptive' and 'pre-emptive' self-defence.[485]

Early in this chapter, it was asserted that a small, but significant distinction exists between the two notions, in that 'interceptive' self-defence imposes a slightly narrower timeframe and a heavier burder of evidence than its 'pre-emptive' counterpart. Indeed, while the latter only requires an 'imminent' threat of attack, the former presupposes that the opponent's *capacity* and *intention* to initiate a concrete armed attack has resulted in concrete measures of *implementation*: the opponent must have crossed the legal Rubicon – the point of no return.[486] While this is the general point of departure, 'interceptive self-defence' arguably necessitates a different approach on the tactical level and on the strategic level. At the strategic level, the irreversibility of the course of actions embarked upon appears to be the determining factor. By contrast, at the tactical level, i.e., the level of on-the-spot reaction to small-scale incidents, what matters most is arguably the ascertaining of the opponent's 'hostile intent'.[487] This is exactly why the example of the incoming missile is so uncontested: once the missile has been detected, the issue of hostile intent normally becomes moot. In other situations, establishing the opponent's hostile intent presupposes a rather complex series of actions, belonging to the realm of military Rules of Engagement. Two main scenarios can be discerned.

4.3.3.a Territorial incursions by land, sea or air

A first border case – both figuratively and literally – concerns (unlawful) territorial incursions by land, sea or air. We have already elaborated on this scenario in Section 3.3, where we examined how, in spite of their sometimes minor scale, such incursions may trigger the right of self-defence under certain conditions. For present purposes, it may be added

---

[485] Compare for example: Waldock, 'The regulation of the use of force', 498; Dinstein, *War, aggression and self-defence*, 4th edn, p. 182. Consider also: Brownlie, *The use of force by States*, p. 368; Shaw, *International law*, p. 1030.

[486] Dinstein, *War, aggression and self-defence*, 4th edn, p. 191; Sicilianos, *Des contre-mesures à la légitime défense*, p. 403.

[487] See, e.g., Fleck, 'Rules of engagement', 181; K.-G. Park, *La protection de la souveraineté aérienne* (Paris: Pedone, 1991), p. 317; J. Sundberg, 'Legitimate responses to aerial intruders: the view from a neutral State', (1985) 10 AASL 251–73, at 266.

that territorial incursions are not only a border case from a *ratione materiae* perspective, but also from the *ratione temporis* perspective. Indeed, as explained before, customary practice accepts that States may undertake proportionate *on-the-spot* military action against (even small-scale) unlawful incursions on their territory, if there are strong indications of a hostile intent on behalf of the intruding State. In such situations, military action may exceptionally be undertaken before the intruding unit(s) have in fact opened fire, in other words before there has been an armed attack in the literal or military sense of the word.

Few scholars will deny that a large-scale incursion, e.g., the unauthorized entry of entire panzer brigades or fighter squads, triggers the territorial State's right of self-defence.[488] Indeed, even if the opponent has not (yet) engaged in actual combat, it is generally accepted that such incursion amounts to an 'armed attack', even if, technically, the military response of the territorial State would constitute a form of 'interceptive' self-defence. This is hardly surprising, since such invasion will generally leave no doubt that the opponent is in the process of launching an attack, and that there is indeed evidence of the required '*animus aggressionis*'. Nonetheless, when dealing with small-scale incursions, several scholars feel uncomfortable with applying the Charter rules on the use of force and bringing a possible military response under the umbrella of self-defence, allegedly because of the lack of actual use of force or actual attack.[489] However, as explained earlier, in the present author's view, any active use of lethal or potentially lethal force by forces of State A against military or police personnel of State B acting in their official capacity, *including within its own borders*, is covered by the prohibition of Article 2(4) UN Charter and must be justified on the basis of Article 51 UN Charter.[490] Accordingly, it seems more logical, and more faithful to customary practice, to construe States' leeway of action in response to small-scale territorial incursions in terms of a continuum between measures short of the use of force and the use of force in self-defence.

What action may be chosen from the continuum of measures strongly depends on the absence or presence of hostile intent. At times, clear indications of hostile intent may exist. This will be the case, for example, if a fighter jet of a rival nation crosses the border and approaches a military installation at full speed (certainly when a radar detects a missile

---

[488] E.g., Constantinou, *The right of self-defence*, p. 125; Dinstein, *War, aggression and self-defence*, 4th edn, p. 189.
[489] See *Infra* Section 3.3.   [490] *Ibid.*

target lock). A similar situation – if one follows the version of the facts presented by the United Arab Republic – concerns the sinking of the Israeli destroyer *Eilat*, which was detected speeding in UAR territorial waters in contravention of the ceasefire.[491] In light of the hostile relationship between the two States at the time of the incident and the fact that the vessel had previously been involved in the sinking of two vessels in UAR waters, the '*animus aggressionis*' could arguably be presumed.

When the subjective element is apparently lacking or uncertain, the territorial State can engage in a number of graduated measures that – initially – fall short of the actual use of force and that shift the onus onto the trespassing unit(s) and force it to either terminate its unlawful behaviour or to reveal a hostile intent. Such measures include the use of verbal warnings, the firing of warning shots, interposition and other manoeuvres, et cetera. If the intruder persists and thereby adopts a threatening posture, the required hostile intent will again be present, implying that proportionate defensive measures can lawfully be undertaken. It may be observed that customary practice is more flexible vis-à-vis forcible action against intrusions by air than against intrusions of the territorial sea. This is probably explained by the high speed and destructive potential of modern aircraft – a modern fighter jet will have crossed the territory of a small State in a manner of minutes (if not seconds) – as well as by the fact that unauthorized aerial incursions are by definition unlawful (the situation is more complex under the law of the sea).

Important factors that influence the detection of the intruder's hostile intent include the political context and the relationship between the States concerned the gravity of the incursions and their isolated or recurring nature. Numerous other, more specific factors can be identified. Possible examples are the intruder's proximity to sensitive targets, the type of unit (e.g., fighter jet versus transport plane), the speed and the track followed, the weather situation at the time, et cetera.

Hostile intent in the present context is not strictly limited to an evident intention to commit an actual attack – in the military sense – against the State's territory, but may exceptionally extend to unlawful and persistent intrusions which can be regarded as preparations for future attacks or which otherwise threaten the State's security. Thus, in relation to aerial intrusions, Brownlie correctly suggests that military intelligence flights and tactics of 'psychological warfare' may – depending on the context – be regarded by the State which is their object as 'circumstantial evidence

---

[491] *Ibid.*

of an intention to attack or preparation for further attacks'.[492] In a similar vein, in light of the difficulty of establishing the objectives and state of readiness of a submerged submarine, the persistent presence of such vessel in a State's territorial waters may sometimes be regarded as an 'armed attack', in the (legal) sense of Article 51 UN Charter.[493]

In any event, it will have to be determined on a case-by-case basis whether the recourse to force could reasonably be regarded as a 'last resort' and whether it was proportionate to the intrusion.

4.3.3.b Hostile encounters between military units and 'unit self-defence'

Mutatis mutandis, one might expect the same principles to apply vis-à-vis hostile encounters between military units *outside the State's territory*, in particular in international waters or airspace. National military manuals appear to offer some support for the thesis that military units are exceptionally permitted to use force in self-defence against an approaching military unit when there is an unequivocal display of hostile intent, even if the latter unit has not (yet) opened fire. Thus, the US Commander's *Handbook of the Law of Naval Operations* repeatedly asserts that: 'Unit commanders always retain the inherent right and obligation to exercise unit self-defense in response to a hostile act or demonstrated hostile intent.'[494] Logic dictates that 'hostile intent' is identified along the lines of the factors listed above. Apart from the political context and the repeated nature of the incidents, evidence of '*animus aggressionis*' can be deduced from the locking of fire control radars, the opening of bomb bay doors, the acoustic detection of torpedo or missile tube doors, the distance and speed of the opposing unit, the unit's manoeuvring into a weapon launch profile, et cetera.[495] At the same time, when dealing with hostile encounters outside the State's own territory, 'hostile intent' must be taken to refer exclusively to the intention to launch an actual attack against the military unit or, for example, a

---

[492] Brownlie, 'The use of force in self-defence', 257. See also US Department of the Navy and US Department of Homeland Security, *The Commander's Handbook of the Law of Naval Operations*, July 2007, NWP 1-14M, available at www.nwc.navy.mil/cnws/ild/documents/1-14m_(jul_2007)_(nwp).pdf (accessed 11 May 2009), 4-4.

[493] Also Dinstein, *War, aggression and self-defence*, 4th edn, p. 198.

[494] NWP 1-14 M, 4-6, 4-9.

[495] See, e.g., D. Stephens, 'Rules of engagement and the concept of unit self-defense', (1998) 45 Naval L Rev 126–51, at 148; Sicilianos, *Des contre-mesures à la légitime défense*, p. 403.

member of its convoy. Military intelligence activities, such as the overflight of a reconnaissance aircraft in international airspace, do not justify the recourse to force outside the State's borders.

Admittedly, upon closer examination of State practice, there appears to be very little public and corroborating evidence for this type of interceptive self-defence. Generally, States involved in such incidents have claimed that their vessels or aircraft were first fired upon before opening fire in self-defence, and have questioned the legality of the opposing unit's presence. An impartial investigation has often proved impossible. A first example concerns the downing of two US military aircraft by the Soviet Air Force on 4 September and 7 November 1954.[496] On both occasions, the US claimed: (1) that the incident took place while its units were located either in Japanese territorial air space (with the consent of the Japanese authorities), or in international airspace over the Sea of Japan; and (2) that the US aircraft – a Neptune and a B-29 respectively – had been attacked by Soviet fighters without advance warning and without any prior provocation on their account. With regard to the first incident, it was stated that the crew of the Neptune only returned fire (in vain) after first having been fired upon and while seeking disengagement.[497] As for the second incident, the US denied that the B-29 had at any time fired upon its attackers.[498] By contrast, according to the Soviet version of the incidents, it was asserted that the two US aircraft had violated the territory of the Soviet Union, and 'without provocation opened fire on Soviet interceptors guarding the State border'.[499]

Again, in relation to the 1964 Gulf of Tunkin incident, the United States insisted that its units were in international waters at the time of the

---

[496] See ICJ, *Aerial incident of 4 September 1954* (*United States of America* v. *Union of Soviet States Republic*), US application instituting proceedings, 25 July 1958, available at www.icj-cij.org/docket/files/40/9187.pdf; ICJ, *Aerial incident of 7 November 1954* (*United States of America* v. *Union of Soviet States Republic*), US application instituting proceedings, 8 June 1959, available at www.icj-cij.org/docket/files/44/10821.pdf; (1954) UNYB 47–50 (websites accessed on 11 May 2009).

[497] ICJ, *Aerial incident of 4 September 1954*, US application, 16.

[498] ICJ, *Aerial incident of 7 November 1954*, US application, 23.

[499] ICJ, *Aerial incident of 4 September 1954*, US application, 22; ICJ, *Aerial incident of 7 November 1954*, US application, 13–14.

Remark: while the US filed two separate claims with the International Court of Justice, both cases were withdrawn as a result of the Soviet Union's refusal to accept jurisdiction. ICJ, *Aerial incident of 4 September 1954*, Order of Removal, 9 December 1958, available at www.icj-cij.org/docket/files/40/2389.pdf; ICJ, *Aerial incident of 7 November 1954*, Order of Removal, 7 October 1959, available at www.icj-cij.org/docket/files/44/2415.pdf (accessed 11 May 2009).

hostile encounters, and North Vietnamese torpedo boats had been first to open fire.[500] Unsurprisingly, the Democratic Republic of Vietnam rejected the US version. Instead, it drew attention to previous US attacks on Vietnamese territory, affirmed that the incidents took place within Vietnamese territorial waters, and objected that US units had initiated the exchange of fire.[501] An independent investigation was never commissioned, yet it has recently been suggested that the account of the incidents was at least partially manipulated by US personnel.[502]

Similarly, in relation to the 1981 Gulf of Sidra incident, during which American aircraft shot down two Libyan aircraft, the States concerned disagreed as to whether the incident took place within or without Libyan territorial airspace, which party was the first to open fire and which party had provoked the incident.[503]

---

[500] With regard to the incident of 2 August the following account was submitted: '[T]he United States destroyer *Maddox* was on routine patrol in international waters in the Gulf of Tonkin... The *Maddox* was approached by three high-speed North Vietnamese torpedo boats in attack formation. When it was evident that these torpedo boats intended to take offensive action, the *Maddox*, in accordance with naval practice, fired three warning shots across the bows of the approaching vessels. At approximately the same time, the aircraft carrier *Ticonderoga*, which ... had been alerted to the impending attack, sent out four aircraft to provide air cover for the *Maddox*. The pilots were under orders not to fire unless they or the *Maddox* were fired upon first. Two of the attacking craft fired torpedoes which the *Maddox* evaded by changing course. All three attacking vessels directed machine-gun fire at the *Maddox*. One of the attacking vessels approached for close attack and was struck by fire from the *Maddox*.' UN Doc. S/PV.1140, 5 August 1964, §§ 36–8. For a similar account of the 4 August 1964 incident: UN Doc. S/PV.1141, 7 August 1964, §§ 45–6 (US).

[501] See UN Doc. S/5907, 19 August 1964 (Democratic Republic of Vietnam).
Remark: the Soviet Union and Czechoslovakia similarly questioned the accuracy of the US version: UN Doc. S/PV.1140, § 56 (USSR); UN Doc. S/PV.1141, §§ 29–31.

[502] See R. J. Hanyok, 'Skunks, bogies, silent hounds, and the flying fish: the Gulf of Tonkin mystery, 2–4 August 1964', (2000–1) 19 *Cryptologic Quarterly*, available at www.nsa.gov/vietnam/releases/relea00012.pdf (accessed 11 May 2009) (The author is a historian who worked for the National Security Agency. The article was unclassified in the course of 2005); S. Shane, 'Vietnam War intelligence "deliberately skewed", Secret Study says', *NY Times* 2 December 2005.

[503] UN Doc. S/14632, 19 August 1981 (US, referring to an unprovoked attack against American naval aircraft operating in international airspace and participating in a routine naval exercise in international waters; stating that 'acting in self-defence, American aircraft returned fire, and two Libyan aircraft were shot down'); UN Doc. S/14636, 20 August 1981 (Libya, referring to the aggressive and provocative nature of the US naval exercises in the Gulf of Sidra; claiming that the incident took place within Libyan airspace; and stating that the Libyan aircraft were shot down 'while conducting reconnaissance duties over our territorial waters and air space'). See also (1981) UNYB 360–1; S R. Ratner, 'The Gulf of Sidra incident of 1981: a study of the lawfulness of peacetime aerial engagements', (1984) 10 YJIL 58–76, at 68.

Ironically, the only incident that was subject to international scrutiny and in which a State relied on interceptive self-defence in relation to a (perceived) hostile encounter between military units beyond its own territory concerns the shooting by the USS *Vincennes* of Iran Air Flight 655 in the Persian Gulf in 1988.[504] *In casu*, the USS *Vincennes* detected what was perceived as a hostile Iranian military aircraft. When, despite repeated warnings by radio transmission, the aircraft continued to approach its location, the vessel launched two surface-to-air missiles, destroying the civilian airliner Iran Air Flight 655 and killing all passengers on board. Shortly after the incident, the US reported to the Security Council that, although it regretted the 'terrible human tragedy', its forces had acted lawfully in accordance with Article 51 UN Charter.[505]

Admittedly, the incident hardly constitutes a very helpful example of the type of interceptive self-defence under consideration. First, the US self-defence claim was not purely based on the need to intercept a perceived attack by the approaching aircraft. It was argued that at the time of the incident, the USS *Vincennes* and another US naval vessel were already engaged in the exchange of fire with a number of Iranian patrol boats in order to protect neutral merchant shipping from attack.[506] This factor not only strengthened the perception on board the USS *Vincennes* that the aircraft had a hostile intent – it was feared that an Iranian plane would render air support for the surface engagements with US warships – but could also be taken to imply that the US was subject to an *ongoing*, rather than a merely incipient armed attack. Second, the incident is of course a perverse example, since it resulted from a series of miscalculations by US military personnel and led to the destruction of a civilian aeroplane, which did not in any event have the potential to launch an attack.

Still, the international response reveals some implicit support for interceptive self-defence vis-à-vis hostile encounters between military units. Thus, throughout a series of Security Council debates, most UN Members accepted that the United States had committed a tragic, yet honest mistake (even if some regretted that the presence of Western naval powers in the Persian Gulf had contributed to a highly ignitable situation).[507] None of the intervening States felt inclined to refute the

---

[504] (1988) UNYB 199–200.   [505] UN Doc. S/19989, 6 July 1988 (US).
[506] *Ibid.*; UN Doc. S/PV.2818, 14 July 1988, 56.
[507] See UN Docs. S/PV.2818-21, 14–20 July 1988 (States criticizing the presence of Western naval powers in the Gulf included the USSR, Libya, Syria, Cuba and Nicaragua).

argument that a military unit could ward off an incipient attack before it had actually been subject to enemy fire.[508] The Security Council did not qualify the US actions as a violation of the Charter provisions on the use of force, but '[expressed] its deep distress at the downing of an Iranian civil aircraft by a missile fired from a [US] warship'.[509]

A Fact-Finding Investigation of the International Civil Aviation Organization (ICAO) supported the thesis that '[the] aircraft was perceived as a military aircraft with hostile intentions'.[510] According to the report, the misidentification of the plane was based on a number of factors, including the fact that it had taken off from a joint civil/military aerodrome; the possibility of Iranian use of air support in the exchange of fire with Iranian patrol boats; the appearance of an unidentified radar contact that could not be related to a scheduled time of departure of a civil flight; the lack of response to challenges and warnings by radio contact; the absence of detection of civil weather radar and radio altimeter emissions from the contact; and reports by some personnel on USS *Vincennes* of changes in flights profile which gave the appearance of manoeuvring into an attack profile.[511] Following receipt of the report, the ICAO adopted a resolution which 'deeply [deplored] the tragic incident which occurred as a consequence of events and errors in identification of the aircraft which resulted in the accidental destruction of an Iran Air airliner and the loss of 290 lives'.[512]

It must also be observed that in the course of the ICJ proceedings on the matter, Iran in its memorial implicitly accepted the possibility of interceptive self-defence against a military unit with hostile intent.[513] It criticized the ICAO Fact-Finding Report for seemingly giving credence to the US argument that it had used force in self-defence. According to Iran, even if Flight 655 had been an F-14, 'it still would have been

---

[508] Remark: Iran came close to arguing exactly this (UN Doc. S/PV.2818, 36–7), but appeared to accept a degree of interceptive self-defence in its ICJ Memorial (*infra*, note 513).

[509] SC Res. 616 (1988) of 20 July 1988.

[510] 'Report of the ICAO Fact-finding Investigation on the Destruction of Iran Airbus A300', November 1988, (1989) 28 ILM 900–43, § 3.2.1.

[511] *Ibid.*, §§ 3.1.23–24.

[512] Resolution adopted by the Council of the International Civil Aviation Organization at the 20th meeting of its 126th Session of 17 March 1989, available at www.icj-cij.org/docket/files/79/9699.pdf (accessed 11 May 2009) (attachment C).

[513] ICJ, *Aerial incident of 3 July 1988 (Islamic Republic of Iran v. United States of America)*, Memorial submitted by Islamic Republic of Iran, 24 July 1990, available at www.icj-cij.org/docket/files/79/6629.pdf (accessed 11 May 2009), § 4.58.

unlawful to shoot the plane down since it would have been operating legitimately within its own airspace. ... The only question that [remained] therefore [was] whether the [US] not only misidentified the plane as an F-14, but also reasonably believed that it was about to be attacked by that F-14.'[514] There was, however, 'no factual basis for a belief that any [US] warship was about to be attacked. The Airbus was behaving normally for a commercial flight; it was descending at a speed far slower than a fighter plane would descend in a dive attack; and it was operating in the regular commercial air corridor.' According to Iran, '[the] lack of either offensive tactics (illumination) or defensive measures (evasion) by IR 655 provided further evidence that the plane had no hostile intent'.[515] Following negotiations between the US and Iran, the *Aerial Incident* case was eventually removed from the list of the ICJ.[516]

In the end, while interceptive self-defence in relation to hostile encounters between military units cannot be excluded, experiences in customary practice recommend a very cautious approach. Incidents of this type will usually take place in highly inflammable security contexts; objective information will often be hard to collect. Rash decisions may lead to unwarranted escalation, or to tragic miscalculations. For these reasons, military commanders should proceed carefully in establishing hostile intent. In principle, warnings should be issued so as to give the hostile unit an opportunity to break off the incipient attack. In addition, whenever reasonably possible, the threatened unit should seek to de-escalate and disengage. Self-defence can only be exercised during the last window of opportunity to ward off an attack.

4.3.3.c Interceptory and pre-emptive self-defence at the strategic level: the great unknown?

What then about the possibility of recourse to force against the threat of a large-scale assault against the State's territory? Can such attack be intercepted or can the threat be pre-empted? In light of our analysis of the Charter's *travaux* and customary practice, the first question ought to be answered in the affirmative, the latter in the negative. Indeed, authors generally agree that if the US military at Pearl Harbour had detected the Japanese air squadrons prior to the attack, it would have been allowed to use force in self-defence to intercept the incoming aircraft before they

---

[514] *Ibid.*, §§ 4.56–60.   [515] *Ibid.*, § 4.61.
[516] ICJ, *Aerial incident of 3 July 1988*, Order of Removal, 22 February 1996, available at www.icj-cij.org/docket/files/79/6783.pdf (accessed 11 May 2009).

entered American airspace.[517] The same reasoning would arguably apply vis-à-vis the advance of German panzer divisions in 1939. On the other hand, it may be recalled that US Governor Stassen – who must nonetheless have been familiar with the attack on Pearl Harbour four years earlier – in 1945 declared that if a fleet had 'started from abroad' against the US but had not yet attacked, the US *'could not under this provision attack the fleet but we could send a fleet of our own and be ready in case an attack came'*.[518]

At the strategic level, the distinction between (admissible) interceptive and (inadmissible) pre-emptive self-defence is determined by and large by the irreversibility of the opponent's conduct. A mere capacity to attack, combined with a professed hostile intent (deduced from bellicose statements and the like) will be insufficient to justify a recourse to force.[519] In such situation there still exists a possibility for de-escalation, for example, by means of troop withdrawal from the border region.[520] Irreversibility does not mean that an incipient attack can never be aborted, yet it certainly presupposes that the opponent has proceeded from the planning stage to the attacking stage. In other words, the *'animus aggressionis'* must be met with actual measures of implementation that demonstrate that a concrete attack has commenced. If not, the threatened State must confine itself to other démarches, such as taking military preparations, adopting countermeasures, or bringing the issue to the attention of the Security Council. Accordingly, had the Americans sought to destroy the Japanese fleet before it sailed – while it was still training for its mission, war-gaming it or otherwise making advance preparations – this would not have been a (lawful) interceptive response to an armed attack.[521]

It cannot be overstated that, if the threat of a large-scale assault on a State's territory is the main concern of States and scholars advocating the possibility of pre-emptive self-defence, the only case in customary practice post 1945 that comes close to the scenario under consideration is the

---

[517] E.g., Brownlie, *The use of force by States*, p. 368; Constantinou, *The right of self-defence*, p. 127.
[518] *Foreign Relations of the United States, Diplomatic Papers* (1945), p. 709 (emphasis added).
[519] In this sense, UN Doc. A/PV.1530, §§ 57–8 (Sudan); UN Doc. A/PV.1541, § 72 (Cyprus).
[520] E.g., Constantinou, *The right of self-defence*, pp. 116–17.
[521] Dinstein, *War, aggression and self-defence*, 4th edn, p. 191.

Six Day War.[522] *In casu*, Israel in its initial statements before the UN Security Council developed a line of reasoning that seemed to build to some extent on the idea of interceptive self-defence: it claimed that 'Egyptian armoured columns moved in an offensive thrust against Israel's borders' and that 'Egyptian planes had taken off from airfields in Sinaï and struck out towards Israel'.[523] If this account were accurate, it could indeed be asserted that Article 51 UN Charter was applicable. However, closer examination of the facts indicates that Israel may well have acted before its opponents had actually *initiated* an armed attack. Whether Israel acted 'interceptively' or 'pre-emptively' will remain contested.[524] Back in 1967, the UN Secretary-General conceded that the UN had no means of ascertaining how the hostilities were initiated.[525]

In the end, the Six Day War illustrates the difficulty of establishing an incipient armed attack at the strategic level as well as the dangers arising from accepting a broader right of pre-emptive self-defence against imminent threats. Without engaging in an in-depth policy evaluation, some considerations are due. First, States and scholars supporting self-defence against 'imminent' threats generally appear to ignore the notion that Article 51 UN Charter itself allows for a limited possibility of 'interceptive' self-defence. Second, adherents of a broad reading of self-defence often frame pre-emptive self-defence in terms of action against an 'imminent threat' without adding the phrase 'of an armed attack'. This is not entirely coincidental. It illustrates that, despite the imminence requirement, many expansionists still link the doctrine to a possible rather than a concrete attack and that there is little clarity on what scenarios would qualify as 'imminent threats'. Admittedly, in its most narrow reading, pre-emptive self-defence would not differ that much from interceptive self-defence in practical terms. This, however, would presuppose a very strict application of the necessity and proportionality criteria, which, given the fluid nature of the two parameters, is rather

---

[522] Constantinou, *The right of self-defence*, p. 117: according to Constantinou, 'the practice of States that have resorted to the use of force in anticipatory self-defence ... evinces that no expected attack exhibited so high a degree of imminence to justify a pre-emptive strike under the *Caroline* doctrine'.

[523] UN Doc. S/PV.1347, §§ 30–2.   [524] See *supra*, under Section 4.1.2.b.

[525] UN Doc. S/PV.1347, § 10. No independent investigation was undertaken after hostilities had subsided. It begs the question what international reaction would have been like had Israel's Arab neighbours commenced hostilities on the basis of an alleged need to thwart an impending Israeli attack against Syria. On the alleged concern among Arab States that Israel was likely to attack Syria, see Quigley, 'The United Nations action against Iraq', 208–11.

unrealistic. If pre-emptive self-defence were to be accepted, States would probably be able successfully to invoke it to justify the recourse to force against an opponent with open hostile intentions and an apparent capacity to attack.[526] In such context, it may be expected that third States' appraisal of the imminence of the security threat will more easily be guided by their friendly or antagonistic relationship with the State concerned than when the acting State would have to demonstrate that it was responding to an attack which had already commenced.[527] The implication is that while potential cases of interceptive self-defence at the strategic level are extremely rare, potential cases of pre-emptive self-defence can be envisaged much more easily. In this regard, one should not forget that inter-State border disputes are a common feature in today's world. Examples of open or latent conflicts between neighbouring countries include those between Malaysia and Indonesia, between Peru and Ecuador, between India and Pakistan, between Thailand and Cambodia, between Russia and Georgia, between North and South Korea, between Azerbaijan and Armenia, and between China and India. In such settings, military threats are occasionally uttered and threatening troop deployments may take place from time to time. Ergo, pre-emptive self-defence carries a serious risk of escalation. The NSS warning that countries should not use pre-emption 'as a pretext for aggression' is hardly reassuring.

It might be objected that this interpretation suffices when it comes to conventional threats, but fails to provide adequate protection against threats involving weapons of mass destruction, most notably nuclear weapons. Even Henkin, nonetheless a strong opponent of anticipatory self-defence, argued that there may be a 'small and special exception for the special case of the surprise nuclear attack'.[528] In general, however, State practice does not support a broad right of anticipatory self-defence

---

[526] Greenwood, for example, finds that an 'imminent threat of attack' presupposes 'evidence not only of the possession of weapons but also of an intention to use them.' Greenwood, 'The pre-emptive use of force', 16. Remark: supporters of pre-emptive self-defence would arguably accept that the US could have destroyed the Japanese naval fleet before it set sail for Pearl Harbour, while it was still training/preparing for the attack.

[527] Brownlie, *The use of force by States*, pp. 259–60; Constantinou, *The right of self-defence*, p. 116.

[528] Henkin, *How nations behave*, p. 140–4. See also the statement from the representative of Pakistan, (ruling out anticipatory action, but conceding that, because of their devastating impact, 'the threat of the use of [nuclear] weapons would entitle the intended victim to the full exercise of the right of self-defence.'). Contra, Constantinou, *The right of self-defence*, pp. 118–19; Sicilianos, *Des contre-mesures à la légitime défense*, p. 405.

against nuclear threats. During the 1962 Cuban missile crisis, the US deliberately avoided the self-defence rationale as a legal basis for its naval quarantine. And in relation to the 1981 strike against Iraq's Osiraq reactor, Israel's self-defence claim was unanimously rejected. It could of course be argued that this was due to the apparent lack of evidence that Iraq was developing a nuclear weapons programme and that this programme was directed against Israel. Along the same lines, one might wonder whether States would be more receptive of an invocation of self-defence, for example, if intelligence indicated that Iran, which has repeatedly threatened Israel with annihilation,[529] would be about to acquire a nuclear device. Threats of this kind undeniably constitute a breach of Article 2(4) UN Charter as well as a major threat to international peace and security. At the same time, while it is not the aim to elaborate on the dangers of nuclear proliferation and/or the strengths and weaknesses of the existing non-proliferation regime,[530] caution is needed. First of all, it must be noted that in principle nothing prohibits States from developing nuclear technology for peaceful purposes. This was stressed by many developing countries in the Council debate following the Osiraq strike.[531] In resolution 487 (1981) the Security Council similarly recognized 'the inalienable sovereign right of . . . all States . . . to develop their economy and industry for peaceful purposes'.[532]

Second, even if the Security Council has labelled the proliferation of nuclear, chemical and biological weapons a threat to international peace and security,[533] there is no rule in general international law which prohibits a State from developing and/or possessing nuclear weapons per se.[534] Article II of the Non-Proliferation Treaty *inter alia* requires non-nuclear weapon States Parties to the Treaty 'not to manufacture or otherwise acquire nuclear weapons or nuclear explosive devices' and 'not to seek or receive any assistance in the manufacture of nuclear weapons

---

[529] See, e.g., 'Israel asks U.N. to expel Iran', *The Hindu*, 28 October 2005; UN Security Council Press Statement on Iran, 28 October 2005, UN Doc. SC/8542.
[530] See the contributions in (2006–7) 39 NYUJILP 929 *et seq.*; and (2006–7) 22 American Un ILRev 361 *et seq.*
[531] See UN Doc. S/PV.2280–7.   [532] SC Res. 487 (1981) of 19 June 1981.
[533] SC Res. 1540 (2004) of 28 April 2004. See also: SC Res. 1887 (2009) of 24 September 2009.
[534] E.g., M E. O'Connell, 'Preserving the peace: the continuing ban on war between States', (2007–8) 38 California Western ILJ 41–62, at 51–2; Wedgwood, 'The military action in Iraq', p. 585 (observing that despite its opposition to nuclear proliferation, the US has never claimed that customary law prohibits the development, acquisition or possession of these weapons).

or other nuclear explosive devices'.[535] Article VI moreover requires nuclear weapon States to pursue diplomatic negotiations in order to achieve nuclear disarmament. On the other hand, Article X affirms that States Parties have the right to withdraw from the treaty by giving three-months' notice when they are faced with 'extraordinary events' that 'jeopardize their supreme interests'. States that have properly withdrawn from the Treaty or that have not joined the regime in the first place (e.g., India, Pakistan and Israel) are probably not bound by any international legal duty not to develop or acquire nuclear weapons.[536]

Third, there is some difficulty in equating the development of a nuclear weapons programme by an enemy State to an imminent threat of an armed attack. Indeed, from a military–strategic perspective, nuclear weapons are in principle not offensive weapons, but rather 'safety devices' intended to deter large-scale attacks against the possessing State. Put differently, States presumably do not seek to acquire nuclear weapons to carry out concrete attacks, but rather to shift the strategic and geopolitical balance to their advantage. In Charter terms, this falls within the framework of collective security rather than that of self-defence.[537] No State has ever deployed nuclear weapons in combat since the notorious bombings of Hiroshima and Nagasaki on 6 and 9 August 1945.[538] Every Head of State is aware that a first use of nuclear weapons would not only make it a pariah in the international community, but would most likely entail a massive military response.[539] As Bobbit acknowledges:

---

[535] Treaty on the Non-Proliferation of Nuclear Weapons, New York, 1 July 1968, 729 UNTS 161.

[536] The ICJ found in the Advisory Opinion on the *Legality of the Threat or Use of Nuclear Weapons*, that '[t]here is in neither customary nor conventional international law any comprehensive prohibition of the threat or use of nuclear weapons as such.' ICJ, *Legality of the threat or use of nuclear weapons*, Advisory opinion of 8 July 1996, (1996) ICJ Rep 226–67, at 266. *A fortiori*, one might add that there is no comprehensive prohibition of the possession of such weapons. On the *Nuclear Weapons* advisory opinion, see: L. Boisson de Chazournes and P. Sands (eds.), *International law, the International Court of Justice and nuclear weapons* (Cambridge University Press, 1999). See also the contributions in (1997) 37 IRRC 6 *et seq.*

[537] Remark: even the US Legal Adviser recognized in 2003 that '[o]ne may not strike another merely because the second might someday develop an ability and desire to attack it.' Taft and Buchwald, 'Preemption, Iraq, and international law', 557.

[538] Remark: Iraq did nonetheless deploy chemical weapons on a large scale during the Iran–Iraq War.

[539] In 2000, Condoleezza Rice in an article in *Foreign Affairs* asserted that if Iraq or North Korea were to acquire WMD, 'their weapons will be unusable because any attempt to use them will bring national obliteration'. C. Rice, 'Promoting the national interest', (2000) 79-1 *Foreign Affairs* 45–62, at 61. In a similar vein: G. Perkovich, J.T. Mathews,

It is now possible for the U.S. to determine within seconds the origin of any ballistic missile launch within an accuracy of ten meters. The leadership of a State that ordered such an attack would face the certainty of an immediate and annihilating retaliatory response. It would require of that leadership not mere irrationality, but something approaching a mass suicide pact to account for such an order.[540]

Some have nonetheless warned that a 'rogue State' acquiring WMD could transfer such weapons to non-State actors in order to be used in a terrorist attack abroad. However, leaving aside the fact that the military usefulness of a dirty bomb has always been in dispute,[541] it seems questionable whether a State that finally manages to collect clandestinely all the necessary ingredients for a nuclear device would be willing to relinquish possession by passing it on to a non-State actor beyond its strict control. More importantly, the same consideration as before applies: the large-scale retaliation that would follow if such attack were to be traced back to a State sponsoring terrorism presumably constitutes a powerful deterrent to abstain from such actions. What appears more troublesome in the present-day security context is that a terrorist group might be able to obtain a weapon of mass destruction by buying assets on an international clandestine market or by breaking into poorly secured military facilities. Military experts strongly disagree on the likelihood of

---

J. Cirincione, R. Gottemoeller and J. B. Wolfstahl, *Universal compliance; a strategy for nuclear security* (Washington, DC: Carnegie Endowment for International Peace, 2005), p. 78 (arguing that Saddam Hussein was clearly deterrable after 1991); R S. McNamara, 'The military role of nuclear weapons: perceptions and misperceptions', (1983–4) 62 *Foreign Affairs* 59–80, at 79 ('[N]uclear weapons serve no military purpose whatsoever. They are totally useless – except to deter one's opponent from using them'). Interestingly, Israeli military historian Van Creveld in 2007 suggested that US and Israeli officials exaggerated the threat of a nuclear Iran, stressing that 'in every place where nuclear weapons were introduced, large-scale wars between their owners have disappeared.' M. Van Creveld, 'The world can live with a nuclear Iran', *Forward (Jewish Daily)* 24 September 2007, available at www.forward.com/articles/11673/ (accessed 11 May 2009). Still, some authors have cautioned that some leaders may be more 'irrational' and may accordingly be harder to deter than others: e.g., C D. Walton and C S. Gray, 'The second nuclear age: nuclear weapons in the twenty-first century', in J. Baylis, J. Wirtz, C S. Gray and E. Cohen (eds.), *Strategy in the contemporary world*, 2nd edn (Oxford University Press, 2007), pp. 209–27, at 214 *et seq.*

[540] P. Bobbitt, *Terror and consent: the wars for the twenty-first century* (London: Penguin Books, 2008), p. 8.

[541] See, e.g., T. Karon, 'The "dirty bomb" scenario', *The Times* 10 June 2002. A 'dirty bomb' is a conventional explosive salted with radioactive isotopes in order to spew out that nuclear material and contaminate a wide area.

such scenario.[542] In any event, the growing risk of a WMD attack by non-State actors provides a potent incentive to strengthen multilateral counter-proliferation efforts and cooperation between law enforcement agencies, to upgrade the safety regimes of nuclear facilities (whether they be in Russia, India, Pakistan or elsewhere), and to reduce existing stocks of nuclear and other weapons of mass destruction around the globe. Yet, it hardly creates a carte blanche for preventive strikes against nuclear facilities abroad under the guise of self-defence.

A fourth element that urges a reserved approach with regard to nuclear threats is the obvious difficulty of obtaining reliable intelligence on the progress of a State's nuclear programme and its intention to engage in a nuclear attack against another State. Shortly after the 9/11 attacks, Glennon claimed that 'modern methods of intelligence collection, such as satellite imagery and communications intercepts, now make it unnecessary to sit out an actual armed attack to await convincing proof of a State's hostile intent.'[543] Subsequent developments have at least partially shattered this illusion. Indeed, the manipulation of evidence brought forward by the US and the UK in the run-up to the Iraq intervention and the presentation in the Security Council of the various allegations regarding Iraq's WMD arsenal and presumed links to terrorist groups[544]

---

[542] On the one hand, a 2005 Adelphi Paper of the International Institute for Strategic Studies concluded *inter alia* that 'there is no evidence ... of a true international black market in nuclear materials'; that 'the detailed plans and engineering drawings necessary to build a [nuclear] bomb are not easily available'; that 'nuclear weapon States, even "rogues," are most unlikely to be foolish enough to hand nuclear weapons, which are among their dearest national treasures, over to ... terrorists, especially when the chances of a suspected State sponsor suffering nuclear retaliation and annihilation are so good, and so blindingly obvious'; and that '[n]either Al Qaeda nor any of the organizations linked to it has ever used WMD, and the evidence that they have the will or the technical capacity to do so is limited and unconvincing'. See: R M. Frost, *Nuclear terrorism after 9/11* (London: IISS Adelphi Paper No. 378), 88 pages.

On the other hand, Bobbit draws attention to a number of disturbing signs of the past few years, such as: (1) the 1995 nerve gas attack by a Japanese sect on the Tokyo subway, killing twelve and injuring hundreds of others; (2) the fact that Bin Laden has publicly acknowledged trying to obtain WMD for his jihad against the US; (3) British intelligence suggesting that Al Qaeda has successfully built a small dirty bomb; (4) the fact that Dr A. Q. Khan, the director the Pakistani nuclear program, confessed to having been involved in a clandestine international network of nuclear weapons technology proliferation from Pakistan to Libya, Iran and North Korea. See Bobbit, *Terror and consent*, in particular at pp. 9, 59, 95, 99 *et seq.*

[543] M.J. Glennon, 'Preempting terrorism: the case for anticipatory self-defense', *Weekly Standard* 28 January 2002, 24.

[544] See, e.g., S. McLellan, *What happened: inside the Bush White House and Washington's culture of deception* (Washington, DC: Public Affairs, 2008), pp. 119–48.

illustrate the importance of having a qualified and impartial organization – the IAEA – monitoring events relating to nuclear proliferation. Although the US had strongly contested the efficiency of the UN weapons inspections, it was unable to find any noteworthy WMD-related materiel after the overthrow of Saddam Hussein: the Iraqi Survey Group declared in September 2004 that it had not 'found evidence that Saddam possessed WMD stocks in 2003'.[545] The result is that, far from demonstrating the need for a broader reading of self-defence in relation to WMD threats, the Iraq intervention has demonstrated the abuse such interpretation could lead to.[546] Fifth and last, it has been argued that, for various reasons, preventive strikes against nuclear facilities have limited chance of operational success and would arguably strengthen the determination of the targeted States to pursue a nuclear weapons programme.[547]

Nonetheless, it is worth noting that in September 2007, Israel carried out an aerial strike in northern Syria (Operation 'Orchard'), the features of which closely resembled those of the 1981 Osiraq strike. While Israeli (and American) officials refused to comment publicly on the nature or target of the operation – let alone offer a legal justification – anonymous sources suggested that the strike had destroyed a presumed nuclear facility that North Korea was helping to equip.[548] North Korea denied the allegations

---

[545] Comprehensive Report of the Special Advisor to the DCI on Iraq's WMD, 30 September 2004, available at www.cia.gov/library/reports/general-reports-1/iraq_wmd_2004/index.html (accessed 11 May 2009). Remark: the report did leave open the possibility 'that some weapons existed in Iraq, although not of a militarily significant capability'.

[546] E.g., Anghie, 'The Bush Administration preemption doctrine', 328.

[547] In 2007, for instance, Barnaby argued that Israeli or US strikes against Iranian nuclear facilities would have limited chance of success because of the large number of targets, the well-protected and hidden nature of the facilities concerned, the lack of adequate intelligence, and the likely survival of key scientists and technicians. Barnaby warned that a strike might moreover be counter-productive insofar as it would strengthen Iran's determination to develop a nuclear arsenal as well as popular support thereof. See F. Barnaby, 'Would air strikes work? Understanding Iran's nuclear programme and the possible consequences of a military strike', March 2007, London, Oxford Research Group, at www.oxfordresearchgroup.org.uk/publications/briefing_papers/pdf/wouldairstrikeswork.pdf, 23 pages (accessed 19 June 2009). In relation to Israel's Osiraq strike, it has similarly been suggested that it may have had the paradoxical effect of strengthening the nuclear ambitions of Arab States. E.g., Fischer, 'Le bombardement par Israël', 167.

[548] See, e.g., T. Butcher, 'US confirms Israeli air strike on Syria', *The Telegraph* 12 September 2007; B. Ravid and A. Harel, 'Syria: there are no N. Korea–Syria nuclear facilities whatsoever', *Haaretz* 16 September 2007; T. Butcher, 'N Korean ship "linked to Israel's strike on Syria"', *The Telegraph* 18 September 2007; T. Butcher, 'N Korean denies link to Israel's strike on Syria', *The Telegraph* 19 September 2007; S. L. Myers and S. Erlanger, 'Bush declines to lift veil of secrecy over Israeli airstrike on Syria', *NY Times* 21 September 2007; 'Report: IDF raid seized nuclear material before Syria air strike', *Haaretz* 23

and condemned the raid as 'a very dangerous provocation'. Syria similarly rejected accusations that it was engaged in a covert nuclear weapons programme and instead claimed that the contested site was in fact a disused military building. In a letter of complaint to the Security Council it condemned the Israeli actions as 'an aggression in clear and brazen defiance of international law'.[549] Commenting on the mysterious bombing run, IAEA Director-General El-Baradei criticized the tendency 'to bomb first and then ask questions later', and regretted that it had not received any information about any clandestine nuclear activities in Syria.[550] Key figures within the US administration were divided on the credibility of the Israeli intelligence.[551] The IAEA determined that the features of the building in question were 'similar to what may be found in connection with a reactor site' and acknowledged that uranium particles were found at the site. At the same time, it stressed that the destruction of the building and the subsequent removal of the debris made verification work very difficult, 'rendering the results so far inconclusive'.[552] In all, the uncertainty of the precise facts, the absence of legal justification on the part of Israel and the lack of a third-State reaction by and large disqualify Operation 'Orchard' as a valid customary precedent.[553]

September 2007; 'Israel admits air strike on Syria', *BBC News* 2 October 2007; H. Naylor, 'Syria tells journalists Israeli raid did not occur', *N.Y. Times* 11 October 2007.

[549] UN Doc. S/2007/537, 9 September 2007 (Syria). According to the statement: '[T]he Israeli air force, after midnight on 6 September 2007, committed a breach of the airspace of the Syrian Arab Republic ... As the Israeli aircraft were departing they dropped some munitions but without managing to cause any human casualties or material damage.' In an interview with the BBC, the Syrian President later told that Israel had bombed an abandoned military construction site and asserted that Syria had 'the right to retaliate', 'maybe politically, maybe in other ways'.

[550] 'IAEA Chief criticizes Israel over Syria raid', *Reuters* 28 October 2007.

[551] M. Mazzetti and H. Cooper, 'An Israeli strike on Syria kindles debate in the U.S.', *NY Times* 9 October 2007.

[552] See the Introductory Statements of IAEA Director-General El Baradei to the Board of Governors of 22 September 2008, 27 November 2008 and 2 March 2009 (under 'Implementation of safeguard in the Syrian Arab Republic'), Vienna, available at www.iaea.org/NewsCenter/Statements/ (accessed 11 May 2009).

[553] Still, it may be observed that a group of US Congress Members introduced a House Resolution expressing 'unequivocal support ... for Israel's right to self defense in the face of an imminent nuclear or military threat from Syria'. The draft resolution was not voted upon, but was referred to the House Committee on Foreign Affairs. US House of Representatives, Draft Resolution Expressing the Unequivocal Support of the House of Representatives for Israel's Right to Self-defence in the Face of an Imminent Nuclear or Military Threat from Syria, introduced by Mr Wexler, referred to the Committee on Foreign Affairs, 110th Congress, 1st Session, H.Res. 674, 24 September 2007, available at http://bulk.resource.org/gpo.gov/bills/110/hr674ih.txt.pdf (accessed 11 May 2009).

THE 'ARMED ATTACK' REQUIREMENT *RATIONE TEMPORIS* 365

In the end, while the threat of WMD proliferation should not be underestimated, the proper way to address it is through multilateral negotiations, the IAEA and the UN Security Council. Even though the club of nuclear-weapon States has expanded in recent years, these mechanisms have worked reasonably well. It may be recalled that during the 1960s no fewer than twenty-three countries had nuclear weapons, were conducting weapons-related research, or were discussing the pursuit of nuclear weapons.[554] In the meantime, Ukraine and South Africa have given up nuclear weapons, and Libya and Brazil terminated their weapons programmes.[555] As of 2008, no fewer than 189 States had signed up to the Non-Proliferation Treaty (even though the credibility of the NPT regime is undermined by the lack of progress on the nuclear weapons States' promise of nuclear disarmament). Since 2003, diplomatic negotiations have been pursued (through the so-called Six-nation talks) in order to convince North Korea to end its nuclear weapons programme.[556] Despite occasional hints at the possibility of military action,[557] attempts to tackle Iran's nuclear ambitions have also been conducted through peaceful negotiations (via the P−5+1)[558] in combination with Security Council

---

[554] See Perkovich *et al.*, *Universal compliance*, 19.

[555] M.E. O'Connell, 'Preserving the peace', 54.

[556] See 'Q&A: North Korea nuclear stand-off', *BBC News* 11 October 2008; 'Timeline: North Korea', *BBC News* 20 November 2008; 'Q&A: North Korea nuclear test', *BBC News* 12 June 2009. Remark: in December 2002 North Korea threw out international inspectors. One month later it withdrew from the NPT. In February 2005, North Korea announced that it had built nuclear weapons for self-defence. Following a nuclear test in late 2006, Pyongyang in February 2007 agreed as a result of Six-party talks to halt its nuclear programme in exchange for fuel aid and other benefits (including a removal from the US terrorism blacklist). Several months later, IAEA inspectors verified the shutdown of the Yongbyon reactor. In June 2008, North Korea submitted a declaration of its nuclear assets. A full resolution of the issue was thought to take several more years. On 25 May 2009, North Korea conducted a second nuclear test, leading to heightened diplomatic and military tension, and giving rise to additional Security Council sanctions (SC Res. 1874 (2009) of 12 June 2009). See also on the démarches of the UN Security Council: G. S. Carlson, 'An offer they can't refuse?: the Security Council tells North Korea to re-sign the nuclear Non-Proliferation Treaty', (2007–8) 46 Columbia JTL 420–67.

[557] Among the many news reports, see, e.g.: U. Mahnaimi, 'Israel readies forces for strike on nuclear Iran', *The Sunday Times* 11 December 2005; 'Iran's nuclear capacity "can be destroyed"', *Toronto Star* 3 January 2006; 'Reports on US to launch attack on Iran are false', *Hürriyet* 4 January 2006; P. Sherwell, 'US prepares military blitz against Iran's nuclear sites', *The Telegraph* 12 February 2006; 'German government divided over military action against Iran', *Deutsche Welle* 14 February 2006; 'Israel primed to strike Iran nuclear sites: report', AFP 18 April 2009.

[558] Remark: these are the five permanent members of the Security Council plus Germany.

sanctions.[559] This is as it should be. It seems undesirable to carve out a broad right of anticipatory self-defence vis-à-vis nuclear threats. To move beyond interceptory self-defence would give powerful States a blank cheque to decide unilaterally which States would be permitted to develop nuclear weapons and which would not – all this while maintaining and upgrading their own nuclear arsenals.[560] Yet, as US President Obama recognized in 2009: 'No single nation should pick and choose which nations hold nuclear weapons.'[561] The better view appears to be that if a

---

[559] See SC Res. 1803 (2008) of 3 March 2008; SC Res. 1747 (2007) of 24 March 2007; SC Res. 1737 (2006) of 23 December 2006. Separate sanctions have also been adopted by the EU and the US. See: 'Q&A: Iran and the nuclear issue', *BBC News* 7 October 2008; W. J. Broad and D. E. Sanger, 'Iran said to have nuclear fuel for one weapon', *NY Times* 20 November 2008.

Remark: While Iran is a Party to the NPT, the IAEA in 2003 reported that it had had a hidden uranium enrichment programme for eighteen years. Iran insisted (and continues to insist) that it is merely exercising its right under the NPT to enrich uranium to be used as fuel for civil nuclear power and has asserted that it will continue to do so despite calls from the UN Security Council to halt uranium enrichment. In July 2008, the Non-Aligned Movement issued a statement supporting Iran's right to develop peaceful nuclear power (15th Ministerial Conference of the Non-Aligned Movement, Tehran, 27–30 July 2008, Statement on the Islamic Republic of Iran's Nuclear Issue, Doc. NAM 2008/Doc.3/Rev.1. The US, Israel and many other Western States are nonetheless concerned that Iran intends to develop a nuclear arsenal. The IAEA has reported that while Iran is continuing to enrich uranium contrary to the decisions of the Security Council, it has not found evidence that Iran has diverted material for weapons purposes. A number of outstanding issues remain on which the IAEA awaits clarification from Iran. See: Report by the IAEA Director-General, 'Implementation of the NPT Safeguards Agreement and relevant provisions of Security Council resolutions 1737 (2006), 1747 (2007) and 1803 (2008) in the Islamic Republic of Iran', 15 September 2008, Doc. GOV/2008/38, available at www.iaea.org/Publications/Documents/Board/2008/gov2008-38.pdf (accessed 11 May 2009). See also: US National Intelligence Estimate, 'Iran: Nuclear intentions and capabilities', November 2007, available at www.dni.gov/press_releases/20071203_release.pdf (accessed 11 May 2009). See also: M. E. O'Connell and M. Alevras-Chen, 'The ban on the bomb – and bombing: Iran, the U.S., and the international law of self-defense', (2006–7) 57 Syracuse LRev 497–517.

[560] See, e.g., Gray, 'The US National Security Strategy', 443 (noting that the US has adopted a selective approach to non-proliferation, exempting Pakistan, India and Israel from criticism); F. Z. Ntoubandi, 'Reflections on the USA–India Atomic Energy Cooperation', (2008) 13 JCSL 2732–871 (on the consequences on the NPT regime of the conclusion of a civilian nuclear cooperation deal between India and the US in spite of India's nuclear weapons programme).

[561] US President Obama, Speech at Cairo University on 4 June 2009: 'I understand those who protest that some countries have weapons that others do not. *No single nation should pick and choose which nations hold nuclear weapons.* That is why I strongly

State feels compelled to resort to military action against a nuclear threat, its actions will be judged by the international community. Ultimately, one can only be grateful that in the darker days of the Cold War none of the two superpowers felt inclined to first push the button. The need for moderation is all the greater in a world with nine nuclear powers.

> reaffirmed America's commitment to seek a world in which no nations hold nuclear weapons. And any nation – including Iran – should have the right to access peaceful nuclear power if it complies with its responsibilities under the nuclear Non-Proliferation Treaty' (emphasis added).

5

The 'armed attack' requirement
ratione personae

The final aspect of the 'armed attack' requirement is at the same time the most complex one: from *whom* must an armed attack emanate in order to trigger the right of self-defence? Clearly, attacks by States' regular forces come within the purview of Article 51 UN Charter. *In extenso*, it is accepted that non-recognized de facto regimes can mount 'armed attacks'.[1] But are cross-border actions also warranted if a certain nexus exists between armed bands carrying out attacks and the State from whose territory they operate? And what about situations where there is no clear link between the two or where a State is simply *unable* to prevent a non-State actor from launching the attacks?

The present chapter is divided in two sections, reflecting the different *Zeitgeist* governing the first four decades of the Charter era and more recent years. As for the former period (Section 5.1), the debate on 'indirect military aggression' was strongly influenced by the struggle for decolonization, in particular by the question whether States could extend armed support to national liberation movements. Throughout the 1980s, this issue – which was never authoritatively settled – has gradually become moot. Instead, today, the growing support for a flexible reading of the *ratione personae* aspect is by and large inspired by the increasingly prominent threat of international terrorism, manifested by deadly attacks on innocent civilians in New York, London, Madrid, Mumbai, Istanbul, Casablanca, Bali and elsewhere (Section 5.2). It is

---

[1] See on this: J. A. Frowein, *Das de facto-regime im Völkerrecht: eine Untersuchung zur Rechtstellung nichtanerkannter Staaten und ähnlicher Gebilde* (Cologne: Heymanns, 1968), pp. 6–7, 52–4, 67–8, 91. For two recent applications of the concept, see (1) in relation to the status of the Taleban in Afghanistan in 2001: R. Wolfrüm and C. E. Philipp, 'The status of the Taleban: their obligations and rights under international law' (2002) 6 MPYBUNL 559–601, at 577–86; (2) in relation to the status of South Ossetia during the Russian–Georgian conflict in 2008: O. Luchterhandt, 'Völkerrechtliche Aspekte des Georgien-Krieges' (2008) 46 *AdV* 435–80.

not so much that terrorism is a new phenomenon, yet the availability of modern technology in terms of transportation, weaponry and communication technology, has undeniably increased its destructive potential and global outreach.

As one author warns:

> The worst incidents of terrorism in the 1970s caused fatalities in the tens. In the 1980s, fatalities from the worst incidents were measured in the hundreds. By the 1990s, attacks on this scale had become more frequent. On September 11, 2001, fatalities ascended to the thousands – and the toll could easily have been higher. This is an order-of-magnitude increase almost every decade. We now look ahead to plausible scenarios in which tens of thousands could die.[2]

5.1 Indirect military aggression in the decolonization era

5.1.1 Formulation of the problem

5.1.1.a Indirect military aggression and intersecting norms

When the delegations of the UN's founding Members met in San Francisco in 1945, the common perception of international peace and security was based on the sad experience of the past years and decades. Armed aggression was construed primarily in terms of large columns of tanks rolling across an international border. Nothing in the Charter's *travaux* suggests that the drafters paid any attention to possible cross-border attacks carried out by irregulars or armed bands.[3] True, some official statements and some draft versions of Article 51 speak of 'attacks by one State against another'.[4] On the whole, however, the problem of irregular attacks was widely overlooked. The final version of Article 51 simply refers to 'armed attacks', without further ado. Even if the Article constitutes an exception to the prohibition on the use of force *between States* laid down in Article 2(4) UN Charter, the implication seems to be

---

[2] B. M. Jenkins, 'Combating global war on terrorism', in P. Katona (ed.), *Countering terrorism and WMD: creating a global counter-terrorism network* (London: Routledge, 2006), pp. 181–98, at 182.
 See also: P. Bobbitt, *Terror and consent: the wars for the twenty-first century* (London: Penguin Books, 2008), pp. 46 *et seq.*

[3] Also R. S. J. Macdonald, 'The *Nicaragua* case: new answers to old question?' (1986) 24 Can YBIL 127–60, at 145.

[4] United Nations, *Documents of the Conference on International Organization*. Vol. I, p. 483 (Turkey); US Department of State, *Foreign Relations of the United States, Diplomatic Papers*. (1945) *General: the United Nations* (1967), pp. 664, 674, 834 (emphasis added).

that the *ratione personae* aspect was left to be worked out in customary practice, without establishing a Charter baseline.

Many early works on the Charter regime on the use of force are equally silent on the matter.[5] Occasionally, it was argued that Article 51 essentially related to attacks carried out by States, but that this notion could exceptionally extend to certain situations whereby a State was involved in (large-scale) attacks by irregulars. According to Kunz, an armed attack 'must not only be directed against a State, it must also be made *by* a State or *with the approval of* a State'.[6] The 1949 Report of the US Senate Committee on Foreign Relations on the North Atlantic Treaty contains the following observation:

> [T]he words 'armed attack' clearly do not mean an incident created by irresponsible groups or individuals, but rather an attack by one State upon another. ... However, if a revolution were aided and abetted by an outside power such assistance might possibly be considered an armed attack.[7]

These general statements[8] are ultimately of limited use in determining the scope for lawful recourse to force in the face of a broad spectrum of potential situations. Different relationships may indeed exist between States and armed bands: a State may itself organize or otherwise control armed bands of irregulars engaging in cross-border incursions; it may give various forms of support, including provision of weapons, training or intelligence; it may tolerate the presence of these bands within its national territory; it may neglect to undertake the necessary enforcement action; or it may simply be unable to control their activities.[9] Apart from

---

[5] See, e.g., H. Kelsen, *The law of the United Nations: a critical analysis of its fundamental problems* (London: Stevens, 1950), pp. 791 *et seq.*; H. Wehberg, 'L'interdiction du recours à la force. Le principe et les problèmes qui se posent' (1951-I) 78 RdC 1–121 at 68 *et seq.*; C. H. M. Waldock, 'The regulation of the use of force by individual States in international law' (1952-II) 81 RdC 451–517, at 495 *et seq.*; D. W. Bowett, *Self-defence in international law* (Manchester University Press, 1958), pp. 187 *et seq.*

[6] J. L. Kunz, 'Individuals and collective self-defense in Article 51 of the Charter of the United Nations', (1947) 41 AJIL 872–79, at 878 (emphasis added).

[7] US Senate, Report of the Committee on Foreign Relations on the North Atlantic Treaty, Executive Report No. 8, 6 June 1949, at 13, quoted in I. Brownlie, *International law and the use of force by States* (Oxford University Press, 1963), p. 278.

[8] See also *ibid.*, pp. 278–9 (Brownlie: 'Sporadic operations by armed bands would also seem to fall outside the concept of "armed attack". However, it is conceivable that a coordinated and general campaign by powerful bands of irregulars, with obvious or easily proven complicity of the government of a State from which they operate, would constitute an "armed attack" ...').

[9] E.g. I. Brownlie, 'International law and the activities of armed bands', (1958) 7 ICLQ 712–35, at 712–13.

the last two categories, these situations are often labelled as 'indirect military aggression'.[10] This generic term is admittedly useful insofar as it reflects the idea that States occasionally use irregulars as an instrument of 'proxy warfare'[11] – this was indeed the main concern throughout the decolonization era. On the other hand, it has been objected that the situations at the lower and the higher end of the spectrum do not really fit the denominator.[12] At the higher end of the spectrum, the nexus between the irregulars and the State may be so close that they become de facto agents of the State, implying that the resulting attacks would better be regarded as 'direct' aggression. At the lower end of the spectrum, one might wonder whether the failure of a State to take sufficient measures against armed bands operating from its territory is sufficiently grave to be qualified as 'indirect military aggression' on its part.

Whatever the label, it must be stressed that we are dealing with a variety of situations with different legal connotations. The legal complexity is fully revealed if we test this typology against three intersecting (sets of) norms, namely the secondary rules pertaining to the imputability of private conduct to a State, the prohibition on the use of force of Article 2(4) UN Charter and the 'due diligence rule'.[13] First, the rules on the imputability of private conduct are particularly relevant at the higher end of the spectrum. They establish when the link between private agents and the State is sufficiently close as to attribute the former's acts to the State, implying that they may be equated to internationally wrongful conduct of the State itself, for which it bears legal responsibility. The attributability or imputability[14] of irregular attacks to a State has long been used as an important indicator to determine the permissibility of a forcible cross-border response. Brownlie notes, for example, that:

[10] Remark: the phrase 'indirect aggression' was used in the 1952 Report of the UN Secretary-General as referring to cases where a State 'without itself committing hostile acts as a State, operates through third parties who are either foreigners or nationals seemingly acting on their own initiative'. Report of the UN Secretary-General, 3 October 1952, UN Doc. A/2211, 56.
[11] Cf. P. Lamberti Zanardi, 'Indirect military aggression', in A. Cassese (ed.), *The current legal regulation of the use of force* (Dordrecht: Martinus Nijhoff, 1986), pp. 111–19, at 111.
[12] Lamberti Zanardi prefers to reserve the term for States giving assistance to armed bands or acquiescing in their activities, rather than actually sending them, *ibid.*, p. 112. See also: R. Pisillo-Mazzeschi, 'The due diligence rule and the nature of the international responsibility of States', (1993) 35 GYBIL 9–51 at 31, 33; UN Doc. A/AC.134/SR.52–66, 19 October 1970, at 36 (France).
[13] See also: Pisillo-Mazzeschi, 'The due diligence rule', 31–6.
[14] The terms 'imputability' and 'attributability' are used interchangeably in the present chapter.

> [i]f rebels are effectively supported and controlled by another State that State is responsible for a 'use of force' as a consequence of the agency.... However, in cases in which aid is given but there is no agency established, and there is no exercise of control over the rebels by the foreign government, it is very doubtful if it is correct to describe the responsibility of that government in terms of ... [an] armed attack.[15]

In principle, it is uncontroversial that when substantial cross-border attacks by irregular forces can be imputed to a State (*sensu stricto*), there is an 'armed attack' against which the victim State may – subject to the necessity and proportionality criteria – exercise defensive measures extending to the territory of the former State. Two observations must, however, be made. First, the precise content of the rules on State responsibility has only recently been clarified as a result of the ICJ's case law and the work of the ILC. The logical inference is that references to 'imputability', 'attributability' and 'State agency' in earlier scholarly writings and official statements must be treated with circumspection. Second, as we will see, the criteria spelled out in the ILC Draft Articles on State Responsibility[16] are rather strict. The crux of the matter is therefore whether and/or to what extent the victim State may exercise the right of self-defence *absent* State imputability. This brings us to the second intersecting norm.

It may be that the active or passive support to armed bands carrying out cross-border attacks is not sufficiently intense to give rise to State attributability, but nonetheless amounts to a violation of Article 2(4) UN Charter. Indeed, if the inclusion of non-State attacks in Article 51 UN Charter is subject to controversy, it is widely accepted that 'indirect use of force' is fully covered by the Charter prohibition on the use of force.[17] International instruments, such as the 1954 Draft Code of Offences

---

[15] Brownlie, *The use of force by States*, p. 370.
[16] See: International Law Commission, 'Commentary on the Draft Articles on the Responsibility of States for Internationally Wrongful Acts', (2001-II) YBILC, at 31 *et seq.*
[17] E.g., P. Cahier, 'Changements et continuité du droit international', (1985-VI) 195 RdC 9–374, at 68–9; R. Higgins, *Problems and process: international law and how we use it* (Oxford: Clarendon Press, 1994), p. 249; Lamberti Zanardi, 'Indirect military aggression', p. 111; P. Malanczuk, 'Countermeasures and self-defence as circumstances precluding wrongfulness in the International Law Commission's Draft Articles on State Responsibility', (1983) 43 GYBIL 705–812, at 765; A. Randelzhofer, 'Article 51', in B. Simma in collaboration with M. Mosler, A. Randelzhofer, C. Tomuschat and R. Wolfrüm (eds.), *The Charter of the United Nations: a commentary.* Vol. I (Oxford University Press, 2002), pp. 788–806, at 800; M. Virally, 'Article 2: paragraphe 4', in J.-P. Cot and A. Pellet, *La Charte des Nations Unies*, 2nd edn (Paris: Economica, 1991), pp. 115–28, at 123; H. Wehberg, 'L'interdiction du recours à la force. Le principe et les

against the Peace and Security of Mankind,[18] have consistently opposed indirect hostile uses of force. The 1965 UNGA Declaration on the Inadmissibility of Intervention, for example, stipulates that 'no State shall organize, assist, foment, finance, incite or tolerate subversive, terrorist or armed activities directed towards the violent overthrow of the régime of another State or interfere in civil strife in another State.'[19] The most important instrument in this context is undeniably the 1970 Friendly Relations Declaration, which lists seven principles of international law relating to friendly relations and co-operation among States.[20] The first principle dealt with is the obligation of States to refrain in their international relations from the threat or use of force. Paragraph 8 of the section concerned states that '[e]very State has the duty to refrain from organizing or encouraging the organization of irregular forces or armed bands including mercenaries, for incursion into the territory of another State'. Paragraph 9 adds that '[e]very State has the duty to refrain from organizing, instigating, assisting or participating in acts of civil strife or terrorist acts in another State or acquiescing in organized activities within its territory directed towards the commission of such acts, when the acts referred to in the present paragraph involve a threat or use of force.' These two provisions can be regarded as an authoritative interpretation of Article 2(4) UN Charter, extending its scope to a wide array of 'indirect' uses of force.[21] In *Nicaragua*, the ICJ confirmed that the Friendly Relations Declaration equates support for subversive or terrorist armed activities within another State with the use of force when the

---

problèmes qui se posent', (1951-I) 78 RdC 1-121, at 68-9. See also: Brownlie, 'The activities of armed bands', 729, 734.

[18] ILC, Draft Code of Offences against the Peace and Security of Mankind, 30 April 1954, UN Doc. A/2693, Article 2 (4)-(6).

[19] GA Res. 2131 (XX), Declaration on the Inadmissibility of Intervention in the Domestic Affairs of States and the Protection of their Independence and Sovereignty, 21 December 1965.

[20] GA Res. 2625 (XXV), Declaration on Principles of International Law Concerning Friendly Relations and Cooperation among States in accordance with the Charter of the United Nations, 24 October 1970.

[21] E.g., ICJ, *Case concerning military and paramilitary activities in and against Nicaragua (Nicaragua v. United States* of America) (Merits), Judgment of 27 June 1986, (1986) ICJ Rep 14-150, §§ 188, 191, 205, 228; R. Rosenstock, 'The Declaration on Principles of International Law Concerning Friendly Relations: a survey', (1971) 65 AJIL 713-35, at 714-15, 720; Virally, 'Article 2: paragraphe 4', p. 123. See also: UN Doc. A/AC.125/SR.110-14, 31 March-1 May 1970, 47 (France); 68 (India), 81 (US); UN Doc. A/C.6/25/SR.1178, 23 September 1970, 9 (Australia); UN Doc. A/C.6/25/SR.1180, 24 September 1970, 19 (US).

acts committed abroad 'involve a threat or use of force'.[22] In *DRC v. Uganda*, the ICJ regarded the two aforementioned paragraphs as declaratory of customary international law.[23] At the same time, this broad interpretation cannot simply be copied vis-à-vis Article 51 UN Charter. Thus, the resolution cautions that '[n]othing in the foregoing paragraphs shall be construed as enlarging or diminishing in any way the scope of the provisions of the Charter concerning cases in which the use of force is lawful'.[24] In this context, it is worth stressing that at the exact moment States agreed to include a wide list of 'indirect uses of force' in the Friendly Relations Declaration, there was strong disagreement among UN Members as to which of these activities could possibly be regarded as 'aggression' and/or trigger the right of self-defence.[25]

With respect to those forms of 'indirect use of force' that involve a breach of a duty to protect rather than a duty to abstain – viz. the tolerating of or acquiescing in cross-border attacks – a third norm comes into play, namely the 'due diligence rule'. This basic principle of

---

[22] ICJ, *Nicaragua* case (Merits), § 205. Remark: there is something ambiguous about the Court's construction of 'indirect use of force'. In §§ 205, 228 and 238 the Court suggests that activities of the type described in paragraphs 8 and 9 of the Friendly Relations Declaration qualify as 'indirect use of force' *if* the subversive or terrorist acts committed abroad (by armed bands, not by State agents themselves) 'involve a threat or use of force'. Yet, in § 228 *in fine*, the Court seems to imply that it is the assistance itself (and not the acts of the irregulars to which assistance is given) that must involve a 'threat or use of force'. The Court thus finds that: 'while the arming and training of the contras can certainly be said to involve the threat or use of force against Nicaragua, this is not necessarily so in respect of all the assistance given by the [US]. In particular, the Court considers that the mere supply of funds to the contras, while undoubtedly an act of intervention in the internal affairs of Nicaragua ... does not in itself amount to a use of force' (in a similar vein: Malanczuk, 'Countermeasures and self-defence', 765–6). The Court's reasoning is not entirely convincing from an analytical point of view. Nonetheless, it is not the present study's ambition to examine directly the scope of the prohibition on the use of force. See also A. Randelzhofer, 'Article 2(4)', in B. Simma (eds.), *The Charter of the United Nations* 115, footnote 63.

[23] ICJ, *Case concerning armed activities on the territory of the Congo (Democratic Republic of the Congo v. Uganda)*, Judgment of 19 December 2005, (2005) ICJ Rep 116–220, § 162.

[24] See also: UN Doc. A/AC.125/SR.110-14, at 77 (UAR: 'With regard to the eighth and ninth paragraphs ..., [the UAR representative] wished to recall that his delegation had in the past expressed its doubt ..., because it feared that their inclusion might be misinterpreted as loosening the restriction embodied in Article 51 of the Charter with regard to the right of self-defence ... That doubt had, however, been dispelled by the inclusion of the last paragraph, which affirmed that nothing in the statements on the use of force should be construed as enlarging or diminishing the scope of Article 51'); Rosenstock, 'Principles of International Law Concerning Friendly Relations', 720, 723–4.

[25] See *infra*, Section 5.1.2 (on the *travaux* of the Definition of Aggression).

international law[26] establishes that States have a duty to prevent their territory from being used to the detriment of other States. This 'duty of vigilance' is recognized amongst others in the *Trail Smelter* and *Corfu Channel* cases,[27] and is applicable to all sorts of primary obligations, ranging from human rights law to environmental protection or diplomatic protection.[28] In relation to attacks by terrorist groups and other non-State actors, the 'due diligence rule' is affirmed by the Friendly Relations Declaration and several other UN documents, such as Security Council resolution 1373 (2001).[29] Although this is sometimes overlooked,[30] it must be noted that there is a qualitative difference between these and situations where harmful private conduct is directly imputable to the State. Indeed, while non-compliance with the due diligence standard raises the State's legal responsibility, *in casu* it is the omission on the part of the State, and not the injurious act by the private actor itself, for which the State may be responsible.[31] Thus, in the *Tehran Embassy* case the Court determined that the original attack on the US embassy could not be imputed to the Iranian authorities, but nonetheless found that Iran's inaction violated its international obligations.[32]

The 'due diligence rule' is not absolute: it presupposes an obligation of means, not an obligation of result. In *DRC* v. *Uganda*, for example, the Court found that the Democratic Republic of the Congo had not violated its duty of vigilance – as Uganda had claimed – by failing to prevent rebel

---

[26] E.g., R. P. Barnidge Jnr., 'The due diligence principle under international law', (2006) 8 ICL Rev 81–121, at 121. See also: R. P. Barnidge, *Non-State actors and terrorism: applying the law of State responsibility and the due diligence principle* (The Hague: TMC Asser Press, 2008), pp. 55–110.

[27] E.g., *Trail Smelter* decision (*United States of America* v. *Canada*), Arbitral award of 11 March 1941, reprinted in (1941) 35 AJIL 684–736, at 713–14; ICJ, *Corfu Channel* (*United Kingdom* v. *Albania*), Judgment of 9 April 1949, (1949) ICJ Rep 4–38, at 22; ICJ, *Case concerning United States diplomatic and consular staff in Tehran* (*United States of America* v. *Islamic Republic of Iran*), Judgment of 24 May 1980, (1980) ICJ Rep 3–46, at 32–3.

[28] See Pisillo-Mazzeschi, 'The due diligence rule', 22–41.

[29] E.g., GA Res. 49/60 of 9 December 1994, Declaration on Measures to Eliminate Terrorism; SC Res. 1373 (2001) of 28 September 2001; SC Res. 1189 (1998) of 13 August 1998.

[30] E.g., R. B. Lillich and J. M. Paxman, 'State responsibility for injuries to aliens occasioned by terrorist activities', (1976–7) 26 American Un LRev 217–313, at 236.

[31] B. A. Frey, 'Small arms and light weapons: the tools used to violate human rights', (2004) 37 *Disarmament Forum* 37–46, at 42; Barnidge, *Non-State actors and terrorism*, p. 6.

[32] ICJ, *Tehran Embassy* case, §§ 56–68. See also: ICJ, *Nicaragua* case (Merits), § 116.

groups in eastern Congo from carrying out cross-border attacks.[33] In light of the remoteness of the area and the complete absence of central government presence, the Court accepted that the DRC's lack of action was not tantamount to 'tolerating' or 'acquiescing' in the rebels' activities, in the sense of the Friendly Relations Declaration.[34] Whether or not a State has taken 'all reasonable measures' must be determined on a case-by-case basis, taking account of the specific circumstances and the primary rules involved.[35] Two criteria seem of paramount importance, namely whether or not the State has the necessary 'means' to suppress the acts concerned; and whether the State is aware of them.[36] Furthermore, a State's failure to exercise due diligence in preventing cross-border attacks arguably does not automatically qualify as 'indirect use of force'. Consider, for instance, a situation in which law enforcement personnel of State A failed to act appropriately against terrorists within its borders despite indications that an attack against State B was about to be committed. It could be that this inaction resulted from neglect rather than from any desire to see the terrorist schemes succeed. In such case, State A would possibly have committed internationally wrongful conduct, yet it would appear unlikely for this to constitute a breach of Article 2(4) on its part.[37] *A fortiori*, it is of course perfectly possible that a State's territory

---

[33] ICJ, *DRC v. Uganda*, §§ 300–2 (according to the Court, neither the DRC nor Uganda were in a position to put an end to the rebel groups' activities). But see the declaration of Judge Tomka, §§ 1–6.

[34] Remark: elsewhere, the Court found that Uganda had failed to live up to its 'duty of vigilance' as an occupying power by not taking appropriate measures to prevent the looting, plundering and exploitation of natural resources in the Ituri region. *Ibid.*, §§ 247–50.

[35] See, e.g., Lillich and Paxman, 'State responsibility for injuries to aliens', in particular at 241–6, 250, 269–70; Pisillo-Mazzeschi, 'The due diligence rule', 44–5.

[36] These two factors clearly surface in the relevant case law of the ICJ: e.g., ICJ, *Tehran Embassy* case, § 68 (finding that Iran was fully aware of its international obligations; was fully aware of the urgent need for action on its part; and had the means at its disposal to perform these obligations); ICJ, *Nicaragua* case (Merits), §§ 157–8 (considering Nicaragua's duty to exercise due diligence in tackling the flow of arms from its territory into El Salvador; referring to the 'resources for subduing this traffic' and the possible lack of knowledge); ICJ, *DRC v. Uganda*, § 301 (focusing on the DRC's lack of means); ICJ, *Corfu Channel* case, §§ 16–22 (dealing with the question whether Albania had knowledge of the mine-laying in the Corfu Channel). Also Lillich and Paxman, 'State responsibility for injuries to aliens', 241–6, 250, 269–70; Pisillo-Mazzeschi, 'The due diligence rule', 44.

[37] Remark: the gap between the due diligence rule and 'indirect use of force' ultimately depends on how one interprets the scope of Article 2(4) UN Charter (whether there is need for a certain gravity, a *mens rea*, et cetera). Again, however, the latter topic is beyond the scope of our study.

is used as a basis for launching cross-border attacks without it having committed any internationally wrongful conduct at all.

5.1.1.b Forcible responses and alternative legal bases

As long as forcible action against armed bands is confined to the State's own territory no problems arise under the *Ius ad Bellum*: since Article 2(4) only applies to inter-State relations, the Charter framework does not come into play. Instead, the State's actions are governed by human rights law and/or international humanitarian law (if the situation qualifies as an 'armed conflict').[38] The same is true *mutatis mutandis* in the unlikely case military force is directed against individuals staying on a *res nullius*. By contrast, as soon as the (unauthorized and deliberate)[39] employment of military means is directed against individuals on the territory of another State, there is a prima facie breach of the latter's sovereignty and of the prohibition on the use of force enshrined in Article 2(4) UN Charter.[40] This will be so even if the intervening State strictly limits its actions to the armed group which is responsible for the cross-border attack(s), and refrains from targeting other civilian or military infrastructure. In order to be lawful, such recourse to force must either be sanctioned by the UN Security Council, or it must qualify as self-defence against an 'armed attack' in the meaning of Article 51.

---

[38] Also J. Kammerhofer, 'The *Armed Activities* case and non-State actors in self-defence law', (2007) 20 Leiden JIL 89–113, at 105; Y. Dinstein, *War, aggression and self-defence*, 4th edn (Cambridge University Press, 2005), p. 244.

[39] Remark: when the use of force is authorized by the territorial State (in accordance with the limits pertaining to 'intervention by invitation'), the *Ius ad Bellum* does not come into play. The implication is that counter-terrorist operations in other countries with the consent of those countries do not count as instances of self-defence, but must instead abide by the demands of international human rights law – in particular the prohibition on the arbitrary deprivation of life – and (in cases of armed conflict) international humanitarian law. For this reason, the US strike against a number of Al Qaeda suspects in Yemen in November 2002, and carried out in cooperation with Yemeni authorities, could not be justified on the basis of Article 51 UN Charter. In this sense: F. Naert, 'The impact of the fight against terrorism on the *Ius ad Bellum*', (2004) 11 *Ethical Perspectives* 144–60, at 151; T. Ruys, 'License to kill? State-sponsored assassination under international law', in (2005) 44 RDMDG 15–49, at 22. Contra: N. G. Printer Jnr., 'The use of force against non-State actors under international law: an analysis of the US predator strike in Yemen', (2003) 8 UCLA JILFA 331–83.

[40] Also L. Condorelli, 'Les attentats du 11 Septembre et leurs suites: où va le droit international?', (2001) 105 RGDIP 829–48, at 838; Kammerhofer, 'The *Armed Activities* case', 105; C. Stahn, 'Terrorist acts as "armed attack": the right to self-defence, Article 51 (1/2) of the UN Charter, and international terrorism', (2003) 27 *Fletcher Forum* 35–54, at 38.

Taking account of the three sets of intersecting norms, the phrase 'armed attack' could theoretically be interpreted in different ways. First, it could be argued that it is limited to attacks which can be imputed to the State concerned. Second, the notion could be extended to cover some or all forms of 'indirect use of force'. A third possibility is that certain other forms of internationally wrongful conduct – e.g., a State's failure to exercise due diligence in preventing cross-border attacks, or the provision of support not amounting to indirect use of force[41] – suffice to transmute non-State attacks into 'armed attacks'. Fourth and last, it could be argued that (large-scale) attacks by non-State actors qualify as 'armed attacks' of their own even if the State has not committed any wrongful conduct.

Some have attempted to circumvent this conundrum by suggesting alternative legal bases distinct from the Charter framework. The first (and fairly unpopular) alternative concerns the so-called 'hot pursuit' doctrine. This is originally a law of the sea doctrine according to which coastal States have the right to pursue ships guilty of offences in territorial waters into areas of the sea beyond national jurisdiction.[42] By analogy, it has sometimes been argued that States have a right to respond to hit-and-run tactics by irregulars by pursuing retreating bands over a frontier.[43] There are, however, several reasons why this argument cannot be upheld. First, the analogy with the law of the sea is mistaken, since a crucial precondition of 'hot pursuit at sea' is that it cannot justify infringements of another State's territory.[44] According to Article 111 (3) UNCLOS, '[t]he right of hot pursuit ceases as soon as the ship pursued enters the territorial sea of its own State or of a third State'.[45] Second, it is clear that (unilateral) hot pursuit on land lacks support in State practice: (1) it has virtually never been invoked as a legal basis; (2) unauthorized cross-border pursuit of armed individuals has consistently led to complaints of breaches of State sovereignty; and (3) numerous

---

[41] See *supra*, note 22 (on the provision of weapons in the *Nicaragua* case).
[42] C. Gray, *International law and the use of force*, 3rd edn (Oxford University Press, 2008), p. 137.
[43] See Brownlie, 'The activities of armed bands', 733–4 (referring to US expeditions into Mexico in 1916 to disperse the bands of Pancho Villa).
[44] E.g., G. Abi-Saab, 'Cours général de droit international public', (1987-III) 207 RdC 9–463, at 374; Dinstein, *War, aggression and self-defence*, 4th edn, p. 246; C. Antonopoulos, 'The Turkish military operation in Northern Iraq of March–April 1995 and the international law on the use of force', (1996) 1 JACL 33–58, at 49.
[45] Article 111 United Nations Convention on the Law of the Sea, Montego Bay, 10 December 1982, (1982) 21 ILM 1261.

bilateral and multilateral agreements have been adopted allowing for cross-border pursuit of criminals or armed bands under specific conditions[46] (if 'hot pursuit' on land were accepted as a customary right, such agreements would in principle be redundant). Poulantzas concludes that hot pursuit on land possesses no status as a customary rule; 'it is simply based on the explicit consent of the States concerned, on the ground in most cases of reciprocity and under strict and specific conditions'.[47] Throughout the Charter era, South Africa was apparently the only country to openly invoke 'hot pursuit' as a legal basis for cross-border intervention. This argument was nonetheless rejected by the international community.[48] In resolution 568 (1985), the Security Council explicitly denounced South Africa's 'racist practice of "hot pursuit" to terrorize and destabilize countries in southern Africa'.[49]

A second alternative justification that enjoys far greater support among legal scholars concerns the so-called 'state of necessity'. The existence of this 'ground precluding wrongfulness' has long been extremely contested because of its vague criteria and the concomitant risk of abuse.[50] In *Gabčíkovo-Nagymaros*, the ICJ recognized it as a norm of customary international law.[51] Its contours are defined in Article 25 DASR.[52] The idea that a 'state of necessity' may somehow be relied upon to justify certain limited breaches of Article 2(4) UN Charter builds on the interpretation of this concept in the Eighth Report on State Responsibility by Special Rapporteur Ago.[53] Ago accepted 'without a shadow of doubt' that it could never preclude the wrongfulness of State conduct not in conformity with the obligation to refrain from any *use of*

---

[46] See: N. M. Poulantzas, *The right of hot pursuit in international law*, 2nd edn (Dordrecht: Martinus Nijhoff, 2002), p. 12, footnote 7; Brownlie, 'The activities of armed bands', 734. Also: Section 3.3.
[47] Poulantzas, *The right of hot pursuit*, pp. 11–35 (examination of State practice), 347.
[48] E.g., UN Doc. S/PV.1944, 27 July 1976, §§ 22 (Zambia), 79 (Mauritania); UN Doc. S/PV.2606, 20 September 1985, §§ 52 (India), 103 (Senegal), 134 (Burkina Faso); UN Doc. S/PV.2607, 20 September 1985, § 46 (Trinidad and Tobago).
[49] SC Res. 568 (1985) of 21 June 1985. After 1985, South Africa abandoned this argument. Gray, *The use of force*, p. 137; (1985) UNYB 186; (1986) UNYB 166.
[50] See, e.g., M. Sørensen, 'Principes de droit international public', (1960-III) 101 RdC 1–254, at 219–20; Cahier, 'Changements et continuité', 290–1.
[51] ICJ, *Case concerning the Gabčíkovo-Nagymaros project* (*Hungary* v. *Slovakia*), Judgment of 25 September 1997, (1997) ICJ Rep 7–84, §§ 51–2.
[52] ILC, 'Commentary on the Draft Articles', 194. See also Malanczuk, 'Countermeasures and self-defence', 779–85.
[53] R. Ago, 'Addendum to the 8th Report on State Responsibility', (1980-II) 32 YBILC, Part One, 14–51, especially § 38 *et seq.*

force constituting an act of aggression against another State.[54] He hesitated, however, to ascribe the same peremptory character of the prohibition of aggression to the prohibition against *less grave uses of force* covered by Article 2(4).[55] Consequently, Ago wondered whether or not the state of necessity might 'exceptionally preclude the wrongfulness of an assault which proved to be less serious', such as 'incursions into foreign territory to forestall harmful operations by an armed group which was preparing to attack the territory of the State, or in pursuit of an armed band or gang of criminals who had crossed the frontier and perhaps had their basis in the foreign territory.'[56] After observing that UN practice did not seem 'to be sufficiently copious and conclusive on this point to enable ... a sure and definitive answer', he concluded that there was no need for the ILC to take a position on this specific point.[57]

If Ago ultimately left the matter undecided, several scholars have copied his reasoning by actually applying the 'state of necessity' to cross-border pursuit of criminals, counter-terrorist operations or 'protection of nationals' abroad.[58] For a variety of reasons, however, this reasoning must be rejected.[59] An authoritative rebuttal is offered by

---

[54] *Ibid.*, § 55.
[55] Also L. Hannikainen, *Peremptory norms (jus cogens) in international law. Historical development, criteria, present status* (Helsinki: Lakimiesliiton Kustannus, 1988), p. 356.
[56] Ago, 'Addendum to the 8th Report on State Responsibility', § 56.
[57] *Ibid.*, § 66. Ago explained that he was 'referring in particular to certain actions by States in the territory of other States which, although they may sometimes be coercive in nature, serve only limited intentions and purposes bearing no relation to the purposes characteristic of a true act of aggression.' He also mentioned incursions for the 'protection of nationals' as a concrete example.
[58] See in particular: G. Cahin, 'L'Etat défaillant en droit international: quel régime pour quelle notion?', in X., *Droit du pouvoir, pouvoir du droit* (Brussels: Bruylant, 2007), pp. 177–209, at 207–9 ; T. Christakis, 'Vers une reconnaissance de la notion de guerre pré ventive?', in K. Bannelier, T. Christakis, O. Corten and P. Klein (eds.), *L'intervention en Irak et le droit international* (Paris: Pedone, 2004), pp. 9–45, at 29 *et seq.*; T. Gazzini, *The changing rules on the use of force in international law* (Manchester University Press, 2005), pp. 204–10; A. Laursen, 'The use of force and (the state of) necessity', (2004) 37 Vanderbilt JTL 485–526; J. Raby, 'The state of necessity and the use of force to protect nationals', (1988) 26 Can YBIL 253–72; O. Schachter, *International law in theory and practice* (Dordrecht: Martinus Nijhoff, 1991), pp. 169–73. Also: I. Johnstone, 'Plea of necessity in international legal discourse: humanitarian intervention and counter-terrorism', (2004–5) 43 Columbia JTL 337–88; M. Romano, 'Combatting terrorism and weapons of mass destruction: reviving the doctrine of state of necessity', (1999) 87 Georgetown LJ 1023–57.
[59] See, e.g., Cahier, 'Changements et continuité', 74; J. Mrazek, 'Prohibition on the use and threat of force: self-defence and self-help in international law', (1989) 27 Can YBIL 81–111 at 106–7; A. C. Müller, 'Legal issues arising from the armed conflict in

THE 'ARMED ATTACK' REQUIREMENT *RATIONE PERSONAE* 381

Corten.⁶⁰ The relevant arguments can be summarized as follows. First, it appears credible that the peremptory character of Article 2(4) is not confined to some purported core. Rather, the prohibition arguably forms part of *ius cogens* in its entirety.⁶¹ Hence, the various grounds precluding wrongfulness listed cannot in principle be relied upon (Article 26 DASR).⁶² Second, the Charter provisions on the use of force inherently deal with extreme situations. They constitute a closed system, which excludes exceptions other than the occurrence of an 'armed attack' or authorization by the Security Council. This reading is confirmed by a considerable number of UNGA resolutions, which *inter alia* state that '[n]o consideration of whatever nature may be invoked to warrant resorting to the threat or use of force in violation of the Charter'.⁶³ In other words, the primary rules implicitly exclude the possibility of invoking necessity in accordance with Article 25(2)(a) DASR.⁶⁴ Third, as even supporters of this alternative legal basis admit, there is a complete lack of support in State practice.⁶⁵ Applications of the so-called 'protection of nationals' doctrine have by and large been justified by reference to the right of self-defence.⁶⁶ Likewise, as will be demonstrated below, the

---

Afghanistan', (2004) 4 *Non-State Actors and International Law* 239-76, at 254-5; C. Stahn, 'International law at crossroads?: the impact of September 11', (2002) 62 ZaöRV 183-255, at 212; J. Verhoeven, 'Les "étirements" de la légitime défense', (2002) 48 AFDI 49-80, at 75.

⁶⁰ See O. Corten, 'L'état de nécessité peut-il justifier un recours à la force non constitutif d'agression?', (2004) 1 *Global Community* 11-50.

⁶¹ *Ibid.*, at 15-16. See also *supra*, Section 1.1.2.b.

⁶² According to Article 26 DASR: 'Nothing in this chapter precludes the wrongfulness of any act of a State which is not in conformity with an obligation arising under a peremptory norm of general international law.'

⁶³ E.g., GA Res. 42/22 of 18 November 1987, Declaration on the Enhancement of the Effectiveness of the Principle of Refraining from the Threat or Use of Force in International Relations, Section I, § 3.

⁶⁴ Corten, 'L'état de nécessité', 17, 24-32. Remark: according to Article 25(2)(a) DASR, necessity may not be invoked if 'the international obligation in question exlcudes the possibility of invoking necessity'.

⁶⁵ *Ibid.*, 23-7, 42-7; Raby, 'The state of necessity', 269-70; Ago, 'Addendum to the 8th Report on State Responsibility', §§ 64-5. Neither the *Caroline* incident (1837) nor the bombing of the *Torrey Canyon* (1967) qualify as valid precedents, the first because it predates the adoption of the UN Charter, the second because it arguably did not involve a breach of Article 2(4).

⁶⁶ See *supra*, Section 3.4.4. Remark: the only pertinent example where 'necessity' was invoked concerns the Belgian intervention in the Congo in 1960. Even here, Belgian statements were confused and imprecise. The term 'necessity' was used more in its ordinary meaning than as a legal concept. Belgium primarily founded its legal case on (1) the consent of the Congolese government, and (2) the responsibility to protect its nationals abroad. See *supra*, Section 3.4.b.i.

incontrovertible fact is that States resorting to force against attacks by non-State actors abroad have expressly employed the language of self-defence.[67] In addition, before the UNGA Sixth Committee, numerous States explicitly objected that the state of necessity could not justify a recourse to force in contravention of the UN Charter.[68] Not a single State adopted the opposite view.[69] Fourth, contrary to 'counter-measures', the 'state of necessity' essentially relates to situations where the other State has not committed an internationally wrongful act.[70] Yet, questions of forcible response to attacks by non-State actors are generally raised when the other State has engaged in 'indirect use of force' and/or has breached the 'due diligence rule'. In other words: even if one were to accept its applicability, the state of necessity would not solve the problem under consideration. The conceptual autonomy of the different grounds precluding wrongfulness would even lead to manifestly absurd results. In case the other State had *not* committed internationally wrongful conduct, recourse to force could exceptionally be justified by reference to the state of necessity. By contrast, if it had breached an international legal obligation, the victim State would only be able to adopt counter-measures falling short of an actual use of force (Article 50 (1)(a) DASR).[71] Fifth and last, the ILC has implicitly rejected Ago's suggestion in its *travaux* after 1980.[72]

5.1.2 The debate on 'indirect aggression' within the Fourth Special Committee on the Question of Defining Aggression

5.1.2.a Article 3(g)

When in the 1950s, negotiations on a Definition of Aggression first commenced, there was – as in San Francisco – relatively little attention on the concept of 'indirect aggression'.[73] By the late 1960s, however,

---

[67] Also: Dinstein, *War, aggression and self-defence*, 4th edn, p. 247.
[68] For references, see: Corten, 'L'état de nécessité', 27–31. Also: S. P. Jagota, 'State responsibility: circumstances precluding wrongfulness', (1985) 16 NYBIL 249–300, at 270.
[69] Corten, 'L'état de nécessité', 30.
[70] E.g., Ago, 'Addendum to the 8th Report on State Responsibility', § 15; Raby, 'The state of necessity', 258–9.
[71] See: Corten, 'L'état de nécessité', 18–23.
[72] *Ibid.*, 31–5. See especially: ILC, 'Commentary on the Draft Articles', 205; J. Crawford, 'Second Report on State Responsibility. Addendum', 3 May–23 July 1999, UN Doc. A/CN.498/Add.2, § 287 (also footnote 557).
[73] See: O. Corten, *Le droit contre la guerre; l'interdiction du recours à la force en droit international contemporain* (Paris: Pedone, 2008), pp. 673–4.

many States had come to realize that indirect aggression was as much a challenge to international peace and security as traditional forms of inter-State conflict, and much more widespread at that.[74] Following the creation of the Fourth Special Committee, the controversy proved to be one of the main stumbling blocks towards a successful conclusion of the negotiations. The immediate cause for this was the explicit exclusion of self-defence against indirect aggression in the Thirteen-Power proposal. Article 3 emphasized that self-defence could be exercised only against armed attacks *by another State*.[75] And according to Article 7:

> When a State is a victim in its own territory of subversive and/or terrorist acts by irregular, volunteer or armed bands organized or supported by another State, it may take all reasonable and adequate steps to safeguard its existence and its institutions, without having recourse to the right of individual or collective self-defence against the other State under Article 51 of the Charter.

Against this, the Six-Power draft[76] defined aggression as 'the use of force in international relations, overt or covert, *direct or indirect*, by a State against the territorial integrity or political independence of any other State, or in any other manner inconsistent with the purposes of the United Nations' (Article 2 (emphasis added)). Article 2B (non-exhaustively) listed the following examples of indirect aggression:

(6) organizing, supporting or directing armed bands or irregular or volunteer forces that make incursions or infiltrate into another State;
(7) organizing, supporting or directing violent civil strife or acts of terrorism in another State;
(8) organizing, supporting or directing subversive activities aimed at the violent overthrow of the Government of another State.

Within the Fourth Special Committee and the UNGA Sixth Committee, the Six Powers strongly objected to the unequivocal exclusion of self-defence in response to indirect aggression.[77] Italy, for example, observed

---

[74] E.g., UN Doc. A/AC.134/SR.52–66, 19 October 1970, 39 (Australia), 44 (Turkey), 109 (UK), 114 (Indonesia); UN Doc. A/AC.134/SR.67–78, 19 October 1970, 111 (Australia); UN Doc. A/AC.134/SR.79–91, 7 June 1971, 31 (Australia), 42 (Italy).
[75] UN Doc. A/AC.134/L.16 (and Corr. 1). Proposal submitted by Colombia, Cyprus, Ecuador, Ghana, Guyana, Haiti, Iran, Madagascar, Mexico, Spain, Uganda, Uruguay and Yugoslavia.
[76] UN Doc. A/AC.134/L.17 (and Corr. 1). Proposal submitted by Australia, Canada, Italy, Japan, the UK and the US.
[77] E.g., UN Doc. A/AC.134/SR.67–78, 106–7 (UK).

that the acts listed in Article 2B, paragraphs 6 to 8, implied a use of force prohibited by Article 2(4) UN Charter.[78] It explained that '[t]he Six-Power proposal was based on the idea that indirect aggression should be treated in the same way as direct aggression'. It 'differed on that point from ... the Thirteen-Power proposal, which did not concede the right of self-defence to a State subjected on its own territory to acts of subversion or terrorism by armed bands or irregular or volunteer forces organized or supported by another State'. Italy found it 'difficult to understand why the application of Article 51 of the Charter had been deliberately excluded ... It was not clear, incidentally, what reasonable and adequate steps to safeguard its existence and its institutions could be taken, under [that] proposal, by a State which was a victim of [indirect] aggression.' Japan agreed that it would be 'unjustifiable to deny a State which was a victim of subversive or terrorist acts by irregular, volunteer or armed bands organized, supported or directed by another State, the lawful recourse to the right of self-defence'.[79] The United States suggested that there was a simple answer to the conundrum: 'to be legitimate, the use of force in self-defence must be proportionate; the same cardinal principle would apply whether the use of force was by direct or indirect means'.[80]

By contrast, the Thirteen Powers insisted during the debates that direct armed aggression was the only form which activated Article 51 of the Charter.[81] According to Ecuador, for example, the activities listed

---

[78] UN Doc. A/AC.134/SR.52–66, 20–1. Also: UN Doc. A/AC.134/SR.67–78, 107; UN Doc. A/AC.134/SR.79–91, 43.

[79] UN Doc. A/AC.134/SR.52–66, 40–1. Also: UN Doc. A/AC.134/SR.67–78, 7.

[80] UN Doc. A/AC.134/SR.52–66, 116. Also at 66 (US, noting that the Thirteen-Power draft could not be the one to rally general support since 'it deprived States of their right under the Charter and under general international law to have recourse to individual or collective self-defence when they [are] the victims of subversive or terrorist acts by irregular bands').

Remark: a number of other States supported the idea that 'indirect aggression' could at least sometimes be regarded as 'armed attack triggering the right of self-defence. E.g., UN Doc. A/AC.134/SR.52–66, 114–15 (Indonesia); UN Doc. A/AC.134/SR.67–78, 52 (DRC, referring to the sending of mercenaries); UN Doc. A/C.6/26/SR.1272, 2 November 1971, § 29 (El Salvador).

[81] E.g., UN Doc. A/AC.134/SR.52–66, 32 (Uruguay: 'direct armed aggression was the only form which justified exercise of the right of self-defence'), 55 (Ecuador), 57 (Colombia), 61 (Yugoslavia), 86 (Mexico), 90 (Cyprus: 'There was no doubt that infiltration and subversion violated the Charter, but they could not be termed aggression in the sense of the armed attack for which provision was made in that Article; in other words, they could not be countered with military action by the victim State'), 113 (Colombia), 117

in Article 2B, paragraphs 6 to 8 of the Six-Power draft, ought to be brought to the attention of the UN: '[T]o use force in those cases would not only be contrary to the letter and the spirit of the Charter, but would violate the obligations laid down in Article 51.'[82] Mexico argued that '[a] State's reaction to indirect aggression could not be the same as its reaction to an armed attack, since, in the latter case, it would be authorized by the Charter to repel the aggression by exercising the right of self-defence'.[83] More specifically:

> A State which was the object of indirect aggression should take all the necessary domestic measures to safeguard its political institutions. If those measures proved inadequate, it could, under Chapters VI or VII of the Charter, request the United Nations to intervene if it considered that there was a threat to peace.[84]

The position of the Thirteen Powers on the matter was shared to varying extent by several other States, such as Syria, the United Arab Republic, Romania, the Soviet Union and even Norway.[85]

In a purportedly accommodating gesture, the Thirteen Powers suggested that States should first focus on negotiating a definition of direct aggression and should postpone the attempt to draft a (separate) definition of indirect aggression to a later stage.[86] Unsurprisingly, however, the Six Powers rejected this démarche as derisory: a Definition of Aggression that would not include a reference to indirect

---

(Uruguay); UN Doc. A/AC.134/SR.67–78, 17 (Cyprus), 112 (Colombia); UN Doc. A/AC.134/SR.79–91, 55 (Uruguay).

[82] UN Doc. A/AC.134/SR.52–66, 55.   [83] UN Doc. A/AC.134/SR.52–66, 86.   [84] Ibid.

[85] (1) Syria: UN Doc. A/AC.134/SR.52–66, 98; (2) UAR: UN Doc. A/AC.134/SR.52–66, at 59–60, 92, 110–11, 119; (3) Romania: UN Doc. A/AC.134/SR.79–91, 79; (4) USSR: The Soviet draft definition of aggression (UN Doc. A/AC.134/L.12 (and Corr. 1)) did not explicitly rule out self-defence against these acts, but Soviet statements during the debates appear to reject it. See: UN Doc. A/AC.134/SR.79–91, 35; UN Doc. A/C.6/26/SR.1272, 2 November 1971, § 7; (5) Norway: UN Doc. A/AC.134/SR.52–66, 37 ('The definition should be limited exclusively to aggression resulting from the direct use of armed force. ... [A]ny enlargement of the definition of aggression would entail a corresponding enlargement of the concept of self-defence'). But: UN Doc. A/AC.134/SR.67–78, 113–14 (suggesting that the permissibility of self-defence should be determined on the basis of the proportionality principle).

Consider also: UN Doc. A/C.6/25/SR.1208, 27 October 1970, § 60 (Sweden).

[86] E.g., UN Doc. A/AC.134/SR.52–66, 32 (Uruguay), 57 (Colombia), 86 (Mexico), 113 (Colombia), 114 (Guyana); UN Doc. A/AC.134/SR.67–78, 17, 48, 106 (Cyprus), 107 (Colombia), 112 (Uruguay). Also: UN Doc. A/AC.134/SR.52–66, 46 (Bulgaria), 78 (Iraq), 114 (Indonesia); UN Doc. A/AC.134/SR.67–78, 50, 52 (Syria); UN Doc. A/AC.134/SR.79–91, 35 (USSR), 39 (Syria).

aggression would be fundamentally incomplete, unbalanced and unacceptable.[87]

In the early 1970s, there were some signs indicating that the deadlock began to disentangle.[88] Whereas there was general agreement that aggression referred in principle to the use of force *by one State against another State* – an idea enshrined in Article 1 of the Definition – the Thirteen Powers, together with several other developing countries, began to recognize that certain forms of indirect aggression could exceptionally give rise to defensive measures.[89] Conversely, the Thirteen Powers conceded that not all forms of indirect aggression would activate Article 51.[90]

A number of variables steered the discussion. First, there was a growing acceptance of the idea that only 'manifest' cases of 'indirect

---

[87] See especially: UN Doc. A/AC.134/SR.52-66, at 66-7, 117 (US: 'The argument that the Committee should restrict itself to defining direct aggression at the present stage because direct aggression was relatively easy to define was derisory; efforts to define it had already lasted for more than thirty years and, moreover, if indirect aggression was a more difficult subject, there was no knowing how long it would take to define. . . . The [US] Government would oppose any definition of aggression from which indirect uses of force were excluded'); UN Doc. A/AC.134/SR.67-78, 48 (US), 111 (Australia). Also: UN Doc. A/AC.134/SR.52-66, 25 (Canada), 40 (Japan), 99 (Australia), 100 (Italy), 101 (US); UN Doc. A/AC.134/SR.67-78, 107 (US); UN Doc. A/AC.134/SR.79-91, 18 (US), 42 (Italy); UN Doc. A/AC.134.SR/92-9, 32 (Australia).

Remark: if the Six Powers had accepted this proposal, this would have affirmed the impression that self-defence was only available in relation to direct aggression, and would have left the Six Powers with little bargaining power to effect a separate and appropriate definition of indirect aggression. Also: UN Doc. A/AC.134/SR.52-66, 115 (Turkey).

[88] According to Broms, then Chairman of the Special Committee: 'Until 1973 some members of the Special Committee . . . had been strongly against any inclusion into the definition of provisions on indirect acts of aggression. . . . In 1973 opposition to the insertion of a provision on indirect aggression was, however, somewhat unexpectedly dropped, and this change had a profound effect on the chances of reaching an overall solution.' B. Broms, 'The definition of aggression', (1977-I) 154 RdC 299-400, at 353.

[89] E.g., UN Doc. A/AC.134/SR.52-66, 99 (Ghana), 118-19 (Cyprus); UN Doc. A/AC.134/SR.79-91, 13 (Cyprus), 60 (Madagascar).

[90] E.g., UN Doc. A/AC.134/SR.52-66, 41 (Japan: '[Japan] did not claim that in each and every case of such indirect aggression a victim State was invariably justified in exercising the right of self-defence under Article 51, but a State should not be deprived of its lawful recourse to the right of self-defence simply because of the "indirect" nature of the acts of aggression of which it was a victim'); UN Doc. A/AC.134/SR.67-78, 108 (Canada); UN Doc. A/AC.134/SR.52-66, 79-91, 33 (Japan). Consider also: UN Doc. A/C.6/SR.1205, 22 October 1970, § 16 (Italy, warning that 'if the definition of the so-called indirect aggression was drafted too widely, it might lead to unacceptable interpretations of Article 51 of the Charter').

aggression' would give rise to self-defence.[91] This is not to say that States' appraisal of the required 'intensity' was entirely parallel. The United States, for example, tended to emphasize that the permissibility of self-defence should be determined by means of the proportionality threshold, and conceded that a relatively minor act of subversion could generally be contained by other methods than through recourse to force.[92] Others stressed that the large majority of subversive and infiltration activities fell under the category of minor acts, and at the worst constituted a threat or a breach of the peace, but not an 'armed attack'.[93] In all, however, it was agreed that the gravity or magnitude of the actions of the armed bands was an important determinant. According to France, 'serious flagrant cases of subversion could be placed on the same footing as direct armed attack within the meaning of Article 51 of the Charter'.[94] This idea was eventually incorporated in the final text of Article 3(g) of the Definition of Aggression, which requires that the acts of armed force carried out by the armed bands, groups, irregulars or mercenaries concerned be of 'such gravity as to amount to' the various examples of (direct) aggression listed in the other paragraphs of Article 3.

A second key aspect concerned the link between the State and the armed bands. Indeed, States generally agreed that the acts contemplated should not only be of sufficient gravity, but also asserted that the participation of the other State therein be fully established.[95] Which activities would establish the required link, however, was subject of disagreement. In 1973, the US began making concessions by dropping its condemnation of 'organizing', 'encouraging', 'assistance to', 'knowing acquiescence in' or 'lending support to' armed bands, and was prepared to settle for the more objective criterion of the actual 'sending' of armed bands against

---

[91] E.g., UN Doc. A/AC.134/SR.67–78, 107 (Turkey, referring to 'cases of manifest aggression'), 118 (Cyprus, referring to the 'degree of danger' emanating from the armed bands), 118–19 (France), 120 (Canada); UN Doc. A/AC.134/SR.79–91, 96 (Indonesia); UN Doc. A/AC.134/SR.100–9, 16 (USSR), 37 (Syria); UN Doc. A/AC.134/SR.110–13, 51 (Mexico).
[92] E.g., UN Doc. A/AC.134/SR.52–66, 116 (US); UN Doc. A/AC.134/SR.67–78, 117 (US). Also: UN Doc. A/AC.134/SR.52–66, 113 (Norway). Consider also: UNGA Sixth Committee, 26th Session, 1270th meeting, 28 October 1971, UN Doc. A/C.6/26/SR.1270, § 6 (Ghana), §§ 26–9 (Burma). Contra: UN Doc. A/AC.134/SR.52–66, 119 (Cyprus); UN Doc. A/C.6/26/SR.1271, 1 November 1971,§ 30 (France).
[93] E.g., UN Doc. A/AC.134/SR.79–91, 13 (Cyprus, admitting there were 'marginal cases in which the infiltration was so substantial and the danger so great that they were tantamount to an armed attack'); UN Doc. A/AC.134/SR.100–9, 37 (Syria).
[94] UN Doc. A/AC.134/SR.67–78, 119.
[95] E.g., UN Doc. A/AC.134/SR.110–13, 44 (Canada), 51 (Mexico).

another State.[96] On the other hand, it insisted that the provision on indirect aggression also refer to cases of 'open and active participation' in the proscribed activities.[97] Numerous States expressed concern about the use of the latter phrase, which was considered imprecise and prone to an overly broad interpretation.[98] France argued that 'the sending by or on behalf of a State' was as far as it was possible to go if interference in the domestic affairs of States was to be avoided.[99] Indonesia, on the other hand, preferred to include the 'supporting' of armed bands but agreed to drop this proposal due to a lack of support.[100] In the end, a compromise was found in the replacement of the phrase 'open and active participation' by States' 'substantial involvement' in the activities of the armed bands. The final version of Article 3(g) thus covers essentially two situations. The first situation, viz. the 'sending by or on behalf of' the State, involves acts of armed bands for which a State is considered directly responsible.[101] This presupposes the actual dispatching of armed bands; 'the mere fact of organizing or preparing armed bands did not of itself constitute an act of aggression'.[102] In addition, the concept of 'substantial involvement' envisages a somewhat broader type of interaction between the State and the armed group, to be

[96] B. B. Ferencz, *Defining international aggression. The search for world peace: a documentary history and analysis*. Vol. II (Dobbs Ferry, NY: Oceana, 1975), p. 39. See also: Report of the Special Committee, 25 April–30 May 1973, UN Doc. A/9019, Appendix B, at 23 (restated in Ferencz, Defining intenational aggression, p. 534.). See also: T. Bruha, *Die Definition der Aggression* (Berlin: Duncker & Humblot, 1980), pp. 228–39.

[97] Ferencz, *Defining international aggression*, p. 39.

[98] *Ibid.*, pp. 39–40. E.g., UN Doc. A/AC.134/SR.100-9, 31 (Algeria), 33 (Egypt), 39–40 (France), 40 (Iraq), 47 (USSR). Also: UN Doc. A/C.6/28/SR.1441, 19 November 1973, 235 (German Democratic Republic).

[99] UN Doc. A/AC.134/SR.100-9, 40 (France). See also: UN Doc. A/C.6/28/SR.1442, 20 November 1973, 248 (Ghana, arguing that the majority of States accepted that only the sending of armed bands by or on behalf of a State constituted an act of aggression, provided that the gravity of the attack was sufficiently substantial); UN Doc. A/C.6/28/SR.1443, 20 November 1973, 253 (USSR, insisting that indirect aggression required 'the presence of a direct link between the sending of the armed bands and the State sending them and a certain degree of intensity of the actions of such bands'); UN Doc. A/C.6/SR.1442, 20 November 1973, § 66 (Ghana).

[100] E.g., UN Doc. A/AC.134/SR.79-91, 95; UN Doc. A/AC.134/SR.100-9, 24; UN Doc. A/AC.134/SR.110-13, 10–11; UN Doc. A/C.6/28/SR.1442, 20 November 1973, 246. Consider also: UN Doc. A/C.6/25/SR.1206, 26 October 1970, § 37 (India: arguing that the organizing or encouraging of acts of civil strife or territorist acts in the territory of another State also constituted aggressive acts).

[101] Broms, 'The definition of aggression', 354.

[102] UN Doc. A/AC.134/SR.110-14, 2 (France); UN Doc. A/C.6/29/SR.1474, 11 October 1974, § 29 (France).

determined on the basis of all relevant circumstances.[103] The reluctance to include 'assistance' or 'support' do, however, indicate that its scope must be interpreted restrictively.[104] France again made clear that:

> it could not accept the idea that the mere fact that the receiving State organized, helped to organize or encouraged the formation of armed bands constituted an act of aggression, independently of whether or not it also participated in sending them on the incursions. Nor could [it] accept *a fortiori* that by making its territory available to such armed bands a State committed an act of aggression.[105]

Even if resolution 3314 (XXIX) asserts that it in no way 'enlarges or diminishes the scope' of the Charter provisions on the use of force (Article 6), one cannot ignore the fact that the toilsome discussion on 'indirect aggression' was in part an exercise to find a compromise on the scope of Article 51 UN Charter.[106] For this reason, the two aforementioned elements of the resulting text, namely the need for at least substantial involvement of the State and for the attacks themselves to be of a certain gravity, can be presumed to represent States' attitude vis-à-vis self-defence in response to attacks by non-State actors at the time.[107] More concretely, States generally accepted that isolated and/or small-scale attacks by armed bands would not allow a forcible cross-border response by the victim State.[108] Furthermore, the discrepancy between the list of State activities in Article 3(g) and the much broader construction of 'indirect use of force' in the 1970 Friendly Relations Declaration (referring to 'organizing', 'encouraging', 'instigating', 'assisting' and even 'acquiescing within its territory') suggests that a close relationship

---

[103] See Ferencz, *Defining international aggression*, p. 40.
[104] Also Corten, *Le droit contre la guerre*, p. 677; O. Corten and F. Dubuisson, 'Opération "liberté immuable": une extension abusive du concept de légitime défense', (2002) 106 RGDIP 51–77, at 56. The authors set strict conditions for 'substantial involvement' under Article 3(g): (1) the State must have had knowledge of the attacks being prepared, and (2) it must itself have participated in a substantial manner. Incidental or accessory participation is deemed insufficient.
[105] UN Doc. A/C.6/28/SR.1441, 239. See also: UN Doc. A/C.6/26/SR.1271, 1 November 1971, § 30 (France: 'Vague concepts such as support for acts of subversion should be excluded, however, since a State might use them as a pretext for aggression under the guise of self-defence').
[106] E.g., UN Doc. A/AC.134/SR.52–66, 100 (Italy: '[T]he main concern was whether the right of self-defence should apply in cases of indirect aggression ...'), 110 (UK), 116 (US); UN Doc. A/AC.134/SR.67–78, at 50 (UAR: 'the real issue was the applicability of Article 51 of the Charter').
[107] See, e.g., Randelzhofer, 'Article 51', p. 800; Abi-Saab, 'Cours général', 363.
[108] Also Broms, 'The definition of aggression', 354.

between the State and the armed group was considered a prerequisite under Article 51 UN Charter.[109] The impression is that relatively minor forms of assistance, and *a fortiori* the tolerating of the group's presence within the State's territory may well constitute a breach of Article 2(4), but remain insufficient to justify an exercise of self-defence.[110] As far as the latter type of conduct is concerned, it is moreover striking that even the Six-Power proposal never listed it as a form of indirect aggression (instead referring only to 'organizing, supporting or directing').[111]

5.1.2.b   Use of force and the right of self-determination

Finally, in order to gain a more comprehensive understanding of the debate, it is imperative to shed some light on a related matter, namely the discussion on the use of force in the context of self-determination. Indeed, during the negotiations on the 1970 Friendly Relations Declaration there was concern among many developing and socialist countries that paragraphs 8 and 9 (dealing with indirect use of force) could be interpreted as unduly restricting people's right to self-determination. More precisely, numerous States insisted that 'oppressed' and/or 'colonial' peoples had the right to use armed force in the exercise of this right as well as the concomitant right to seek and receive support, possibly including armed assistance, from other States.[112] Accordingly,

---

[109] Also: Abi-Saab, 'Cours général', 363; Macdonald, 'The *Nicaragua* case', 148–9.
[110] Remark: Israel was apparently the only country to draw attention to the problem of the tolerance of armed bands within a State's territory. It warned that 'the all too common attitude of passivity towards acts of indirect aggression and terrorism might be found not to have been adequately treated [by Article 3(g)].' UNGA Sixth Committee, 28th Session, 1443rd meeting, 20 November 1973, § 51.
[111] L.-A. Sicilianos, *Les réactions décentralisées à l'illicité: des contre-mesures à la légitime défense* (Paris: Librairie générale de droit et de jurisprudence, 1990), p. 326.
[112] States held differing views on the precise scope of this right. Some stressed that only peoples under colonial domination could use force in self-determination. Others extended it to all 'oppressed' peoples. Some insisted that force could only be used if all other alternatives had been exhausted. Furthermore, some States explicitly accepted that these peoples could receive armed support from third States, while others referred more cautiously to 'assistance' in general terms. See, e.g., UN Doc. A/AC.125/SR97–109, 18 August–19 September 1969, 24–7 (USSR), 39 (Romania), 44–5 (Czechoslovakia), 59 (Madagascar), 89, 101 (Kenya); UN Doc. A/AC.125/SR.110–14, 51 (Yugoslavia), 59 (Kenya), 62–3 (USSR), 64–5 (Syria), 78 (UAR). Also: UN Doc. A/C.6/25/SR.1178, 23 September 1970, § 13 (Zambia); UN Doc. A/C.6/25/SR.1179, 24 September 1970, § 19 (Pakistan, stressing that 'the duty of States not to organize armed bands or to instigate civil strife and terrorist acts had to be viewed in the light of the right of a dependent people to take armed action to secure its right to self-determination.'); UN Doc. A/C.6/

this right could not be curtailed by the aforementioned paragraphs. In the words of the Syrian delegate:

> The provisions in the eighth and ninth paragraphs of the principle of non-use of force ... should not be expanded in scope to the extent that they could be used as a pretext to deny peoples who were suffering from colonialism, military occupation, oppression or any other form of foreign domination, the right of individual and collective self-defence and the right to seek and receive all forms of assistance in their struggle for ... self-determination.[113]

The Soviet delegate, observing that the struggle of colonial peoples had already been 'legitimized' by the decisions of the General Assembly and the Security Council, argued that the negotiations on the Friendly Relations Declaration offered an opportunity to finally 'legalize' this struggle 'in the juridical sense'.[114]

As could be expected, other States were not particularly eager to recognize a right to use force and to seek and receive armed support as a corollary of self-determination. Australia and the UK held that the UN Charter was neutral in this respect and did not confer upon, or deny to, colonial peoples the right of rebellion.[115] Both countries were convinced that States could not intervene by giving military support or arms in a Non-Self-Governing or Trust Territory.[116] The US stressed that the right of peoples to seek and receive support in their quest for self-determination 'did not constitute a general license for international traffic in arms' and 'did not give States the right to intervene by military

---

25/SR.1182, 25 September 1970, § 16 (Afghanistan); § 47 (Libya: 'the principle prohibiting the threat or use of force should not affect the right to self-defence of peoples under colonial rule'). More reserved: UN Doc. A/AC.125/SR.97–109, 66 (France); UN Doc. A/AC.125/SR.110–14, 49 (France).

[113] UN Doc. A/AC.125/SR.110–14, 64.   [114] UN Doc. A/AC.125/SR.97–109, 104.

[115] UN Doc. A/AC.125/SR.97–109, 40 (UK), 76–7 (Australia, on the inapplicability of the right of self-defence to peoples under colonial domination); UN Doc. A/AC.125/SR.110–14, 63 (Australia), 74 (UK). Both countries moreover asserted that the proscription of the use of force against people seeking self-determination did not preclude such limited police action as might be essential to maintain or restore law and order with a view to establishing conditions in which the peoples of a Non-Self-Governing Territory would be enabled to proceed to the exercise of their right to self-determination.

[116] Japan and the Netherlands urged that the legitimate frustrations of peoples under colonial domination should generally be dealt with through peaceful meachanisms, first and foremost within the UN Framework: UN Doc. A/AC.125/SR.97–109, 52–3 (Japan, but conceding that in the face of imminent and overwhelming danger to their existence, dependent peoples might have no choice but to resist by force), 86 (Netherlands).

means in the territories concerned'.[117] Finally, according to South Africa, the UN Charter did not entitle States to intervene by giving military support or armed assistance in Non-Self-Governing Territories or elsewhere.[118]

In the end, ambiguity was the price for consensus. Paragraph 5 of the Friendly Relations Declaration's section on the 'principle of equal rights and self-determination of peoples' declared that:

> Every State has the duty to refrain from any forcible action which deprives peoples referred to above in the elaboration of the present principle of their right to self-determination and freedom and independence. In their actions against, and resistance to, such forcible action in pursuit of the exercise of their right to self-determination, such peoples are entitled to seek and to receive support in accordance with the purposes and principles of the Charter.[119]

While this paragraph indicates considerable sympathy for the struggle of colonial peoples and accepts in general terms that they are entitled 'to seek and to receive support', the circular catch-phrase inserted at the end is *incontournable*: by demanding that acts of resistance and support by other States must be conducted 'in accordance with the purposes and principles of the Charter', the provision ultimately refrains from pronouncing on the legal validity of the possibility of using armed force and of providing armed support.[120]

During the debates on the Definition of Aggression, the controversy regarding self-determination was raised in a slightly different context. *In casu*, a number of States feared that if a provision on indirect aggression was included, support to peoples struggling for self-determination could hypothetically be brought within its ambit and be regarded as triggering the right of self-defence.[121] In order to exclude such abusive

---

[117] UN Doc. A/AC.125/SR.110–14, 83; UN Doc. A/C.6/25/SR.1180, 24 September 1970, § 25.
[118] UN Doc. A/C.6/25/SR.1184, 28 September 1970, §§ 15–16.
[119] GA Res. 2625 (XXV) of 24 October 1970.
[120] See, e.g., C. Don Johnson, 'Towards self-determination – a reappraisal as reflected in the Declaration on Friendly Relations', (1973) 3 Georgia JICL 145–63, at 150–1; Rosenstock, 'Principles of International Law Concerning Friendly Relations', 732–3. See also: A. Tanca, 'The prohibition of force in the UN Declaration on Friendly Relations of 1970', in Cassese (ed.), *The use of force*, pp. 397–412, at 404–8.
[121] See in particular: UN Doc. A/AC.134/SR.52–66, 60 (UAR); UN Doc. A/AC.134/SR.67–78, 97 (Ghana: 'the definition might be misinterpreted as meaning that a State which gave its support to a dependent people must be considered as indirectly supporting aggression'), 101 (UAR). Also: UNGA Sixth Committee, 28th Session, 1442nd meeting, 20 November 1973, § 43 (Yugoslavia). See also: Bruha, *Die Definition der Aggression*, p. 228.

interpretation, several developing and socialist countries insisted on a specific provision, exempting dependent peoples and the States aiding them from the obligation not to use force in their international relations. Others warned against the risks of an explicit rule of this kind.[122] Australia, for example, somewhat prophetically warned that 'it would be rash to resort to a formula which might be turned against its authors and constitute a threat to the security and integrity of States everywhere'.[123]

Again, in a spiritr of compromise, Article 7 of the Definition of Aggression tried to bridge the diverging views:

> Nothing in this definition ... could in any way prejudice the right to self-determination ... as derived from the Charter, of peoples forcibly deprived of that right and referred to in the [Friendly Relations Declaration] in accordance with the [UN Charter], particularly peoples under colonial and racist regimes or other forms of alien domination; nor the right of these peoples to struggle to that end and to seek and receive support, in accordance with the principles of the Charter and in conformity with the above-mentioned Declaration.[124]

While a number of States explicitly declared that the provision should be interpreted as including the right of peoples subject to alien domination to resort to force and to obtain support, including armed support, from other States,[125] the text ultimately refrains – like the Friendly Relations

---

[122] See: Ferencz, *Defining international aggression*, pp. 47–9. For an overview of States' respective positions, see especially: UN Doc. A/AC.134/SR.67-78, 93-105. E.g., *ibid.*, 94 (UK: '[T]he [UK] could not accept a provision, the effect of which would be that an act, which would otherwise be defined as aggression by one State against another, would not be considered aggression simply because it had been accomplished in a "self-determination context"'). See also the following statements arguing that the Definition of Aggression did not restrict the right of peoples to struggle for self-determination or their right to seek and receive assistance for that purpose: UN Doc. A/C.6/25/SR.1202, 16 October 1970, § 18 (Iraq); UN Doc. A/C.6/25/SR.1203, 20 October 1970, § 11 (Uganda); UN Doc. A/C.6/25/SR.1204, 21 October 1970, § 5 (Syria); UN Doc. A/C.6/25/SR.1205, 22 October 1970, § 38 (Gabon), § 40 (Ghana); UN Doc. A/C.6/25/SR.1206, 26 October 1970, § 50 (Afghanistan), § 71 (Cuba); UN Doc. A/C.6/28/SR.1442, 20 November 1973, § 21 (Kenya), § 52 (Indonesia). But: UN Doc. A/C.6/25/SR.1207, 27 October 1970, § 50 (Portugal).
[123] UN Doc. A/AC.134/SR.92-100, 33. Contrast with: UN Doc. A/AC.125/SR.97-109, 62 (USSR).
[124] GA Res. 2625 (XXV) of 24 October 1970.
[125] E.g., UN Doc. A/AC.134/SR.110-114, 47 (USSR), 49 (Algeria), 52 (Egypt). Also: UN Doc. A/C.6/29/SR.1472, 9-23 October 1974, § 5 (USSR), § 43 (Bulgaria); UN Doc. A/C.6/29/SR.1474, § 24 (Kenya); UN Doc. A/C.6/29/SR.1478, 41 (Hungary); UN Doc. A/C.6/29/SR.1479, § 33 (Algeria), § 42 (Cuba); UN Doc. A/C.6/29/SR.1480, § 49 (Belarus); UN Doc. A/C.6/29/SR.1483, § 32 (Egypt).

Declaration – from pronouncing on the legality of the actual recourse to force. Instead, the wording was left so vague that the opposing parties might each interpret it to their own advantage should the need arise.[126] Even if the negotiations were thus inconclusive in this respect, it must be kept in mind that the inclusion of Article 7 was of pivotal importance to persuade particularly the Arab States to assent to Article 3(g).[127] As we will see below, the controversy on the use of force for self-determination also surfaced in UN debates regarding concrete self-defence claims.

5.1.3 State practice

5.1.3.a Early cases

State practice confirms that the application of Article 51 UN Charter is not limited exclusively to attacks by regular troops. Already in the 1950s and 1960s, well before the move towards a compromise within the Fourth Special Committee, States on occasion invoked the right of self-defence against attacks by armed bands. At the same time, these claims were construed in cautious terms, relying on very close links between the armed bands and the State concerned.

In 1956, for example, Israel invoked the inherent right of self-defence in order to justify a large-scale ground offensive into Egypt resulting in the occupation of the whole Sinaï Peninsula.[128] According to Israel, the object of the operations was to eliminate the Egyptian *fedayeen* bases from which armed units carried out recurring raids into its territory.[129] In the preceding ten months alone, these raids had killed twenty-eight Israelis and wounded 127.[130] Interestingly, Israel put considerable emphasis on the close link between the Nasser regime and the *fedayeen*. Citing a number of statements by Egyptian officials as well as by the Commander of UNTSO, it insisted that the *fedayeen* bands were used by Egypt as an instrument for Israel's destruction. In the words of the Israeli UN representative, Egypt had 'sent' these units into Israeli territory to murder and plunder, and raids were carried out 'under the responsibility

---

[126] Ferencz, *Defining international aggression*, p. 49.
[127] See *ibid.*, p. 40; UN Doc. A/AC.134/SR.92–100, 74 (US, recognizing that the key to securing agreement on indirect aggression 'might well be in the inclusion in the definition of a reference to the right of self-determination').
[128] UN Doc. S/PV.749, 30 October 1956, § 33 (Israel). [129] *Ibid.*
[130] *Ibid.*, §§ 49 *et seq.*, 93.

THE 'ARMED ATTACK' REQUIREMENT *RATIONE PERSONAE* 395

and control of Mr Nasser'.[131] Egypt's involvement was clearly considered to go beyond the mere harbouring or assisting of the *fedayeen:*

> While other Arab Governments shared the responsibility for sheltering, feeding and training these units on their soil, we never doubted for a single moment that the original guilt and the *active responsibility of command* rested with Nasser. It is he who presses the button; it is others who suffer the impact of the explosion.[132]

Israel's version of the facts was apparently shared by France. Before the UN Security Council, the latter country observed that the 'Egyptian High Command long ago *organized* special commando units of *fedayeen* trained to attack property, communications and people in Israel territory. ... At the same time, official statements have boasted of the activities of these fellaghas'.[133] For these reasons, France felt that it was not possible to condemn Israel.[134] Other Council Members refrained from discussing the relationship between the *fedayeen* and the Egyptian authorities. Several expressed understanding for Israel's security concerns and condemned the *fedayeen* raids.[135] The general attitude was, however, that Israel's response was in any event disproportionate to the wrongs suffered.[136] A draft resolution expressing 'grave concern at this

---

[131] *Ibid.*, §§ 33 ('under the special care and authority of Mr Nasser'), 37 ('The Government of Egypt made no secret of these activities or of its responsibility for them'), 38–44 (referring to Egyptian statements), 45, 91–2 (referring to statements by the UN commander), 98 (referring to 'responsibility and control of Mr Nasser'), 103, 105 (referring to the 'sending' of armed units by Egypt).

[132] *Ibid.*, § 48 (emphasis added).

[133] UN Doc. S/PV.749, §§ 156, 164 (also referring to 'rebellions instigated by Cairo', the holding of 'courses of terrorism' in Egyptian camps, and the sending of arms in ever-growing quantities) (emphasis added).

[134] *ibid.*, §§ 172–3.

[135] UN Doc. S/PV.748, 30 October 1956, § 22 (Yugoslavia: 'None of us, I am sure, condones [these raids]. They could, however, have been dealt with through the armistice machinery .... They can in no way provide a pretext or an excuse for the course of naked aggression upon which Israel has embarked'), § 37 (Australia: 'It is true that Israel has suffered *at the hands of Egypt* in various ways ... But that, in our view, does not justify what has been taking place in recent hours' (emphasis added)); UN Doc. S/PV.749, § 3 (UK, referring to 'renewed raids by guerrillas, culminating in the incursion of Egyptian commandos'), § 132 (Republic of China: 'While I do not accept [Israel's] thesis, I must confess that I have a certain measure of sympathy with his country's dilemma').

[136] E.g., UN Doc. S/PV.748, § 8 (US), § 21–2 (Yugoslavia), § 29 (USSR), § 37 (Australia); UN Doc. S/PV.749, § 16 (US), § 29 (USSR), § 133 (Republic of China). Also: T. M. Franck, *Recourse to force: State action against threats and armed attacks* (Cambridge University Press, 2002), p. 55.

violation of the Armistice Agreement' and calling for Israel's immediate withdrawal failed only owing to British and French vetoes.[137] Whether the international community would have accepted a more limited intervention directed specifically against individual *fedayeen* bases remains a hypothetical question.[138]

Issues concerning 'indirect aggression' again surfaced in 1958 in relation to US and British interventions in Lebanon and Jordan respectively.[139] *In casu*, the latter countries had requested the help of the former governments in order to protect their integrity and independence in the face of acts of infiltration allegedly orchestrated by the United Arab Republic. Both States expressly relied on Article 51 UN Charter.[140] Lebanon accused the UAR of 'massive, illegal and unprovoked intervention' in its domestic affairs, through the supply of arms on a large scale to subversive elements in Lebanon; the inciting, training and sending of these elements to overthrow the Lebanese government; and the participation of UAR governmental elements in subversive and terrorist activities and in the direction of rebellion in Lebanon.[141] Jordan, in addition to complaining of threatening troop movements along its northern borders, accused the UAR of 'the smuggling of saboteurs and agents into the country, together with clandestine supplies of arms, ammunition and explosives' as well as 'the mustering and bribing of subversive elements within Jordan with the intent to overthrow the existing regime'.[142] In response to objections that neither country had been the victim of an 'armed attack',[143] others warned that 'indirect' aggression could be just as dangerous as 'direct' aggression.[144] According to Lebanon:

> Article 51 is ... intended to cover all cases of attack, whether direct or indirect, provided it is armed attack. ... What real difference is there

---

[137] See UN Doc. S/PV.749, § 186; UN Doc. S/3710, 30 October 1956 (US draft). The resolution obtained seven votes in favour (Belgium and Australia abstained).
[138] Higgins, *Problems and process*, p. 202.
[139] See UN Docs. S/PV.827–38, 15 July – 7 August 1958.
[140] E.g., UN Doc. S/PV.827, § 84 (Lebanon); UN Doc. S/PV.831, § 24 (Jordan); UN Doc. S/PV.832, § 33 (Jordan); UN Doc. S/PV.836, § 7 (Lebanon).
[141] E.g., UN Doc. S/PV.827, § 71. Also: UN Doc. S/PV.828, §§ 54–5; UN Doc. S/PV.833, §§ 13–30; UN Doc. S/PV.835, §§ 91–101 (referring to the 'sending', 'recruiting' and 'instructing' of the *fedayeen*).
[142] E.g., UN Doc. S/PV.831, §§ 19–24.
[143] E.g., UN Doc. S/PV.827, § 116 (USSR); UN Doc. S/PV.828, § 33 (UAR); UN Doc. S/PV.829, § 40 (USSR); UN Doc. S/PV.830, § 4 (UAR); § 48 (Sweden); UN Doc. S/PV.831, § 72 (USSR), § 109 (UAR),
[144] E.g., UN Doc. S/PV.827, §§ 45, 49, 53 (US); UN Doc. S/PV.829, § 13 (US); UN Doc. S/PV.831, § 32 (UK), § 99 (Republic of China).

between armed soldiers in uniform making a frontal attack on a certain part of a certain country and these same soldiers, armed but not in uniform, secretly infiltrating into the area to regroup there and engage in the same sort of armed attack as soldiers in uniform? It would seem obvious that this distinction between direct and indirect attack is purely verbal and wholly factitious in this instance.[145]

It does not appear from the Council debates that any State challenged the idea that self-defence could be exercised against irregulars sent from abroad per se.[146] Rather, States held different perceptions of the allegations of infiltration under consideration. A number of States – including France, China and Canada – accepted the charges of large-scale indirect aggression on the part of the UAR.[147] Others, especially the UAR and the Soviet Union, denounced the allegations as unsubstantiated and/or fabricated, and pointed out that the UN Observer Group in Lebanon had been unable to confirm reports of infiltration.[148] In relation to Lebanon, it was moreover submitted that this country was embroiled in a civil war and that the US was simply trying to protect an unpopular puppet

---

[145] UN Doc. S/PV.833, § 10. [146] Also Gray, *The use of force*, p. 174.
[147] E.g., UN Doc. S/PV.827, §§ 32–44 (US), §§ 71–82 (Lebanon), §§ 87–9 (UK); UN Doc. S/PV.828, §§ 2–9 (France, regarding the US intervention in Lebanon as justified under Article 51 UN Charter), § 16 (Canada, *idem*), §§ 25–6 (Republic of China), §§ 54–5 (Lebanon); UN Doc. S/PV.829, §§ 57–64 (US); UN Doc. S/PV.831, §§ 19–24 (Jordan), § 99 (Republic of China, accepting Jordan's reliance on self-defence); UN Doc. S/PV.832, §§ 2–4 (France), § 34 (Jordan); UN Doc. S/PV.833, §§ 13–30 (Lebanon); UN Doc. S/PV.835, §§ 91–101 (Lebanon); UN Doc. S/PV.836, § 2 (Lebanon). Also: UN Doc. S/PV.833, § 47 (Colombia).
[148] E.g., UN Doc. S/PV.827, § 96 (USSR); UN Doc. S/PV.828, §§ 40–2 (UAR), § 59 (USSR); UN Doc. S/PV.829, § 22 (USSR); UN Doc. S/PV.831, § 78 (USSR); UN Doc. S/PV.835, § 106 (UAR); UN Doc. S/PV.838, §§ 27–9 (USSR), 129–31 (UAR).
Remark: the UN observers had indeed concluded that the extent of the infiltration '[could not] be on anything more than a limited scale, and [was] largely confined to small arms and ammunition'. In no case had the observers, who had been 'vigilantly patrolling the opposition-held areas and [had] frequently observed the armed bands there, been able to detect the presence of persons who [had] indubitably entered from across the border for the purposes of fighting'. See: Second Report of the United Nations Observation Group in Lebanon, 30 July 1958, UN Doc. S/4069, §§ 62–3. The report also found that there was no coordinated military planning and control of these forces (§ 64). Remark: Lebanon went to great lengths to discard the findings of the UN Observer Group. It argued that observation had been ineffective, *inter alia* because the UN observers had been denied access to parts of the border area and because observation had been confined to the daylight hours. See, e.g., UN Doc. S/PV.827, §§ 75–9; UN Doc. S/PV.828, §§ 64–6; UN Doc. S/PV.833, §§ 1–3; UN Doc. S/PV.835, § 102; UN Doc. S/PV.838, §§ 109–26. Also: UN Doc. S/PV.828, § 6 (France); UN Doc. S/PV.838, §§ 62–4 (US).

regime.[149] In addition, the intervention was criticized for interfering with the action already undertaken by the Security Council.[150]

In any event, no military action was undertaken against the UAR, neither by American and British troops, nor by Jordan and Lebanon themselves.[151] Hence, one might wonder whether it would not have been more appropriate to frame the situation in terms of 'intervention by invitation' rather than by reference to Article 51.[152] The situation was eventually passed on to the Third Emergency Special Session of the General Assembly, which in turn requested the UN Secretary-General to propose practical arrangements for reducing tension in the region.[153]

In the case of Vietnam, the US again justified its ever-increasing military involvement as an exercise of collective self-defence. In a legal memorandum of 1966, it claimed that South Vietnam had been the victim of an 'armed attack', taking the forms of 'externally supported subversion, clandestine supply of arms, infiltration of armed personnel, and most recently the sending of regular units of the North Vietnamese army into the South'.[154] According to the US, by the end of 1964, North Vietnam might well have moved over 40,000 armed and unarmed guerrillas into South Vietnam. Such 'infiltration of thousands of armed men clearly constitute[d] an "armed attack" under any reasonable definition'. In a letter to the Security Council, it alleged that Viet Cong attacks were 'directed, staffed and supplied in crucial respects' by the North.[155] States did not deny that the actions of irregular troops could be attributed to a State, but doubted whether in fact there was an invasion of one State by armed bands from another, rather than an internal uprising throughout Vietnam.[156] The reports of the International Control Commission

---

[149] E.g., UN Doc. S/PV.827, §§ 99–103, 114–15 (USSR); UN Doc. S/PV.830, § 2 (UAR).
[150] E.g., UN Doc. S/PV.827, § 116 (USSR); UN Doc. S/PV.828, § 33 (UAR); UN Doc. S/PV.830, § 4 (UAR).
[151] E.g., Corten, *Le droit contre la guerre*, p. 686; A. Constantinou, *The right of self-defence under customary international law and Article 51 of the UN Charter* (Brussels: Bruylant, 2000), p. 108.
[152] See, e.g.: UN Doc. S/PV.831, § 29 (UK); UN Doc. S/PV.832, § 29 (Iraq).
[153] SC Res. 129 (1958) of 7 August 1958; GA Res. 1237 (ES-III) of 21 August 1958.
[154] US Department of State, 'The legality of United States participation in the defense of Viet-Nam', 4 March 1966, reprinted in (1966) 60 AJIL 564–85, at 565–6.
[155] E.g., UN Doc. S/6174, 7 February 1965 (US), § 7.
[156] Gray, *The use of force*, p. 174. See also: Q. Wright, 'Legal aspects of the Viet-Nam situation', (1960) 66 AJIL 750–69, at 756–67; R. A. Falk, 'International law and the United States role in the Viet Nam War', (1966) 75 Yale LJ 1122–60; J. N. Moore, 'International law and the United States role in Viet Nam: a reply', (1967) 76 Yale LJ 1051–94; R. A. Falk, 'International law and the United States role in Viet Nam: a reply to

indicated a gradual increase in violations of the 1954 Geneva ceasefire accord by both sides after 1958, but apparently did not permit a clear judgment on which side began 'armed attacks'.[157]

5.1.3.b Interventions in neighbouring countries by Israel, Portugal, South Africa and Southern Rhodesia

Regardless of the particularities of the different situations, the aforementioned cases all signal an acceptance that self-defence is not strictly contingent upon attacks being carried out by *regular* forces of another State, but may also apply to certain attacks by irregulars. At the same time, the States concerned consistently relied on a very close link between the armed bands and the other State, exceeding the mere supply of arms, money and logistical support.[158] In addition to the latter elements, it was claimed – rightly or not – that the other State was somehow responsible for the attacks by these armed groups because it recruited, sent, directed and/or controlled these elements. More generally, the armed bands were by and large regarded as an 'instrument' in the hands of the other State.

From the late 1960s onwards, however, there have been many occasions where States relied on self-defence to justify forcible responses against States with a far less intense relationship with armed bands allegedly carrying out cross-border attacks.[159] The overwhelming majority[160] of these interventions were conducted by Israel, South

---

Professor Moore', (1967) 76 Yale LJ 1095–158; (1965) UNYB 186–8; (1966) UNYB 146–60. Remark: the US position was expressly approved in 1966 by the Council of the South-East Asian Treaty Organization, with the French Representative abstaining and the Pakistan representative reserving (*NY Times*, 30 June 1966).

[157] See: Wright, 'Legal aspects of the Viet-Nam situation', 767.

[158] See also: Constantinou, *The right of self-defence*, pp. 106–8 ('The fact that the U.S. based its arguments on infiltration [from North Vietnam] rather than on material support, is sufficient to show that material assistance was not regarded as the activity which constituted an armed attack. . . .'); Lamberti Zanardi, 'Indirect military aggression', p. 114 (observing that the US 'only considered that there had been an armed attack when North Vietnam had sent thousands of armed infiltrators, followed by regular troops'); Gray, *The use of force*, pp. 175–7.

[159] See *Ibid.*, pp. 136–40; Corten, *Le droit contre la guerre*, pp. 688–9; A. Cassese, 'Article 51', in J.-P. Cot and A. Pellet, *La Charte des Nations Unies*, 2nd edn. (Paris: Economica, 1991), pp. 771–95, at 780–2; T. Ruys and S. Verhoeven, 'Attacks by private actors and the right of self-defence', (2005) 10 JCSL 289–320, at 292–4.

[160] One exception relates to the French military operations against Tunisia in 1958. *In casu*, France accused Tunisia of 'aiding and abetting' rebels carrying out cross-border raids into Algeria. See: (1958) UNYB 77–9. See in particular: UN Doc. S/3954, 14 February 1958 (France); UN Doc. S/PV.819, 2 June 1958, §§ 70 *et seq.* (France). Following negotiations, the two countries agreed that French troops stationed in Tunisia would leave the country.

Africa, Southern Rhodesia and Portugal, and were aimed against national liberation movements operating from abroad.[161] As a common point of departure, it was argued that neighbouring States deliberately allowed 'hostile elements' or 'terrorists' to use their territory as a base of operations. Thus, Portugal accused Zambia, Guinea and Senegal of giving sanctuary to hostile elements carrying out cross-border raids.[162] After the Six Day War, Israel made similar accusations vis-à-vis 'terrorist bases' located on Lebanese[163] and, exceptionally, on Jordanian[164] and Tunisian[165] territory. Analogous justifications were used in relation to interventions by South Africa and Southern Rhodesia into Zambia, Botswana, Lesotho, Angola and Mozambique.[166]

It is true that on occasion, the intervening States added allegations of different forms of support for or even participation in the attacks on the part of the States concerned. In 1968, for example, Israel argued that there was 'full operational coordination between the Jordanian Army and the raider commandos' and that the latter received instructions from Jordan *inter alia* to determine the best timing and route for crossing the

---

[161] See: (1) Interventions by Portugal: (1963) UNYB 24–6; (1964) UNYB 120–1; (1965) UNYB 134–7; (1966) UNYB 121–2; (1967) UNYB 131–2; (1968) UNYB 159–60; (1969) UNYB 135–45; (2) Interventions by Israel: (1968) UNYB 191–215, 228–32; (1970) UNYB 223–4, 227–40; (1971) UNYB 177–8; (1972) UNYB 157–71; (1973) UNYB 178–82; (1978) UNYB 295 *et seq.*; (1979) UNYB 325 *et seq.*; (1980) UNYB 348 *et seq.*; (1982) UNYB 428 *et seq.*; (1985) UNYB 285–93; (1988) UNYB 217–20; (3) interventions by South Africa and Southern Rhodesia: (1976) UNYB 163–7, 171; (1977) UNYB 206, 216–21; (1979) UNYB at 218 *et seq.*; (1980) UNYB 252–6, 263–6; (1981) UNYB 214–22; (1982) UNYB 310–18; (1983) UNYB 169–80; (1984) UNYB 177–84; (1985) UNYB 178–96; (1986) UNYB 155–67; (1987) UNYB 163–76; (1988) UNYB 158–61.

[162] E.g., (1965) UNYB 134; (1966) UNYB 122; (1967) UNYB 123; (1969) UNYB 136, 138, 141.

[163] E.g., (1968) UNYB 228–9; (1970) UNYB 223, 227–8 (arguing that Lebanon had concluded an agreement with the terrorist organizations, by which they were permitted to operate in and from Lebanese territory), 229, 239–40; (1971) UNYB 177–8; (1972) UNYB 157–9 (stating that Lebanon had long permitted terrorist organizations not only to set up their headquarters in Beirut but also to establish bases and encampments in or near Lebanese villages from which to carry out attacks against Israel), 161, 170; (1973) UNYB 178–9; (1978) UNYB 297.

[164] E.g., (1968) UNYB 191–3, 200, 205, 211.   [165] (1985) UNYB 288, 290.

[166] E.g., (1976) UNYB 164, 171; (1977) UNYB 217; (1979) UNYB 221, 225; (1980) UNYB 263, 264; (1981) UNYB 218–22; (1982) UNYB 312, 315; (1983) UNYB 175, 178; (1984) UNYB 181, 183; (1985) UNYB 189, 193–4; (1986) UNYB 166; (1987) UNYB 174; (1988) UNYB 161. See also: F.M. Higginbotham, 'International law, the use of force in self-defence, and the southern African conflict', (1986–7) 25 Columbia JTL 529–92, at 561 *et seq.*; E. Kwakwa, 'South Africa's May 1986 military incursions into neighbouring African States', (1987) 12 YJIL 421–43.

ceasefire line.[167] At times, Israel also suggested that Lebanon cooperated with terrorist organizations 'in the installation of supplies, and rest and aid posts',[168] or that it 'officially encouraged' terrorist attacks.[169] South Africa drew attention to the fact that the 'terrorists' of the South West Africa People's Organization (SWAPO) were 'actively supported' by Zambian armed forces,[170] and were provided with 'facilities and arms' by Angola.[171] Portugal in turn claimed that Senegalese troops had sometimes participated in attacks by anti-Portuguese elements[172] – an allegation vigorously denied by Senegal.[173] Yet, even absent indications (or at least allegations) of active State support or participation, the intervening States insisted that by *deliberately allowing* armed groups to use their territory as a springboard for cross-border attacks, neighbouring States exposed themselves to a forcible response in self-defence.[174]

Throughout the 1970s, Israel gradually adopted a broader version of the 'harbouring' rationale, and began to argue that even if Lebanon did not 'actively support' the Palestinian terrorists operating on its soil, and did not 'willingly' provide them with a safe haven, Israel could nonetheless exercise its right of self-defence when Lebanon was either unwilling *or unable* to prevent cross-border attacks from taking place.[175] Israel asserted that it did not wish to impair Lebanon's sovereignty or territorial integrity; rather it saw Lebanon's inability to control its territory as the root of the problem.[176] At the same time, it left no doubt that as long as

---

[167] (1968) UNYB 211.　[168] (1970) UNYB 239.
[169] (1968) UNYB 229; (1971) UNYB 177.　[170] (1979) UNYB 221.
[171] (1984) UNYB 181. Also: (1985) UNYB 181.　[172] (1969) UNYB 138.
[173] *Ibid.*, 139. See also: (1964) UNYB 121; (1965) UNYB 134.
[174] Remark: as mentioned earlier, South Africa sometimes relied on a more general right of 'hot pursuit' vis-à-vis armed bands fleeing across the border. However, this doctrine was widely condemned by the international community, after which South Africa abandoned it and reverted to the 'harbouring' rationale. See, e.g., (1985) UNYB 186; SC Res. 568 (1985) of 21 June 1985.
[175] See, e.g., (1970) UNYB 239; (1972) UNYB 158 ('as long as Lebanon was unwilling or unable to prevent armed attacks from its territory against Israel, it could not complain against actions taken in self-defence'); (1979) UNYB 332; (1982) UNYB 434. But see e.g., (1972) UNYB 159 (France, arguing that Lebanon was undoubtedly doing all it could to control the activities of the *fedayeen* in its territory, and could not be held responsible for what happened in Israeli territory); (1973) UNYB 180 (France, stating that it would be asking the impossible to expect Lebanon to be able to control the legitimate aspirations of some 300,000 refugees living on its territory).
[176] E.g., (1978) UNYB 297 ('[T]he aim of the Israeli operation was not retaliation ... but to clear PLO from the area of southern Lebanon ... and to create conditions in which the Government of Lebanon could restore control and re-establish its sovereign right in the area'); (1980) UNYB 349; (1982) UNYB 430; (1982) UNYB 437; (1988) UNYB 218–19.

Lebanon failed to abide by its international obligations to put an end to cross-border terrorist attacks, Israel would take action in self-defence.[177]

How were these claims received by the international community? At the outset, the incontrovertible fact is that the vast majority of interventions were denounced by the Security Council,[178] albeit for a variety of reasons. Many were regarded as reprisals that were punitive and/or disproportionate in nature.[179] Even if the intervening States generally insisted that their operations were directed solely against terrorist bases or 'hostile elements' abroad,[180] many were criticized for resulting in large numbers of civilian casualties.[181] A subsidiary motivation for denouncing certain interventions was that the State allegedly harbouring hostile

---

[177] E.g., (1972) UNYB 162. In relation to the Israeli raid against the PLO headquarters in Tunisia in 1985, Israel argued that the Friendly Relations Declaration and the Definition of Aggression 'clearly spelt out that an act of aggression occurred when a country failed to fulfil its duty to refrain from organizing or encouraging the organization of irregular forces or armed bands for incursion into the territory of another State; they also required that States must not acquiesce in organized activities within its territory directed towards the commission of terrorist acts.' Also: (1985) UNYB 290.

[178] E.g., (1) resolutions condemning Portugal: SC Res. 178 (1963) of 24 April 1963; SC Res. 204 (1965) of 19 May 1965; SC Res. 268 (1969) of 28 July 1969; SC Res. 273 (1969) of 9 December 1969; SC Res. 275 (1969) of 22 December 1969; (2) resolutions condemning Israel: SC Res. 248 (1968) of 23 March 1968; SC Res. 256 (1968) of 16 August 1968; SC Res. 262 (1968) of 31 December 1968; SC Res. 280 (1970) of 12 May 1970; SC Res. 316 (1972) of 26 June 1972; SC Res. 332 (1973) of 19 April 1973; SC Res. 450 (1979) of 14 June 1979; SC Res. 467 (1980) of 24 April 1980; SC Res. 573 (1985) of 4 October 1985; (3) resolutions condemning South Africa or Southern Rhodesia: SC Res. 393 (1976) of 30 July 1976; SC Res. 403 (1977) of 14 January 1977; SC Res. 455 (1979) of 23 November 1979; SC Res. 447 (1979) of 28 March 1979; SC Res. 454 (1979) of 2 November 1979; SC Res. 475 (1980) of 27 June 1980; SC Res. 466 (1980) of 11 April 1980; SC Res. 527 (1982) of 15 December 1982; SC Res. 545 (1983) of 20 December 1983; SC Res. 546 (1984) of 6 January 1984 (quite unusually, the resolution also 'reaffirms' Angola's right of self-defence); SC Res. 567 (1985) of 20 June 1985; SC Res. 571 (1985) of 20 September; SC. Res. 574 (1985) of 7 October 1985 (again reaffirming Angola's right of self-defence); SC Res. 577 (1985) of 6 December; SC Res. 568 (1985) of 21 June 1985; SC Res. 580 (1985) of 30 December 1985; SC Res. 581 (1986) of 13 February 1986; SC Res. 602 (1987) of 25 November 1987; SC Res. 606 (1987) of 22 December 1987. Numerous interventions were also condemned by the UNGA. Some examples are: GA Res. 36/172 of 17 December 1981; GA Res. 37/101 of 14 December 1982.

[179] E.g., (1965) UNYB 135; (1968) UNYB 193-8, 208-9, 229-31; (1970) UNYB 231-3 (inter alia statements of Finland, Zambia, Burundi, Nepal), 236 (statement by the US); (1972) UNYB 158-9 (USSR, Italy, Belgium), 163; (1978) UNYB 298-9; (1982) UNYB 434-6; (1985) UNYB 186, 288-9.

[180] E.g., (1968) UNYB 204-5; (1970) UNYB 229; (1973) UNYB 179; (1979) UNYB 329; (1985) UNYB 288; (1980) UNYB 253, 264; (1981) UNYB 218-19, 222.

[181] (1971) UNYB 178; (1978) UNYB 298; (1979) UNYB 219-20 (US), 225; (1982), UNYB 311-12, 315.

elements was not found complicit in the cross-border raids, but was to the contrary considered to have played a moderating role or to have behaved in a peaceful manner.[182] Furthermore, *inter alia* in relation to South African interventions in Lesotho, several States questioned whether any cross-border raids had actually taken place at all.[183]

Apart from this, a crucial factor that affected the international community's response concerns the fact that the intervening countries were regarded as being in illegal occupation of the territory which they were purporting to defend.[184] In this context, it must be recalled that numerous socialist and developing countries believed that people under colonial or alien domination were entitled to use force in their struggle for self-determination, and that support – including, according to some, armed support – from other States did not constitute 'indirect aggression' giving rise to self-defence. Consequently, many objected that Portugal, South Africa and Israel could not invoke Article 51 UN Charter to perpetuate colonialism or to consolidate the illegal occupation of territory.[185] As in the General Assembly,[186] Western States generally adopted a guarded approach, merely affirming in general terms the right of self-determination. Still, it is clear that international reactions were strongly influenced by the underlying issues of colonialism, occupation and self-determination.[187] This is most evident from a number of Security Council resolutions which not only condemned the acts of

---

[182] E.g., (1968) UNYB 230; (1970) UNYB 234; (1972) UNYB 159; UN Security Council, 2611th meeting, 2 October 1985, §§ 22, 40; (1986) UNYB 166 (US, stressing that South Africa's neighbours had made efforts to limit cross-border violence directed at South Africa).

[183] E.g., UN Doc. S/PV.2407, 15 December 1982, § 89 (Ireland); UN Doc. S/PV.2408, 16 December 1982, § 77 (Sierra Leone).

[184] See, e.g. Gray, *The use of force*, p. 138.

[185] E.g., (1968) UNYB 194–202; (1969) UNYB 136–7, 139 (e.g., the UAR representative 'pointed out that the attacks alleged by Portugal could not be considered attacks on Portuguese Guinea: they were attacks on the forces of colonialism and the occupiers of Guinea (Bissau)'), 142 ('It was stated that the right of self-defence could not be invoked to perpetuate colonialism and to flout the right of self-determination and independence'); (1970) UNYB 230–1, 235; (1972) UNYB 158; (1973) UNYB 179–81 (PRC); (1976) UNYB 165; (1977) UNYB 220; (1978) UNYB 298–301; (1979) UNYB 219–20, 227–32, 331–2; (1980) UNYB 255, 264–5; (1981) UNYB 219–21 (e.g., France (at 220)); (1982) UNYB 311–12, 315–16, 438; (1983) UNYB 175–6; (1984) UNYB 181–12; (1985) UNYB 182–4, 191–3, 285–6; (1987) UNYB 169–70.

[186] See *supra*, Section 4.1.2.b.

[187] Cf. (1972) UNYB 163 (France: 'It was of course up to the Lebanese government to control the activities of the *fedayeen* on its territory as best as it could, but the situation was the direct result of Israel's occupation of territories conquered by force').

aggression by the 'illegal regime' of Southern Rhodesia and the 'racist regime' of South Africa, but also 'commended' neighbouring States for their continued support to peoples under colonial domination 'in their just and legitimate struggle for the attainment of freedom and independence and for their scrupulous restraint in the face of unwarranted armed provocations.'[188] In light of these factors – viz. the diversity of legal arguments for rejecting the self-defence claims, as well as the inextricable link between legal and political objections – it is extremely difficult to detract from these incidents any conclusive or generalizable findings as to the *'ratione personae'* aspect of self-defence.[189]

On the whole, there were virtually no statements directly dealing with the applicability of Article 51 to cross-border attacks by non-State actors. This finding cuts both ways. On the one hand, apart from a handful of statements stressing that 'acts of terrorism could not be used as an excuse for launching armed attacks on a third country',[190] there is very little *opinio iuris* explicitly dismissing self-defence in response to armed bands per se. On the other hand, apart from a single exception,[191] there was no genuine support for the self-defence argument either. Indeed, even if a number of (mainly Western) States sometimes abstained or voted against resolutions condemning an intervention, this voting behaviour did not signal an acceptance of the self-defence claims involved. States at times considered that the Council did not have objective and sufficiently

---

[188] E.g., SC Res. 455 (1979) of 23 November 1979; SC Res. 447 (1979) of 28 March 1979. Also, e.g., SC Res. 577 (1985) of 6 December 1985. Remark: the General Assembly repeatedly '[called] upon all States ... to provide moral and material support' to independent African States subject to acts of aggression by South Africa (e.g., GA Res. 36/172 of 17 December 1981). In another resolution, the General Assembly even called upon States to provide 'military assistance': GA Res. 37/233 of 20 December 1982. See also: SC Res. 546 (1984) of 6 January 1984). And in the face of South African allegations that its neighbours were 'harbouring' terrorists, the General Assembly and the Security Council recognized these States' right to give sanctuary to South African refugees or to victims of the apartheid regime. E.g., GA Res. 37/101 of 14 December 1982; SC Res. 527 (1982) of 15 December 1982; SC Res. 580 (1985) of 30 December 1985; SC Res. 568 (1985) of 21 June 1985; SC Res. 572 (1985) of 30 September 1985; SC Res. 581 (1986) of 13 February 1986 ('reaffirms the right of all States ... to give sanctuary to the victims of apartheid)'. South Africa objected that the neighbouring States were not giving sanctuary to genuine refugees but rather to 'terrorists'.

[189] Cf. Cahier, 'Changements et continuité', 75 (rejecting the relevance of this practice altogether).

[190] E.g., UN Doc. S/PV.2613, 3 October 1985, § 115 (Greece).

[191] One notable exception concerns the US position in relation to the Israeli attack on the PLO headquarters in Tunisia in 1985. UN Doc. S/PV.2615, 4 October 1985, § 252. See *infra* Section 5.2.1.b.

complete information on the conflicting allegations to proceed to a condemnation.[192] In relation to Israeli interventions, Council Members occasionally objected that a proposed resolution was imbalanced insofar as it did not simultaneously condemn attacks against Israeli civilians.[193] The United States in particular stressed that it could not but oppose all acts of violence from either side and even vetoed a number of resolutions for this reason.[194]

5.1.3.c   Other cases

Finally, questions involving the use of force against attacks by irregulars or armed bands have arisen in two other contexts.[195] First of all, as discussed above, a number of States have repeatedly claimed a right to intervene abroad for the purpose of the 'protection of nationals'.[196] Insofar as this right has generally been framed as a special form of self-defence, it is a rather atypical application of Article 51, both from a *ratione temporis* dimension – in that it is sufficient that nationals abroad are threatened – and from a *ratione personae* dimension – in that the threats/attacks will often emanate from armed bands (e.g., the rebel forces in the Congo in 1964) or terrorists (e.g., the hijackers at Entebbe airport in 1976). Because of the exceptional nature of this doctrine, however, it appears inappropriate to regard the relevant cases as general evidence of a broad right of self-defence vis-à-vis attacks by non-State actors. Furthermore, as explained above, the permissibility of unilateral 'protection of nationals' remains contested *de lege lata*.

Finally, the Security Council has exceptionally used the term 'armed attack' or 'armed aggression' in resolutions condemning mercenary attacks aimed at the overthrow of the regime in Congo (1967),[197] Benin (1977)[198] and the Seychelles (1981).[199] In each case, there were allegations that the mercenaries had received varying degrees of support

---

[192] E.g., (1969) UNYB 137, 140, 143; (1986) UNYB 164.
[193] See, e.g., (1970) UNYB 232, 236; (1972) UNYB 163; (1973) UNYB 180; (1979) UNYB 333, 335; (1980) UNYB 353. Also, in relation to interventions by South Africa and Southern Rhodesia: (1979) UNYB 220, 228, 232 (UK).
[194] See, e.g., (1982) UNYB 436; (1988) UNYB 218, 220. Also, in relation to South Africa: (1981) UNYB 218.
[195] For other examples, see Constantinou, *The right of self-defence*, pp. 94 *et seq.*
[196] See Section 3.4.4.
[197] SC Res. 241 (1967) of 15 November 1967. See also SC Res. 239 (1967) of 10 July 1967.
[198] SC Res. 405 (1977) of 14 April 1977; SC Res. 419 (1977) of 24 November 1977.
[199] SC Res. 496 (1981) of 15 December 1981; SC Res. 507 (1982) of 28 May 1982 ('commending the Seychelles for successfully repulsing the mercenary aggression and

from third States. Congo, for instance, *inter alia* accused Belgium and Portugal of colliding with the mercenaries.[200] Benin submitted comparable allegations vis-à-vis France and several African neighbours.[201] And in relation to the mercenary attack against the Seychelles, a UN Commission of Inquiry found corroborating evidence of involvement on the part of South Africa.[202] The Security Council repeatedly condemned the permitting or tolerating of the recruitment of mercenaries and the provision of facilities to them, and called upon States to ensure that their territory not be used for the recruiting, training or transit of mercenaries.[203] Portugal and South Africa were reprimanded *ad nominatim*.[204] In any event, each attack was rebuffed by military action by the victim State within its own territory. There was never any hint of a cross-border military response, nor was there any reference to Article 51 UN Charter in the complaints of the victim States or in the Council debates.[205] Accordingly, the incidents concerned arguably do not teach us anything about the permissibility of self-defence against indirect aggression.[206]

5.1.4 Indirect aggression in the wake of the ICJ's Nicaragua *case*

5.1.4.a The *Nicaragua* judgment (1986)

The International Court of Justice was first confronted with questions pertaining to indirect aggression in the *Nicaragua* case. *In casu*, the US had, directly and indirectly, resorted to the use of force against

---

defending its territorial integrity and independence'). See also Corten, *Le droit contre la guerre*, pp. 239–42.

[200] See (1967) UNYB 123–30.
[201] See (1977) UNYB 207–14. See also: Report of the Special Mission to the People's Republic of Benin, New York, 1977, UN Doc. S/12294/Rev.1, § 145.
[202] Supplementary Report of the Security Council Mission of Inquiry established under Resolution 496 (1981), New York, 17 November 1982, UN Doc. S/15492/Rev.1, § 78. See also (1982) UNYB 321–7.
[203] SC Res. 239 (1967) of 10 July 1967; SC Res. 241 (1967) of 15 November 1967; SC Res. 405 (1977) of 14 April 1977; SC Res. 419 (1977) of 24 November 1977; SC Res. 496 (1981) of 15 December 1987; SC Res. 507 (1982) of 28 May 1982.
[204] SC Res. 241 (1967) of 15 November 1967; SC Res. 507 (1982) of 28 May 1982.
[205] E.g., UN Doc. S/8031, 5 July 1967 (DRC); UN Doc. S/8218, 3 November 1967 (DRC); UN Doc. S/12278, 26 January 1977 (Benin); UN Doc. S/14769, 26 November 1981 (Seychelles).
[206] Contra: Y. Dinstein, *War, aggression and self*-defence, 3rd edn (Cambridge University Press, 2001), p. 214 (regarding the reference to 'armed attack' in SC Res. 241 (1967) as evidence that armed attacks by non-State actors can be armed attacks regardless of State involvement).

Nicaragua[207] and needed to justify its actions by reference to the (customary) right of (collective) self-defence. To this end, it was necessary to verify whether Nicaragua had committed an 'armed attack' against El Salvador, Honduras and/or Costa Rica.

On the one hand, the Court found that certain trans-border military incursions into the territory of Honduras and Costa Rica were imputable to Nicaragua.[208] Yet, due to a lack of information regarding the precise circumstances, the Court eventually left open the question whether they could be treated 'as amounting, singly or collectively, to an "armed attack"'.[209] The Court next examined the support by Nicaragua to the armed opposition in El Salvador. In its Declaration of Intervention of 15 August 1984, El Salvador had asserted that 'terrorists' seeking to overthrow the Government were '*directed, armed, supplied and trained* by Nicaragua'.[210] Nicaragua denied each and every allegation and objected that they were not supported by any proof of evidence.[211] On the basis of a series of concordant indications,[212] the Court was satisfied that between July 1979 and early 1981, Nicaragua had provided support for the armed opposition in El Salvador: an intermittent flow of arms was routed via its territory to the latter movement.[213] There was, however, insufficient evidence to demonstrate that assistance had continued on any significant scale after this period.[214]

The question next arose to what extent this support qualified as an 'armed attack'. Interestingly, the Court used Article 3(g) of the Definition of Aggression, which was taken to reflect customary international law, as the relevant legal threshold.[215] Hence, an 'armed attack' should be understood as including 'not merely action by regular armed forces across an international border, but also "the sending by or on behalf of a State of armed bands, groups, irregulars or mercenaries, which carry out acts of armed force against another State of such gravity as to amount to" an actual armed attack conducted by regular forces, "or its substantial involvement therein"'.[216] In accordance with the Definition of Aggression, the Court stressed the need for a certain gravity of the 'acts of armed force' of the armed bands:

> The Court sees no reason to deny that, in customary law, the prohibition of armed attacks may apply to the sending by a State of armed bands to

---

[207] For the factual overview, see: ICJ, *Nicaragua* case (Merits), §§ 75 *et seq.*
[208] Ibid., § 164. [209] Ibid., § 231. [210] Ibid., § 132 (emphasis added). [211] Ibid., § 133.
[212] See: ibid., §§ 150, 152. [213] Ibid., §§ 152, 160. [214] Ibid., § 160. [215] Ibid., § 195.
[216] Ibid.

the territory of another State, if such an operation, *because of its scale and effects, would have been classified as an armed attack rather than as a mere frontier incident* had it been carried out by regular armed forces.[217]

At the same time, the Court adopted a restrictive interpretation of the notion of 'substantive involvement':

> But the Court does not believe that the concept of 'armed attack' includes not only acts by armed bands where such acts occur on a significant scale but also assistance to rebels in the form of the provision of weapons or logistical or other support.

Assistance of the latter type could be regarded as a threat or use of force, or amount to intervention in the internal affairs of other States, but did not warrant an exercise of self-defence.[218] Hence, even assuming the participation of the Nicaraguan Government, the intermittent flow of arms via its territory to the armed opposition in El Salvador did not constitute an 'armed attack'.

On the basis of the *Nicaragua* judgment, the required nexus between the State apparatus and the armed bands carrying out cross-border attacks can be established in two different ways. First, when the attack(s) can be imputed to the State, the victim can act in self-defence as long as it complies with the remaining conditions. This principle is as such uncontroversial. The concept of the 'sending by or on behalf of a State' of armed bands is generally considered to convey this idea of imputability/attributatibility.[219] Accordingly, it is appropriate to clarify the precise meaning of this notion as well as other imputability mechanisms by means of the secondary rules on State responsibility, as developed/codified by the ICJ and the ILC. Second, the concept of 'substantial involvement' suggests that – even absent State imputability – certain forms of 'indirect use of force' can be equated to 'armed attacks' in the sense of Article 51. The Court's narrow interpretation of this concept has, however, been heavily criticized by legal scholars.

5.1.4.b Option 1: imputability or attributability of attacks by non-State actors

In general, international law is very restrictive in attributing private conduct to a State. As a rule, only the acts of State organs and other

---

[217] *Ibid.* (emphasis added)   [218] *Ibid.*
[219] Also: Corten, *Le droit contre la guerre*, p. 672; Lamberti Zanardi, 'Indirect military aggression', p. 112; A. Cassese, 'The international community's "legal" response to terrorism', (1989) 38 ICLQ 589–608, at 598–9.

persons empowered by national law to exercise elements of governmental authority are imputable to a State.[220] By contrast, actions of private actors are normally not regarded as acts of a State under international law. The case law of the ICJ and the ILC Draft Articles on State Responsibility[221] nonetheless make clear that a number of exceptions exist.

First, according to the ICJ, persons, groups of persons or entities may, for purposes of international responsibility, be equated with State organs even if that status does not follow from internal law, 'provided that in fact the persons, groups or entities act in "complete dependence" on the State, of which they are ultimately merely the instrument'.[222] The relevant dicta cover a highly exceptional situation, where because of the 'particularly great degree of State control over them', the individuals concerned are regarded as de facto organs of the State.[223] In *Nicaragua*, the Court eventually found that there was no clear evidence of the US having actually exercised *such a degree of control in all fields* as to justify the Contras as acting on its behalf.[224] And in *Prevention of genocide*, it rejected the idea that the Bosnian Serb Army was 'completely dependent' on the Federal Republic of Yugoslavia, since 'the latter had some qualified, but real, margin of independence'.[225]

---

[220] According to Article 4 DASR: 'The conduct of any State organ shall be considered an act of that State under international law, whether the organ exercises legislative, executive, judicial or any other functions ...'. A State organ includes 'any person or entity which has that status in accordance with the internal law of the State' (Article 4(2) DASR). Article 5 adds a second category, constituted of persons or entities which are not organs of the State but which are nevertheless 'empowered by the law of that State to exercise elements of the governmental authority.' Article 6 refers to organs placed at the disposal of a State by another State and acting in the exercise of elements of the governmental authority of the former State. Finally, Article 7 makes clear that the conduct of State organs or persons empowered to exercise elements of governmental authority will be considered acts of the State, even if the aforementioned persons or entities act *ultra vires*. See ILC, 'Commentary on the Draft Articles', 45–7.

[221] Remark: in GA Res. 56/83 of 12 December 2001 and GA Res. 59/35 of 2 December 2004, the UN General Assembly has 'taken note of' and 'commended' the Draft Articles. At least some provisions have been recognized by the ICJ to reflect customary international law. See: ICJ, *Application of the Convention on the Prevention and Punishment of the Crime of Genocide (Bosnia and Herzegovina v. Serbia and Montenegro)*, Judgment of 26 February 2007, reprinted in (2007) 46 ILM 188–310, § 414.

[222] ICJ, *Nicaragua* case (Merits), § 109; ICJ, *Prevention of Genocide* case, § 392.

[223] See: M. Milanović, 'State responsibility for genocide', (2006) 17 EJIL 553–604, at 576–7, 582.

[224] ICJ, *Nicaragua* case (Merits), § 109.   [225] ICJ, *Prevention of Genocide* case, § 394.

Second, if 'complete dependency' cannot be established, acts of private individuals can still be imputed to the State along the lines of Article 8 DASR. The latter provision constitutes a rule of customary international law[226] and states that:

> The conduct of a person or group of persons shall be considered an act of a State under international law if the person or group of persons is in fact acting on the instructions of, or under the direction of control of, that State in carrying out the conduct.[227]

According to the ILC Commentary, the three terms 'instruction', 'direction' and 'control' are disjunctive; it is sufficient to establish any one of them.[228] The first situation is fairly straightforward and covers situations where the State gives the individual(s) *specific instructions* to commit internationally wrongful conduct.[229] More complex issues arise in determining whether conduct was carried out 'under the direction or control' of a State. In the *Nicaragua* case, the Court held that the litmus test was whether the State had 'effective control' over the operations in the course of which the wrongful conduct was committed.[230] It is clear from the application of this standard that it is a fairly restrictive one. Thus, the ICJ argued that 'United States participation, even if preponderant or decisive, in the financing, organizing, training, supplying and equipping of the contras, the selection of its military or paramilitary targets, and the planning of the whole of its operation, [was] still insufficient in itself, on the basis of the evidence in the possession of the Court, for the purpose of attributing to the [US] the acts committed by the *contras* in the course of their ... operations against Nicaragua'.[231] For this to be the case, there had to be evidence that the US 'directed or enforced the perpetration of the acts', *quod non*.[232] Accordingly, the US was not responsible for the actions of the Contras, but only for its own conduct vis-à-vis Nicaragua, including conduct related to the acts of the Contras.[233]

In the *Tadić* case, the Appeals Chamber of the International Criminal Tribunal for the Former Yugoslavia (ICTY) questioned the validity of

---

[226] *Ibid.*, § 398.   [227] ILC, 'Commentary on the Draft Articles', 47.   [228] *Ibid.*, 48.
[229] According to the ILC Commentary, if a State gives lawful instructions to persons who are not its organs, it does not normally assume the risk that the instructions will be carried out in an internationally unlawful way. *Ibid.*, 48.
[230] ICJ, *Nicaragua* case (Merits), §§ 93–116.   [231] *Ibid.*, § 115.   [232] *Ibid.*
[233] *Ibid.*, § 116.

the 'effective control' threshold.[234] According to the ICTY, the reasoning of the *Nicaragua* case went against the very logic of State responsibility by allowing States to escape such responsibility by having private individuals carry out certain tasks.[235] Furthermore, the Appeals Chamber claimed that the 'effective control' test was at variance with judicial and State practice on the matter.[236] Instead, practice supported a distinction between two scenarios, namely that of private individuals engaged by a State to perform specific illegal acts in the territory of another State; and that of individuals making up an organized and hierarchically structured group, such as a military unit or, in case of war or civil strife, armed bands of irregulars or rebels.[237] As for the former category, the ICTY required that the individuals be acting on the 'specific instructions' of the State for their conduct to be imputable. As for the latter category, however, the ICTY replaced the 'effective control' test by a more flexible 'overall control' test. Such control was considered to come about when a State 'has a role in organizing, coordinating or planning the military actions of the military group, in addition to financing, training and equipping or providing operational support to that group'.[238] By contrast, it was not necessary that specific acts should have been instructed.[239]

The *Tadić* case raises a number of difficult questions. One might wonder, for instance, where activities of State-sponsored terrorist cells would fit into the framework. It also appears that the Appeals Chamber's interpretation of *Nicaragua* is at variance with the way in which the ICJ has (re-)interpreted the sometimes vague dicta in the more recent

---

[234] ICTY Appeals Chamber, *Prosecutor v. Dusko Tadić*, Case No. IT-94-1-A, Judgment of 15 July 1999, §§ 68 *et seq*. The question before the Court was whether the conflict under consideration was an international armed conflict in the sense of the Geneva Conventions. Observing that IHL lacked criteria in this respect, the Appeals Chamber found that the phrase 'belonging to a Party to the conflict' in Article 4 of the Third Geneva Convention had to be construed in accordance with the general rules on State responsibility.

[235] *Ibid.*, §§ 116 *et seq*. Remark: the ICJ did condemn the US for *encouraging the commission* of acts contrary to general principles of IHL (ICJ, *Nicaragua* case (Merits), Dispositif, § 9).

[236] ICTY Appeals Chamber, *Tadić* case, §§ 124 *et seq*.   [237] *Ibid.*, §§ 118–20.

[238] *Ibid.*, § 137, 145.

[239] *Ibid.*, § 131, 137: 'it is by no means necessary that the controlling authorities should plan all the operations of the units dependent on them, choose their targets, or give specific instructions concerning the conduct of military operations and any alleged violations of international humanitarian law.'

Prevention of Genocide case.[240] The present study has no ambition to enter the fray.[241] Instead, we will confine ourselves to the observation that both the ILC and the ICJ have confirmed the 'effective control' test after *Tadić*. First, according to the ILC Commentary, conduct will be attributable to the State only if it directed or controlled *the specific operation* and the conduct complained of was an integral part of that operation.[242] By contrast, Article 8 DASR did not extend to conduct which was only incidentally or peripherally associated with an operation and which escaped from the State's direction or control.[243] Second, in *Prevention of Genocide*, the ICJ returned the favour to the ICTY by deciding that the argument in favour of the 'overall control' test as a general imputability threshold was 'unpersuasive':[244] 'The major drawback ... was that it broadened the scope of State responsibility

---

[240] Remark: In the *Tadić* case, for instance, the ICTY Appeals Chamber found that the references in *Nicaragua* to 'effective control' and 'complete dependence' are part of a single test (*ibid.*, § 112). In *Prevention of Genocide*, however, the ICJ neatly separates the two concepts (ICJ, *Prevention of Genocide* case, § 397). Furthermore, the ICTY seems to interpret the *Nicaragua* case as requiring 'specific instructions', even under the 'effective control' test – implying that the three disjunctive standards would somehow merge into one (e.g., ICTY Appeals Chamber, *Tadić* case, § 131). The ICJ itself nonetheless makes a clear distinction between 'effective control' and 'specific instructions' (ICJ, *Prevention of Genocide* case, § 400).

For a convincing criticism of the *Tadic* judgment, see Milanović, 'State responsibility for genocide', 581, 585–7.

[241] For references, see *infra*, note 244. See also: C. Kreß, 'L'organe de facto en droit international public: réflexions sur l'imputation à l'Etat de l'acte d'un particulier à la lumière des développements récents', (2001) 105 RGDIP 93–141.

[242] ILC, 'Commentary on the Draft Articles', 47–8, § 3–5. After dealing consecutively with *Nicaragua* and *Tadić*, the Commentary in § 8 sticks to the concept of 'effective control'. Also: Milanović, 'State responsibility for genocide', 583; Corten and Dubuisson, 'Opération "liberté immuable"', 65–6.

[243] ILC, *Commentary on the Draft Articles*, 47, § 3.

[244] ICJ, *Prevention of Genocide* case, §§ 403–4. Like the ILC, the Court stressed that the ICTY's jurisdiction is criminal and extends over persons only.

See especially: R. J. Goldstone and R. J. Hamilton, '*Bosnia v. Serbia*: Lessons from the encounter of the International Court of Justice with the International Criminal Tribunal for the Former Yugoslavia', (2008) 21 Leiden JIL 95–112; A. Cassese, 'The *Nicaragua* and *Tadić* tests revisited in light of the ICJ judgment on genocide in Bosnia', (2007) 18 EJIL 649–68; Milanović, 'State responsibility for genocide'. On the *Prevention of Genocide* case, see also: M. Spinedi, 'On the non-attribution of the Bosnian Serbs' conduct to Serbia', (2007) 5 JICJ 829–38; A. B. Loewenstein and S. A. Kostas, 'Divergent approaches to determining responsibility for genocide', (2007) 5 JICJ 839–57; A. Abass, 'Proving State responsibility for genocide: the ICJ in *Bosnia v. Serbia* and the International Commission of Inquiry for Darfur', (2008) 31 Fordham ILJ. 871–910; V. Dimitrijević and M. Milanović, 'The strange story of the Bosnian *Genocide* case', (2008) 21 Leiden JIL 65–94.

well beyond the fundamental principle governing the law of international responsibility: a State is responsible only for its own conduct, that is to say the conduct of persons acting, on whatever basis, on its behalf'.[245] The Court reiterated that Article 8 DASR applied to situations 'where an organ of the State gave the *instructions* or provided the *direction* pursuant to which the perpetrators of the wrongful act acted or where it exercised *effective control over the action* during which the wrong was committed'.[246] Since none of these thresholds were met in the case at hand, it concluded that the genocide in Srebrenica could not as such be attributed to the Federal Republic of Yugoslavia.[247]

It is important to stress that the ICJ believed that in the absence of a clearly expressed *lex specialis* the rules for attributing private conduct to a State did not vary with the nature of the wrongful act in question.[248] Hence, in principle, the rules also apply to the question whether an attack must be considered an attack *by a State*. Whether the notion of 'substantial involvement' must be regarded as a *lex specialis* warranting a broader interpretation of 'armed attack' for purposes of Article 51 is examined below.

Before going into the latter issue, reference must briefly be made to a third mechanism of imputability. According to Article 11 DASR, private conduct will be considered an act of the State 'if and to the extent that the State acknowledges and adopts the conduct as its own'. As the ILC Commentary explains, both requirements – acknowledgment and adoption – have to be fulfilled cumulatively and must be clear and unequivocal.[249] A general acknowledgement of a factual situation or mere support or endorsement of actions by private actors is insufficient.[250] In the *Tehran Embassy* case, the ICJ found that the attack and subsequent overrunning of the US embassy by Iranian militants was not itself imputable to Iran.[251] The fact that the authorities refused to intervene and uttered statements of official approval (including congratulations from Ayatollah Khomeini) did not alter this finding.[252] At the same time, the Court concluded that through a decree of 17 November 1979, Iran

---

[245] ICJ, *Prevention of Genocide* case, § 406. According to the Court, 'the "overall control" test ... stretches too far, almost to breaking point, the connection which must exist between the conduct of a State's organs and its international responsibility'.
[246] *Ibid.* (emphasis added).
[247] *Ibid.*, §§ 413–15. Remark: the Court did find the Federal Republic of Yugoslavia guilty of failing to prevent the genocide at Srebrenica (dispositif, § 5).
[248] *Ibid.*, § 401.   [249] ILC, 'Commentary on the Draft Articles', 53.   [250] *Ibid.*
[251] ICJ, *Tehran Embassy* case, § 57.   [252] *Ibid.*, §§ 58–9.

had acknowledged and adopted the *subsequent occupation* of the embassy premises as its own conduct.[253] The decree *inter alia* declared that the embassy and the hostages would remain as they were until the US had handed over the former Shah for trial and returned his property to Iran. In the words of the ICJ, '[t]he approval given to these facts ... and the decision to perpetuate them, translated continuing occupation of the Embassy and detention of the hostages into acts of that State'.[254]

We will later come back to a fourth possible tool of imputability, vis-à-vis conduct carried out 'in the absence or default of the official authorities' (Article 9 DASR), and examine its possible relevance for the *Ius ad Bellum*.[255] For now, however, it suffices to note that the aforementioned venues offer little prospect in dealing with indirect aggression.[256] First, considering the underlying philosophy of covert proxy warfare, it is of course highly unlikely that a State would unequivocally acknowledge and adopt an armed attack by non-State actors as its own and make itself liable to counter-attack. Second, the 'complete dependence' test is so strict that it actually requires the actors concerned to be State agents in all but name: they can have no real autonomy from the controlling State. Third, Article 8 DASR similarly leaves little leeway, since States will seldom give 'specific instructions' to armed bands to carry out attacks, nor will they normally 'direct' or exercise 'effective control' over the actual operations during which these attacks are executed. This is not to say that these standards will never be reached. In 1993, for example, most Security Council Members appeared to accept the US plea that Iraq had 'planned, equipped and launched the terrorist operation' aimed at the assassination of former President Bush Snr.[257] Yet, in most cases, indirect aggression will distinctly fall below this threshold and take the form of the provision of assistance, training, funds, logistical support and intelligence. Even under the ICTY's 'overall control' test, such forms of involvement are insufficient as long as the State does not have a role in the 'organizing, coordinating or planning' of the attacks.[258] Moreover, the ICJ's firm rebuttal of this test in the *Prevention of Genocide* case makes it uncertain whether it has any future in the realm of State responsibility.

---

[253] *Ibid.*, §§ 73–5.   [254] *Ibid.*, § 74.   [255] See *infra*, Section 5.2.3.b.
[256] See, e.g., H. Hofmeister, '"To harbour or not to harbour?": Die Auswirkungen des 11 September auf das Konzept des "bewaffneten Angriffs" nach Art 51 UN-Charta', (2007) 62 ZÖR 475–500, at 490; Stahn, 'International law at crossroads?', 221 *et seq.*
[257] See UN Doc. S/PV.3245, 27 June 1993, 3 *et seq.*
[258] ICTY Appeals Chamber, *Tadić* case, § 137, 145.

5.1.4.c Option 2: 'substantial involvement'

While the notion 'sending by or on behalf of the State' strongly conveys the idea of imputability/attributability to the State, the reference to 'substantial involvement' in the remainder of Article 3(g) Definition of Aggression should not be overlooked. Indeed, the *effet utile* principle implies that it has a different content than 'sending',[259] one that is not necessarily governed by the secondary rules on the imputability of private acts.[260]

In *Nicaragua*, the ICJ did not provide positive indications as to what types of behaviour might qualify under this notion. It is, however, generally agreed that the Court implicitly excluded the mere tolerating of an armed group's presence within the State's territory.[261] Furthermore, the Court's restrictive interpretation is evident from the exclusion of '*assistance to rebels in the form of the provision of weapons or logistical or other support*'.[262] This finding caused a deep rift between the different Hague judges and provoked a storm of scholarly criticism.

First, the Court's interpretation was strongly opposed by Judges Jennings and Schwebel. Judge Jennings agreed with the Court that the 'mere provision of arms' did not amount to an armed attack, but claimed that it could nonetheless constitute an 'important element in what might be thought to amount to an armed attack, where it is coupled with other kinds of involvement'.[263] Accordingly, he could not support the finding that the provision of arms, coupled with 'logistical or other support' fell outside the concept of 'armed attack':

> Logistical support may itself be crucial. ... [It] covers the 'art of moving, lodging, and supplying troops and equipment' ... If there is added to all this 'other support', it becomes difficult to understand what it is, short of direct attack by a State's own forces, that may not be done apparently without a lawful response in the form of ... self-defence.

---

[259] E.g., Corten, *Le droit contre la guerre*, p. 672; Sicilianos, *Les réactions décentralisées à l'illicité*, p. 322.

[260] See, e.g., J. Verhoeven, *Les réactions décentralisées à l'illicité*, pp. 57–9 (criticizing the confusion between the rules on imputability and the 'substantial involvement' threshold).

[261] E.g., Gray, *The use of force*, pp. 132–3; T. J. Farer, 'Drawing the right line', (1987) 81 AJIL 112–16, at 113. Also: Cassese, 'The international community's "legal" response to terrorism', 599.

[262] ICJ, *Nicaragua* case (Merits), § 195 (emphasis added).

[263] *Ibid.*, Dissenting opinion of Judge Jennings, 543.

In a similar vein, Judge Schwebel strongly regretted that the the Court ignored – or reduced *ad absurdum* – the notion of 'substantial involvement':[264]

> [L]et us assume ... that the Court is correct in holding that provision of weapons or logistical support of themselves may not be tantamount to armed attack (an assumption which I do not share, not least because the term 'logistical support' is so open-ended, including, as it may, the transport, quartering and provisioning of armies). It does not follow that a State's involvement in the sending of armed bands is not to be construed as tantamount to armed attack when, cumulatively, it is so substantial as to embrace not only the provision of weapons and logistical support, but also participation in the re-organization of the rebellion; provision of command-and-control facilities on its territory ...; provision of sanctuary ...; provision of training facilities ...; and permitting rebels to operate broadcasting and other communication facilities from its territory in pursuance of their subversive activities.[265]

Contrary to the Court, Schwebel found that the Nicaraguan support for Salvadorian insurgents, taking the form of 'providing arms, munitions, other supplies, training, command-and-control facilities, sanctuary and lesser forms of assistance' undeniably qualified as 'substantial involvement' in acts of force by insurgents against another State, which were, in turn, of sufficient gravity in the sense of Article 3 of the Definition of Aggression.[266] As a result, even if Nicaragua had not 'sent' the rebels, its conduct fell within the scope of Article 3(g) and triggered the right of self-defence.

The objections of the two judges were echoed in the academic writings of several scholars.[267] Moore, for instance, argued that the ICJ's finding was not only 'flatly wrong as a principle of international law', but also constituted a 'tragedy for world order' since it would simultaneously encourage secret aggressive attack through support for terrorists and

---

[264] *Ibid.*, Dissenting opinion of Judge Schwebel, §§ 154 *et seq.* (esp. § 171).
    Interestingly, Schwebel agreed with the Court that Article 3(g) was the appropriate standard to evaluate the legality of self-defence against indirect aggression: 'This resolution ... is an interpretation by the General Assembly of the meaning of the provisions of the United Nations Charter governing the use of armed force' (§ 168).
[265] *Ibid.*, § 171.   [266] *Ibid.*, § 166.
[267] E.g., J. L. Hargrove, 'The *Nicaragua* Judgment and the future of the law of force and self-defense', (1987) 81 AJIL 135–43; Higgins, *Problems and process*, p. 251; Dinstein, *War, aggression and self-defence*, 4th edn, pp. 202–4; Cahier, 'Changements et continuité', 76–7; Macdonald, 'The *Nicaragua* case', 149.

guerrillas and discourage effective defence in response.[268] Franck regretted that States supporting armed bands were made 'legally invulnerable to individual or collective response against their own territory, even if the insurgency [was] planned, trained, armed and directed from there'.[269]

Others have rendered a more positive appraisal of the Court's verdict.[270] In his separate opinion, President Singh affirmed that even if the flow of arms from Nicaragua to El Salvador would have been regular and substantial, as well as spread over a number of years, it could still not amount *as such* to an 'armed attack' against the latter country.[271] Judge Ruda defended the view that 'juridically, the concept of "armed attack" [did] not include assistance to rebels'.[272] Against the criticism that a restrictive construction of Article 3(g) would deprive States of meaningful protection against indirect aggression, some authors objected that the Court's interpretation prevented an unfettered proliferation of the number and type of situations in which force might lawfully be used.[273]

In all, the large majority of scholars accepted that some form of State involvement was needed to transform attacks by non-State actors into 'armed attacks', and most agreed that the mere provision of weapons or the harbouring of armed bands or terrorists was insufficient.[274] As for

---

[268] J. N. Moore, 'The *Nicaragua* case and the deterioration of world order', (1987) 81 AJIL 151–9, at 152, 154–5. See also: J. N. Moore, 'The secret war in Central America and the future world order', (1986) 80 AJIL 43–127.

[269] T. M. Franck, 'Some observations on the ICJ's procedural and substantive innovations', (1987) 81 AJIL 116–21, at 120. Remark: Franck warned that given the nature of proliferating proxy wars and international terrorist networks, it was inconceivable that the US would agree to go along with such a grant of immunity (at 121).

[270] E.g., Randelzhofer, 'Article 51', p. 674; H. W. Briggs, 'Appraisals of the ICJ's decision: Nicaragua v. United States (merits)', (1987) 81 AJIL 78–86, at 78, 84–5; J. P. Rowles, '"Secret Wars," self-defense and the Charter – a reply to Professor Moore', (1986) 80 AJIL 568–83; P. S. Reichler and D. Wippman, 'United States armed intervention in Nicaragua: a rejoinder', (1986) 11 YJIL 462–73, at 470–1; Kwakwa, 'South Africa's May 1986 military incursions', 442 ('This holding ... is not only consistent with, but also dictated by, the requirements for the maintenance of minimum world order'). Remark: Mrazek even argued that the Court adopted an *overly broad* interpretation of 'armed attack': Mrazek, 'Prohibition on the use and threat of force', 98.

[271] ICJ, *Nicaragua* case (Merits), Separate opinion of Judge Singh, 154.

[272] *Ibid.*, Separate opinion of Judge Ruda, § 13.

[273] E.g., Rowles, 'Secret wars', 579; Gray, *The use of force*, p. 131; Lamberti Zanardi, 'Indirect military aggression', p. 116.

[274] E.g., Lamberti Zanardi, 'Indirect military aggression', pp. 112–16; Randelzhofer, 'Article 51', p. 674; Sicilianos, *Les réactions décentralisées à l'illicité*, p. 326; Gray, *The use of force*, pp. 175–7; Constantinou, *The right of self-defence*, pp. 94 *et seq.*; Brownlie, *The use of force by States*, p. 370; Higginbotham, 'The southern African conflict', 546–50;

complaints that the Court's unqualified exclusion of 'logistical or other support' emptied the residual meaning of the phrase 'substantial involvement',[275] it is admittedly difficult to conceive of concrete actions – apart from the 'directing or controlling' of attacks in the sense of Article 8 DASR, or the actual participation of State agents alongside private individuals – that would be covered by its interpretation of Article 3(g). The residual role of 'substantial involvement' was clearly construed in a very limited fashion. One possible reading would be that State involvement, which would fall below the 'effective control' test but which would nonetheless constitute 'overall control' as interpreted by the ICTY, would transform attacks by non-State actors into 'armed attacks'.[276]

In the end, several scholars point out that the ICJ's interpretation in *Nicaragua* was consistent with the *travaux* of the Definition of Aggression and accurately reflected the practice of States in preceding decades.[277] This appears to be by and large correct. First, as discussed earlier, the preparatory works of the Definition and the gap between Article 3(g) and the Friendly Relations Declaration command a restrictive interpretation, excluding minor forms of assistance, and *a fortiori* the tolerating of an armed group's presence. Conversely, customary practice does not render support to the idea that the 'harbouring' or 'assisting' of armed bands triggers Article 51. In the 'early cases' mentioned above, States invoking the right of self-defence generally claimed that the other State had somehow 'sent' the perpetrators of the attacks. By

---

Schachter, *International law*, pp. 164–5. Also Kammerhofer, 'The *Armed Activities* case', 100 *et seq.* (Kammerhofer observes that even among the minority of scholars that have argued for the right of self-defence against an 'armed attack' not attributable to a State, most still uphold the need for some connection between the behaviour of the State and that of the private actor.). Remark: Judges Jennings and Schwebel in their dissenting opinions implicitly acknowledge the need for some degree of State involvement. One of the rare authors regarding State involvement as irrelevant is Dinstein: *War, aggression and self*-defence, 3rd edn, p. 214.

[275] E.g., Sicilianos, *Les réactions décentralisées à l'illicité*, pp. 324–5. Sicilianos speaks of a justification that is available in theory, but excluded in practice; ICJ, *Nicaragua* case (merits), Dissenting opinion of Judge Jennings, 543.

[276] See, e.g., Dinstein, *War, aggression and self-defence*, 4th edn, p. 204; Stahn, 'Terrorist acts as "armed attack"', 47.

[277] E.g., Gray, *The use of force*, pp. 130–2 ('the Court's judgment is consistent with State practice'), 143–4; Constantinou, *The right of self-defence*, pp. 94, 103–10; Sicilianos, *Les réactions décentralisées à l'illicité*, p. 325. Also: Cassese, 'Article 51', p. 781; Lamberti Zanardi, 'Indirect military aggression', pp. 113–15; Corten, *Le droit contre la guerre*, p. 689; Corten and Dubuisson, 'Opération "liberté immuable"', 56–62; Kwakwa, 'South Africa's May 1986 military incursions', 441.

contrast, self-defence claims relying on active or passive support to armed bands or 'terrorists' operating on a more autonomous basis, did not meet with legal acceptance from third States.[278]

5.2 Self-defence against non-State actors in the age of international terrorism and State failure

5.2.1 Prelude to 9/11: shifting context, shifting practice?

5.2.1.a The end of the decolonization era

If, despite scholarly criticism, the ICJ's approach accurately reflected existing State practice, it could nonetheless be argued that the *Nicaragua* judgment was pronounced at a time when the international community's position vis-à-vis rebel movements and terrorist violence was undergoing a marked evolution. Two predominant trends can be singled out: the (quasi-)completion of the decolonization process, and the growing recognition of terrorism as a threat to international security.

As far as the first issue is concerned, it must be recalled that ever since the adoption of the UNGA Declaration on the Granting of Independence to Colonial Peoples,[279] there had been a vigorous debate as to whether people under colonial rule were permitted to use force in the pursuit of self-determination. Even more contested was the question whether third States were allowed to extend armed support for such purposes. We have already observed that the Friendly Relations Declaration and the Definition of Aggression were deliberately vague on this issue:[280] reference was made to the legitimacy of the 'struggle' of peoples under colonial rule and to the need to provide 'material and moral assistance' to national liberation movements. Whether this meant '*armed* struggle' and '*armed* assistance' was left to the eye of the beholder.[281]

From 1973 onwards, the annual UNGA resolution on 'the universal realization of the right of peoples to self-determination' explicitly '[reaffirmed] the legitimacy of the peoples' struggle for liberation from colonial and foreign domination and alien subjugation by all available means, *including armed struggle*'.[282] In spite thereof, the legal controversy has

---

[278] However, *supra*, note 191.   [279] GA Res. 1514 (XV) of 14 December 1960.
[280] See Section 5.1.2.b.
[281] Similar provisions were included in several other UN resolutions. See *supra*, note 188.
[282] E.g., GA Res. 3070 (XXVIII) of 30 November 1973; GA Res. 3246 (XXIX) of 29 November 1974; GA Res. 3382 (XXX) of 10 November 1975; GA Res. 31/34 of 30 November 1976 (emphasis added).

never been authoritatively settled. On the one hand, the response of the international community to the cited attacks on neighbouring countries by Portugal, Israel and South Africa was undeniably affected by feelings of solidarity with national liberation movements and/or disapproval of these States' policies of repression or occupation (cf. *supra*). On the other hand, it is equally true that these neighbouring countries refrained from explicitly claiming a legal right to provide support – armed or other – to liberation movements.[283] Rather, they framed their actions in terms of the resisting of aggression. Involvement in the activities of armed bands was generally denied. As a result, there was no theoretical discussion of the conflicting views during these debates.[284] In *Nicaragua*, the Court merely noted *en passant* that it was 'not concerned with the process of decolonization'.[285] Neither have legal scholars been very supportive of the idea orginally launched by some developing countries[286] that colonialism qualified as a 'permanent armed attack', bringing it within the purview of Article 51.[287] The provision of armed support has generally been held to be unlawful. As for the provision of material support and the giving of sanctuary, scholarly opinion has been divided.[288]

In any event, at the time the ICJ pronounced its judgment, the decolonization process was by and large complete. The vast majority of former colonies had obtained independence. Four years after the ruling, Namibia became independent and the apartheid regime in South Africa was finally brought to an end. Following the demise of the colonial era, the controversy

---

[283] E.g., Kwakwa, 'South Africa's May 1986 military incursions', 441; Gray, *The use of force*, p. 63.

[284] E.g., *ibid.* p. 63.   [285] ICJ, *Nicaragua* case (Merits), § 206.

[286] E.g., UN Doc. A/AC.134/SR.67–78, 96 (Syria: the use of force by dependent peoples 'stemmed directly from the notion of self-defence, as they were the victims of a permanent attack ...'), 98 (Guyana).

[287] E.g., Randelzhofer, 'Article 2(4)', p. 121 (see also the references under footnote 123); L. Henkin, *How nations behave. Law and foreign policy*, 2nd edn (New York: Columbia University Press, 1979), p. 144; Malanczuk, 'Countermeasures and self-defence', 766–7; Rosenstock, 'Principles of International Law Concerning Friendly Relations', 733; Abi-Saab, 'Cours général', 413.

[288] E.g., condemning the provision of weapons, and logistical and other support: ICJ, *Nicaragua* case (Merits), Dissenting opinion of Judge Schwebel, § 180; Schachter, *International law*, pp. 119–20. Accepting material assistance and the granting of sanctuary: H. Bokor-Szegö, 'The attitude of socialist States towards the international regulation of the use of force', in Cassese (ed.), *The use of force*, pp. 453–77, at 469 (accepting 'material' and 'political' assistance, but excluding direct assistance, for example, via their regular armed forces); Abi-Saab, 'Cours général', 414 (accepting even military support falling short of direct intervention of troops). Unclear: Tanca, 'The prohibition of force', p. 407.

lost most of its practical signifance in that it was generally confined to 'dependent people'. As for the potential application of an alleged right to use force in self-determination beyond the colonial context, it appears that those countries that originally backed such right gradually came to denounce it as an unguided projectile. It is unsurprising then that the idea of use of force in self-determination and that of forcible assistance to liberation movement has since retreated to the background.[289] Significantly, after 1991, the annual UNGA resolution on 'the universal realization of the right of peoples to self-determination' abandoned the reference to 'armed struggle'.[290] Certainly, self-determination is and remains well-established as a universal human right,[291] and considerations of self-determination continue to influence the international appraisal of conflicts around the globe.[292] On the whole, however, the concept has lost its impact vis-à-vis the *ratione personae* dimension of the 'armed attack' requirement. Even if it is famously stated that 'one man's terrorist is another man's freedom fighter', the lists of 'terrorist organizations' have grown considerably longer in recent years. Few armed groups are nowadays recognized as 'liberation movements'.

5.2.1.b A new focus on terrorism: the 'Shultz doctrine' and beyond

The *Nicaragua* judgment was not only passed during the closing stages of the decolonization era, it also came at a time of growing awareness of the threat of international terrorism.[293] One of the first symptoms thereof

---

[289] Also: L. Henkin, *International law: politics and values* (Dordrecht: Martinus Nijhoff, 1995), p. 117 ('With colonialism essentially eliminated and no longer an important concern, the pressure for a "self-determination exception" to the law of the Charter subsided and the significance of such an exception, if recognized, is sharply reduced.'); Gray, *The use of force*, pp. 63–4; Dinstein, *War, aggression and self-defence*, 4th edn, p. 70.

[290] E.g., GA Res. 46/87 of 16 December 1991; GA Res. 47/82 of 16 December 1992; GA Res. 48/94 of 20 December 1993; GA Res. 49/151 of 23 December 1994 (this was the last such resolution). See Gray, *The use of force*, p. 62 (footnote 125).

[291] See, e.g., Article 1 of the International Covenant on Civil and Political Rights (UN Doc. A/6316 (1966); 999 UNTS 171) as well as Article 1 of the International Covenant on Economic, Social and Cultural Rights (U.N. Doc. A/6316 (1966); 993 UNTS 3).

[292] Remark: the issue of self-determination also plays an important role in the debates on the legality of humanitarian intervention as well as so-called pro-democratic intervention. These controversial topics are, however, beyond the scope of our analysis. The concept of 'wars of national liberation' also has a special legal purport under IHL (cf. Article 1(4) of the First Additional Protocol of 1977).

[293] Cf. S. Regourd, 'Raids "anti-terroristes" et développements récents des atteintes illicites au principe de non-interventione', (1986) 32 AFDI 79–103, at 79.

was the adoption by the US, two years prior to the *Nicaragua* judgement, of the so-called 'Shultz doctrine'. This doctrine copied the reasoning hitherto defended by Israel, according to which a State unwilling to prevent terrorist attacks from its territory would be liable to a forcible response in self-defence.

The genesis of the doctrine was strongly influenced by a series of incidents, such as the Entebbe hijacking (1976) and the seizure of the US embassy in Tehran (1979). Two terrorist attacks against US targets in Lebanon in 1983 were the proverbial last straw.[294] In April 1983, sixty-three people were killed in a suicide attack against the US embassy. Six months later, a truck packed with explosives drove straight into the barracks of the US marines in Beirut, reducing the barrack's headquarters to shambles. No fewer than 242 Americans lost their lives.[295]

Shortly afterwards, the Reagan administration adopted a number of classified national security directives which foresaw the possibility of unilateral military action against State-sponsored terrorist activity.[296] This new policy was subsequently made public through a number of speeches by Secretary of State Shultz. In 1984, for example, Shultz called for military action aimed at the prevention and deterrence of future terrorist acts.[297] Two years later, he called it

> absurd to argue that international law prohibits us from capturing terrorists in international waters or airspace; from attacking them on the soil of other nations, even for the purpose of rescuing hostages; or from using force against States that support, train, and harbor terrorists or guerrillas. International law requires no such result. A nation attacked by terrorists

---

[294] See M. Byers, 'Terrorism, the use of force and international law after September 11', (2002) 51 ICLQ 401–14, at 406–7; J. N. Maogoto, 'Walking an international law tightrope: use of military force to counter terrorism – willing the ends', (2005–6) 31 Brooklyn JIL 405–61, at 428 *et seq.*; W. M. Reisman and A. Armstrong, 'The past and future of the claim of preemptive self-defense', (2006) 100 AJIL 525–50, at 527–9.

[295] US Department of Defence, Report of the Commission on Beirut International Airport Terrorist Act, 20 December 1983, available at http://ibiblio.org/hyperwar/AMH/XX/MidEast/Lebanon-1982-1984/DOD-Report/index.html (accessed 15 May 2009) (stressing the need for 'a wide range of timely military response capabilities' to tackle State-sponsored terrorism).

[296] National Security Decision Directive 138, 3 April 1984, available at www.gwu.edu/~nsarchiv/NSAEBB/NSAEBB55/nsdd138.pdf; National Security Decision Directive 207, The National Program for Combatting Terrorism, 20 January 1986, available www.gwu.edu/~nsarchiv/NSAEBB/NSAEBB55/nsdd207.pdf (websites accessed 15 May 2009).

[297] US Secretary of State George Shultz, 'Terrorism and the modern world', New York, 25 October 1984, reprinted in Department of State Bulletin, December 1984, 12–17.

is permitted to use force to prevent or preempt future attacks, to seize terrorists, or to rescue its citizens when no other means is available. ... [T]his nation has consistently affirmed the right of States to use force in exercise of their right of individual or collective self-defence.[298]

As the language indicates, this was not merely a policy statement. It also intended to reflect the administration's interpretation of the law of the Charter. Significantly, the 'Shultz doctrine' was expressed at the international level in the course of the Security Council debates on the Israeli raid against the PLO headquarters in Tunis in 1985. Explaining why the US had abstained from voting on a resolution condemning the raid,[299] the US representative declared as follows:

[W]e recognize and strongly support the principle that a State subjected to continuing terrorist attacks may respond with appropriate use of force to defend itself against further attacks. This is an aspect of the inherent right of self-defence recognized in the [UN] Charter. ... It is the collective responsibility of sovereign States to see that terrorism enjoys no sanctuary, no safe haven, and that those who practice it have no immunity from the responses their acts warrant. Moreover, it is the responsibility of each State to take appropriate steps to prevent persons or groups within its sovereign territory from perpetrating such acts.[300]

It does not appear from the debate, however, that the US position obtained significant approbation from other States.[301] All other participants explicitly denounced the operation as a breach of Tunisia's sovereignty and territorial integrity. A multitude of factors were introduced, including the disproportionate character of the raid, the loss of civilian lives, the moderating role of Tunisia and the Palestinian struggle for self-determination. At the same time, many States stressed that the Israeli concept of self-defence stood far from the law of the UN Charter. In the majority view, even if the PLO was indeed responsible for the murder of three Israeli citizens in Cyprus a few days earlier – as Israel

---

[298] US Secretary of State George Shultz, 'Low-intensity warfare: the challenge of ambiguity', 15 January 1986, reprinted in (1986) 25 ILM 204.
[299] SC Res. 573 (1985) of 4 October 1985.
[300] UN Doc. S/PV.2615, 4 October 1985, § 252. Remark: the argument was implicitly repeated in relation to the situation in southern Lebanon in the late 1980s. Thus, in 1988, explaining why it vetoed a resolution condemning Israeli interventions into Lebanon, the US declared that 'in requesting that Israel cease all attacks against Lebanese territory regardless of provocation, this draft resolution would deny to Israel its inherent right to defend itself.' UN Doc. S/PV.2832, 14 December 1988, 29.
[301] See UN Docs. S/PV.2610-11, S/PV.2613, S/PV.2615, 2–4 October 1985.

contended – this did not justify the action undertaken against Tunisia.[302] Resolution 573 (1985), adopted by fourteen votes to none, vigorously condemned the Israeli action as an 'act of armed aggression in flagrant violation of the [UN] Charter'.[303]

It has been observed that the US itself applied the 'Shultz doctrine' when it carried out military strikes against Libya and Iraq in 1986 and 1993 respectively.[304] In the former case, the US reported that it had exercised its right of self-defence in response to 'an ongoing pattern' of terrorist attacks by Libya targeting US citizens and installations, including the bombing of a Berlin discotheque, killing one US soldier and injuring numerous others.[305] In the latter case, it argued that Iraq had 'planned, equipped and launched the terrorist operation' aimed at the assassination of former President Bush Snr.[306] Upon closer reading, however, it seems misguided to regard these precedents as a novel trend in State practice overstepping the *Nicaragua* threshold. First and foremost, the US insisted that the attacks had been conducted not by non-State actors, but by two States – Libya and Iraq. In other words, it by and large framed its claims along the classical lines of State imputability. Thus, Libya was accused of 'openly targeting American citizens and US installations', and was held 'directly responsible' for the Berlin bombing.[307] The US claimed to possess 'direct, precise and irrefutable evidence' that Libya had ordered its agents to carry out the latter attack, and that it was planning a multitude of future attacks.[308] Again, in 1993, the US asserted that it had 'clear and compelling evidence' that Iraq bore

---

[302] See in particular: UN Doc. S/PV.2611, § 18 (Denmark), § 40 (Turkey), § 52 (Australia), §§ 111–12 (UK: '[E]ven if there had been demonstrable responsibility by the PLO, this would not have justified the retaliation taken against Tunisia on 1 October.'); UN Doc. S/PV.2613, §§ 16–18 (Madagascar), § 115 (Greece: '[A]cts of terrorism cannot in any way serve as an excuse for a Government to launch an armed attack on a third country').

[303] SC Res. 573 (1985) of 4 October 1985.

[304] See, e.g., Stahn, 'Terrorist acts as "armed attack"', 36.

[305] UN Doc. S/17990, 14 April 1986 (US). See: M. N. Leich, 'Contemporary practice of the United States relating to international law', (1986) 80 AJIL 612–44, at 632–6.

[306] See UN Doc. S/PV.3245, 27 June 1993, 3 *et seq.*

[307] UN Doc. S/17990, 14 April 1986 (US).

[308] UN Doc. S/PV.2674, 15 April 1986, 16–17. 'More than a week before the attack, orders were sent from Tripoli to the Libyan People's Bureau in East Berlin to carry out a terrorist attack against Americans, an attack designed to cause maximum and indiscriminate casualties. Libya's agents then planted the bomb. On 4 April, the People's Bureau alerted Tripoli that the attack would be carried out the following morning. The next day, the People's Bureau reported back to Tripoli on the "great success" of the mission.'

'direct responsibility' for the failed assassination attempt.[309] Evidence included forensic data on the explosives and firing systems used, as well as information retrieved from the interrogation of the suspects, indicating that the ringleaders were recruited and received orders from the Iraqi intelligence services.[310] Second, the question of State responsibility had a direct impact on the reactions of third States. In 1986, most States regarded the US raid on Tripoli as unlawful *inter alia* because the United States had failed to provide convincing evidence that Libya had a hand in the Berlin bombing or other attacks.[311] According to Ghana, for instance:

> Clearly the use of force in self-defence can only be directed against the party that has perpetrated the armed attack. The fact of the matter is that the Council has not been presented with evidence establishing to its satisfaction linkage between the perpetrators of the various incidents and the Government of Libya such as would render them official acts of that Government.[312]

By contrast, those Western States that accepted Libya's responsibility adopted a more neutral or even supportive appraisal of the US actions.[313] In relation to the raid against Baghdad, the reaction of the Security Council Members was fairly positive, or at least condoning, as most agreed that the evidence brought forward by the US – far more elaborate than in 1986 – satisfactorily illustrated Iraq's responsibility for the

---

[309] UN Doc. S/26003, 26 June 1993 (US).
[310] See UN Doc. S/PV.3245, 27 June 1993, 3–6 ('From all the evidence available ... we are therefore highly confident that the Iraqi Government, at its highest levels, directed its intelligence services to carry out an assassination attempt against President Bush').
[311] See, e.g., UN Doc. S/PV.2675, 15 April 1986, 18 (Syria), 24–5 (Oman); UN Doc. S/PV.2680, 18 April 1986, 32–4 (Ghana), 47 (Nicaragua); UN Doc. S/PV.2682, 21 April 1986, 16 (Uganda), 41 (Thailand); UN Doc. S/PV.2683, 24 April 1986, 7 (India), 33 (Ghana). Remark: Libya denied any connection with attack against US targets (e.g., UN Doc. S/PV.2673, 4–6).
[312] UN Doc. S/PV.2680, 32–365: 'Instead ... reference has been made to secret communications emanating from unidentified sources going to further unidentified parties. ... The so-called tapes ... linking President Qadhafi to the discotheque bombing have not been subjected to any impartial examination ...'. Also: UN Doc. S/PV.2683, 33.
[313] France and Australia refrained from condemning or supporting the operation: UN Doc. S/PV.2676, 17–18 (Australia), UN Doc. S/PV.2682, 33–6 (Australia), 42 (France). Denmark accepted the evidence of Libyan involvement but denounced the US raid as disproportionate in nature: UN Doc. S/PV.2682, 32–3 (Denmark). The UK was the only country explicitly to support the US self-defence claim: UN Doc. S/PV.2679, 21–7 (UK). Each of these four countries, as well as the US itself – voted against a Council resolution condemning the US (see UN Doc. S/PV.2682, 43), which was consequently vetoed. On 20 November 1986, the General Assembly did, however, condemn the US raid (GA Res. 41/38).

murder plot.³¹⁴ If anything, these two precedents therefore affirm, rather than question, the need for a close link with the State for an 'armed attack' to materialize.³¹⁵

A more relevant application of the Shultz doctrine and a more straightforward challenge of the *Nicaragua* threshold concerns the US response to the bombings by Al Qaeda of the American embassies in Kenya and Tanzania (1998), which resulted in the death of twelve US citizens and over 250 other persons and which injured more than five thousand. *In casu*, the US reported to the Security Council that it had exercised its right of self-defence and had struck at a series of camps and installations used by the Bin Laden organization, more precisely a facility used to produce chemical weapons in Sudan, as well as terrorist training and base camps in Afghanistan.³¹⁶ In contrast with the previous incidents, the US did not hold Sudan and Afghanistan directly responsible for the embassy bombings. Rather, it accused both countries of giving sanctuary to Al Qaeda and declared that the air strikes 'were carried out only after repeated efforts to convince the Government of the Sudan and the Taliban regime in Afghanistan to shut these terrorist activities down and to cease their cooperation with the Bin Ladin organization'.³¹⁷ Amidst evidence that further terrorist attacks were under preparation, the US 'had no choice but to use armed force to prevent these attacks from continuing'.³¹⁸

The international response to Operation 'Infinite Reach' was mixed. A number of Western States, such as the UK, Israel, Australia, Germany, France and Spain, approved the US actions without elaborating on their legal basis, or simply expressed understanding.³¹⁹ On the other hand,

---

[314] See UN Doc. S/PV.3245, 27 June 1993, 13 (France), 16 (Japan), 17–18 (Brazil), 18–20 (Hungary), 21–2 (UK, explicitly supporting the self-defence claim), 22 (Russia, *idem*), 23 (New Zealand), 24–5 (Spain). China reacted negatively (21).

[315] See also: UN Doc. S/PV.2675, 53 (PRC: 'we are against encroachment upon the territory of a sovereign State under the pretext of striking terrorism'); UN Doc. S/PV.2677, 8 (Qatar).

[316] UN Doc. S/1998/780, 20 August 1998 (US).

[317] *Ibid.* In a press statement, President Clinton, moreover emphasized that 'Afghanistan and Sudan had been warned for years to stop harbouring and supporting terrorist groups'. Cited in 'U.S. fury on 2 continents; Clinton's words: "There will be no sanctuary for terrorists"', *NY Times* 21 August 1998.

[318] UN Doc. S/1998/780.

[319] See, e.g., 'Annan "concerned" over US air strikes', *BBC News* 20 August 1998; S. D. Murphy, 'Contemporary practice of the United States relating to international law', (1999) 93 AJIL 161–94, at 164–5; J. Lobel, 'The use of force to respond to terrorist attacks: the bombing of Sudan and Afghanistan', (1999) 24 YJIL 537–57, at 538.

several other States, including Iran, Iraq, Libya and Russia condemned the strikes.[320] Interestingly, both the Non-Aligned Movement and the League of Arab States denounced the strike against the El-Shifa pharmaceutical plant in Khartoum as an act of aggression, but offered no comment on the strikes against Afghanistan.[321] The main criticism undoubtedly related to the lack of reliable intelligence vis-à-vis the target in Khartoum.[322] Sudan indeed went to great lengths to demonstrate that the El-Shifa plant was not in any way involved in the development of chemical weapons but merely produced medicines for human and veterinary use, and called for a fact-finding mission to be sent *in situ*, a plea supported by numerous African and Arab States.[323]

Schmitt regards the international response to the strikes as 'implied acceptance of a State's right to react forcefully to terrorism pursuant to the law of self-defence, so long as the action is based on reliable information'.[324] This may be a bridge too far: when taking account of the lack of debate on the merits of the US self-defence claim, it remains difficult to deduce the *opinio iuris* required to proceed to such assertion. On the other hand, when comparing the mixed and muted reaction to the widespread condemnation of, for example, the Israeli strike against the PLO headquarters in Tunis (1985), the events of 1998 do seem to reflect an emerging shift in the attitude of States vis-à-vis the permissibility of recourse to force against terrorist attacks. In retrospect, the 1998 strikes constitute an important step in the transition from the classical view that terrorist attacks must be dealt with through law enforcement mechanisms[325] to the acceptance that the

---

[320] Murphy, 'Contemporary practice of the United States', 164. Criticism was also expressed by Pakistan and the Federal Republic of Yugoslavia. See: UN Doc. 1/53/285, 25 August 1998 (Yugoslavia); UN Doc. S/1998/794, 24 August 1998 (Pakistan).

[321] See UN Doc. S/1998/879, 22 September 1998 (Sudan: containing extracts from the final document of the summit meeting of Heads of State and Government of the Movement of Non-Aligned Countries, Durban, 3 September 1998); UN Doc. S/1998/800, 24 August 1998 (Kuwait); UN Doc. S/1998/894, 28 September 1998 (Lebanon).

[322] See on this Lobel, 'The use of force', 544 *et seq.*; R. Wedgwood, 'Responding to terrorism: the strikes against bin Laden', (1999) 24 YJIL 559–76, at 569–75. Also S. L. Myers and T. Weiner, 'After the attack: the chemicals; possible benign use is seen for chemical at factory in Sudan', *NY Times* 27 August 1998.

[323] See (1998) UNYB 1219.

[324] M. N. Schmitt, 'Responding to transnational terrorism under the *Ius ad Bellum*: a normative framework', in M. N. Schmitt and J. Pejic, *International law and armed conflict: exploring the faultlines: essays in honour of Yoram Dinstein* (Leiden: Martinus Nijhoff, 2007), pp. 157–95, at 165.

[325] Cf. S. D. Murphy, 'Terrorism and the concept of "armed attack" in Article 51 of the UN Charter', (2002) 43 HILJ 41–51, at 46.

recourse to military force may exceptionally be warranted to deal with transnational terrorism.

5.2.1.c Other manifestations of shifting custom

Before examining the impact of 9/11, reference must be made to a number of other cases where States resorted to cross-border use of force in response to attacks by terrorist groups or other non-State actors.[326] Insofar as the *Nicaragua* standard was apparently not met in most of these cases,[327] and insofar as intervening States escaped condemnation from the UN Security Council, they provide relevant customary practice illustrating a move towards a more flexible interpretation of Article 3(g) Definition of Aggression. At the same time, the general lack of international scrutiny or legal argumentation, as well as the limited information as to allegations of State involvement in the attacks concerned temper their precedential value.

In 1992 and 1995, Senegalese warplanes bombed suspected rebel bases in Guinea-Bissau alleged to be safe havens for Casamance rebels.[328] Interestingly, in 1992, when Guinea-Bissau protested that it had not supported rebel incursions, Senegal apologized for its action.[329] In 1993, Tajikistan and Russia were involved in extensive military actions against irregular forces operating from Afghanistan.[330] Both countries invoked Article 51 UN Charter in their reports to the UN Security Council.[331] According to Tajikistan, Tajiki opposition forces were supported by Afghan *mujaheddin* and sub-units from the Afghan Ministry of Defence.[332] The (de facto) Afghan authorities rejected allegations of involvement in the attacks as completely unfounded.[333] Again in 1996, Sudan complained of armed aggression perpetrated by Eritrea because

---

[326] See Franck, *Recourse to force*, pp. 63–7; Gray, *The use of force*, pp. 140–3; Ruys and S. Verhoeven, 'Attacks by private actors', 294–5.
[327] Remark: occasionally, however, there were allegations of direct participation of regular armed forces in attacks by non-State actors. *Infra*, notes 332, 334, 335.
[328] (1992) 38 *Keesing's* 39228.   [329] Gray, *The use of force*, p. 140.
[330] (1993) UNYB 383–4.
[331] UN Doc. S/16091, 14 July 1993 (Tajikistan); UN Doc. S/16092, 15 July 1993 (Tajikistan); UN Doc. S/26110, 15 July 1993 (Russia, invoking collective self-defence).
[332] Tajikistan also suggested that Afghan forces had directly participated in the attacks. UN Doc. S/16091; UN Doc. S/16092 ('The situation is further aggravated by the fact that units led by Afghan field commanders from a subunit of the 55th Infantry Division of the Ministry of Defence of the Islamic State of Afghanistan are participating ... in these armed provocations'; also referring to support by 'Afghan mujahidin and subunits under the [Afghan] Ministry of Defence').
[333] UN Doc. S/26145, 22 July 1993 (Afghanistan). Also: UN Doc. S/26814, 11 November 1993 (Afghanistan).

Eritrea was sponsoring and hosting elements of the rebel movement in southern Sudan, with a view to overthrowing the Sudanese government.[334] One year later, Burundi attempted to justify territorial incursions into Tanzania on the ground that Tanzania had provided Burundian exiles with military training and weapons.[335] Accusations of State involvement were also made in relation to border tension between Burma and Thailand,[336] between the Central African Republic and Chad,[337] and between Liberia, Guinea, Burkina Faso and Sierra Leone.[338] In the latter case, the Security Council issued a Presidential Statement which expressed serious concern over reports of external military support to rebel groups and called upon all States to refrain from such support and to prevent armed individuals from using their national territory to prepare and commit attacks in neighbouring countries.[339]

Of particular interest are the repeated incursions by Turkey, and to lesser extent by Iran, against Kurdish fighters operating from Iraqi territory following the 1990–1 Gulf War.[340] Well before 1991, Turkey already undertook cross-border action against PKK hideouts on a regular

---

[334] (1996) UNYB 133; (1996) 42 *Keesing's* 42112; UN Doc. S/1996/358, 17 May 1996 (Sudan, accusing Eritrea of 'sponsoring and hosting' rebel forces); UN Doc. S/1996/1007, 5 December 1996 (Sudan, referring to 'flagrant support of the Eritrean regime to Sudanese terrorist groups', as well as listing several incidents where Eritrean forces directly participated in attacks). Similar allegations were made in 2002: (2002) UNYB 217; UN Doc. S/2002/1117, 8 October 2002 (Sudan).

[335] (1997) 43 *Keesing's* 41851, 41897; (1997) UNYB 89–90. In a letter of 28 October 1997, Burundi also accused the Tanzanian army of having launched a series of attacks against its territory (UN Doc. S/1997/822). These accusations were denied by Tanzania, which in turn invoked Article 51 UN Charter against attacks by Burundi (UN Doc. S/1997/850, 5 November 1997).

[336] (1995) 41 *Keesing's* 40554.   [337] (2002) UNYB 145; (2002) 48 *Keesing's* 44926.

[338] (2000) UNYB 182–3, 188; (2000) 46 *Keesing's* 43781, 43984–5. See also: UN Doc. S/2001/474, 11 May 2001 (Liberia: 'The Government of Guinea has openly, blatantly and with impunity allowed Liberian dissidents ... to carry out armed attacks against Liberia ... with the intention of overthrowing the Government .... In addition, the Guinean Army has provided and continues to provide military support to these dissidents.... The Liberian Government reserves the right to defend itself pursuant to [Article 51 UN Charter]'); UN Doc. S/2001/562, 4 June 2001 (Liberia); UN Doc. S/2001/851, 6 September 2001 (Liberia).

[339] Presidential Statement UN Doc. S/PRST/2000/41, 21 December 2000.

[340] See: C. Gray and S. Olleson, 'The limits of the law on the use of force: Turkey, Iraq and the Kurds', (2001) 12 Finnish YBIL 357–408; M. Bothe and T. Lohmann, 'Der türkische Einmarsch im Nordirak: neue Probleme des völkerrechtlichen Gewaltverbots', (1995) 5 SZIER 441–54; Antonopoulos, 'The Turkish military operation in Northern Iraq'; Gray, *The use of force*, pp. 141–2; Franck, *Recourse to Force*, pp. 63–4.

basis. In general, these operations were approved, or at least condoned by the Hussein regime.[341] However, relations between the two countries deteriorated when Turkey sided with the allied forces in the Gulf War. As a result, after 1991, Iraq began denouncing Turkish incursions and filed numerous complaints with the Security Council to protest against repeated violations of its sovereignty and territorial integrity.[342] On most occasions, Turkey avoided the spotlights and refrained from communicating on or offering any legal justification for its actions. Exceptionally, it presented its arguments to the Security Council in relation to a number of fairly large-scale operations in 1995 and beyond.[343] Without expressly invoking Article 51 UN Charter, Turkey seemed to rely on a reading of the right of self-defence similar to that employed by Israel vis-à-vis Palestinian attacks emanating from Lebanese territory (cf. *supra*).[344] On the one hand, it emphasized that in light of the de facto *autonomy* of Iraqi Kurds resulting from the Gulf War and the instalment of the no-fly zones, Iraq was unable to exercise its sovereign authority over the northern part of its territory. Accordingly, Turkey 'could not ask the Government of Iraq to fulfil its obligation, under international law, to prevent the use of its territory for the staging of terrorist acts against Turkey'. On the other hand, Turkey stressed that its operations solely targeted terrorist targets without intending to diminish Iraq's territorial integrity, and were limited in time and scope. Iraq protested that Turkey was itself responsible for the absence of any legitimate authority in northern Iraq, since its support for the no-fly zones had helped to consolidate the power vacuum in that

---

[341] See Gray and Olleson, 'The limits of the law on the use of force', 378 (footnotes 113, 115); Antonopoulos, 'The Turkish military operation in Northern Iraq', 49.
[342] See references in Gray and Olleson, 'The limits of the law on the use of force', 378 *et seq*.
[343] See in particular the communications by Turkey: UN Doc. S/1995/605, 24 July 1995 ('As Iraq has not been able to exercise its authority over the northern part of its country since 1991 for reasons well known, Turkey cannot ask the Government of Iraq to fulfil its obligation, under international law, to prevent the use of its territory for the staging of terrorist acts against Turkey. Under these circumstances, Turkey's resorting to legitimate measures which are imperative to its own security cannot be regarded as a violation of Iraq's sovereignty. No country would be expected to stand idle when its own territorial integrity is incessantly threatened by blatant cross-border attacks of a terrorist organization based and operating from a neighbouring country, if that country is unable to put an end to such attacks. The recent operations of limited time and scope were carried out within this framework'); UN Doc. S/1996/479, 27 June 1996; UN Doc. S/1997/7, 3 January 1997; UN Doc. S/1996/836.
[344] Gray and Olleson, 'The limits of the law on the use of force', 383, 387.

region.³⁴⁵ Hence, Turkey could not 'justify its practices by citing the principle of the need for or legitimate right of self-defence, since it had itself directly and actively contributed to the creation and perpetuation of the anomalous situation in northern Iraq'. The international reaction to Turkey's actions was extremely muted and limited.³⁴⁶ The US and the UK were reluctant to pronounce on the legal merits, but occasionally expressed approval. In 1995, the US asserted that a country has the right to use force in self-defence 'to protect itself from attacks from a neighbouring country if the neighbouring State is *unwilling or unable to prevent the use of its territories for such attack*' (emphasis added).³⁴⁷ At the same time, it expressed concern that the Turkish operations be 'limited in scope and duration'. The UK responded in a broadly similar manner: while acknowledging Turkey's right to defend its territorial integrity, it insisted that the action taken in northern Iraq must be proportionate to the threat.³⁴⁸ Although the issue was not put on the Security Council's agenda, some of the major cross-border operations did attract international criticism. In relation to a large-scale offensive in 1995, several EU Member States expressed strong concern.³⁴⁹ In 1996, the League of Arab States denounced the creation of a 'danger zone' by Turkish forces as a violation of Iraq's territorial integrity.³⁵⁰ One year later, it condemned a large-scale invasion of Iraqi territory as a 'flagrant violation of the rules of international law and the [UN] Charter'.³⁵¹ Last

---

³⁴⁵ E.g., UN Doc. S/1996/561, 15 July 1996 (Iraq); UN Doc. S/1997/129, 13 February 1997 (Iraq).
³⁴⁶ Gray and Olleson, 'The limits of the law on the use of force', 355. Remark: in response to parliamentary questions, the German government in 1995 and 1998 expressed cautious approval for the Turkish operations. See Deutscher Bundestag, Drücksache 13/1246, 2 May 1995, at 2; Drücksache 14/218, 10 December 1998, 1.
³⁴⁷ See US State Department, Daily Press Briefings of 28 March 1995, 31 March 1995, 17 April 1995, 7 July 1995, 5 September 1996, 6 November 1996 and especially of 11 February 1998.
³⁴⁸ See the statements cited in (1995) 66 BYBIL 725; (1997) 68 BYBIL 630; (1998) 69 BYBIL 586.
³⁴⁹ See, e.g., 'Turks attack Kurds in Iraq for a 2nd day; 200 reported killed', *NY Times* 22 March 1995; 'Turks reported likely to keep troops in Iraq for weeks', *NY Times* 23 March 1995; 'Turk sees foray in Iraq ending in few weeks', *NY Times* 7 April 1995; Gray and Olleson, 'The limits of the law on the use of force', 402 (footnotes 235–7); (1995) 41 *Keesing's* 40474, 40522. It appears that European States were mainly concerned with the size and duration of the operation.
³⁵⁰ UN Doc. S/1996/796, 24 September 1996 (League of Arab States).
³⁵¹ UN Doc. S/1997/416, 30 May 1997 (Lebanon). Remark: the Gulf Cooperation Council also expressed 'strong disquiet' at these operations (UN Doc. A/52/168, 2 June 1997).

but not least, the Non-Aligned Movement in 2000 adopted the following statement:

> We strongly condemn the repeated actions of Turkish armed forces violating the territorial integrity of Iraq under the pretext of fighting guerrilla elements hiding inside Iraqi territory. ... We also reject the so-called 'hot pursuit' measures adopted by Turkey to justify such actions that are abhorrent to international law and to the norms of practice amongst States.[352]

Like Turkey, Iran occasionally engaged in cross-border operations against Kurdish fighters based in Iraq in the mid 1990s. Contrary to the former country, however, Iran relatively consistently reported its operations to the Security Council, couching them as applications of Article 51 UN Charter.[353] On most occasions, Iran accused Iraq of providing terrorist groups with active support, such as military training, financial and logistical support and intelligence services. Exceptionally, in 1996, it copied Turkey's reasoning that it was forced to take defensive measures due to the inability of Baghdad to exercise control over its territory.[354] All the while, Iran stressed that its actions were proportionate and targeted exclusively against 'terrorist groups'. Although the incidents were again not subject to debate within the Security Council, it is remarkable that the United States claimed that Iran's cross-border actions had 'no justification whatsoever'.[355] In explaining the difference between the position of Turkey and Iran, the spokesperson of the US State Department could only declare that 'Iran was an outlaw State' and

---

[352] UN Doc. S/2000/580, 6 June 2000 (South Africa).
[353] See Gray and Olleson, 'The limits of the law on the use of force', 395–400. See in particular the following communications by Iran: UN Doc. S/25843, 25 May 1993; UN Doc. S/1994/1273, 9 November 1994; UN Doc. S/1996/602, 29 July 1996; UN Doc. S/1999/420, 13 April 1999; UN Doc. S/1999/781, 12 July 1999; UN Doc. S/2000/216, 14 March 2000; UN Doc. S/2001/271, 26 March 2001; UN Doc. S/2001/381, 19 April 2001. Like Turkey, Iran argued that it had no intention of undermining Iraq's sovereignty or territorial integrity. See, e.g., UN Doc. S/2001/381: 'The Government of [Iran] emphasizes that this limited and proportionate operation was carried out to stop cross-border attacks against [Iran] from Iraqi territory by the MKO terrorist organization harboured in Iraq ... [Iran] expects the Government of Iraq to take appropriate measures ... to put an end to the use of its territory for cross-border attacks and terrorist operations against [Iran], which would render unnecessary measures in self-defence in accordance with Article 51 of the Charter of the United Nations.'
[354] UN Doc. S/1996/602.
[355] US State Department, Daily Press Briefings, 30 July 1996, 18 September 1996. See Gray and Olleson, 'The limits of the law on the use of force', 399–400 (the authors observe that Iran actually had a stronger case for invoking self-defence than Turkey).

that the US '[did] not have the type of relationship with Iran – far from it – that we do with Turkey'.

What to conclude from all this? Franck tentatively observes that the Turkish interventions in Iraq may indicate that 'the international system, at least in practice if not yet in theory, was growing more accepting of the (proportionate) use of force by a State against neighbouring States that persist in providing safe havens for the cross-border incursions of irregular forces'.[356] Some elements seem to back this conclusion. Most notably, Turkey, Iran, the US and the UK explicitly or implicitly accepted the principle that defensive measures are permissible when a neighbouring State is *unwilling or unable* to prevent cross-border attacks. Furthermore, criticism seems mainly to have been directed against the allegedly disproportionate character of some operations. On the other hand, one should not overlook the fact that the international reaction was mixed; that support for the Turkish actions was often expressed in ambiguous terms; that the general lack of international scrutiny was probably influenced by the pariah status of the Hussein regime after the Gulf War; and that the US itself adopted a rather inconsistent position vis-à-vis the Iranian actions.[357] In sum, while in retrospect, the Turkish actions constitute another step in the evolution in customary practice towards a more flexible position on the *ratione personae* controversy, they also illustrate that such a flexible position was by no means well-established before 2001. This is also evident from the rejection by the Security Council in 2000 of the Rwandan authorities' claim to a right to attack Hutu insurgents operating out of neighbouring territory.[358] In resolution 1304 (2000), the Council expressed 'unreserved condemnation' of this violation of the sovereignty and territorial integrity of the DRC.[359]

5.2.2 9/11: awakening to a new security environment

5.2.2.a Security Council resolutions 1368 and 1373 (2001) and the US intervention in Afghanistan

5.2.2.a.i Chronology and international response On the noon of 12 September 2001, a little over twenty-four hours after a group of nineteen

---

[356] Franck, *Recourse to force*, p. 63.
[357] *Ibid.*; Gray and Olleson, 'The limits of the law on the use of force', 407.
[358] Franck, *Recourse to force*, p. 66; Corten and Dubuisson, 'Opération "liberté immuable"', 60.
[359] SC Res. 1304 (2000) of 16 June 2000.

Al Qaeda terrorists killed almost 3,000 civilians – the highest number of casualties in the United States in a single day since the American Civil War[360] – the fifteen Members of the Security Council convened at UN Headquarters.[361] Following a brief meeting, the Council unanimously adopted resolution 1368 (2001), which 'unequivocally condemned the horrifying terrorist attacks' and, 'like any act of international terrorism', held the attacks to constitute 'a threat to international peace and security'.[362] Interestingly, although much remained unknown as to the source of the attacks – the US had only just commenced the largest criminal investigation in its history – the resolution's preamble recognized in general terms 'the inherent right of individual or collective self-defence in accordance with the Charter'.

The same reference to self-defence was included in resolution 1373 (2001) of 28 September 2001,[363] a remarkable piece of quasi-legislation[364] spelling out a whole list of obligations and recommendations to States in order to tackle international terrorism. Elaborating on States' duty to exercise due diligence in preventing harm to other countries, the Council *inter alia* called upon States to 'refrain from providing any form of support, active or passive, to entitities or persons involved in terrorist acts, including by suppressing recruitment of members of terrorist groups and eliminating the supply of weapons to terrorists'; to 'deny safe haven to those who finance, plan, support, or commit terrorist acts, or provide safe havens'; to 'prevent the movement of terrorists . . . by effective border controls', et cetera.

In the meantime, the US and the UK pursued their investigation into the source of the attacks. On 4 October, the UK publicized its findings in a document entitled 'Responsibility for the Terrorist Atrocities in the United States'.[365] While emphasizing that the document did not purport to provide a prosecutable case in a court of law, it left no

---

[360] Murphy, 'Terrorism and the concept of "armed attack"', 47.
[361] UN Doc. S/PV.4370, 12 September 2001.
[362] SC Res. 1368 (2001) of 12 September 2001.
[363] SC Res. 1373 (2001) of 28 September 2001.
[364] See, e.g., M. Happold, 'Security Council Resolution 1373 and the Constitution of the United Nations', (2003) 16 Leiden JIL 593–610.
[365] UK Press Release, Office of the Prime Minister, 'Responsibility for the terrorist atrocities in the United States, 11 September 2001', 4 October 2001, available at www.independent.co.uk/news/uk/politics/official-document-responsibility-for-the-terrorist-atrocities-in-the-united-states-11-september-2001-748317.html. The document was updated on 14 November 2001 (www.number10.gov.uk/Page3807) (websites accessed 15 May 2009).

THE 'ARMED ATTACK' REQUIREMENT *RATIONE PERSONAE* 435

doubt that the 9/11 attacks were headed, planned and carried out by Al Qaeda.[366] It found that Al Qaeda had carried out other terrorist attacks in the past, including the bombings of the US embassies in Nairobi and Dar es Salaam in 1998 and the attack against the USS *Cole* in the harbour of Aden in 2000, and that it had the motivation and capability to carry out more attacks in the future.[367] Although the document did not accuse the Taleban regime – at the time the de facto government of Afghanistan – of being directly involved in the attacks, it observed that a close symbiosis existed between the two structures.[368] Bin Laden provided financial support, military training, infrastructure assistance and humanitarian aid to the Taleban. In turn, the Taleban provided Al Qaeda with a safe haven in which to operate and protected its drugs stockpiles. The British data were later confirmed by the US.[369]

Once the source of the attacks had been convincingly established, the United States issued an ultimatum, demanding that the Taleban hand over all Al Qaeda leaders, immediately close every terrorist training camp and allow the US to verify that these camps were no longer operating.[370] President Bush made clear that these demands were 'not open to negotiation or discussion': 'The Taleban must act and act immediately. They will hand over the terrorists, or they will share in their fate.'[371]

Following a rejection of the ultimatum, the US and the UK on 7 October 2001 launched Operation 'Enduring Freedom'. Both countries reported to the Security Council on the exercise of their right of self-defence pursuant to Article 51 UN Charter. The US letter stated that there was clear and compelling information that the Al Qaeda organization, 'which is supported by the Taleban regime in Afghanistan, had a central role' in the 'armed attacks' against the United States.[372] The attacks and the ongoing threat had been 'made possible by the decision of the Taleban regime to allow the parts of Aghanistan that it controls to be used by this organization as a base of operation'. Since the Taleban had refused to change its policy, US forces had initiated actions 'designed

---

[366] *Ibid.*, § 1. [367] *Ibid.*, §§ 35 *et seq.* [368] *Ibid.*, §§ 4, 10 *et seq.*
[369] D. E. Sanger, 'White House approved data Blair released', *NY Times* 6 October 2001.
[370] US President, Address before a Joint Session of the US Congress, 20 September 2001, cited in Murphy, 'Contemporary practice of the United States', 243.
[371] *Ibid.* Remark: the UN Security Council had already called upon the Taleban regime to stop providing sanctuary and training for terrorist organizations. See SC Res. 1193 (1998) of 28 August 1998; SC Res. 1214 (1998) of 8 December 1998; SC Res. 1267 (1999) of 15 October 1999; SC Res. 1333 (2000) of 19 December 2000.
[372] UN Doc. S/2001/946, 7 October 2001 (US).

to prevent and deter further attacks on the United States', including 'measures against Al Qaeda terrorist training camps and military installations of the Taleban regime'. The UK letter argued by analogy that in order 'to avert the continuing threat of attacks', it had undertaken military action 'directed against [Al Qaeda] and the Taleban regime that is supporting it'.[373]

Operation 'Enduring Freedom' was approved almost unanimously by the international community and received unprecedented offers of airspace and landing rights. On 2 October, well before the operation was launched, NATO determined that since the attacks of 9/11 were 'directed from abroad', they would be regarded as an action covered by the collective self-defence provision of Article 5 of the NATO Treaty.[374] The OAS similarly adopted a ministerial declaration according to which the attacks were regarded as 'attacks against all American States'.[375] The EU declared its "wholehearted support for the action that is being taken in self-defence and in conformity with the [UN Charter] and Security Council resolution 1368 (2001)'.[376] Several individual members, such as Canada, France, Australia, Germany, the Netherlands, New Zealand and Poland, notified the Security Council that 'in accordance with Article 51 UN Charter', they had adopted

---

[373] UN Doc. S/2001/947, 7 October 2001 (UK).

[374] Statement by NATO Secretary-General Lord Robertson, Brussels, 2 October 2001, reprinted in (2001) 41 ILM 1267. The North Atlantic Council had already issued a statement on 12 September 2001, deciding that '*if* it was determined that the attack was directed from abroad against the United States,' it would be regarded as an action covered by Article 5 NATO Treaty (emphasis added). Statement by the North Atlantic Council, 12 September 2001, NATO Press Release No. 124, available at www.nato.int/docu/pr/2001/p01-124e.htm (accessed 15 May 2009).

[375] 'Terrorist threat to the Americas', resolution adopted at the 24th Meeting of Consultation of Ministers of Foreign Affairs, Washington DC, 21 September 2001, Doc. OEA/Ser.F/II.24 RC.24/Res.1/01. The preamble also 'recalls' the inherent right of individual or collective self-defence.

After the commencement of the military campaign, another OAS declaration proclaimed that '[the] measures being applied by the [US] and other States in the exercise of their inherent right of individual and collective self-defence have the full support of the States parties to the Rio Treaty.' Support for the Measures of Individual and Collective Self-defence established in Resolution RC.24/Res.1/01, Meeting of Consultation of Ministers of Foreign Affairs, Committee for Follow-up to the 24th Meeting of Consultation of Ministers of Foreign Affairs, 16 October 2001, Doc. OEA/Ser.F/II.24-CS/TIAR/Res.1/01. The Members of the OAS also 'reiterated their willingness to provide additional assistance and support' to the US 'to prevent future armed attacks by terrorists'.

[376] UN Doc. S/2001/967, 8 October 2001 (Belgium, on behalf of the EU).

various measures in support of Operation 'Enduring Freedom'.[377] Support was furthermore expressed by Russia, China, Norway, Mexico, Egypt and many others.[378] While some expressed concern at the fate of the Afghan people, condemnation of the operation as such was highly exceptional.[379] The Organization for the Islamic Conference urged the US not to extend its military response beyond Afghanistan, but made no criticism of the military actions against Afghanistan.[380]

5.2.2.a.ii Precedential value: instant custom or unique exception? The launching of Operation 'Enduring Freedom' and the adoption of Security Council resolutions 1368 and 1373 has inspired an avalanche of academic analysis,[381] addressing a variety of legal questions under the *Ius*

---

[377] UN Doc. S/2001/1005, 24 October 2001 (Canada); UN Doc. S/2001/1103, 23 November 2001 (France); UN Doc. S/2001/1104, 23 November 2001 (Australia); UN Doc. S/2001/1127, 29 November 2001 (Germany); UN Doc. S/2001/1171, 6 December 2001 (Netherlands); UN Doc. S/2001/1193, 17 December 2001 (New Zealand); UN Doc. S/2002/275, 15 March 2002 (Poland).

[378] UN Doc. S/2001/1091, 16 November 2001 (Chile, on behalf of the Rio Group, approving of the exercise of the right of self-defence); UN Doc. S/PV.4413, 13 November 2001, 7 (France), 10 (Norway); UN Doc. S/PV.4414, 13 November 2001, 13 (Norway, acknowledging the right of self-defence). See also the references in Murphy, 'Terrorism and the concept of "armed attack"', 49 (footnotes 47–52); Murphy, 'Contemporary practice of the United States', 248 (footnotes 79–88); Byers, 'Terrorism', 410, footnote 46.

[379] C. Gray, 'The use of force and the international legal order', in M. D. Evans (ed.), *International law* (Oxford University Press, 2003), pp. 589–619, at 604 (noting that only Iran and Iraq expressly challenged the legality of the operation); S. R. Ratner, '*Jus ad Bellum* and *Jus in Bello* after September 11', (2002) 96 AJIL 905–21, at 910, footnotes 24–7.

[380] Murphy, 'Contemporary practice of the United States', 248.

[381] For a tip of the iceberg, see, e.g., G. Abraham and K. Hopkins, 'Bombing for humanity: the American response to the 11 September attacks and the plea of self-defence', (2002) 119 South African LJ 783–801; Y. Arai-Takahashi, 'Shifting boundaries of the right of self-defence: appraising the impact of the September 11 attacks on *Jus ad Bellum*', (2002) 36 *International Lawyer* 1081–102; R. Bermejo García, 'El Derecho internacional frente al terrorismo: ¿nuevas perspectivas tras los atentados del 11 de Septiembre?', (2001) 17 ADI 5–24; T. Bruha, 'Gewaltverbot und humanitäres Völkerrecht nach dem 11. September 2001', (2002) 40 AdV 383–421; Byers, 'Terrorism'; J. I. Charney, 'The use of force against terrorism and international law', (2001) 95 AJIL 835–9; Corten and Dubuisson, 'Opération "liberté immuable"'; O. Corten and F. Dubuisson, 'La guerre "antiterroriste" engagée par les Etats-Unis a-t-elle été autorisée par le Conseil de Sécurité?', (2001) 120 *Journal des Tribunaux* 889–95; B. A. Feinstein, 'Operation Enduring Freedom: legal dimensions of an infinitely just operation', (2002) 11 JTLP 201–95; T. M. Franck, 'Terrorism and the right of self-defense', (2001) 95 AJIL 839–42; J. A. González Vega, 'Los atentados del 11 de septiembre, la operación "Libertad Duradera" y el derecho de legitíma defensa', (2001) 53 REDI 247–71; C. Greenwood, 'International law and the

ad Bellum.[382] Undoubtedly, scholarly attention has focused first and foremost on the potential impact of the incident on the *ratione personae* dimension of Article 51. Reactions from international lawyers have varied wildly. Scholars that believed that Article 51 extended to attacks by non-State actors well before 9/11, as well as scholars that believed that customary law was evolving in such direction, have tended to regard the response to the 9/11 attacks as an unequivocal confirmation of this view[383] – with some labelling it as 'instant custom'.[384] Those who

> pre-emptive use of force: Afghanistan, Al-Qaida, and Iraq', (2003) 4 San Diego ILJ 7–37; Hofmeister, 'To harbour or not to harbour?'; M. Krajewski, 'Selbstverteidigung gegen bewaffnete Angriffe nicht-staatlicher Organisationen – Der 11.September 2001 und seine Folgen', (2002) 40 AdV 183–214; J. N. Maogoto, 'War on the enemy: self-defence and State-sponsored terrorism', (2003) 4 Melbourne JIL 406–38; Müller, 'Legal issues'; Murphy, 'Terrorism and the concept of "armed attack"'; Murphy, 'Contemporary practice of the United States'; E. P. J. Myjer and N. D. White, 'The Twin Towers attack: an unlimited right to self-defence?', (2002) 7 JCSL 5–17; F. Naert, 'The impact of the fight against international terrorism on the *Ius ad Bellum* after "11 September"', (2004) 43 RDMDG 55–107; M. E. O'Connell, 'Lawful self-defense to terrorism', (2002) 63 Un. Pittsburgh L.Rev. 889–908; J. J. Paust, 'Use of armed force against terrorists in Afghanistan, Iraq, and beyond', (2002) 35 Cornell ILJ 533–57; N. Quénivet, 'The legality of the use of force by the United States and the United Kingdom against Afghanistan', (2003) 6 ARIEL 205–40; C. Ramón Chornet, 'La lucha contra el terrorismo internacional después del 11 de septiembre de 2001', (2001) 53 REDI 273–88; Ratner, '*Jus ad Bellum* and *Jus in Bello* after September 11'; W. M. Reisman, 'In defense of world public order', (2001) 95 AJIL 833–5; K. Schmalenbach, 'The right of self-defence and the "war on terrorism" one year after September 11', (2002) 3 German LJ, available at www.germanlawjournal.com/article.php?id=189 (accessed 15 May 2009); N. Schrijver, 'Responding to international terrorism: moving the frontiers of international law for "Enduring Freedom"?', (2001) 48 NILR 271–91; Stahn, 'Terrorist acts as "armed attack"'; Stahn, 'International law at crossroads?'; J. Verhoeven, 'Les "étirements" de la légitime défense'; G. K. Walker, 'The lawfulness of Operation Enduring Freedom's self-defense responses', (2003) 37 Valparaiso Un L Rev 489–540; S. Yee, 'The potential impact of the possible US responses to the 9-11 atrocities on the law regarding the use of force and self-defence', (2002) 1 Chinese JIL 287–93.

[382] See *supra*, Section 2.2.1.b (in relation to the application of the 'until clause') and Section 2.2.2.c. (on the conformity with the proportionality principle). As is well-known, the war in Afghanistan and the overarching US 'war on terror' have also raised numerous questions from the perspective of international humanitarian law and international human rights law, related to combatant and POW status, qualification of armed conflicts, torture, 'extraordinary rendition', et cetera. These issues are beyond the scope of our study.

[383] E.g., Dinstein, *War, aggression and self-defence*, 4th edn, pp. 206–8; Franck, 'Terrorism and the right of self-defense'; Greenwood, 'International law and the pre-emptive use of force', 16–17; Paust, 'Use of armed force against terrorists', 535. Also: Stahn, 'Terrorist acts as "armed attack"', 35–6.

[384] See, e.g., B. Langille, 'It's "instant custom": how the Bush doctrine became law after the terrorist attacks of September 11, 2001', (2003) 26 Boston College ICL Rev 145–56.

regarded the *Nicaragua* threshold as the appropriate standard prior to 9/11[385] have construed the precedent more divergently. While most concede that it renders support to a more flexible application of the *ratione personae* dimension, many have stressed that it remains unclear how far exactly the existing threshold has been loosened, and have warned that the highly 'exceptional' context surrounding 'Enduring Freedom' should not be ignored.[386]

There is merit in both views. On the one hand, a number of factors support the idea of a sweeping departure from pre-existing custom. First, the legal basis invoked by the US and the UK was clear. They did not claim that Operation 'Enduring Freedom' was authorized by the Security Council, nor did they make any attempt to obtain such authorization for that matter.[387] Whether or not this attitude was inspired by a deliberate policy of seeking to 'overthrow' the *Nicaragua* threshold,[388] the fact remains that the intervening countries relied on Article 51 UN Charter. Second, the self-defence claim obtained widespread international support. The objection that third-State responses were ambiguous in terms of *opinio iuris*[389] is not convincing. If a considerable number of UN Members refrained from pronouncing on the legal merits, it is no less true that NATO, the OAS, the EU and individual States such as Canada and Australia explicitly framed the operation in terms of individual or collective self-defence. This view is further reinforced by the fact that in

---

Consider also: Arai-Takahashi, 'Shifting boundaries of the right of self-defence', 1094–5. Contra: J. Verhoeven, 'Les "étirements" de la légitime défense', 64.

[385] E.g., authors adopting a more conservative approach in relation to the status of the law as it existed prior to 9/11: Arai-Takahashi, 'Shifting boundaries of the right of self-defence', 1087; Byers, 'Terrorism', 407–8; Condorelli, 'Les attentats du 11 Septembre et leurs suites', 838; Krajewski, 'Der 11.September 2001 und seine Folgen', 188; Müller, 'Legal issues', 245; Myjer and White, 'The Twin Towers attack', 7; Naert, 'The impact of the fight against terrorism on the *Ius ad Bellum*', 146; Schmalenbach, 'The right of self-defence and the "war on terrorism"', §§ 6–7; Schrijver, 'Responding to international terrorism', 284.

[386] E.g., Murphy, 'Terrorism and the concept of "armed attack"', 51; Corten and Dubuisson, 'Opération "liberté immuable"', 53.

[387] E.g., Greenwood, 'International law and the pre-emptive use of force', 21. Several authors have been critical, saying that it would have been more in conformity with the Charter regime to have obtained an explicit authorization from the Security Council. E.g., Charney, 'The use of force against terrorism and international law', 838; Corten and Dubuisson, 'Opération "liberté immuable"', 75; Y. Sandoz, 'Lutte contre le terrorisme et droit international: risques et opportunités', (2002) 3 RSDI 319–54, at 339; J. Verhoeven, 'Les "étirements" de la légitime défense', 76.

[388] In this sense, e.g., Byers, 'Terrorism', 401–2, 410.

[389] E.g., Corten, *Le droit contre la guerre*, pp. 694–5.

resolutions 1368 and 1373 (2001), the UN Security Council for the first time in its existence made a reference to the right of self-defence in connection to attacks by terrorists (or by other non-State actors for that matter).[390] Third, support for the US action was overwhelming *despite* the fact that the nexus between Al Qaeda and the Taleban fell prima facie below the *Nicaragua* threshold. Based on the information available it was generally accepted that the 9/11 attacks were not attributable to the Taleban within the meaning of the ILC DASR.[391] The operation was not 'directed or controlled' by the latter entity as envisaged in Article 8 DASR. Nor did the refusal of the Taleban to extradite Osama Bin Laden amount to the 'acknowledging and adopting' of the attacks as their own as provided for in Article 11 DASR. Even if we concede that certain other forms of operational collaboration vis-à-vis the attacks would be covered by the residual phrase 'substantial involvement' as interpreted by the ICJ, documents such as the Downing Street Report[392] do not offer any significant indications to this end.[393] Rather, the US mainly accused the Taleban of 'allowing the Afghan territory to be used as a base of operation' by Al Qaeda – in other words: it relied on a 'harbouring' doctrine. As pointed out before, such doctrine was implicitly rejected in the *travaux* on the Definition of Aggression and by the ICJ. Comparable claims were generally defeated by the international community in the past. Fourth, Operation 'Enduring Freedom' also presented a departure from earlier practice to the extent that military operations were also directed against the Taleban as such. This would not have posed additional legal problems if the intervening States had merely responded selectively and defensively to attacks by Taleban on US military personnel and installations in the course of the operation.[394] *In casu*, however, the US and the UK made it clear from the very outset that the Taleban was as much a direct target as Al Qaeda itself. This

---

[390] Gray, 'The use of force and the international legal order', p. 604.
[391] Also: Arai-Takahashi, 'Shifting boundaries of the right of self-defence', 1096–8; Corten and Dubuisson, 'Opération "liberté immuable"', 55–70; Krajewski, 'Der 11.September 2001 und seine Folgen', 189–95; Müller, 'Legal issues', 246–7; Ratner, '*Jus ad Bellum* and *Jus in Bello* after September 11', 908. Contra: Murphy, 'Terrorism and the concept of "armed attack"', 50–1; Stahn, 'International law at crossroads?', 223–7 (relying on Article 9 DASR and the ICTY's 'overall control' standard); Wolfrüm and Philipp, 'The status of the Taleban', 595–6 (relying on an application by analogy of Article 16 DASR).
[392] UK Government Press Release, *supra* n. 365.
[393] Contra: Stahn, 'Terrorist acts as "armed attack"', 47.
[394] Paust, 'Use of armed force against terrorists', 543.

policy was criticized by numerous scholars[395] and strongly contrasts with prior assertions by States such as Israel and South Africa that their alleged recourse to self-defence was strictly confined to targeted terorists or rebel groups.

On the other hand, the aforementioned features are counterbalanced by a number of factors calling for a cautious handling of the 9/11 precedent. A first such element is exactly the contrast with previous customary practice. Even if one accepts that the text of Article 51 does not exclude 'armed attacks' by non-State actors, and even if one were to argue that the refutation of analogous self-defence claims in the past was due to considerations of proportionality and self-determination, a 'harbouring' doctrine is still difficult to reconcile with the consensus that emerged as a result of the negotiations on the Friendly Relations Declarations and the Definition of Aggression. A second element concerns the legal ambiguity surrounding the debates and the adoption of resolutions 1368 and 1373. There was no in-depth discussion as to the responsibility of the Taleban regime for the acts of Al Qaeda before the Security Council. Similarly, it remains unclear why the Council Members decided to include a general recognition of the right of self-defence 'in accordance with the UN Charter' in the preambles of resolutions 1368 and 1373 (2001), without at the same time labelling the 9/11 attacks as 'armed attacks'.[396] Third, the fact that the intervening States placed considerable emphasis on the fact that the Taleban was 'harbouring' and/or 'supporting' Al Qaeda[397] could be taken to imply that the nexus between the non-State actors and the territorial State has not become completely redundant for the purpose of determining the applicability or scope of the right of self-defence. Last but not least, Ratner draws attention to what he identifies as the 'Eiffel Tower factor', i.e., the idea that the unprecedented scale and effects of these horrendous attacks may well discount the effect of law

---

[395] *Ibid.*; Krajewski, 'Der 11.September 2001 und seine Folgen', 214; Müller, 'Legal issues', 253–6; Naert, 'The impact of the fight against terrorism on the Ius ad Bellum', 147–8; Schrijver, 'Responding to international terrorism', 290. Contra: Greenwood, 'International law and the pre-emptive use of force', 25 (according to Greenwood, the Taleban exposed its own forces to lawful attack in self-defence by declaring that it would oppose any foreign forces entering its territory to root out Al Qaeda bases).

[396] E.g., Hofmeister, 'To harbour or not to harbour?', 483; Maogoto, 'Walking an international law tightrope', 452; Myjer and White, 'The Twin Towers attack', 9–11; Naert, 'The impact of the fight against terrorism on the *Ius ad Bellum*', 148–9.

[397] Also D. Jinks, 'Remarks', (2003) 97 ASIL Proc 144–6, at 144.

completely.[398] In such context, it could be argued that States reacted as they did on the basis of emotion and empathy, without necessarily endorsing a modification of existing customary law.

These sometimes conflicting reflections suggest a wide range of possible interpretative outcomes depending on one's point of view. At one extreme, the 9/11 precedent could be held to constitute 'instant custom', amounting to a blank cheque vis-à-vis the exercise of self-defence against non-State actors, regardless of State involvement. At the other extreme, 9/11 could be regarded as an exception without precedential value, leaving unaffected the traditional customary threshold.[399] In between these extremes, a variety of options can be identified. One possibility would be that the *Nicaragua* threshold remains relevant only to determine whether the exercise of self-defence should be confined to the hideouts of the non-State actor concerned or could also extend to the infrastructure of the territorial State.[400] Another possibility is that customary law now accepts a flexible interpretation of 'substantial involvement', encompassing the 'harbouring', or 'aiding and abetting' of non-State actors that conduct cross-border attacks.[401] On a more restrictive reading, it could be argued that self-defence is only permissible in response to non-State attacks that are of a similar magnitude as the attacks on the Twin Towers,[402] or can only be exercised when the Security Council has sanctioned it in the concrete case.[403] Which of

---

[398] Ratner, '*Jus ad Bellum* and *Jus in Bello* after September 11', 908 (The reasoning goes that it is 'simply unimaginable that France, Russia, China, or India, … would have responded otherwise had Al Qaeda crashed planes into the Eiffel Tower, the Kremlin, the Forbidden City, or the Taj Mahal'). Also Hofmeister, 'To harbour or not to harbour?', 484.

[399] This is the view apparently adopted by Corten: Corten, *Le droit contre la guerre*, pp. 692–7.

[400] E.g., Müller, 'Legal issues', 257; Paust, 'Use of armed force against terrorists', 540 *et seq*. Apparently using a more flexible threshold: Franck, 'Terrorism and the right of self-defense', 841; J. Brunnée and S. Toope, 'The use of force: international law after Iraq', (2004) 53 ICLQ 785–806, at 795–6; Stahn, 'Terrorist acts as "armed attack"', 50–1.

[401] Arguably falling within this broad category, e.g.: Arai-Takahashi, 'Shifting boundaries of the right of self-defence', 1082; Byers, 'Terrorism', 408–9; Cassese, 'Article 51', p. 1350 (concluding that since 9/11 it is accepted that self-defence may be exercised against attacks by terrorist groups which are tolerated or assisted by a sovereign State); Hofmeister, 'To harbour or not to harbour?', 494–9; Schmalenbach, 'The right of self-defence and the "war on terrorism"', §§ 20–1.

[402] E.g., Cassese, 'Article 51', p. 1352 (referring to 'massive attacks').

[403] Gray, 'The use of force and the international legal order', p. 604 (noting that the right of self-defence against terrorism may exist only in cases where the right has been asserted by the Security Council, since several States regarded the backing of this body as crucial

these scenarios best reflects the shifting trends in customary practice is impossible to determine on the basis of this single incident. Indeed, while the 9/11 attacks offer irrefutable proof of the global threat and increased destructive potential of international terrorism, they do not provide a conclusive answer as to possible changes in the customary boundaries of self-defence. To find such answer, it is imperative to look beyond Operation 'Enduring Freedom'.

5.2.2.b Security doctrines post 9/11

Already in the immediate aftermath of the 9/11 attacks, there were indications that the impact on the law of self-defence would reverberate beyond the Afghan context. In his address to US Congress on 20 September 2001, President Bush issued an unequivocal threat to State sponsors of terrorism around the globe: 'From this day forward, *any nation that continues to harbour or support terrorism will be regarded by the United States as a hostile regime*'.[404] US Congress adopted a Joint Resolution authorizing the use of force against States which 'planned, authorized, committed or aided the terrorist attacks ... or harboured such organizations'.[405] The US self-defence claim as reported to the UN Security Council did not use such broad phrasing, yet warned that '[w]e may find that our self-defence requires further action with respect to other organizations and other States'.[406]

Interestingly, officials on the other side of the Atlantic also paid lip-service to the idea of a radical modification of the customary rules. On 19 September 2001, the German Chancellor acknowledged that NATO 'now also [regarded] a terrorist attack as an attack on a Party to the [Washington]Treaty'.[407] He added that 'under the terms of [Security Council resolution 1368 (2001)], *which further develops international law*, [the US] can and may take equally resolute action against States which support and harbour the perpetrators [of the 9/11 attacks]'.[408]

---

to the US claim of self-defence); Condorelli, 'Les attentats du 11 Septembre et leurs suites', 843.

[404] US President, Address before a Joint Session of the US Congress, 20 September 2001, cited in Murphy, 'Contemporary practice of the United States', 244 (emphasis added).

[405] US Congress, Joint Resolution to Authorize the Use of United States Armed Forces against those Responsible for the Recent Attacks Launched against the United States, 18 September 2001, reprinted in (2002) 40 ILM 1282.

[406] UN Doc. S/2001/946.

[407] Deutscher Bundestag, Plenarprotokoll 14/187, 19 September 2001, 18302.

[408] *Ibid* (emphasis added). See also: S. Talmon, 'Changing views on the use of force: the German position', (2005) 5 Baltic YBIL 41–76, at 53–4.

Two days later, the Council of the European Union explicitly accepted that the US action could also be directed 'against States abetting, supporting or harbouring terrorists' (albeit that the Council seemed to rely on Security Council resolution 1368 instead of Article 51 UN Charter).[409]

The impact of the 9/11 attacks has continued past the launch of Operation 'Enduring Freedom'. Most notably, the promulgation of the US *National Security Strategy* (NSS) of September 2002 can be regarded as a further codification of the 'harbouring and supporting' approach in US doctrine, completing a shift in strategic thinking that was set in motion more than fifteen years earlier by President Reagan and Secretary of State Shultz. In the words of the NSS, the US will make 'no distinction between terrorists and those who knowingly harbour or provide aid to them'.[410] Furthermore, the document proclaims that the US will exercise its 'right of self-defence by acting preemptively against [terrorist groups], to prevent them from doing harm against our people and our country'.[411] In a similar vein, action will be undertaken in order to '[deny] further sponsorship, support, and sanctuary to terrorists by convincing or compelling States to accept their sovereign responsibilities'.[412]

While few countries have gone as far as the US in this respect, several other examples are worth mentioning. In December 2002, for instance, following the suicide attacks against two nightclubs on Bali that killed over eighty Australian tourists, Australian Prime Minister Howard claimed that his country should have the right to attack terrorist groups in neighbouring countries where there was credible evidence that these groups were planning to attack Australia or Australian citizens abroad.[413] In September 2002, President Putin announced that Russia

---

[409] Council of the European Union, Extraordinary Meeting of 21 September 2001, Conclusions and Plan of Action, SIC (2001)990, at http://ec.europa.eu/external_relations/cfsp/doc/concl_21_09_01.htm. See also: NATO Parliamentary Assembly, 2001 Ottawa Fall Session: Declaration on the Fight Against Terrorism, available at www.nato-pa.int/Default.asp?SHORTCUT=331 (websites accessed 15 May 2009).

[410] White House, *National Security Strategy of the United States of America*, 17 September 2002, available at http://georgewbush-whitehouse.archives.gov/nsc/nss/2002/index.html (accessed 15 May 2009), 5.

[411] *Ibid.*, 6.

[412] *Ibid.* See also White House, *National Security Strategy of the United States of America*, March 2006, available at http://georgewbush-whitehouse.archives.gov/nsc/nss/2006/ (accessed 15 May 2009), 12.

[413] See *supra*, Section 4.2.2.c.

reserved the right to defend itself against attacks by pro-Chechen rebels operating from Georgia, warning military actions if the Georgian authorities failed to prevent incursions.[414] Following the Beslan school siege in 2004, Russia moreover declared that it might strike terrorist bases 'in any region of the world'.[415] A press statement of the Ministry of Foreign Affairs of February 2005 states as follows:

> Article 51 of the [UN Charter] confirms the inalienable right of a State to self-defence. This right as now understood in light of new threats to international and national security undoubtedly includes the right to self-defence in the case of a large-scale terrorist attack on a State. That the right to self-defence arises not only in relation to classical armed attacks, that is attacks by one State on another, but also in the case of an attack by terrorists, is confirmed, in particular, by the resolutions of the [UN] Security Council adopted after September 11, 2001.
>
> Where a country has been subjected to a terrorist attack and there are serious grounds to believe that a repetition of this attack from an identified source is inevitable, the State by way of the exercise of its right of self-defence can take necessary measures to liquidate or reduce that lingering threat.[416]

Several European States have also recognized the extension of Article 51 to attacks by non-State actors in the years following the Twin Towers attacks. In 2004, the German Government repeated before the Bundestag that 'in the meantime it is recognized' that non-State actors can commit 'armed attacks'.[417] The Netherlands Defence Doctrine, adopted in September 2005, notes that '[a]n armed attack primarily involves operations by regular forces in the territory of another nation', but acknowledges that '[o]ther cases, such as terrorist actions, can also be regarded as

---

[414] E.g., 'Putin warns of "self-defence" strikes', *BBC News* 11 September 2002; UN Doc. S/2002/1012, 12 September 2002 (Russia). But see: UN Doc. S/2002/1033, 16 September 2002 (Georgia). See also *infra*.

[415] E.g., 'Russia targets top Chechen rebels', *BBC News* 8 September 2004; E. Piper, 'Russia set to hit 'terror' worldwide', *Reuters* 8 September 2004.

[416] Russian Foreign Ministry, 'Information and Press Department Commentary regarding a Russian Media Question concerning Possible Preventive Strikes at Terrorists' Bases', 3 February 2005, available at www.ln.mid.ru/brp_4.nsf/sps/504A679ED357240EC32 56F9D00347AEF (accessed 15 May 2009).

[417] Deutscher Bundestag, Antwort der Bundesregierung, 'Bilanz deutscher VN-Politik in der Zeit der Mitgliedschaft Deutschlands im VN-Sicherheitsrat 2003 und 2004', Drucksache 15/3635, 3 August 2004, 17. However, in a speech in 2003, the Minister of Justice conceded that a broad interpretation of self-defence also ran the risk of blurring concepts. 'Vortrag Bundesjustizministerin Zypries – Friedrich-Ebert-Stiftung', Berlin, 22 September 2003.

such under certain circumstances'.[418] A similar approach can be found in the 2006 White Paper on Terrorism of the French Government:

> Si [une] action terroriste n'a pu être empêchée contre notre territoire ou contre nos intérêts à l'étranger, notre pays pourra recourir à une réponse militaire dans le cadre de l'article 51 de la charte des Nations Unies relatif à la légitime défense. Les modalités et l'intensité de la riposte seront adaptées à la gravité de l'acte commis ainsi qu'aux cibles choisies.[419]

Another interesting document is the African Union Non-Aggression and Common Defence Pact, adopted on 31 January 2005.[420] Although the latter document does not explicitly pronounce on the right of self-defence, Article 1(c) spells out a broad definition of 'aggression', extending to 'the use, intentionally and knowingly, of armed force or any other hostile act by a State, a group of States, an organization of States *or non-State actor(s)* ... (emphasis added)'. The Article includes a list of examples of 'aggression', modelled after Article 3 of the Definition of Aggression. Apart from a provision copying *grosso modo* the text of Article 3(g) Definition of Aggression, it refers to 'the encouragement, support, harbouring or provision of any assistance for the commission of terrorist acts and other violent trans-national organized crimes against a Member State' (Article 1(c)(xi)).

Contrary to the controversy on anticipatory self-defence, the question of self-defence against attacks by terrorist groups or other non-State actors was not addressed in the report of the UN High-Level Panel on Threats, Challenges and Change.[421] Neither was there any discussion on

---

[418] Dutch Ministry of Defence, *Netherlands Defence Doctrine,* 1 September 2005, available at www.defensie.nl/onderwerpen/beleid_en_financien/defensie_doctrine/ (accessed 15 May 2009), 33.
[419] Secrétariat Général de la Défense Nationale, *La France face au terrorisme: Livre Blanc du Gouvernement sur la sécurité intérieure face au terrorisme* (Paris: La Documentation française, 2006), p. 95.
[420] African Union Non-Aggression and Common Defence Pact, Abuja, 31 January 2005, available at www.africa-union.org/root/au/Documents/Treaties/treaties.htm (accessed 15 May 2009).
[421] Remark: the EU submission to the Panel suggests that military action may in certain circumstances be required to deal effectively with terrorist groups, for instance 'when a State is unwilling or unable to deal with the threat posed by a non-State actor on its territory.' Whether such action would be covered by Article 51 or presupposes Security Council authorization is not made explicit. EU General Affairs and External Relations Council, 'Paper for the submission to the High-Level Panel on Threats, Challenges and Change', 17–18 May 2004, available at http://consilium.europa.eu/uedocs/cmsUpload/EU%20written%20contribution2.pdf (accessed 15 May 2009), § 37

the matter in the course of the meeting of Heads of States and Heads of Government during the September 2005 World Summit.[422]

5.2.3 Customary practice after 9/11

5.2.3.a Israel–Syria 2003

The aforementioned statements indicate a fundamental shift in States' *opinio iuris* in that the recourse to force is not automatically excluded in response to attacks by non-State actors and that the right to territorial integrity must in some instances yield to the exercise of another State's right to protect itself under the rubric of self-defence.[423] At first sight, this evolution is corroborated by the occasional invocation of Article 51 UN Charter in such context in more recent years. However, as we will see, the response of the international community vis-à-vis concrete self-defence claims has been anything but coherent.

A first noteworthy incident concerns the Israeli strike on Syrian territory carried out on 5 October 2003.[424] This strike, the first direct attack on Syria since the 1973 War, followed shortly after a suicide attack in Haifa killed nineteen Israeli civilians and wounded at least sixty others. Responsibility was claimed by Islamic Jihad, a notorious terrorist group which had conducted numerous other attacks in previous months and years, and which held its headquarters in Damascus.[425]

Before the Security Council, Israel went to great lengths to detail Syria's support to Islamic Jihad and other terrorist groups.[426] Apart from facilitating the transfer of arms to Palestinian terrorist organizations and glorifying suicide bombings through its State-run media and official institutions, it accused Syria of providing safe harbour and training facilities. Well-known terrorists, such as the Secretary-General of Islamic Jihad, were allowed to operate freely in Damascus. Recruits at government-sponsored training camps were taught how to assemble

---

[422] See, e.g., Corten, *Le droit contre la guerre*, pp. 684–5. However, consider the following exception: UN Doc. A/60/PV.12, 18 September 2005, 11 (Russia, referring to the right of self-defence *inter alia* against external terrorist attacks).
[423] Cf. Stahn, 'Terrorist acts as "armed attack"', 44.
[424] See, e.g., K. Ghattas, 'Syria warns Israel of retaliation', *BBC News* 11 October 2003; D. Jehl, 'Construction was spotted at Syrian camp hit by Israel', *NY Times* 10 October 2003; N. MacFarquhar, 'New rules for Israel and Syria', *NY Times* 13 October 2003. See also: Cassese, 'Article 51', p. 1352; Corten, *Le droit contre la guerre*, pp. 249–50; Gray, *The use of force*, pp. 236–7.
[425] See UN Doc. S/PV.4836, 5 October 2003, 5. [426] UN Doc. S/PV.4836, 5–7.

bombs, conduct kidnappings, gather intelligence, et cetera. Israel even alleged that Syrian officials had coordinated and/or instructed a number of past terrorist attacks. In light of Syria's persistent refusal to end its support for terrorism, Israel had decided to conduct a strike against the Ein Saheb base, a terrorist training camp, located some fifteen miles from Damascus. This was justified as a 'measured defensive response' 'in accordance with Article 51 UN Charter', 'designed to prevent further armed attacks against Israeli civilians in which Syria was complicit'.[427] Israel also made cursory reference to Security Council resolution 1373 (2001), which made 'absolutely clear that States must prevent acts of terrorism and refrain from any form of financing, support, safe harbour for or toleration of terrorist groups'.[428]

In turn, Syria argued that the Israeli strike had caused material damage to 'a civilian site' and denounced the operation as an act of aggression and a serious escalation threatening regional and international security.[429] Future breaches of Syrian territorial integrity would result in a defensive response by Syria.[430] The Arab world unequivocally joined Syria in condemning the Israeli 'aggression'.[431]

In stark contrast with the broad support for the intervention in Afghanistan, most Security Council Members condemned the Israeli raid. In spite of the dreadful attack in Haifa, the operation was denounced as contrary to the UN Charter by twelve out of fifteen Council Members, namely Pakistan, Spain, China, Germany, France, Bulgaria, Chile, Mexico, Angola, Guinea, Cameroon and, of course, Syria itself.[432] The UK regarded the Israeli operation as 'unacceptable', yet adopted a somewhat ambiguous position.[433] While criticizing Israel for undermining the peace process and escalating the situation, it recognized 'that terrorists are continuing to attack Israel and that they are being permitted to do so'. It was nonetheless clear from resolution 1373 (2001) that there was a 'heavy responsibility on all those who are in a position to act against terrorism to do so'. Russia merely cautioned

---

[427] Ibid., 7. [428] Ibid., 6.
[429] UN Doc. S/2003/940, 5 October 2003 (Syria, requesting an emergency meeting of the Security Council).
[430] See, e.g., N. MacFarquhar, 'New rules for Israel and Syria', NY Times 13 October 2003.
[431] UN Doc. S/2003/949 (League of Arab States), 7 October 2003. See also the statements by the representatives of the OAS, Lebanon, Algeria, Morocco, Jordan, Egypt, Tunisia, Palestine, Kuwait, Saudi Arabia, Iran, Bahrain, Libya, Yemen, Qatar and Sudan in UN Doc. S/PV.4836, 14 et seq.
[432] UN Doc. S/PV.4836, 8–13. [433] Ibid., 9.

against increased confrontation in the Middle East.[434] Finally, the US called for restraint, but emphasized that 'Syria [was] on the wrong side of the war on terrorism': 'We have been clear of the need for Syria to cease harbouring terrorist groups. Specific directions for terrorist acts continue to be issued from terrorist groups based in Syria. ... [T]his was unacceptable and intolerable'.[435] In the end, even if Israel escaped a formal condemnation by the Security Council – no resolution was put to the vote – it is striking that no general support was expressed for a wide right to use force against terrorist camps in a third State.[436] Implicit support for such right can, however, be deduced from the international response to the Second Lebanon War in the summer of 2006.

5.2.3.b   Israel–Lebanon 2006 [437]

In 2000, Israel pulled back its troops from southern Lebanon and retreated behind the UN-monitored 'Blue Line'. In subsequent years, relations between the two countries remained tense yet relatively stable. Occasionally, Lebanon complained of violations of its airspace by Israeli fighters; Israel, in turn, reserved the right to act in self-defence in response to repeated rocket attacks by Hezbollah.[438] In general, military confrontations were limited and not subject to significant international scrutiny.

All this changed when on 12 July 2006, Hezbollah militants attacked an Israeli military patrol, capturing two soldiers and killing three.[439] In

---

[434] *Ibid.*, 10.
[435] *Ibid.*, 14. Remark: although initially there existed some uncertainty as to the nature of the target of the Israeli operation, US intelligence also indicated that the Ein Saheb camp had been used as a training base for various Palestinian organizations. Syria contended that the camp was a civilian area but nonetheless denied the media access to the site. See: K. Ghattas, 'Syria warns Israel of retaliation', *BBC News*, 11 October 2003; D. Jehl, 'Construction was spotted at Syrian camp hit by Israel', *NY Times* 10 October 2003.
[436] Gray, *The use of force*, p. 237.
[437] See also: T. Ruys, 'Crossing the Thin Blue Line: an inquiry into Israel's recourse to self-defense against Hezbollah', (2007) 43 Stanford JIL 265–94.
[438] See, e.g., Israeli communications: UN Doc. S/2000/512, 31 May 2000; UN Doc. S/2003/603, 2 June 2003; UN Doc. S/2003/758, 24 July 2003; UN Doc. S/2003/976, 9 October 2003; UN Doc. S/2004/465, 8 June 2004 (reporting that Israel had responded to rocket attacks by the PFLP by 'measured defensive action, in accordance with its right and duty of self-defence'). Lebanese communications: UN Doc. S/2002/135, 31 January 2002; UN Doc. S/2002/1038, 17 September 2002; UN Doc. S/2003/147, 4 February 2003.
[439] See: Report of the Secretary-General on the United Nations Interim Force in Lebanon, 21 July 2006, UN Doc. S/2006/560, §§ 2 *et seq.*; A. Harel, 'Hezbollah kills 8 soldiers, kidnaps two in offensive on northern border', *Haaretz*, 13 July 2006; G. Myre and

response, Israel engaged in military operations to retrieve the captured soldiers while carrying out air strikes against several targets in Lebanon, including Beirut airport. The incident escalated in the following days, as aerial bombardments by the Israeli Defence Forces (IDF) were answered by a rainstorm of Katyusha rockets targeting Haifa and other cities in northern Israel, and Israeli ground forces clashed with Hezbollah militants in southern Lebanon.[440] The so-called 'Second Lebanon War' ended one month later, when a frail ceasefire was put in place at the order of the UN Security Council.[441] In all, 116 Israeli soldiers and forty-three Israeli civilians lost their lives. On the Lebanese side, some 1,109 people – mostly civilians – were killed, as well as twenty-eight Lebanese soldiers.[442] Scores of people on both sides were injured or forced to flee their homes.

While Israel reported its action to the Security Council as an exercise of the right of self-defence,[443] there was some ambiguity in relation to its legal argumentation.[444] On the one hand, it argued that 'responsibility' for the 'act of war' lay with the government of Lebanon and that the attack of 12 July was the 'action of a sovereign State'.[445] On the other

---

S. Erlanger, 'Israelis Enter Lebanon after attacks' *NY Times* 13 July 2006; A. Shadid and S. Wilson, 'Hezbollah raid opens 2nd front for Israel', *Washington Post* 13 July 2006.

[440] See, e.g., E. Cannizzaro, 'Entités non-étatiques et régime international de l'emploi de la force: une étude sur le cas de la réaction israélienne au Liban', (2007) 111 RGDIP 333–53; F. Dubuisson, 'La guerre du Liban de l'été 2006 et le droit de la légitime défense', (2006) 39 RBDI 529–64; G. Redsell, 'Illegitimate, unnecessary and disproportionate: Israel's use of force in Lebanon', (2007) 3 Cambridge Student L Rev 70–85; N. Ronzitti, 'The 2006 conflict in Lebanon and international law', (2007) 16 Italian YBIL 3–19; R. Van Steenberghe, 'La légitime défense en droit international: une evolution à la suite du conflit israélo-libanais?', (2007) *Journal des Tribunaux* 421–4; S. Weber, 'Die israelischen Militäraktionen im Libanon und in den besetzten palästinensischen Gebieten 2006 und ihre Vereinbarkeit mit dem Völkerrecht', (2006) 44 AdV 460–80; A. Zimmerman, 'The Second Lebanon War: *Jus ad Bellum, Jus in Bello* and the issue of proportionality', (2007) 11 MPYBUNL 99–141.

[441] UN SC Res. 1701 (2006) of 11 August 2006.

[442] 'Middle East crisis: facts and figures', *BBC News* 31 August 2006, available at http://news.bbc.co.uk/2/hi/middle_east/5257128.stm (accessed 15 May 2009).

[443] UN Doc. S/2006/515, 12 July 2006 (Israel).

[444] On the ambiguity of the legal claims of Israel and Lebanon, see Dubuisson, 'La guerre du Liban de l'été 2006', 545–9.

[445] See UN Doc. S/2006/515; 'PM Olmert: Lebanon is responsible and will bear the consequences', 12 July 2006, available at www.mfa.gov.il/MFA/Government/Communiques/2006/PM+Olmert+-+Lebanon+is+responsible+and+will+bear+the+consequences+12-Jul-2006.htm; 'Statement by FM Livni on Hizbullah attack from Lebanon', 12 July 2006, available at www.mfa.gov.il/MFA/About+the+Ministry/MFA+Spokesman/2006/Statement+by+FM+Livni+on+Hizbullah+attack+from+Lebanon+12-Jul-2006.htm; 'Statement by Foreign Ministry Deputy DG Gideon Meir', 13 July 2006, available at

hand, while Israel accused Iran and Syria of 'supporting and embracing those who carried out this attack',[446] it refrained from identifying any actual support to Hezbollah on the part of the Lebanese Government. Rather, it stressed that its 'ineptitude and inaction ... [had] led to a situation in which it [had] not exercised its jurisdiction for many years'.[447] In other words, Israel relied on the incapability of the Lebanese authorities to disarm and dismantle Hezbollah in accordance with Security Council Resolution 1559 (2004)[448] to justify 'appropriate actions to secure the release of the kidnapped soldiers and bring an end to the shelling that [terrorized] [its] citizens'.[449] Interestingly, while Israel 'held the government of Lebanon responsible', it asserted that it was 'concentrating its response carefully, mainly on Hezbollah strongholds, positions and infrastructure'.[450] Observing that Lebanon had long been held hostage by Hezbollah, Israel even argued that its military operations, if successful, would benefit the Lebanese authorities.[451]

Unsurprisingly, the latter argument did not entirely convince the principal addressee. On 13 July, Lebanon called for an urgent meeting of the Security Council. It declared that it was 'not aware of the events that occurred and are occurring on the international Lebanese border' and did not endorse them.[452] Refuting responsibility for the actions of Hezbollah, Lebanon strongly condemned 'the Israeli aggression that targeted ... the vital and civil Lebanese infrastructure'.[453]

In the course of a first Security Council debate, it became clear that many Council members supported Israel's invocation of self-defence in principle even though they refrained from speaking out on Lebanon's possible responsibility for the Hezbollah attacks.[454] Only China and

---

www.mfa.gov.il/MFA/About+the+Ministry/MFA+Spokesman/2006/Statement+by +Foreign+Ministry+Deputy+DG+Gideon+Meir+13-Jul-2006.htm (websites accessed 15 May 2009). Remark: several official statements stressed that Hezbollah was a member of the Lebanese Government.

[446] UN Doc. S/2006/515.   [447] Ibid.
[448] SC Res. 1559 (2004) of 2 September 2004; SC Res. 1680 (2006) of 17 May 2006.
[449] UN Doc. S/2006/515. Also: 'Statement by FM Livni'.
[450] UN Doc. S/PV.5489, 14 July 2006, 6.
[451] UN Doc. S/PV.5489, 7; UN Doc. S/PV.5493, 21 July 2006, 11.
[452] UN Doc. S/2006/518, 13 July 2006 (Lebanon).
[453] Ibid. UN Doc. S/2006/529, 17 July 2006 (Lebanon); UN Doc. S/PV.5489, 4–5; UN Doc. S/PV.5493, 13.
[454] UN Doc. S/PV.5489, 14 July 2006, 9 (Argentina), 10 (US), 12 (Japan), 12 (UK), 14 (Peru), 15 (Denmark), 17 (France).

Qatar identified Israel's response as 'armed aggression'.[455] Most Council members showed sympathy for the Lebanese authorities and stressed the need for them to exercise full control over the entire territory. Virtually all expressed concern at the targeting of civilians and civilian infrastructure in Lebanon and called for restraint, with several countries, such as Russia and France, expressly condemning the disproportionate nature of Israel's campaign.

In the following days, Israel's claim received implicit and explicit support from several corners, although often in combination with deep concern at the loss of civilian life. The applicability of Article 51 UN Charter was recognized implicitly or explicitly by the G8,[456] the US Senate,[457] the Australian Prime Minister,[458] and even by UN Secretary-General Annan.[459]

The open debate in the Security Council of 21 July shows a broadly similar picture. Notwithstanding deep concern at or outright condemnation of the excessive use of force, a majority of participants agreed as a matter of principle that Israel had the right to defend itself against the attacks by Hezbollah. This position was held *inter alia* by the United States, the (then) twenty-five Member States of the European Union, eleven other UN Members aligning themselves with the EU Statement, Russia, Canada, Australia, Norway, Brazil, Argentina, Peru, Guatemala and Ghana.[460] On the other hand, the twenty-two member League of Arab States[461]

---

[455] *Ibid.*, 10 (Qatar), 11 (PRC). Other States labelled the actions as retaliatory: 7 (Russia), 13 (DRC).
[456] G8 St. Petersburg Summit Declaration, Middle East, 16 July 2006, available at http://en.g8russia.ru/docs/21.html (accessed 15 May 2009).
[457] US Senate, Resolution Condemning Hezbollah and Hamas and their State Sponsors and Supporting Israel's Exercise of its Right to Self-defense, 18 July 2006, 109th Congress, 2nd Session, S. Res. 534.
[458] 'Israel Acting in Self-Defence, Says Howard', *ABC News Online* 16 July 2006.
[459] See, e.g., UN Secretary-General Press Release, 'Secretary-General says "Immediate Cessation of Hostilities" needed in Lebanon, describes package aimed at lasting solution, in Security Council briefing', UN Doc. SG/SM/10570, SC/8781, 20 July 2006.
[460] UN Doc. S/PV.5493, 16–17 (US), 19 (Slovakia); UN Doc. S/PV.5493 (Resumption 1), 2 (Russia), 3 (Greece), 4 (Peru), 6 (UK), 7 (Denmark), 8 (Ghana), 9 (Argentina), 16 (EU plus Bulgaria, Romania, Turkey, Croatia, the former Yugoslav Republic of Macedonia, Albania, Bosnia-Herzegovina, Serbia, Iceland, Ukraine and the Republic of Moldova), 18 (Switzerland), 19 (Brazil), 23 (Norway), 27 (Australia), 28 (Turkey), 39 (Canada), 40 (Guatemala).
[461] While the permanent observer of the LAS explicitly referred to 'Israeli acts of aggression', most Member States submitted statements of their own in which they vehemently condemned the Israeli aggression. Some, such as Egypt, took a more moderate stance. E.g., UN Doc. S/PV.5493 (Resumption 1), 22–3 (Egypt), 32 (Djibouti).

condemned the Israeli aggression, as did China, Iran, Cuba and Venezuela. Other countries, such as India and Indonesia, merely condemned the disproportionate character of Israel's action. Again, while some Western countries were openly critical of the involvement of Syria and Iran in the activities of Hezbollah,[462] all States expressed support for Lebanon's sovereignty and territorial integrity. The consensus was that the crisis could only be solved through a fully fledged extension of Lebanese authority over its southern territory as envisaged in Security Council resolution 1559 (2004). Resolution 1701 (2006) clearly reflects this consensus insofar as it 'welcomed' the decision of the Lebanese Government to deploy 15,000 troops in South Lebanon following the withdrawal of the Israeli army, and 'emphasized' 'the importance of the extension of the control of the Government of Lebanon over all Lebanese territory ... for it to exercise its full sovereignty, so that there will be ... no authority other than that of the Government of Lebanon'.[463]

In the end, scrutiny of third-State reactions teaches us that (1) a majority of the international community regarded the self-defence claim as valid in principle; and (2) that criticism focused almost exclusively on the obviously disproportionate character of Israel's Operation 'Just Reward'.[464] The implication seems to be that many States not only regarded the Hezbollah attack of 12 July as sufficiently 'grave' to trigger Article 51 UN Charter,[465] but also saw no problems from a 'ratione personae' dimension. Nonetheless, the traditional rules on State responsibility enshrined in Articles 4, 8 and 11 DASR clearly did not allow the attack of 12 July to be imputed to Lebanon. First, even if – as Israel emphasized – Hezbollah held a number of seats in the Lebanese Parliament and was a minority partner in the Cabinet,[466] the Hezbollah

---

[462] E.g., UN Doc. S/PV.5489, 10 (US); UN Doc. S/PV.5493 (Resumption 1), at 6 (UK), 39 (Canada).
[463] SC Res. 1701 (2006) of 11 August 2006.
[464] E.g., Cannizzaro, 'Entités non-étatiques et régime international de l'emploi de la force', 341; Y. Ronen, 'Israel, Hizbollah, and the Second Lebanon War', (2006) 9 YBIHL, at 385, 390; Van Steenberghe, 'La légitime défense en droit international', 423. Also, more cautiously: Dubuisson, 'La guerre du Liban de l'été 2006', 549–53. Remark: the United States was probably the only country not to express criticism at the lack of proportionality in Israel's conduct.
[465] See also: Dubuisson, 'La guerre du Liban de l'été 2006', 539; Ronen, 'The Second Lebanon War', 370–4; Weber, 'Die israelischen Militäraktionen', 464; Zimmerman, 'The Second Lebanon War', 109. Seemingly contra: Redsell, 'Israel's use of force in Lebanon', 72–4; Van Steenberghe, 'La légitime défense en droit international', 422.
[466] Hezbollah had participated as a political party in Lebanese elections since 1992 and at the time of the crisis held fourteen seats in the 128 member Parliament. It held two

fighters that launched the attack did not qualify as formal organs of the States within the meaning of Articles 4–5 DASR: they were not formally incorporated into the State structure, nor were they empowered by virtue of the law to act on behalf of the State.[467] They were not de facto State agents either: Lebanon was in no position to exercise 'effective' or even 'overall' control over the activities of Hezbollah, let alone was the latter organization 'completely dependent' on Lebanon.[468] Furthermore, rather than 'adopting and acknowledging' Hezbollah's conduct as its own, the Lebanese Government immediately denied responsibility and denounced the attack.[469]

Again, if Syria and Iran were accused of providing material support, weapons supplies and financial aid to Hezbollah,[470] no such allegations were made vis-à-vis the Lebanese authorities. Rather, *in casu* it was Lebanon's failure to prevent attacks by non-State actors that was held to activate Israel's right of self-defence. Whether Lebanon had breached its legal duty to exercise 'due diligence' in preventing cross-border harm stands open to debate.[471] In the end, the widespread international support for the Lebanese authorities and the implicit recognition in resolution 1701 (2006) that Lebanon had so far been unable to exercise jurisdiction over all of its territory reinforce the view that it was not in any way directly responsible for or complicit in the attack of 12 July.[472]

Against this background, the acceptance of Israel's right of self-defence renders support to the idea that the international response to the 9/11 attacks marked a new departure for the interpretation of Article 51 UN Charter *ratione personae*. More concretely, it appears to constitute an important precedent recognizing that attacks by non-State actors

---

ministerial posts (Energy and Water, and Labour), and had 'endorsed' the position of Fawzi Salloukh, Minister for Foreign Affairs.

[467] See Cannizzaro, 'Entités non-étatiques et régime international de l'emploi de la force', 335–6; Redsell, 'Israel's use of force in Lebanon', 77; Ronen, 'The Second Lebanon War', 379; Ruys, 'Crossing the Thin Blue Line', 276–7; Zimmerman, 'The Second Lebanon War', 110–11.

[468] See Cannizzaro, 'Entités non-étatiques et régime international de l'emploi de la force', 335–6; Redsell, 'Israel's use of force in Lebanon', 77–8; Zimmerman, 'The Second Lebanon War', 111–15.

[469] Also: Ronen, 'The Second Lebanon War', 380–1. [470] See *supra*, notes 446, 462.

[471] Ronen suggests that any attempt on behalf of the Lebanese armed forces to disband Hezbollah would probably have led to an all-out civil war. Since the 'due diligence' rule only requires a State to take 'reasonable measures', such demand might have been a bridge too far. See Ronen, 'The Second Lebanon War', 383–4.

[472] *Ibid.*, 384–5.

may exceptionally constitute 'armed attacks' in the sense of Article 51 UN Charter, warranting defensive measures when the territorial State is unwilling or unable to prevent cross-border attacks.[473]

Two reservations must, however, be made. First of all, the ambiguity of State reactions makes it difficult to deduce clear *opinio iuris* with respect to possible shifts in customary practice.[474] States that recognized Israel's right of self-defence did not explain why the right was applicable in the present circumstances and refrained from elaborating on the legality of self-defence against attacks by non-State actors. No express reference was made to resolutions 1368 or 1373 (2001). This is all the more problematic when taking into account the unique characteristics of the situation in southern Lebanon (our second reservation), most notably the considerable degree of territorial control exercised by Hezbollah.[475] Indeed, Hezbollah has often been described as 'a State within the State'.[476] In those areas with a large Shiite majority – namely the south of Lebanon, the Bequaa valley, as well as several Shiite suburbs of Beirut – Hezbollah exercised a range of functions traditionally borne by the government. In contrast with the official authorities, it acted as the primary military and security provider in the south, maintaining a visible presence in the vicinity of the Blue Line and organizing observation posts and checkpoints.[477] In addition, in the aforementioned Shiite areas it '[exercised] almost exclusive control and [maintained] a dense social network [providing] food, medicine, education, and basic services'.[478] According to UN sources, it was at the time operating at least four hospitals, twelve clinics, twelve schools and two agricultural centres at the time, in addition to operating its own television station and radio station.[479]

---

[473] In this sense Ronen, 'The Second Lebanon War', 385; Van Steenberghe, 'La légitime défense en droit international', 423.

[474] Also Corten, *Le droit contre la guerre*, p. 698; Dubuisson, 'La guerre du Liban de l'été 2006', 551–3; Gray, *The use of force*, p. 239.

[475] Emphasizing the degree of territorial control: Cannizzaro, 'Entités non-étatiques et régime international de l'emploi de la force', 338 *et seq.*; Zimmerman, 'The Second Lebanon War', 120.

[476] See Ruys, 'Crossing the Thin Blue Line', 287–90.

[477] *Ibid.*, 288–9. See also: Report of the Secretary-General on the United Nations Interim Force in Lebanon, 21 July 2006, UN Doc. S/2006/560, §§ 27–8.

[478] D. Byman, 'Should Hezbollah be next?', (2003) 82 *Foreign Affairs* Nov/Dec 54–66, at 60.

[479] See references in Ruys, 'Crossing the Thin Blue Line', 289. According to one source: 'Hezbollah [was doing] everything a government should do, from collecting the garbage, to running hospitals and repairing schools.' See H. Schuster, 'Hezbollah's secret weapon', *CNN News* 25 July 2006.

In such peculiar circumstances, one might wonder whether Hezbollah's conduct could not be imputed to the Lebanese government by virture of the somewhat neglected rule laid down in Article 9 DASR.[480] Under that provision: 'The conduct of a person or group of persons shall be considered an act of a State ... if the person or group of persons is in fact exercising elements of the governmental authority in the absence or default of the official authorities and in circumstances such as to call for the exercise of those elements of authority'. According to the ILC Commentary, it presupposes that a partial or total collapse of the regular government has occurred, which led to individuals performing conduct which would normally be exercised by governmental authorities.[481] The situation envisaged is not that of a general de facto government. Rather it presupposes the existence of a government in office and of 'State machinery whose place is taken by irregulars or whose action is supplemented in certain cases'.[482] This may happen on part of the territory of a State which is for the time being out of control, or in other specific circumstances. While much remains unclear with regard to the principles governing this scenario,[483] some elements suggest that the rule could be applicable in the Lebanese context. Especially when looking at the preponderant military role of Hezbollah in the South, in combination with the near absence of the official Lebanese authorities, one might say that Hezbollah exercised 'elements of governmental authority in the default of the official authorities' in the sense of Article 9 DASR.[484] On the other hand, the application of Article 9 DASR meets with a number of obstacles.[485] First, according to the ILC Commentary, it requires that the State concerned had knowledge of the operations of the private persons or groups of persons and did not specifically object to

---

[480] See Ruys, 'Crossing the Thin Blue Line', 287–90.
[481] ILC, 'Commentary on the Draft Articles', 49.   [482] Ibid.
[483] See, e.g., J. A. Hessbruegge, 'The historical development of the doctrines of attributability and due diligence in international law', (2004) 36 NYU JILP 265–306, at 275.
[484] This leaves open a third precondition, viz. the presence of 'circumstances such as to call for the exercise of those elements of [governmental] authority'. This is arguably the vaguest of the three criteria. The ILC Commentary suggests that it conveys the idea that some exercise of governmental functions was called for, though not necessarily the conduct in question. According to Ronen, '[t]he Lebanese position, advocated more enthusiastically by Hezbollah than by the government but nonetheless agreed between the two, is that the defence of the border with Israel is vital against Israel's aggression'. See Ronen, 'The Second Lebanon War', 380.
[485] See also Cahin, 'L'Etat défaillant en droit international ', pp. 202–4.

them.[486] The rule of Article 7 DASR, according to which ultra vires conduct of State organs remains imputable to the State, does not apply. Hence, even if one would accept that the Lebanese Government had de facto outsourced national defence to a paramilitary group, the fact remains that the 12 July attack was arguably in excess of whatever tacit permission Hezbollah might have received from the government.[487] Second, a creative and somewhat unorthodox application of Article 9 DASR imputing the attack to the State of Lebanon may not be justified in light of the fact that States generally did not hold Lebanon responsible for the actions of Hezbollah. Third, it must be recognized that Article 9 DASR is in any event only applicable in highly exceptional circumstances and therefore does little to 'defuse' the broader controversy on self-defence against attacks by non-State actors. Its limited 'reach' is easily demonstrated when we look at another recent instance of State practice, namely the Turkish intervention in northern Iraq in 2007–8.

5.2.3.c   Turkey–Iraq 2007–8[488]

After 2004, Turkey suffered an intensifying campaign of Kurdish separatist violence, claiming over 1,500 lives in a period of a few years.[489] Attacks mainly originated from a group of some estimated 3,000–3,500 PKK fighters, operating from bases in the mountainous border region in northern Iraq. Against growing Turkish frustration at the lack of action undertaken by Iraqi authorities or by US forces present in Iraq, a series of attacks in October 2007 proved to be the straw that broke the camel's back. On 7 October, thirteen Turkish soldiers were killed in an ambush, days after PKK gunmen had shot dead thirteen village guards on a bus. On 21 October, another cross-border attack resulted in the killing of twelve soldiers and the capture of eight others.

After the Grand National Assembly overwhelmingly gave the green light for military incursions into northern Iraq, Turkey initiated aerial

---

[486] ILC, 'Commentary on the Draft Articles', 49 (referring to the *Yeager* case of the Iran–US Claims Tribunal). Authors holding Article 9 DASR to be inapplicable to the Lebanese context: Cannizzaro, 'Entités non-étatiques et régime international de l'emploi de la force', 336; Redsell, 'Israel's use of force in Lebanon', 77; Ronen, 'The Second Lebanon War', 380.

[487] ibid., 380.

[488] The present section is based on: T. Ruys, '*Quo vadit Ius ad Bellum?*: A legal analysis of Turkey's military operations against the PKK in Northern Iraq', (2008) 9 Melbourne JIL 334–64.

[489] See, e.g., H. J. Barkey, 'Turkey and the PKK' in R. J. Art and L. Richardson, *Democracy and counterterrorism: lessons from the past* (Washington, DC: USIP, 2007), pp. 343–81.

bombardments and artillery attacks, combined with a small-scale hot pursuit operation to retrieve the captured soldiers.[490] Subsequently, on 21 February 2008, the Turkish military launched a major ground offensive (Operation 'Sun'), sending several thousand troops into northern Iraq. Following the conclusion of the ground operation one week later, the Turkish military again shifted its focus to similar operations within Turkey's own south-eastern provinces.[491]

Despite the magnitude of the operations, Turkey felt little need to provide a clear legal basis for its conduct. President Gül spoke of his country's 'readiness and right' to intervene in northern Iraq.[492] Stressing that the goal of the operation was to 'prevent the region from being a permanent and safe base for the terrorists',[493] he warned that Turkey would 'not tolerate those who help and harbour terrorists'.[494] No formal justification was made public, nor was the Security Council informed. One of the more elaborate statements was delivered after the conclusion of Operation 'Sun', when Turkey submitted a *note verbale* to the Human Rights Council, declaring that:

> The counter-terrorism operation carried out ... in northern Iraq was limited in scope, geography and duration. It targeted solely the PKK ... terrorist presence in the region. Turkish military authorities took all possible measures to ensure the security of civilians and to avoid collateral damage. As a result, there has been no civilian casualty. Turkey remains a staunch advocate of the territorial integrity and sovereignty of Iraq.[495]

---

[490] (2007) 53 *Keesing's* 48219–20.
[491] Nonetheless, in subsequent months, air raids were still being launched occasionally against PKK targets within northern Iraq. See, e.g., 'Turkey hits rebel targets in Iraq', *BBC News* 29 March 2008; 'Military: Turkish jets have struck Kurdish rebel target in northern Iraq', *IHT* 8 June 2008; 'Turkish jets target PKK in Iraq', *BBC News* 24 July 2008. Remark: in October 2008, the Turkish Parliament extended the army's mandate to carry out cross-border raids against Kurdish rebels in northern Iraq by one year: 'Turkey extends Iraq raid window', *BBC News* 8 October 2008.

On a more positive note, see: 'Iraqi leader gives PKK ultimatum', *BBC News* 23 March 2009; C. Recknagel, 'Iraq, Turkey nearing deal to deprive PKK of bases', *Radio Free Europe* 24 March 2009.
[492] See 'Turkey "right to intervene" in Iraq', *Al Jazeera* 3 December 2007.
[493] See S. Tavernise and S. Arsu, 'Turkey says it has sent ground troops into Iraq', *NY Times* 22 February 2008.
[494] See 'Europe again warns against Turkish intervention in Iraq', *Deutsche Welle* 22 October 2007.
[495] Note verbale from the Permanent Mission of Turkey to the Human Rights Council, 26 March 2008, UN Doc. A/HRC/7/G/15.

THE 'ARMED ATTACK' REQUIREMENT *RATIONE PERSONAE* 459

The Turkish actions ostensibly add to the evidence in customary practice suggesting a more flexible construction of the *ratione personae* requirement. First, the nexus between the Iraqi authorities and the PKK presence in northern Iraq fell below the *Nicaragua* threshold.[496] Rather than endorsing the PKK attacks, Iraq denounced them. Iraq was not exercising 'overall' or 'effective' control over the PKK, let alone giving specific instructions for attacks against a friendly neighbour. Furthermore, even if Iraq was undoubtedly aware of the presence of the PKK fighters and even if the (Iraqi) Kurdish regional authorities arguably displayed a degree of sympathy with their actions, there was no evidence of active support to the PKK. Rather, it appears that – in spite of the conclusion of a new security arrangement between the countries concerned in September 2007[497] – Iraq simply failed to take appropriate action to prevent cross-border attacks from its territory. This is illustrated by Iraq's public refusal to extradite suspects to Turkey or to directly combat the PKK, as well as by the long overdue closure of PKK offices.[498] It may finally be observed that contrary to Hezbollah in Lebanon, the PKK was not exercising any significant form of territorial control in northern Iraq, nor was it exercising elements of governmental authority.

Second, while the international community urged Turkey to pursue a diplomatic solution to the conflict, the response to the actual operations in northern Iraq was surprisingly muted. The United States consistently labelled the PKK 'a common enemy' and promised to step up efforts to combat the terrorist group.[499] More concretely, the US actually aided Turkey by supplying actionable military intelligence about PKK whereabouts and by clearing northern Iraqi airspace to enable Turkish strikes.[500] With regard to Operation 'Sun', the US merely insisted that the Turks needed 'to move quickly, achieve their objective and get out',

---

[496] See Ruys, '*Quo vadit Ius ad Bellum?*', 353–5.   [497] See (2007) 53 *Keesing's* 48151.
[498] See, e.g., Iraqi Ministry of Foreign Affairs Press Release, 'Foreign Minister receives his Turkish counterpart in Baghdad', 23 October 2007; Iraqi Ministry of Foreign Affairs Press Release, Republic of Iraq, 'Steps taken by Iraqi government to handle the last developments on the Iraqi–Turkish borders', 11 November 2007, available at www.mofa.gov.iq/index.aspx (accessed 15 May 2009); Report of the Secretary-General pursuant to Paragraph 6 of Resolution 1770 (2007), 14 January 2008, UN Doc S/2008/19; T. Daloglu, 'Kurdish terror and the West: a terrorist is a terrorist, plain and simple', *Washington Times* 30 October 2007; 'Iraq warns Turkey over incursion', *BBC News* 23 February 2008.
[499] See 'US labels Kurdish group as terrorist', *CNN News* 11 January 2008; (2007) 53 *Keesing's* 48265.
[500] See (2007) 53 *Keesing's* 48316.

and that the incursion 'should be as short and precisely targeted as possible'.[501] The EU's reaction was a mixture of sympathy and concern. On the one hand, it expressed understanding for Turkey's need to protect its citizens.[502] At the same time, it called on Turkey 'to exercise restraint, to respect the territorial integrity of Iraq and refrain from any military action that could undermine regional peace and stability'. Following the launch of Operation 'Sun', the EU issued another statement which resorted to the following ambiguous formula:

> While recognizing Turkey's need to protect its population from terrorism, the Presidency calls on Turkey to refrain from taking any disproportionate military action and to respect Iraq's territorial integrity, human rights and the rule of law. It also calls on Turkey to limit its military activities to those which are absolutely necessary for achieving its main purpose – the protection of the Turkish population from terrorism.[503]

In sum, like the US, the EU refrained from taking a clear stance on the legal merits of the intervention, instead emphasizing the need for proportionality and – eventually – for a political solution. Reactions from other States were largely analogous.[504] It may be observed in this context that – contrary to the Israeli intervention in Lebanon – Turkey complied reasonably well with the proportionality criterion. Military operations were directed against PKK hideouts and do not seem to have exceeded this objective. The civilian population and infrastructure was kept out of

---

[501] See 'Turkey must end Iraq raid – Bush', *BBC News* 28 February 2008. Remark: the Turkish ground offensive was terminated one day after the aforementioned statements by President Bush and US Defence Secretary Gates. This striking conjunction of circumstances fuelled speculations that the withdrawal was a concession to American demands. Turkish authorities nonetheless denied rumours of foreign pressure and claimed that Operation 'Sun' was terminated because it had achieved its objective.

[502] See 'Europe again warns against Turkish intervention in Iraq', *Deutsche Welle* 22 October 2007; Presidency of the EU, Press Release, 'EU Presidency Statement on the terrorist attacks of the PKK in Turkey over the weekend', 22 October 2007, available at www.eu2007.pt/UE/vEN/Noticias_Documentos/Declaracoes_PESC/20071022PESC PKK.htm; Presidency of the EU, Press Release, 'EU Presidency Statement on the military actions undertaken by Turkey on Iraqi territory', 17 December 2007, available at www.eu2007.pt/UE/vEN/Noticias_Documentos/Declaracoes_PESC/20071217Iraque.htm (websites accessed 15 May 2009).

[503] Presidency of the EU, Press Release, 'EU Presidency Statement on the military action undertaken by Turkey in Iraqi territory', 25 February 2008, available at www.eu2008.si/en/News_and_Documents/CFSP_Statements/February/0225MZZturkey.html (accessed 15 May 2009).

[504] See Ruys, '*Quo vadit Ius ad Bellum?*', 344 (referring to statements by China, Japan, Russia, as well as by UN Secretary-General Ban Ki-Moon).

harm's way. There were no reports of attacks resulting in large numbers of civilian casualties. Apart from Iraqi complaints that a few bridges had been destroyed,[505] there were no significant excesses. Interestingly, a number of States explicitly accepted that the Turkish operations were not disproportionate.[506] Even Iraq, while formally condemning the violation of its sovereignty,[507] conceded in the aftermath of Operation 'Sun' that the Turkish withdrawal 'indicate[d] the credibility of the ... government's statements that the military operation [would] be limited and temporary'.[508]

Must we conclude from this that there is no longer any need for a nexus between the non-State actor and the State from whose territory the group operates, and that proportionate and targeted defensive measures can be undertaken when the former is 'unwilling or unable' to prevent the attacks? This is certainly a *possible* interpretation of the precedent under consideration. Interestingly, some States accepted that in the given circumstances Turkey was acting pursuant to its right of self-defence. Belgium, for instance, 'condemn[ed] the terrorist acts of the PKK on Turkish territory and [understood] Turkey's right to defend itself'.[509] More explicitly, the Dutch Foreign Minister declared before Parliament that:

> The Iraqi government has the primary duty to make sure that its territory is not used for launching terrorist attacks. As it appears that Iraq has continuously failed to effectively counter them, Turkey has the right to defend itself against these attacks by military means.[510]

---

[505] 'Iraq warns Turkey over incursion', *BBC News* 23 February 2008.

[506] See, e.g., Statement by Belgian Foreign Minister De Gucht, Questions et réponses écrites, Chambres des Représentants de Belgique, 21 February 2008, QRVA 52 010 1357, available at www.dekamer.be/QRVA/pdf/52/52K0010.pdf (noting that the operation 'was precisely targeted and aimed only at PKK targets, without harming the population of northern Iraq or local factions' (author's translation)); Statement by Dutch Foreign Minister Verhagen, 'Beantwoording vragen van het lid Van Bommel over een Turkse invasie in Noord-Irak', 3 March 2008, available at www.minbuza.nl/nl/actueel/brievenparlement,2008/03/Beantwoording-vragen-van-het-lid-Van-Bommel-over-e.html ('the Turkish actions appear to be restricted to specific actions against PKK targets in the border area of northern Iraq' (author's translation)) (websites accessed 15 May 2009).

However, it could be argued that, absent new cross-border PKK attacks, the continuation of Turkish aerial raids continued well beyond the conclusion of Operation 'Sun' exceeded the proportionate duration of lawful self-defence. Ruys, '*Quo vadit Ius ad Bellum?*', 363.

[507] See (2007) 53 *Keesing's* 48316, 48427.

[508] See 'Turkey urges PKK to end struggle', *BBC News* 1 March 2008.

[509] Statement by Belgian Foreign Minister De Gucht, *supra* note 506 (author's translation).

[510] Statement by Dutch Foreign Minister Verhagen, *supra* note 506 (author's translation).

On the other hand, it is difficult to ignore the general lack of international legal scrutiny. Turkey did not report to the Security Council, nor did it explicitly frame its actions as an application of the right of self-defence. The Council did not convene to discuss the situation. And apart from a few exceptions, States generally refrained from pronouncing on the legal merits of the Turkish conduct. Yet, acquiescence is a fickle barometer of *opinio iuris*. The muted reaction of the international community might as well indicate that States felt uncomfortable about setting a new precedent. Our next case would seem to support the latter interpretation.

5.2.3.d   Colombia–Ecuador 2008

On 1 March 2008, Colombia conducted a military raid on a camp of the Revolutionary Armed Forces of Colombia (FARC) located within Ecuadorian territory, some 1,800 metres from the frontier with Colombia.[511] Operation 'Phoenix' resulted in the killing of twenty-five guerrillas, including senior FARC commander Raúl Reyes. Although Colombia did not report its action to the Security Council, the Foreign Ministry asserted that Colombia 'had not violated Ecuador's sovereignty, but had instead acted according to the principle of self-defence'.[512] Colombia stressed that FARC 'terrorists' were accustomed to seeking refuge in neighbouring countries after carrying out attacks on Colombian soil and accused Ecuador of failing to take appropriate action to secure its borders.[513] Furthermore, it alleged that evidence obtained from computers seized during the raid indicated that the FARC had received financial support (and weapons supplies from Venezuela, and that the Ecuadorian government had maintained communications with FARC commanders.[514]

---

[511] See, e.g., G. Marcella, 'War without borders: the Colombia–Ecuador crisis of 2008', December 2008, available at www.strategicstudiesinstitute.army.mil/pdffiles/PUB891.pdf; T. Waisberg, 'Colombia's use of force in Ecuador against a terrorist organization: international law and the use of force against non-State actors', ASIL Insight No. 17, 22 August 2008, available at www.asil.org/insights080822.cfm (websites accessed 15 May 2009); Remark: Colombian planes first bombed the camp. Subsequently, armed forces moved in and clashed with some FARC members that had survived the aerial raid. Colombia at first denied that its planes had violated Ecuadorian airspace, but later changed its version of the facts.

[512] Comunicado No. 081 del Ministeria de Relaciones Exteriores de Colombia, Bogotá, 2 March 2008, at http://web.presidencia.gov.co/comunicados/2008/marzo/archivo.html (accessed 15 May 2009).

[513] *Ibid.*

[514] Interpol confirmed the authenticity of the seized computer files, without however certifying their content. 'Forensic report on FARC computers and hardware seized by

Ecuador and Venezuela responded furiously to the Colombian 'aggression' and called for regional condemnation.[515] Both countries broke off diplomatic relations with Colombia and sent troops to the border. While labelling the FARC as 'irregular forces' rather than as 'terrorists', both denied allegations of support. They admitted having been in contact with FARC commanders, but solely for the purpose of negotiating the release of hostages.[516] Ecuador insisted that it did not tolerate the presence of irregular forces on its soil. Instead, it complained that it was the victim of the Colombian conflict, since 'the incapacity of Colombia to prevent some members of the irregular FARC group from crossing the border and establishing themselves clandestinely in Ecuador' had forced it to deploy 11,000 members of the Armed Forces and police to the border, 'at a high economic cost to the Ecuadorian State, necessitating the diversion of considerable resources from other urgent social needs'.[517]

On 5 March 2008, in a meeting of the group's foreign ministers, the OAS considered that the conducting of the operation without the express consent of the government of Ecuador constituted 'a violation of the sovereignty and territorial integrity of Ecuador and of principles of international law'.[518] It reaffirmed the principle, enshrined in Article 21 of the OAS Charter, 'that the territory of a State is inviolable and may not be the object, even temporarily, of military occupation or of other measures of force taken by another State, directly or indirectly, on any grounds whatsoever' and decided to establish a fact-finding mission to investigate the circumstances of the raid. Two days later, the Members of the Rio Group adopted another declaration 'denouncing the violation of the territorial integrity of Ecuador'.[519] The Rio Group 'noted with satisfaction

---

Colombia', 15 May 2008, available at www.interpol.int/Public/ICPO/PressReleases/PR2008/pdfPR200817/Default.asp (accessed 15 May 2009).

[515] See, e.g., 'Ecuador seeks to censure Colombia', *BBC News* 5 March 2003; 'Colombia raid "must be condemned"', *BBC News* 6 March 2003; S. Romero, 'Crisis at Colombia border spills into diplomatic realm', *NY Times* 4 March 2008; UN Doc. S/2008/146, 3 March 2008 (Ecuador); UN Doc. S/2008/177, 14 March 2008 (Ecuador).

[516] See, e.g., 'FARC rebel link files "genuine"', *BBC News* 16 May 2008.

[517] UN Doc. S/2008/177. See however Marcella, 'War without borders', 9 *et seq.*

[518] OAS, 'Convocation of the meeting of consultation of ministers of foreign affairs and appointment of a commission', 5 March 2008, Doc. OEA/Ser.G, CP.RES.930 (1632/08). Also S. Romero, 'Regional bloc criticizes Colombia raid in Ecuador', *NY Times* 6 March 2008.

[519] Rio Group, Declaration of the Heads of State and Government of the Rio Group on the recent events between Ecuador and Colombia, Santo Domingo, 7 March 2008, Annex 2 to the Report of the OAS Commission that visited Ecuador and Colombia, 16 March 2008, Doc. OEA/Ser.F/II.25, RC.25/doc.7/08. See also 'War of words opens LatAm summit', *BBC News* 7 March 2008; 'In quotes: Rio summit sparring', *BBC News* 7 March 2008.

the full apology' offered by the Colombian President and 'acknowledged' his pledge that the events would not be repeated under any circumstances. Subsequent to the completion of the report of the OAS fact-finding Commission,[520] the OAS again adopted a resolution 'rejecting' the incursion by Colombian military forces in 'clear violation of Articles 19 and 21 of the OAS Charter'.[521] At the same time, the resolution '[reiterated] the firm commitment of all Member States to combat threats to security caused by the actions of irregular groups or criminal organizations, especially those associated with drug trafficking'.

In the end, it is striking that in spite of the targeted nature of the operation – directed strictly against a FARC hideout in a remote border area – the United States was the hemisphere's only nation to give explicit and unqualified support to Colombia.[522] Even if the OAS Members were inspired first and foremost by the desire to ease the diplomatic crisis in the Andes and even if they did not directly address the scope of self-defence, the fact nonetheless remains that they adhered to a more conservative reading of territorial integrity and State sovereignty than is conceived by proponents of a flexible application of Article 51 UN Charter vis-à-vis non-State actors.

5.2.3.e   Other examples

Apart from the aforementioned examples, the permissibility of recourse to force against non-State attacks was raised in several other cases. In 2002, for instance, Georgia addressed the Security Council to complain of Russian aerial raids within its territory, which it regarded as 'barefaced aggression' in violation of its sovereignty.[523] Russia repeatedly denied

---

[520] See Report of the OAS Commission that visited Ecuador and Colombia. Remark: the report merely includes a restatement of the Colombian and Ecuadorian versions of the facts. It does not contain an analysis of FARC presence on Ecuadorian territory or of alleged links between the FARC and Ecuador.

[521] OAS, Resolution of the Twenty-fifth Meeting of Consultation of Ministers of Foreign Affairs, 17 March 2008, Doc. OEA/Ser.F/iI.25, RC.25/RES.1/08 rev.1.

[522] See US State Department, Daily Press Briefings by T. Casey, Deputy Spokesman, 3–5 March 2008, available at http://2001–2009.state.gov/r/pa/prs/dpb/2008/mar/index.htm (accessed 15 May 2009). See also 'Colombia raid "must be condemned"', *BBC News* 6 March 2003. By contrast, the raid was reportedly condemned by several individual States, including Brazil, Chile, Argentina, Nicaragua and Peru. See: Romero, 'Crisis at Colombia border spills into diplomatic realm'; H. Murphy and J. Goodman, 'Uribe seeks trial for Chávez in International Court (update 3)', *Bloomberg.com* 4 March 2008.

[523] See the following communications by Georgia: UN Doc. S/2002/250, 8 March 2002; UN Doc. S/2002/950, 23 August 2002; UN Doc. S/2002/1033, 15 September 2002; UN Doc. S/2002/1035, 13 September. Also (2002) UNYB. 395–6.

allegations of attacks – even though incursions were verified by the OSCE.[524] On the other hand, exactly one year after 9/11, Russia did explicitly invoke Article 51 UN Charter to threaten military actions against Georgia.[525] According to Russia, it was a well-known fact that Chechen fighters and international terrorists had established bases in the Pankisi Gorge from which they mounted attacks on the Russian Federation.[526] Nonetheless, in contravention of its obligations under Security Council resolution 1373 (2001) the Georgian authorities proved unable and unwilling to undertake appropriate actions, and refused practical cooperation with Russia.[527] According to the Russian UN representative:

> If the Georgian leadership is unable to establish a security zone in the area of the Georgian–Russian border, continues to ignore United Nations Security Council resolution 1373 (2001) ..., and does not put and end to the bandit sorties and attacks on adjoining areas in the Russian Federation, we reserve the right to act in accordance with Article 51 [UN] Charter ...[528]

Georgia strongly protested against Russia's threats. First, while it did not deny the presence of foreign fighters within its territory, it insisted that it fully complied with its obligations under Security Council Resolution 1373 (2001), that it was a loyal member of the global anti-terrorist coalition, and that it had informed Russian services of recent efforts to step up counter-terrorist operations.[529] In addition, echoing an

---

[524] See, e.g., S. L. Myers, 'Russia: more fighting along Georgian Border', *NY Times* 31 July 2002; S. L. Myers, 'Georgia hearing heavy footsteps from Russia's war in Chechnya', *NY Times* 15 August 2002; S. L. Myers, 'Russia: denial on airstrikes', *NY Times* 27 August 2002.
[525] See UN Doc. S/2002/1012, 11 September 2002 (Russia).
[526] Remark: Russia *inter alia* asserted that those responsible for three apartment bombings that killed more than 300 people in 1999 were hiding in Georgia. See: UN Doc. S/2002/1012; S. L. Myers, 'Vigilance and memory: Russia; Putin warns Georgia to root out Chechen rebels within its borders or face attacks', *NY Times* 12 September 2002.
[527] UN Doc. S/2002/1012; UN Doc. S/2002/854, 31 July 2002 (Russia).
[528] UN Doc. S/2002/1012. In the statement, President Putin also asked the Russian General Staff 'to announce proposals on the possibility and expediency of carrying out strikes against reliably identified terrorist bases during pursuit operations'. Remark: in a previous letter to the Secretary-General, Russia had made similar threats without, however, explicitly referring to Article 51 UN Charter. UN Doc. S/2002/854.
[529] UN Doc. S/2002/854; UN Doc. S/2002/1033; UN Doc. S/2002/1035. Remark: in August 2002, Georgia announced that it would reinforce its security presence in the Pankisi Gorge to step up counter-terrorist efforts, yet this initiative was apparently ridiculed by Russia. See: S. L. Myers 'Echoing Bush, Putin asks U.N. to back Georgia attack', *NY*

argument that was also used by Ecuador in relation to the Colombian raid in 2008, Georgia stressed that it was the victim of a situation that was ultimately created by Russia itself: the situation in the Pankisi Gorge was the 'result of the military operation conducted in Chechnya, during which Russian armed forces ... allowed the "spreading" of the conflict onto the territory of a ... neighbouring nation'.[530] Georgia claimed that the 'far-fetched pretext of fighting terrorists' was merely invoked to exert political pressure on Georgia.[531] Interestingly, it rejected as 'totally unacceptable the liberal, if mildly put, interpretation of Article 51 [UN Charter]' invoked by Russia.[532]

The Russian actions/threats were not addressed by the Security Council. It appears, however, that the US did not accept the Russian claims, but instead deplored the violations of Georgian sovereignty and spoke of actions 'under the guise of anti-terrorist operations' – even though it acknowledged that Georgia had not been able to establish effective control over the eastern part of the country and accepted a link between Chechen forces and Al Qaeda.[533]

Cross-border use of force by non-State actors has also been a key catalyst in the deadly conflict that has held the Great Lakes region hostage ever since the mid 1990s and that has killed and displaced millions of innocent civilians.[534] While we will examine below the ICJ's appraisal of the situation in *DRC* v. *Uganda*, it may be observed that *inter alia* in 2004, the DRC addressed the Security Council to protest against the unauthorized presence of Rwandan soldiers in eastern Congo.[535] Rwanda's reaction was by and large comparable to that of Russia with reference to Georgia.[536] On the one hand, it denied allegations of

---

Times 13 August 2002; 'Georgia to send troops to Pankisi Gorge', *NY Times* 20 August 2002; S. L. Myers, 'Georgia moves against rebels and accuses Russia of airstrikes', *NY Times* 24 August 2002.

[530] UN Doc. S/2002/1033. [531] UN Doc. S/2002/950; UN Doc. S/2002/1033.

[532] UN Doc. S/2002/1035. Also: UN Doc. S/2002/1033.

[533] Gray, *The use of force*, pp. 230–1. See also: US State Department, Office of the Coordinator for Counterterrorism, 'Eurasia Overview – Patterns of Global Terrorism', 21 May 2002, available at www.state.gov/s/ct/rls/crt/2001/html/10239. htm (accessed 15 May 2009); S. L. Myers, 'Georgia seeks to ease tensions with Russia over Chechens', *NY Times* 14 September 2002.

[534] See F. Reyntjens, *The Great African War: Congo and regional geopolitics, 1996–2006* (Cambridge University Press, 2009), 340 pages.

[535] See UN Doc. S/2004/327, 26 April 2004 (DRC); UN Doc. S/2004/935, 30 November 2004 (DRC). Also (2004) UNYB 123 *et seq.* Consider also *supra*, notes 358, 359.

[536] See the following communications by Rwanda: UN Doc. S/2004/652, 16 August 2004 ('Rwanda once again calls upon the international community to take action against this

territorial incursions[537] – even if the UN Organisation Mission in the Democratic Republic of the Congo (MONUC) declared otherwise.[538] On the other hand, Rwanda persistently accused the Congo and MONUC of failing to live up to their obligations to disarm and demobilize the ex-FAR/Interahamwe forces, which were responsible for the 1994 genocide in Rwanda, and which continued to carry out cross-border attacks from Congolese territory. Rwanda left no doubt that if this threat to its security was not removed, it would 'take appropriate measures in self-defence'.[539]

The response of the international community was twofold. On the one hand, States recognized that the presence of the Interahamwe in eastern Congo posed a genuine threat to regional peace and security and ought to be dealt with adequately. Thus, the Security Council recognized:

> that the continued presence of ... Interahamwe elements in the eastern [DRC] is a source of instability, a threat to civilian populations and an impediment to good neighbourly relations between the [DRC] and Rwanda. It considers [their] armed presence and activities ... to be unacceptable and demands that they disarm and disband without delay, with a view to their repatriation and resettlement.[540]

The European Union and the African Union similarly expressed understanding for the Rwandese security concerns.[541]

On the other hand, the international community unequivocally reiterated its support for the territorial integrity of the DRC and objected to unauthorized operations by Rwandan forces. The EU pointed out that the presence of foreign troops on Congolese territory violated international law.[542] The AU 'urge[d] Rwanda to refrain from any unilateral

> incipient ethnic cleansing now taking root in the region and especially in the eastern [DRC]. We also reiterate our demand for the forcible disarmament, demobilization and repatriation of the Ex-FAR/Interahamwe now deployed along Rwanda's border and in many cases co-located with armed forces of the [DRC]; failure to do so may force Rwanda to take appropriate measures in self-defence. Rwanda is not prepared to accept or tolerate the status quo'); UN Doc. S/2004/933, 30 November 2004; UN Doc. S/2004/951, 6 December 2004.

[537] E.g., UN Doc. S/2004/951.
[538] See, e.g., M. Wines, 'U.N. reports a possible push into Congo by Rwandans', *NY Times* 3 December 2004; 'Congo tells Rwanda troops to stay out', *NY Times* 4 December 2004.
[539] E.g., UN Doc. S/2004/652; UN Doc. S/2004/951 ('If the [DRC] does not remove the threat of this genocidal force to Rwanda ... then Rwanda reserves the right to respond as she deems fit in defence of her people, her sovereignty, and territorial integrity').
[540] UNSC Presidential Statement of 7 December 2004, UN Doc. S/PRST/2004/45. See also: UNSC Presidential Statement of 14 May 2004, UN Doc. S/PRST/2004/15.
[541] See UN Doc. S/2004/385, 11 May 2004 (Ireland, on behalf of the EU); UN Doc. S/2004/966, 8 December 2004 (Nigeria, on behalf of the AU).
[542] UN Doc. S/2004/385.

action'.[543] Last but not least, the Security Council 'expresse[d] its very deep concern at multiple reports of military operations by the Rwandan arm in the eastern [DRC] and at threats of the Government of Rwanda in this regard'.[544] It 'strongly condemn[ed] any and all such military action', and 'demand[ed] that ... Rwanda withdraw without delay any forces it [might] have in the territory of the [DRC]'.

The reserved position of the international community may well have been inspired by fears that military action by Rwanda would again flare up violent conflict in the region, causing renewed humanitarian catastrophe.[545] Still, it is significant that in spite of the recognized failure to prevent cross-border attacks against Rwanda, there was no support whatsoever for any right to respond through targeted measures in self-defence.[546]

A similar dispute arose in late 2005 between the DRC and Uganda in relation to attacks by the notorious Lord's Resistance Army (LRA) emanating from Congolese territory.[547] On 3 October, the DRC notified the Security Council that Uganda had threatened cross-border action if the DRC and MONUC failed to disarm the LRA within a period of two months.[548] The Congolese UN ambassador asserted that his country had 'demonstrated sufficient commitment to disarm the [LRA] rebels so as not to expose itself to new pretexts for justifying the dangerous and negative interference of Uganda in the [DRC]'.[549] He stressed that the

---

[543] UN Doc. S/2004/966.   [544] UN Doc. S/PRST/2004/45.
[545] See, e.g., M. Wines, 'U.N. reports a possible push into Congo by Rwandans', *NY Times* 3 December 2004; M. Lacey, 'Strife in Congo town sows fear of return to all-out war', *NY Times* 19 December 2004.
[546] Remark: in December 2008, a Group of Experts established by the Security Council found evidence of Rwandan support to the CNDP (a Congolese rebel group led by renegade general Laurent Nkunda) and of collaboration with Congolese commanders with the FDLR (ex-Interahamwe). See: Letter from the Chairman of the Security Council Committee Established pursuant to Resolution 1533 (2004) concerning the DRC to the Security Council, 10 December 2008, UN Doc. S/2008/773. Rwanda, however, vigorously rejected the allegations ('Rwanda: support for rebels denied', *NY Times* 17 December 2008). Shortly afterwards, Rwanda and the DRC launched a joint offensive against Rwandan Hutu rebels in eastern Congo. E.g., 'Hutu rebels killed in Congo raid', *BBC News* 13 February 2009.
[547] (2005) UNYB 184–5; 'DR Congo troops to Uganda border', *BBC News* 4 October 2005; 'MONUC deploys into East DR of Congo where Ugandan-based soldiers briefly seen', *UN News Service* 9 November 2005.
[548] UN Doc. S/2005/620, 3 October 2005 (DRC).
[549] *Ibid.* The statement also stressed that the DRC had given an ultimatum to the LRA to leave the country. It warned of the risk of human suffering if Ugandan troops were to take action, and claimed that the LRA 'did not at present have the capability to harm the government of Uganda'.

Ugandan threat constituted a violation of Article 2(4) UN Charter and that, if acted upon, the DRC would exercise its right of self-defence. In response, Uganda declared that:

> As a responsible and sovereign State, Uganda is expected to guarantee peace and security of her citizens, who, for an extended period of time, have been terrorized by ... armed groups, using the territory of some neighbouring States as bases from which to attack Uganda. Uganda has an obligation to defend itself if attacked, in accordance with Article 51 of the [UN] Charter ...[550]

At the same time, it stressed that there was 'no planned attack' against the DRC.[551] The Security Council, for its part, did not pronounce on the Ugandan threats, but merely 'noted with concern the incursion of the LRA', while 'welcoming the intention of the DRC to disarm this group'.[552]

One year later, Ethiopia sent several thousands of troops into Somalia to support the Transitional Federal Government (TFG) in its fight against the Islamist forces of the Union of Islamic Courts (UIC).[553] While Ethiopia initially denied the presence of combat troops, it eventually justified the intervention by reference to the right of self-defence. According to Prime Minister Zenawi, his country had 'taken self-defensive measures and started counter-attacking the aggressive extremist forces of the Islamic Courts and foreign terrorist groups.'[554] The purport was not to meddle in Somalia's internal affairs, but to protect the sovereignty of Ethiopia against the UIC, which had allegedly begun infiltrating its territory and had declared a 'holy war' against it.[555]

In light of the justification invoked, the conflict again raises interesting questions regarding the permissibility of self-defence against non-State

---

[550] UN Doc. S/2005/645, 7 October 2005 (Uganda).   [551] Ibid.
[552] UNSC Presidential Statement of 4 October 2005, UN Doc. S/2005/46. Remark: in December 2008, the DRC, Sudan and Uganda launched a joint offensive against LRA fighters hiding in eastern Congo. See 'UN backs action on Uganda rebels', *BBC News* 18 December 2008; 'Uganda "strikes LRA rebel camps"', *BBC News* 21 December 2008.
[553] See O. Corten, 'La licéité douteuse de l'action militaire de l'Ethiopie en Somalie et ses implications sur l'argument de l'"intervention consentie"', (2007) 111 RGDIP 513–37; Gray, *The use of force*, pp. 244–52; Z. W. Yihdego, 'Ethiopia's military action against the Union of Islamic Courts and others in Somalia: some legal implications', (2007) 56 ICLQ 666–76.
[554] Quoted by UN Special Representative Fall, UN Doc. S/PV.5614, 26 December 2006, 3.
[555] See in particular Ethiopian Ministry of Foreign Affairs, Newsletter 21, available at www.mfa.gov.et/Press_Section/Newsletter21/NewsFeature21.pdf (accessed 15 May 2009). Also: Gray, *The use of force*, pp. 248, 250; Corten, 'La licéité douteuse de l'action militaire de l'Ethiopie en Somalie', 515–16; Yihdego, 'Ethiopia's military action', 667 et seq.

actors. Nonetheless, the failure of the States involved adequately to explain their actions in legal terms and the reluctance of other States to enter into the legal debate impede the analysis.[556] Ethiopia did not file a report with the Security Council. Nor was there any debate within the Security Council.[557] The public silence of China, Russia and the Non-Aligned Movement was striking.[558] The African Union initially seemed sympathetic,[559] but subsequently issued a joint communiqué together with the Leage of Arab States and the Intergovernmental Authority on Development (IGAD) calling upon Ethiopia to withdraw its troops.[560] A handful of individual States pronounced in favour of or against the intervention through declarations in the media, yet by and large refrained from addressing the self-defence claim.[561] Furthermore, it must be kept in mind that the Ethiopian intervention was approved by and coordinated with the Somali Transitional Federal Government, which enjoyed the backing of the Security Council, the AU, the League of Arab States and IGAD.[562] Hence, even if the TFG was rapidly losing ground to the UIC, the implication seems to be that it better fits the 'intervention by invitation' denominator than that of self-defence.[563]

---

[556] Gray, *The use of force*, p. 244.

[557] See *ibid.*, 251. Yihdego, 'Ethiopia's military action', 671. Qatar circulated a draft Presidential Statement calling for an immediate withdrawal of all international forces, specifically Ethiopian troops, yet this initiative garnered little support among other Council Members.

[558] Gray, *The use of force*, p. 244.   [559] See *ibid.*, 251.

[560] Joint Communiqué of the African Union, the League of Arab States and the Inter-Governmental Authority on Development, On the Current Situation in Somalia, Addis Ababa, 27 December 2006, www.africa-union.org/root/au/News/Press/2006/December/Joint_Communique_on_Somalia.doc (accessed 15 May 2009). See also the statements cited in Corten'La licéité douteuse de l'action militaire de l'Ethiopie en Somalie', 533–5.

[561] The US, the UK, Egypt and Yemen expressed understanding for the actions. Conversely, Eritrea denounced it, whereas Djibouti insisted on the immediate withdrawal of Ethiopian troops. See Yihdego, 'Ethiopia's military action', 672–3.

[562] See, e.g., (2004) UNYB 261; UNSC Presidential Statement of 13 July 2006; Yihdego, 'Ethiopia's military action', 667.

[563] Also Gray, *The use of force*, p. 250. In light of the resolutions previously adopted by the UN Security Council, Corten nonetheless concludes that the invitation of the TFG was insufficient as a legal basis for the operation. See Corten, 'La licéité douteuse de l'action militaire de l'Ethiopie en Somalie', 521 *et seq.*

Remark: this is all the more so since Ethiopia failed to provide any tangible information on alleged infiltrations and attacks by Islamist forces, and instead seemed to rely on a broad right of preventive self-defence. See on this aspect of the Ethiopian claim: Corten, 'La licéité douteuse de l'action militaire de l'Ethiopie en Somalie', 516–20. It may also be noted that the Ethiopian intervention began long before the UIC announced its 'holy war'.

Indeed, in light of the complexity of the Somali situation – with the TFG and the UIC allegedly receiving support from the US and Ethiopia, and from Eritrea and a number of Arab States respectively[564] – it would seem to be a classical case testing the limits of intervention and counter-intervention in the context of a civil war. Undeniably, the TFG approval had an important influence on the international community's (lack of) response. Statements of the US, the TFG and Egypt in support of the operation all made express reference to this element.[565] In January 2009, Ethiopian troops finally pulled out of Somalia, allegedly after having ended the threat from the Islamists.[566]

It must be noted that the aforementioned list of incidents is not exhaustive and continues to grow longer.[567] In many cases, however, the facts are unclear, the intervening States refrain from explaining the legal basis of their actions, and international scrutiny is minimal if not wholly absent. A final example that might briefly be mentioned in order to conclude our overview of State practice relates to the troubled relationship between Afghanistan and the United States on the one hand, and Pakistan on the other hand, resulting from the security problems in Pakistan's Federally Administered Tribal Areas. More precisely, throughout 2008 and 2009, the US and Afghanistan repeatedly accused Pakistan of failing to undertake appropriate actions to prevent Taleban fighters and Al Qaeda operatives from using its border region as a springboard for mounting attacks in Afghanistan.[568] According to press reports, the US in 2008 repeatedly carried out cross-border strikes by means of remotely piloted Predator drones.[569] Following a major Taleban assault, Afghan President Karzai moreover threatened to send

---

[564] See, e.g., Report of the Security Council Committee established under resolution 751 (1992), 21 November 2006, UN Doc. S/2006/913, §§ 56 et seq. Also: Gray, *The use of force*, pp. 246, 249; Yihdego, 'Ethiopia's military action', 668.

[565] See Corten, 'La licéité douteuse de l'action militaire de l'Ethiopie en Somalie', 521, footnotes 37–9. On the other hand, a US spokesperson also framed the Ethiopian intervention as a response to 'aggression' by the Islamists. See: M. Mazetti, 'U.S. signals backing for Ethiopian incursion into Somalia', *NY Times* 27 December 2006.

[566] 'Ethiopia completes Somali pull-out', *BBC News* 25 January 2009. But see: M. O. Hassan, 'Ethiopia troops "back in Somalia"', *BBC News* 19 May 2009.

[567] E.g., 'Iraq protests Iran air raid on Kurd villages', *AFP* 5 May 2009; UN Doc. S/2009/38, 15 January 2009 (Israel, vis-à-vis rocket attacks from Lebanese territory); R. F. Worth, 'Yemeni Rebels and Saudis clash at border', *NY Times*, 6 November 2009.

[568] Less publicly, there have also been allegations of clandestine support by Pakistan's Inter-Services Intelligence Directorate (ISI).

[569] See, e.g., E. Schmitt and M. Mazzetti, 'Bush said to give orders allowing raids in Pakistan', *NY Times* 11 September 2008; J. Perlez, 'Pakistan's military chief criticizes

troops into Pakistan, for 'Afghanistan has the right to cross the border and destroy terrorist nests ... in order to defend itself, its schools, its peoples and its life'.[570]

On the other hand, Pakistan denounced the aforementioned accusations. It presented itself as the victim of the internal turmoil in Afghanistan and warned that military action by the US would merely strengthen domestic support for extremist armed groups on its soil. Pakistani officials occasionally condemned US strikes as violations of their country's territorial integrity. Although it has sometimes been suggested that such protests merely intended to placate domestic factions, it appears that opposition to territorial incursions gradually grew stronger and has, to some extent, forced the US military to back away from launching small-scale ground raids against suspected militants.[571] Significantly, the United States typically kept a low profile, refraining from officially commenting on alleged airstrikes, let alone from putting forward a legal justification.[572]

5.2.4 The response of the International Court of Justice

In light of the evolution in *opinio iuris* and State practice following the adoption of its *Nicaragua* judgment in 1986 and especially following the 9/11 attacks, it is worth considering to what extent the ICJ has reaffirmed or reviewed its earlier dicta. On two occasions, the Court had an opportunity to pronounce on the matter, namely in its advisory opinion of 9 July 2004 on the *Palestinian Wall*,[573] and in its judgment of 19 December 2005 in the *DRC* v. *Uganda* case.[574] Those who had hoped for

---

U.S. over a raid', *NY Times* 11 September 2008; M. Mazzetti and E. Schmitt, 'U.S. takes to air to hit militants inside Pakistan', *NY Times* 27 October 2008; J. Perlez and P. Zubair Shah, 'U.S. strike reportedly killed five in Pakistan', *NY Times* 20 November 2008; 'Pakistan protests over U.S. missile strikes', *NY Times* 20 November 2008.

[570] Cited in C. Gall, 'Karzai threatens to send soldiers into Pakistan', *IHT* 16 June 2008.

[571] See, e.g., M. Mazzetti and E. Schmitt, 'U.S. takes to air to hit militants inside Pakistan', *NY Times* 27 October 2008; 'Pakistan protests over U.S. missile strikes', *NY Times* 20 November 2008.

[572] Following the collapse of a peace deal with the Taleban militants in the north-western part of its territory, the Pakistani army in May 2009 launched a major offensive against the Taleban. Cooperation between Pakistan and the US had also increased. E.g., E. Schmitt and M. Mazzetti, 'In a first, U.S. provides Pakistan with drone data', *NY Times* 14 May 2009; A. Kannapell, 'From air and ground, Pakistan strikes back at Taliban', *NY Times* 10 May 2009.

[573] ICJ, *Legal consequences of the construction of a wall in the Occupied Palestinian Territory*, Advisory opinion of 9 July 2004, (2004) ICJ Rep 136–203.

[574] ICJ, *DRC* v. *Uganda*.

a visionary analysis of the *ratione personae* controversy nonetheless came home empty-handed. In all, the Court stuck to a restrictive and State-centric construction of Article 51 UN Charter. At the same time, it did so in a rather confusing manner that is bound to exacerbate legal uncertainty. The considerable number of separate and dissenting opinions illustrate the lack of agreement at the Peace Palace and further calls in question the authority of the Court's findings.[575]

5.2.4.a   The *Palestinian Wall* advisory opinion (2004)

On 8 December 2003, the UN General Assembly adopted a resolution requesting that the ICJ render an opinion on the 'legal consequences of the construction of the wall being built by Israel, the Occupying Power, in the Occupied Palestinian Territories' (hereafter: OPT).[576] Seven months later, the Court handed down its reply. After having determined that the construction violated IHL and international human rights law,[577] it examined whether there were any possible justifications for Israel's conduct. The Court observed that Israel had argued that the construction of the 'barrier' was 'consistent with the right of States to self-defence enshrined in Article 51 of the Charter'.[578] According to Israel, Security Council resolutions 1368 (2001) and 1373 (2001) '[had] clearly recognized the right of States to use force in self-defence against terrorist attacks', and therefore surely recognize the right to use non-forcible measures to that end.[579]

The self-defence argument was rejected with surprising – and perhaps disturbing – brevity. The Court needed no more than a single paragraph (§ 139) to conclude that:

> Article 51 ... recognizes the existence of an inherent right of self-defence in the case of armed attack by one State against another State. However, Israel does not claim that the attacks against it are imputable to a foreign State. The Court also notes that Israel exercises control in the Occupied Palestinian Territory and that, as Israel itself states, the threat which it regards as justifying the construction of the wall originates within, and not outside, that territory. The situation is thus different from that contemplated by Security Council resolutions 1368 (2001) and 1373

---

[575] See also: C. J. Tams, 'Note analytique: swimming with the tide or seeking to stem it? Recent ICJ rulings on the law of self-defence', (2005) 18–2 RQDI 275–90, at 285, 288, 290.
[576] GA Res. A/RES/ES-10/14 of 8 December 2003, adopted by ninety votes against eight, with seventy-four abstentions.
[577] ICJ, *Palestinian Wall* case, §§ 115–37.   [578] *Ibid.*, § 138.   [579] *Ibid.*

(2001), and therefore Israel could not in any event invoke those resolutions in support of its claim to be exercising a right of self-defence. Consequently, the Court concludes that Article 51 ... has no relevance in this case.[580]

The dictum contains two separate arguments that are altogether difficult to reconcile. At first, the Court seems to indicate boldly that an armed attack has to be imputable to a State, *end of story*. So shortly after the 9/11 attacks, this is certainly a remarkable statement, especially since it seems to further narrow down the interpretation of Article 3(g) of the Definition of Aggregation spelt out in the *Nicaragua* case. Indeed, as we saw earlier, in *Nicaragua*, the Court regarded the formula of that provision as the customary threshold determining the permissibility of self-defence against attacks by irregulars and armed bands. As the Court excluded from its scope 'logistical or other support', it was, as Judge Jennings indicated,[581] difficult to understand what it was, short of an attack actually attributable to a State in accordance with the rules on State responsibility, that could trigger the right of self-defence. Still, at least theoretically, the Court at the time did not per se rule out the possibility that the concept of 'substantial involvement' had a residual meaning beyond the rule enshrined in Article 8 DASR. By contrast, this appears to be exactly what the Court did by restricting Article 51 to 'attacks imputable to a foreign State'.

The Court's approach is, however, obfuscated by its second argument. Indeed, if the Court wished to limit the scope of application of Article 51 exclusively to attacks 'imputable to a foreign State' – as most scholars have deduced from the phrasing[582] – it is unclear why it felt compelled to declare that Israel 'could not in any event' rely on resolutions 1368 and 1373 (2001). By so doing, the Court implicitly renders support to those who regard these resolutions as affecting the interpretation of Article 51.[583] No clues whatsoever are given, however, in relation to their

---

[580] *Ibid.*, § 139.
[581] ICJ, *Nicaragua* case (Merits), Dissenting opinion of Judge Jennings, 543.
[582] E.g., A. Bianchi, 'Dismantling the wall: the ICJ's advisory opinion and its likely impact on international law', (2005) 47 GYBIL 343–91 374–5; Cannizzaro, 'Entités non-étatiques et régime international de l'emploi de la force', 342; I. Canor, 'When *Jus ad Bellum* meets *Jus in Bello*: the occupier's right of self-defence against terrorism stemming from occupied territories', (2006) 19 Leiden JIL 129–49, at 132; Dubuisson, 'La guerre du Liban de l'été 2006', 541; C. J. Tams, 'Light treatment of a complex problem: the law of self-defence in the Wall Case', (2006) 16 EJIL 963–78, at 967; Waisberg, 'Colombia's use of force in Ecuador'; Zimmerman, 'The Second Lebanon War', 115–16.
[583] Also, e.g., Ronen, 'The Second Lebanon War', 376.

possible purport. The Court arguably does not hold them to constitute a blank cheque for (proportionate) self-defence against non-State actors – this would make the first two sentences of the aforementioned quote meaningless. What then is the decisive trigger? Is the relevance of the resolutions limited to cases of *'international' terrorist attacks*; to non-State attacks *of extreme magnitude*; or to *cases where the Security Council has explicitly recognized* the victim State's right of self-defence? Must there still be some degree of State involvement? Or is mere failure to prevent (recurring?) non-State attacks sufficient? The Court's view remains shrouded in mystery.

If the separate opinions of Judges Kooijmans and Higgins and the declaration of Judge Buergenthal illustrate the controversial nature of the Court's findings, they hardly make it easier to read the mind of the majority. Significantly, all three judges criticized the Court's State-centric reading of Article 51. Judge Kooijmans, for instance, conceded that it had been the generally accepted interpretation for more than fifty years that 'armed attacks' should be committed by another State.[584] In his view, however, resolutions 1368 and 1373 (2001) had introduced a completely new element vis-à-vis 'acts of international terrorism'.[585] Judges Buergenthal and Higgins in turn emphasized that nothing in Article 51 stipulates that self-defence is available only when an armed attack is made by a State.[586] Judge Higgins stressed that *that* qualification was rather the result of the Court so determining in *Nicaragua* and grudgingly accepted that this ought to be regarded as a statement of the law as it now stands.[587] Judge Buergenthal noted that resolutions 1368 and 1373 supported a more flexible construction of Article 51.[588]

In light of the objections of the three judges it appears that the first sentences of the paragraph concerned should not simply be understood as restating the obvious – that an armed attack by a State warrants the exercise of self-defence – but rather as having a *limitative* effect, implying

---

[584] ICJ, *Palestinian Wall* case, Separate opinion of Judge Kooijmans, § 35.
[585] Paradoxically, and in spite of the Court's explicit reference to the documents, Kooijmans regretted that the Court had 'by-passed' this new element which 'undeniably marked a new approach to the concept of self-defence', while simultaneously observing that their legal implications 'could not as yet be assessed.' *Ibid.*
[586] ICJ, *Palestinian Wall* case, Declaration of Judge Buergenthal, § 6; Separate opinion of Judge Higgins, § 33.
[587] *Ibid.*, Separate opinion of Judge Higgins, § 33.
[588] *Ibid.*, Declaration of Judge Buergenthal, § 6.

that 'armed attack' must in principle emanate from a State.[589] On the other hand, the individual opinions do not clarify to what extent the advisory opinion's reference to resolutions 1368 and 1373 (2001) signals a deviation from this State-centric approach. In the end, the advisory opinion has rightly been criticized for raising more questions than it solves and for constituting a missed opportunity to clarify the *ratione personae* contoversy.[590]

Apart from adding to the existing confusion vis-à-vis self-defence against non-State attacks, the Court's reasoning also raises the issue of the applicability of Article 51 to occupied territories. More precisely, the Court's objection that the attacks emanated from territory over which Israel exercised control (thus distinguishing the situation from that envisaged in resolutions 1368 and 1373), has been understood as ruling out the exercise of self-defence by occupying powers against territories occupied by them in the meaning of the Hague Regulations and the Fourth Geneva Convention. This view has been criticized by a number of authorities, not so much because they discard the need for an 'external element' in order to activate the right of self-defence – surely terrorism occurring wholly within the State does not implicate the right of self-defence[591] – but rather because they argue that this 'external element' is not necessarily absent in relation to occupied territory. Thus, while Judge Kooijmans followed the Court's view on this matter,[592] Judges Buergenthal and Higgins rejected the Court's analysis as overly formalistic.[593] Similarly, a number of scholars have

---

[589] Cf. a number of scholars have observed that the Court did not expressly state that Article 51 recognizes self-defence *only* against attacks by one State against another, but nonetheless accept that the criticism of Judges Kooijmans, Buergenthal and Higgins indicates that this was indeed the majority view. E.g., Gray, *The use of force*, pp. 135–6; Hofmeister, 'To harbour or not to harbour?', 485–7; Murphy, 'Self-defense and the Israeli wall advisory opinion: an *ipse dixit* from the ICJ?', (2005) 99 AJIL 62–76, at 63.

[590] E.g., Bianchi, 'Dismantling the wall', 376; S. C. Breau, '*Legal consequences of the construction of a wall in the Occupied Palestinian Territory*: advisory opinion, 9 July 2004', (2005) 54 ICLQ 1003–13, at 1007; Canor, 'When *Jus ad Bellum* meets *Jus in Bello*', 132; R. Kahan, 'Building a protective wall around terrorists – how the International Court of Justice's ruling in the *Legal consequences of the construction of a wall in the Occupied Palestinian Territory* made the world safer for terrorists and more dangerous for Member States of the United Nations', (2004–05) 28 Fordham ILJ 827–78, at 877–8; Murphy, 'Self-defense and the Israeli *Wall* advisory opinion', 62–3, 76; Tams, 'The law of self-defence in the *Wall* case', 966, 973 *et seq.*

[591] M. N. Schmitt, 'Responding to transnational terrorism under the *Ius ad Bellum*', 169.

[592] ICJ, *Palestinian Wall* case, Separate opinion of Judge Kooijmans, § 36.

[593] ICJ, *Palestinian Wall* case, Declaration of Judge Buergenthal, § 6; Separate opinion of Judge Higgins, § 34.

criticized the Court's approach.[594] Insofar as the Court's reasoning might (incorrectly) be read as barring an occupying power from undertaking any forcible action in relation to occupied territories, this concern is understandable. In this context, it stands to reason why the Court did not follow a far less controversial road to obtain the same result, by holding that the general rules of the *Ius ad Bellum* are superseded by the *lex specialis* of the *Ius in Bello* relating to situations of belligerent occupation.[595]

This argument was raised before the Court by the representatives of Palestine[596] and the League of Arab States.[597] Thus, on behalf of Palestine, Abi-Saab duly observed that by relying on the right of self-defence, Israel made an 'impermissible confusion between the two branches of the law of war that have to be kept radically apart'.[598] The relevant rules of IHL establish certain limits within which an occupying power may engage in belligerent reprisals and may use forcible measures to maintain order and protect its own citizens and military personnel from attacks.[599] It was by reference to these rules that the Israeli High Court of Justice in *Beit Sourik Village Council v. Israel* (2004)[600] and in *Mara'abe v. Prime Minister of Israel* (2005)[601] decided to order the Israeli

---

[594] E.g., R. Rivier, 'Conséquences juridiques de l'édification d'un mur dans le Territoire Palestinien Occupé – Court Internationale de Justice, Avis Consultatif du 9 Juillet 2004', (2004) 50 AFDI 292–336, at 306; M. N. Schmitt, 'Responding to transnational terrorism under the *Ius ad Bellum*', 169.

[595] In this sense: V. Kattan, 'The legality of the West Bank Wall: Israel's High Court of Justice v. the International Court of Justice', (2007) 40 Vanderbilt JTL 1425–517, at 1468, 1482–9 ('Self-defence is not available to an occupying power when it has already subdued its enemy and taken control of its territory; it is only available at the start of hostilities, not when they come to an end. Once the occupied territory is under the effective control of the occupying power, the right of self-defence is no longer applicable'); J. M. Gomez-Robledo, 'L'Avis de la C.I.J. sur les Conséquences juridiques de l'édification d'un mur dans le Territoire Palestinien Occupé: timidité ou prudence?', (2005) 109 RGDIP 521–37, at 529–31 ; I. Scobbie, 'Words my mother never taught me – "in defense of the International Court"', (2005) 99 AJIL 81–4; Tams, 'The law of self-defence in the *Wall* case', 969–70;. Unclear: Murphy, 'Self-defense and the Israeli *Wall* advisory opinion', 71; R. Wedgwood, 'The ICJ advisory opinion on the Israeli security fence and the limits of self-defense', (2005) 99 AJIL 52–61, at 58–9.

[596] Written Statement submitted by Palestine, 30 January 2004, § 534.

[597] Written Statement of the League of Arab States, January 2004, § 9.6.

[598] George Abi-Saab, Oral pleading, 23 February 2004.

[599] See in particular Article 43 of the 1907 Hague Regulations, and Articles 27(4) and 64 of the Fourth Geneva Convention.

[600] Israeli Supreme Court, sitting as High Court of Justice, 30 June 2004, reprinted in (2004) 43 ILM 1099 (e.g., § 34).

[601] Israeli Supreme Court, sitting as High Court of Justice, 15 September 2005, available at http://elyon1.court.gov.il/files_eng/04/570/079/A14/04079570.a14.pdf (accessed 15 May 2009).

government to consider alternative paths for its 'security barrier'. By applying the same legal framework, the Court could have avoided pronouncing on the scope of self-defence[602] – which would have been preferable to issuing such a confusing dictum – while shedding some light on the scope and limits of the rights of occupying powers.[603]

---

[602] Also Murphy, 'Self-defense and the Israeli *Wall* advisory opinion', 71.

[603] Also Tams, 'The law of self-defence in the *Wall* Case', 970.

Remark: Despite the ICJ's advisory opinion, Israel has continued to invoke the right of self-defence to justify military operations against the OPT, in particular against Gaza (see, e.g., the following communications by Israel: UN Doc. S/2005/609, 26 September 2005; UN Doc. S/20025/756, 5 December 2005; UN Doc. S/2006/798, 3 October 2006; UN Doc. S/2006/891, 15 November 2006; UN Doc. S/2006/916, 22 November 2006; UN Doc. S/2007/285, 16 May 2007; UN Doc. S/2007/316, 29 May 2007; UN Doc. S/2007/524, 4 September 2007; UN Doc. S/2008/816, 27 December 2008; UN Doc. S/2009/131, 6 March 2009). Increasingly, other UN Members have similarly come to use the language of 'self-defence' in their appraisal of these operations (see, e.g., EU Presidency Statement, The ICJ Resolution – Explanation of Vote, 20 July 2004, available at www.europa-eu-un.org/articles/en/article_3693_en.htm; UN Doc. S/PV.5481, 30 June 2006, 10 (France), 13 (Slovakia), 22 (EU); UN Doc. S/PV.5488, 13 July 2006, 5 (UK); UN Doc. S/PV.6060, 31 December 2008, 9 (South Africa), 13 (Italy, Vietnam). Contra, e.g., UN Doc. S/PV.5481, 28 (Libya: 'self-defence cannot take place in occupied territories'), 30 (Lebanon)). While it is not always clear whether the concept of 'self-defence' is used in its legal meaning, the situation has become particularly murky in the wake of Israel's unilateral disengagement from Gaza in September 2005. On the one hand, despite the military withdrawal, Israel still controls the Gaza airspace, the adjacent seawaters and all but the Rafah border crossing (over which it exercises indirect power). These and other elements indicate that Israel still acts as the occupying power (see, e.g., A. Bockel, 'Le retrait israélien de Gaza et ses consequences sur le droit international', (2005) 51 AFDI 16–26, at 21–3; Statement of UN Special Rapporteur Richard Falk to the Special Session of the Human Rights Council of 9 January 2009, available at www.unhchr.ch/huricane/huricane.nsf/view01/14B004C3AE39004BC125 753900599B5D?opendocument. Contra: Israeli Supreme Court, sitting as High Court of Justice, *Bassiouni* v. *Prime Minister*, Judgment of 30 January 2008, available at http://elyon1.court.gov.il/files_eng/07/320/091/n25/07091320.n25.pdf, § 12). On the other hand, it could be argued that the Gaza Strip has come to constitute a de facto regime, making it subject to the *Ius ad Bellum* (e.g., R. A. Caplen, 'Rules of "disengagement": relating to the establishment of Palestinian Gaza to Israel's right to exercise self-defense as interpreted by the International Court of Justice at the Hague', (2006) 18 Florida JIL 679–716, at 709–14). See also: Y. Shany, 'Faraway so close: the legal status of Gaza after Israel's disengagement', (2007) 8 YBIHL 369–83. (websites accessed 15 May 2009).

To some extent, the discussion on the applicability of the *Ius ad Bellum* might be seen as an exercise in legal acrobatics, since the underlying parameters largely overlap with the constraints on the recourse to force under the law of belligerent occupation, and since the exercise of the right of self-defence must in any event respect the rules of the *Ius in Bello* (e.g., Canor, 'When *Jus ad Bellum* meets *Jus in Bello*', 145–6). It may be observed in this respect that international scrutiny of Israel's operations against Gaza has by and large focused on its compliance with the basic rules of IHL pertaining to

5.2.4.b The 'Tangled Web': *DRC* v. *Uganda* (2005)

The ICJ was presented with another opportunity to address the matter under consideration in the *DRC* v. *Uganda* (or *Armed Activities*) case.[604] In this highly complex and multi-faceted case, set against the background of the Great African War, the Court examined whether the presence of Ugandan troops on Congolese territory between 1998 and 2003 amounted to a breach of Article 2(4) UN Charter. Uganda did not deny that its troops had carried out military operations – as part of Operation 'Safe Haven' – and had penetrated deep into Congolese territory, but invoked a twofold legal justification. On the one hand, it insisted that the Congolese authorities had consented to its military presence from May 1997 (when President Kabila – backed by Uganda – assumed power in Kinshasa) until 11 September 1998, and again from 10 July 1999 onwards (as a result of the Lusaka Agreement). As for the period in-between, Uganda portrayed its actions as lawful self-defence.

Interestingly, while both parties considered the provision of Article 3(g) of the Definition of Aggression to define the scope of self-defence in relation to attacks by irregulars and armed bands, they held a different conception of its meaning. According to the DRC, self-defence against indirect aggression was only available if the following four criteria were *cumulatively* fulfilled:

- irregular forces undertake military action against their own government of such gravity as to amount to genuine aggression;
- the irregular's actions are tolerated or even encouraged by the other State;

---

targeting and distinction. In the end, however, in light of the complexities of the Israeli–Palestinian situation, it would appear inappropriate to add the Israeli operations against Gaza to the general list of precedents supporting a more flexible reading of the *ratione personae* dimension.

[604] ICJ, *DRC* v. *Uganda*. See: S. A. Barbour and Z. A. Salzman, '"The Tangled Web": the right of self-defense against non-State actors in the *Armed Activities* case', (2007–8) 40 NYU JILP 53–106; J. T. Gathii, 'Armed Activities on the territory of the Congo', (2007) 101 AJIL 142–9; Kammerhofer, 'The *Armed Activities* case'; P. N. Okowa, 'Case concerning armed activities on the territory of the Congo (*Democratic Republic of the Congo* v. *Uganda*)', (2007) 56 ICLQ 742–53; R. Van Steenberghe, 'L'arrêt de la Cour Internationale de Justice dans l'affaire des Activités Armées sur le Territoire du Congo et le recours à la force', (2006) 39 RBDI 671–702; S. Verhoeven, 'A missed opportunity to clarify the modern *Ius ad Bellum*: Case concerning armed activities on the territory of the Congo', (2006) 45 RDMDG 355–63.

– the latter State provides the irregulars with *military and logistical assistance*; and,
– it is *substantially and actively involved* in the activities of these forces.[605]

The DRC argued that Uganda's self-defence claim met *none* of these criteria.[606] It stressed that it had not 'tolerated' or 'supported' anti-Ugandan forces present in the north-eastern part of its territory, but had simply been unable to exercise its authority over the region concerned for several years.

Against this, Uganda accused the DRC of setting the legal standard too high.[607] It drew attention to a 'powerfully expressed alternative view according to which the formulation of the majority of the Court in the *Nicaragua* case was excessively narrow in its approach to the interpretation of the phrase "armed attack"', and according to which 'the *giving of logistical support to armed bands with knowledge of their objectives* may constitute an armed attack'.[608] Relying on the ideas of Judges Jennings and Schwebel, Uganda concluded that

> the concept of 'armed attack' include[d] the following elements, taken both separately and cumulatively:
> a. The *sending by a State* of armed bands to the territory of another State . . .;
> b. The *sponsoring of armed bands by a State by the provision of logistical support in the form of weapons, training or financial assistance*; in these circumstances, and *in the presence of a shared purpose*, the armed bands become agents, or 'de facto organs,' of the sponsoring State;
> c. The *operations of armed groups which form part of the command structure of the armed forces of the State* concerned . . .; and
> d. In other circumstances in which there is *evidence of a conspiracy between the State concerned and the armed bands* fighting against the State taking action in self-defence.[609]

Uganda subsequently argued that *each* of these triggers was met in the present case: it claimed, for instance, that Sudanese forces and anti-Ugandan rebels had been incorporated in the Congolese army, and

---

[605] ICJ, *DRC v. Uganda*, Memorial of the Democratic Republic of the Congo, 6 July 2000, § 5.17.
[606] Ibid., §§ 5.08–5.24. [607] Ibid., Rejoinder of Uganda, 6 December 2002, § 242.
[608] Ibid., Counter-memorial of Uganda, 21 April 2001, § 350 (emphasis added). Contra: Reply of the Democratic Republic of Congo, 29 May 2002, §§ 3.127 et seq.
[609] Ibid., Counter-memorial of Uganda, 21 April 2001, § 359 (emphasis added).

that meetings between Congolese officials and rebel leaders further attested to the existence a conspiracy against Uganda.[610]

Two observations are in order. First, the written proceedings show a clear discrepancy between the Parties' reading of Article 3(g) Definition of Aggression. While the DRC relied on an orthodox reading based on the *Nicaragua* judgment, Uganda openly advocated a more liberal approach, keenly emphasizing that the ICJ 'does not adhere to a rigid doctrine of precedent'.[611] Second, while the Parties strongly disagreed on the extent to which mere 'support' was sufficient for purposes of self-defence, it is striking that – notwithstanding the DRC's insistence that it had been unable to exercise its authority over the volatile border region – Uganda did not directly challenge the assertion that the 'mere tolerance' within a State's borders of armed groups carrying out cross-border attacks was insufficient to activate Article 51.[612] Indeed, Uganda's cited enumeration of scenarios seemingly starts from the assumption that an 'armed attack' still requires *some degree* of State complicity. Put differently: mere failure to prevent cross-border attacks is implicitly ruled out as a justification for self-defence. Only in the oral proceedings did Professor Brownlie, Counsel for Uganda, suggest *en passant* that 'there is a separate, a super-added standard of responsibility, according to which a failure to control the activities of armed bands, creates a susceptibility to action in self-defence by neighbouring States'.[613]

How did the Court respond to the claim that Uganda had acted in self-defence between August 1998 and June 2003? First, the Court observed that the stated objectives of Uganda's Operation 'Safe Haven' were not consonant with the concept of self-defence as understood in international law.[614] Indeed, the 'High Command document', which had provided the basis for the operation, referred to security needs that were essentially preventative. Only one of the five listed objectives (viz. the neutralization of 'Ugandan dissident groups') referred to a response to acts that had already taken place. Second, Uganda had failed to report its actions to the Security Council.[615] Third, having rejected allegations of a tripartite conspiracy against Uganda between the DRC, the anti-Ugandan rebels of the ADF and Sudan, and having found that there

---

[610] *Ibid.*, §§ 360–71.   [611] *Ibid.*, Rejoinder of Uganda, 6 December 2002, § 268.
[612] *Ibid.*, Reply of the Democratic Republic of Congo, 29 May 2002, §§ 3.124.
[613] *Ibid.*, Public sitting held on Monday 18 April 2005, CR 2005/7, § 80.
[614] *Ibid.*, §§ 109, 119, 143. Remark: these dicta can be read as an implicit rebuttal of 'preventive' self-defence. See also *supra*, Section 4.2.2.c.
[615] *Ibid.*, § 145.

was no satisfactory proof of Congolese involvement, directly or indirectly, in cross-border attacks by the ADF, the Court observed that the attacks of which Uganda had been the victim 'did not emanate from armed bands or irregulars sent by the DRC or on behalf of the DRC, within the sense of Article 3(g) [Definition of Aggression]'.[616] Thus, even if this proven series of attacks could be taken cumulatively, 'they still remained non-attributable to the DRC'.[617]

The Court goes on to conclude that *'for all these reasons,* ... the legal and factual circumstances for the exercise of a right of self-defence by Uganda against the DRC were not present'.[618] Strangely enough, it subsequently states that 'accordingly, the Court has no need to respond to the contentions of the Parties as to whether and under what conditions contemporary international law provides for a right of self-defence against large-scale attacks by irregular forces'.[619] The Court's analysis of the self-defence claim is concluded by the observation, admittedly *obiter dicta*, that the taking of airports and towns many hundreds of kilometres from Uganda's border would in any event not have been proportionate to the series of transborder attacks.[620]

What is the unsuspecting reader to make of this reasoning? Despite the Court's dictum that it need not pronounce on the legality of self-defence against large-scale attacks by irregular forces, several scholars have objected that the ICJ answers in the negative the contentions it vows not to respond to.[621] Indeed, on the one hand, the Court seems to agree that Uganda has been the victim of a series of cross-border attacks by irregulars operating from Congolese territory and that the Congo was unable to control the events along its border.[622] Yet, on the other hand, the only 'legal and factual circumstances' identified by the Court in its rebuttal of Uganda's self-defence claim are, first, the lack of a report to the Security Council – which, according to previous case law and State practice, is *not an absolute precondition* for the lawful recourse to self-defence[623] – and, second, the lack of attributability of the ADF attacks to

---

[616] Ibid., § 146.   [617] Ibid., §§ 132, 146.   [618] Ibid., § 147 (emphasis added).   [619] Ibid.
[620] Ibid.
[621] See Kammerhofer, 'The *Armed Activities* case', 651. Also: Barbour and Salzman, 'The Tangled Web', 61–70; Corten, *Le droit contre la guerre*, pp. 702–3 (especially footnote 468); Dubuisson, 'La guerre du Liban de l'été 2006', 542; Okowa, 'Case concerning armed activities on the territory of the Congo', 748–9; Ronen, 'The Second Lebanon War', 376, note 93; S. Verhoeven, 'A missed opportunity to clarify the modern *Ius ad Bellum*', 358.
[622] ICJ, *DRC* v.*Uganda*, §§ 132, 135, 302–3.   [623] See *supra*, Section 2.2.1.a.

the DRC. Seen from this perspective, it is difficult to escape the impression that the Court not only rejected self-defence in response to non-State attacks which a State *fails to prevent*, but also reaffirmed the restrictive State-centric approach developed in *Nicaragua*.[624] It may moreover be noted that the Court's citation of Article 3(g) Definition of Aggression is incomplete: it only mentions the first 'link', viz. the 'sending by or on behalf of a State' of armed bands, while omitting the second element, namely the 'substantial involvement' of a State in attacks by non-States. Whether or not this omission was deliberate remains uncertain, yet at face value it would further seem to strictly limit the scope of Article 51 UN Charter to attacks that are imputable to a State in the meaning of the secondary rules on State responsibility.

On the other hand, at least theoretically, it remains possible to construe the Court's dicta as a somewhat artificial attempt to avoid pronouncing on the legality of self-defence against attacks by non-State actors in the absence of (substantial) direct or indirect State involvement.[625] Thus, Gray observes that the Court was able to circumvent this delicate issue because Uganda had not clearly argued for a wider view of 'armed attack beyond substantial involvement'.[626] It may be that the majority of the Court considered the Ugandan self-defence claim inadmissibile because Operation 'Safe Haven' was not directed solely against rebels carrying out cross-border raids.[627] Alternatively, it is possible that the judges believed the attacks of the ADF were not sufficiently large-scale to trigger Article 51 UN Charter.[628] Whether or not these factors played a role remains a matter of speculation, which cannot be determined on the basis of the judgment alone.

As in the *Palestinian Wall* advisory opinion, however, the individual opinions of a number of judges reinforce the view that the Court implicitly reaffirmed the *Nicaragua* threshold.[629] First and foremost,

---

[624] See, e.g., Corten, *Le droit contre la guerre*, pp. 702–3.

[625] In this sense, e.g., Zimmerman, 'The Second Lebanon War', 116. Arguably also: Gray, *The use of force*, p. 134.

[626] See *Ibid.*, p. 134, footnote 80.

[627] Cf. ICJ, *DRC v.Uganda*, § 110 ('Uganda was not in August 1998 engaging in military operations against rebels who carried out cross-border raids. Rather, it was engaged in military assaults that resulted in the taking of the town of Beni ..., followed by the taking of the town of Bunia ..., and the town of Watsa ...'.

[628] Cf. *ibid.*, § 147 ('the Court has no need to respond to the contentions of the Parties as to whether and under what conditions contemporary international law provides for a right of self-defence *against large-scale attacks by irregular forces*') (emphasis added).

[629] Also Van Steenberghe, 'L'affaire des activités armées sur le territoire du Congo', 686.

Judge Kooijmans observed that the Court 'implicitly reject[ed] Uganda's argument that mere tolerance of irregulars "creates a susceptibility to action in self-defence by neighbouring States"'.[630] He agreed with the Court that if the activities of armed bands present on a State's territory cannot be attributed to that State, the victim State is not the object of an armed attack *by it*. However, even absent substantial State involvement, if attacks by irregulars would, because of their scale and effects, have to be classified as an armed attack had they been carried out by regular armed forces, there is nothing in the language of Article 51 that prevents the victim State from exercising its inherent right of self-defence.[631] Kooijmans drew attention to a phenomenon which in present-day relations had unfortunately become as familiar as terrorism, 'viz. the almost complete absence of government authority in the whole or part of the territory of a State'.[632] He stressed that if irregular bands carried out cross-border attacks from such territory, the permissibility of self-defence should not be made contingent upon any concept of State attributability, but should be judged on the basis of the gravity of the attacks and the necessity and proportionality of the response.[633] Kooijmans regretted that the Court had foregone an opportunity to fine-tune the much-criticized threshold set out in its *Nicaragua* judgment.[634] Judge Simma fully agreed with his honourable colleague and accepted that when armed attacks were carried out by irregular forces operating from territory falling beyond the State's governmental authority, these activities still qualified as 'armed attacks', even if they could not be attributed to the territorial State.[635] Simma also regretted that the ICJ had missed the opportunity to clarify the state of the law on a highly controversial matter which is marked by great controversy and confusion – 'not the least because it was the Court itself that . . . substantially contributed to this confusion by its *Nicaragua* judgement'.[636] While the Court's approach in *Nicaragua* might well have reflected the prevailing interpretation of the law for a long time, recent developments in State practice and *opinio iuris* indicated that it ought to be reconsidered 'also by the Court'.[637] Both Simma and Kooijmans believed that the initial

---

[630] ICJ, *DRC v. Uganda*, Separate opinion of Judge Kooijmans, §§ 20–35, especially 22.
[631] *Ibid.*, § 29.   [632] *Ibid.*, § 30.
[633] *Ibid.*, § 31 (Remark: Kooijmans argued it was irrelevant whether the victim State's reaction would be termed self-defence, necessity or 'extra-territorial law enforcement'. What was clear that the criteria to be applied were those of self-defence).
[634] *Ibid.*, §§ 25, 35.   [635] *Ibid.*, Separate opinion of Judge Simma, §§ 4–15, especially 12.
[636] *Ibid.*, § 8.   [637] *Ibid.*, § 11.

response to ADF attacks in the DRC's border region in August 1998 fell within the limits of lawful self-defence, but found that Uganda had grossly overstepped these limits when it marched on Kisangani.[638] Criticism of the ruling was also expressed by Judge ad hoc Kateka, who observed that the gist of the Court's language had the same effect as that in *Nicaragua*, and that the Court apparently stuck to its limited interpretation of Article 3(g) Definition of Aggression.[639] Interestingly, Judge Tomka accepted in principle that 'the absence of central government presence in certain areas of a State's territory ... coupled with the attacks originating in that territory, would have justified the neighbouring State, victim of attack, to step in and put an end to the attacks'.[640] On the other hand, Judge Koroma argued that if a State merely enabled armed groups to act against another State, this would constitute 'no more than a "breach of the peace", enabling the Security Council to take action, *without, however, creating an entitlement to unilateral response based on self-defence*'.[641] As with *Palestinian wall*, most scholars expressed regret that the Court missed another opportunity consistently to address the legal issues surrounding the law of self-defence 'in a time in which a clear and unequivocal answer is highly desirable'.[642]

5.2.5 Conclusion: can non-State actors commit 'armed attacks'?

5.2.5.a *De lege lata*: legal uncertainty

Having examined the relevant customary practice and ICJ case law, we must again confront our key question: to what extent do cross-border attacks by non-State actors amount to 'armed attacks', warranting a defensive response against the non-State presence abroad and possibly against the infrastructure of the State from whose territory the attacks were prepared, directed and/or launched? In the past, as we have seen, this question was answered in a restrictive manner. A general right of hot pursuit was never recognized, and – despite the open-ended phrasing of Article 51 – purely 'private' attacks were excluded from its scope. Rather,

---

[638] *Ibid.*, § 14;, Separate opinion of Judge Kooijmans, §§ 32–4.
[639] *Ibid.*, Dissenting opinion of Judge ad hoc Kateka, §§ 13–15, 24 *et seq.*, esp. 14, 34.
[640] *Ibid.*, Declaration of Judge Tomka, § 4.
[641] *Ibid.*, Declaration of Judge Koroma, § 9 (emphasis added).
[642] E.g., Barbour and Salzman, 'The Tangled Web' 57; Okowa, 'Case concerning armed activities on the territory of the Congo', 752; S. Verhoeven, 'A missed opportunity to clarify the modern *Ius ad Bellum*', 360. Contra: Van Steenberghe, 'L'affaire des Activités Armées sur le Territoire du Congo', 702 (praising the prudence of the Court).

it was agreed that Article 51 only applied when close links existed between the non-State actor and the latter State, which in fact employed it as an instrument of proxy warfare. Article 3(g) of the Definition of Aggression identified two possible nexus, namely (1) the 'sending' by a State of non-State actors carrying out attacks, or (2) the 'substantial involvement' in these acts. The precise meaning of 'substantial involvement' was not specified, but the *travaux* indicate that logistical support and *a fortiori* the harbouring or tolerating of non-State actors was held insufficient. In 1986, the ICJ affirmed the relevance of Article 3(g) while excluding from its scope the provision of weapons and 'logistical or other support'. The latter limitation caused consternation among a number of legal scholars, yet it could be said to properly reflect customary practice prior to the mid 1980s.

Does this interpretation still correspond to State practice as it has developed in the past quarter of a century? It appears not. To hold otherwise would ignore the considerable number of interventions that exceed its strict parameters, as well as the numerous security doctrines and official statements that support a more permissive interpretation of Article 51.[643] Indeed, if we look *inter alia* at the US interventions in Afghanistan (1998 and 2001) and Sudan (1998), the Israeli intervention in Lebanon (2006) and the Turkish intervention in Iraq (2007–8), or at the *opinio iuris* expressed by States such as the US, Russia, Australia, France, the Netherlands, Rwanda, Ethiopia and Iran, it is difficult to avoid the impression that both State practice and *opinio iuris* have undergone important shifts since 1986, and especially since 2001.

At the same time, it appears premature to conclude that this shift in customary practice has crystallized in the unequivocal emergence of a new *ratione personae* threshold, replacing the traditional one. First and most importantly, as explained above, State practice since 2001 has been far from coherent.[644] While some claims of self-defence against non-State attacks have been accepted in principle, others have encountered a less favourable treatment: Israel's intervention in Syria in 2003 was denounced by a majority of Security Council Members; one year later,

---

[643] Consider also: Tams, 'Recent ICJ rulings on the law of self-defence', 289.
[644] Also urging caution: Corten, *Le droit contre la guerre*, pp. 694–9, 704; Corten and Dubuisson, 'Opération "liberté immuable"' (vis-à-vis 'Enduring Freedom'); Dubuisson, 'La guerre du Liban de l'été 2006', 562–3 (in relation to the Israeli–Lebanese conflict of 2006); Naert, 'The impact of the fight against terrorism on the *Ius ad Bellum*', 155 (referring to the Israeli strike against Syria in 2003); J. Verhoeven, 'Les "étirements" de la légitime défense', 50, 79.

Rwanda was condemned for intruding on Congolese territory; again, in 2008, Colombia was criticized by the OAS for raiding a FARC camp within Ecuadorian territory. It is not entirely clear from the discussions what distinctive features account for this differential treatment, thus generating the impression that the international response is primarily steered by political motives, rather than by legal considerations. Furthermore, while Russia and Rwanda claimed a broad right of self-defence against non-State attacks emanating from Georgia and the DRC respectively, both denied actual implementation of this claim. And if several security doctrines deviate from the *Nicaragua* threshold, few explicitly pronounce on the applicable criteria. For example, the assertion in the Netherlands Defence Doctrine that terrorist actions can also be regarded as armed attacks 'under certain circumstances'[645] is hardly helpful in clarifying the state of the law. Similarly, academic debate has so far failed to cut the Gordian Knot: while a majority of scholars accept that a strict insistence on State imputability is no longer tenable, alternative formulae vary wildly. Finally, recent ICJ case law has further embroiled the matter by combining an ostensible reaffirmation of the *Nicaragua* threshold with a smoke screen of ambiguity.

For now, the only thing that can be said about proportionate transborder measures of self-defence against attacks by non-State actors in cases falling below the *Nicaragua* threshold is that they are 'not unambiguously illegal'.

In light of the current legal uncertainty, one is forced to rely primarily on the proportionality and necessity criteria when assessing the exercise of self-defence in response to non-State attacks – this was for instance the focus of the debate during the Israeli intervention in Lebanon (2006) and the Turkish intervention in northern Iraq (2007–8). However, as the incoherent attitude of the international community amply reveals, these general parameters leave too much room for subjectivity and politicization, and fail to provide the minimal *Rechtssicherheit* that is indispensable for a credible and effective legal regime on inter-State recourse to force. *De lege lata*, further refining and complementing of these standards is needed.

Before returning to the drawing board, it is important briefly to re-emphasize the delicacy of balancing the national security interests of a State that falls victim to non-State attacks and the fundamental right to sovereignty and territorial integrity of the State from whose territory the

---

[645] Dutch Ministry of Defence, Netherlands Defence Doctrine, 33.

attacks are prepared, launched and/or directed. On the one hand, while non-State violence is not a new fact, the destructive potential of these groups has increased considerably – as illustrated by the 9/11 attacks. Modern means of transportation and communication allow them to travel and coordinate their actions under the radar, with little bother of national borders.[646] Explosives training is readily available on the Internet, and shadowy websites and media outlets provide a useful forum to recruit new members or instigate attacks. Many non-State groups continue to receive funding, military training, intelligence or other support from official authorities. This remains a notorious phenomenon in the Great Lakes Region[647] and the Middle East. Allegations of third-State support have also been made vis-à-vis the FARC, the Taleban, the Union of Islamic Courts, et cetera. The degree of support may vary considerably, and reliable evidence is often extremely difficult to collect. At times, non-State groups may establish a military presence within States that are incapable – for political, military or geographical reasons – of exercising full governmental authority throughout their entire territory. In such situations, law enforcement measures or military action within the victim State's own soil will not always suffice appropriately to protect it from further attacks.

At the same time, sovereign inviolability remains a fundamental tenet of international law, which cannot be set aside by reason of any given case of internationally wrongful conduct. Respect for the State's territorial integrity appears all the more pivotal when it has ostensibly not committed any wrong, but is instead the victim of a non-international conflict that has spilled over from a neighbouring country. Cross-border operations against non-State groups may gain little military advantage and cause important adverse side effects, such as an increased legitimacy of the non-State group or a further degradation of the governmental authority of the 'host State'. Last but not least, military escalation often looms over the horizon. The Colombian raid in Ecuador (2006) produced a blazing diplomatic rift, with Ecuador and Venezuela sending troops to the border. A genuine risk of escalation also existed in relation to the Turkish intervention in Iraq (2007–8). In a similar vein, one may

---

[646] Consider, for instance, the story of the 'shoe bomber' Richard Reid as recounted in Bobbitt, *Terror and consent*, pp. 67–70.
[647] See, e.g., Letter from the Chairman of the Security Council Committee Established pursuant to Resolution 1533 (2004) concerning the DRC to the Security Council, 10 December 2008, UN Doc. S/2008/773.

speculate what would have happened had India regarded the terrorist attacks in Mumbai of November 2008 – which left 170 dead and hundreds injured – as 'armed attacks' warranting a defensive response against Lashkar-i-Taiba targets within Pakistan.[648] In sum, while modern security needs urge a reappraisal of the *ratione personae* dimension, one must avoid embarking on a slippery slope to chaos and escalation, or reverting to a situation where 'might makes right'.

5.2.5.b The quest for a new threshold – some tentative criteria

5.2.5.b.i A modification of primary or secondary rules? A first – somewhat theoretical – question that needs to be tackled is whether the evolution towards a more flexible interpretation of the *ratione personae* threshold is a matter of 'primary' or 'secondary' law. 'Primary' law refers to the substantive rights and obligations of States in international law; 'secondary' law regulates the interpretation, modification and sanctioning of the primary rules.[649] In general, the rules that determine when private conduct is attributed to a State fall within the second category.

In relation to self-defence against non-State attacks, a number of authors argue that while the traditional interpretation of the concept – as developed by the ICJ and the ILC – is no longer satisfactory, 'State attributability' of armed attacks remains indispensable. More concretely, these authors argue that 'State attributability' should be interpreted in a more flexible manner, so that an armed attack *by* a State is no longer confined to situations where the non-State group is 'completely dependent' on the State, where the State itself 'sends', 'directs' or 'controls' the perpetrators of the attack in the (strict) sense of Article 8 DASR, or where it 'adopts and acknowledges' the attacks as its own in the (strict) sense of Article 11 DASR. Rather, it ought to include certain other forms of action or inaction on the part of the State.[650] Kammerhofer, for instance, insists that 'attribution is a necessary requirement of legal theory: armed attacks

---

[648] Remark: the attacks, which lasted from 26 until 29 November 2008, were traced back to the Lashkar-i-Taiba movement in Pakistan. According to US and Indian sources, this militant group allegedly maintained contacts with the Pakistani Inter-Services Intelligence (ISI). Pakistan denied all allegations. See, e.g., 'Pakistanis wary of Mumbai claims', *BBC News* 1 December 2008; 'Mumbai dossier is not evidence', *BBC News* 14 January 2009; 'Pakistan admits India attack link', *BBC News* 12 February 2009; 'India urges more action on Mumbai', *BBC News* 13 February 2009.
[649] See A. Cassese, *International law*, 2nd edn (Oxford University Press, 2005), 244; L. H. A. Hart, *The concept of law*, 2nd edn (Oxford University Press, 1994), 81, 91–8, 232–7.
[650] See *infra*, note 658.

need to be attributed to a State'.[651] At the same time, he finds that while for a long time the ILC DASR have 'simply been assumed to be the correct route', it has become uncertain whether they remain the appropriate standard.[652]

Others travel the road of primary law.[653] According to these scholars, recourse to self-defence is not, or no longer, absolutely contingent upon the imputability of cross-border attacks to the State whose territory is the *locus* of the defensive riposte. The implication is that – even if most of these scholars still hold State action to be *relevant* for purposes of Article 51 – they do not confine that provision to attacks (directly or indirectly) *by* a State, but accept that, legally speaking, 'armed attacks' may be committed *by* non-State actors. This possibility, it must be reiterated, is not excluded by the text of Article 51 UN Charter.

This difference of approach is not purely an academic exercise; it may entail certain consequences, both from a symbolic point of view (is the State the author of the attack?) and in terms of liability for the consequences of an attack.[654] A complicating factor is that Article 51 has characteristics of both 'primary' and 'secondary' law.[655] It constitutes a qualification to an obligation to abstain (viz. Article 2(4) UN Charter), and it couples a sanction to a factual occurrence (an armed attack) that does not constitute an autonomous breach of an international obligation (Article 51 does not *prohibit* an 'armed attack' as such). Article 21 DASR moreover identifies self-defence as a 'ground precluding wrongfulness'.

At least from a theoretical perspective, it is possible that the evolution towards a broader right of self-defence vis-à-vis attacks executed by non-State actors takes place through the emergence of a new and special imputability regime. Article 55 DASR recognizes that the Draft Articles do not apply where and to the extent that the content or implementation

---

[651] Kammerhofer, 'The *Armed Activities* case', 105, 110.   [652] *Ibid.*, 110.
[653] E.g., Brunnée and Toope, 'International law after Iraq', 794–5; Greenwood, 'International law and the pre-emptive use of force', 17; D. Jinks, 'State responsibility for the acts of private armed groups', (2003) 4 *Chicago JIL* 83–95; Krajewski, 'Der 11. September 2001 und seine Folgen', 196 *et seq.*; Maogoto, 'War on the enemy', 427; Müller, 'Legal issues', 257; Ronen, 'The Second Lebanon War', 384–5; Stahn, 'Terrorist acts as "armed attack"', 42–3.
[654] See, e.g., Lillich and Paxman, 'State responsibility for injuries to aliens', 308–9.
[655] See Kammerhofer, 'The *Armed Activities* case', 107–9. On the distinction between primary and secondary law, see: D. Bodansky and J. R. Cook, 'Symposium: the ILC's State Responsibility articles: introduction and overview', (2002) 96 AJIL 773–91, at 780; J. Crawford, 'The ILC's Articles on Responsibility of States for Internationally Wrongful Acts: a retrospect', (2002) 96 AJIL 874–90, at 876–9.

of the international responsibility of a State is governed by special rules of international law.[656] Furthermore, in the *Prevention of Genocide* case, the ICJ asserted that '[t]he rules for attributing alleged internationally wrongful conduct to a State do not vary with the nature of the wrongful act', *unless there is a 'clearly expressed* lex specialis'.[657] Against this background, one might argue that recent shifts in customary practice warrant a more flexible interpretation of the imputability regime in relation to cross-border attacks. *In concreto*, one might – hypothetically – suggest that (1) Article 8 DASR should be extended to attacks carried out under the 'overall control' of a State; (2) when a State willingly harbours a non-State group committing cross-border attacks, this would transmute the actual attacks into conduct 'acknowledged and adopted by the State as it's known' in the sense of Article 11 DASR; and/or (3) Article 9 DASR should extend to certain non-State attacks carried out in situations of partial or complete absence of governmental authority.[658]

In the end, however, apart from the obvious lack of *'clearly expressed'* lex specialis (considering the incoherence of recent practice), the attempt to change the limits of self-defence through a revision of the imputability standards appears artificial and counter-intuitive. Indeed, while there is a narrow margin to discuss the precise degree of 'direction or control' that

---

[656] An example of such *lex specialis* regime can be found in the Convention on the International Liability for Damage caused by Space Objets, GA Res. 2777 (XXVI) of 29 March 1972.

[657] § 401 (emphasis added).

[658] See, e.g., G. Travalio and J. Altenburg, 'Terrorism, State responsibility, and the use of military force', (2003) 4 *Chicago JIL* 97–119, at 102, 107, 110–11 ('[T]he very restrictive approach to State accountability advocated in the *Nicaragua* and *Iran Hostages* cases does not represent the current state of international law. ... Rather, the standard for State responsibility is one of sanctuary or support, and it has been accepted by the world community'); Murphy, 'Terrorism and the concept of "armed attack"', 50–1 (supporting a flexible reading of Articles 4,5, 9 and 11 DASR); Randelzhofer, 'Article 51', p. 802; Ruys and S. Verhoeven, 'Attacks by private actors', 318–19 (possible application of Article 9 DASR in the context of failed States); Stahn, 'Terrorist acts as "armed attack"', 37, 51 (suggesting that the 'effective control' test has been replaced by the 'overall control' test when it comes to determining the permissibility of self-defence *against* States); Stahn, 'International law at crossroads?', 223–6 (*idem* and supporting a flexible application of Article 9 DASR); S. Verhoeven, 'A missed opportunity to clarify the modern *Ius ad Bellum*', 359–60 (regarding the possible application of Article 9 DASR in the context of the *DRC* v. *Uganda* case); Wolfrüm and Philipp, 'The status of the Taleban', 595–6 (supporting an application by analogy of Article 16 DASR to non-State actors). Zimmerman suggests that there may be a 'specific norm of attribution' in case a State fails to comply with a request from the UN Security Council to take certain actions and its territory is then used by a non-State group for launching attacks against another State. See Zimmerman, 'The Second Lebanon War', 120.

is needed to impute private conduct to States, the axiom remains the same, whether we are dealing with human rights violations, acts of genocide, trans-boundary pollution or cross-border attacks:

> a State is only responsible for its own conduct, that is to say the conduct of persons acting, on whatever basis, on its behalf.[659]

Extending imputability for non-State attacks to cases where a State has provided military training and funding, has granted a non-State group access to its territory or has simply failed to prevent the attacks destroys this basic premise and stretches to breaking point the connection which must exist between the conduct of a State's organs and its international responsibility (to paraphrase the *Prevention of Genocide* case).[660] It completely overlooks the distinction that exists between (1) private conduct that is attributable to a State; (2) State actions in relation to non-State actors that themselves amount to internationally wrongful conduct; and (3) State omissions in relation to non-State actors that may or may not amount to internationally wrongful conduct.[661] Thus, it

---

[659] ICJ, *Prevention of Genocide* case, § 406. Remark: the ILC justifies this approach 'both with a view to limiting responsibility to conduct which engages the State as an organization, and also so as to recognize the autonomy of persons acting on their own account and not at the instigation of a public authority.' Quoted in Barnidge, *Non-State actors and terrorism*, pp. 4–5.

[660] *Ibid.*

[661] See in particular: Jinks, 'State responsibility for the acts of private armed groups', 83–4; Milanović, 'State responsibility for genocide', 583–4, 602 ('[T]*he law on state responsibility and the law on the use of force have their own separate logic and can simply develop independently*. . . . [The State] is responsible for . . . allowing the terrorists to operate from its territory; it is not, however, responsible for the acts of the terrorists themselves unless it controls them' (emphasis added)); Pisillo-Mazzeschi, 'The due diligence rule', 32–6; See also: Barnidge, *Non-State actors and terrorism*, p. 6; Lillich and Paxman, 'State responsibility for injuries to aliens'; S. Verhoeven, 'A missed opportunity to clarify the modern *Ius ad Bellum*', 359.

Remark: It is worth drawing the comparison with Article 16 DASR, which finds that '[a] State which aids or assists a State in the commission of an internationally wrongful act by the latter is internationally responsible for doing so if (a) that State does so with knowledge of the circumstances of the internationally wrongful act; and (b) the act would be internationally wrongful if committed by that State.' Here too, the ILC Commentary distinguishes between the different kind of responsibility of the States concerned: 'Under Article 16, aid or assistance by the assisting State is not to be confused with the responsibility of the acting State. In such a case, the assisting State will only be responsible to the extent that its own conduct has caused or contributed to the internationally wrongful act. Thus, in cases where that internationally wrongful act would clearly have occurred in any event, the responsibility of the assisting State will not extend to compensating for the act itself.' ILC, 'Commentary on the Draft Articles,' 66. See also Travalio and Altenburg, 'Terrorism, State responsibility, and the use of military force', 104.

may be recalled that in the *Tehran* judgment the ICJ did not deem Iran responsible for the acts of private individuals in seizing an embassy, but nonetheless held it responsible for failing to take all necessary steps to protect the embassy from seizure or to regain control over it.[662] Again, in *Prevention of genocide*, the Court determined that although Serbia had not committed genocide through its organs or persons whose acts engaged its responsibility, it had violated the obligation to prevent genocide in respect of the massacres at Srebrenica.[663] A similar distinction surfaces in other branches of international law.[664] It is submitted that it should also be upheld in the *Ius ad Bellum*.

Recent practice confirms that a complete alteration of the imputability regime vis-à-vis non-State attacks is inappropriate. Regardless of possible breaches of international obligations on the part of the States involved, it is clear that the 1998 US embassy bombings and the 9/11 attacks were regarded as 'armed attacks' *by* Al Qaeda, not *by* Afghanistan and Sudan; that the attacks against the Israeli border patrol in July 2006 was regarded as an 'armed attack' *by* Hezbollah and not *by* the State of Lebanon; and that cross-border attacks against Turkish security forces in 2007 were regarded as 'armed attacks' *by* the PKK and not *by* Iraq. In conclusion, the present author believes that it is the primary rules that are undergoing a process of modification, not the secondary ones, and that today non-State actors can (exceptionally) commit 'armed attacks' in the international legal meaning of that phrase.

5.2.5.b.ii The exercise of self-defence *within* and *against* a State

Does this mean that State imputability no longer bears *any* relevance for purposes of determining the permissibility of self-defence? Interestingly, a number of scholars argue that while imputability of attacks to a State is, indeed, no longer a prerequisite to allow an exercise of self-defence on its soil, only attacks that are imputable to a State, properly speaking, permit the defending State actually to *target* that

---

[662] ICJ, *Tehran Embassy* case.   [663] ICJ, *Prevention of Genocide* case.
[664] In international criminal law, for instance, a commander incurs criminal responsibility for crimes committed by forces under his command when he was, or should have been, aware of the acts, yet failed to take the necessary measures to prevent or repress their commission or to submit the matter for investigation and prosecution. This command responsibility is distinct from the direct penal responsibility for committing certain war crimes. See especially Article 28 Rome Statute of the International Criminal Court, 17 July 1998, UN Doc. A/CONF.183/9, reprinted in (1998) 37 ILM 1002–69.

State's infrastructure.[665] In other words, a distinction is made between the exercise of self-defence *within* the territory of another State, and the exercise of self-defence directed *against* that State.

Substantial support for this approach is found in State practice. In those cases where States responded to cross-border non-State attacks by mounting interventions within other States that either failed to prevent attacks from their territory or that allegedly 'harboured' or 'assisted' the non-State group concerned, the intervening States consistently emphasized that their actions solely targeted fighters and facilities belonging to the non-State group. Throughout the 1970s and 1980s, Israel, South Africa and Southern Rhodesia insisted that their incursions in neighbouring territories were directed solely against terrorist bases or 'hostile elements' abroad.[666] The same line of reasoning was followed by the US in relation to the strikes against 'the Bin Laden organization' in Sudan and Afghanistan (1998),[667] or by Turkey and Iran in relation to incursions in Iraqi territory throughout the 1990s.[668] In 2003, Israel claimed to have struck a terrorist training facility in Syria.[669] In July 2006, Israel asserted that it was 'concentrating its response carefully, mainly on Hezbollah strongholds, positions and infrastructure'.[670] The majority conviction expressed within the Security Council was that Israel could indeed take action against Hezbollah militants, but should refrain from attacking the Lebanese military or infrastructure. Again in 2007–8, the international community put considerable emphasis on the need for Turkish incursions into northern Iraq to be as precisely targeted as possible, and Turkey itself declared that it 'targeted solely the PKK presence in the region'.[671]

---

[665] See, to varying extents: Greenwood, 'International law and the pre-emptive use of force', 23–4; Krajewski, 'Der 11.September 2001 und seine Folgen', 203, 207; Maogoto, 'War on the enemy', 413; Müller, 'Legal issues', 253–7; Naert, 'The impact of the fight against terrorism on the *Ius ad Bellum*', 155; Paust, 'Use of armed force against terrorists', 533–43; Ronen, 'The Second Lebanon War', 385–6; Stahn, 'Terrorist acts as "armed attack"', 42–3; Wolfrüm and Philipp, 'The status of the Taleban', 590 *et seq*. However, several authors envisage a broader possibility for using force against the territorial State absent imputability: e.g., Brunnée and Toope, 'International law after Iraq', 795–6; M. N. Schmitt, 'Responding to transnational terrorism under the *Ius ad Bellum*', 182–7; Travalio and Altenburg, 'Terrorism, State responsibility, and the use of military force', 112.
[666] See *supra*, note 180.   [667] See UN Doc. S/1998/780.   [668] See *supra* Section 5.2.1.c.
[669] UN Doc. S/PV.4836, 7.   [670] UN Doc. S/PV.5489, 6.
[671] See *supra* Section 5.2.3.c; UN Doc. A/HRC/7/G/15.

By contrast, on those occasions where States directly targeted the infrastructure of the other State, they deemed it necessary to demonstrate in one form or another that the actual perpetrators of the attack were sent, directed or controlled by the former State. In 1956, for example, Israel claimed that Egypt not only harboured and assisted the *fedayeen*, but that active responsibility of command of these fighters rested with President Nasser.[672] In 1986, the US claimed to possess irrefutable evidence that Libya had ordered its agents to carry out the Berlin bombing, and that it was planning a multitude of future attacks.[673] Similarly, in relation to the strikes against Baghdad in 1993, the US argued that Iraq had 'planned, equipped and launched the terrorist operation' aimed at the assassination of former President Bush Snr.[674]

The only notable exception that does not fit this schism relates to Operation 'Enduring Freedom'.[675] Here, the US and the UK accused the Taleban – the de facto regime of Afghanistan – of having harboured and assisted Al Qaeda, yet they did not go as far as to accuse it of having 'sent, directed or controlled' the perpetrators of the 9/11 attacks. Nonetheless, the intervening States did not limit their actions to Al Qaeda targets within Afghanistan, instead launching an all-out war on Al Qaeda and the Taleban. Should we infer from the quasi-unanimous support for the intervention that customary practice now accepts that the mere 'harbouring' of armed groups makes a State's infrastructure liable to attack in self-defence? Probably not. Apart from the fact that numerous scholars criticized the extension of the operation to the Taleban regime,[676] one should not lose sight of the extraordinary context, viz. the extreme magnitude of the 9/11 attacks, the unique symbiosis between Al Qaeda and the Taleban, and the express recognition of the right of self-defence by the Security Council.[677] Apart from Operation 'Enduring Freedom', State practice has never accepted that the provision of military or logistical support, or the harbouring of non-State armed groups, make a State a lawful object of attack. These actions are all forms of internationally wrongful conduct which make a State liable to countermeasures. They do not, however, warrant an exercise of self-defence *against* – as opposed to *within* – that State. One *possible* reading of *Nicaragua* and

---

[672] E.g., UN Doc. S/PV.749, § 48.   [673] E.g., UN Doc. S/PV.2674, 16–17.
[674] E.g., UN Doc. S/PV.3245, 3 *et seq.*
[675] In this sense: K. N. Trapp, 'Back to basics: necessity, proportionality, and the right of self-defence against non-state terrorist actors', (2007) 56 ICLQ 141–56, at 152–6.
[676] See *supra*, note 395.   [677] Also Stahn, 'International law at crossroads?', 228.

DRC v. Uganda is that this is ultimately why the Court rejected the self-defence claims of the United States and Uganda: both countries had obviously gone beyond the targeting of the non-State presence abroad (by mining Nicaraguan ports, by taking numerous Congolese villages by force, et cetera).[678]

In a sense, these considerations flow from the overarching necessity and proportionality criteria, which require that self-defence be directed *against the actual source of the attack*. When the State does not itself 'send', 'direct' or 'control' the cross-border attacks, and the attacks are not otherwise imputable to the State in the sense of the DASR, it should not be considered the 'source' of the attack. On the other hand, even if non-State attacks are not imputable to it, a State may under certain conditions (cf. *infra*) be obliged to tolerate the exercise of self-defence *within* its territory. If, in such situation, the territorial State actively opposes incursions against terrorist groups or other armed bands, the State engaged in self-defence is permitted to take selective action against it insofar as needed to protect its military personnel and installations.[679] This brings us to the next question: when can self-defence be exercised against non-State actors *within* another State?

5.2.5.b.iii The irrelevance of the 'terrorist' label In examining the evolution of self-defence post 9/11, many authors have concluded that a special regime has emerged vis-à-vis 'terrorist' attacks or attacks by 'terrorist groups'.[680] This focus on the terrorist label is to a certain extent understandable since it is by and large the growing threat and destructive potential of trans-national terrorist groups as well as the increased awareness thereof that has led to the questioning of the scope of Article 51. Security Council resolution 1368 (2001), adopted on 12 September 2001, identified all acts of international terrorism as 'threats to international peace and security'. Resolution 1373 (2001) added an ambitious list of measures to eliminate international terrorism. Still, the

---

[678] E.g., ICJ, *DRC v. Uganda*, § 110. In this sense: Trapp, 'Back to basics', 142–5, 150.

[679] E.g., Dinstein, *War, aggression and self-defence*, 4th edn, pp. 250–1; Paust, 'Use of armed force against terrorists', 543; Stahn, 'Terrorist acts as "armed attack"', 50 ('The use of force against the host State might . . . be permissible to the extent that forces of the host State obstruct the use of force by the defending State against terrorist targets, or if they even join units of the terrorist group that launched the attack').

[680] E.g., Cassese, 'Article 51', pp. 1350–2; Naert, 'The impact of the fight against terrorism on the ius ad bellum'; Randelzhofer, 'Article 51', p. 802; Stahn, 'Terrorist acts as "armed attack"'; Travalio and Altenburg, 'Terrorism, State responsibility, and the use of military force', 112–13.

idea that there is a separate category of self-defence for 'terrorist attacks' is a misconception.

Despite continuous efforts, the international community has not (yet) succeeded in adopting an overarching legal definition of what constitutes 'terrorism'.[681] Today, States and regional organizations tend to adopt separate lists of groups that are identified as 'terrorist organizations'. Such lists are *inter alia* used by the EU, the US, Russia, India, Australia, Canada and the UK.[682] The content of the lists varies to a considerable extent. Hezbollah, for instance, is identified as a terrorist group by Canada and the US, whereas the Australian and British lists refer to the Hezbollah External Security Organisation and the Military Wing of Hezbollah respectively. By contrast, the lists of the EU, Russia and India make no reference to it. Similarly, while the FARC figures on the lists of the EU, Canada and the US, others fail to mention it, and several Latin American countries deliberately refuse to denounce it as a 'terrorist' group. The same is true *mutatis mutandis* in relation to other groups, such as the PKK. Against this background, making the application of self-defence contingent upon the recognition of the perpetrator of the attack as a 'terrorist' group is unrealistic and undesirable. It stands to wonder by whom such recognition should be issued. Certainly not by the intervening State itself, since that would grant it *carte blanche*. By a majority of the international community? Could it be argued that Turkey can engage in cross-border action against the PKK because many States have denounced it as a terrorist group, while Rwanda is prohibited from undertaking comparable action against ex-Far/Interahamwe fighters

---

[681] See e.g., Barnidge, *Non-State actors and terrorism*, pp. 13–51. Remark: work on a Comprehensive Convention on International Terrorism continues within the framework of the Ad Hoc Committee established by GA Res. 51/210 of 17 December 1996. For updates, see: www.un.org/law/terrorism/index.html or www.reformtheun.org/index.php (websites accessed 15 May 2009).

[682] As of 15 May 2009: European Union, Council Common Position 2009/67/CFSP of 26 January 2009, (2009) OJ 27 January 2009, L-23/37; US Bureau of Coordinator for Counterterrorism, 'Foreign Terrorist Organizations', 8 April 2008, at www.state.gov/s/ct/rls/other/des/123085.htm; 'Russia names "terrorist" groups', *BBC News* 28 July 2006 (the Russian list is available through the website of the Federal Security Service (FSB), www.fsb.ru/); Indian Ministry of Home Affairs, 'Banned Organisations', at www.mha.gov.in/uniquepage.asp?Id_Pk=292; Australian Government, 'Listing of Terrorist Organizations', available at www.ag.gov.au/agd/www/nationalsecurity.nsf/AllDocs/95FB057CA3DECF30CA256FAB001F7FBD?OpenDocument; Public Safety Canada, 'Currently listed entities', available at www.publicsafety.gc.ca/prg/ns/le/cle-en.asp; UK Home Office, 'Proscribed terrorist groups', at http://security.homeoffice.gov.uk/legislation/current-legislation/terrorism-act-2000/proscribed-groups.

operating from the DRC because they are not officially listed as 'terrorists' by third States? Of course not. Such approach would end in sheer subjectivity and would run against the entire rationale of self-defence. By comparison, it is worth recalling that self-defence against attacks by regular armed forces is not dependent upon the official recognition by the victim of the rival State and/or government, but equally applies to de facto regimes.[683] By analogy, the *ratione personae* conundrum must be tackled in a functional, rather than a formalist manner.

Two further considerations are warranted. First, 'terrorism' is often framed in terms of acts intended to cause death or serious bodily harm *to civilians or non-combatants*.[684] Hence, if one were to link the permissibility of self-defence against non-State actors to the 'terrorist' nature of the attack, it could be argued that (non-State) cross-border attacks against civilians would sanction the lawful recourse to self-defence, whereas attacks against military targets would not. This is an absurd suggestion, which flatly ignores exigencies of national security and the realities of State practice. Thus, the Israeli intervention in Lebanon in 2006 was essentially a response to a Hezbhollah attack against an Israeli border patrol (even though the Hezbollah had simultaneously launched rockets against Israeli villages). Likewise, the Turkish intervention in northern Iraq in 2007–8 was provoked by PKK attacks against Turkish security forces in south-eastern Turkey, not against civilians. Second, the idea that the recognition of the attacker as a 'terrorist group' is indispensable for the exercise of self-defence does not correspond to State practice. For example, in 2006, the EU and Russia recognized Israel's right of self-defence, even though neither officially listed Hezbollah as a terrorist organization. Conversely, even if Islamic Jihad is widely regarded as a terrorist group, the Israeli strike against a training camp in Syria in 2003 was denounced by most Security Council members.[685] Finally, it may be observed that while the Security Council has qualified numerous terrorist attacks as 'threats to international peace and

---

[683] See *supra*, note 1.
[684] See, e.g., the definitions used in Article 2(1)(b) of the Terrorism Financing Convention (reprinted in (2000) 39 ILM 270), in the Report of the UN-High Panel on Threats, Challenges and Change ('A More Secure World: Our Shared Responsibility', 2 December 2004, UN Doc. A/59/565, § 164), and in the UNSG Report 'In Larger Freedom' ('In Larger Freedom: towards Development, Security and Human Rights for All', 21 March 2005, UN Doc. A/59/2005, § 91). See also Maogoto, 'War on the enemy', 412.
[685] See *supra* Section 5.2.3.a.

THE 'ARMED ATTACK' REQUIREMENT *RATIONE PERSONAE* 499

security',[686] it has never explicitly labelled terrorist attacks as 'armed attacks' in the sense of Article 51. Resolutions 1368 and 1373 (2001) are so far the only occasions where the Council recognized the right of self-defence in the face of a terrorist attack.[687] In sum, while the terrorist nature of attacks may have important repercussions for purposes of law enforcement and criminal prosecution, it does not determine the permissibility of self-defence. For this reason, it is more appropriate to speak of self-defence against 'non-State actors',[688] and abandon the notion of 'self-defence against terrorist attacks'.

5.2.5.b.iv **Gravity and substantial external link** Having discarded a formalist approach based on the allegedly 'terrorist' nature of the attack, two functional elements are crucial in determining the applicability of Article 51 UN Charter, namely the gravity of the attack(s) and the external link. First, gravity matters. Strikingly, while several authors have challenged the wisdom of imposing a *de minimis* threshold on self-defence against armed attacks by regular armed forces,[689] there is a broad consensus on the importance of such threshold in relation to non-State attacks.[690] As mentioned elsewhere, this element received particular attention in the course of the debate on indirect aggression within the Fourth Special Committee and is emphasized in the final text of Article 3(g) of the Definition of Aggression. The implication is that isolated or sporadic acts of violence are excluded from the scope of Article 51.[691] For example, occasional terrorist attacks against individual diplomats have

---

[686] See, e.g., SC Res. 1438 (2002) of 14 October 2002; SC Res. 1440 (2002) of 24 October 2002; SC Res. 1450 (2002) of 13 December 2002; SC Res. 1465 (2003) of 13 February 2003; SC Res. 1516 (2003) of 20 November 2003; SC Res. 1530 (2004) of 11 March 2004; SC Res. 1566 (2004) of 8 October 2004.
[687] See also Hofmeister, 'To harbour or not to harbour?', 483–4.
[688] E.g., authors using this label: Hofmeister, 'To harbour or not to harbour?'; Kammerhofer, 'The *Armed Activities* case'; Krajewski, 'Der 11.September 2001 und seine Folgen'; E. Wilmshurst, 'Principles of international law on the use of force by States in self-defence', Chatham House International Law Working Paper 05/01, October 2005, 11.
[689] See *supra* Section 3.2.1.
[690] Especially Arai-Takahashi, 'Shifting boundaries of the right of self-defence', 1101; Cassese, 'Article 51', p. 1352; Krajewski, 'Der 11.September 2001 und seine Folgen', 199–201; Müller, 'Legal issues', 250–1; M.N. Schmitt, 'Responding to transnational terrorism under the *Ius ad Bellum*', 170; Stahn, 'Terrorist acts as "armed attack"', 45–6; Wilmshurst, 'The use of force by States in self-defence', 11, 13; Wolfrüm and Philipp, 'The status of the Taleban', 590.
[691] Travalio and Altenburg, 'Terrorism, State responsibility, and the use of military force', 100.

generally been framed in terms of 'crimes' punishable before a court of law, rather than as 'armed attacks', warranting the exercise of self-defence.[692] Likewise, in 1985, the murder of three Israeli citizens on a yacht in Cyprus, was not considered sufficiently grave to justify the strike against the PLO headquarters in Tunis.[693] The rationale behind this criterion is clear: in principle, attacks by non-State actors (terrorist or other) fall within the realm of law enforcement and criminal justice.[694] It is only when these attacks come to pose a genuine threat to national security that they also enter the sphere of the *Ius ad Bellum* and sanction the recourse to the military option. This certainly does not mean that only attacks of 9/11-like proportions give rise to self-defence. The immediate cause for the Turkish intervention in Iraq in 2007–8, for instance, consisted in three PKK attacks resulting in the killing of thirty-eight security personnel and the capture of eight others.[695] In turn, the Israeli intervention in Lebanon (2006) was provoked by the killing by Hezbollah of two Israeli soldiers and the capture of two others, this in combination with a series of diversionary rocket attacks. Upon closer scrutiny, there must either be one or more truly large-scale attacks, or else a protracted campaign of possibly smaller attacks.[696] In both cases, there must be evidence – in the form of statements by representatives of the non-State group and corroborating intelligence information – that further attacks are imminent.

A second requirement is that the armed attack(s) must present an external link to the State victim of the attack. Purely internal matters are of course excluded. The external link must moreover be substantial, in the sense that the *source* of the attack(s) and of the threat of future attacks falls beyond the State's own territory.[697] Thus, the fact that non-State

---

[692] E.g., UN Doc. S/14951, 3 April 1982 (Israel, regarding the shooting of an Israeli diplomat in Paris); UN Doc. S/15158, 4 June 1982 (Israel, regarding the shooting of the Israeli ambassador in London).

[693] Stahn, 'Terrorist acts as "armed attack"', 46.

[694] *Ibid.*, 45–6: 'The boundaries of law enforcement and self-defense can only be defined on the basis of a gravity threshold, which is determined on the basis of a variety of criteria, such as the duration and severity of the injury caused by the terrorist acts to the State.' See also Travalio and Altenburg, 'Terrorism, State responsibility, and the use of military force', 98–9.

[695] See *supra* Section 5.2.3.c.

[696] See also Dinstein, *War, aggression and self-defence*, 4th edn, p. 202; Stahn, 'Terrorist acts as "armed attack"', 46.

[697] Also Stahn, 'Terrorist acts as "armed attack"', 43. Unlike Stahn, however, the present author does not believe that the required external link is established simply by virtue of the fact that an attack is launched and directed by foreign nationals.

armed groups (terrorist or other) – think of the Irish Republican Army (IRA), the Euskadi Ta Askatasuna (ETA) or the Liberation Tigers of Tamil Eelam (LTTE) – receive money from diaspora abroad, have sympathizers or even recruiters in third countries, or acquire weapons outside their own country generally does not provide the necessary external link. Neither does the fact that individual members from time to time travel to or seek refuge in third countries. Instead, the proper link is reflected in the statements of NATO in the wake of the 9/11 attacks, where it held that Article 5 of the North Atlantic Treaty was activated if it was demonstrated that the attacks were 'directed from abroad'.[698] In other words, there must be a settled non-State presence abroad, from which attacks are instructed and/or launched, and from which future attacks are being prepared.

When dealing with an organized military group that is actively engaged in a campaign of hit-and-run attacks across a border (e.g., the PKK in 2007–8), the application of the aforementioned criteria is fairly straightforward. The task is, however, far more complex when confronted with isolated terrorist attacks that do not simply take the form of bullets or rockets being launched from territory A into territory B. *In casu*, thorough investigation must determine whether it was the work of a disparate group of individuals, acting on their own initiative, or whether it was coordinated by a structured non-State group, with quasi-military features, such as the existence of a clear chain of command and training camps for its members.[699] Consider the difference between the following incidents. On 12 October 2000, a small boat laden with explosives attacked the USS *Cole*. The blast ripped a hole in the side of the vessel, killing seventeen members of the crew and wounding at least forty others.[700] Subsequent investigation revealed that the suicide attack was supervised directly by Bin Laden: 'He chose the target and location of the attack, selected the suicide operatives, and provided the money needed to purchase explosives and equipment.'[701] In a similar vein, the 9/11 Commission Report reveals that the 9/11 hijackers were selected, trained and funded by Bin Laden and his aides, and that preparations for the

---

[698] See references *supra* note 374.
[699] In a similar vein: Krajewski, 'Der 11.September 2001 und seine Folgen', 200. Remark: this task may be facilitated when a known organization claims responsibility for the attack, yet the victim State is still obliged to verify the reliability of the claim.
[700] 'The 9/11 Commission Report', 22 July 2004, available at www.9-11commission.gov/report/911Report.pdf (accessed 15 May 2009).
[701] See *ibid*., 190–1.

attacks were closely coordinated by key Al Qaeda figures in Afghanistan.[702] By contrast, the Madrid train bombings of 11 March 2004, which killed 191 people and left at least 1,800 injured, were organized by a small group of Moroccan, Syrian and Algerian Muslims, with no ostensible link to Al Qaeda.[703] In relation to the London bombing of 7 July 2005, which killed fifty-two people and injured more than 770,[704] an official report explicitly posed the question whether the attacks were 'directed from abroad'.[705] While it found that several of the suicide bombers had travelled to Pakistan prior to the attacks, the report concluded that there was no firm evidence of Al Qaeda support or coordination.[706]

5.2.5.b.v Manifest and persistent unwillingness or inability to prevent non-State attacks – exhaustion of peaceful means

Once non-State attacks reach a sufficient gravity and there is a substantial external link, they can arguably be qualified as 'armed attacks' under Article 51. This, however, does not mean that such attacks automatically warrant the exercise of self-defence *within* the State of the external link. Indeed, in accordance with the necessity principle, which prescribes that self-defence only be used as a last resort, an additional safeguard is arguably needed before proceeding to a breach of the latter's territorial integrity. This safeguard pertains to the relationship between the territorial State and the non-State group within its borders, an element which has consistently influenced the international community's appraisal and which has attracted considerable attention in scholarly writings. The key question of course is what relationship is needed. As mentioned earlier, State imputability for the attacks, while certainly *sufficient*, is not *necessary* in order to justify coercive action *within* the State. In subsidiary order, must the State somehow be complicit in the attacks? Must it have committed an internationally wrongful conduct connected to the attacks?

---

[702] See *ibid.*, 153–73, 215–53. See also: UK Press Release, 'Responsibility for the terrorist atrocities in the United States', §§ 61–73.
[703] See: J. Burke, 'What role did Al-Qaida play?', *The Guardian* 31 October 2007; 'Timeline: Madrid investigation', *BBC News* 28 April 2004.
[704] See BBC News Special Report, 'London attacks', available at http://news.bbc.co.uk/2/hi/in_depth/uk/2005/london_explosions/default.stm (accessed 15 May 2009).
[705] UK House of Commons, Report of the Official Account of the Bombings in London on 7th July 2005, 11 May 2006, available at http://news.bbc.co.uk/2/shared/bsp/hi/pdfs/11_05_06_narrative.pdf (accessed 15 May 2009), §§ 42–55.
[706] *Ibid.*, §§ 50, 55.

In the wake of Operation 'Enduring Freedom', many authors have developed some form of 'harbouring' doctrine, the essence of which consists in the fact that a State allows a non-State actor to use its territory to launch or prepare armed attacks.[707] This approach echoes the US plea that the attacks of 9/11 had been 'made possible by the decision of the Taleban regime to allow the parts of Afghanistan that it controls to be used by [Al Qaeda] as a base of operation'.[708] It shares some resemblance with Article 3(f) of the Definition of Aggression which refers to 'the action of a State in allowing its territory, ... to be used by [another] State for perpetrating an act of aggression against the third State'.[709] An analogy can also be drawn with the law of neutrality, which states that 'neutral powers' may not permit belligerents to move troops, munitions or supplies across their territory, nor may they allow their territory to be used to form 'corps of combatants' nor 'recruiting agencies'.[710] Should a neutral State violate these proscriptions, the other belligerent State is justified in attacking the enemy forces in the territory of the neutral State.[711] 'Harbouring' not only presumes a material element, viz. the presence of an armed group within the State's territory. It also presupposes a subjective element, a *'mens rea'*, in that the State must have *willingly* granted access to and use of its territory even if it knew the non-State group was carrying out armed attacks or planned to do so. Some authors add as an additional requirement that the harbouring State should have provided different forms of support (training, weapons...) to the non-State group within its territory and/or that its support/harbouring should have 'enabled' or 'substantially contributed to' the commission of the non-State attacks.[712]

---

[707] E.g., Brunnée and Toope, 'International law after Iraq', 795; Gray, 'The use of force and the international legal order', p. 604; Hofmeister, 'To harbour or not to harbour?'; Randelzhofer, 'Article 51', p. 801; Stahn, 'Terrorist acts as "armed attack"', 49; S. Verhoeven, 'A missed opportunity to clarify the modern *Ius ad Bellum*', 359.

[708] UN Doc. S/2001/946.   [709] GA Res. 3314 (XXIX).

[710] Articles 2–5 Hague Convention V (1907) respecting the Rights and Duties of Neutral Powers and Persons in Case of War on Land, reproduced in A. Roberts and R. Guelff (eds.), *Documents on the laws of war*, 3rd edn (Oxford University Press, 2000), pp. 87–94.

[711] In this sense: Krajewski, 'Der 11.September 2001 und seine Folgen', 203; Travalio and Altenburg, 'Terrorism, State responsibility, and the use of military force', 111.

[712] See, e.g., Hofmeister, 'To harbour or not to harbour?', 494–9 (listing the following cumulative criteria: (1) the harbouring by a State of a non-State group; (2) the attacks could not be carried out without this 'harbouring' (*conditio sine qua non*); (3) clear and compelling evidence; and (4) the awareness of the harbouring State that the non-State group is carrying out attacks or is planning to do so); Randelzhofer, 'Article 51', p. 801

Although there is significant value in these approaches, the 'harbouring' model only offers a partial response to the challenge emanating from non-State armed groups. More precisely, it does not tackle what Judge Kooijmans described as a 'phenomenon which in present-day relations has unfortunately become as familiar as terrorism', namely the 'almost complete absence of government authority in the whole or part of the territory of a State', or – put differently – State failure.[713] In order to deal with such situations, several scholars accept a second trigger for self-defence against armed attacks by non-State actors. They agree that while a failed State is in principle protected by the rule of Article 2(4) UN Charter,[714] its failure to prevent cross-border attacks by non-State groups exceptionally justifies the recourse to proportionate defensive measures within its territory.[715]

Admittedly, 'harbouring' of non-State actors and 'failure to prevent' attacks are the two key scenarios where non-State attacks may give rise to self-defence. At the same time, one should not exaggerate in singling out these two settings. On the one hand, the two scenarios are not neatly separated in practice. Thus, while the attitude of the Taleban vis-à-vis Al Qaeda could quite unequivocally be characterized as 'harbouring' and while the DRC's impotence vis-à-vis armed groups in eastern Congo at the beginning of the twenty-first century could arguably be described as 'failure to prevent', it seems more complex to classify the position of Hezbollah in southern Lebanon in 2006, or that of the PKK in northern Iraq in 2007–8. On the other hand, the common rationale underlying these two scenarios is the same: before breaching another State's territory

('Decisive is, to what extent State support has enabled private groups to commit acts of military force . . .'); S. Verhoeven, 'A missed opportunity to clarify the modern *Ius ad Bellum*', 359. Others use the 'aiding and abetting' formula: e.g., Arai-Takahashi, 'Shifting boundaries of the right of self-defence', 1099; Ruys and S. Verhoeven, 'Attacks by private actors', 314–16 (drawing an analogy with 'aiding and abetting' in international criminal law). But: Stahn, 'Terrorist acts as "armed attack"', 227–8. Travalio and Altenburg refer to 'sanctuary or support': Travalio and Altenburg, 'Terrorism, State responsibility, and the use of military force', 111.

[713] ICJ, *DRC v. Uganda*, Separate opinion of Judge Kooijmans, § 30.
[714] M. Bothe, 'Terrorism and the legality of pre-emptive force', (2003) 14 EJIL 227–40, at 233; Cahin, 'L'Etat défaillant en droit international', pp. 192–3; Schmalenbach, 'The right of self-defence and the "war on terrorism"', § 7; J. Verhoeven, 'Les "étirements" de la légitime défense', 60.
[715] E.g., Bothe, 'Terrorism and the legality of pre-emptive force', 233; Brunnée and Toope, 'International law after Iraq', 795, footnote 58; Dinstein, *War, aggression and self-defence*, 4th edn, p. 245; Randelzhofer, 'Article 51', p. 802; Schmalenbach, 'The right of self-defence and the "war on terrorism"', § 7; J. Verhoeven, 'Les "étirements" de la légitime défense', 60.

by engaging in military action against a non-State group abroad, the State acting in self-defence should exhaust all peaceful means. In other words, it should offer the other State the opportunity to redress the situation by taking appropriate action against the non-State actor.[716] Only when there is clearly no prospect of the other State removing the threat to national security emanating from the non-State group, can the victim State take action on its own initiative.

In this context, rather than linking self-defence against non-State actors to two juxtaposed models – viz. the 'willful harbouring' model and the 'failed State' scenario – it may be more appropriate and more realistic to link the exercise of self-defence to a single overarching precondition, namely the *manifest and persistent unwillingness or inability to prevent non-State attacks*.[717] This precondition can be construed as a continuum with at one extreme situations where the territorial State provides active support to the non-State group (e.g., training, weapons, transportation, funding, accommodation, intelligence), and at the other extreme situations where the State has completely lost control over that part of its territory from which the group operates.

Evidently, the burden of proof lies with the State allegedly acting in self-defence. A valuable tool in discharging the *onus probandi* arguably consists in the existence of previous Security Council resolutions which may, for instance, label the situation as a threat to international peace and security; which may condemn the territorial State for supporting a terrorist organization; or which may call upon the territorial State to exercise its governmental authority throughout its entire territory. In the case of Afghanistan, for example, resolution 1267 (1999) insisted that the Taleban cease the provision of sanctuary and training to international terrorists and their organizations, take effective measures to ensure that the territory under its control is not used for terrorist installations and camps, and demanded that the Taleban turn over Osama Bin Laden to the appropriate authorities in a country where he had been indicted.[718] By comparison, resolution 1583 (2005) called upon Lebanon fully to extend and exercise its authority throughout the south, including

---

[716] E.g., Naert, 'The impact of the fight against terrorism on the *Ius ad Bellum*', 147, 155.
[717] Consider also: Dinstein, *War, aggression and self-defence*, 4th edn, p. 247; Müller, 'Legal issues', 256; Stahn, 'Terrorist acts as "armed attack"', 44; Wilmshurst, 'The use of force by States in self-defence', 11.
[718] SC Res. 1267 (1999) of 15 October 1999. These demands were reiterated in 2000: SC Res. 1333 (2000) of 19 December 2000.

through the deployment of its armed forces, and to exert control over the use of force on its territory and from it.[719]

Insofar as possible, even in extreme cases of unwillingness and inability to prevent non-State attacks, the territorial State should be granted some possibility to rectify the abuse. Thus, it may be recalled that in the wake of the 9/11 attacks, the US issued a threefold ultimatum to the Taleban: it had to hand over all Al Qaeda leaders to the US; it had to immediately close all terrorist camps; and it had to allow the US to verify that the camps were no longer operating.[720]

Again, a subtle difference exists between isolated 'Al Qaeda-like' terrorist attacks and repeated hit-and-run attacks across a border. In the former case, the territorial State may be expected to cooperate with the victim State in the field of law enforcement, that is, by arresting and prosecuting or extraditing suspected terrorists, through the exchange of information, by confiscating or 'freezing' the assets of the group in accordance with resolution 1373 (2001), et cetera. In the latter case, what matters is whether the territorial State takes credible steps to deploy its regular armed forces to volatile areas in order to re-establish law and order, or whether it steps up efforts to control its side of the border. Possible compromises may consist in the organization of joint border patrols or the conduct of a joint military operation. Alternatively, the States concerned may adopt a 'hot pursuit' agreement which defines the terms under which the victim State is allowed to engage in cross-border action.

In any event, in light of the need to strike an acceptable balance between the security needs of the victim State and the sovereign integrity of the territorial State, a genuine commitment to exhaust all peaceful means is even more important than in relation to attacks by regular armed forces. True, if a State is aware that its territory is used for launching or preparing attacks and manifestly and persistently fails to take action against the non-State group, it cannot perpetually hide behind its sovereign inviolability. On the other hand, if the State acts in good faith and takes reasonable steps to remove the non-State threat – possibly brokered or monitored by the international community – the victim State must refrain from having recourse to unilateral force.

---

[719] SC Res. 1583 (2005) of 28 January 2005. Similar provisions were included in SC Res. 1614 (2005) of 29 July 2005 and SC Res. 1655 (2006) of 31 January 2006.
[720] US President, Address before a Joint Session of the US Congress, 20 September 2001.

5.2.5.b.vi Other criteria? Should there be additional variables conditioning the permissibility of self-defence in response to non-State armed attacks? In light of the risk of escalation and other possible adverse side effects, one might be inclined to argue that further limitations are desirable to avoid over-application of Article 51 UN Charter. Two possible criteria come to mind. First, it could be argued that self-defence against non-State actors is only permissible if there is a 'reasonable chance of success'. This criterion has a long history in the *bellum justum* doctrine: already in the seventh century, Grotius identified it as one of the basic principles of just war theory.[721] It is closely related to the broader proportionality assessment in that it not only presupposes that military action stands a reasonable chance of success, but requires that the adverse consequences should not outweigh the possible benefits. It is therefore best framed in terms of a 'balance of consequences'. According to the UN High-Level Panel on Threats, Challenges and Change the key question here is whether there is 'a reasonable chance of the military action being successful in meeting the threat in question, with the consequences of the action not likely to be worse than the consequences of inaction'.[722] A second possible criterion could be that the victim State should not itself have contributed to the situation which gave rise to self-defence. This factor forms part of the definition of 'necessity' as a circumstance precluding wrongfulness in Article 25 DASR. In the past, it has also been used by some authors to distinguish allegedly reasonable from unreasonable reprisals.[723]

The problem with both criteria is that, while intuitively making sense, they are extremely difficult to operationalize in the present context, making them prone to subjectivity. First, it is often hard to predict the

---

[721] See, e.g., N. Fotion and B. Coppieters, 'Likelihood of Success', in B. Coppieters and N. Fotion (eds.), *Moral constraints on war: principles and cases* (Lanham: Lexington Books, 2002), pp. 79–91, at 79.

[722] Report of the Secretary-General's High-Level Panel on Threats, Challenges and Change, 'A More Secure World: Our Shared Responsibility', 1 December 2004, UN Doc. A/59/565, § 207. The High-Level Panel mentions this 'balance of consequences' as one of the criteria to determine the legitimacy of military action by the UN Security Council. The Panel probably found its inspiration in the reference thereto in the Report of the International Commission on Intervention and State Sovereignty: 'The Responsibility to Protect', December 2001, available at www.iciss.ca/pdf/Commission-Report.pdf (accessed 15 May 2009), 37.

[723] See D. Bowett, 'Reprisals involving recourse to armed force', (1972) 66 AJIL 1–36, at 15 *et seq.*; R. Falk, 'The Beirut raid and the international double standard', (1969) 63 AJIL 415–43, at 441–2.

likelihood of success of military operations against non-State actors, especially when the latter are dug-in in impenetrable areas such as mountainous or densely forested border regions. States have no crystal ball to predict how an intervention will turn out. Interestingly, in the aftermaths of the Israeli operation in Lebanon in 2006 and Turkey's Operation 'Sun' in Iraq (2008), both intervening States claimed to have at least partially secured their objectives. Conversely, Hezbollah and the PKK declared they were the actual victors of the respective showdowns.[724] An impartial account is not readily available. Furthermore, apart from the direct military outcome, there may be substantive negative 'fall-out'. The Pakistani government in 2008 repeatedly warned the US that predator strikes against Taleban fighters on its soil would further radicalize part of its population and weaken its domestic clout. The Israeli intervention of 2006 dramatically raised the stature of Hezbollah both in Lebanon and in the broader Arab world.[725] In March 2009, in response to a joint military operation by Rwanda and the DRC, FDLR rebels in eastern Congo launched a campaign of retaliation against the civilian population.[726] Do such elements influence the 'balance of consequences'? The better view appears to be that the 'likelihood of success' can only play a marginal role, as part of the broader necessity and proportionality assessment, and should not be regarded as a separate requirement of its own.

Examining whether the intervening State itself contributed to the situation giving rise to self-defence produces even greater uncertainty. In many cases, the State from whose territory the non-State group launches its attacks is itself the victim of an internal conflict which has spilled over its border. This was partially the case in relation to the presence of Chechen fighters, FARC members, ex-Interhamawe rebels, PKK and Taleban militants in Georgia, Ecuador, the DRC, Iraq and Pakistan respectively. And to what extent did Israel itself 'contribute' to the 2006 conflict through its continued occupation of the disputed

---

[724] See, e.g., A. Saikal, 'Limits of force: Israel's hollow victory in Lebanon', *IHT* 15 August 2006; 'Hezbollah leader: militants "won't surrender arms"', *CNN.com* 22 September 2006; 'Iraq incursion finished, Turkey says', *CNN.com* 29 February 2008. According to Mearsheimer and Walt, '[i]t was clear to most independent experts ... that Hezbollah had come out ahead in the fight' in 2006. See: J. J. Mearsheimer and S. M. Walt, *The Israel lobby and US foreign policy* (London: Penguin Books, 2007), p. 315 (especially footnotes 49 and 50).

[725] E.g., A. Saikal, 'Limits of force: Israel's hollow victory in Lebanon', *IHT* 15 August 2006.

[726] E.g., 'Congolese flee new Hutu attacks', *BBC News* 20 March 2009. Consider also: 'Uganda army says LRA rebels weakened', *AFP* 12 May 2009.

Shebaa farms and other areas? Again, this criterion raises more questions than it answers. It confuses the legal evaluation of the intervention with the political context and impedes an objective approach to the problem under consideration.

In the end, over-application and escalation is best avoided by strictly applying the necessity and proportionality principles, rather than by devising additional criteria beyond objective verification. The implication is that self-defence against non-State actors can only be a last resort, after peaceful means have been exhausted and it has been established that the territorial State is manifestly and persistently unwilling or unable to prevent attacks. No cross-border action is justified if the non-State threat can sufficiently be dealt with through action within the victim State's own territory (e.g., increased border patrols) or if the Security Council is able and willing to take effective action.[727] Furthermore, the defensive response must be strictly targeted against the actual source of the attack and should be strictly limited in scope, duration and intensity.[728] Temporary occupation of a neighbouring country's territory is excluded. Widespread damage to State infrastructure or large numbers of civilian casualties are unacceptable. Turkey's Operation 'Sun' in northern Iraq (2008) to some extent offers an example of an action that is indeed proportionate in nature. By contrast, Israel's large-scale intervention in Lebanon in 2006 arguably offers a demonstration of how States should not act.[729]

Apart from a strict application of the proportionality and necessity standards, abusive recourse to self-defence may be avoided by taking more seriously the evidentiary burden of the State claiming the exercise of self-defence. Simply submitting a formal report to the Security Council invoking Article 51 UN Charter is not sufficient. Instead, the intervening State must provide 'clear and compelling' evidence that (1) it

---

[727] Travalio and Altenburg, 'Terrorism, State responsibility, and the use of military force', 113–14. According to Travalio and Altenburg, 'it may be that mere public exposure of their support or sanctuary, or other diplomatic measures, may cause a State to cease its sanctuary or support. In other cases, economic sanctions by the threatened State and others will be enough. Resort to international bodies, such as the [UN] Security Council, must also have proven to be impractical or unavailing. Simply stated, a State cannot use force against a State providing sanctuary or support to terrorist groups unless that State has been given the opportunity to remove the terrorist threat from its soil or cease its support.'

[728] E.g., M. N. Schmitt, 'Responding to transnational terrorism under the *Ius ad Bellum*', 182.

[729] See, e.g., UNSG, Report of the Secretary-General on the Application of Resolution 1701 (2006), 12 September 2006, UN Doc. S/2006/730, 2.

has suffered one or more substantial attacks by a non-State group; (2) the attack(s) was/were directed from abroad; (3) further attacks are imminent; (4) the other State is manifestly and persistently unwilling or unable to prevent these attacks; (5) the action taken is necessary to tackle the non-State threat; and (6) the action is strictly targeted against and proportionate to the non-State threat.[730] Available evidence must be made public and subject to international scrutiny.

By way of conclusion it must be emphasized that while the present author does not believe that cross-border action against non-State actors *always* presupposes an authorization from the territorial State or from the UN Security Council, unilateral recourse to force risks generating only a placebo effect without rooting out the security threat. Ultimately, positive peace cannot be enforced; it must be 'built.' For this reason, bilateral and multilateral cooperation between law enforcement authorities remains the proper venue to thwart the threat of trans-national terrorist organizations. Likewise, diplomatic efforts to re-establish the authority of failed and failing States are likely to offer more promising and more durable outcomes than military intervention. Dealing with rebel groups and renegade fighters may require the creation of ambitious disarmament, demobilization and reintegration (DDR) programmes or the adoption of far-reaching amnesty laws. More generally, recourse to force can never serve as an excuse to ignore the political context and underlying root causes (think, for example, of the link between the Turkish Kurds' cultural and social rights and the success of the PKK). A more proactive attitude of the Security Council and regional organizations can go a long way in meeting the threat emanating from non-State armed groups and in reducing the need for unilateral recourse to force.

---

[730] Also: Charney, 'The use of force against terrorism', 836 (warning that the US failure to disclose the factual basis for its self-defence claim following the 9/11 attacks 'makes it easier for others to take unjustifiable military actions based on unsupported assertions of self-defence'); Arai-Takahashi, 'Shifting boundaries of the right of self-defence', 1088, 1095; Hofmeister, 'To harbour or not to harbour?', 497–8; Maogoto, 'War on the enemy', 408; Stahn, 'Terrorist acts as "armed attack"', 51; Stahn, 'International law at crossroads?', 234–5. See also: M. E. O'Connell, 'Lawful self-defense to terrorism', (2002) 63 Un Pittsburgh L Rev 889–908, at 895 *et seq*.; M. E. O'Connell, 'Evidence of terror', (2002) 7 JCSL 19–36.

6

What future for the 'armed attack' criterion?

6.1 The customary boundaries of self-defence

In this Section, we again confront the research question posed at the outset of our study: to what extent have recent evolutions in the international security environment, and reactions thereto in terms of State practice and *opinio iuris,* altered the customary boundaries of self-defence, both *de lege lata* and *de lege ferenda*? To answer it, we will bring together the different pieces of the puzzle, while keeping footnotes to a healthy minimum.

6.1.1 A word of caution

First, a word of caution. Throughout this study we have proceeded on the conviction that the primary material for interpreting and supplementing Article 51 UN Charter consists in relevant customary practice. We have made extensive use of 'concrete' custom, viz. States' physical practice and the concomitant exchanges of legal claims and counter-claims, but also of 'abstract' evidence – in particular the *travaux* of the UNGA Definition of Aggression. The case law of the ICJ and legal doctrine have been employed as a subsidiary source of interpretation.

While we believe this is the proper (positivist) method, its application is not without difficulties for various reasons. First, in spite of the abundance of verbal practice in the records of the UN Security Council and General Assembly, the idenfication and weighing of State practice and *opinio iuris* is not a matter of exact science. There is no mathematical formula that allows us to derive (the content of) a customary rule from a specific quantity of practice in combination with a fixed degree of *opinio iuris*. As an unwritten source of law, custom inevitably implies a greater degree of uncertainty than treaty law. In the realm of the *Ius ad Bellum*, this uncertainty is increased by the fact that States tend to mix legal and political considerations – the international response to South African and Israeli incursions in neighbouring countries serves as a good example.[1] Often, support for or opposition to concrete interventions is influenced by States' friendly or inimical relations with one another. This is illustrated, for example, by the different response of the United States to cross-border interventions against Kurdish separatists from Turkey and Iraq respectively.[2] States have also been far from consistent over time in interpreting the rules on the use of force. For example, whereas Pakistan seemed to rely on the notion of anticipatory self-defence to justify its troop deployment in Kashmir in 1950, it repeatedly rejected this doctrine on subsequent occasions.[3] In a similar vein, if the United States sometimes seemed sympathetic to the 'pre-existing custom' paradigm' in its attempt to have the Nicaraguan complaint before the ICJ declared inadmissible, it was keen on stressing that the Charter provisions on the use of force had 'subsumed and supervened' customary law.[4] Uncertainty over the precise circumstances of concrete instances of recourse to force is another factor complicating the analysis. This is especially the case with regard to small-scale incidents, which for this reason frequently escape international scrutiny. Yet, the lingering confusion over the outbreak of the 1967 Six Day War illustrates that the same may also be true for larger scale interventions.[5] Finally, while a significant amount of both physical and verbal practice has been amassed during the Charter era, the resulting picture remains fragmentary in certain respects. For instance, the invocation of Article 51 in response to the attacks against the US embassies in Nairobi and Dar es Salaam[6] has indicative value in determining whether large-scale attacks against embassies fall under the rubric of 'armed attack'. At the same time, due to a lack of generality, it is hardly irrefutable evidence. The same is true *mutatis mutandis* vis-à-vis the impact of the 1993 Baghdad raid on the extension of Article 51 to attacks against heads of State. This is not to say that analysing customary practice amounts to little more than discerning shapes in clouds – an honest and in-depth evaluation of the available material certainly does produce valuable insights. Still, grey spots remain.

---

[1] See *Supra* Section 5.1.3.b.   [2] See *Supra* Section 5.2.1.c.   [3] See *Supra* Section 4.1.2.c.
[4] ICJ, *Case concerning military and paramilitary activities in and against Nicaragua (Nicaragua v. United States of America)* (Merits), Judgment of 27 June 1986, (1986) ICJ Rep. 14–150, § 173.

Remark: another important example is the changed attitude of Russia in relation to self-defence against non-State actors (cf. the Soviet position during the negotiations on the UNGA Definition of Aggression to Russian statements after 9/11).

[5] See *Supra* Section 4.1.2.b.   [6] See *Supra* Section 5.2.1.b.

While the *Ius ad Bellum* framework has been clarified in important respects by the International Court of Justice, reliance on its case law does not remove all outstanding issues. It can be observed, for instance, that the Court has not settled the controversies on the permissibility of forcible counter-measures against 'lesser uses of force' or on the relationship between the right of self-defence in conventional and customary law, and may even have intensified them. As far as the interpretation of the 'armed attack' requirement is concerned, the ICJ deliberately refrained from pronouncing on the legality of self-defence against 'imminent' threats. *Ratione materiae*, the Court did pronounce in favour of a *de minimis* threshold, but gave little positive guidance for the purpose of establishing an 'armed attack'. Most problematically, recent rulings of the ICJ have exacerbated the confusion over the applicability of self-defence in *ratione personae* terms. If the *Nicaragua* case was long considered the Bible of the *Ius ad Bellum*, it must nevertheless be understood to be the Old Testament. So far, the apostles of the Peace Palace have been unable to come up with a new manual. The implication is a growing gap between the 'law in practice' and the 'law in the books', which is further accentuated by the various separate or dissenting opinions addressing the law on the use of force.

An in-depth analysis of legal doctrine is hardly more satisfactory. First, even if shifts in the positions of 'highly qualified publicists' indicate that the customary boundaries of self-defence are undergoing important changes, doctrinal disagreement remains as wide and deeply entrenched as ever. A proper mapping of the different views is impeded by the diverging meaning ascribed to key concepts, such as 'pre-emptive' and 'preventive' self-defence, or 'imputability/attributability' of private conduct. Another complicating factor is that positions vis-à-vis the scope of self-defence cannot be understood without taking into account scholars' broader approach to the applicability of the *Ius ad Bellum*. For example, an author may reject the legality of pre-emptive self-defence, but nonetheless believe that pre-emptive strikes can be excused by reference to a 'state of necessity'. It is also possible that an author combines a very narrow reading of the 'armed attack' requirement of Article 51 UN Charter with the view that limited cross-border operations against terrorist groups fall beyond the prohibition of Article 2(4) UN Charter. In other words, one must examine both the substantive outcome envisaged by the scholars concerned as well as the legal grounds in which it is couched. Scholarly attention has unsurprisingly tended to focus on the most large-scale and controversial cases, to the detriment of less 'visible' practice. The implication is that one risks creating a distorted picture of the *Ius ad Bellum*. Finally, more than in any other branch of international law, when dealing with the law on the use of force, members of the 'invisible college of international lawyers' find it difficult to set aside their own values, allegiances and perceptions of what is 'fair' in international relations. It is a known fact that the 'just war' theories of the past were strongly coloured by the bias of their respective authors. Vittoria, for instance, argued in the sixteenth century that the refusal of the native Americans to allow the Spaniards to travel freely among them and to propagate Christianity justified the Spanish war in the New World.[7] Even if not expressed openly, hints of apologetism or utopianism continue to underly present day assessments of concrete recourses to force. The present author does not pretend to be wholly impervious to such elements, yet it must be stressed that we have scrutinized concrete interventions for the purpose of deducing customary evidence rather than for the purpose of passing judgment. Arguments *de lege ferenda* have moreover explictly been cast in such terms.

These considerations are not intended to serve as a 'disclaimer', reneging the findings spelt out in previous chapters. Yet, it must be stressed that if an analysis of customary practice is both necessary and useful, it remains a work in progress. There is no simple QED – *quod erat demonstrandum* – at the end. Several questions remain unanswered *de lege lata*.

6.1.2 *The correlation between Article 51 UN Charter and other primary or secondary rules, and the 'pre-existing custom' paradigm*

Throughout our analysis, we have identified various sources of disagreement that have essentially existed since the adoption of the UN Charter. A first controversy concerns the relationship between the right of self-defence and other primary and secondary rules of international law. Second, ever since 1945, a major schism has existed between those scholars (sometimes dubbed the 'expansionists' or 'counter-restrictionists') who claim that Article 51 does not in any way diminish the pre-existing customary right of self-defence, and those scholars (the 'restrictionists') who find that the provision authoritatively regulates self-defence. Finally,

---

[7] See Y. Dinstein, *War, aggression and self-defence*, 4th edn (Cambridge University Press, 2005), p. 65.

both between and within these two blocs, scholars hold divergent interpretations on the precise requirements of self-defence, and, in particular, the precise purport of the 'armed attack' requirement. Although the latter issue has been the main object of our attention, for reasons of interrelatedness, the former questions should not be glossed over. A number of observations are due.

First, as Ago points out, 'it is right to dismiss at the outset so unconvincing an idea as that two really divergent notions of self-defence, based respectively on general international law and on the [UN] system, could co-exist'.[8] On the one hand, the suggestion that pre-existing custom has remained valid regardless of substantial differences with the Charter provisions on the use of force is theoretically unsustainable insofar as it ignores the equal normative power of treaty law and custom and the primacy of the *lex posterior*. On the other hand, the claim that the phrase 'if an armed attack occurs' in Article 51 UN Charter should be construed in a declaratory rather than a limitative fashion is unconvincing. All the primary means of interpretation show that the 'armed attack' requirement forms an integral part of the right of self-defence. The Charter's *travaux* contain no credible indications to the contrary. Furthermore, the continued reliance on 'pre-existing custom' by a number of scholars – and on rare occasions by States – has become all the more anachronistic and absurd in light of the considerable amount of customary practice generated over the past six decades. Claims pertaining to a broad interpretation of self-defence must not be rejected per se, yet they must be tested against customary practice as it has evolved throughout the Charter era, not as it stood before the San Francisco Conference. The 'expansionists' for their part would do better to abandon the 'pre-existing custom' discourse altogether, including the far-fetched assertion that the 1837 *Caroline* incident authoritatively explains the contours of a twenty-first century right of self-defence.

Second, it was argued that the use of force in breach of Article 2(4) UN Charter cannot be justified on any legal basis other than self-defence or Security Council authorization. Article 50(1)(a) DASR confirms that the recourse to force is excluded from the ambit of permissible countermeasures.[9] There is no support whatsoever in customary practice for any

---

[8] R. Ago, 'Addendum to the 8th Report on State Responsibility', (1980-II) 32 YBILC, Part One, 63.

[9] ILC, 'Commentary on the Draft Articles on the Responsibility of States for Internationally Wrongful Acts', (2001-II) YBILC at 75, 84–5, 131–2.

right of cross-border 'hot pursuit' absent the consent of the territorial State,[10] nor is there credible support that a 'state of necessity' can preclude the wrongfulness of violations of Article 2(4).[11]

The foregoing inevitably raises the question what acts constitute a threat or use of force in violation of Article 2(4) UN Charter, and what gap exists between the concept of 'use of force' in that provision and that of 'armed attack' surfacing in Article 51. We have not attempted a direct and comprehensive definition of the scope of 'use of force' under Article 2(4) UN Charter. Thus, we have not dwelled on whether or not humanitarian or pro-democratic interventions are uses of force 'consistent with the Purposes of the United Nations'. What we have asserted, however, is that the scope of Article 2(4) must be construed in a comprehensive manner, and is not restricted to interventions aimed specifically against the territorial integrity or political independence of the State.[12] Limited counter-terrorist operations, for example, are equally covered when they do not enjoy the consent of the territorial State. Furthermore, Article 2(4) may also apply to acts by a State within its own territory. This is particularly the case where a State actively uses lethal or potentially lethal force within its own borders against military personnel of another State.[13] In other situations, the answer is less clear-cut. For instance, while in certain circumstances the firing of shots against a merchant vessel comes within the rubric of law enforcement, in other situations it may amount to violation of Article 2(4) UN Charter.[14] The criteria which determine the applicable legal framework (cf. the amount of force used, the context or the intention of the parties) are not clearly established and certainly merit further scrutiny.[15] In any event, it must be emphasized that the concepts of 'use of force' and 'armed attack' are not identical, and that the latter has an autonomous denotation. Certain acts may constitute a 'use of force', but

---

[10] Cf. SC Res. 568 (1985) of 21 June 1985; N. M. Poulantzas, *The right of hot pursuit in international law*, 2nd edn (Dordrecht: Martinus Nijhoff, 2002), p. 12, footnote 7.

[11] See *Supra* Section 5.1.1.b; O. Corten, 'L'état de nécessité peut-il justifier un recours à la force non constitutif d'agression?', (2004) 1 *Global Community* 11–50, at 23–7, 42–7.

[12] This view is shared by a broad majority of legal doctrine. See Section 2.1.2.

[13] E.g., Dinstein, *War, aggression and self-defence*, p. 198, footnote 117; J. Kammerhofer, 'The *Armed Activities* case and non-State actors in self-defence law', (2007) 20 *Leiden JIL* 89–113, at 105.

[14] See, e.g., P. Jimenez Kwast, 'Maritime law enforcement and the use of force: reflections on the categorization of forcible action at sea in the light of the *Guyana/Suriname* award', (2008) 13 JCSL 49–91.

[15] For a rare in-depth analysis, see: O. Corten, *Le droit contre la guerre; l'interdiction du recours à la force en droit international contemporain* (Paris: Pedone, 2008), pp. 63–121.

not an armed attack. Assistance to rebels in the form of provision of weapons or logistical support probably falls within this category.[16] Other acts may of course qualify both as a 'use of force' and an 'armed attack' – this is certainly true with regard to large-scale cross-border interventions by one State against another. More controversially, while in general every 'armed attack' will *a fortiori* constitute a 'use of force', it is exceptionally possible to conceive of 'armed attacks' that do not simultaneously qualify as a breach of Article 2(4). Indeed, as discussed in Chapter 5, customary practice increasingly accepts that substantial cross-border attacks by non-State actors may be regarded as 'armed attacks' that trigger the right of self-defence within certain parameters, even if, technically, they are not a 'use of force' *by one State against another* as envisaged by Article 2(4). In other words, the relationship between the two concepts is not strictly linear.

6.1.3 Preconditions of individual self-defence other than the 'armed attack' requirement

In Section 2.2, we dealt with the preconditions of self-defence other than the 'armed attack' requirement. We found that Article 51 UN Charter contains two 'procedural' requirements, the objective of which is to guarantee that self-defence is only an exceptional and temporary deviation from the UN collective security framework, pending appropriate measures by the Security Council. As far as the reporting obligation is concerned, State practice as well as legal doctrine generally support the idea that a failure to comply does not automatically render the recourse to force unlawful. Rather, it provides a *rebuttable* indication that the State concerned does not believe itself to be acting in self-defence. If Gray identifies a growing compliance with the duty to report,[17] the record remains far from satisfactory, most notably in relation to small-scale incidents, but also with regard to more substantial interventions. This remains a worrisome situation, since proper reporting is crucial to facilitate international scrutiny of concrete interventions and to enable the Security Council to act at an early stage for the purpose of defusing latent or open conflicts.

In accordance with the 'until clause', the exercise of self-defence is terminated when the Security Council has taken 'measures necessary to

---

[16] Cf. ICJ, *Nicaragua* case (Merits), § 195.
[17] C. Gray, *International law and the use of force*, 3rd edn (Oxford University Press, 2008), pp. 122–3.

maintain international peace and security'. Due to the inertia of the Council throughout the Cold War era, there is relatively little practice on the matter. Still, an analysis of the available practice and of legal doctrine suggests that the rule only applies when the Council has actually taken concrete and effective measures to deal with the situation under consideration. The inclusion of an item on its agenda or the promulgation of measures of general purport are insufficient. By contrast, the adoption of military enforcement measures under Article 42 abrogates the right of self-defence, unless (1) the Council itself indicates otherwise; or (2) a new and significant *casus foederis* occurs. The same arguably applies when the Council adopts sanctions under Article 41 UN Charter. In other cases, it is probably up to States themselves – subject to the judgment of the international community and possibly to judicial scrutiny – to decide in good faith whether the Council's actions have been adequate.

Of paramount importance for the purpose of assessing self-defence claims are the customary standards of necessity and proportionality. These overarching principles are closely related and jointly hold that the exercise of self-defence must be geared towards the halting and repelling of an armed attack, and should not exceed this goal. In accordance with the necessity criterion, self-defence can only be exercised as a last resort, i.e., when peaceful means have reasonably been exhausted or would clearly be futile. Practice nonetheless indicates that the need to exhaust peaceful means only plays a subsidiary role when there is a prior attack, and that unlawfulness will only result when a manifest unwillingness to address diplomatic channels can be demonstrated. Another component of the necessity principle concerns the 'immediacy' of action undertaken in self-defence, viz. the requirement that such action should in principle be undertaken while the original armed attack which triggered it is still in progress and that there should be a close proximity in time between the start of the latter attack and the response in self-defence. Again, however, this condition must be interpreted with a certain degree of flexibility. Precedents illustrate that a limited time lapse may be justified in light of the need to make military preparations, to conduct an investigation into the origins of the attack(s), or to give peaceful negotiations a chance.

A second reservation concerns the idea that self-defence may exceptionally be lawful after an attack is 'factually over' insofar as it aims at preventing further attacks from being launched (this is the 'prospective' dimension of the necessity assessment, to be distinguished from the controversy pertaining to anticipatory self-defence). The underlying rationale is that when successive attacks are interlinked in time, source and nature, they can be assimilated to an 'ongoing' attack under Article 51 UN Charter. This is particularly relevant in the context of attacks by non-State actors, since these groups will often rely on hit-and-run tactics. If this qualification may seem fairly straightforward in the context of an unrelenting campaign of cross-border attacks, the risk of abuse is more troublesome in relation to attacks that are less frequent and more dispersed in time. For this reason, it is imperative that the intervening State produce compelling evidence that the acts complained of are related and that further attacks are imminent. A final aspect of the necessity criterion holds that action in self-defence must in principle be directed against the actual source(s) of the armed attack(s).

As far as the proportionality principle is concerned, a considerable majority of legal doctrine has asserted that it must be construed in a functional manner. In other words, most scholars believe that the proportionality of a concrete intervention must be assessed not by comparing the attack and the response thereto in terms of the relative casualties and damage caused, the weapons used and the number of troops deployed, but by testing the defensive action against the objective of 'halting and repelling the attack(s)'. If a rigid quantitative approach must indeed be discarded, customary practice nonetheless appears to give preference to a combined approach, differentiating on the basis of the intensity and the frequency of the armed attacks. In other words, when dealing with a relatively small-scale and isolated attack, the scale and effects of the defensive action ought to be reasonably proportionate (*eiusdem generis*) to the provocation. If, however, the armed attack were to assume a much larger scale, or if it were to form part of a series of successive attacks, then a more flexible and functional evaluation of the proportionality criterion becomes incumbent. Apart from the intensity of the defensive action and the range of targets, the proportionality evaluation is influenced by its geographical scope and duration. In accordance with the former factor, self-defence should normally be confined to the area of the attacks that they are designed to repel.[18] The latter parameter presupposes that self-defence should not continue past the point in time that is necessary to deal effectively with the attack(s).

---

[18] E.g., C. Greenwood, 'Self-defence and the conduct of international armed conflict', in Y. Dinstein (ed.), *International law at a time of perplexity: essays in honour of Shabtai Rosenne* (Dordrecht: Martinus Nijhoff, 1989), pp. 273–88, at 274–6.

Clearly, application of the necessity and proportionality criteria must take place on a case-by-case basis and is strongly determined by the various aspects of the 'armed attack' requirement.

6.1.4 Ratione materiae: *the basic ingredients of an 'armed attack'*

Contrary to the temporal and personal dimension of the armed attack requirement, the *ratione materiae* aspect has raised relatively little direct attention in recent years and appears to be unaffected by the shockwaves of 9/11. There is no recent physical practice which radically alters the traditional views vis-à-vis the basic ingredients of an 'armed attack'. Nonetheless, upon a closer look, there still exists considerable misunderstanding in this area, most notably in relation to the *de minimis* threshold.

A significant part of legal doctrine holds that Article 51 is only triggered by very large scale (or even massive) uses of force. This view – which is rejected by a growing number of scholars – is founded on an unwarranted focus on a number of ICJ dicta, and tends to ignore less visible instances of State practice as well as self-evident military exigencies. First, it appears to be inspired by the Court's distinction in *Nicaragua* between 'the most grave forms of the use of force (those constituting an armed attack)' and 'less grave forms', as well as on the exclusion from the scope of Article 51 of 'mere frontier incidents'.[19] Yet, while these findings indeed point to the existence of a gravity gap between 'use of force' and 'armed attack' and do impose a *de minimis* threshold on Article 51, they do not necessarily exclude the exercise of self-defence in response to small-scale attacks. Contrary to the Ethiopia–Eritrea Claims Commission,[20] the ICJ has never ruled out the fact that small-scale border incursions could 'singly or collectively' amount to an armed attack.[21] And in *Oil platforms*, the Court '[did] not exclude the possibility that the mining of a single military vessel might be sufficient to bring into play the "inherent right of self-defence"'.[22] Second, State

---

[19] ICJ, *Nicaragua* case (Merits), §§ 191, 195.
[20] Ethiopia–Eritrea Claims Commission, Partial Award *Jus ad Bellum*, Ethiopia Claims 1–8, 19 December 2005, reprinted in (2006) 45 ILM 430, §§ 11–16.
[21] In *Nicaragua*, it could not decide the question due to lack of information on the circumstances and motivations of the attacks (ICJ, *Nicaragua* case (Merits), § 231). Again, in *DRC v. Uganda*, the issue was circumvented for various reasons (ICJ, *Case concerning armed activities on the territory of the Congo (Democratic Republic of the Congo v. Uganda)*, Judgment of 19 December 2005, (2005) ICJ Rep 116–220, § 146).
[22] ICJ, *Case concerning oil platforms (Islamic Republic of Iran v. United States of America)*, Judgment of 6 November 2003, (2003) ICJ Rep 161–219, § 72.

practice contains considerable evidence demonstrating that self-defence equally applies to smaller scale attacks. Thus, when in the summer of 2006, an Israeli border patrol was ambushed by Hezbollah fighters, a majority of States accepted that Israel was permitted to act in self-defence.[23] Numerous other incidents involving hostile encounters between military units or border patrols have similarly been framed in terms of Article 51 UN Charter.[24] Although episodes such as the Gulf of Tunkin (1964) or the Gulf of Sidra (1981) incidents illustrate that the States concerned tend to present wholly different accounts of the facts, the underlying rationale is clear: in principle, a military unit that is subject to attack is permitted to take appropriate 'on-the-spot-reaction' in self-defence. This brings us to a third consideration, namely that it would be absurd and counter-intuitive to hold that military units are prohibited from defending themselves when attacked. In fact, no author has been willing to take such stance. Proponents of a high *de minimis* threshold either close their eyes to the problem of small-scale hostile encounters or else devise alternative legal mechanisms to create the same result. Thus, some have argued that although small-scale attacks cannot give rise to self-defence, they may nonetheless justify forcible counter-measures, or that forcible responses thereto may be justified on the basis of a 'state of necessity' or simply fall beyond the reach of Article 2(4) UN Charter. With respect, this approach not only seems inconsistent with the comprehensive and peremptory character of the Charter provisions on the use of force, but also ignores the fact that State practice has repeatedly framed these responses as applications of the right of self-defence.

This is not to say that there is no *de minimis* threshold whatsoever and that any 'use of force' automatically qualifies as an 'armed attack'. Both physical practice and the *travaux* of the Definition of Aggression do indeed support the need for a minimal gravity, depending on the circumstances. Again, the provision of weapons to a non-State group that is engaged in attacks against another State may qualify as an (indirect) use of force under Article 2(4), but will not as such trigger Article 51 UN Charter. In a similar vein, the firing of a single rifle shot across a border, hitting a tree or a cow may or may not constitute an infringement of

---

[23] See *Supra* Section 5.2.3.b.
[24] E.g., (1976) 22 *Keesing's* 27548; UN Doc. S/2000/49, 24 January 2000 (Pakistan); UN Doc. S/2007/69, 8 February 2007 (Israel); UN Doc. S/2008/653, 15 October 2008 (Cambodia); UN Doc. S/2008/657, 16 October 2008 (Thailand).

Article 2(4), but can hardly be regarded as an 'armed attack'.[25] Yet, the gravity gap should be construed in a narrow manner. An appropriate definition of the material element is provided by Dinstein, who finds that an armed attack requires '*a use of force producing (or liable to produce) serious consequences, epitomized by territorial intrusions, human casualties or considerable destruction of property*. When no such results are engendered by (or reasonably expected from) a recourse to force, Article 51 does not come into play.'[26]

Apart from this objective element, the present author believes that an 'armed attack' also presupposes a subjective element, a certain '*animus aggressionis*'. This argument finds support in the negotiations of the UNGA Definition of Aggression and in the case law of the ICJ.[27] It is crucial to emphasize, however, that the concept of '*animus aggressionis*' does not imply an analysis of the specific *motives* or *purposes* of the State using armed force (if such analysis is feasible at all). Rather, it must be understood more narrowly, as requiring the *deliberate* use of armed force against another State. In other words, it mainly serves to exclude the recourse to self-defence against acts committed by accident or by mistake (e.g., when an infantry unit accidentally crosses into neighbouring territory). In relation to more substantive uses of force, the '*animus aggressionis*' is normally implicit in the act itself unless there are clear indications to the contrary (States generally do not bomb or invade one another by accident). By contrast, in the context of isolated encounters between military units and small-scale territorial incursions, the permissibility of defensive action is strongly influenced by the subjective element. More specifically, practice suggests that in case of uncertainty, States should first opt for a series of measures that essentially aim at de-escalating the situation or at forcing the other side to betray its hostile intention. In situations such as these, the subjective element in principle consists in the actual *intent to attack*. When dealing with territorial incursions, however, it may exceptionally be interpreted as extending to certain incursions which threaten the national security and which can be seen as a harbinger of an impending attack. This is particularly the case when a State is the victim of repeated unauthorized surveillance flights or when foreign submarines are found submerged in the vicinity of military installations. Even so, any forcible response must be both necessary and proportionate under the concrete circumstances.

---

[25] Dinstein, *War, aggression and self-defence*, p. 195. [26] *Ibid.*, p. 193 (emphasis added).
[27] ICJ, *Nicaragua* case (Merits), § 231; ICJ, *Oil Platforms* case, §§ 61, 64.

Both State practice and ICJ case law[28] render support to the idea that different attacks that are linked in time and source may be 'accumulated' for the purpose of assessing self-defence claims. Since we have concluded that the *de minimis* threshold should be set relatively low, however, 'accumulation of events' is arguably not all that relevant for determining the existence of an 'armed attack' under Article 51 UN Charter. Still, it may be important in the sense that, in cases of doubt, the accumulated nature of the attacks can provide evidence of the '*animus aggressionis*'.[29] Otherwise, the recurring nature of the attacks suffered is probably more relevant from a necessity and proportionality perspective. As regards the former aspect, it may be recalled that successive attacks exceptionally permit the recourse to self-defence after the last attack is factually over, insofar as there is compelling evidence that further attacks are imminent (i.e., the 'prospective' dimension of the necessity criterion). As regards the latter aspect, practice suggests that the proportionality of defensive action should not be tested simply against the attack which ultimately provoked the response, but must equally take account of the fact that it was only the latest in a string of attacks (this may be regarded as the 'retroactive' dimension of the proportionality analysis).

If an 'armed attack' is commonly associated with an attack against a State's territory, it equally extends to certain attacks against 'external manifestations' of the State. This is first and foremost the case for attacks against military units or military installations abroad. The scope of Article 51 could moreover be expanded to large-scale attack against a State's embassies (although customary evidence is admittedly not conclusive in this respect). Exceptionally, States may also undertake on-the-spot reaction to protect civilian vessels or aircraft from attack (without, however, interfering with law enforcement measures by third States).[30] Finally, whether or not a State may forcibly intervene abroad to protect its nationals from harm when the territorial State is unable or unwilling to do so continues to give rise to disagreement. The debate on diplomatic protection within the UNGA Sixth Committee in 2000 amply reveals that

---

[28] ICJ, *Nicaragua* case (Merits), § 231; ICJ, *Oil Platforms* case, § 64; ICJ, *DRC v. Uganda*, §§ 146–7.

[29] Cf. in relation to the 1964 Gulf of Tunkin incident, for instance, the UK representative observed in the Security Council that: 'In the present case, there has not been merely one isolated attack on United States warships in international waters; we have been told that there have been repeated attacks, the nature of which is such as to indicate that they were deliberately mounted.' UN Doc. S/PV.1140, 5 August 1964, § 80.

[30] See *supra* Section 3.4.3.

many (mostly developing) States still perceive 'protection of nationals' as a pretext for domestic interference and 'gunboat diplomacy'.[31] On the other hand, an overview of concrete incidents reveals that condemnations have mainly focused on the abusive application of the doctrine rather than its validity as such. In addition, recent practice suggests a growing tolerance vis-à-vis limited military interventions to rescue foreigners abroad. In light hereof, the present author has pleaded for a conditional acceptance of so-called 'non-combatant evacuation operations'. Such operations could *de lege ferenda* be regarded as special applications of Article 51 UN Charter if the following conditions are cumulatively fulfilled: (1) there is an imminent threat of injury to nationals abroad; (2) the territorial sovereign is manifestly unable or unwilling to step in; (3) the national State has first attempted to obtain the consent of the host State; (4) the intervention is strictly limited to the objective of evacuating the threatened nationals; (5) force is used only insofar as necessary to protect the lives of persons entitled to evacuation as well as the personnel involved in the operation; and (6) like any other application of Article 51 UN Charter, the operation is reported to the Security Council.

6.1.5 The 'armed attack' ratione temporis

Contrary to the *ratione materiae* ingredients, the *ratione temporis* dimension has generated widespread public attention in the wake of the 9/11 attacks, both in political circles, in the media and in legal doctrine. The immediate cause for this was the promulgation in 2002 of the new US National Security Strategy, which falsely declared that the legality of self-defence against imminent threats was widely taken for granted, and suggested the need for 'temporal imminence' be abandoned.[32] If the NSS has succeeded in producing a certain shift in *opinio iuris* (and legal doctrine), it must be recognized that this shift is only partial, and has not been met by a concomitant trend in actual (physical) practice.

Since the academic debate on the *ratione temporis* controversy has long been clogged by terminological confusion, a first step to understanding the conundrum is to clarify the key concepts. In accordance with the 2004

---

[31] See *supra* Section 3.4.4.
[32] The National Security Strategy of the United States of America, Washington DC, 17 September 2002, at http://georgewbush-whitehouse.archives.gov/nsc/nss/2002/index.html (accessed 6 June 2009), 15.

report of the UN High-Level Panel on Threats, Challenges and Change,[33] the present study has used the term 'pre-emptive' self-defence as referring to self-defence against 'imminent' threats of attack, and 'preventive' self-defence as referring to action in response to 'non-imminent' threats. 'Pre-emptive' and 'preventive' self-defence are both subcategories of 'anticipatory'– as opposed to 'reactive' – self-defence. A final category that has generally been overlooked by States, but has attracted growing attention in legal doctrine, concerns 'interceptive' or 'interceptory' self-defence. This category lies on the fault line between 'anticipatory' and 'reactive' action and envisages situations where a concrete attack has been set in motion, but has not yet struck the defending State. While the distinction is not easy to make, 'interceptive' self-defence imposes a slightly narrower timeframe and a heavier burder of evidence than its 'pre-emptive' counterpart. Indeed, while the latter only requires an 'imminent threat' of attack, the former presupposes that the opponent's *capacity* and *intention* to initiate an armed attack has resulted in concrete measures of *implementation*. Uttering bellicose statements and/or making preparations for attack are insufficient under this rubric.

Proceeding on this basis, an analysis of relevant material prior to the events of 9/11 leads to the following conclusions:

- A substantial group of international lawyers has consistently spoken out in favour of defensive action against imminent threats of attack. Still, anticipatory self-defence has long been rejected by a majority of legal doctrine.
- Throughout the *travaux* of the Definition of Aggression, a majority of States refuted the legality of anticipatory self-defence. Statements to the contrary were strikingly rare (and lukewarm).
- Concrete customary practice confirms that Article 51 does not sanction preventive self-defence against 'non-imminent' threats. This flows from the reluctance of the US and the OAS to invoke this justification during the 1962 Cuban missile crisis, and, more importantly, from the widespread condemnation of Israel's strike against the Iraqi Osiraq reactor in 1981.
- Finally, despite the absence of a formal UN condemnation, the exchange of claims and counter-claims relating to the Six Day War reveals the reluctance of States to establish a precedent in favour of pre-emptive self-defence as well as the explicit dismissal of such doctrine by several others.

---

[33] Report of the Secretary-General's High-level Panel on Threats, Challenges and Change, 'A More Secure World: Our Shared Responsibility', 2 December 2004, UN Doc. A/59/565, § 189.

As mentioned earlier, this *status questionis* has undergone important shifts since the 9/11 attacks. The United States, determined to adapt its security strategy to the challenges of trans-national terrorism, State failure and WMD proliferation, publicly affirmed its support for self-defence against imminent threats and urged that it should be expanded to include certain non-imminent threats. While the US and its allies refrained from relying on a broad doctrine of anticipatory self-defence to justify the intervention in Iraq in 2003, the promulgation of the NSS has not gone unnoticed. On the one hand, the attempt to broaden the scope of Article 51 UN Charter to threats that are not temporally imminent has widely been defeated by States and legal scholars alike, as well as by the ICJ.[34] On the other hand, the NSS arguably initiated a chain reaction insofar as support for self-defence against imminent threats has increased considerably. On both sides of the Atlantic, a growing number of scholars has pronounced in favour of pre-emptive self-defence. Two important symbolic documents, the report of the UN High-Level Panel on Threats, Challenges and Change[35] and the UNSG report 'In Larger Freedom',[36] have subscribed to the US view that 'a threatened State, according to long established international law, can take military action as long as the threatened attack is imminent'. Last but certainly not least, apart from the United States, several other States have embraced the concept of pre-emptive self-defence in press statements, military doctrines or communications to the United Nations.[37]

Two reservations are due. First, in the run-up to the 2005 World Summit, numerous UN Members explicitly resisted the attempt to broaden Article 51 UN Charter to imminent threats. The implication is that there continues to be an important gap in *opinio iuris* within the international community. Second, the shift in *opinio iuris* and verbal practice has so far not been met by a comparable shift in physical State practice. Put differently: there still has not been any concrete precedent which convincingly demonstrates the community's acceptance of some form of anticipatory self-defence. For these reasons, it is premature to argue that Article 51 UN Charter has evolved to accept the legality of pre-

---

[34] ICJ, *DRC v. Uganda*, §§ 119, 143, 148.
[35] 'A More Secure World: Our Shared Responsibility', § 189.
[36] UN Secretary-General Kofi Annan, 'In Larger Freedom: Towards Development, Security and Human Rights for All', 21 March 2005, UN Doc. A/59/2005, § 122.
[37] See *supra* Section 4.2.2.c.

emptive self-defence (let alone that it has been modified to include preventive action against non-imminent threats).

In conclusion, the present author believes that *de lege lata*, Article 51 only allows minimal leeway for 'interceptive' self-defence, in response to attacks which have actually been launched, even if the consequences have not fully materialized.[38] This concept plays a role both at the tactical level – vis-à-vis small-scale territorial incursions by land, sea or air, as well as isolated hostile encounters between military units – and at the strategic level – vis-à-vis large-scale attacks against a State's territory. In the former situation, what matters most is the ascertaining of the opponent's 'hostile intent'. In the latter scenario, the irreversability of the course of actions embarked upon appears to be determinative. Thus, it is generally accepted that the US could have taken defensive action when it discovered that the Japanese fleet was sailing in the direction of Pearl Harbour. It must nonetheless be stressed that this scenario is extremely exceptional. The only notable example after 1945 that comes close to it concerns the Six Day War. The continuing confusion regarding the outbreak of that conflict nonetheless makes clear that an 'incipient' armed attack is particularly difficult to establish and illustrates the dangers of supplanting the 'armed attack' requirement by the much more indeterminate notion of 'imminent threat'. It should finally be noted that States are not completely forced to stand idle as threats emerge: they can of course engage in military preparations of their own, adopt non-forcible counter-measures or bring the situation to the attention of the Security Council.

On a final note, it may be observed that many proponents of a more liberal reading *ratione temporis* seem to agree that the threat of a *conventional* attack by another State does not permit the threatened State to take the initative and to actually open hostilities. By contrast, they believe that such reactive posture is not warranted when it comes to nuclear proliferation since a surprise nuclear attack can lead to complete annihilation. While this doom scenario appeals to the imagination, some reservations must nonetheless be made. First, from a military–strategic perspective, it is a fallacy to present 'pre-emptive strikes' against (suspected) nuclear facilities in a third country as a form of national self-defence. In such settings, the intervening State does not respond to pre-empt a concrete attack against it, but rather to prevent an adverse shift in the strategic and geopolitical balance. Indeed, as any use of

---

[38] See *supra* Sections 4.3.3–4.3.4.

nuclear weapons is most likely to result in massive retaliation, nuclear weapons are essentially instruments of deterrence. Second, upon close scrutiny, the 1962 Cuban missile crisis, the 1981 Osiraq raid and the 2003 Iraq intervention all illustrate that Article 51 UN Charter does not justify military action that simply aims at preventing States from developing nuclear programmes. The manipulation of the evidence regarding Iraq's WMD programme in the run-up to the 2003 Iraq intervention has moreover severely weakened the case of those favouring a 'nuclear' exception to Article 51. The mysterious Israeli raid against Syria in 2003 can hardly be regarded as a new trend in State practice and *opinio iuris*. In the end, although the threat of WMD proliferation must not be underestimated, the proper way to address it is through multilateral negotiations, through IAEA inspections and Security Council action.

6.1.6 Ratione personae: *attacks by non-State actors and the right of self-defence*

This brings us to the final and most complex aspect of the 'armed attack' requirement. If the *ratione materiae* dimension has not been subject to considerable changes after 9/11 and if the evolution pertaining to the *ratione temporis* dimension has been limited to a shift in *opinio iuris*, we now touch upon a dimension that has undergone fundamental challenges *both* in terms of *opinio iuris* and (physical) State practice.

Throughout the decolonization era, it was generally agreed that, in spite of the open-ended wording of Article 51 UN Charter, attacks by non-State actors could not in themselves qualify as 'armed attacks' in the legal sense, but only did so by virtue of a link with a State.[39] Furthermore, if the assisting or harbouring of non-State groups carrying out cross-border attacks was regarded as a form of 'indirect' use of force in breach of Article 2(4) UN Charter, so-called 'indirect aggression' was construed much more narrowly. After lengthy negotiations, Article 3(g) of the UNGA Definition of Aggression defined the latter concept as: '[t]he sending by or on behalf of a State of armed bands, groups, irregulars or mercenaries, which carry out acts of armed forces against another State of such gravity as to amount to the acts [of direct aggression listed in the Definition], or its substantial involvement therein'.[40] In its 1986 *Nicaragua* judgment, the ICJ concluded that this provision constituted

---

[39] See *supra* Section 5.1.
[40] Definition of Aggression, Annex to GA Res. 3314 (XXIX) of 14 December 1974.

a norm of customary international law and regarded it as the appropriate threshold to determine the legality of self-defence against attacks by irregulars and armed bands.[41] At the same time, the Court asserted that it did not extend to 'the provision of weapons or logistical or other support'. A *fortiori*, it implicitly excluded the mere harbouring or tolerating of non-State armed groups within the State's territory. The Court's restrictive interpretation was passionately decried by a considerable group of scholars, who criticized the Court for emptying the residual meaning of the notion of 'substantial involvement'. In the words of Judge Jennings, 'it [became] difficult to understand what it [was], short of direct attack by a State's own forces, that [might] not be done apparently without a lawful response in the form of . . . self-defence'.[42] Still, it could be argued that the Court's approach by and large reflected the compromise that emerged during the *travaux* on the Definition of Aggression. Furthermore, State practice throughout this era did not contain credible evidence to the contrary. On several occasions where States invoked Article 51 in response to infiltrations by armed bands, they insisted that the latter were 'sent' or 'directed' by the other State concerned. By contrast, the self-defence claims of Israel, Portugal, South Africa and Southern Rhodesia relying on active or passive support to armed bands or 'terrorists' operating on a more autonomous basis were generally refuted by the international community. In the end, the implication is that self-defence was by and large restricted to attacks that could be imputed or attributed to a State (in other words: attacks *by* a State in the legal sense). In accordance with the secondary rules on State responsibility, as developed by the ICJ and the ILC, this meant that attacks by irregulars were regarded as 'armed attacks' in the following situations: (1) when the irregulars were 'completely dependent' on the State; (2) when they were 'sent' by the State; (3) when they were acting under its 'direction or control'; or (4) if and to the extent that the State acknowledged and adopted the conduct as its own.

Amidst growing concern over the threat of trans-national terrorism and along with the fading of the colonial era, the *Nicaragua* threshold has increasingly been called into question in more recent years. Interestingly, critics have not only called for a more flexible reading of the required nexus between the State and the non-State actor, but have also queried whether such link is needed at all. While there were already indications of

---

[41] ICJ, *Nicaragua* case (Merits), § 195.
[42] ICJ, *Nicaragua* case (Merits), Dissenting opinion of Judge Jennings, 543–4.

a shift in customary practice prior to 2001 – most notably the surfacing of the US 'Shultz doctrine' in the 1980s – the real watershed coincided with the events of 9/11. Indeed, the horrendous attacks against the World Trade Center not only confronted the international community in an inescapable manner with the heightened threat of trans-national terrorism in a globalized world, they also sparked a US-led intervention in Afghanistan, directed against Al Qaeda and its patron, the Taleban regime. Despite the fact that the situation fell below the *Nicaragua* threshold, support for the intervention was quasi-unanimous.[43] Both NATO and the OAS invoked their respective collective defence provisions. Numerous individual States explicitly supported the applicability of Article 51 UN Charter. Even more remarkable, the Security Council in two subsequent resolutions referred to 'the inherent right of individual or collective self-defence in accordance with the Charter'.[44]

In the wake of Operation 'Enduring Freedom' several authors were quick to identify an 'instant' change in customary law, overturning the traditional conception of the *ratione personae* conundrum. Nonetheless, the overall picture is more complex. Thus, while several countries have adopted statements recognizing that attacks by terrorists or other non-State actors might be regarded as 'armed attacks' in the sense of Article 51 UN Charter, the international response to concrete incidents has been far from coherent.[45] In 2006, for instance, most States agreed in principle that the Hezbollah attack against an Israeli border patrol activated Israel's right of self-defence. When, some eighteen months later, Turkey launched an intervention against PKK hideouts in northern Iraq, the international reaction was characterized by widespread tolerance. By contrast, an Israeli strike against an Islamic Jihad training camp in Syria in 2003 and a Columbian attack on a FARC camp in Ecuadorian territory in 2008 gave rise to predominantly negative reactions. Furthermore, it must be observed that in two recent cases, the ICJ seems to have reiterated that self-defence is only available against attacks that are attributable to States – albeit in a highly ambiguous manner, which has evoked criticism from several individual judges.[46] Finally, whereas numerous scholars agree that the *Nicaragua* threshold has become untenable or invalid, opinions widely diverge as to the precise content of the new *ratione personae* regime.

---

[43] See *supra* Section 5.2.2.
[44] SC Res. 1368 (2001) of 12 September 2001; SC Res. 1373 (2001) of 28 September 2001.
[45] See *supra* Section 5.2.3. [46] See *supra* Section 5.2.4.

In the end, we must admit that this is an area which is characterized by significant legal uncertainty. *De lege lata*, the only thing that can be said about proportionate trans-border measures of self-defence against attacks by non-State actors in cases falling below the *Nicaragua* threshold is that they are 'not unambiguously illegal'. *De lege ferenda*, we believe that customary law is evolving towards a different application of Article 51 UN Charter in relation to defensive action *against* a State – viz. coercive action that directly targets the State's military or infrastructure – and defensive action *within* a State – viz. recourse to force against a non-State group present within the territory of another State. Action of the former type arguably remains conditional upon the imputability of the attack(s) to the State along the classical lines of the secondary rules on State responsibility. As far as action of the latter type is concerned, we believe that, absent State imputability, attacks by non-State actors may exceptionally qualify as 'armed attacks' in the legal sense and give rise to self-defence if and to the extent that the following conditions are cumulatively fulfilled:[47]

- The non-State actor has committed one or more truly large-scale attacks or is engaged in a protracted campaign of (possibly less substantial) attacks.
- There is a substantial external link to the State on whose territory defensive action is undertaken. This presupposes that there is a settled non-State presence in the latter country, from which attacks are instructed and/or launched. In addition, the attack(s) must have been coordinated by a structured non-State group, with (quasi-) military features, rather than being the work of a disparate group of individuals.
- There is compelling evidence that further attacks are imminent.
- There must be a manifest and persistent unwillingness or inability on the part of the territorial State to prevent the non-State attacks. This will in particular be the case when the State itself provides active support to the non-State group (e.g., training, weapons, transportation, accomodation, intelligence), or when it has completely lost control over that part of its territory from which the group operates (this is the 'failed State' scenario). Insofar as possible, even in extreme cases of unwilingness or inability to prevent cross-border attacks, the territorial State should be granted some possibility to rectify the abuse.
- The non-State threat cannot appropriately be dealt with by other means, such as action within the victim State's own territory.

---

[47] See *supra* Section 5.2.5.

– The defensive action is strictly targeted against and proportionate to the non-State threat. Only if the territorial State actively opposes defensive action that is compatible with the aforementioned conditions is the defending State permitted to take selective action against it (insofar as needed to protect its military personnel and installations).

Whether the perpetrator of the armed attacks can or cannot be regarded as a 'terrorist group' is irrelevant for present purposes: it is the nature of the acts committed, rather than the formal recognition of an entity as a terrorist group (by individual States or regional organizations) that is decisive. In any event, it must be stressed that this form of self-defence is to remain the exception. Bilateral and multilateral cooperation between law enforcement authorities remains the proper venue to thwart the threat of terrorist organizations. Likewise, diplomatic efforts to re-establish the authority of 'failing' States is likely to offer more promising outcomes than military intervention.

6.1.7 The slippery slope of self-defence

The picture we have sketched in the foregoing pages is likely to upset some scholars or politicians for being overly permissive. Others may reject it for being too rigid. The present author believes that the legal framework drafted throughout this study properly reflects customary evolutions *de lege lata* and *de lege ferenda* and represents a balance between national security concerns and the need for international stability and respect for territorial integrity. This, however, is not to say that it is immune from abuse. Indeed, while we have discarded a broad possibility of anticipatory self-defence, other challenges remain.

First, the acceptance that small-scale attacks may come within the ambit of Article 51 could be said to risk escalation, especially in highly contested border regions. This concern is not wholly unfounded, yet it must be stressed that in such situations, defensive action is governed by a very strict application of the proportionality and necessity standards. In principle, a small-scale attack can only give rise to on-the spot reaction aimed at the halting and repelling of that particular attack. To the extent feasible, the attacked unit should seek to disengage. On the other hand, denying such unit the right to undertake on-the-spot reaction is not only counter-intuitive, but also incompatible with actual State practice. It moreover seems illusory to think that simply denying this right would remove the threat of escalation.

A second hazard flows from the acceptance that States may exceptionally act in self-defence after the original attack is factually over in order to prevent further attacks from being launched. As examined elsewhere, this possibility seriously blurs the distinction between (lawful) self-defence and (unlawful) reprisals. Indeed, we have in recent years witnessed several interventions which have dangerously flirted with, or even overstepped, this fine line of demarcation. A notable example concerns the 1993 US raid against Baghdad. Even accepting that Iraq was behind the assassination attempt against former President Bush Snr, it is difficult to see the intervention as anything but a punitive expedition. Nonetheless, in spite of the absence of credible evidence that further attacks against the US were impending, a majority of Security Council members approved the operation.[48] The apparent acceptance that, in the absence or unlikelihood of effective Security Council sanctioning, individual States – or at least the United States as sole remaining superpower – should be given free reign to take the law in their own hands is a worrying development. It is submitted that States intervening in the Security Council or General Assembly should act more consistently in order to uphold the distinction between self-defence and reprisals. Again, absent Security Council authorization, *post facto* action is only allowed if the intervening State offers compelling evidence that further attacks are imminent.

Third and last, the prospect of defensive action in response to attacks by non-State actors could also be said to create a slippery slope to abuse and escalation. It might draw various actors into violent conflict, or be used as a pretext for domestic interference or territorial annexation. Prior to the Turkish intervention in northern Iraq in 2007–8, for instance, many States feared that a Turkish offensive would destabilize the (then) only stable part of Iraq. The President of the Iraqi Kurdistan Regional Government (KRG) explicitly warned that 'if the Turkish military [targeted] any Kurdish civilian citizens or any civilian structures', the KRG would order a large-scale resistance.[49] In the end, however, under pressure from the international community, Turkey's action was strictly targeted against the PKK presence in the Iraqi border region. This outcome sharply contrasts with the tragic events surrounding the Great African War (1996–2003). *In casu*, Rwanda, Uganda and Burundi shared legitimate security concerns vis-à-vis rebel groups that used the volatile regions in eastern Congo as a springboard for cross-border incursions. Uganda and especially Rwanda invoked

---

[48] See UN Doc. S/PV.3245, 27 June 1993.
[49] 'Iraq warns Turkey over incursion', *BBC News* 23 February 2008.

this argument as one of the main justifications to support their large-scale intervention in Congolese territory.[50] The results are well-known: apart from taking military action against hostile rebel groups, the intervening countries used the opportunity to oust President Mobutu and instal Laurent-Désiré Kabila in Kinshasa.[51] In a second chapter of the war, they occupied sizeable parts of Congolese territory (a multiple of their own territory) and began capitalizing on the extraction of natural resources (giving them little incentive to abandon the battlefield). As both countries effectively exported their civil war to neighbouring Congo, numerous other African States were drawn in on both sides of the conflict. The remainder of the international community stood by the sidelines as millions of civilians were killed or displaced.

The Great African War serves as a painful reminder that self-defence against non-State attacks must be approached with extreme caution. At the same time, the situation in Central Africa illustrates the power and detrimental impact of many non-State armed groups. The reports of the UN Groups of Experts on the DRC contain disturbing evidence on the facility with which rebel groups established control over parts of Congolese territory, their substantial financial resources, and the massive inflow of weapons by clandestine flights as well as overland.[52] In 2004, the Group of Experts found that:

> The [DRC] Government exerts little or no authority over extended parts of the eastern border. For instance, in Ituri, cross-border trade is controlled by armed groups that reap substantial benefits, in terms of both tax-generated revenue and easy access to commodities, both licit and illicit, from abroad. Controlling border areas is also of major strategic relevance, because it allows for a timely retreat to neighbouring countries when needed. ...
>
> As an institutionally weak State, the [DRC] significantly lacks control over both custom and immigration at its 83 formal border posts ... In some instances, State administration and authority is not present at all.[53]

---

[50] See F. Reyntjens, *The Great African War: Congo and regional geopolitics. 1996–2006* (Cambridge University Press, 2009).

[51] Remark: the love between Kabila and his patrons soon faded. Less than two years after his rise to power, Kabila found himself at war with the very States that had installed him in Kinshasa.

[52] The periodic reports of the Group of Experts to the UN Security Council are available at www.un.org/sc/committees/1533/egroup.shtml (accessed 1 June 2009).

[53] Letter from the Chairman of the Security Council Committee established pursuant to Security Council Res. 1533 (2004) concerning the Democratic Republic of the Congo to the Security Council, UN Doc. S/2004/551, 15 July 2004, §§ 27, 30.

The features of these non-State armed groups – like those of Hezbollah, the Taleban or Al Qaeda – demonstrate that an exclusively State-centred approach to the *Ius ad Bellum* is no longer appropriate.

6.2 Towards a UNGA 'Definition of Armed Attack'?

6.2.1 Resuming an ancient project

The present study holds that although it is premature to declare the death of the Charter provisions on the use of force,[54] recent events have nonetheless diminished the 'determinacy' of Article 51 UN Charter. The latter term is coined by Franck as the ability of a rule to generate an ascertainable meaning of what is permitted and what is prohibited.[55] For a rule to be determinate, it is not to be expected that it should provide a ready-made answer for each and every scenario possibly conceivable. Still, it must be possible to come to a reasoned consensus on its application in the great majority of cases. The determinacy of a rule strongly influences the efficiency of the justificatory discourse process, i.e., the exchange of claims and counter-claims at the international level, which in turn catalyses the 'compliance pull' of the rule concerned.[56] The more determinate a given norm, the easier it becomes to distinguish lawful and unlawful behaviour, and, consequently, the costlier it becomes to commit a breach.

As far as the right of self-defence is concerned, we have seen that many aspects of Article 51 have long given rise to fundamental disagreement among legal scholars. This is most notably the case with regard to the *de minimis* threshold, the doctrine of anticipatory self-defence, and the legality of self-defence in response to attacks by non-State actors. In light of the growing threat emanating from non-State armed groups and the growing number of nuclear States, these controversies are no longer limited to academic circles, but have increasingly left their marks on the public debate, giving rise to new security doctrines and shifts in

---

[54] Cf. T. M. Franck, 'Who killed Article 2(4)? Or: changing norms governing the use of force by states', (1970) 64 AJIL 809–37. See also: M. J. Glennon, 'The rise and fall of the U.N. Charter's use of force rules', (2003–04) 27 Hastings ICLRev 497–510, at 497.

[55] T. M. Franck, *Fairness in international law and institutions* (Oxford: Clarendon Press, 1995), pp. 30–4.

[56] See on this: I. Johnstone, 'Security Council deliberations: the power of the better argument', (2003) 14 EJIL 437–80; T. Ruys, 'When law meets power: the limits of public international law and the recourse to force', in E. Claes, W. Devroe and B. Keirsbilck (eds.), *Limits of the law* (Berlin: Springer, 2009), pp. 253–72.

State practice. Given the inability and/or lack of competence of the ICJ and legal doctrine to cut the Gordian Knot and given the resulting legal uncertainty, the present author believes that States should take these matters up directly and engage in a comprehensive effort to clarify the content of Article 51 UN Charter. Simply circumventing difficult legal questions by relying on the overarching necessity and proportionality standards is no longer tenable. Rather, what is needed is a genuine 'Definition of Armed Attack', by analogy with the UNGA Definition of Aggression, to be incorporated in a General Assembly resolution, and providing an authoritative interpretation of Article 51 UN Charter.[57]

If this proposal may appear somewhat radical, if not utopian, it is not entirely novel. Indeed, as we have seen elsewhere, from the very outset, the efforts to negotiate a UNGA definition of 'aggression' were inspired not only by the desire to define States' legal responsibility for 'aggression', but also to clarify the scope for lawful self-defence. Just as during the negotiations on the UN Charter at San Francisco, the terms were widely regarded as two sides of the same coin.[58] Moreover, discussions on specific aspects of 'aggression', such as the meaning of 'indirect aggression' or the impact of the 'first use' criterion, were inextricably linked to considerations of self-defence. In 1952, for example, UK representative Fitzmaurice admitted that:

> The whole problem resides precisely in knowing when the war is being waged as a matter of self-defence and when it is being waged as a matter of aggression. Until you have defined what self-defence consists of, and what are the cases in which the use of force is use of force in self-defence, you are no nearer precise definition than you were before. If there is no definition of self-defence, there is no definition of aggression.[59]

As the negotiations developed, however, a group of Western States sought to detach the quest for a definition of 'aggression' from the scope of self-defence. On the one hand, the Thirteen-Power proposal expressed the conviction 'that armed attack (armed aggression) is the most serious and dangerous form of aggression and that it is proper at this stage to proceed to a definition of this form of aggression'.[60] By contrast, the Six-Power proposal made clear that it aimed at a

---

[57] Consider also: T. Gazzini, 'The expanding law of self-defence', (2006) 11 JCSL 343–59.
[58] See *supra* Sections 3.1.1–3.1.2.
[59] Extracts from a speech delivered before the UNGA Sixth Committee by UK representative G. G. Fitzmaurice, 9 January 1952, reprinted in (1952) 1 ICLQ 137–44, at 142.
[60] Preamble, UN Doc. A/AC.134/L.16 (and Corr.1).

clarification of the term 'act of aggression', as used in Article 39 of the UN Charter, dealing with the enforcement powers of the UN Security Council.[61] Throughout the debates, the Six Powers strongly objected to the mingling of 'aggression' and 'self-defence'. Referring to the schism between two schools of thought – one seeing Article 51 UN Charter as part of a broader customary right of self-defence, and another viewing Article 51 as the exclusive regulation of self-defence – they stressed that it was unrealistic to believe in a definition of 'armed attack' acceptable to both. Furthermore, it was considered unnecessary to examine the scope of self-defence in any detail, since it was only of incidental relevance for the purpose of defining 'aggression' as understood in Article 39 UN Charter. In the end, as part of a broader political compromise, the Six Powers succeeded in defusing the endeavour to obtain a joint definition of 'aggression' and 'self-defence'. Instead, Article 6 of resolution 3314 (XXIX) simply observes that: 'Nothing in this Definition shall be construed as in any way enlarging or diminishing the scope of the Charter, including its provisions concerning cases in which the use of force is lawful'.[62]

Taking account of the extreme length of the negotiation process, it is difficult not to perceive the outcome as a disillusionment. Rather than achieving a legal definition of 'aggression' or 'self-defence', the resolution simply offers non-binding guidance to the UN Security Council for the purpose of clarifying its own enforcement powers. Moreover, it does not appear to have had significant impact on the practice of that body. In the overwhelming majority of cases, the Security Council has based its enforcement action on (a broad interpretation of) the notion of 'threat to the peace', rather than 'breach of the peace' or 'act of aggression'. References to '(acts of) aggression' have been rare in the practice of the Security Council,[63] and the Definition of Aggression has so far not been mentioned a single time.[64] On the other hand, it must be admitted that (part of) the Definition of Aggression was somewhat 'rehabilitated' as a result of the ICJ's *Nicaragua* judgment. In addition, it may be observed that the definition of the 'crime of aggression' adopted by consensus at the thirteenth plenary meeting of the ICC Assembly of States Parties on 11 June 2010 (Resolution RC/ Res. 6, Annex I, 'Amendments to the Rome

---

[61] Article 1, UN Doc. A/AC.134/L.17 (and Corr.1).
[62] Definition of Aggression, Annex to GA Res. 3314 (XXIX) of 14 December 1974.
[63] See N. Weisbord, 'Prosecuting aggression' (2008) 49 HILJ 161–220, at 169.
[64] See O. Solera, *Defining the crime of aggression* (London: Cameron May, 2007), pp. 201–2.

Statue of the International Criminal Court on the Crime of Aggression') expressly relies on the content of Resolution 3314 (XXIX). Thus the new Article 8*bis* (1) of the amended Rome Statute of the International Criminal Court declares that:

> For the purpose of this Statute, 'crime of aggression' means the planning, preparation, initiation or execution, by a person in a position effectively to excersise control over or to direct the political or military action of a State, of an act of aggression which, by its character, gravity and scale, constitutes a manifest violation of the Charter of the United Nations.

Article 8 *bis* (2) moreover copies the text of Articles 1 and 3 of the General Assembly Definition of Aggression.

Whatever the contemporary significance of resolution 3314 (XXIX), it is submitted that States ought to recapture its original ambition, and strive towards a full-fledged 'Definition of Armed Attack', to take the form of a General Assembly Resolution. If successful, this project would result in a consensus resolution providing authoritative guidance on the interpretation and application of Article 51 UN Charter.

While such endeavour will not be a walk in the park, the present author does not believe that a 'Definition of Armed Attack' is completely unattainable. First, already during the preparatory works of resolution 3314 (XXIX), there was a certain convergence of positions vis-à-vis issues relating to self-defence. The primary example was the compromise on 'indirect aggression' incorporated in Article 3(g). Another illustration was the growing recognition throughout the negotiations that the criteria of 'priority' and 'intent' were not incompatible. Interestingly, there was also a promising in-depth discussion of anticipatory self-defence throughout the 1950s (although the topic was by and large avoided in subsequent years).[65] There is no reason to believe that what was possible then should be impossible nowadays. Second, an additional factor which may facilitate negotiations is that there exists today a considerable body of State practice interpreting the Charter rules and that the International Court of Justice has given valuable guidance on a range of issues. In the past, some Western delegations tended to frame the controversy on self-defence in terms of a binary choice between Article 51 UN Charter and the 'pre-existing custom' approach. Today, it is clear that such picture is overly simplistic and that a more nuanced analysis of post-1945 customary practice is long overdue. Third, if disagreement on the scope of

---

[65] See *supra* Section 4.1.3.

self-defence has never been so open and widespread, the paradox is that the time may actually be ripe to achieve a global consensus. As for the *ratione temporis* aspect, for instance, it should be fairly uncontroversial to decree that self-defence cannot be exercised against non-imminent threats. Moreover, in light of the shift in *opinio iuris* towards greater recognition of pre-emptive self-defence (against imminent threats), States that have traditionally insisted on a restrictive interpretation of Article 51 UN Charter may now be more inclined to meet half-way and explicitly recognize the legality of interceptive self-defence. As for the *ratione personae* conundrum, the fading of the colonial era may allow for a more politically detached approach to the legality of self-defence in response to attacks by non-State actors. Another factor that could catalyse a more flexible reading of this topic is the heightened zero-tolerance in the post-9/11 era of State support for armed groups and in particular terrorist organizations. On a more general level, negotiations on the Definition of Aggression were often split along classical Cold War lines. Clearly, such schism no longer exists.

Of course, certain issues are bound to provoke fierce opposition among UN Members. In light of its concern over Iran's nuclear ambitions, a State such as Israel may show little proclivity to recognize that security threats do not warrant unilateral recourse to force. In a similar vein, States whose territory is on occasion used as a springboard for cross-border attacks by non-State armed groups (e.g., Iraq, Pakistan, the DRC, Ecuador) may feel reluctant to extend the scope of Article 51 UN Charter to cover such situations. In the end, however, even if unanimity would prove beyond reach, a UNGA resolution adopted by a large majority of UN Members would still have significant interpretative authority. If, in the worst case scenario, no resolution would be adopted, the negotiation process itself could – like the *travaux* of resolution 3314 (XXIX) – nevertheless serve as a valuable pool of abstract customary evidence.

6.2.2 *A blueprint*

The quest for a 'Definition of Armed Attack' need not start from scratch. Past UNGA resolutions, in particular the Definition of Aggression, obviously provide helpful guidance to steer the process. Furthermore, it is worth noting that the Institut de Droit International (IDI) during its Session in Santiago in October 2007 adopted a resolution on self-defence.[66] Apart from illustrating that the long-standing controversies are not insurmountable, this ten-paragraph resolution provides an excellent point of departure for drafting a General Assembly resolution. The following are some of the strong points of the IDI resolution:

- By referring to 'Article 51 [UN] Charter as supplemented by customary international law' (§ 1), it does away with the idea of two separate legal frameworks, one enshrined in Article 51 UN Charter and another part of customary international law.
- It explicitly acknowledges that there is no basis in international law for the doctrine of 'preventive self-defence' (§ 6).
- It makes a distinction between self-defence 'against' and 'within' a State and recognizes that attacks by non-State actors that are not imputable to a State may exceptionally give rise to measures of self-defence (§ 10).

Other provisions, however, are more problematic. First, despite a lack of support in State practice, the IDI resolution affirms the legality of pre-emptive self-defence (against a 'manifestly imminent armed attack', § 3).[67] Second, whereas the resolution asserts that an armed attack must be 'of a certain degree of gravity', it adds that '[i]n case of an attack of lesser intensity the target State may ... take strictly necessary police measures to repel the attack' (§ 5). As explained earlier, however, the present author believes it is inappropriate to exclude 'attacks of lesser intensity' from the scope of Article 51 UN Charter. Rather, insofar as necessary, such attacks may give rise to self-defence, be it in the form of limited on-the-spot reaction. Third, although the resolution recognizes that armed attacks by non-State actors may exceptionally trigger the right of self-defence absent State imputability, it only refers to situations where the attacks are launched 'from an area beyond the jurisdiction of any State' (i.e., the extreme 'failed State' scenario). Hence, it offers an incomplete answer to the challenge of non-State attacks.

A number of provisions could moreover be added or elaborated. For instance, it would seem useful explicitly to affirm the peremptory

---

[66] Institut de Droit International, Tenth Commission – Present Problems of the Use of Armed Force in International Law – Self-defence, Resolution of 27 October 2007, available at www.idi-iil.org/idiF/resolutionsF/2007_san_02_fr.pdf. For the provisional draft of Rapporteur Emmanuel Roucounas and the Comments of the Institute's Members, see: (2007) Ann IDI, pp. 67–165, available at www.idi-iil.org/idiF/annuaireF/10th_commission_a.pdf (websites accessed 1 June 2009).
[67] Preferring a more limited acceptance of interceptive self-defence, *ibid.*, p. 149 (Conforti), p. 156 (Torres Bernárdez).

character of Articles 2(4) and 51 UN Charter, or to elaborate on the meaning of the necessity and proportionality criteria (the IDI resolution simply confirms that the latter criteria 'are essential components of the normative framework of self-defence' (§ 2)). An explicit reaffirmation that peacetime reprisals are prohibited is also desirable.

In the end, on the basis of the UN Charter, the Definition of Aggression, the Friendly Relations Declaration, the ICJ case law, the 2007 IDI resolution and the various findings spelt out in the present study, the following blueprint could be put forward:

Draft Definition of Armed Attack

The General Assembly,

Recalling the obligation of States to settle their international disputes by peaceful means,

Recalling that all States shall refrain in their international relations from the threat or use of force against the territorial integrity or political independence of any State, or in any other manner inconsistent with the Purposes of the United Nations,

Recalling, in particular, that all States must refrain from organizing, assisting, or harbouring armed groups engaged in terrorist acts or armed incursions into the territory of another State,

Recalling the primary responsibility of the UN Security Council for the maintenance of international peace and security,[68]

Reaffirming the principle of equal rights and self-determination of peoples,

Reaffirming that aggression constitutes a crime against the peace, for which there is responsibility under international law,

Reaffirming that no territorial acquisition or special advantage resulting from aggression is or shall be recognized as lawful,[69]

Recognizing the peremptory character of Articles 2(4) and 51 of the Charter of the United Nations,

Mindful of the controversies concerning the scope of the right of self-defence,

---

[68] Remark: preambular paragraphs 1, 2 and 4 restate the fundamental provisions of Articles 2(3), 2(4) and 24(1) UN Charter. In addition, building on paragraphs 8 and 9, Section 1 of the Friendly Relations Declaration, paragraph 3 draws attention to the unacceptability of State-sponsored terrorism and proxy warfare.

[69] Paragraphs 6 and 7 restate Articles 5(2) and 5(3) of the Definition of Aggression.

Convinced that the adoption of a Definition of Armed Attack ought to have the effect of deterring potential aggressors and would contribute to the strengthening of international peace and security,

Believing that, although the question whether a recourse to force meets the requirements of lawful self-defence must be considered in the light of all the circumstances of each particular case, it is nevertheless desirable to formulate basic principles as guidance for such determination,[70]

Recognizing that Article 51 of the Charter of the United Nations, as supplemented by customary international law,[71] allows for the exercise of the right of individual or collective self-defence only when a State is the victim of an armed attack,

Adopts the following Definition of Armed Attack:

1. An armed attack consists in the deliberate use of armed force against a State, producing, or liable to produce, serious consequences, epitomized by territorial intrusions, human casualties or considerable destruction of property.[72]
2. (a) An armed attack must normally be of substantial gravity or consist in a protracted campaign of interlinked attacks.
   (b) In the context of hostile encounters between military units or small-scale territorial incursions, States may, as a last resort, respond to armed attacks of lesser intensity by means of limited on-the-spot reaction.
3. (a) An armed attack normally consists in the cross-border use of force against the territory of a State.
   (b) At the same time, it includes attacks against certain external manifestations of the State, most notably military personnel and military installations abroad.
   (c) Exceptionally, States may undertake limited on-the-spot reaction to protect civilian vessels or aircraft from armed attack, without, however, interfering with law enforcement measures by third States.

---

[70] Paragraphs 9–11 build on the preambles of the Definition of Aggression and the IDI resolution.

[71] The phrase 'Article 51 . . . as supplemented by customary international law' is taken from Article 1 of the IDI resolution and reflects the idea that Article 51 must be interpreted by reference to customary practice.

[72] Article 1 uses the definition suggested by Dinstein (Dinstein, *War, aggression and self-defence*, p. 193), while adding the term 'deliberate'.

4. (a) An armed attack primarily refers to attacks by States. This includes attacks that are carried out by non-State actors at the instructions, direction or control of a State. In such cases, and subject to the other requirements spelled out in this Definition, the latter State can become the object of action in self-defence.[73]
   (b) Absent State imputability, cross-border attacks by non-State actors will only qualify as armed attacks if and to the extent that the following conditions are cumulatively fulfilled:
      i. the attack or attacks meet the requirement of Section 3(a);
      ii. the attack or attacks are instructed and/or launched from abroad;
      iii. the attack or attacks are the work of an organized armed group that maintains a settled presence abroad, rather than a disparate group of individuals.
   Defensive action within the territory of another State against armed attacks of this type is permitted only within the strict confines set out in Section 7.
5. (a) When concrete measures of implementation indicate that an armed attack has actually been set in motion, the targeted victim State need not await its consequences, but may exceptionally act in self-defence to intercept the incoming attack.
   (b) Threats of attack do not give rise to a right to self-defence, but shall be brought to the attention of the UN Security Council.[74]
6. Every recourse to self-defence shall be geared towards the halting and repelling of an armed attack, and shall not exceed this goal.
   (a) In accordance with the necessity principle:
      i. Self-defence shall be a last resort, and peaceful means should reasonably have been exhausted.
      ii. The time lapse between the start of the armed attack and the recourse to self-defence shall be reasonably short, taking account of the need for conducting investigations and peaceful negotations, as well as the need to make necessary military preparations.
      iii. Defensive action shall not be initiated after an armed attack is factually over, unless the victim State provides compelling evidence that further attacks are imminent.

---

[73] See also: paragraph 10(2)(i) of the IDI resolution.
[74] Article 2 recognizes the legality of interceptive self-defence, while rejecting pre-emptive or preventive action. Alternatively, one might simply state in paragraph b that 'threats of attack shall be brought to the attention of the UN Security Council'.

         iv. Defensive action shall be directed against the actual source or sources of the armed attack.
    (b) The nature, intensity, geographical scope and duration of the defensive action shall be reasonably proportionate to the armed attack(s) that triggered it. This must be evaluated in light of the gravity and frequency of the armed attack(s), as well as the objective to be achieved by the recourse to self-defence.
7. Armed attacks by non-State actors as defined in Section 4(b) justify the recourse to self-defence against the non-State presence in the State from which the attack or attacks are instructed and/or launched if and to the extent that the following conditions are cumulatively fulfilled:
    (a) There is compelling evidence that further attacks are imminent.
    (b) The State from whose territory the non-State actor operates is manifestly and persistently unwilling or unable to prevent the cross-border non-State attacks. This will in particular be the case when the State itself provides active support to the non-State actor, or when it has completely lost control over that part of its territory from which the group operates.
    (c) Peaceful means have fully been exhausted.
    (d) The non-State threat cannot appropriately be dealt with by other means, such as action within the victim State's own territory.
    (e) The defensive action is strictly targeted against and proportionate to the non-State threat. Only if the territorial State actively opposes action that is compatible with the aforementioned conditions, is the defending State permitted to take selective action against it insofar as needed to protect its military personnel and installations.
8. (a) Any action purportedly undertaken in self-defence, regardless of its scale or duration, shall immediately be reported to the Security Council. Failure to do so will constitute an indication that the State does not consider itself to be acting in self-defence.
    (b) Unless the Security Council holds otherwise, defensive action shall be discontinued when the Security Council has adopted measures necessary to maintain or restore international peace and security.
    (c) The right of collective self-defence shall be exercised only at the request of the victim State.[75]

---

[75] Article 8(c) copies paragraph 8 of the IDI resolution. Alternatively, one could use the notion of 'collective defence' instead of 'collective self-defence'. See *supra*, Section 2.2.1.c.

9. States may exceptionally conduct non-combatant evacuation operations abroad without the consent of the territorial State if and to the extent that the following conditions are cumulatively fulfilled:
   (a) There is an imminent threat of injury to nationals abroad;
   (b) The territorial State is manifestly unable or unwilling to protect them;
   (c) Insofar as possible, the national State has first attempted to obtain the consent of the territorial State;
   (d) The operation is strictly limited to the objective of evacuating the threatened nationals;
   (e) Force is used only insofar as necessary to protect the lives of persons entitled to evacuation as well as the personnel involved in the operation.
   Article 8(a) fully applies to the operations under consideration.
10. (a) States have a duty to refrain from acts of reprisal involving the use of force.[76]
    (b) Any recourse to self-defence must comply with the relevant and applicable rules of the law of armed conflicts, in particular those pertaining to the selection of targets and the distinction between combatants and non-combatants.

6.2.3 Post-scriptum: strengthening the compliance pull of the Ius ad Bellum

The present author is convinced that the adoption of a UNGA Definition of Armed Attack would ultimately benefit the compliance pull of the Charter regime on the use of force in a twofold way. First, by strengthening the 'determinacy' of Article 51 UN Charter, it would facilitate the justificatory discourse on the legality of concrete interventions, making it easier to identify and denounce breaches of the prohibition on the use of force. Second, by forging a new global security consensus, taking account of the twenty-first century threats to international peace and security, it would simultaneously enhance the substantive 'fairness' of the rules concerned.[77]

At the same time, this would only be a first step in the right direction, pending several others. For example, one of the requirements to sustain a workable justificatory discourse is that the facts on the basis of which decisions are taken must be truthful and complete as informed by the

---

[76] See Friendly Relations Declaration, Section 1, paragraph 7.
[77] See Franck, *Fairness in international law and institutions*, pp. 8–9.

best evidence available.[78] Yet, as we have seen, in reality information regarding the circumstances of concrete recourses to force is often manipulated, contradictory, incomplete or simply unavailable. To counter this trend, there should be greater pressure within the international community to comply with the reporting obligation of Article 51 UN Charter, including with regard to small-scale interventions. In accordance with the *actori incumbit probatio* principle, States allegedly acting in self-defence must explain why they have been the victim of an armed attack and why their reaction is necessary and proportionate. States should be encouraged to provide the UN Secretariat and the UN Security Council with relevant intelligence. In addition, in order to come to a more even-handed approach, there is a need to clarify the standard of proof concerning self-defence claims. A number of scholars have rightly pleaded in favour of a standard of 'clear and compelling' evidence[79] and have suggested that the ICJ do more to articulate such evidentiary standard.[80] When the facts remain clouded, the UN Security Council should seriously consider setting up commissions of inquiry or fact-finding missions (as it has occasionally done in the past).[81]

Efforts to strengthen the compliance pull cannot be limited to facilitating the justificatory discourse process, but must equally address the so-called 'sticks' and 'carrots' of the *Ius ad Bellum* framework. As the supreme body endowed with the oversight of self-defence claims and with the maintenance of international peace and security, the Security Council Members should have the courage to call a spade a spade, and identify and condemn 'acts of aggression' or breaches of Article 2(4) UN Charter when appropriate. At the same time, as the Security Council is – and always will be – an inherently political body, stronger judicial

---

[78] See C. Bjola, 'Legitimating the use of force in international politics: a communicative action perspective', (2005) 11 EJIRel 266–97.

[79] See, e.g., J. Lobel, 'The use of force to respond to terrorist attacks: the bombing of Sudan and Afghanistan', (1999) 24 YJIL 537–57; M. E. O'Connell, 'Rules of evidence for the use of force in international law's new era', (2006) 100 ASIL Proc 44–7; M. E. O'Connell, 'Evidence of terror', (2002) 7 JCSL 19–36.

[80] See, e.g., J. A. Green, 'Fluctuating evidentiary standards for self-defence in the International Court of Justice, (2009) 58 ICLQ 163–79.

[81] Remark: in his report to the Institut de Droit International, Special Rapporteur Roucounas raised the question whether it was advisable to propose the establishment by the Security Council of a subsidiary Permanent Fact-Finding Body. Yet, two IDI members objected that the 'experience of such bodies was dismal'. See IDI, Present Problems of the Use of Armed Force in International Law – Self-defence', 147, 151 (Conforti), 153 (Crawford).

WHAT FUTURE FOR THE 'ARMED ATTACK' CRITERION? 547

enforcement remains a 'consummation devoutly to be wish'd'.[82] A powerful development in this regard is the adoption at the ICC Review Conference in Kampala in June 2010 of a resolution, amending the ICC Rome Statute by (finally) rendering explicit the 'Elements of Crime' of the 'crime of aggression' and by identifying the different ways in which the International Criminal Court could in principle exercise jurisdiction over this crime (State referral, *proprio motu*, Security Council referral).[83] The resolution brings us a step closer to the long-awaited activation of the ICC's embryonic jurisdiction over 'crimes of aggression',[84] albeit that further steps are still needed (viz. the ratification of the amendments by thirty States Parties as well as the adoption of a complementary decision by the Assembly of States Parties after 1 January 2017).[85] Should this jurisdiction eventually be 'activated', it would certainly offer a powerful sanction against aggression and a deterrent from future abuse. At the same time, the Prosecutor and Judges of the ICC will have to exercise the utmost caution to avoid accusations of political interference and double standards. To this end, a strict insistence on the 'manifest' character of crimes of aggression seems preferable.[86] As far as the

---

[82] Remark: it may be observed that national courts have traditionally been very reluctant to deal with inter-State recourse to force. See, e.g., UK House of Lords, *R* v. *Jones*, Judgment of 29 March 2006, (2006) UKHL, 16; US Court of Appeals, District of Columbia Circuit, *El-Shifa Pharmaceutical Industries Co.* v. *US*, 27 March 2009, 559 F.3d 578. By contrast, see: Judgment of the Bundesverwaltungsgericht of 21 June 2005, BVerwG, 2 WD 12.04.

[83] ICC Assembly of States Parties, Resolution RC/Res.6, 13th plenary meeting, 11 June 2010 (adopted by consensus). Three Annexes are added to the Resolution: (1) Annex I contains the actual amendments to the Rome Statute (viz. Article 8*bis* (definition of the crime of aggression) and 15*bis-ter* (exercise of jurisdiction)); (2) Annex II contains the amendments to the Elements of Crime; and (3) Annex III contains a series of understandings regarding the amendments to the Rome Statute. See also: www.icc-cpi.int/Menus/ASP/Crime+of+Aggression/; www.icc-cpi.int/Menus/ASP/ReviewConference/Crime+of+Aggression.htm.

[84] Remark: when States adopted the Rome Statute in 1998, they failed to reach an agreement on the exercise of jurisdiction by the ICC over the crime of aggression as well as on the definition of that crime. For this reason, the following language was inserted in Article 5(2) of the Rome Statute: 'The Court shall exercise jurisdiction over the crime of aggression once a provision is adopted ... defining the crime and setting out the conditions under which the Court shall exercise jurisdiction with respect to this crime. Such a provision shall be consistent with the relevant provisions of the [UN]Charter.'

[85] See Articles 15*bis*(2)–(3) and 15*ter*(2)–(3).

[86] Cf. ICC Assembly of States Parties, Resolution RC/Res.6, Annex II, 'Amendments to the Elements of Crimes'. Remark: it is noted that Resolution RC/Res.6 does not itself pronounce on the scope of Articles 2(4) or 51 UN Charter. Annex III ('Understandings regarding the amendments to the Rome Statute') moreover asserts that '[t]he amendments shall, in accordance with article 10 of the Rome Statute, not be interpreted as

'carrots' are concerned, there are no direct and easily implementable measures to strengthen States' interest in a peaceful international order. In the long term, history illustrates that this objective is best pursued through economic cooperation and integration – the European post-War project is the best proof of this. On a different level, concrete confidence-building measures may go a long way to mitigate the detrimental effects of the realist 'security dilemma'. A noteworthy initiative in this respect is the 1990 Treaty on Conventional Armed Forces in Europe,[87] which provides for comprehensive limits on conventional military equipment and installed a verification regime.[88] Increased openness and public debate on military manuals and peacetime Rules of Engagement could also contribute to greater objectivity in assessing hostile confrontations and reduce the risk of escalation.[89]

Finally, the perceived fairness of the Charter rules on the recourse to force is inextricably linked to the perceived fairness of the special position of the UN Security Council. As a result, the Council should not only become more (pro-)active, but also more representative of current demographic and power balances. This presupposes an expansion of the Council's membership, albeit in a way that would not altogether reduce its effectiveness (a further expansion of the veto power seems objectionable).

The end of the Cold War era raised the hope of a more peaceful world order. Twenty years later, however, this prospect has been reduced to a shambles *inter alia* as a result of the wars in Central Africa and the Balkans, or the advance of trans-national terrorism. The forces of globalization have made the world a 'smaller' place, but unfortunately not a safer one. Latent and open border conflicts – between Sudan and Chad, between Thailand and Cambodia, between India and Pakistan, to name but a few – continue to threaten regional stability in many parts of the world. Nuclear proliferation has not been halted. At the time of writing, North Korea had just launched a second nuclear test, following an earlier test in October 2006,[90] and Israel and the United States refused to rule

---

limiting or prejudicing in any way existing or developing rules of international law for purposes other than this Statute.'

[87] Treaty on Conventional Armed Forces in Europe, 19 November 1990, Paris, (1991) 30 ILM 1.

[88] Remark: Russia in 2007 decreed a suspension of the treaty in protest to US plans to build a missile defence system in eastern Europe. 'Russia suspends arms control pact', *BBC News* 14 July 2007.

[89] Also D. Fleck, 'Rules of engagement of maritime forces and the limitation of the use of force under the UN Charter', (1989) 31 GYBIL 165–86, at 181–2.

[90] C. Sang-Hun, 'North Korea claims to conduct 2nd Nuclear Test', *NY Times* 24 May 2009.

out a preventive military strike against nuclear facilities in Iran. In several States, e.g., Somalia, Afghanistan and the Democratic Republic of the Congo, there existed a notable lack of governmental authority over substantial parts of the territory. Such power vacuums allow non-State armed groups to flourish. Often, these groups commit gross human rights abuses against the civilian population (consider, for instance, the atrocities by the Lord's Resistance Army or the ex-Interahamwe, ranging from murder and rape to the abduction of child soldiers), or engage in widespread criminal activities (the FARC, for instance, has been estimated to supply more than 50 per cent of the world's cocaine).[91] Especially when they receive support from third States, non-State armed groups are forces to be reckoned with. The ultimate doom scenario is that of a trans-national terrorist group acquiring nuclear, biological or chemical weapons, and using them to inflict catastrophic harm in a major world city. This scenario is something of a cliché, yet it is not completely out of touch with reality. It may be noted, for instance, that in May 2009, when Taleban fighters battled the Pakistani army, some US officials expressed genuine concern that the Taleban would sooner or later get their hands on Islamabad's nuclear arsenal.[92]

Against such background, it is hardly surprising that the tumultuous period since the 9/11 attacks has inspired some to throw overboard the Charter regime on the use of force. A number of legal scholars have been keen to deliver funeral orations of the *Ius ad Bellum* or have called for some form of hegemonial exceptionalism.[93] Likewise, several foreign policy experts and political figures have fundamentally called its validity into question. The argument goes that in today's security environment, abiding by the legal rules dramatically exposes States to the threats of asymmetric warfare and that in the twenty-first century confrontation between 'post-modern' and 'pre-modern' States,[94] or between 'States of

---

[91] US Drug Enforcement Administration, 'United States charges 50 leaders of narco-terrorist FARC in Colombia with supplying more than half of the world's cocaine', DEA News Release, 22 March 2006, available at www.usdoj.gov/dea/pubs/pressrel/pr032206a.html (accessed 6 June 2009).
[92] I. Wilkinson, 'US "concerned Taliban will snatch Pakistan's nuclear weapons"', *The Telegraph* 4 May 2009.
[93] Some have indeed suggested that the international law on the use of force applies differently to powerful countries, in particular the US, and others. See on this: G. J. Simpson, *Great powers and outlaw states: unequal sovereigns in the international legal order* (Cambridge University Press, 2004), pp. 326–51.
[94] See R. Cooper, *The breaking of nations: order and chaos in the twenty-first century* (London: Atlantic Books, 2003).

consent' and 'States of terror',[95] the former should be given free reign. According to one renowned British expert, 'in the jungle, one must use the laws of the jungle', 'following well-established legal norms and relying on self-defence will not solve the problem.'[96]

If the latter approach reflects an underlying belief that unilateral recourse to force is a viable policy instrument in the domain of 'high politics', this myth has largely been dispelled by the sobering lessons of Afghanistan and Iraq. True, a normative framework on the recourse to force does not in itself guarantee peaceful relations between States. There is no simple *'paix par le droit.'* Yet, if anything, recent events have taught us that the proper road to a more stable and secure world is through proactive and multilateral action, such as efforts aimed at the strengthening of ailing governmental structures or at increased international cooperation between law enforcement agencies. The *Ius ad Bellum* is not a nuisance to this end, but rather the essential legal groundwork upon which such multilateral efforts are engrafted. It is not part of the problem, but part of the solution.

Claims that the Charter regime on the use of force is fundamentally maladjusted to current security needs are grossly exaggerated. Admittedly, there is a need for a cautious revision of the applicability of self-defence to attacks by non-State actors, and, above all, a need for clarification and reaffirmation of the Charter norms. Yet, as the international community of States acknowledged in September 2005, the relevant provisions of the United Nations Charter remain in essence adequate to address the full range of threats to international peace and security.[97]

Even if States were to succeed in forging a consensus on Article 51 UN Charter – whether or not along the lines of the proposed 'Definition of Armed Attack' – breaches will continue to take place from time to time. Any legal norm that constrains behaviour inherently involves a risk of non-compliance. Yet, as Judge Simma observes, as long as claims behind the disregard for the law are being met not with resigned silence but with firm counterclaims for a return to legality, international law will not give way to the short-sighted arbitrariness and apologetism aspired to by a powerful few.[98]

---

[95] See P. Bobbitt, *Terror and consent: the wars for the twenty-first century* (London: Penguin Books, 2008).
[96] Cooper, *The breaking of nations*, pp. 62, 64.
[97] 'World Summit Outcome', GA Res. 60/1, 16 September 2005, UN Doc. A/RES. 60/1, § 79.
[98] B. Simma, 'Foreword', in E. Cannizzaro and P. Palchetti (eds.), *Customary international law on the use of force* (Leiden: Martinus Nijhoff, 2005), pp. ix–x.

INDEX

9/11 attacks
  anticipatory self-defence, and 250–1, 305–42
  carrying out of 305–6
  changes in approach to non-State actors prior to ix, 419–33
  compared to Pearl Harbour attack 250
  customary law and practice following ix, 447–72
  effect on international law and practice ix, 2–3, 433–47
  endorsement of necessary measures 78
  international support for US response 306
  preventive justification for responses 104
  revised security strategies following ix, 443–7
  UNSC resolutions ix, 433–43
  US and UK investigation 434–5
  US NSS, and *see* National Security Strategy (NSS)
  US reaction as 'instant custom' 2

'abstract' evidence, meaning 511
'accumulation of events' doctrine
  application 168–9
  colonialism, issues of 171
  de minimis threshold, and 4–5, 115, 116
  Dinstein's classification, and 182
  disproportionate response to attacks 170–1
  evidence for 174–5
  frequent use of 171–2
  ICJ support for 173–4
  inevitability of response to attacks 170
  overview viii, 168–75
  proportionality, and 175
  purpose 115, 116
  relevance to armed attack 177
  self-determination, issues of 171
  support for 169–70, 523
Act of Chapultepec 1945
  accordance with UN Charter 62
  implementation 84
actions by States *see* exceptional measures
Afghanistan
  intervention in
    attacks on Al Qaeda *see* Al Qaeda, attacks on
    legal weight of international approval 35, 38
    maritime interdiction operation 121
    operations by Russia and Tajikistan 428
    proportionality 120–1
    support for 117
    Taleban, operations against *see* Al Qaeda, attacks on
  tension with Pakistan
    Afghan and US claims 471–2
    background 471–2
    Pakistani claims 472
African Union
  Non-Aggression and Common Defence Pact, definition of aggression 446
  Rwandan operations against Hutu insurgents, and 467

552   INDEX

aggression *see also* Definition of
    Aggression 1974; indirect
    aggression
  armed attack, relation to viii, 67–8,
    127–39
  crime of, ICC jurisdiction 547
  defining relationship to armed attack
    127–8
  definition
    African Union 446
    detachment from self-defence 536–7
    drafting of UN Charter, in 129
    pre-Charter concepts 128–9
    presumption of 160
    prohibited goals 158–9
    prohibition as *ius cogens* 26–7
    rebuttal of presumption 160
    UN Charter definitions 130–1
    UN Charter terminology 127
  aggressive intention *see animus*
    aggressionis
aircraft
  civil aircraft *see* civil aircraft
  military aircraft *see* military aircraft
aircraft incursions
  animus aggressionis, and 192–3
  graduated response to trespass by
    191–2
  private aircraft 198–9
  proportionality of response 193–4
  ROEs as to 191–2
Al Qaeda, attacks by, control of
    501–2 *see also* 9/11 attacks
Al Qaeda, attacks on
  academic analysis 437–9
  application of Shultz doctrine 426
  chronology ix, 433–7
  clarity of legal basis 439
  contrast with previous custom 441–2
  cooperation from Yemen 377
  delayed launch of 101
  differing interpretations 442–3
  example of distinction of self-
    defence within and against a
    State, as 495–6
  instant custom, as ix, 437–43, 530
  international response ix, 117, 306,
    426–7, 433–7, 435–6, 439–40

justification for 202, 377
launch of 'Enduring Freedom' 435–6
link between Al Qaeda and Taleban
    440–1
precedential value ix, 437–43
protection of nationals, as 225–6
unique exception, as ix, 437–43
UNSC resolutions 433–4
US ultimatum to Taleban 435
Albania, evacuation of foreign
    nationals 231
Algeria
  intervention in Iraq, and 317
  rejection of pre-emptive self-defence
    340–1
Angola, alleged support for SWAPO
    401
animus aggressionis
  constituent element of armed attack,
    as 177, 522
  de Brouckère Report as to 166–8
  Definition of Aggression 1974,
    and 158
  first debates 158
  hostile intent, and *see* hostile intent
  lack of hostile intent 165
  military aircraft 192–3
  motives or purposes of use of force,
    and 160–1
  need for *mens rea* 158
  Nicaragua judgment 161–2
  Oil Platforms judgment 162–3
  overview viii, 158–68
  priority (first use) principle, and 158
  small-scale attacks, and 166–8,
    192–3
  subjective element 163–5
Annan, Kofi
  highlights dangers of anticipatory
    use of force 327–8
  'In Larger Freedom' Report *see* 'In
    Larger Freedom' Report
  sets up High-Level Panel 327
anticipatory self-defence
  academic support 263–4, 331–6
  alternative measures 261–2
  analysis of content of States'
    statements on 334–6

INDEX 553

arguments in favour
  continuance of customary right 255–6
  greater threat from modern military capability 257
  overview viii, 255–7
  scope of analysis 255
  subsidiary arguments 256–7
arguments opposing
  avoidance of military escalation, need for 262
  Caroline incident irrelevant 258–9
  impact of Article 51 259
  no customary right 260–1
  overview viii, 258–62
  weakness of subsidiary arguments for pre-existing custom 261
  whether anticipatory self-defence desirable 261–2
Article 51, and 259
assessment of claims 261
balance of majority and minority opinion 338–41
calls for clarification of issue of 303
Caroline incident, and *see Caroline* incident
categories 252
content of chapter 251
continuing controversy 250
customary law and practice
  evidence in specific incidents viii, 267–94
  lack of precedent 293–4
customary right
  continuance of 255–6
  limitations 255–6
development of doctrine post-1945 viii, 255–305
difference of views 267
difficulty of assessing necessity and proportionality 279–80
doctrinal debate viii, 255
effect of 9/11 250–1, 526
extent of doctrinal divide viii, 263–7
further attacks viii, 342–3
gap between *opinio iuris* and practice 526–7
ICJ's approach viii, 262–3

imminent attacks *see* imminent attacks
increased support for 336
lack of concrete precedent 250
necessity standard, and 4–5
non-imminent attacks *see* non-imminent attacks
nuclear weapons, and 257, 527–8
prevention of further attacks 290–1
reactive self-defence distinguished 251–2
scope of analysis viii, 250–4
State's statements as *opinio iuris* 334
summary of pre-9/11 legal doctrine 525
terminology
  application to Pearl Harbour attack 254
  importance of correct usage 254
  issues 251–3
  time frame 253–4
US NSS, and *see* anticipatory self-defence
Webster formula *see* Webster formula
Argentina
  Belgian intervention in the Congo, and 218–20, 241, 244–5
  Falklands War *see* Falklands War
  ILC Draft Articles on State Responsibility, and 304–5
  Israeli intervention in Lebanon, and 115, 116
  policy for submarine incidents 196
  rejection of pre-emptive self-defence 339
armed attack
  accumulation of events *see* 'accumulation of events' doctrine
  aggression, and *see* aggression
  animus aggressionis see animus aggressionis
  consistency of ingredients over time 175–7
  context, role of 175–7
  Corten's criteria 185–6

554 INDEX

armed attack (cont.)
  de minimis threshold *see de minimis* threshold
  definition *see* definition of armed attack
  different interpretations 378
  elements ix, 480–1, 520–4
  error or accident, resulting from 166–8
  factors for existence of viii, 139–84
  future for armed attack criterion
    overview ix, 511–50
    scope of analysis 511
  hostile intent *see* hostile intent
  integral part of Article 51, as vii, 53–68
  mens rea see animus aggressionis
  necessity, and *see* necessity standard
  objective element as essence 175–7
  other forcible acts not self-defence distinguished 139
  panoply of scenarios viii, 175–84
  personnel aspect *see* personnel aspect of armed attack requirement (*ratione personae*)
  perspectives on meaning of requirement 3
  proportionality, and *see* proportionality standard
  small-scale attacks *see* small-scale attacks
  threshold level *see de minimis* threshold
  timing aspect *see* timing aspect of armed attack requirement (*ratione temporis*)
  types of act aspect *see* types of act aspect of armed attack requirement (*ratione materiae*)
  UN Charter terminology 127
armed bands *see* non-State actors
armed force, meaning of force restricted to 55–6
armed reprisals, self-defence distinguished 183

Article 2(4) UN Charter
  Article 51, and 1, 58–60, 516–17
  challenges to determinacy of 4
  customary status 16, 17–8
  effect on previous customary law 9
  general nature of 22
  inclusion in other instruments 15–6
  ius cogens, as 26–7
  modification 27–8
  peremptory norm, as 25
  supplementary provisions 57
Article 51 UN Charter vii, 83–91
  adherence pre-9/11 1–2
  anticipatory self-defence, and 259
  armed attack confirmed as integral 67
  armed attack requirement as integral vii, 53–68
  Article 2(4), and 1, 58–60, 516–17
  challenges to determinacy of 4
  collective self-defence, and *see* collective self-defence
  continued sufficiency 2–3
  controversy over scope 1
  customary law and practice as primary material for interpreting 511
  customary right, and 1, 4
  customary status 9, 18–9
  determinacy 535
  disagreement, sources of 514–15, 535–6
  drafting of 260
  effect on previous customary law 9
  imminent threats, and 526–7
  inclusion in other instruments 15–6
  inherent right of self-defence, and *see* inherent right of self-defence
  interpretation
    absurd results from literal 260
    primary sources vii, 55–60
    UN Charter drafting documents vii, 60–8
  ius cogens, as 26–7
  location in Charter, interpretative significance 63–4
  modification 27–8

INDEX

non-State actors, as to 404–5
pre-existing custom, and ix, 514–17
'primary law', as 490
protection of substantive rights 58–9
raison d'être 62–8
relationship to other rules ix, 514–17
reporting obligation *see* reporting obligation
'secondary' law, as 490
study limitations ix, 511–14
text 57–8
'until clause' *see* 'until clause'
assistance, right to request 87–91
Australia
  amendment to Article 2(4) 57
  Australian national pursued by German police into France 191
  Definition of Aggression 1974, and 296, 393
  dominance of 'counter-restrictionist' views 325
  Friendly Relations Declaration 1970, and 391–2
  intervention in Iraq, and 314–15
  Israeli airstrike on Tunis, and 424
  NEO doctrine 246
  reaction to Bali bombing 330, 444
  rejection of preventive self-defence 322, 337
  Suez crisis, and 395
  US operations against Libya, and 425
Austria, Definition of Aggression 1974, and 300–2
'axis of evil' 310–11

Bali bombing, reaction to 330, 444
Bangladesh, rejection of pre-emptive self-defence 340–1
'Baxter paradox' as to treaty law and customary law 17
Belarus
  Definition of Aggression 1974, and 297–8
  rejection of pre-emptive self-defence 340–1

Belgium
  Definition of Aggression 1974, and 294–6, 300
  intervention in the Congo 218–20, 381
  mercenary attack on DRC, and 405–6
Benin, mercenary attack 405–6
blockade, use of 276–7
border incidents *see* small-scale attacks
Brazil
  Suez Canal dispute 1951, and 290
  termination of nuclear weapons programme 365–7
Bulgaria, Definition of Aggression 1974, and 299
burden of evidence
  attacks by non-State actors 505–6, 509–10
  clarification of standard 546
  interceptive and pre-emptive self-defence 265–6
  prevention of further attacks 518–19
Burkina Faso, border tensions 429
Burundi, Tanzania dispute 429
Bush, George *see also* 'Bush doctrine'
  assassination attempt 202–3, 414, 533
  'axis of evil' speech 310–11
  case against Iraq 310–11
'Bush doctrine' *see also* National Security Strategy (NSS)
  assertion as 'instant custom' 2
  essence 308–9
  exposition of 306
  rebuttal of 317–18
  similar statements by other States 330–1, 333–4

Cambodia
  border incidents 156
  evacuation by Thailand 232
  Mayaguez incident 211, 224–5
Cameroon, dispute with Nigeria 173–4
Canada
  Definition of Aggression 1974, and 151, 160
  drafting of Article 51, and 64

Canada (cont.)
  NEO doctrine 245–6
  rejection of preventive self-defence 322
Caroline incident *see also* Webster formula
  background 255–6
  example of anticipatory self-defence, as 258–9
  necessity and proportionality, and *see* necessity standard; proportionality standard
  proof of continuing right of anticipatory self-defence, as 10–11, 258–9, 515
case law *see* International Court of Justice (ICJ); *opinio iuris*
Chechen rebels, Russian self-defence claims 444–5
Chile
  Definition of Aggression 1974, and 294–6
  Osiraq nuclear reactor strike, and 285–6
China
  border incidents 156
  Definition of Aggression 1974, and 295–6
  destruction of Belgrade embassy 165
  intervention in Iraq, and 312, 313
  protection of nationals, and 237–8
  rejection of pre-emptive self-defence 340–1
  submarine incident in Japanese waters 196–7
  Suez crisis, and 395
civil aircraft
  Definition of Aggression 1974 as to 204–5
  external manifestations of the State, as 204
  right of self-defence viii, 204–13
  shooting down of 291
  used as weapons 199
civilians as targets of terrorism 498
collective self-defence
  Article 51, and 9, 62
  conceptual difficulties 85–9
  criteria 83–4
  customary status, lack of evidence for 84
  defence of 'self' rather than 'other' 85–9
  formal request for assistance 89–91
  mandatory request for assistance 91
  overview vii, 83–91
  proximate relationship, need for 85–9
  right to request assistance 87–91
colonialism *see also* decolonization
  'accumulation of events' doctrine, and 171
  illegal occupation of territory, as 403–4
  legality of use of force
    opposition to 391–2
    support for 390–1
  permanent attack, as 420
Colombia
  drafting of Article 51, and 64
  Operation 'Phoenix'
    Colombian claims 462
    Ecuadorian and Venezuelan claims 463
    OAS response 463–4
    overview ix, 462–4
    US response 464
'complete dependence' on State of non-State actors 409
'computer network attack' (CNA) as armed attack 176–7
conflict of laws
  interpretation and modification of treaties, and 23
  settlement techniques 13–14
  treaties and peremptory norms 13
  UN Charter, and 13
Congo (Belgian)
  Belgian intervention 218–20, 381
  US intervention 220
Congo (DRC)
  mercenary attack 405–6
  Rwandan operations *see* Rwandan operations against Hutu insurgents
  Uganda dispute *see* DRC v Uganda

Contras *see Nicaragua* judgment
Corfu Channel case
  anticipatory self-defence, and 262–3
  UK claims 56
Corten's criteria of armed attack 185–6
Costa Rica, rejection of pre-emptive self-defence 340–1
'counter-restrictionist' views
  anticipatory self-defence viii, 255–7
  Article 51 and customary right, as to 514–15
  dominance 325, 326–7, 329–30, 331–6
  'imminence' standard, and 320, 337
  Nicaragua judgment 10–11
  subsidiary arguments 256–7
  suggested precedents for anticipatory self-defence, 287
  summary of argument with 'restrictionists' 514–15
criminals *see* law enforcement response to attacks
Cuba
  rejection of pre-emptive self-defence 340–1
  US intervention in Dominica, and 221
Cuban missile crisis
  imminence of threat 271–2
  overview 267
  precedent for anticipatory self-defence, as 270–1
  rejection of preventive self-defence, as 286
  UNSC debate 268–70
  US response to Soviet deployment 267–8
custom
  balanced approach to quest for, need for vii, 51–2
  conditions for creating 44
  dynamic nature of process 34
  hierarchy with treaty law 12–13
  identification
    elements of custom 29–30
    methodological debate vii, 29–31
    methodology 30–1
    problem of 29
    science of 30
  pre-existing
    anticipatory self-defence 261
    Article 51, and ix, 514–17
    grounds for claim of continuing validity 11
    UN Charter, and 30–1
  quest for vii, 6
  UN Charter, and *see* United Nations Charter
  undisclosed acts 34–5
customary law and practice
  absolute consistency of, need for 44, 49
  'abstract' evidence, meaning 511
  analysis as work in progress 514
  anticipatory self-defence *see* anticipatory self-defence
  boundaries
    overview ix, 511–35
    scope of research 52, 511
  'concrete' custom, meaning 511
  conflicts *see* conflict of laws
  contribution by all State organs 43–4
  de minimis threshold, and viii, 149–57
  density of vii, 44–51
  derogation *see* derogation
  element of custom, as 29–30
  exceptional measures *see* exceptional measures
  extensiveness of 44–7
  incompatible with UN Charter *see* United Nations Charter
  inconsistency *see* inconsistent conduct
  inherent right of self-defence as affirming 8
  legal weight of policy declarations 41–2
  legal weight of theoretical debates 42–3
  non-State actors *see* non-State actors
  opinio iuris, and vii, 29–51
  oral and written statements, importance of 32–4
  overlap with treaty law 7–8
  physical acts, importance of 32
  post-9/11 ix, 447–72

customary law and practice (cont.)
    primary material for interpreting
        Article 51 511
    protection of overseas nationals see
        nationals protection of
    range of verbal practice 43–4
    source for interpretation, as 2–3, 4
    source of definition of armed attack,
        as 8
    study methodology, in vii, 6
    time taken for practice to become
        47–9
    treaty interpretation and
        modification, and see
        interpretation, treaty law
    UN Charter, and see United Nations
        Charter
    UNGA resolutions as 49–51
    uniformity of 44
    UNSC resolutions as 49
customary right of self-defence see also
        instant custom
    Article 51 right, and 1, 4
    Article 51 right as part 9
    necessity standard as part of 8
    proportionality standard as part of 8
Cyprus
    Definition of Aggression 1974, and
        344–5, 384–5, 387
    Larnaca airport operation 229
    Six Day War, and 279
Czechoslovakia, Definition of
        Aggression 1974, and 297–8

de Brouckère Report 1926 166–8
de minimis threshold
    'accumulation of events' doctrine,
        and 4–5, 115, 116, 168–9
    any armed force requirement 145
    attacks liable to cause damage
        reaching 152–3
    customary law and practice, and viii,
        149–57
    Definition of Aggression 1974, and
        viii, 149–57
    disagreement over 535–6
    existence of viii, 139–57
    ICJ approach viii, 140–3, 407–8

    indirect aggression 140, 150
    interim reflections on 146–9
    less grave uses of force, and 145–6
    misunderstanding over 520
    'most grave' forms of use of force,
        and viii, 139–57
    options 145
    small-scale attack requirement 145
    study focus 3
    substantial attack requirement 145
Declaration on the Enhancement of the
        Effectiveness of the Principle
        of Refraining from the Threat
        or Use of Force 1987,
        application 17
declarations of war
    acts of aggression, as 133, 344–5
    exception to prohibition of pre-
        emptive self-defence, as
        344–5
    omission from Definition of
        Aggression 1974 345–6
decolonization
    attacks by non-State actors 528–9
    completion 420–1
    end of, changing approach to non-
        State actors ix, 419–21
    indirect military aggression and
        formulation of problem ix, 369–82
    intersecting norms ix, 369–77
    overview ix, 369–419
'defensive armed reprisals'
    Dinstein's classification 181–2
    necessity standard, and 107–8
Definition of Aggression 1974
    'abstract' evidence for interpreting
        Article 51, as 511
    animus aggressionis, and 158, 159–60
    anticipatory self-defence
        arguments against 297–8
        compromise resolution 298–9
        early negotiations viii, 294–8
        final negotiations viii, 298–303
        opposition to 297
        overview 299
        priority (first use) principle see
            priority (first use) principle
        support for 296, 299–303

INDEX

application 27
circumstantial evidence of scope of permissible self-defence, as 149
civil aircraft and shipping, as to 204–6
critique 136–7
declarations of war *see* declarations of war
first use of force as self-defence 343–4
Fourth Special Committee negotiations
  anticipatory self-defence 298–9
  awareness of importance of 132
  convergence of positions 135–6
  de minimis threshold 150
  debate over kind of concept to define 133–4
  declarations of war 133
  different opinions 129–30
  'first use' principle *see* priority (first use) principle
  indirect aggression *see* indirect aggression *below*
  options 134–5
  overview viii, 129–36
  priority (first use) principle *see* priority (first use) principle
  prohibited goals of aggression 158–9
  proportionality criterion 133
  required gravity of acts 133
  Six-Power proposal 131, 158–9, 383–4
  Small-scale attacks 155
  Thirteen-Power proposal 130, 382–3, 384–5
  USSR proposal 131–2
'gravity', and *see* gravity of forms of use of force
indirect aggression 131–2, 134–5, 135–6, 150
  agreement on 'manifest' cases 386–7
  Article 3(g) ix, 382–90
  compromise 386
  compromise on scope of Article 51 389–90
  definition 528
  Fourth Special Committee debate ix, 382–94
  inclusion in Definition 125
  link between State and non-State actors 387–9
  proposal for separate definition 385–6
  Six-Power proposal 383–4
  Thirteen-Power proposal 382–3, 384–5
limitations 537
military units and installations abroad, as to 200
Nicaragua judgment, and 407–8
on-the-spot defensive measures for shipping, regulation of 209
presence of forces continuing beyond agreed timescale 343–4
protection of nationals viii, 233–5
relationship between 'use of force', 'aggression' and 'armed attack', on 149–50
relevance 149–50
self-determination
  ambiguity 393–4
  compromise 393
  controversy 392–3
'substantial involvement' of States with non-State actors 415
use of term 'State' 16
usefulness 137–9
value viii, 136–9
Western powers' approach to project 137
definition of armed attack
  attainability 538–9
  Charter negotiations, in 536–7
  clarification of lawful self-defence 536
  draft text 541–5
  existing guidance ix, 539–41
  need for 536
  Nicaragua judgment 8–9
  objective 538
  potential conflict areas 539
  proposal for ix, 535–50
  source in customary law and practice 8

Denmark
  Red Crusader incident 209
  US operations against Libya, and 425
derogation
  allowability in principle 13
  from *ius cogens* 24–6
  recognition of derogatory regime 38
determinacy, meaning 4
Dinstein's classification
  'accumulation of events' doctrine, and 182
  critique 182
  'defensive armed reprisals' 181–2
  definition of material element 521–2
  hostile intent, and 182
  'modalities' of self-defence 181
  'on-the-spot' reaction 181
  separation of categories 184
  use of category of 'war' 183–4
  value 182–4
  'war' 182
diplomacy, use of vii, 95–8
diplomatic envoys
  external manifestations of the State, as 202–4
  gravity of attacks on 203–4
  ILC Draft Articles on protection of 235–9
  law enforcement response to attacks on 203
divergent frameworks *see* use of force (*Ius ad Bellum*)
Dominican Republic, US operation 115, 119–22
Draft Articles on State Responsibility (DASR)
  anticipatory self-defence, and 303–5
  attributability of private conduct to State 410
  confirmation of 'effective control' test 412
  private conduct in absence or default of official authority 414
  'state of necessity', as to 379–82
DRC v Uganda
  accumulation of events 173–4
  background 468–9
  comparison of claims 481
  criteria for self-defence 479–80
  critique 482–3
  DRC claims 468–9, 479–80
  'due diligence rule', and 375–7
  duration of action 119–20
  element of armed attack 480–1
  escalation of conflict 533–4
  findings 481–2
  Friendly Relations Declaration, as to 374
  Group of Experts reports 534
  international response 469
  issue 479
  overview ix, 479–85
  proportionality 114, 119
  reporting obligation 69
  separate opinions 483–5
  Ugandan claims 469, 479, 480–1
'due diligence rule'
  application 374–5, 454
  obligation of means, as 375–7
  UNSC resolution 434
duration of action and proportionality standard 119–21

East Germany, Osiraq nuclear reactor strike, and 286
Ecuador
  Definition of Aggression 1974, and 344, 384–5
  Operation 'Phoenix', and *see* Colombia
  Suez Canal dispute 1951, and 290
'effective control' threshold as to non-State actors 410–13
Egypt
  Larnaca operation 229
  rejection of pre-emptive self-defence 340–1
  sinking of *Eilat* 194–5, 348–9
  Six Day War *see* Six Day War
  Suez Canal dispute with Israel 1951
    background 288
    Egypt's justification 288–9
    importance of resolution 290
    overview 288–90
    UNSC debate 289

Suez Canal incident with USA 165
Suez crisis *see* Suez crisis
Eilat, sinking of 194–5, 348–9
embassies, attacks on
　gravity of force 152
　hostile intent 165
　large-scale attacks 202
　overview viii, 201–4
　protection of nationals doctrine 225–6
　right of self-defence 201
'Enduring Freedom', Operation *see* Al Qaeda attacks on
Entebbe operation
　international response 241, 249
　legality 98
　ongoing negotiations 96–7
　protection of nationals doctrine 226–9
　range of targets 122
Eritrea
　Ethiopia dispute *see* Ethiopia
　Sudan dispute 428–9
escalation of conflict ix, 532–5
Ethiopia
　Eritrea dispute
　　critique of findings 179
　　findings 178–9
　Somalia operation
　　background 469–71
　　Ethiopian claims 469
　　international response 469–71
European Union (EU)
　European Security Strategy 330–1, 335
　Operation 'Enduring Freedom', and 436–7
　Osiraq nuclear reactor strike, and 284–5
　rejection of preventive self-defence 323
　Rwandan operations against Hutu insurgents, and 467
　support for US action against terrorism 443–4
　Turkish operations in Iraq, and 459–60

exceptional measures
　evidentiary raw material, as 41
　evidentiary weight of justification 35–6
　expressions of acceptance or opposition 38–41
　influence of undisclosed acts on custom 34–5
　legal character of justification 36
　'meaningful silence' in response to 38
　reaction of other States 37–41
　right to take 34–7
　State's responsibility 34–5
　treaty law modification as 24
　UN responses 39–40
expansionist views *see* 'counter-restrictionist' views
external manifestations of the State, attacks against
　scope of analysis viii, 199–249
　scope of Article 51 523–4

failing States, non-State actors and ix, 419–510
Falklands War
　delayed response by UK 101–2
　proportionality 118–19
　sinking of *General Belgrano* 122
　'until clause', effectiveness of 81
fedayeen see Suez crisis
fishing vessels, attacks on 204–5
force, meaning 55–7
France
　Belgian intervention in the Congo, and 218–20, 241, 244–5
　contributions to debates 259
　Definition of Aggression 1974, and 160, 344–5, 387, 388–9
　German police pursuit into 191
　intervention in Iraq, and 312, 313
　Israeli operations in Lebanon, and 401, 403
　mercenary attack on Benin, and 405–6
　NEO doctrine 246
　non-State actors, and 446
　operations against Somali pirates 188

France (cont.)
  protection of neutral vessels 211–12
  protection of overseas nationals in Africa viii, 229–30, 233
  rejection of preventive self-defence 336–7
  security strategy 330–1, 335–6
  Six Day War, and 277, 278
  Suez Canal dispute 1951, and 289
  Suez crisis *see* Suez crisis
  Tunisia operation 344, 399
  US operations against Libya, and 425
Friendly Relations Declaration 1970
  ambiguity as to self-determination and use of force 392
  application 16–17
  non-State actors, as to 372–4
  self-determination, and 390–1
further attacks
  danger of escalation as to 533
  prevention of viii, 342–3, 518–19

General Belgrano, sinking of 122
Georgia, Russian operations 232–3
Germany
  Albania evacuation (Operation '*Libelle*') 231
  non-State actors, and 445
  police pursuit into France 191
  rejection of preventive self-defence 336–7
  revised security strategy 443–4
  support for pre-emptive self-defence 331–2
Ghana
  contributions to debates 272
  Definition of Aggression 1974, and ix, 300, 344–5, 388, 392
  US operations against Libya, and 425
gravity of forms of use of force *see also* de minimis threshold; proportionality standard
  'accumulation of events' doctrine, and 168–9
  consideration of 152
  de minimis threshold, and viii, 139–57
  diplomatic envoys, attacks on 203–4
  distinction of more and less grave forms questioned 143–4
  equation with defensive response 110, 111
  general relevance of 150, 151
  importance for *de minimis* threshold 151–2
  minimal gravity requirement 155, 521–2
  non-state actors 499–500
  small-scale attacks *see* small-scale attacks
  spontaneous reactions *see* spontaneous reactions to attacks
  testing of 118–19
gravity threshold *see de minimis* threshold
Great African War *see DRC v Uganda*, Rwandan operations against Hutu insurgents
Greece
  Definition of Aggression 1974, and 294–6
  Israeli airstrike on Tunis, and 424
Grenada, US operation 120, 222–4
Guatemala
  Definition of Aggression 1974, and 300–2
  fishing boats dispute with Mexico 206, 210–11
Guinea
  border tensions 429
  M/V Saiga case 198–9
Guinea-Bissau, Senegal dispute 428
Gulf of Sidra incident
  account of incident 353
  Libyan action 194
  Libyan claims 195
  'unit self-defence', as example of 352

Harib Fort action
  'accumulation of events' doctrine 170
  de minimis threshold 152–3
  immediacy criterion 99
  international response 95, 108–9, 114
  UK claims 100–1, 108–9

INDEX

Hezbollah *see* Lebanon
High-Level Panel
  non-State actors, and 446–7
  presentation of Report 328–9
  rejection of preventive self-defence 329–30
  Report viii, 327–30
  setting up 327
Hostage Convention 1979
  protection of nationals 234–5
  territorial State obligations 249
hostage rescues viii, 225–9, 248–9 *see also* Entebbe operation
hostage taking as armed attack 201
'hostile' environment for NEOs 245–6
hostile intent
  animus aggressionis, as 160–1
  ascertaining of 347
  Dinstein's classification, and 182
  examination 189–90
  lack of 165
  relevance to armed attack 166–8
  ROE, and 166
  territorial incursions 349, 350
  'unit self-defence' against demonstrated 350–1
'hot pursuit agreements' in response to small-scale attacks 187–9
'hot pursuit' doctrine
  application 378–9
  support in customary law and practice 515–16
'hot pursuit' operations 457–8
human rights law and incursions by non-State actors 198–9
humanitarian law
  incursions by non-State actors 198–9
  protection of nationals 213

'if an armed attack occurs', interpretation 58–60, 256–7, 260
'imminence' standard, 'counter-restrictionist' views 320, 337
imminent attacks, pre-emptive self-defence to 524–5
imminent threats

anticipatory self-defence 252
customary right of self-defence
  limited to 255–6
  inclusion in Article 51 526–7
  nuclear weapons development 360–2
  pre-emptive self-defence to 287
imputability to State
  application 371–2, 407, 408–14, 424–5, 490–1
  appropriateness of revision 493
  claims 424–5, 456–7
  Draft Articles on State Responsibility (DASR) and 490–1
  new imputability regime 490–1
  revision of standard 491–3
'In Larger Freedom' Report
  findings 329
  rejection of preventive self-defence 329–30
inconsistent conduct
  analytical approaches 31
  assessment 30–1
  evidentiary weight of vii, 31–44
  importance of analysis 32
incursions by non-State actors 198–9
India
  border incidents 156
  Definition of Aggression 1974, and 388
  Goa dispute 118–19
  intervention in Iraq, and 317
  Kashmir dispute 77–8, 80–1, 287–8
  rejection of pre-emptive self-defence 340–1
  Six Day War, and 277
  threat of anticipatory action 330, 333–4
indirect aggression
  criteria for self-defence 479–80
  de minimis threshold 140, 150
  decolonization, and *see* decolonization
  Definition of Aggression 1974 *see* Definition of Aggression
  ICJ judgments as to *see* International Court of Justice (ICJ)
  inclusion in analysis viii, 126
  meaning 370

indirect aggression (cont.)
  Nicaragua judgment *see Nicaragua* judgment
  State practice 529
Indonesia
  Definition of Aggression 1974, and 297–8, 388–9
  rejection of pre-emptive self-defence 340–1
'Infinite Reach', Operation *see* Al Qaeda attacks on
inherent right of self-defence
  affirming relevance of customary law, as 8
  debate over 260
  interpretation 58–60, 64–7
  Oil Platforms judgment 200
  pre-UN Charter 11–12
  scope 9, 11
  study limitations 3
  vesting in States 58–60
'innocent passage' by warships, UNCLOS provisions 188–9
instant custom
  attacks on Al Qaeda as ix, 437–43, 530
  'Bush doctrine' as 2
  from single UNSC resolution 44, 49
Institut de Droit International (IDI)
  resolution on self-defence ix, 325–6, 539–41, 545
intelligence as basis for action 427–8
interceptive self-defence
  academic acceptance 264
  burden of evidence 265–6
  compatibility with UN Charter 266–7
  dividing line with pre-emptive self-defence 265
  on-the-spot measures viii, 346–67
  permissibility 527
  pre-emptive self-defence distinguished 265–7, 347, 524–5
  strategic level
    overview viii, 355–67
    pre-emptive self-defence distinguished 356
  tactical level
    ascertaining of hostile intent 347
    overview viii, 346–67
    scope of analysis 346–7
    territorial incursions *see* territorial incursions
    'unit self-defence' *see* 'unit self-defence'
  terminological time frame 253
  time frame 265–6
  use of term 253
International Atomic Energy Agency (IAEA)
  importance of role 362
  intervention in Iraq, and 312–13
  Operation 'Orchard', and 363–4
  Osiraq nuclear reactor, and 281–2
International Civil Aviation Organization (ICAO)
  investigation of USS *Vincennes* incident viii, 258–62
  regulations on interception of civil aircraft 198–9
International Court of Justice (ICJ)
  absolute consistency of practice, on need for 44, 49
  'accumulation of events' doctrine, and 173–4
  anticipatory self-defence, and viii, 262–3
  attributability of private conduct to State, and 409
  case law as source of interpretation 4, 52
  clarification of use of force framework 513
  confirmation of 'effective control' test 412–13
  Corfu Channel case *see Corfu Channel* case
  critique of approach to *de minimis* threshold viii, 143–9
  de minimis threshold, and viii, 140–3
  hierarchy of customary law and practice, on 12–13
  indirect aggression, on 127–8
  Nicaragua judgment *see Nicaragua* judgment
  non-State actors, and

opportunities to pronounce 472–3
overview ix, 472–85
Oil Platforms judgment *see Oil Platforms* judgment
Palestinian Wall see Palestinian Wall advisory opinion
rejection of preventive self-defence 338
timing aspects of interpretation, on 21
USS *Vincennes* proceedings 258–9
International Criminal Court (ICC), crime of aggression 547
International Law Association (ILA)
formation of customary law, on 32–3, 44, 48
treaties as customary rules, on 17–18
International Law Commission (ILC)
animus aggressionis, and 158
Draft Articles on Diplomatic Protection 235–9
Draft Articles on State Responsibility *see* Draft Articles on State Responsibility (DASR)
interpretation and modification distinguished 22
ius cogens, on 27–8
modification of treaties, on 27–8
peremptory norms, on 25
relation between Charter and customary law, on 10
treaty interpretation, on 20
interpretation
Article 51 *see also* Article 51 UN Charter
conflict of laws, and 23
division from modification 23
inherent right of self-defence 58–60, 64–7
modification distinguished 22
role of custom vii, 19–22
sliding scale with modification 28–9
source materials 4
timing aspects *see* timing aspects of interpretation
interventions outside scope of study

alternative approaches to study, as vii, 6
examples 3
Iran
Definition of Aggression 1974, and 297–8
intervention in Iraq, and 317
Iraq
Gulf War 292–3
operations against Kurds 432–3
negotiations on nuclear weapons programme 365–7
Oil Platforms judgment *see Oil Platforms* judgment
rejection of pre-emptive self-defence 340–1
shooting down of airliner by US 291
'Tanker War' 206–7
threat of anticipatory action 330, 333–4
US Embassy occupation *see Tehran Embassy* case
Iraq 512
'axis of evil' 310–11
intervention in
academic analysis
extent 318
focus 318–19
overview 318–27
support for self-defence viii, 320–1, 322
alternative justifications 33
application of Shultz doctrine 424–5
commencement of military action 313
de minimis threshold 152–3
'defensive armed reprisals' 107–8
distinction of political and legal arguments 314–16
events leading to viii, 310–13
immediacy 101
international response viii, 314–18, 425
legal justifications viii, 314–18
necessity justification 96
'novel right shared in principle', whether 314

Iraq (cont.)
   overview viii, 310
   political signals for 310–11
   precedent for anticipatory self-defence, as viii, 314–18
   preventive justification 104
   rebuttal of 'Bush doctrine' 317–18
   search for evidence of WMDs 362–3
   shifts in approaches to viii, 318–42
   targeting justification 109
   UNSC resolution
      adoption 311–12
      debate over weapons inspections 312–13
      focus of debate 316–17
      international responses to 312
      provision for use of force 312
   UNSC resolution as justification 293
   US attack on intelligence HQ 202–3, 512
   involvement in George Bush assassination attempt 129–30, 414, 533
Iran
   Gulf War 292–3
   operations against Kurds 432–3
   Israeli nuclear reactor airstrike 56, 96–7
   Kuwait invasion 75, 79–80
   'Tanker War' 206–7
   Turkish operations *see* Turkey
Ireland, Osiraq nuclear reactor strike, and 285
irregulars *see* non-State actors
Israel
   airstrike against Syria, declaring responsibility for 35, 38
   allegations of Jordanian support for raiders 400–1
   Definition of Aggression 1974, and 300–2, 390
   Draft Articles on State Responsibility, and 304–5
   Entebbe operation *see* Entebbe operation
   intervention in Lebanon *see* Lebanon
   Iraqi nuclear reactor airstrike 56, 96–7
   Lake Tiberias incident 170–1
   non-State actors, operations against 394–6
   Operation 'Orchard' 363–4
   operations against non-State actors ix, 399–405
   Qibya incident 95
   rejection of preventive self-defence 337
   sinking of *Eilat* 194–5, 348–9
   Six Day War *see* Six Day War
   Suez Canal dispute with Egypt 1951 *see* Egypt
   Suez crisis *see* Suez crisis
   Syria operation vii, 53–5
      background 447
      international response 448–9
      Israeli claims 447–8
      overview ix, 447–9
      Syrian claims 448
   Tunis air raid 114–15, 402, 404, 423–4
Italy
   Belgian intervention in the Congo, and 218–20, 241, 244–5
   Definition of Aggression 1974, and 344–5, 383–4, 386
   protection of nationals, and 237–8
   security strategy 330–1
ius cogens
   application 26–7
   derogation from 24–6
   UN Charter as 24–6

Japan
   Chinese submarine incident 196–7
   Definition of Aggression 1974, and 384, 387–6
   Friendly Relations Declaration 1970, and 391
   proposals to include attacks on fishing vessels in Definition of Aggression 1974 204–5
   rejection of preventive self-defence 323
   Soviet nuclear submarine incident 189–90

support for pre-emptive self-defence 331–2
Jordan
　alleged support for raids into Israel 400–1
　assistance from UK 88, 396–8
　Six Day War, and 277
'just war' theories, bias within 512

Kellogg–Briand Pact *see* Pact of Paris 1928 (Kellogg–Briand Pact)
Korea *see* North Korea, South Korea
Kurds, operations against *see* Turkey
Kuwait, Iraqi invasion 75, 79–80

large-scale attacks *see also* gravity of forms of use of force
　as armed attacks 145
　de minimis threshold, as 520–1
　interceptive or pre-emptive self-defence? 355–6
　merchant vessels, on 205–6
　self-defence against 151–2
large-scale responses
　proportionality 115
　support for 117
Larnaca airport operation 229
law enforcement response to attacks
　diplomatic envoys 203
　'hot pursuit agreements' 187–9
　non-State actors 510
　scope 185–6
　'state of necessity' as to cross-border pursuit of criminals 380–2
League of Arab States
　intervention in Iraq, and 312
　Turkish operations in Iraq, and 431–2
Lebanon
　2006 Israeli operation
　　analysis 453–4
　　background 449–50
　　Draft Articles on State Responsibility, application of 456–7
　　international response 451–3
　　Israeli claims 450–1
　　Lebanese claims 451
　　Lebanon's 'due diligence' failure 454
　　opinio iuris 455
　　overview ix, 449–57
　　precedential value 454–5
　　retreat to 'Blue Line' 449
　　support for Israel 452
　intervention in Iraq, and 317
　Israeli intervention
　　after attacks on diplomats 203
　　armed attack, status as viii, 126
　　intern 402–3
　　international response 39
　　necessity and proportionality 92–3, 94
　　preventive justification 103
　　proportionality 111, 115, 117, 119–20
　　self-defence claims 401–2
　　small-scale attacks 156–7, 166–8
　　targeting justification 109
　　'until clause', use of 75
　US intervention
　　indirect aggression, and 396–8
　　justification as protection of overseas nationals 217–18
　　reporting obligation 74
　　'until clause', use of 81
legal doctrine *see opinio iuris*
Lesotho, South African raid 103, 403
lex posterior, application 13–14
lex specialis
　application 13–14
　'substantial involvement' as 413
lex superior, absence of 13–14
Liberia, border tensions 429
Libya
　Friendly Relations Declaration 1970, and 391
　Gulf of Sidra incident *see* Gulf of Sidra incident
　termination of nuclear weapons programme 365–7
　US operations 96, 102–3, 104, 154, 171–2, 291–2
　　application of Shultz doctrine 424–5
　　international response 425

Liechtenstein, support for pre-emptive self-defence 332–3
localized disputes, geographical aspect of proportionality standard applied to 119

Malaysia
  intervention in Iraq, and 317
  rejection of pre-emptive self-defence 340–1
massive attacks *see* large-scale attacks
Mayaguez incident 211, 224–5
'measures necessary', meaning 75–81
mens rea see animus aggressionis
mercenary attacks, condemnation of 405–6
merchant vessels
  customary law and practice 206–7
  Definition of Aggression 1974 as to 204–5
  external manifestations of the State, as 204
  halting of 80, 121
  massive attacks 205–6
  on-the-spot defensive measures 209
  protection of neutral vessels 211–13
  right of self-defence viii, 204–13
  ROEs as to attacks on 206
  'Tanker War' in Gulf 206–7
Mexico
  Definition of Aggression 1974, and 302, 384–5
  fishing boats dispute with Guatemala 206, 210–11
  Osiraq nuclear reactor strike, and 285–6
  rejection of pre-emptive self-defence 339
military aircraft
  right of unit self-defence 200
  self-defence against intruding *animus aggressionis* 192–3
  proportionality standard 193–4
  ROEs as to 191–2
military units and installations abroad
  Definition of Aggression 1974 as to 200

  external manifestations of the State, as 200
  overview viii, 199–200
  scope of analysis 199–200
Mongolia, ILC Draft Articles on State Responsibility, and 304–5
Morocco, Six Day War, and 277
M/V Saiga case 198–9

national liberation movements *see* non-State actors
National Security Strategy (NSS) *see also* 'Bush doctrine'
  academic analysis viii, 324–7
  adoption 2, 41–2, 250–1
  analysis of threats 307–8
  anticipatory self-defence
    broadening of 309–10
    endorsement of 309
    use of 308–9
  covering letter 307
  drafting of viii, 305–10
  effect on *opinio iuris* and practice 524
  impact 251
  preventive self-defence against non-imminent threats 309–10
  promulgation 444
  ratione temporis dimension 308–9
  reassessment of strategy 306
  response to 9/11 attacks, as 305–18
  scope 307–8
nationals, protection of *see also* non-combatant evacuation operations (NEOs)
  abuse of doctrine 240–2
  baselines for agreement on 243–4
  cumulative conditions (Waldock) 213–14
  customary law and practice
    overview viii, 216–33
    scope of analysis 216
    statements indicating viii, 233–9
  doctrinal debate viii, 213–16
  evidence for permissibility of use of force for 239–40
  exception to prohibition of pre-emptive self-defence, as 346

existence of customary right 243
hostage rescues 248–9
humanitarian intervention, as 213
international large-scale operations 230–2
justification for large-scale military operations, as 244
legal bases 214–15
non-combatant evacuation, as 247
against non-State actors 405
not reported to UNSC viii, 229–30, 233
overview viii, 213–49
peaceful means, use of 244
principle for non-use of armed force for 243–4
proposed parameters 243–9
recent State practice
  evidence of custom in viii, 242
  importance of viii, 242–3
scope for use of force viii, 244–5
'state of necessity' as to 380–2
sufficiency of evidence for customary right 240
universal doctrine 233
unlawfulness 215
whether compatible with Charter 215–16
NATO
  collective self-defence against terrorism 443–4
  destruction of Chinese embassy in Belgrade 165
  Operation 'Enduring Freedom', and 436–7
  provisions for response to attacks on merchant vessels 206
naval law enforcement, use of force distinguished 209
naval operations *see also* Falklands War; merchant vessels; United Nations Convention on the Law of the Sea (UNCLOS)
  forcible action against private ships 198
  geographical aspect of proportionality standard applied to 118–19
  graduated response to 194
  halting of shipping 80, 121
  'innocent passage' by warships, UNCLOS provisions 188–9
  proportionate lethal force in response 194–5
  submarines 195–7
naval vessels, right of self-defence 200 *see also* submarines
necessity standard *see also* 'state of necessity'
  academic interest 94–5
  anticipatory self-defence 4–5, 279–80
  application 518
  armed attack criterion, and 3
  authority 91–2
  case-by-case determination 520
  controversy 92–4
  'defensive armed reprisals' 107–8
  distinction between premeditated and spontaneous action 100–2
  distinction of self-defence within and against a State, and 496
  exceptions to prohibition of pre-emptive self-defence viii, 342–3
  'failure to prevent' attacks, and 502
  flexible interpretation 98
  immediacy of self-defence action vii, 99–108
  isolated attacks of short duration 102
  non-State actors, as to 487, 507, 509
  overview vii, 91–123
  part of customary right of self-defence, as 8
  prevention of further attacks 102–8, 518–19
  proportionality standard linked 123–5
  self-defence as last resort vii, 95–8
  small-scale attacks 157
  targeting vii, 108–10
Netherlands
  Definition of Aggression 1974, and 296

570 INDEX

Netherlands (cont.)
  Friendly Relations Declaration 1970, and 391
  non-State actors, and 445–6
  revised security strategy 445–6
  Suez Canal dispute 1951, and 290
Nicaragua judgment
  'accumulation of events' doctrine, and 173–4
  animus aggressionis 161–2
  arguments 7–10
  assessment of inconsistent conduct 30–1
  Bible of use of force, as 513
  Charter as peremptory norm 25
  clarification of meaning of armed attack 8–9
  controversy 1
  'counter-restrictionist' views 10–11
  critique of collective security findings vii, 83–91
  critique of *de minimis* findings 143
  critique of less grave force findings 144–5
  de minimis threshold, and viii, 140–3, 407–8
  Definition of Aggression 1974, use of 407–8
  definition of armed attack 8
  dissenting opinions 98
  duration of action 119–20
  Friendly Relations Declaration 17, 373–4
  identicality of Charter and custom 260–1, 263
  indirect aggression
    findings ix, 406, 528–9
    overview ix, 406–19
  infringement of sovereignty, as to 185
  inherent right of self-defence 8
  link between State and non-State actors, determination of 408, 529–30
  necessity standard 8, 99
  Nicaraguan claims 9–10
  overlap of custom and treaty law 7–8, 11–12, 19, 22
  proportionality 8
  proportionate countermeasures by direct victim of less grave force, on 141
  question of whether armed attack occurring ix, 406–7
  relationship of use of force and armed attack, on 140
  reporting obligation 8, 68, 71–2
  'restrictionist' views 9–10
  significance 7, 8–9
  substantive involvement, as to 408, 415–19
  summary of main findings 7–8
  US claims 7, 9–10, 16, 68, 512
  US control of Contras 409, 410
  US withdrawal from case 8
  uses of force other than armed attack, on 140–1
  'Vandenberg reservation', and 7, 8–9
Niger, Osiraq nuclear reactor strike, and 285–6
Nigeria, dispute with Cameroon 173–4
Non-Aligned Movement
  rejection of pre-emptive self-defence 341
  Turkish operations in Iraq, and 431–2
non-combatant evacuation operations (NEOs)
  host state approval requirement 247–8
  protection of nationals as 247
  technical guidelines 245–6
  types of threat environments 245
non-combatants as targets of terrorism 498
non-imminent attacks
  academic support for action against
    European commentators 321–2
    US commentators viii, 320–1, 322
  anticipatory self-defence 252
  lack of support for action against 336–8
  preventive self-defence 524–5
  US NSS, and *see* National Security Strategy (NSS)

INDEX 571

non-Member States
  acknowledgement of customary status of Article 2(4) 16
  application of UN Charter to 15
  treaties with 16
Non-Proliferation Treaty 365–7
non-State actors *see also* terrorism
  acknowledgement of private conduct by States 413–14
  additional variables governing self-defence ix, 507–10
  allegations of State support for 400–1
  attacks as armed attacks, conditions 531–2
  attributability of attacks 372–4, 408–14, 489–90
  balance of State security with sovereignty and territorial integrity 487–8
  challenges to *opinio iuris* and practice 528
  changes in approach pre-9/11 ix, 419–33
  co-operative law enforcement against 510
  'complete dependence' on State 409
  covert proxy-warfare 414
  danger of escalation as to 533–4
  decolonization era 528–9
  distinction of self-defence within and against a State *see* self-defence
  'due diligence rule' as to 374–5
  'effective control' threshold 410–13
  end of decolonization ix, 419–21
  evolution of approach to 419
  external link to victim State
    application of criteria 501–2
    overview 500–1
  failing States ix, 419–510
  failure to prevent attacks by
    burden of evidence of defending State 505–6
    commitment to peaceful means 506
    differing approaches to 506
    'harbouring' doctrine 503
    limitations of 'harbouring' doctrine 504
    link to State 502
    necessity standard 502
    opportunity to rectify abuse 506
    overview ix, 502–6
    relationship of 'harbouring' and 'failure to prevent' 504–5
    State failure 504
  gravity of forms of use of force 499–500
  'harbouring' doctrine
    application 401
    'failure to prevent' attacks, and 503
    harbouring as indirect force 528
    international response 402–3
  'hot pursuit' doctrine, and 378–9
  ICJ, and *see* International Court of Justice (ICJ)
  imputability *see* imputability to State
  incursions 198–9
  instruments of State, as 399, 409
  international terrorism ix, 419–510
  intersecting norms as to 371–2
  interventions in neighbouring countries against ix, 399–405
  key question as to 485–6
  lack of attention to problem of
    academic analysis, in 370–1
    Article 51, by 369–70
  legal complexity as to 371–2
  legal uncertainty as to ix, 485–9, 531
  legality of proportionate measures against 487
  legality of support for 419
  link to State 387–9, 408, 440–1, 461–2, 502, 528
  mercenary attacks 405–6
  necessity standard as to 487, 507, 509
  notion of self-defence against 499
  operations against national liberation movements 399–400
  opinio iuris as to 404–5
  other cases of action against ix, 405
  placebo effect of self-defence 510

non-State actors (cont.)
  private conduct in absence or default of official authority 414
  proportionality standard as to 487, 509
  protection of nationals from 405
  'reasonable chance of success' of self-defence
    applicability 507–8
    criteria 507
  responses to attacks by, legal bases for ix, 377–82
  self-determination, and *see* self-determination
  shifts in approaches to 486
  signs of shift in custom as to ix, 428–33
  State-centred approach, appropriateness 535
  'state of necessity' as to responses to 379–80
  State practice
    early cases 394–9
    overview ix, 394–406
    reliance on link between non-State actors and State 394
  statements as to applicability of Article 51 404–5
  'substantial involvement' of States
    Definition of Aggression 1974, and 415
    Nicaragua judgment as to 408, 415–19
    overview ix, 415–19
    whether *lex specialis* 413
  summary of analysis ix, 528–32
  summary of Charter framework 377
  victim state not having contributed to situation
    applicability 508–9
    criteria 507
  whether able to commit 'armed attacks' ix, 485–510
North Korea
  alleged assassination of South Korean ministers 203
  Operation 'Orchard', and 363–4
  termination of nuclear weapons programme 365–7
  threat of anticipatory action 330, 333–4
  USS *Pueblo* incident 187
Norway
  Definition of Aggression 1974, and 132, 297, 300
  proposals on use of force 61
  submarine incidents 196
nuclear weapons
  anticipatory self-defence, and 257, 527–8
  development as imminent threat 360–2
  intelligence on programmes 362–3
  need for avoidance of military escalation 262
  Non-Proliferation Treaty 365–7
  pre-emptive self-defence 358–9
  termination of programmes 365–7
Nuremburg Military Tribunal, acceptance of legality of anticipatory self-defence 256–7

Oil Platforms judgment
  'accumulation of events' doctrine, and 173–4
  animus aggressionis 162–3
  armed attack against merchant ship 207–9
  collective self-defence 90–1
  critique 142–3
  de minimis threshold, and 142
  immediacy 100
  inherent right of self-defence 200, 520
  Iran's claims 207–9
  prevention of further attacks 105–6, 210–11
  proportionality 110, 111, 113–14
  protection of neutral vessels 212–13
  self-defence as last resort 98
  targeting 109–10
  US claims 153, 207–9
Oman, Osiraq nuclear reactor strike, and 285–6

INDEX 573

on-the-spot measures
  Definition of Aggression 1974 209
  Dinstein's classification 181
  interceptive self-defence viii, 346–67
  merchant vessels 209
Operation 'Phoenix' *see* Colombia
opinio iuris
  acceptance of Article 2(4) as peremptory norm 25–6
  customary law and practice, and vii, 29–51
  element of custom, as 29–30
  non-State actors, as to 404–5
  shift as to pre-emptive self-defence 341–2
  source for interpretation, as 2–3, 4, 513–14
  State's statements on anticipatory self-defence as 334
  study methodology, in vii, 6
  UN Charter as 'negative' 14–15
  UNGA resolutions as 49–51
Organization of American States (OAS)
  Operations 'Enduring Freedom', and 436–7
  Operation 'Phoenix', and 463–4
Osiraq nuclear reactor strike
  international attitudes to lawfulness 285–6
  international response 284–5
  Israeli justification 280–1
  Israel's reliance on preventive self-defence justification 283–4
  overview viii, 280–7
  precedent for anticipatory self-defence, as 282–3
  rejection of pre-emptive self-defence claim 287, 358–9
  UNSC debate 281–2

Pact of Paris 1928 (Kellogg–Briand Pact)
  customary law and practice, as 11–12
  self-defence provision 54

Pakistan
  border incidents 156
  Definition of Aggression 1974, and 300–2
  Friendly Relations Declaration 1970, and 390
  Kashmir dispute 77–8, 80–1, 287–8, 512
  Osiraq nuclear reactor strike, and 285–6
  rejection of pre-emptive self-defence 339
Palestinian Wall advisory opinion
  critique 475–8
  findings 473
  overview ix, 473–8
  self-defence argument finding 473–5
  separate opinions 475
Panama
  Definition of Aggression 1974, and 297
  US operation 222–4
peace and security
  maintenance or restoration of *see* 'until clause'
  measures to ensure greater 546
  multilateralism as means to greater 550
  post-Cold War threats 548
peaceful means, use of
  diplomacy vii, 95–8
  prevention of attacks by non-State actors 505–6, 509–10
Pearl Harbour attack
  anticipatory self-defence, hypothetical use 254
  compared to 9/11 attacks 250
  possible self-defence against 355–6
peremptory norms
  conflicts *see* conflict of laws
  listing of 25
  non-recognition of situations created by breach of 26
  'permissive' environment for NEOs 245–6

personnel aspect of armed attack requirement (*ratione personae*) *see also* non-State actors
　content of chapter 368–9
　criteria for new threshold ix, 489–510
　modification of primary or secondary rules ix, 489–93
　question of who must attack come from 368
　scope 3
　scope of analysis ix, 368–9
　summary of analysis ix, 528–32
　whether new threshold 486–7
Philippines, Osiraq nuclear reactor strike, and 285, 286
physical force, meaning of force restricted to 55–6
'pin prick attacks'
　accumulation *see* 'accumulation of events' doctrine
　response to 115, 116
Poland, Belgian intervention in the Congo, and 218–20, 241, 244–5
Portugal
　allegations against Senegal 401
　Goa dispute 118–19
　mercenary attack on DRC, and 405–6
　operations against non-State actors ix, 399–405
　Samine attack in Senegal 171
positivist method of analysis, application of 511–12
pre-emptive self-defence
　academic support for viii, 324–7
　borderline cases *see* exceptions to prohibition *below*
　burden of evidence 265–6
　compatibility with UN Charter 266–7
　dangers of accepting broader right of 357–8
　dividing line with interceptive self-defence 265
　exceptions to prohibition
　　declarations of war 344–5

　　interceptive self-defence *see* interceptive self-defence
　　necessity standard, and viii, 342–3
　　overview viii, 342–67
　　possible exceptions viii, 343–6
　　presence of forces continuing beyond agreed timescale 343–4
　　protection of nationals 346
　　scope of analysis 342
　imminent threats, and 287
　interceptive self-defence distinguished 265–7, 347, 524–5
　nuclear weapons 358–9
　preventive self-defence distinguished 524–5
　rejection 287, 339
　shift in *opinio iuris* 341–2
　shifts in approaches to viii, 318–42
　Six Day War as closest example 356–7
　State support viii, 330–42
　strategic level
　　interceptive self-defence distinguished 356
　　overview viii, 355–67
　　terminological time frame 253–4
　　time frame 265–6
　　use of term 252–3
　　WMDs 358–9, 527–8
pre-existing custom *see* custom
prevention of further attacks
　anticipatory self-defence 290–1
　necessity standard 102–8
　Oil Platforms judgment 210–11
Prevention of Genocide case
　'complete dependence' issue 409
　'effective control' threshold 412–13
　imputability to State ruling 491–3
preventive self-defence
　majority academic opinion against 322
　pre-emptive self-defence distinguished 524–5
　rebuttal of viii, 322–4
　rejection 286, 287, 329–30, 336–8

rejection by international lawyers 322
shifts in approaches to viii, 318–42
State support viii, 330–42
terminological time frame 254
US NSS, and *see* National Security Strategy (NSS)
use of term 252–3
'primary' law
  Article 51 as 490
  meaning 489
priority (first use) principle
  animus aggressionis, and 158
  anticipatory self-defence 294, 299
  debate over 132–3, 158–9
  factors 160–1
  objections 294–6
  presumption of aggression 160
  provision 159–60
  rebuttal of presumption of aggression 160
private conduct *see* non-State actors
private ships, forcible action against 198
proportionality standard
  academic interest 94–5
  'accumulation of events' doctrine, and 170–1, 175
  anticipatory self-defence 279–80
  application 460–1, 518, 519
  armed attack criterion, and 3
  assessment vii, 116–23
  authority 91–2
  case-by-case determination 520
  controversy 92–4
  distinction of self-defence within and against a State, and 496
  duration of action 119–21
  Fourth Special Committee negotiations 133
  geographical aspect 118–19
  less grave uses of force 141
  military aircraft 192–3
  naval vessels 194–5
  necessity standard linked 123–5
  non-State actors, as to 487, 509
  opposition to 92–3, 94
  overview vii, 91–123

part of customary right of self-defence, as 8
quantitative vs. functional approach vii, 110–16
range of targets aspect 121–3
small-scale attacks 157
weapons types as factor 123

reactive self-defence
  anticipatory self-defence distinguished 251–2
  terminological time frame 253
Red Crusader incident 209
reporting obligation
  compliance over small-scale incidents 73–4
  existence in customary law and practice 8
  failure to report and legality of measures 71–2, 517
  mandatory nature 69–70
  observance 72
  over-reporting 72
  overview vii, 68–74
  purpose 68
  strengthening 545–6
  text 68
  whether norm creating 69
  whether substantive or procedural 70, 72
request for assistance, right to make 87–91
'restrictionist' views
  abandonment 325
  anticipatory self-defence viii, 258–62, 263–4, 265–6
  Article 51 and customary right, as to 514–15
  dominance 325
  Nicaragua judgment 9–10
  summary of argument with 'counter-restrictionists' 514–15
Rhodesia, operations against non-State actors ix, 399–405
Rules of Engagement (ROEs)
  aircraft 191–2
  hostile intent, and 166
  merchant vessels, attacks on 206

576   INDEX

Rules of Engagement (ROEs) (cont.)
    national self-defence and unit self-
        defence distinguished 180
    openness and public debate 548
    'unit self-defence' 350–1
Russia
    Afghanistan operations 428
    Chechen rebels, and 444–5
    claims to right of pre-emptive strike
        330, 334–5
    Georgia operations
        Georgian claims 359–60
        international response 360–2
        overview 357–8
        protection of nationals 232–3
        Russian claims 358–9
    intervention in Iraq, and 312, 313
    Israeli operation against Syria, and
        448–9
Rwandan operations against Hutu
        insurgents
    escalation of conflict with DRC
        533–4
    international response 467–8
    overview 466–8
    rejection of Rwandan claims 433
    Rwandan claims 466–7

Saint Vincent and the Grenadines, *M/V
        Saiga* case 198–9
'secondary' law
    Article 51 as 490
    meaning 489
security and peace, maintenance or
        restoration of *see* 'until
        clause'
security strategies
    preventive deployment 330–1
    revision ix, 2, 41–2, 443–7
self-defence *see also* collective self-
        defence
    anticipatory *see* anticipatory self-
        defence
    armed attack requirement 51 UN
        Charter *see* Article
    armed reprisals distinguished 183
    Article 51 right *see* Article 51 UN
        Charter

    clarification in definition of armed
        attack 536
    conditions other than armed attack
        vii, 68–125
    customary boundaries ix, 511–35
    customary right *see* customary right
        of self-defence
    danger of escalation ix, 532–5
    de minimis threshold *see de minimis*
        threshold
    'defensive armed reprisals' 107–8
    definition of aggression detached
        from 537
    dichotomy of legal and military
        frameworks 179–80
    differentiated application of
        parameters 180–1
    Dinstein's classification *see*
        Dinstein's classification
    distinction between premeditated
        and spontaneous action
        100–2
    divergent frameworks *see* use of
        force (*Ius ad Bellum*)
    effect of restrictive meaning 60
    elements of evidentiary norm
        177–8
    equation with gravity of armed
        attack 110, 111
    forcible acts not triggering right of,
        armed attacks distinguished
        139
    immediacy vii, 99–108
    inherent right *see* inherent right of
        self-defence
    interlinking of aspects 4–5
    isolated attacks of short duration 102
    large-scale attacks, against 151–2
    last resort, as vii, 95–8
    national self-defence and unit self-
        defence distinguished 180
    necessity standard *see* necessity
        standard
    preconditions other than armed
        attack ix, 517–20
    preconditions, scope of analysis
        vii, 53
    pre-UN Charter vii, 53–5

INDEX 577

prevention of further attacks *see* prevention of further attacks
proportionality standard *see* proportionality standard
reliable information as basis for action 427–8
reporting obligation *see* reporting obligation
small-scale attacks *see* small-scale attacks
   against a State and within a State, distinction 368
      attacks on infrastructure of other State 495
      attacks on terrorists and bases 494
      distinction made 493–4
      necessity and proportionality, and 496
      Operation 'Enduring Freedom' as example 495–6
      overview ix, 493–6
      support for distinction 494
suspension *see* 'until clause'
targeting vii, 108–10
temporary measure, as 57–8
'until clause' *see* 'until clause'
self-determination
   'accumulation of events' doctrine, and 171
   affirmation of right to armed struggle 419–20
   Definition of Aggression 1974 *see* Definition of Aggression
   Friendly Relations Declaration 1970 *see* Friendly Relations Declaration
   right to use force against colonial occupation 403–4
   support for legality of use of force 390–1
   UNSC resolutions supporting 403–4
   use of force, and ix, 390–4
Senegal
   Guinea-Bissau dispute 428
   Portuguese allegations against 401
   Portuguese attack on Samine 171
Seychelles, mercenary attack 405–6

Shultz doctrine
   adoption 421–2
   application 424–5
   expression 423
   genesis 422
   interpretation of Charter law, as 422–3
   overview ix, 421–8
   publication 422–3
Sierra Leone
   border tensions 429
   Osiraq nuclear reactor strike, and 285–6
Singapore, support for pre-emptive self-defence 332–3
Six Day War
   arguments against precedential impact 274–8
   closest example of pre-emptive self-defence, as 356–7
   course of war 272–3
   international response 278–9
   overview viii, 272–80
   precedent for anticipatory self-defence, as 272, 274, 279–80
   prior armed attack, as 274–8
   rejection of pre-emptive self-defence, as 287
   response to blockade, as 276–7
   UNSC debate 273–4
skirmishes *see* small-scale attacks
Slovenia, protection of nationals, and 237–8
Small-scale attacks
   accumulation *see* 'accumulation of events' doctrine
   animus aggressionis, and 166–8, 192–3
   application of parameters for analysis 178
   armed attacks, as 155, 156
   border incidents 155
   clandestine presence of ununiformed agents 185–6
   consistency of applicable legal parameters for responses 198
   danger of escalation as to 532

Small-scale attacks (cont.)
  examples where self-defence invoked 187
  graduated response to
    generally 190
    land incursions 190–1
    naval vessels 194–5
    submarines 195–8
    trespassing military aircraft 191–2
  gravity 189–90
  hostile intent 189–90
  'hot pursuit agreements' 187–9
  inclusion in Charter provisions 184–7
  infringement of sovereignty 184–7
  isolated attacks of short duration 102
  law enforcement response 185–6
  necessity standard 157
  no automatic exemption for 157
  overview viii, 184–99
  'pin prick attacks', response to 115, 116
  proportionality of response 193–4
  proportionality standard 157
  proportionate lethal force 194–5
  qualifying as use of force 185–6
  scope of analysis 184
  skirmishes 155
  spontaneous reactions to attacks 157
  unlawfulness requirement 187–9
Somalia
  Ethiopian operation *see* Ethiopia
  French anti-piracy operations, 188
South Africa
  allegations of foreign support for SWAPO 401
  Friendly Relations Declaration 1970, and 391–2
  intervention in Iraq, and 317
  Lesotho raid 103, 403
  mercenary attack on Seychelles, and 405–6
  operations against non-State actors ix, 399–405
  termination of nuclear weapons programme 365–7
South Korea
  alleged assassination of ministers by North Korea 203
  shooting down of airliner by USSR 198–9
  support for pre-emptive self-defence 332–3
sovereignty
  infringement by small-scale attacks 184–7
  inviolability as fundamental international law 488–9
Spain
  Definition of Aggression 1974, and 300–2
  Madrid bombings 502
  Osiraq nuclear reactor strike, and 285
spontaneous reactions to attacks
  gravity of incident 154
  small-scale attacks 157
'State', use of term 16
'state of necessity'
  applications 380–2
  customary law and practice, as 379–80, 515–16
  responses to actions by non-State actors, as to 379–80
State practice *see* customary law and practice
States *see* specific countries
  acceptance of Article 2(4) as peremptory norm 25
  acknowledgement of private conduct as own 413–14
  actions *see* exceptional measures
  all State organs contributing to formation of customary law 43–4
  analysis of content of statements on anticipatory self-defence 334–6
  atttributability of private conduct to 408–9
  balance of security with sovereignty and territorial integrity 487–8
  balance of State security with sovereignty and territorial integrity 532

INDEX 579

distinction of self-defence within and against a State *see* self-defence
'due diligence rule' as to 374–5
echoing of 'Bush doctrine' 330–1, 333–4
external manifestations, attacks against *see* external manifestations of the State, attacks against
failing States and non-State actors ix, 419–510
imputability *see* imputability to State
inconsistent conduct *see* inconsistent conduct
inherent right of self-defence vested in 58–60
non-State actors, and *see* non-State actors
prerogative to judge adequacy of UNSC measures 82
sovereignty *see* sovereignty
support for pre-emptive and preventive self-defence viii, 330–42
study
  application of positivist method of analysis 511–12
  focus 3
  limitations ix, 3–4, 511–14
  methodology
    content of chapter vii, 6–7
    scope of analysis vii, 6–7
  opinio iuris as evidence 513–14
  quest for custom vii, 6
  scope 3
submarines
  lawful use of force against 197–8
  unlawful intrusions by 195–7
subsequent developments in law, treaty interpretation, and 21–2
'substantial involvement' *see* non-State actors
Sudan
  Eritrea dispute 428–9
  Six Day War, and 279
  US attacks on Al Qaeda *see* Al Qaeda, attacks on

Suez crisis
  action against *fedayeen*
    international response 96, 114, 170
    Israeli claims 276–7, 394–6, 495
  diplomacy, use of 96
  effectiveness of UNSC resolutions 82
  proportionality 114, 170
  protection of nationals doctrine 216–17
'Sun', Operation *see* Turkey
Sweden
  Definition of Aggression 1974, and 300–2
  Osiraq nuclear reactor strike, and 284–5
  Soviet submarine incident 195–6
Switzerland, support for pre-emptive self-defence 332–3
Syria
  Definition of Aggression 1974, and 344–5
  Israeli airstrike *see* Israel
  Israeli operation vii, 53–5 *see* Israel
  Lake Tiberias incident 170–1
  Operation 'Orchard' 363–4
  rejection of pre-emptive self-defence 340–1
  self-determination, and 420
  Six Day War *see* Six Day War
  support for legality of use of force against colonialism 391

Tadić case, 'effective control' threshold 410–13
Tajikistan, Afghanistan operations 428
Taleban, operations against *see* Al Qaeda, attacks on
Tanzania
  Burundi dispute 429
  intervention in Iraq, and 317
targeting
  necessity standard vii, 108–10
  proportionality of range of targets 121–3
Tehran Embassy case
  'due diligence rule', and 375
  imputability to State ruling 491–3

Tehran Embassy case (cont.)
  international response 225–6
  labelling as 'armed attack' 201
territorial acquisition by force, non-recognition 26
territorial incursions
  choice of actions against 348–9
  continuum of measures against 348
  hostile intent
    case-by-case determination 350
    detection of 349
    scope 349–50
  measures short of force 349
  overview viii, 347–50
  ratione temporis dimension 347–8
terrorism
  authorization of force against 443
  civilians as targets of 498
  increased threat from use of modern technology 368–9
  irrelevance of 'terrorist' label ix, 496–9, 532
  legal definition 497–8
  more flexible approach to 428
  non-combatants as targets of 498
  non-State actors ix, 419–510
  notion of self-defence against 499
  special regime as to 496–7
  'state of necessity' as to operations against 380–2
  State practice as to recognition of terrorist groups 498–9
Thailand
  border incidents 156
  Cambodia evacuation 232
threshold level of attack *see de minimis* threshold
time taken for practice to become customary 47–9
timing aspect of armed attack requirement (*ratione temporis*) *see also* anticipatory self-defence
  key concepts 524–5
  scope 3
  scope of analysis viii, 250–4

sliding scale of interpretation and modification, and 28–9
summary of analysis ix, 524–8
timing aspects of interpretation
  ICJ 21
  subsequent developments in law 21–2
  VCLT 20
Tokyo Military Tribunal, acceptance of legality of anticipatory self-defence 256–7
Tunkin incident 71, 104, 154
  account of incident 352
  UK reaction 174–5, 523
  'unit self-defence', as example of 351–2
treaty law
  'Baxter paradox' 17
  conflicts *see* conflict of laws
  customary rules, as 17–18
  derogation *see* derogation
  hierarchy with customary law and practice 12–13
  interpretation *see* interpretation
  modification
    division from interpretation 23
    draft VCLT 23–4
    evidentiary standard 29
    exceptional measure, as 24
    interpretation distinguished 22
    overview vii, 22–9
    sliding scale with interpretation 28–9
  overlap with customary law and practice 7–8
  void treaties 13
Tunisia
  Belgian intervention in the Congo, and 218–20, 241, 244–5
  French operations 344, 399
  Israeli airstrike 114–15, 402, 404, 423–4
Turkey
  Definition of Aggression 1974, and 160, 387
  Kurdish operations
    analysis 433, 459
    background 429–31

danger of escalation 533
'hot pursuit' operation 457–8
immediacy 101
increased Kurdish activity 457
international response 71, 431–2, 459–60, 512
launch of 'Operation Sun' 458
link between Kurds and Iraq 461–2
overview ix, 457–62
proportionality 119, 120–1, 460–1
targeting 109
Turkish claims 429–31, 458
rejection of pre-emptive self-defence 339
types of act aspect of armed attack requirement (*ratione materiae*)
Dinstein's classification *see* Dinstein's classification
scope 3
scope of analysis viii, 126–7
summary of analysis ix, 520–4

U-2 incident 164
Uganda
Congo (DRC) dispute *see* DRC v Uganda
Entebbe operation *see* Entebbe operation
intervention in Iraq, and 316
support for pre-emptive self-defence 332–3
Ukraine, termination of nuclear weapons programme 365–7
'uncertain' environment for NEOs 245–6
unilateral recourse to force
meaning 3
study limitations 3
'unit self-defence'
against demonstrated hostile intent 350–1
cautious approach to customary practice 355
evidence in State practice 351
overview viii, 350–5
ROEs as to 350–1

United Arab Republic (UAR), self-determination, and 403
United Kingdom (UK)
assistance to Jordan 88, 396–8
attacks on Al Qaeda *see* Al Qaeda, attacks on
Belgian intervention in the Congo, and 218–20, 241, 244–5
Caroline incident *see Caroline* incident
Corfu Channel case *see Corfu Channel* case
Definition of Aggression 1974, and 135, 136, 296, 299–302, 345
dominance of 'counter-restrictionist' views 325
Draft Articles on State Responsibility, and 304–5
Falklands War *see* Falklands War
Friendly Relations Declaration 1970, and 391–2
intervention in Iraq, and 312, 313, 314–15
Israeli operation against Syria, and 448–9
London bombings 502
NEO doctrine 246
Osiraq nuclear reactor strike, and 285–6
proposals on use of force 65
reaction to uses of force by USA 40
Red Crusader incident 209
rejection of preventive self-defence 322, 337
Suez Canal dispute 1951, and 290
Suez crisis *see* Suez crisis
Tonkin incident, and 174–5, 523
Turkish operations in Iraq, and 431–2, 459–60
US operations against Libya, and 425
Yemen Harib Fort action *see* Harib Fort action
United Nations Charter *see also* Article 2(4) UN Charter; Article 51 UN Charter
abandonment of Charter regime 549–50
application to non-Members 15

United Nations Charter (cont.)
  capability for evolution vii, 6
  commitment to compliance 550
  Conference on International Organization 60–1
  continuing validity of Charter regime 550
  custom, and vii, 7–29
  customary status 15–16
  departure from pre-existing custom, as 11–12
  division of preparatory work 61
  incompatible custom
    continued application to non-Members 14–15
    removal of 12–13, 18
  ius cogens, as 24–6
  'negative' *opinio iuris*, as 14–15
  non-Member States, and *see* non-Member States
  pre-existing custom, and vii, 7–19
  preparatory works and interpretation of Article 51 *see* Article 51 UN Charter
  primacy of obligations 13
  self-defence prior to vii, 53–5
  terminology relating to use of force 127
  whole of use of force regulation, as 7–8, 19, 22
United Nations Convention on the Law of the Sea (UNCLOS)
  forcible action against private ships 198
  graduated response to incursions by warships 194
  'hot pursuit', as to 378
  'innocent passage' by warships 188–9
  unlawful intrusions by submarines 195–7
Definition of Aggression *see also* United Nations General Assembly (UNGA) 1974
  legal weight of responses to use of force 39–40
  non-recognition of forcible territorial acquisition 26
  resolutions affirming applicability of Charter to all States 16–17
  resolutions as custom 49–51
United Nations Security Council (UNSC)
  enforcement powers 57
  fairness as to special position of 548
  intervention in Iraq, and *see* Iraq
  legal weight of responses to use of force 39–40
  need for appropriate condemnation of aggression 546
  primary competence 49
  reporting obligation *see* reporting obligation
  resolutions as custom 49
  resolutions supporting self-determination 403–4
  'until clause', use of *see* 'until clause'
United States (US)
  9/11 attacks *see* 9/11 attacks
  Afghanistan operations *see* Afghanistan
  Afghanistan–Pakistan tension, and *see* Afghanistan
  aircraft losses to Soviet fighters 351
  acknowledgement of customary status of Article 2(4) 16
  attacks on Al Qaeda *see* Al Qaeda, attacks on
  Belgian intervention in the Congo, and 220
  'Bush doctrine' *see* 'Bush doctrine'
  Bush, George, assassination attempt 202–3
  Caroline incident *see Caroline* incident
  claims of right of self-defence against terrorism 443
  Cuban missile crisis *see* Cuban missile crisis
  Definition of Aggression 1974, and 125, 135, 150, 151, 384, 386, 394
  diplomatic papers as interpretative source 64–5
  dominance of 'counter-restrictionist' views 325

Dominican Republic operation 115, 119–20, 220–2
drafting of Article 51, and 64
Friendly Relations Declaration 1970, and 391–2
Grenada operation 120, 222–4
Gulf of Sidra incident *see* Gulf of Sidra incident
ILC Draft Articles on State Responsibility, and 304–5
intervention in Afghanistan *see* Afghanistan
Iran embassy occupation *see* Tehran Embassy case
Iranian airliner incident *see* USS Vincennes incident
Iraq operations *see* Iraq
Israeli operation against Syria, and 448–9
Israeli raid on Tunis, and 172, 423–4
Kurdish operations by Turkey, and 120–1, 512
Lebanon, and *see* Lebanon
Libya operations *see* Libya
Mayaguez incident 211, 224–5
National Security Strategy (NSS), US *see* National Security Strategy (NSS)
Nicaragua judgment, and *see Nicaragua* judgment
Oil Platforms judgment *see Oil Platforms* judgment
Operation 'Phoenix', and 463–4
Panama operation 222–4
Pearl Harbour attack *see* Pearl Harbour attack
protection of neutral vessels 211–12
rejection of preventive self-defence 337–8
response to attacks on embassies 152, 512
ROE 180, 206
Shultz doctrine *see* Shultz doctrine
Suez Canal incident 165
Tehran Embassy occupation *see Tehran Embassy* case
Tunkin incident *see* Tunkin incident
Turkish operations in Iraq, and 431–2, 459–60
U-2 incident 164
USS *Cole* attack 501–2
USS *Pueblo* incident 187
USS *Vincennes* incident *see* USS *Vincennes* incident
'Vandenberg reservation' 7
Vietnam operations 398–9
Yugoslavia operations 165, 187, 192–4
'until clause'
available practice 517–18
drafting 74
interpretation issues 75
meaning of 'measures necessary' 75–81
more frequent use 75
overview vii, 74–83
peace and security, drafting of reference 77
practicality 74–5
scope of 'necessary measures' 78
suspension of self-defence
concrete measures taken, when 79–80
decision on whether measures adequate 81–3
enforcement measures and provisional measures distinguished 82–3
measures effective, if 81–2
peace and security restored, when 77–8
UNSC action other than enforcement, by 80–1
UNSC aware of situation, when 75–6
UNSC resolution, by 76–7
ununiformed agents, clandestine presence of 185–6
Uruguay, Definition of Aggression 1974, and 344–5, 384–5
use of force (*Ius ad Bellum*)
clarification by ICJ 513
danger of escalation ix, 532–5

use of force (*Ius ad Bellum*), law of *see also* unilateral recourse to force
- 9/11, and *see* 9/11 attacks
- acts constituting use of force, question of 516–17
- compliance pull
  - benefit from definition of armed attack 545
  - commitment to compliance 550
  - strengthening ix, 545–50
  - strengthening sanctions and incentives 547–8
- divergent frameworks
  - 'counter-restrictionist' views 10–11
  - existence 515
  - grounds for claim of 11
  - *Nicaragua* judgment 8–9
  - 'restrictionist' views 9–10
  - unsustainability of idea 19
- evolution as State-driven process 4
- exceptions to prohibition *see* exceptional measures
- gravity of forms of *see* gravity of forms of use of force
- gravity threshold *see de minimis* threshold
- implied erosion of 'compliance pull' 4
- inconsistent conduct *see* inconsistent conduct
- interpretation *see* interpretation
- lack of hostile intent 165
- limitations of previous studies vii, 6
- 'most grave' forms *see* gravity of forms of use of force
- naval law enforcement distinguished 209
- *Nicaragua* judgment *see Nicaragua* judgment
- presuppositions for development of law 34
- prohibition not confined to force directed against State's territory or independence 56–7
- self-determination *see* self-determination
- study focus on process of change in law vii, 6
- study limitations 3–4
- theoretical debates 42–3
- UN Charter terminology 127

USS *Cole* attack 501–2

USS *Pueblo* incident 187

USS *Vincennes* incident 291
- account of incident 256–7
- ICAO investigation viii, 258–62
- ICJ proceedings 258–9
- interceptive self-defence, as example of 256–7
- international response 257

USSR
- Belgian intervention in the Congo, and 218–20, 241, 244–5
- Cuban missile crisis *see* Cuban missile crisis
- Definition of Aggression 1974, and 131–2, 160, 233–4, 344–5, 385, 388
- Friendly Relations Declaration 1970, and 391
- Korean airliner incident 198–9
- military interventions by 88, 90–1
- opposition to proportionality standard 92–3, 94
- policy for submarine incidents 196
- priority (first use) principle, proposal *see* priority (first use) principle
- protection of nationals, and 218
- shooting down of US aircraft 351
- Six Day War, and 274, 278
- submarine incident in Japanese waters 189–90
- submarine incident in Swedish waters 195–6
- US intervention in Dominica, and 221

'Vandenberg reservation', *Nicaragua* judgment, and 7, 8–9

Venezuela
- contributions to debates 269
- Operation 'Phoenix', and *see* Colombia

Vienna Convention on the Law of
        Treaties 1969 (VCLT)
    conflict of laws provisions 13
    ius cogens concept, on 24–6
    modification of treaties 23–4, 27–8
    treaty interpretation, on 19–22
Vietnam
    call for assistance 88
    rejection of pre-emptive self-defence
        340–1
    Tunkin incident *see* Tunkin incident
    US operations 398–9

Waldock's cumulative conditions for
        protection of overseas
        nationals 213–14
war
    declarations as acts of aggression 133
    Dinstein's classification *see*
        Dinstein's classification
    meaning 55
weaponry *see also* nuclear weapons
    increased threat from advanced
        weapons 257
weapons of mass destruction
        (WMDs) *see also* nuclear
        weapons
    pre-emptive self-defence 358–9,
        527–8
    proper response to proliferation
        365–7

search for evidence 362–3
threat to international peace and
    security, as 359–60
Webster formula
    acceptance 255–6
    application 250
    critique 265
World Summit vii, 55–60
    non-State actors, and 446–7
    Outcome Document statements 2–3

Yemen
    attacks on Al Qaeda *see* Al Qaeda,
        attacks on
    Harib Fort action *see* Harib Fort
        action
    intervention in Iraq, and 317
Yugoslavia
    Definition of Aggression 1974, and
        134
    Prevention of Genocide case *see*
        Prevention of Genocide case
    Osiraq nuclear reactor strike, and
        285
    Six Day War, and 279
    Suez crisis, and 395
    Tadić case *see Tadić* case
    US operations 165, 187, 192–4

Zambia, alleged support for SWAPO
    401